THE DOCTRINE OF THE WORD OF GOD

CHURCH DOGMATICS

BY

KARL BARTH

VOLUME I

THE DOCTRINE
OF THE WORD OF GOD

PART ONE

EDITORS
REV. PROF. G. W. BROMILEY, D.LITT., D.D.
REV. PROF. T. F. TORRANCE, D.LITT., D.D., D.THEOL.

EDINBURGH: T. & T. CLARK, 38 GEORGE STREET

THE
DOCTRINE OF THE
WORD OF GOD

(Prolegomena to Church Dogmatics, Being Volume I, 1)

BY
KARL BARTH, D. THEOL., D.D., LL.D.

TRANSLATOR
G. W. BROMILEY, D.LITT., D.D.

EDINBURGH: T. & T. CLARK, 38 GEORGE STREET

Original German Edition

DIE KIRCHLICHE DOGMATIK I:

Die Lehre vom Wort Gottes, 1

Published by

EVANGELISCHER VERLAG A.G.

ZOLLIKON—ZÜRICH

Authorised English Translation © 1975

T. & T. CLARK LIMITED

EDINBURGH

PRINTED IN GREAT BRITAIN BY

MORRISON AND GIBB LIMITED

FOR

T. & T. CLARK, EDINBURGH

ISBN 0 567 09013 2

FIRST EDITION	1936
FIRST EDITION LATEST IMPRESSION . .	1970
SECOND EDITION	1975

EDITORS' PREFACE

It was in 1936 that Professor Thomson's translation of this half-volume of Karl Barth's *Church Dogmatics* first appeared. In introducing this new translation, our first word must be one of deep gratitude for what he did. It is only now in the completion of the English edition of the *Church Dogmatics* that we are able properly to appreciate the arduous intellectual as well as linguistic work he had to put in, at that early stage, in breaking into Barth's thought and finding a way of giving it intelligible articulation in English. Without his pioneering work the translation of the succeeding volumes would have been much more difficult and rather less successful. Meantime some 14,000 copies of Thomson's translation have been printed, and their distribution all over the world, not only in English-speaking countries, has done yeoman service in introducing many generations of students and readers to the work which more than any other has changed the direction of the history of theology. The fact that the continued demand for this, and the subsequent volumes, in English, does not abate, belies the ever-recurring rumours (evidently spread by wishful thinking reactionaries!) that Barth's influence is on the wane, and argues rather that modern theology is aware that, far from by-passing Barth, or even passing through him, it has yet to catch up on him. This increasing interest in Barth's dogmatics is also apparent in the persistent demand for a fresh translation of this half-volume, made in the light of the rest and making the English edition of the *Church Dogmatics* uniform throughout. Now that it has been completed the Index Volume will follow shortly.

Readers are referred to the Editors' Preface to *Church Dogmatics* I, 2, for some indication of the difficulties that are posed for translation into English by Barth's characteristic forms of thought as well as by his distinctive German style. Several points of special relevance to this work, however, may be mentioned here. In his discussion of the scientific character of dogmatics, Barth's language clearly reflects the logic and philosophy of science which he encountered in the 1920s, not least through his friend Heinrich Scholz whom he invited to join him in the crucial seminars he held in Bonn in 1930 for the elucidation of the theological method of St. Anselm. His use of technical terms, however, was distinctive, in line with his refusal to divorce form from material content, and his determination to develop the scientific character of dogmatics on its own proper ground. Care has been taken to render his thought as accurately as possible in English, but readers are warned not to interpret his terms (e.g. " analytic ") simply out of their knowledge of current linguistic philosophy but to look to their actual use. It may help to note that Barth reacted strongly against the nominalist and conventionalist tendencies of this philosophy even as represented by Heinrich Scholz himself. Two terms in particular have given us a lot of thought, *Gegenstand* and *Seinsweise*. Quite often the best English rendering of *Gegenstand* would be " subject " rather than " object," but since this lays itself open again and again to serious ambiguity in English, we have kept consistently to the rendering " object," while making it evident that this cannot be taken in an " objectifying " sense. In regard to *Seinsweise* Karl Barth himself once agreed with us that " way of being " might be a better rendering in English than " mode of being," if only to avoid any hint of " modalism," which he completely rejects. Yet his intention here to refer back to the Cappadocian τρόπος ὑπάρξεως and the *modus entis* of Protestant Orthodoxy made it evident that it would be best to preserve the rendering " mode of being " adopted by Thomson. In any case, " way of being " appears in some contexts to detract from Barth's determination to move behind an " economic " to an " immanent " (i.e. an ontological) Trinity.

The lasting significance of this work can be indicated briefly by drawing attention to two of its main features. (1) In it Barth seeks to ground theology as rigorously as possible upon the mutual relation of God and man actualised by divine grace in the being of the Church. At the same time his intention is both to deliver theology from its persistent tendency to become reduced to some form of anthropology, and also to establish the freedom and rationality of the human subject in the creative address of God through his Word. Much of the small print in the Introduction and in the first chapter represents Barth's attempt to establish this position through arguments on two fronts, with Modernistic Protestantism and with Mediaeval Roman Catholicism, each of which, he claims, in its own way wrongly subordinates the knowledge of God to an antecedent and independently grounded system of thought. (2) In it Barth seeks to direct modern theology back to its patristic foundations in the dogma of the Holy Trinity, and to show that the root of the Church's understanding of the Triunity of God is to be found in God's revelation of Himself as the Lord. He consistently attacks the split that developed in Roman Catholic and Protestant theology alike between the being and the activity of God, whether in creation or in redemption, which led to the fatal rift in the basic concept of God evident both in the division between an independent natural theology and revealed theology and also in the separation between the treatise on the one God and the treatise on the Triune God.

Far from being a mere inference or a deduction from a " more basic " position, the doctrine of the Trinity itself belongs to the very basis of the Christian faith and constitutes the fundamental grammar of dogmatic theology.   At this point at least, Karl Barth has been followed by some of the most eminent dogmatic theologians, not least in the Roman Catholic Church.   In introducing his translation of this work Professor G. T. Thomson claimed that it was " undoubtedly the greatest treatise on the Trinity since the Reformation," but when it is studied in connexion with volume two on the doctrine of God, the claim may well be made that it is the greatest treatise of the kind since the *De Trinitate* of St. Augustine.

The Editors wish to express their thanks to Mr. Richard H. Roberts, of New College, Edinburgh, in assisting them with the proofs, and above all to the Publishers and the Printers for their continued patience and courtesy in making this new edition available in English.

PASADENA AND EDINBURGH, *Trinity* 1973.

PREFACE

HUMAN affairs—even those over which we think we have some control—often take a different course from the one planned. *Hominum confusione? Dei providentia?* No doubt the latter too and decisively, and yet in such a way that on the human side everything is primarily and *per se confusio*, many plans being not carried out at all, or carried out in a way which is very different from that envisaged.

When five years ago I published *The Doctrine of the Word of God* as the first volume of a *Christian Dogmatics in Outline*, I had many serviceable materials to hand and thought that I should and could finish the promised whole within the time which has now elapsed. Things turned out differently. When the first volume was before me in print, it showed me plainly—whatever may be the experience of others, much more plainly than a manuscript lying in a cupboard could ever have done—how much I myself have still to learn both historically and materially. The opposition which it encountered at least amongst colleagues was too general and vehement, the intervening changes in the theological, ecclesiastical and general situation gave me so much to think about, and the need for my little work on Anselm of Canterbury was so pressing, that I could not pay any attention to the gradually increasing chorus of friendly or ironical enquiries as to what had happened to the second volume, nor even think of continuing on the level and in the strain of the initial volume of 1927. This first became clear to me, of course, when the four thousand copies of the first edition of what had been published as the first volume began to run out, and I was faced with the task of preparing a second edition. My experience of twelve years ago in re-editing the *Römerbrief* was repeated. I could still say what I had said. I wished to do so. But I could not do it in the same way. What option had I but to begin again at the beginning, saying the same thing, but in a very different way? Hence I must gratify or perhaps in part annoy my readers by giving them a revision of the old book instead of the expected new one. May some at least believe that from my own standpoint at any rate this change of plan has been forced on me by the pressure of outer and inner necessities! And may it be clear to some at least that there are good reasons for this unusual arrest or change of direction!

The alteration which I have made consists first and formally in the fact that I have thought it good to make my exposition much more explicit. This emerges at once in the relationship between the size of the book and the material covered. The book is much larger, and it has been severely compressed in places, but it covers only half the material treated in the first edition, and is thus only a half-volume. But what else can I do ? In the last five years all the problems have assumed for me a far richer, more fluid and difficult aspect. I have had to make more extensive soundings and lay broader foundations. And yet I venture to hope that the result has been to make everything simpler and clearer.

The external growth of the book is also connected with my desire to give more space to an indication of the biblico-theological presuppositions and the historico-dogmatic and polemical relations of my statements. I have condensed all these things into the interposed sections in small print, and have so arranged the dogmatic presentation that non-theologians especially may read connectedly even though they skip these small print sections. Do I have to ask gourmet theologians not to read these sections alone ? At a pinch, though only at a pinch, the text can be understood without them, but not *vice versa*. If for the most part I have reproduced *in extenso* passages adduced from the Bible, the fathers and theologians, this has not merely been for the sake of the many who do not have ready access to the originals, but in order that all readers may have the opportunity, more directly than would be possible by mere references, to hear the voices which were in my own ears as I prepared my own text, which guided, taught, or stimulated me, and by which I wish to be measured by my readers. I never imagine that these voices said exactly what I say, but I do suggest that what has to be said and heard in dogmatics to-day is better understood, and in the last resort can only be understood, if we join in listening to these voices so far as concerns the Bible passages, i.e., the basic text upon which all the rest and everything of our own can only wait and comment. If there are those who think they miss the citation of an authority which they think important, they should consider that dogmatics follows a different principle of selection from that which obtains in historical presentation in the narrower sense. Hence I have not followed up systematically the counter-theses implicitly or explicitly contested by me, not even those of my special and direct adversaries and critics of the day, but have pursued my own course, taking up theses which have made some kind of impression on me, and doing so at the point where it seems that they materially serve to advance or at any rate to clarify the problems.

The facts as to the change in content between the first and this second edition, the reader may gather from the book itself. I may content myself here with some general observations.

In substituting the word Church for Christian in the title, I have tried to set a good example of restraint in the lighthearted use of the great word " Christian " against which I have protested. But materially I have also tried to show that from the very outset dogmatics is not a free science. It is bound to the sphere of the Church, where alone it is possible and meaningful. As laments have accompanied the general course of my development, they will undoubtedly increase at this obvious alteration. But some will see what I have had in view when in recent years, and indeed even in this book, I have often had to speak with some vigour against, or rather on behalf of, the Church. Be that as it may, it will be found that in this new edition the lines are drawn more sharply in the direction indicated by this alteration.

This means above all that I now think I have a better understanding of many things, including my own intentions, to the degree that in this second draft I have excluded to the very best of my ability anything that might appear to find for theology a foundation, support, or justification in philosophical existentialism. " The Word or existence ? " The first edition gave to acumen, or perhaps stupidity, some ground for putting this question. I may hope that so far as concerns my own intentions the answer to it is now clear. In the former undertaking I can see only a resumption of the line which leads from Schleiermacher by way of Ritschl to Herrmann. And in any conceivable continuation along this line I can see only the plain destruction of Protestant theology and the Protestant Church. I can see no third alternative between that exploitation of the *analogia entis* which is legitimate only on the basis of Roman Catholicism, between the greatness and misery of a so-called natural knowledge of God in the sense of the *Vaticanum*, and a Protestant theology which draws from its own source, which stands on its own feet, and which is finally liberated from this secular misery. Hence I have had no option but to say No at this point. I regard the *analogia entis* as the invention of Antichrist, and I believe that because of it it is impossible ever to become a Roman Catholic, all other reasons for not doing so being to my mind short-sighted and trivial.

To say this is to clarify my attitude to the charge which I clearly foresaw five years ago and which has been raised at once all along the line and in every possible tone from friendly concern to downright anger, namely, that historically, formally and materially I am now going the way of scholasticism. It would seem that Church history no longer begins for me in 1517. I can quote Anselm and Thomas with no sign of horror. I obviously regard the doctrine of the early Church as in some sense normative. I deal explicitly with the doctrine of the Trinity, and even with that of the Virgin Birth. The last-named alone is obviously enough to lead many contemporaries to suspect me of crypto-Catholicism. What am I to say ? Shall I excuse myself by pointing out that the connexion between the Reformation and the early Church, trinitarian and christological dogma, and the very concepts of dogma and the biblical Canon, are not in the last resort malicious inventions of my own ? Or shall I oppose to indignation my own indignation at the presumption which seems for its own part to regard the necessity of ignoring or denying these things, and therefore an epigonous fideism, as dogmas whose despisers are at once open to the charge of Catholicism ? Or shall I ask, perhaps mentioning names, why none of the so-called positive theologians of whom there are still supposed to be several in German universities—they or their predecessors ran a fairly lively campaign for the " confession " only twenty years ago—have sprung to my assistance in this matter ? Or shall I ask what or what sort of teaching they now think should be given concerning the Trinity and the Virgin Birth ? Or shall I merely be astonished at the Philistinism which thinks it should bewail " speculation " when it does not recognise its own ethicism, and fails to see that not merely the most important but also the most relevant and beautiful problems in dogmatics begin at the very point where the fable of " unprofitable scholasticism " and the slogan about the " Greek thinking of the fathers " persuade us that we ought to stop ? Or shall I laugh at the phonetically ridiculous talk about *fides quae* and *fides qua* by which many obviously think that they can dismiss the whole concern of scholasticism at a single stroke, promptly dealing with me at the same time ? Or shall I rather bemoan the constantly increasing confusion, tedium and irrelevance of modern Protestantism, which, probably along with the Trinity and the Virgin Birth, has lost an entire third dimension—the dimension of what for once, though not confusing it with religious and moral earnestness, we may describe as mystery—with the result that it has been punished with all kinds of worthless substitutes, that it has fallen the more readily victim to such uneasy cliques and sects as High Church, German Church, Christian Community and religious Socialism, and that many of its preachers and adherents have finally learned to discover deep religious significance in the intoxication of Nordic blood and their political *Führer* ? However right these various courses might be, I can only ignore the objection and rumour that I am catholicising, and in face of the enemy repeat the more emphatically and expressly whatever has been deplored in my book in this respect. It is precisely in relation to this disputed aspect that I am of particularly good courage and sure of my cause.

A final remark may be made concerning the present theological situation. Whether in agreement or opposition this book will be the better understood the more it is conceived, as I have already said in the preface to the first edition, as standing on its own, and the less it is conceived as representing a movement, tendency, or school. In this sense, too, it aims to be a Church dogmatics. I may take it as well known that there exists between Eduard Thurneysen and myself a theological affinity which is of long standing and has always shown itself to be self-evident. Again, among theological colleagues, ministers and non-theologians I know many men and women towards whom I am conscious of being wholeheartedly sympathetic in general outlook. But this does not constitute a school, and I certainly cannot think in this emphatic way of those who are commonly associated with me as leaders or adherents of the so-called " dialectical theology." It is only fair to them as well as to me that in its new form, too, this book should not be hailed as the dogmatics of dialectical theology. The community in and for which I have written it is that of the Church and not a community of theological endeavour. Of course, there is within the Church an Evangelical theology which is to be affirmed and a heretical non-theology which is to be resolutely denied. But I rejoice that *in concreto* I neither know nor have to know who stands where, so that I can serve a cause and not a party, and mark off myself from a cause and not a party, not working either for or against persons. Thus I can be free in relation to both ostensible and true neighbours, and responsible on earth only to the Church. I only wish I could make things clear to those who would like to see me walking arm in arm with X or Y.

I am not unaware that to undertake a dogmatics of the Evangelical Church to-day is intrinsically, and quite apart from specific objections, to expose oneself to difficulties which I cannot easily resolve. For where is to-day the Evangelical Church which desires to be taken seriously and to confess itself in the sense of the present book ? Am I not aware that in the realm of modern Protestantism the very authorities of the Church seem to have no more urgent wish than to give as little heed as possible to the doctrine of the Church ? Am I not aware that even the doctrinal interest which does exist in the Church of to-day is focused on very different matters from those which are treated in this basic study ? Am I not aware of the lack of connexion between what fills the heads and hearts of all to-day and what I seek to set forth as stimulating and important in these pages ? Am I not aware how probable it is that from large circles of those accustomed to take notice of theological work in general the cry will arise afresh that stones are being offered here instead of bread ? Yes, I am aware of all these things, and it might well discourage me to think of them. My only reply can be that I hold myself forbidden to be discouraged by thinking of them. For I believe that to the very day of judgment we shall wait in vain for an Evangelical Church which takes itself seriously unless we are prepared to attempt in all modesty to take the risk of being such a Church in our own situation and to the best of our ability. I believe that I understand the present-day authorities of the Church better than they understand themselves when I ignore their well-known resentment against what should have been their most important task, appealing from authorities badly informed to authorities which are better informed. I am firmly convinced that, especially in the broad field of politics, we cannot reach the clarifications which are necessary to-day, and on which theology might have a word to say, as indeed it ought to have, without first reaching the comprehensive clarifications in and about theology which are our present concern. I believe that it is expected of the Church and its theology—a world within the world no less than chemistry or the theatre—that it should keep precisely to the rhythm of its own relevant concerns, and thus consider well what are the *real* needs of the day by which its own programme should be directed. I have found by experience that in the last resort the man in the street who is so highly respected by many ecclesiastics and theologians will really take notice of us when we do not worry about what he expects of us but do what we are charged to do. I believe in fact that, quite apart from its ethical applications, a better Church dogmatics might well be finally a more significant and solid contribution even to such questions and tasks as that of German liberation than most of the well-meant stuff which even so many theologians think in dilettante fashion that they can and should supply in relation to these questions and tasks. For these reasons I hold myself forbidden to be discouraged. For these reasons I venture upon what is really a venture for me too, addressing myself in the middle of 1932 to a dogmatics, and to a dogmatics of such compass. I could not refrain from saying this in indication of the fact that I have been affected by the many jesting or serious comments made upon it.

At the publishers' desire I willingly, but without obligation, tell my readers how I hope to continue after the beginning made with this half-volume.

First, in a second half-volume of what will I suppose be much the same size I plan to conclude the *Prolegomena to Dogmatics*. As in the first edition, this will be devoted to the finishing of the doctrine of revelation and then to the doctrine of Holy Scripture and the proclamation of the Church.

The second volume should contain the doctrine of God, the third the doctrine of creation, the fourth the doctrine of reconciliation and the fifth the doctrine of redemption.

What is called ethics I regard as the doctrine of the command of God. Hence I do not think it right to treat it otherwise than as an integral part of dogmatics, or to produce a dogmatics which does not include it. In this dogmatics the concept of the command of God in general will be treated at the close of the doctrine of God. The command of God from the standpoint of order will then be discussed at the close of the doctrine of creation, from the standpoint of law at the close of the doctrine of reconciliation, and from the standpoint of promise at the close of the doctrine of redemption.

I need not say that I shall have to have many years to carry out the plan as now envisaged. And all sensible people will realise that in a matter of such wide prospect I cannot commit myself by detailed pronouncements in the light of my preliminary work, but must ask them to believe, on the basis of the indications given, that I do at least know what I am after. " If the Lord will, and we live " (Jas. 4^{15}).

BERGLI, OBERRIEDEN (Canton Zürich)
August, 1932.

CONTENTS

CHAPTER II

THE REVELATION OF GOD

PART I. THE TRIUNE GOD

INTRODUCTION

INTRODUCTION

§ 1.

THE TASK OF DOGMATICS

As a theological discipline dogmatics is the scientific self-examination of the Christian Church with respect to the content of its distinctive talk about God.

1. THE CHURCH, THEOLOGY, SCIENCE

Dogmatics is a theological discipline. But theology is a function of the Church.

The Church confesses God as it talks about God. It does so first by its existence in the action of each individual believer. And it does so secondly by its specific action as a fellowship, in proclamation by preaching and the administration of the sacraments, in worship, in its internal and external mission including works of love amongst the sick, the weak and those in jeopardy. Fortunately the reality of the Church does not coincide with its action. But its action coincides with the fact that alike in its existence in believers and its communal existence as such it speaks about God. Its action is " theology " in both the broader and the narrower sense.

Theology is *de divinitate ratio sive sermo* (Augustine, *De civ. Dei*, VIII, 1). Θεολόγος est ὁ τὸν θεὸν ἐκ θεοῦ ἐνώπιον τοῦ θεοῦ εἰς δόξαν αὐτοῦ λέγων (Coccejus, *Summa theol.*, 1699, 1, 1).

But as it confesses God the Church also confesses both the humanity and the responsibility of its action. It realises that it is exposed to fierce temptation as it speaks of God, and it realises that it must give an account to God for the way in which it speaks. The first and last and decisive answer to this twofold compulsion consists in the fact that it rests content with the grace of the One whose strength is mighty in weakness. But in so doing it recognises and takes up as an active Church the further human task of criticising and revising its speech about God. This brings us to the concept of theology in the third, strictest and proper sense of the word.

Cf. for this threefold concept of theology J. Gerhard, *Loci theol.*, 1610, *Prooem.* 4 : Theology is 1. *fides et religio Christiana, quae omnibus fidelibus doctis aeque ac indoctis communis est, ut sic theologi dicantur;* 2. *functio ministerii*

3

Ecclesiastici ; 3. *accuratior divinorum mysteriorum cognitio, qua ratione theologi dicuntur, qui possunt veritatem divinam solide stabilire, eique oppositam falsitatem potenter destruere.*

Theology as a science, in distinction from the " theology " of the simple testimony of faith and life and the " theology " of the service of God, is a measure taken by the Church in relation to the vulnerability and responsibility of its utterance. It would be meaningless without justifying grace, which here too can alone make good what man as such invariably does badly. But it can be meaningful as an act of obedience to this grace, i.e., of the obedience in which here too man may believe that he is doing well even though he does not see it.

Theology saw this quite early . . . *et hominum officio ipso sancto Spiritu largiente in docendis etiam ipsis doctoribus non debere cessare et tamen neque qui plantat esse aliquid neque qui rigat sed Deum qui incrementum dat* (Augustine, *De doct. christ.,* IV, 16).

The Church produces theology in this special and peculiar sense by subjecting itself to self-examination. It puts to itself the question of truth, i.e., it measures its action, its talk about God, against its being as the Church. Thus theology exists in this special and peculiar sense because before it and apart from it there is in the Church talk about God. Theology follows the talk of the Church to the extent that in its question as to the correctness of its utterance it does not measure it by an alien standard but by its own source and object. Theology guides the talk of the Church to the extent that it concretely reminds it that in all circumstances it is fallible human work which in the matter of relevance or irrelevance lies in the balance, and must be obedience to grace if it is to be well done. Theology accompanies the utterance of the Church to the extent that it is itself no more than human " talk about God," so that with this talk it stands under the judgment that begins at the house of God and lives by the promise given to the Church.

The work in which the Church submits to this self-examination falls into three circles which intersect in such a way that the centre of each is also within the circumference of the other two, so that in view of that which alone can be the centre it is as well neither to affirm nor to construct a systematic centre, i.e., the centre of a circle embracing the other three. The question of truth, with which theology is concerned throughout, is the question as to the agreement of the Church's distinctive talk about God with the being of the Church. The criterion of past, future and therefore present Christian utterance is thus the being of the Church, namely, Jesus Christ, God in His gracious revealing and reconciling address to man. Does Christian utterance derive from Him ? Does it lead to Him ? Is it conformable to Him ? None of these questions can be put apart, but each is to be put independently and with all possible force. Hence theology as biblical theology is the question of the basis, as practical theology the question of the goal and as dogmatic theology the question of the content of the distinctive utterance of the Church.

What is called Church history does not correspond to any independently raised question concerning Christian talk about God, and it cannot therefore be regarded as an independent theological discipline. It is an auxiliary science indispensable to exegetical, dogmatic and practical theology.

When the Church puts to itself the question of truth in its threefold form in a way which is objective and not arbitrary, its self-examination acquires the character of a scientific undertaking which has its own place alongside other human undertakings of the same or a similar kind. It is this particular science, i.e., theological science. Naturally, however, it is only in practice and with reservations that we can claim for it either its character as a science or its distinctiveness among the sciences.

Even the asserted independence of theology in relation to other sciences cannot be proved to be necessary in principle. It is indeed unfortunate that the question of the truth of talk about God should be handled as a question apart by a special faculty, and, while we have to recognise that such a course is unavoidable in practice, we cannot find any final reasons to justify it. Only theological arrogance could argue the point on other than practical grounds. Within the sphere of the Church philosophy, history, sociology, psychology, or pedagogics, whether individually or in conjunction, might well take up the task of measuring the Church's talk about God by its being as the Church, thus making a special theology superfluous. Theology does not in fact possess special keys to special doors. Nor does it control a basis of knowledge which might not find actualisation in other sciences. Nor does it know an object of enquiry necessarily concealed from other sciences. Only by failing to recognise the actualisation of revelation, the possibility of grace and therefore its own nature, could it possibly make any such claim. Similarly, we cannot possibly prove that there is any necessity in principle for a theology of the service of God. Might it not be that Jer. 31³⁴ is in process of fulfilment? Philosophy and secular science generally do not have to be secular or pagan. There might be such a thing as *philosophia christiana*.

Porro si sapientia Deus est, per quem facta sunt omnia sicut divina auctoritas veritasque monstravit, verus philosophus est amator Dei (Augustine, *De civ. Dei*, VIII, 1).

To contest this principle is to combine despair of the world with over-valuation of the Christian world in a way which is incompatible either with Christian hope or Christian humility. Theology as a special science, like the theology of the service of God as special Christian utterance, can be justified only as a relative and factual necessity. As such it is justified.

Absolute et simpliciter Theologia non est necessaria, ne quidem toti Ecclesiae : potest enim Deus homine immediate, h.e. sine ministerio hominum Theologorum informare et convertere—sed ex hypothesi posita scil. Dei voluntate (Quenstedt, *Theol. did.pol.*, 1685, I, *cap.* 1, *sect.* 2, *qu.* 1, *ekth.* 6).

The other sciences have not in fact recognised and adopted the task of theology. To be sure, attempts have always been made on all sides to criticise and correct the Church's talk about God. But what is required is its criticism and correction in the light of the being of the Church, of Jesus Christ as its basis, goal and content. In fact, however, even though we cannot show that this is in accordance with any necessity of principle, even those historians, pedagogues, etc., and especially philosophers who kindly take this aspect into account always miss the real problem by setting it within the sphere of their own sciences, judging the utterance of the Church about God in accordance with alien principles rather than its own principle, and thus increasing rather than decreasing the mischief which makes critical science necessary for the Church. The result is even worse when this is done in the name of " theology." In practice the achievements of the philosopher, historian, etc. can be of only indirect significance to the problem which here confronts us, i.e., by way of a specific interpretation. Directly, in all the three areas of theological enquiry philosophy, history, psychology, etc. have always succeeded in practice only in increasing the self-alienation of the Church and the distortion and confusion of its talk about God. And in the interpretation offered, as the relevant experts at once object, philosophy ceases to be philosophy, or history history. There never has actually been a *philosophia christiana*, for if it was *philosophia* it was not *christiana*, and if it was *christiana* it was not *philosophia*. If, then, the concern of the Church is not to go by default, the special function of a scientific theology, corresponding to the special function of the service of God, is in fact indispensable. Its task, not in fact discharged by other sciences, is that of the criticism and correction of talk about God according to the criterion of the Church's own principle. Theology is the science which finally sets itself this task, and this task alone, subordinating to this task all other possible tasks in the human search for truth.

Non ubique quidquid sciri ab homine potest in rebus humanis . . . huic scientiae tribuens, sed illud tantummodo, quo fides saluberrima, quae ad veram beatitudinem ducit, gignitur, nutritur, defenditur, roboratur (Augustine, *De trin.*, XIV, 1, 3). *Theologia . . . ita est omnium arbitra et domina, ut de ipsis judicet et ipsa a nulla alia scientia judicetur ; omnes enim aliae disciplinae exigendae sunt ad ejus amussim, ut quicquid habent cum Theologia non consonum reiiciatur* (F. Turrettini, *Instit. Theol. elenchth.*, I, 1679, 1, 6, 7). Cf. Thomas Aquinas, *S. theol.*, I, *qu.* 1, *art.* 5.

The other sciences, too, might finally set themselves this task and this task alone, subordinating all other tasks to it. All sciences might ultimately be theology. The fact that they are not is one which we need neither bewail nor justify in the present context. But it is a fact which creates a vacuum intolerable for the Church. The separate existence of theology signifies the emergency measure on which the Church has had to resolve in view of the actual refusal of the other sciences in this respect. It can have no epistemological basis. From the standpoint of the Church itself and therefore of theology, the separate existence of the latter is theoretically very questionable. Of the efforts made to assign it a place in the system of sciences, theology itself must say that the honour is both too great, and too small.

The case is much the same when we ask whether theology is really a science at all. This question is not a vital one for theology. There is no necessity of principle, nor are there any internal reasons, why it should claim to belong to this genus. On the contrary, there are good grounds why it should definitely refrain from doing so.

Among the older orthodox, so far as I am aware, Baier was the first (*Comp. Theol. posit.*, *Prol.* 1, 15), and then Buddeus (*Instit. dogmat.*, 1724, I, 1, 28), emphatically to call theology a *scientia*. Perhaps in the wake of Thomas Aquinas (*S. theol.*, I, *qu.* 1, *art.* 2 and 6) the older Leiden school (e.g., Walæus, *Loci comm.*, 1640, p. 4, *Leidener Synopsis pur. Theol.*, 1624, I, 9) spoke cautiously of *scientia vel sapientia*, while to the best of my knowledge the overwhelming majority of the older (e.g., Wolleb, *Christ. Theol. Comp.*, 1626, *Praecogn.*) and later (e.g., Mastricht, *Theol. theor.-pract.*, 1698, I, 1, 1) Reformed, and even the Lutheran Quenstedt (*Theol. did. -pol.*, 1685, I, *cap.* 1, *sect.* 1, *th.* 28), preferred the term *doctrina*. J. Gerhard expressly rejected the description of theology as *scientia* on the following grounds : 1. *scientiae certitudo ab internis et inhaerentibus principiis, fidei vero ab externis videlicet ab autoritate revelantis pendet ;* 2. *subjectum Theologiae est Christus, cujus cognitio scientifico modo haberi nequit, sed ex divina revelatione eam peti oportet ;* 3. *cujusvis scientiae principium est intellectus, quando ex principiis apte cognitis ad scientiam conclusionem devenitur. At in theologia intellectus non est principium sed finis ;* 4. *scientiis ratiocinando inventis potest subesse falsum* (*Loci theol.*, 1610, *Prooem.* 8). He and later Hollaz (*Ex. Theol. acroam.*, 1707, *Prol.*, 1, 1) chose the term *sapientia*. In the 19th century A. F. C. Vilmar is alone, so far as I am aware, in rejecting the term " science " as one which " for the time being " is too heavily loaded (*Dogmatik*, 1874, I, p. 38. Cf. *Die Theologie der Tatsachen wider die Theologie der Rhetorik*, 4th ed. 1876, p. VI f.). The passion with which G. Wobbermin assures us that " theology has the greatest possible, i.e., a thoroughly existential interest in ranking as a real science, as a science in the strict, and indeed the very strictest sense of the word " (*Richtlinien evang. Theologie*, 1929, p. 25), is exaggerated. For the preceding ancient and mediaeval history of the question, cf. G. Söhngen, " Die kathol. Theologie als Wissenschaft und Weisheit," (*Catholica, Vierteljahrschrift für Kontroverstheologie*, April, 1932).

If theology allows itself to be called, and calls itself, a " science," in so doing it declares 1. that like all other so-called sciences it is a human concern with a definite object of knowledge, 2. that like all others it treads a definite and self-consistent path of knowledge, and 3. that like all others it must give an account of this path to itself and to all others who are capable of concern for this object and therefore of treading this path. But it would make not the slightest difference to its real business if it had to rank as something other than science. If it is ranked as a science, and lays claim to such ranking, this does not mean that it must allow itself to be disturbed or hampered in its own task by regard for what is described as science elsewhere. On the contrary, to the discharge of its own task it must absolutely subordinate and if necessary sacrifice all concern for what is called science elsewhere. The existence of other sciences, and the praiseworthy fidelity with which many of them at least pursue their own axioms and methods, can and must remind it that it must pursue its own task in due order and with the same fidelity. But it cannot allow itself to be told by them what this means concretely in its own case. As regards method, it has nothing to learn from them.

It does not have to justify itself before them, least of all by submitting to the demands of a concept of science which accidentally or not claims general validity.

To the question what is the " science " to which theology must fully adhere G. Wobbermin gives (*op. cit.*, p. 29) the ingenuous answer : " Striving after the most exact and complete possible knowledge of the reality accessible to us." But what good theology will include its object in the " reality accessible to us " ? And will a bad theology which does this really be granted by other sciences the recognition which it seeks ?

What it involves to accommodate oneself to the concept of science which is accepted and holds sway to-day, and probably not only to-day, is made strikingly clear in the essay of Heinrich Scholz " Wie ist eine evangelische Theologie als Wissenschaft möglich ? " (*Z.d.Z.*, 1931, pp. 8–53). In an ascending scale, the demands made upon an undertaking which aspires to rank as " science," and therefore upon theology, are listed by Scholz as follows (*op. cit.*, pp. 18–24, 24–48) : 1. freedom from contradiction in all the propositions to be constructed in the so-called science (" the proposition postulate ") ; 2. unity in the sphere of its object (" the coherence postulate ") ; 3. the possibility that all the propositions presented might be tested by any " sufficiently attentive readers or hearers " (" the verifiability postulate ") ; 4. respect for that which is physically and biologically impossible (" the congruity postulate ") ; 5. freedom from all pre-judgments (" the independence postulate ") ; and 6. the possibility of all pro-positions being broken up into axioms and theorems and demonstrated on this basis (this being the solemn " supreme demand which is made of a science ").* Scholz is undoubtedly right when in answer to the possible objection of theologians that this concept of science is an arbitrary modern invention he argues that it, too, " has a tradition, a great, classical tradition, and that it is a splendid and

---

* Editors' note. These six requirements correspond to what we would think of as (1) formal consistency, (2) inherent consistency, (3) openness to control through a community of verifiers, (4) antecedent credibility, (5) impartiality or, positively stated, according to the principle of sufficient reason, and (6) formalisability.

worthwhile thing to work for the high estimation of this tradition " (*op. cit.*, p. 51). In addition to a theoretical basis in the history of philosophy since Plato and Aristotle, it has on its side the historical development of at least the last two or three hundred years, and its fairly consistent practical application in Berlin, New York and Tokyo. Nor is it meant as a rigid but rather as a flexible principle which readily admits of variations in practical execution. There is thus no point in drawing attention to its internal difficulties or the ways in which it is perhaps always broken when applied, even in the natural sciences. It is still the proper concept of science for our own time. And theology can only say point-blank that this concept is unacceptable to it. Even the minimum postulate of freedom from contradiction is acceptable to theology only when it is given a particular interpretation which the scientific theorist can hardly tolerate, namely, that theology does not affirm in principle that the " contradictions " which it makes cannot be resolved. But the statements in which it maintains their resolution will be statements concerning the free activity of God and not therefore statements whIch " dismiss contradictions from the world " (*op. cit.*, p. 44). The remaining sections of the law as stated by Scholz can only remind the theologian that he ought to know what he is about when he transgresses them, but also that as a theologian he cannot help transgressing them. Not an iota can be yielded here without betraying theology, for any concession at this point involves surrendering the theme of theology. On the other hand, in answer to the question whether relevance or objectivity should not be regarded as one of the main postulates of the concept of science, Scholz replies (*op. cit.*, p. 52) that he has not so far met any criterion " with the help of which it can be decided even in a single seriously controverted issue whether a given line of thought is objective or not." The theologian will perhaps appreciate more than others the importance of this statement. But he will say that objectivity in this aggravatingly indefinite sense is the most general expression of the one distinctive rule to which theology may and must keep. Hence in its dealings with this concept of science it can only make the dry declaration that the concept cannot be that of theology.

An apparently more harmless because more general definition of the concept of science is given by Arthur Titius in his Berlin University address on July 26 1932 : " Ist systematische Theologie als Wissenschaft möglich ? " According to Titius, science is " present or in process of realisation wherever common work exists or is possible in the realm of knowledge. This is only the case where the object behind the knowledge is made accessible to all with the necessary clarity and can be expounded according to the methods which are common to all " (p. 5 f.). The possibility of a fulfilment of this condition by systematic theology Titius sees first (p. 11 f.) in the fact that in the newly exploited notion of the unity of the world it has a point of contact accessible to all who are capable of thinking at all. He then finds it (p. 14 f.) in the possibility of the myth of the direct working of God as an inner causality of a personal and miraculous nature, in the Christian form of which the theologian sees " profound truth," i.e., the truth which even those who reject this myth must recognise in its " significance " etc. He sees it finally (p. 27 f.) in the psychological, sociological and moral significance of the Christian religion as this may be plainly grasped by any man. " Hence theology may be integrated with scholarship " if only there is accorded to it as to all historical and scientific learning the possibility of making appropriate use of the more basic contemplation which is " a kind of intuition in virtue of which aesthetic elements enter into the process of cognition and help to determine it " (p. 30). In this way theology may indeed be integrated into knowledge. But in respect of the very three elements which are supposed to vindicate it as a science, namely, the idea of unity, the possibility of myth, and the humanistic relevance of Christianity, it can only be described as completely empty from the theological standpoint, so that theology integrated along these lines must be flatly disowned as theology. How can it be otherwise if the intention is to make the theme of theology accessible to all men with the requisite clarity and to depict it according to methods which are valid for all ? Whatever may be the concept of science, this object of knowledge cannot be handled in this way.

If theology allows itself to be called, or calls itself, a science, it cannot in so doing accept the obligation of submission to standards valid for other sciences.

Similarly, it cannot justify itself before other sciences on the score of propounding for discussion by them a concept of science which does not exclude but includes a good theology. To set itself in a systematic relationship to other sciences, theology would have to regard its own separate existence as necessary in principle. But this is the very thing which it cannot do. It cannot think of itself as a link in an ordered cosmos, but only as a stop-gap in a disordered cosmos. But how can there possibly be a concept of knowledge common to this stop-gap and the disordered cosmos ? Any attempt of this kind must founder at once upon the conflict of will whether or not to take up the theme of theology. And from the theological standpoint this conflict is no mere problem to be solved by a synthetic construction.

Since the days of Schleiermacher, many encyclopaedic attempts have been made to include theology in the sciences. But the common objection may be made against all of them that they overlook the abnormality of the special existence of theology and therefore essay that which is radically impossible. The actual result of all such attempts has always been the disturbing or destructive surrender of theology to a general concept of science and the mild unconcern with which non-theological science, perhaps with a better sense of realities than theologians with their desire for synthesis, can usually reply to this mode of justifying theology.

Thus even the task of drafting a better concept of science in basic self-justification can only be rejected on the part of theology.

The only way which theology has of proving its scientific character is to devote itself to the task of knowledge as determined by its actual theme and thus to show what it means by true science. No science has any manorial rights to the title, nor does any theory of science have absolute power either to grant or withhold the title. Even conventions brought into currency by a general concept of science have no claim to final respect. Whether or not a person or thing is what it claims to be is always decided by the event which either substantiates or refutes the claim and not by even the most weighty stipulations concerning the justification or non-justification of the claim. We must leave it to this event. Theology has no reason not to call itself a science. It may well prove to be more of a science than many or even all the sciences grouped under the above convention.

There are three practical reasons why we should quietly insist on describing theology as a science.

1. In so doing, theology brings itself into line. As a human concern for truth, it recognises its solidarity with other such concerns now grouped under the name of science. It protests against the idea of an ontological exaltation above them such as might easily be suggested by its emphatic and distinctive designation by older writers as *doctrina* or even *sapientia*. It remembers that it is only a science and therefore that it is secular even as it works in its own relatively special way and in the highest spheres.

2. In not just resigning the title to others, with all due respect to the classical tradition it makes a necessary protest against a general concept of science which is admittedly pagan. It cannot do any harm even to the most stalwart representatives of this concept, or indeed to the whole university, to be reminded by the presence of the theologian among them that the quasi-religious certainty of their interpretation of the term is not in fact undisputed, that the tradition which commences with the name of Aristotle is only one among others, and that the Christian Church certainly does not number Aristotle among its ancestors.

3. Finally, in grouping itself among the sciences for all the radical and indeed indissoluble difference in the understanding of the term, theology shows that it does not take the heathenism of their understanding seriously enough to separate itself under another name, but that it reckons them as part of the Church in spite of their refusal of the theological task and their adoption of a concept of science which is so intolerable to theology. It believes in the forgiveness of sins, and not in the final reality of a heathen pantheon. If there can be no question of establishing this belief, there can be even less of denying it. But such a denial might well underlie too clear-cut a distinction between theology and the sciences.

These are the external and less basic reasons which we have for not making this distinction.

2. DOGMATICS AS AN ENQUIRY

Dogmatics is the self-examination of the Christian Church in respect of the content of its distinctive talk about God. The true content which is sought we shall call dogma. This term, and therefore the word " dogmatics," will be explained in § 7. In this initial approach we may simply say that when we describe the true content of the Church's talk about God as the object of human work or investigation, we presuppose that it has both the capacity and the need to serve as the object of human enquiry. In other words, we presuppose that the " science of dogma " is both possible and necessary. Neither proposition is self-evident. Each must be sustained.

1. Dogmatics as an enquiry presupposes that the true content of Christian talk about God can be known by man. It makes this assumption as in and with the Church it believes in Jesus Christ as the revealing and reconciling address of God to man. Talk about God has true content when it conforms to the being of the Church, i.e., when it conforms to Jesus Christ ... εἴτε προφητίαν, κατὰ τὴν ἀναλογίαν τῆς πίστεως (Rom. 12⁶). It is in terms of such conformity that dogmatics investigates Christian utterance. Hence it does not have to begin by finding or inventing the standard by which it measures. It sees and recognises that this is given with the Church. It is given in its own peculiar way, as Jesus Christ is given, as God in His revelation gives Himself to faith. But it is given. It is complete in itself. It stands by its claim without discussion. It has the certainty which a true standard or criterion must have to be the means of serious measurement. Dogmatics presupposes that, as God in Jesus Christ is the essence of the Church, having promised Himself to it, so He is the truth, not merely in Himself, but also for us as we know Him solely by faith in Jesus Christ. To the extent that dogmatics receives this standard by which it measures talk about God in Jesus Christ, in the event of the divine action corresponding to the promise given to the Church, it is possible for it to be knowledge of the truth. What is or is not the true content of such talk about God is clear at once and with complete fulness and certainty in the light in which we are here set. The fulfilment of this knowledge, the event of human action, the appropriation corresponding to this address in which, through the stages of intuitive apprehension to formulated comprehension, the revelation of the *analogia fidei* and the resultant clarity in dogmatics (in dogmatics too, but not first or solely in dogmatics) take creaturely form, is, of course, a second event compared with the divine action itself, united with it in faith, yet also in faith to be distinguished from it. The second event, however, does not abolish the first. In, with and under the human question dogmatics speaks of the divine answer. It knows even as it seeks. It teaches even as it learns. In human uncertainty like any other science, it establishes the most certain truth ever known. In relation to its subject, every statement in dogmatics, as a statement of faith, must be ventured with the assurance of speaking divine and not just human truth. In distinction from the academic reserve of, e.g., a philosophical proposition, it cannot evade the severity of the dogmatic. The necessary corrective is supplied by the matter itself : " in relation to its object ... as a statement of faith." The intractability of faith and its object guarantees that divine certainty cannot become human security. But

it is this intractable faith and its intractable object which make possible the certain divine knowledge which is at issue in dogmatics.

ὁ δὲ πνευματικὸς ἀνακρίνει μὲν τὰ πάντα, αὐτὸς δὲ ὑπ᾽ οὐδενὸς ἀνακρίνεται. τίς γὰρ ἔγνω νοῦν κυρίου, ὃς συμβιβάσει αὐτόν ; ἡμεῖς δὲ νοῦν Χριστοῦ ἔχομεν (1 Cor. 2¹⁵ f.). *Viderint, qui Stoicum et Platonicum et dialecticum Christianismum protulerunt. Nobis curiositate opus non est post Christum Jesum nec inquisitione post evangelium* (Tertullian, *De praescr.*, 7). *Aliud est, de silvestri cacumine videre patriam pacis et iter ad eam non invenire et frustra conari per invia . . . et aliud tenere viam illuc ducentem curia coelestis imperatoris munitam* (Augustine, *Conf.* VII, 21, 27). *Civitas Dei . . . habens de rebus quas mente et ratione comprehendit etiamsi parvam . . . tamen certissimam scientiam (De civ. Dei, XIX, 18). Tolle assertiones, et Christianismum tulisti* (Luther, *De servo arb.*, 1525, W.A., 18, p. 603, l. 32). *Spiritus sanctus non est scepticus, nec dubia aut opiniones in cordibus nostris scripsit, sed assertiones ipsa vita et omni experientia certiores et firmiores (ibid., p. 605, l. 32). Veritas periclitari potest, perire non potest. Impugnatur quidem, sed non expugnatur, Quia verbum Domini manet in aeternum* (Comm. on Gal. 1⁷, 1535, W.A., 40¹, p. 115, l. 15). *Sic ego omnino nihil audio contrarium meae doctrinae ; sum enim certus et persuasus per Spiritum Christi meam doctrinam de Christiana justitia veram ac certam esse* (Comm. on Gal. 3¹, W.A., 40¹, p. 323, l. 28). *Haec est ratio, cur nostra Theologia certa sit : Quia rapit nos a nobis et ponit nos extra nos, ut non nitamur viribus, conscientia, sensu, persona, operibus nostris, sed eo nitamur, quod est extra nos, Hoc est, promissione et veritate Dei, quae fallere non potest* (Comm. on Gal. 4⁶, W.A., 40¹, p. 589, l. 25). *Ut certa est cuilibet sano haec sententia : bis quattuor sunt octo . . . ita sint certi nobis et immoti articuli fidei, comminationes et promissiones divinae. . . . Quare illam dubitationem philosophicam seu ἐποχὴν nequaquam admittamus ad doctrinam ecclesiae a Deo traditam. . . . Non alenda est hic aut laudanda dubitatio, sed sit fides certa assensio. . . .* (Melanchthon, *Loci comm.*, 1559, C. R. 21, p. 604 f.). The " critical question " with which Eberhard Grisebach thinks it necessary to approach the work of theology has the value of sharpening the insight, not unfamiliar to some theologians, that the statements of dogmatics can have no other certainty than that which may be had by statements of faith with reference to their object, and that neither object nor faith stands at the disposal of the dogmatician. To the extent that such criticism passes from the investigation of theological certainty to its denial, it destroys itself and may be ignored. And theologians of this school may well be asked how long they think they can live on repetition of the " critical question."

It was obviously with reference to this aspect of the possibility of dogmatics as enquiry that the Reformed orthodox adopted the dangerously abbreviated definition of theology as *doctrina revelata* or *patefacta*. Yet among the later writers of this school we also find the more exact statement that *evidentia* and *certitudo* are proper to theological propositions in respect of their *ratio objectiva*, i.e., revelation, and the *habitus*, i.e., faith, in which we affirm them (F. Burmann, *Syn. Theol.*, 1678, I, 2, 60), *Ea cognitio est vera, etiamsi non sit adaequata, quia quae de Deo cognoscuntur . . . carent omni mendacio, licet plus in re ipsa sit, quam a nobis intellegi potest* (Coccejus, *Summa theol.*, 1669, I, 4).

2. Dogmatics as an enquiry presupposes that the true content of Christian talk about God must be known by men. Christian speech must be tested by its conformity to Christ. This conformity is never clear and unambiguous. To the finally and adequately given divine answer there corresponds a human question which can maintain its faithfulness only in unwearied and honest persistence. There corres-

ponds even at the highest point of attainment the open : " Not as though I had already attained." Dogmatics receives even the standard by which it measures in an act of human appropriation. Hence it has to be enquiry. It knows the light which is intrinsically perfect and reveals everything in a flash. Yet it knows it only in the prism of this act, which, however radically or existentially it may be understood, is still a human act, which in itself is no kind of surety for the correctness of the appropriation in question, which is by nature fallible and therefore stands in need of criticism, of correction, of critical amendment and repetition. For this reason the creaturely form which the revealing action of God assumes in dogmatics is never that of knowledge attained in a flash, which it would have to be to correspond to the divine gift, but a laborious movement from one partial human insight to another with the intention though with no guarantee of advance.

Βλέπομεν γὰρ ἄρτι δι' ἐσόπτρου ἐν αἰνίγματι ... ἄρτι γινώσκω ἐκ μέρους (1 Cor. 13¹²). And with a like application we may also recall 2 Cor. 4⁷ : Ἔχομεν δὲ τὸν θησαυρὸν τοῦτον ἐν ὀστρακίνοις σκεύεσιν, ἵνα ἡ ὑπερβολὴ τῆς δυνάμεως ᾖ τοῦ θεοῦ καὶ μὴ ἐξ ἡμῶν. *Diximusne aliquid et sonuimus aliquid dignum Dei ? Imo vero nihil me aliud quam dicere voluisse sentio : Si autem dixi, non hoc est, quod dicere volui* (Augustine, *De doctr. Christ.*, I, 6). *Cur non te sentit, Domine Deus, anima mea, si invenit te ? An non invenit, quem invenit esse lucem et veritatem ? . . . An et veritas et lux est, quod vidit, et tamen nondum te vidit, quia vidit te aliquatenus, sed von vidit te, sicuti es ? Domine Deus meus, formator et reformator meus, dic desideranti animae meae, quid aliud es, quam quod vidit ut pure videat quod desiderat* (Anselm of Canterbury, *Prosl.*, 14). *Et ut omne aenigma est sermo obscurus, nodosus, involutus, intellectu difficilis : ita nostra Theologia ratione obiecti est inevidens, complectens mysteria profundissima et in hac mortalitate cognitu difficillima* (Hollaz, *Examen Theol.* acroam., 1707, *Prol.*, I, 8).

The fact that it is in faith that the truth is presupposed to be the known measure of all things means that the truth is in no sense assumed to be to hand. The truth comes, i.e., in the faith in which we begin to know, and cease, and begin again. The results of earlier dogmatic work, and indeed our own results, are basically no more than signs of its coming. They are simply the results of human effort. As such they are a help to, but also the object of, fresh human effort. Dogmatics is possible only as *theologia crucis*, in the act of obedience which is certain in faith, but which for this very reason is humble, always being thrown back to the beginning and having to make a fresh start. It is not possible as an effortless triumph or an intermittent labour. It always takes place on the narrow way which leads from the enacted revelation to the promised revelation.

. . . ἐκ πίστεως εἰς πίστιν (Rom. 1¹⁷). Augustine in an important passage evolves the doctrine that *credere* must precede *intelligere* to the extent that it is established by the *vox de coelo* (*verbum Dei*), but that it must follow it to the extent that it is to be established by the *sermo propheticus* (*verbum meum*), as in Mark 9²². Faith as faith in God stands on its own feet and is the basis of knowledge. Faith as the faith of man requires knowledge and is established by it (*Sermo*, 43, 4–9).

Here our way diverges from that of Roman Catholic dogmatics, and we must also enter a *caveat* against a certain tendency in the older Protestant tradition. Dogmatics is the science of dogma. Only in a subordinate sense, and strictly in conjunction with the primary, is it also the science of dogmas. The task of dogmatics, therefore, is not simply to combine, repeat and transcribe a number of truths of revelation which are already to hand, which have been expressed once and for all, and the wording and meaning of which are authentically defined.

Even on the Roman Catholic view there does seem to be " a true progress of the teaching Church," namely, in knowledge and understanding in the development, application and expression of revealed truth (Diekamp, *Kath. Dogmatik*, 6th ed., Vol. I, 1930, p. 19 f. Cf. Vincent of Lerins and his doctrine of *profectus religionis*, *Common.*, I, 22 f.). In this context, however, the truth of revelation means the " apostolic deposit " infallibly proposed by the teaching office of the Church in the two forms of Holy Scripture and oral apostolic tradition (Diekamp, *op. cit.*, p. 24 f.). This deposit is thus identical with a sum of sacred texts. The task of dogmatics is " to mediate a fuller understanding of these truths by inferences " (*op. cit.*, p. 76 f.). Moreover it is presupposed that the meaning of these truths or texts has already been mediated and authoritatively proclaimed by the teaching office, so that even in this task of understanding there can be no question of anything but transcription in a rather higher sense : *Hinc sacrorum quoque dogmatum is sensus perpetuo est retinendus, quem semel declaravit sancta mater Ecclesia, nec unquam ab eo sensu altioris intelligentiae specie et nomine recedendum* (*Conc. Vatic., Sess.* III, *Constit. de fide cath.*, c. 4).

This only too practicable view, by its direct equation of divine ascription and human appropriation in the dogmas, fails to recognise the divine-human character of the being of the Church. The being of the Church is Jesus Christ, and therefore an indissolubly divine-human person, the action of God towards man in distinction from which human appropriation as attested in the dogmas believed by the Church may be very worthy and respectable but can hardly be called infallible and therefore withdrawn from further enquiry whether this is how it should be. The concept of truths of revelation in the sense of Latin propositions given and sealed once for all with divine authority in both wording and meaning is theologically impossible if it is a fact that revelation is true in the free decision of God which was taken once for all in Jesus Christ, that it is thus strictly future for us, and that it must always become true in the Church in the intractable reality of faith. The freely acting God Himself and alone is the truth of revelation. Our dogmatic labours can and should be guided by results which are venerable because they are attained in the common knowledge of the Church at a specific time. Such results may be seen in the dogmas enshrined in the creeds. But at no point should these replace our dogmatic labours in virtue of their authority. Nor can it ever be the real concern of dogmatics merely to assemble, repeat and define the teaching of the Bible.

This is how Melanchthon seems to have understood the task (*Loci comm.*, 1559, *C.R.*, 21, p. 601). Rather more crudely Heidanus (*Corp. Theol. christ.*, 1686, *Prol.*, 1 f.) taught that Holy Scripture is *non scripta ut systema quoddam, sed historica nobis facta Ecclesiae ab initio mundi ad finem describit.* Hence it is the task of *Loci communes* to present res. *S. Scriptura contentas certo et concinno ordine . . . ut certo methodo res divinas complecti et eas suo ordine collocare possitis et sicut Pharmacopolae solent medicamenta sua certis capsulis distinguere et disponere, ita vos omnia suis quaque locis digerere possitis.*

Exegetical theology investigates biblical teaching as the basis of our talk about God. Dogmatics, too, must constantly keep it in view. But only in God and not for us is the true basis of Christian utterance identical with its true content. Hence dogmatics as such does not ask what the apostles and prophets said but what we must say on the basis of the apostles and prophets. This task is not taken from us because it is first necessary that we should know the biblical basis.

Although exegesis and dogmatics are constantly interwoven in his work, for Calvin too *Institutio religionis christianae* means the direction of Christian thought and speech to its own contemporary responsibility.

As the Church accepts from Scripture, and with divine authority from Scripture alone, the attestation of its own being as the measure of its utterance, it finds itself challenged to know itself, and therefore even and precisely in face of this foundation of all Christian utterance to ask, with all the seriousness of one who does not yet know, what Christian utterance can and should say to-day.

Nam et ego tecum credo et inconcusse credo . . . sed nunc molimur id quod in fidem recepimus, etiam intelligendo scire ac tenere firmissimum (Augustine, *De lib. arb.*, I, 3 6; cf. 4, 10). *Quod enim hortante ipso quaerimus eodem ipso demonstrante inveniemus, quantum haec in hac vita et a nobis talibus inveniri queat* (*ib.*, II, 2, 6). The purpose of Anselm of Canterbury regarding the question raised by his interlocutor is *non tam ostendere, quam tecum quaerere* (*Cur Deus homo ?*, I, 2). His aim in *intellectus fidei* is not a repetition of the believer's *legere*, but a genuine *intus legere* of Scripture and dogma, though not on the basis of their accepted authoritative givenness : . . . *quatenus auctoritate Scripturae penitus nihil in ea* (scil. *meditatione*) *persuaderetur* (*Monol. Prol.*) . . . *ut quod fide teneamus . . . sine Scripturae auctoritate probari possit* (*Ep. de incarn.*, 6). For the distinction between dogmatic enquiry and authoritative quotation we might also refer to the well-known though not wholly unobjectionable formula of Anselm : *remoto Christo . . . quasi nihil sciatur de Christo* (*Cur Deus homo ?, Prol.*). *Quaedam disputatio ordinatur ad removendam dubitationem an ita sit ; et in tali disputatione theologica maxime utendum est auctoritatibus, quas recipiunt illi, cum quibus disputatur. . . . Quaedam vero disputatio est magistralis in scholis non ad removendum errorem, sed ac instruendum auditores, ut inducantur ad intellectum veritatis quam intendit ; et tunc oportet rationibus inniti investigantibus veritatis radicem et facientibus scire, quomodo sit verum, quod dicitur* (Thomas Aquinas, *Quodlib.*, 4, 18).

This aspect of the matter, i.e., the necessity of dogmatics as an enquiry, was in the minds of the orthodox Lutherans when they used to distinguish theology quite expressly from Holy Scripture as *ex verbo Dei exstructa* (e.g., J. Gerhard, *Loci comm.*, 1610, *Prooem.*, 31) *docens . . . ex divina revelatione* (Baier, *Comp. Theol. pos.*, 1686, *Prol.*, 38), etc. (So, too, among the Reformed writers, Burmann, *Syn. Theol.*, 1678, I, 2, 41.)

3. DOGMATICS AS AN ACT OF FAITH

Dogmatics is a part of the work of human knowledge. But this part of the work of human knowledge stands under a particularly decisive condition. Like all work of human knowledge, it naturally demands the intellectual faculties of attentiveness and concentration, of understanding and appraisal. Like all serious work of human knowledge, it demands the best will to utilise these faculties and ultimately the giving of the whole man to this utilisation. Over and above this, however, it demands Christian faith, which does not simply come of itself even with the deepest and purest surrender to this task. Dogmatics is a function of the Christian Church. The Church tests itself by essaying it. To the Church is given the promise of the criterion of Christian faith, namely, the revelation of God. The Church can pursue dogmatics. Even in the Church dogmatics need not be the work of a special dogmatic science. But there is no possibility of dogmatics at all outside the Church. To be in the Church, however, is to be called with others by Jesus Christ. To act in the Church is to act in obedience to this call. This obedience to the call of Christ is faith. In faith the judgment of God is acknowledged and His grace extolled. In faith self-examination is necessary in view of responsibility before God. Faith grasps the promise that we shall be led into all truth (Jn. 16[13]). Faith knows God. Faith is the determination of human action by the being of the Church and therefore by Jesus Christ, by the gracious address of God to man. In faith, and only in faith, human action is related to the being of the Church, to the action of God in revelation and reconciliation. Hence dogmatics is quite impossible except as an act of faith, in the determination of human action by listening to Jesus Christ and as obedience to Him. Without faith it would be irrelevant and meaningless. Even in the case of the most exact technical imitation of what the Church does, or the most sincere intention of doing what the Church does, it would be idle speculation without any content of knowledge.

H. Scholz (*Z.d.Z.*, 1931, p. 34) poses the question, expressly in relation to dogmatics : " Can we or can we not construct a form of Christianity, and do so in such a way that it is worth our while to contemplate this form and immerse ourselves in it, unless for better or for worse we ourselves actually believe in this

Christianity ? " His own answer, which fortunately is only indirect, is to the effect " that we may confidently evolve from Platonism or Aristotelianism, from Leibniz or Kant, a picture which ought to impress any who are susceptible to such spiritual pictures, and in such a way that for better or for worse we are neither Platonists nor Aristotelians, neither Leibnizians nor Kantians, but what it is our destiny to be." Our comment is that, so long as we understand by Christianity the creaturely and cultural reality of a view of life and the world alongside Platonism, Aristotelianism, etc., and so long as we understand by a form or picture of Christianity the representation of it in its creatureliness according to the laws of the knowledge of such a reality, then the construction of an impressive form of Christianity without believing in it for better or for worse, is certainly an attractive and rewarding possibility. But there can be no question of this in dogmatics. In dogmatics Christianity means the proper content of talk about God ventured in the fear of God. Form means the statements in which we formulate our provisional answers in investigation of this content. The problem of impressiveness for the spiritually susceptible is bluntly replaced by that of responsibility to God. The third point reminds us that in dogmatics there can be no construction outside the real encounter between God and man, which is faith. Nor can the real content, i.e., Jesus Christ, be simply equated with creaturely reality. For He is revelation, divine-human reality. If there is such a reality, and if there is knowledge of it, as the Church and dogmatics presuppose, then this knowledge can only be that of faith, and we have good reason to ask if faith is really faith unless it is for better or for worse. *Omnis recta cognitio Dei ab obedientia nascitur* (Calvin, *Instit.*, I, 6, 2). Plato's claim to make us Platonists might be transformed without loss into an impressive exposition of Platonism. Christ's claim to obedience is identical with the being of the Church and cannot therefore be evaded by any dogmatics which is not prepared to forswear itself and become a mere survey of human thought. Dogmatics does not presuppose that it is our destiny to believe as Christians, but rather that our destiny not to do so is not final, and therefore that we shall not be disobedient to the heavenly voice (Ac. 26[19]),

Faith, however, is not a determination of human action which man can give to it at will or maintain at will once it is received. On the contrary, it is the gracious address of God to man, the free personal presence of Jesus Christ in his activity. Hence, if we say that dogmatics presupposes faith, or the determination of human action by hearing and as obedience to the being of the Church, we say that at every step and with every statement it presupposes the free grace of God which may at any time be given or refused as the object and meaning of this human action. It always rests with God and not with us whether our hearing is real hearing and our obedience real obedience, whether our dogmatics is blessed and sanctified as knowledge of the true content of Christian utterance or whether it is idle speculation.

It is in this light that we have to ponder what was once much discussed as the demand for regeneration or conversion in the theologian and what is to-day being debated afresh as the prerequisite of what is called existentiality in theological thinking. Urgent warnings that theologising is powerless unless there is a relationship between the theme and the theologian in which the true and total man is claimed may be found already in Anselm, who tells us that the *credere* underlying *intelligere* cannot be merely a *credere id* but must be a *credere in id, quod credi debet (Monol.*, 76–78). *Rectitudo fidei et intellectus* necessarily involves a *rectitudo volendi (De concordia, qu.* III, 2 and 6). *Non solum ad intelligendum altiora prohibetur mens ascendere sine fide et mandatorum Dei obedientia, sed etiam aliquando, datus intellectus subtrahitur . . . neglecta bona conscientia (Ep. de incarn.,* 1). *Non est . . . securus transitus a scientia ad sapientiam; oportet ergo medium ponere, scilicet sanctitatem* (Bonaventura, *In Hex.,* XIX, 3). Against certain supposed " mystical " theologians, whose actual experience was the very opposite of all *theologia negativa,* and who knew nothing of the Christian's love for death and hell, the younger Luther wrote the words : *Vivendo, immo moriendo et damnando fit theologus, non intelligendo, legendo aut speculando (Op. in Psalm. W.A.,* 5, p. 163, 1, 28). " Doctors of arts, medicine, law and philosophy, can be made by the pope, the emperor, and the universities ; but be quite sure that no one can make a doctor of Holy Scripture save only the Holy Ghost from heaven, as Christ says in John vi : ' They must all be taught of God himself.' Now the Holy Ghost does not ask after red or brown robes, or what is showy, nor whether a man is young or old, lay or clerical, monastic or secular, virgin or married. Indeed, He once spake by an ass against the prophet that rode on it. Would God we were worthy that such doctors be given us. . . ." (Luther, *An d. chr. Adel deutch. Nation v. d. chr. Standes Besserung,* 1520, *W.A.,* 6, p. 460, 1. 28), Even Melanchthon (e.g., *Apol. Conf. Aug., De justif.,* 9 and 37, *C.R.,* 27, 430 and 434) was ready to insist that true knowledge of salvation is not gained by empty speculations, but only *in agone conscientiae et in acie,* The theological significance of all this is brought out in the age of orthodoxy by the fact that *theologia concretive considerata,* i,e,. as event rather than concept, is described as *habitus* θεόσδοτος *per verbum a Spiritu sancto homini collatus* (J. Gerhard, *Loci theol.,* 1610, *Prooem.,* 31). It can be said : *Post lapsum non nascuntur theologi, sed fiunt scil. a Deo docti per verbum scriptum* (Quenstedt, *Theol. did. pol.,* 1685, I, *cap.* 1, *sect.* 2, *qu.* 2, *ekth.* 2). Thus true theology is an actual determination and claiming of man by the acting God. That there is at this point an acute danger of anthropologising theological knowledge is shown by the rather equivocal assertion of Anselm that if we compare the proclamation and hearing of the Word of God with sowing *(agricultura),* then the *semen,* i.e., the Word of God, is *immo non verbum sed sensus qui percipitur per verbum (de Concordia, qu.* III, 6). For here there is at least the threat of the unfortunate transition from a divine determining to a human determination, if not expressly to a human achievement, as was the opinion of Bonaventura, who understood and could describe that *sanctitas* as a *vita timorata, inpolluta, religiosa, aedificatoria (In Hex.,* XIX, 20 f.). If we follow up this line, then the *sensus,* the human determination, the experience and attitude of the knowing subject are made the criterion of theological knowledge. It was obviously in an attempt to avoid this danger that the middle and later orthodoxy (e.g. Quenstedt, *op. cit., ekth.* 5 ; Hollaz, *Ex. theol. acroam.,* 1707, *Prol.* 1, 18–21 ; Buddeus, *Instit. theol. dogm.,* 1724, I, 1, 49) made a distinction between objective theological *habitus* on the one side and faith or the regeneration of the theologian on the other : *Constat, habitum Theologiae reapse separare posse a fide salvifica* (Heidan, *Corp. Theol. christ.,* 1686, L, 1, p. 3). It hardly need be said that this is not in keeping with the thought of Luther. It carries with it the far worse implication that faith, regeneration and conversion are now to be regarded quite definitely as a human experience and attitude. How little certainty there was in the whole matter is shown by the fact that it was thought necessary to hedge around with every conceivable reservation and restriction the possibility of an unconverted theologian living only by the *habitus,* i.e., of a *theologia irregenitorum,* which had to be admitted on the basis of the distinction. We need not be surprised that Pietism abandoned the distinction and demanded of the student of theology at least a serious striving for personal conversion (A. H. Francke, *Method. stud. theol.*, 1723, *cap.* 2). But the very fact that it can speak only of striving is an indication how self-evident has become the idea that faith is to be decisively regarded as a determination of human reality. So far as concerns this subjective presupposition, Rationalism (e.g., G. J. Planck, *Einl. i. d. theol. Wissensch.*, 1794, Vol. I, p. 62 f.) was not prepared to insist on the need for Christian religiosity, but only for religiosity in general. But this did not help the situation. And when Schleiermacher as a theologian was prepared to speak, " out of the irresistible inner necessity of his nature " (*Reden ü. d. Rel.*, 1799, p. 5), only of that which was " the innermost impulse of his being " (*loc. cit.*), thus expounding " his own view as an object for the rest " (*op. cit.*, p. 182), he had obviously lost altogether any sense of what Anselm, Luther and Melanchthon were after with their demand for *sensus* and *experientia* as the presupposition of true theology. " It may be presupposed that no one becomes a theologian, or makes the science of the Christian religion his calling, without having an inner relation to religion or Christianity, just as no one will pursue any branch of science without a love for its theme "—such is their concern as translated into the language of 19th-century Liberalism (H. Mulert, *Evangelische Kirchen und theologische Fakultäten*, 1930, p. 16 f.). The anthropologising of theology was complete. And it is a serious question whether the same is not to be said of the existential element which is demanded to-day from theological thinking and utterance under the influence of Kierkegaard, but supremely if sometimes unconsciously in continuation of the Pietist tradition. It is perhaps laughable though highly suspicious that in line with the contemporary vogue even G. Wobbermin has set out to reinterpret his theology, which is in no sense either interested in Kierkegaard or orientated to him, as a theology of existential religious psychology (*Wort Gottes und evangelischer Glaube*, 1931, p. 14 f.). If this existential element is sought in the fact that the statements of theology must be accounts of the human situation of the theologian as radically revealed in faith ; if it is demanded that its utterances must be " the cry of a man who like Christophorus breaks under the far too heavy burden of what must now in any circumstances take place in modern Germany " ; if, e.g., the proposition that we are all sinners is not to be a mere phrase, but " I am to speak it for concrete reasons, being brought by a definite occasion to an awareness that this hopeless failure of mine springs from a self-centredness . . . which I share with all my fellows " (K. Heim, *Glaube und Denken*, 1931, p. 409), then these are psychologisms and legalisms under the yoke of which we do not have to bend and should not do so. The time has come to go back with a new understanding to the pre-Pietist doctrine of the theological *habitus* in virtue of which the theologian is what he is by the grace of God quite irrespective of his greater or lesser likeness to Christophorus, and without any need for existential outcry, etc. A reaction in this sense, a new relating of Christophorus to Christ, has indeed appeared already. We have been told afresh that " theological statements are possible only on the basis of the presence of the Gospel, the message and proclamation." A proposition with theological intention is one which is true " quite apart from the existential position of the speaker, receiving its meaning for the hearers only on the basis of this independence " (K. F. Schumann, *Der Gottesgedanke und der Zerfall der Moderne*, 1929, p. 348 f.), Or again with a sharp polemical application : " The ἀκοὴ πίστεως is not to be understood as the existential decision of faith in apprehension of the promise " (H. M. Müller, *Glaube und Erfahrung bei Luther*, 1929, p. 90). " Where the existential element is in any way made the theme of theology, service is offered to the *humanum*. . . . There is only one alternative : Either we understand our own existence as being in faith, or we await God's contingent visitation in the real end of this existence " (*op. cit.*, p. 187). This reaction is timely and useful. Yet the original demand of Anselm, Luther and Melanchthon, in which the older and newer doctrine of the *theologia regenitorum*, of existential theology, has its *particula veri*, must not be lost to view. Even if only from the standpoint of the end, or from without, God's contingent visitation does affect the existence of man, and therefore the gift of its promise by faith is a divine determination and claiming of the concrete being of man, of myself. Without this, theology would become the irrelevant wisdom of spectators outside the Church. There would be knowledge only in the dependent form of an imitative formal participation in the knowledge of the Church and faith. If the latter were to fail, then, as Anselm rightly stated, such a theology would lose its power of knowledge. But theology neither does nor can at any time find human safeguards against the danger of becoming the irrelevant wisdom of spectators outside the Church, and therefore a-theology. Faith, regeneration, conversion, existential thinking on the basis of a preceding existential encounter, are no doubt indispensable prerequisites of dogmatic work, yet not to the extent that they imply an experience and attitude, a desire and activity, a knowledge and achievement of the theologian, so that his theology is a personal cry, an account of his biographical situation, but to the extent that they imply the grace of divine predestination, the free gift of the Word and Holy Spirit, the act of calling the Church, which must always come upon the theologian from the acting God in order that he may really be what he does and what his name suggests.

Naturally, the Church can and should undertake and execute its own self-examination of itself with the human application of human means. But whether in so doing it acts as the Church and therefore knows God in faith ; whether the result of its action is true and important criticism and correction and not a worse perversion of Christian utterance, does not depend upon itself. Clearly, the presence of any distinctive and decisive determination of dogmatics, the decision as to what is or is not true in dogmatics, is always a matter of the divine election of grace. In this respect the fear of the Lord must always be the beginning of wisdom. This is the often discovered difficulty of all theology, especially dogmatic theology.

Cognovi, explicationem dogmatum Ecclesiae propter multas causas opus esse difficillimum et quamquam necessarium est, tamen plenum esse ingentium periculorum (Melanchthon, *Loci communes*, 1559, *C.R.*, 21, 602). It was more than a monkish trick of style when Anselm referred to the *imbecillitas scientiae meae* (*Cur Deus homo ?*, I, 25) and Bonaventura to the *pauper portiuncula scientiolae nostrae* (*Breviloq., Prooem.*), and when on the first page of his *Sentences* Peter Lombard compared his achievement to the widow's mite or the two pence which the Good Samaritan gave to the inn-keeper with the promise to pay him more when he returned. The story is also told of Thomas Aquinas, whose *Summa theologica* obviously remained a torso, that when asked to write more he replied : " Reginald, I cannot, for all that I have written is like chaff to me. I hope that God will soon put an end to my life and thinking " (M. Grabmann, *Das Seelenleben des hl. Thomas v. Aq.*, 1924, p. 51). As against this, the other story that when he was engaged in the christological part of the work Christ appeared to him with the words : *Bene scripsisti de me, Thoma !* seems to be less in accord with the facts ! Thomas himself was rightly prepared to leave it to eschatology to invest the *doctor ecclesiae* with a halo (*S. theol.*, III, qu. 96, art. 6).

C.D.—B *

Dogmatics must always be undertaken as an act of penitence and obedience. But this is possible only as it trusts in the uncontrollable presence of its ontic and noetic basis, in the revelation of God promised to the Church, and in the power of faith apprehending the promise. This is no less true in the case of the teacher than the scholar, of the author of dogmatic works than the reader. The act of faith, which means, however, its basis in the divine predestination, the free act of God on man and his work, is always the condition by which dogmatic work is made possible but by which it is also called in question with final seriousness.

Paul Althaus finds the problem of theology as a science in the conflict between critical attitude and Church connexion, which are both necessary to the theologian but which seem to be irreconcilably opposed (*Grundriss der Dogmatik*, 1929, § 1). There is a lack of true and final seriousness in this problem. As Althaus himself shows, it can be solved on both sides in a comparatively easy and amicable way. The older theologians rightly found the difficulty of theology, and sought to overcome it, on a different level : *Non ego te duco, sed ille, de quo loquimur, sine quo nihil possumus, nos ducit, ubicumque viam veritatis teneamus* (Anselm, *Cur Deus homo ?*, II, 9). *In Theologia . . . datur subiectum plane divinum, quod est . . . omni re prius, ut nullam principiati rationem habere possit, unde . . . fit, ut duas hasce rationes simul contineat, sitque subjectum, de quo agit Theologia et simul etiam ejus principium* (F. Turrettini, *Inst. Theol. el.*, I, 1679, L, 1, qu. 5, 9). *Ille enim solus idoneus est de se testis, qui quod sibi gratum est, docere nos possit et cui nihil gratum esse potest, nisi a se profectum et naturae suae conveniens. Quod quale sit nemo novit nisi ipse. At id quomodo nobis innotescat, nisi nobis ab ipso patefiat et reveletur ?* (Heidanus, *Corp. Theol. chr.*, 1686, L, 1, p. 7). *Quemadmodum in spiritualibus nemo mortalium sibi ipse quidquam absque gratiae viribus aut dare aut tribuere, ita multo minus ea largire potest, quae ad theologiae habitum requiruntur* (Buddeus, *Instit. Th. dogm.*, 1724, I, 1, 51). In his work *Die Entstehung der chr. Theologie und des kirchl. Dogmas*, 1927, p. 54 f., 87 f., A. v. Harnack explains in relation to both past and present that there are and always have been two kinds of theology. The first is a charismatic theology from within. In this, speaking from the standpoint of a believer, the theologian is convinced of its truth by its inner power of persuasion, and is never without an awareness " that he can speak as a theologian only with the assistance of the Spirit of God, and that his work is thus charismatically determined." Paul is the founder of this kind of theology, but it can never become either ecclesiastical or scientific. It shapes confession and preaching, but not fellowship. The second is a theology from without. It " places the relevant religion in the circle of other objects of knowledge, and describes its reality and truth accordingly to generally valid historical, psychological and theoretical principles of knowledge." Its fathers are the 2nd-century apologists, and it alone creates fellowship and can be ecclesiastical and scientific. " We may bewail this, since the inadequacy of such a theology is manifest ; but no one can alter the fact, and he who tries to do so destroys and confuses theology. His proper task is to preach." It is only fitting that this final declaration of one whom I also honour as a teacher should be allowed to speak for itself without either commentary or criticism.

Humanly speaking, there is no way to overcome this fundamental difficulty which afflicts theology alone among the sciences, and dogmatics alone within theology. There is no feasible way of creating this specifically decisive condition of dogmatics. We may summon up good intentions, but even the best of intentions are of no avail at this point. Nor can we evoke of ourselves the Christian faith which decisively constitutes the theological *habitus*. The popular suspicion of theology, and especially of dogmatics, is only too well founded. There always seems to be an element of presumption in it, and all the exertions seem to lead to such meagre results. We always seem to be handling an intractable object with inadequate means. And this appearance is too solidly grounded in the nature of the study itself to be permanently overcome by a mere change of methods.

The mystery of the *ubi et quando visum est Deo* (*Conf. Aug.*, Art. 5 ; cf. for an understanding of this statement the passages adduced by Hans Engelland, *Melanchthon*, 1931, p. 568 f.) has accompanied not only Christian talk about God in general, but dogmatics in particular, through all the stages of its history. Nor can it be any different in the future.

We maintain that humanly speaking there is nothing to alleviate the difficulty. We simply confess the mystery which underlies it, and we merely repeat the statement that dogmatics is possible only as an act of faith, when we point to prayer as the attitude without which there can be no dogmatic work.

Hoc intelligere quis hominum dabit homini ? quis angelus angelo ? quis angelus homini ? A te petatur, in te quaeratur, ad te pulsetur : sic accipietur, sic invenietur, sic aperietur (Augustine, *Conf.*, XIII, 38, 53). *Non solum admonendi sunt studiosi venerabilium Litterarum, ut in scripturis sanctis genera locutionem sciant* . . . *verum etiam, quod est praecipium et maxime necessarium, orent ut intelligant. In eis quippe Litteris, quarum studiosi sunt, legunt quoniam Dominus dat sapientiam et a facie ejus scientia et intellectus a quo et ipsum studium, si pietate praeditum est, acceperunt* (*De doct. chr.*, III, 37). We are already reminded of Anselm's *Proslogion*, 1—a passage to which we shall return in § 6, 4. Thomas Aquinas set the following prayer at the head of his *Summa theologica :* *Concede mihi quaeso, misericors Deus, quae tibi sunt placita ardenter concupiscere, prudenter investigare, veraciter agnoscere et perfecte implere ad laudem nominis tui.* Relevant, too, is the intention of A. H. Francke in his treatment *De oratione* in a whole section of his directions for the study of theology. Nor is it to be regarded as baroque adornment that Hollaz transforms his treatment of each specific *Locus* into a *Suspirium*, his talk about God becoming quite expressly address to God.

Prayer can be the recognition that we accomplish nothing by our intentions, even though they be intentions to pray. Prayer can be the expression of our human willing of the will of God. Prayer can signify that for good or evil man justifies God and not himself. Prayer can be the human answer to the divine hearing already granted, the epitome of the true faith which we cannot assume of ourselves. We do not speak of true prayer if we say " must " instead of " can." According to Rom. 8²⁶ᶠ the way from " can " to " must " is wrapped in the mystery at the gates of which we here stand. With this reference we do not give anyone a means by which he can count on succeeding in his work. It must be said, however, that it is hard to see how else there can be successes in this work but on the basis of divine correspondence to this human attitude : " Lord, I believe ; help thou mine unbelief."

THE TASK OF PROLEGOMENA TO DOGMATICS

Prolegomena to dogmatics is our name for the introductory part of dogmatics in which our concern is to understand its particular way of knowledge.

1. THE NECESSITY OF DOGMATIC PROLEGOMENA

Prolegomena to a science, in so far as they are necessary and possible, will always consist decisively in discussions and expositions of how knowledge is attained in it. By prolegomena to dogmatics (*praecognita Theologiae*, as many older writers called it with even greater fulness of meaning), we understand the attempt to give an explicit account of the particular way of knowledge taken in dogmatics, or, as we might also say, of the particular point from which we are to look, think and judge in dogmatics. It cannot be taken for granted that this question can be explicitly raised and answered, and therefore that there can be such a thing as dogmatic prolegomena. Or again, the question might be answered quite simply by the manner in which dogmatics goes its way. The assumptions made might perhaps emerge and prove themselves in application. What is said might obviate any need for a foreword. The lack of prolegomena, or at least of extensive prolegomena, might well indicate, not a naive attitude, but one which is scientifically mature and well-considered. Nor need such an attitude rest on an illusion. It might well have a solid basis in the simplicity of truth, in supreme scientific soundness. *Ab esse ad posse valet consequentia* might well be its justification. It must be remembered that the great representatives of early and mediaeval dogmatics were sometimes content with the briefest reflections on the way of knowledge taken by them.

For instance, in the Ἔκδοσις ἀκριβὴς τῆς ὀρθοδόξου πίστεως of John Damascene we find two introductory chapters on the knowability of God which might be claimed as prolegomena. Peter Lombard begins his *Sentences* with a short preface in which there is no discussion of method. In the *Summa theologica* Thomas Aquinas has a first *Quaestio* with ten articles on the concept of *doctrina sacra*, and in his *Summa c. gent.* there are 8 introductory sections on faith and knowledge. Among the Reformers Zwingli in his *Comm. de vera et falsa religione*, 1525, kept to the same tradition with a brief discussion of the term *religio*. His *Fidei ratio*, 1530, plunges at once into the doctrine of the Trinity after an address to the

Emperor, and his *Fidei christianae expositio*, 1531, follows up the address to the French king with a development of the concept of God. Among more recent writers A. Schlatter, *Das christliche Dogma*, 2nd ed., 1923, is able to dispense almost completely with prolegomena.

But the phenomenon is not unequivocal. It might be explained by a profound realism, but it might also be explained by a less profound arrogance and self-assurance. From the theological standpoint, both possibilities have to be taken into account, and we must not be over-hasty in deciding between them.

I still think it rash to conclude that in the rapid application of older writers to their main task we have the expression of a *theologia gloriae* which does not see its own difficulties (cf. E. Brunner, *Z.d.Z.*, 1930, p. 397). On the other hand, I fear that in the first edition of the present book (p. 10 f.) I myself was guilty of a romanticising philosophy of history, which I must now reject, when I described the earlier procedure as that of a classical age and our modern approach as that of a decadent age.

The situation of the Church which is the sphere of dogmatic work is not always the same but lays various special conditions on this work. What is now forbidden did not always have to be. On the other hand, what was once permitted may now be forbidden. We are now forbidden to take up the main content of dogmatics without express and explicit discussion of the problem of the way of knowledge. The only question is—and it is decisively important—on what ground this is forbidden, and therefore on what ground dogmatic prolegomena are necessary.

At this point the customary procedure, followed with new zeal in modern work, is to indicate the change in general cultural awareness and the general world-picture which has taken place in the last 300 years and called theology as such in question. Attention is drawn to the wave of paganism which obviously seems to be engulfing everything and to carry with it a particular threat to the Church and theology. Note is taken of the radicalism of rational thought which supposedly distinguishes our age from all others and which negates all revelation as such.

" Already in the second half of the seventeenth century, and even more so in the first half of the eighteenth, so many questions, objections and doubts were brought by naturalists, rationalists and free-thinkers against the doctrines of the Christian faith and their scholarly presentation that a short introduction was not enough and preliminary discussion became indispensable before dogmatics could begin " (Carl Daub, *Prolegomena zur Dogmatik*, 1839, p. 3). " The problem to-day is not the nature of God but His existence, not what is revealed but whether there is such a thing as revelation, not rationalistic corruption at individual points but the questioning of the miracle of revelation as such. It is the problem of the sign and norm of all Christian theology, of the concept of revelation and not its contents. In short, it is the problem of reason and revelation " (E. Brunner, *Z.d.Z.*, 1930, p. 414).

This altered situation, we are told, is what makes dogmatic prolegomena necessary to-day. If dogmatics is to be existential theology and not to fall victim to a " dangerous Chinese Wall mentality," then in addition to its primary task as the reflection of the Church on the Word of God there must be recognised and tackled a second task which arises out of this situation.

In his essay " Die andere Aufgabe der Theologie " (*Z.d.Z.*, 1929, p. 255 f.), to which I particularly refer, E. Brunner proposes to give to this preparatory dogmatic discipline the name of eristics rather than apologetics. But does he not make out the older apologetics to be worse than it was, in order to be able to mark himself off from it, when he characterises it *in toto* as a " feeble and anxious defensive before a tribunal of reason, as the self-justification of Christians before a world which has lost confidence in them " (*op. cit.*, p. 258) ? Is the difference between C. E. Luthardt's *Apologetische Vorträge* (1870 f.), for example, and Karl Heim's *Glauben und Denken* (1931), any other than that between the better and the worse, or the outmoded and the modern ? Would it not be clearer to accept the name apologetics without apology ? Eristics is hardly likely to escape the scourge of Overbeck with which the earlier apologetics is chastised according to Brunner.

On this view the task of dogmatics consists in the " conflict against the self-assurance of the modern spirit," " against the rational axiom of the final efficacy of reason." It consists in the " contesting of this reason which is self-sufficient and therefore opposes the Word," and in the " liberation of the reason which in this illusion and isolation of reason secretly yearns for the divine Thou."

Karl Heim says much the same thing with rather greater restraint (*op. cit.*, p. 433) : " In accordance with the lowly position of service . . . occupied by knowledge in relation to life, only a negative task can be ascribed to Christian philosophy. It must deprive man of assurance. It must mercilessly reveal in its impossibility all that man has always undertaken, and thus point him to a position of reserve in which he is assured in face of the question of eternity constantly posed to him afresh."

Nevertheless, there is " in man a point of contact for the divine message which is not disturbed by sin." There is a " questing after God " which is natural to man.

By this concept of a point of contact, which is so important to him, E. Brunner understands the " self-evident knowledge which man can have even as an unbeliever and which as such is taken up into his believing " (" Theologie und Ontologie," *Z.Th.Z.*, 1931, p. 112).

In connexion with this point of contact it has " to be shown how by the Word of God human reason is partly disclosed to be the source of error which is hostile to life, and partly fulfilled in its own incomplete searching."

E. Brunner, *Z.d.Z.*, 1929, p. 257, 260, 262, 264, 267, 273 f. Cf. also *Z.d.Z.*, 1930, p. 398, 410 ; *Gott und Mensch*, 1930, p. 55 f.

This basis of the necessity of dogmatic prolegomena is to be rejected for three reasons.

1. It is to be rejected because there is no theological foundation for the assumed difference between our own and earlier times. Has there ever been an age in which theology has not basically confronted a radical negation of the revelation believed in the Church? Have not antiquity and the Middle Ages, as theologians realised only too well, had their rationalists, atheists and secularists as forerunners of our specifically modern heathenism? If we are concerned to-day for the tactical situation of belief in revelation, was it not much more seriously threatened in the second half of the 18th century? Above all, did the plenitude of gods, demons and miracles which distinguished the ancient view of the world from our own really signify from the Christian standpoint a true gain as compared with the dedivinisation which marks the present time? Did the pre-Kantian and pre-Copernican cultural consciousness, in which there was more place than in our own for this or that revelation, or for revelation in general, genuinely make easier the situation of the Christian Church and its dogmatics, and thus constitute a serious reason for the paucity of prolegomena in earlier writers? On the other hand, has the modern cultural consciousness and view of the world, with its particular threat to all revelation, to revelation as a whole and in general, really created for Christian dogmatics a situation of greater peril in which there is a very different kind of need for assurance and debate? Both questions could be given an affirmative answer if the revelation believed in the Church were to be understood as a specific instance within the genus of revelation as a whole and in general. But this is not so, if we may provisionally make this simple affirmation. Knowledge of the revelation believed in the Church does not stand or fall with the general religious possibility that is made easier by the ancient view of things and more difficult by the modern. On the contrary, the struggle between the unbelieving reason of man and the revelation believed in the Church has always been with fundamentally the same seriousness the problem of Christian utterance in general and of dogmatics in particular. Hence we need not regard the tragedy of modern godlessness as anything out of the ordinary, nor treat it as tragically as is presupposed in this conception of the necessity of dogmatic prolegomena.

2. This conception is also mistaken, however, because it carries with it a complex of problems for dogmatic prolegomena which results in the abandonment rather than the serious acceptance of the task of dogmatics. In dogmatics the Church has to measure its talk about God by the standard of its own being, i.e., of divine revelation. Its talk about God, however, is that of the intrinsically godless reason of man which is inimical to belief. At every point, therefore, dogmatics is

a struggle between this reason of man and the revelation believed in the Church. This struggle, however, takes place in the Church itself, so that it is not orientated to the contradiction of reason but to the declaration of revelation. Its interest is not in the exhibition of a point of contact for the divine message to man but wholly and utterly in the divine message itself as it has gone out and been received. Even its question of knowledge cannot, then, be put as follows : How is human knowledge of revelation possible ?—as though there were doubt whether revelation is known, or as though insight into the possibility of knowledge of divine revelation were to be expected from investigation of human knowledge. It can only take this form : What is true human knowledge of divine revelation ?—on the assumption that revelation itself creates of itself the necessary point of contact in man. But if this relationship is set aside, if the contradiction of human reason is made the subject of enquiry and its overcoming the goal, the sphere of the Church is abandoned and " another task " is indeed substituted for the task of dogmatics.

" Eristic theology is distinguished from dogmatic by the fact that it has more regard to the one with whom it speaks about faith, that it addresses itself more . . . to his resistance, and that to this extent it speaks more *ad hominem* " (E. Brunner, *Z.d.Z.*, 1929, p. 269). As though dogmatics were speaking rather to angels ! But if there is an emphatic intention of speaking " to men," not merely the dogmatic attitude but the theological attitude in general is jeopardised.

However legitimate or possible this other task may be, the task of dogmatics is set aside when it is pursued. No progress is thus made towards the answering of its own specific question of knowledge nor towards the establishment of its own body of knowledge. Undertaken in relation to this complex of problems, prolegomena to dogmatics do not so much lead up to the real work of dogmatics as lead away from it.

Nor is it merely the zeal of the discoverer which leads Emil Brunner, particularly in his 1929 essay, to set the work of real dogmatics in a very unfavourable light as compared with that of eristics.

3. It must also be asked, however, whether in this conception of the necessity of dogmatic prolegomena too little justice is not done even to the concern in which it clearly has its basis, namely, the " responsibility and relevance " (E. Brunner, *Z.d.Z.*, 1930, p. 397) of theological thinking. Is it really going to protect dogmatics from isolation, and secure for it the undoubtedly desirable connexion with the unbelieving contemporary world, if it loses sight of its theme at the very first step and with mysterious omnipotence applies itself to the strange task of " shattering the axiom of reason " (E. Brunner, *Z.d.Z.*, 1929, p. 265) ? We do not think so. Theological thinking which by the grace of God is truly responsible and relevant, and stands in true connexion with contem-

porary society, will even to-day show itself to be such by not allowing itself to be drawn into discussion of its basis, of the question of the existence of God or of revelation. On the contrary, it will refrain from attempted self-vindication as its theme demands, and thus show its responsibility and relevance by simply fulfilling itself as thinking on this basis, and therefore by simply existing as the witness of faith against unbelief. There can be no question, of course, that with the Christian Church generally dogmatics, too, has everywhere to speak in the antithesis of faith to unbelief and therefore apologetically and polemically. But there has never been any effective apologetics or polemics of faith against unbelief except that which is not deliberately planned, which cannot possibly be planned, which simply happens as God Himself acknowledges the witness of faith. There are three reasons why all planned apologetics and polemics have obviously been irresponsible, irrelevant and therefore ineffective.

(*a*) In such apologetics faith must clearly take unbelief seriously. Hence it cannot take itself with full seriousness. Secretly or openly, therefore, it ceases to be faith. What unbelief expects of faith is quite simply that it should be an event. It is not in our hands to produce this event. But faith is certainly not an event in conscious wrestling with unbelief. Does not the credal statement concerning the remission of sins itself forbid any discussion in which the unbelief of the partner in discussion is taken seriously, and he is therefore addressed as a worldling and riveted to his unbelief ? Is there really any hope even apagogically that in this way he will be taught the injustice of his prejudices against faith ?

(*b*) In all independently ventured apologetics and polemics there may be discerned the opinion that dogmatics has done its work.

Karl Heim begins the preface to his *Glaube und Denken*, 1931, with the astonishing statement : " We have enough dogmatic handbooks, which provide excellent introductions to the teaching of the Evangelical Church." Enough ? Excellent ?

The theologian who gives himself to these crafts is obviously of the opinion that he has both the time and the authority to abandon the concern for dogmatics, and instead of working at the thing itself to begin to discuss it with others. This confident distraction is quite out of place, and cannot in the long run or at bottom succeed in making itself convincing.

(*c*) An independent eristics at least runs the risk that once its task is completed dogmatics will think that its conflict with unbelief has been brought to an end in the form of such prolegomena, and that it will thus lose the necessary awareness of the constant exposure to assault of all its statements. In other words, dogmatics may well come to act as an eristics which is *praenumerando* assured, and thus be guilty of a genuine Chinese Wall mentality, the building of the Great Wall of China being obviously a thoroughly eristic enterprise.

Theology is genuinely and effectively apologetic and polemical to the extent that its proper work, which cannot be done except at the heart of the conflict between faith and unbelief, is recognised, empowered and blessed by God as the witness of faith, but not to the extent that it adopts particular forms in which it finally becomes only too clear to the opposing partner that it is either deceiving him when it proposes to deal with him on the ground of common presuppositions, or that it is not quite sure of its own cause in so doing. Either way, there can be no shattering of the axiom of reason along these lines, but only as theology goes its own way sincerely and with no pretence. Apologetics and polemics can only be an event and not a programme.

It is thus true of theology too : " For this reason we must note that if we do not uphold the Gospel with its own strength, but rather with our own resources, all will be lost, so that no matter how well we defend it, it will crumble to pieces. Let us have no anxiety that the Gospel needs our help. It is sufficiently strong of itself, and may be committed to God alone, whose it is. . . . Hence it is a poor and miserable thing that this feeble rabble of sophists opposes it. For what do these poor bats hope to accomplish with their petty flappings ? Let them come ! By the grace of God they have no true learning. . . . In all these things there is no better counsel than to preach the Gospel simply and purely, praying God that He will direct and lead us " (Luther, *Sermon vom Glauben und guten Werken*, 1522, *W.A.*, 10³, p. 354, l. 15). " It is thus settled that the Word of God can have no other master, judge or protector than God Himself. It is His Word, and therefore, as He utters it quite apart from human merit or counsel, so He Himself will uphold and defend it without human help or strength. If any man seek human protection or comfort in this respect, he will undoubtedly fall and miss both, being abandoned by both God and man " (*Fastenpostille*, 1525, *W.A.*, 17², p. 108, l. 26).

To be truly imperious, the necessity of dogmatic prolegomena, i.e., of an explicit account of the particular way to be taken in dogmatics, must be an inner necessity grounded in the matter itself. If it rests on a conflict in which faith finds itself, then, if this conflict is to be serious, it must be a conflict of faith with itself. The conflict of faith with unbelief can be truly significant only as and when it is a conflict of faith with itself, since in faith unbelief has in some sense expressed itself and claims a hearing. This paradoxical fact is a real fact. Faith does not stand only, or even in the first and most important sense, in conflict with unbelief. It stands in conflict with itself, i.e., with a form or forms of faith in which it recognises itself in respect of form but not of content, in which it so seriously fails to do so in the latter respect that, although in them it must genuinely recognise faith, and even Christian faith, so far as form is concerned, it can only understand this faith as another faith so far as concerns content. This other faith is the faith in which we hear unbelief express itself. As we take up the task of dogmatics, we come up against this fact of another faith. That is to say, as we try to ask about the being of the Church, about Jesus Christ, as the norm of Church action, we find that even in the understanding of this norm, in the knowledge of Jesus Christ as the Lord of the Church, we are so much at one with some that we can at once address ourselves to the task with them, but so little at one with others even in this presupposition, i.e., in the way in which we understand it, that we cannot pursue the dogmatic task together with them. We have to state quite definitely that our own understanding of the being of the Church is in no sense the only one, that alongside it other and quite different understandings are also present, that the only possible fellowship with the representatives of these other understandings is that of conflict with them, and that the different and even alien element in them cannot be regarded by us as another possibility of faith perhaps as yet unknown to us, but only as a possibility which is hostile to faith, and therefore as unbelief, even though it must still be understood as a possibility of faith in virtue of its formal presuppositions. The paradoxical fact to which we refer is that of heresy. By heresy we understand a form of Christian faith which we cannot deny to be a form of Christian faith from the formal standpoint, i.e., in so far as it, too, relates to Jesus Christ, to His Church, to baptism, Holy Scripture and the common Christian creeds, but in respect of which we cannot really understand what we are about when we recognise it as such, since we can understand its content, its interpretation of these common presuppositions, only as a contradiction of faith.

This paradoxical element in the factor of heresy has been finely brought out in the words of Irenaeus : *Similia enim loquentes fidelibus . . . non solum dissimilia sapiunt, sed et contraria et per omnia plena blasphemiis, per quae interficiunt eos, qui per similitudinem verborum dissimile affectionis eorum in se attrahunt venenum ; sicut quis aquae mixtum gypsum dans pro lacte, seducat per similitudinem coloris, sicut quidam dixit superior nobis de omnibus qui quolibet modo depravant quae sunt Dei, et adulterant veritatem : In Dei lacte gypsum male miscetur* (C. o. haer., III, 17, 4).

Because of its paradoxical nature, heresy is for faith an important factor. Or, as we might say, unbelief in the form of heresy is for faith an important factor—which is not the case when it is present as pure unbelief. Because in heresy it is present as a form of faith, it must be taken seriously at this point, and there can and must be serious conflict between faith and heresy.

The early, mediaeval and post-Reformation Church right up to Pietism and the Enlightenment engaged in conflict with Jews, pagans and atheists only for the most part incidentally, and never with anything like the same emphasis or zeal as it did with heretics. Even when this included the by no means laudable nor even necessary mutual abuse or even burnings of those past days, there was meaning in it, since the Church and heretics were talking very differently about the same theme, and therefore not talking past one another but in opposition to one another. There was thus a headlong collision such as can only take place between contending brothers. The much vaunted progress made between the 17th and 18th centuries consisted in the decision to tolerate one another, i.e., to abandon one another to the appropriate fate. This was the first breach in the fellowship hitherto continually maintained in conflict.

In the conflict between the Church and heresy, however, it is a matter of engagement from different angles with the thing itself, and not of mere talk about it condemned at the very outset to be sterile of results. The theme is the same. This is why there can be strife. We have to do with differing interpretations of the same theme. This is why there has to be strife. So different is the interpretation of the Church from that of heretics that the menacing question arises whether they are not really dealing with different themes, and therefore whether the opposing and different faith is not really to be understood as unbelief. The conversation between the Church and heretics would not be so serious if it were conducted elsewhere than under the shadow of this menacing question. But so long and so far as the conversation goes on, this question is not decided in such sort that the Church and heretics can have no further dealings. The conversation itself, and its very sharpness, prove the contrary. In this conversation the Church must wrestle with heresy in such a way that it may itself be the Church. And heresy must attack the Church because it is not sufficiently or truly the Church. Neither can perform its task without recourse to the continually problematical formal presuppositions which they have in common. Though divided in the content of faith, both sides appeal to certain common forms of faith and thus maintain, even if only by raising that menacing question, a common ground of faith which does at least always come into consideration. Only when the Church and heresy no longer confront one another, or have no more to say to one another, is the distant but indisputable bow of peace which overarches them broken or robbed of its significance. In true encounter with heresy faith is plunged into conflict with itself, because, so long and so far as it is not free of heresy, so long and so far as heresy affects it, so long and so far as it must accept responsiblity in relation to it, it cannot allow even the voice of unbelief which it thinks it hears in heresy to cause it to treat it as not at least also faith but simply as unbelief. It must understand it as a possibility of faith. To be sure, it will see it as a profoundly incomprehensible one, which can be regarded only as a possibility of the disruption and destruction of faith, as a possibility against which it must be on guard. Yet it must still understand it as a possibility of faith, and therefore and to this extent—hence the need for powerful defence—as its own possibility, as a possibility within and not without the Church, hard though it may be to think of it as such. This is the reason why this conflict is a serious conflict. This is the reason why the task of giving an explicit account of the way of knowledge taken in dogmatics can and must be an inner necessity grounded in the matter itself.

We stand before the fact of heresy. Concretely, we stand before the fact of Roman Catholicism in the form which it gave itself in the 16th century in the battle against the Reformation. Again, within the organised unities of the Evangelical Churches themselves, we stand before the fact of pietistic and rationalistic Modernism as rooted in mediaeval mysticism and the humanistic Renaissance. The fact of the modern denial of revelation, etc., is quite irrelevant compared with this twofold fact. For here, in its antithesis to Roman Catholicism and Protestant Modernism, the Evangelical faith stands in conflict with itself. For these two things are not irrelevant paganisms, nor do they seek to be such. If we take them for what they purport to be, they encounter us as possibilities of faith, and therefore of our own faith, within and not without the Church. And as we listen to them, not evading the formal justice of their claim, we are forced to say that in them we do not recognise faith and the Church. We so fully fail to recognise faith and the Church in them that the question is unavoidable whether these are not possibilities of simple unbelief, whether the Roman Catholic or Protestant Modernist theologian is not to be regarded as " an heathen man and a publican " (Mt. 18^{17}). But our encounter with heresies would not be a true encounter ; we should be quickly rid of them ; we should not hear them any more, if we were to regard this question as settled. If they really confront us as a fact, and if this question is not therefore settled, it turns against ourselves and there is demanded of us purification, reckoning and responsibility in respect of our own understanding of the being of the Church and our own knowledge of Christ. That we pursue Evangelical and not some other theology is, of course, something that we can as little discuss or establish as that we are baptised and believe. In relation to ourselves, too, we can only start with the fact in so far as it is posited as such. But heresies force us to see clearly to what extent, in what sense and with what inner foundation we stand on the one side and not the other, and thus understand revelation, not in Roman Catholic or Modernist terms, but in Evangelical terms.

That we must hear this demand decisively in the existence of heresies is an ancient insight : *Improbatio quippe haereticorum facit eminere quid Ecclesia tua sentiat et quid habeat sana doctrina* (Augustine, *Conf.*, VII, 19, 25, cf. *De cat. rud.*, 24, 44, *De civ. Dei*, XVI, 2, 1). *Ob hoc haereseon non statim divinitus eradicantur auctores, ut probati manifesti fiant, id est, ut unusquisque, quam tenax et fidelis et fixus catholicae fidei sit amator, appareat* (Vincent of Lerins, *Common.*, I, 20, 25, cf. 19, 24). *Quia perversi homines apostolicam doctrinam et caeteras doctrinas et scripturas pervertunt ad sui ipsorum perditionem . . . ideo necessaria fuit temporibus procedentibus explicatio fidei* (Thomas Aquinas, *S. theol.*, II², *qu. 1, art. 10*).

The purification required of us, however, will at once and necessarily be a purification in respect of the way of knowledge which we take. The ways diverge from the very source of knowledge. Already in relation to this source we must thus be at unity with ourselves in respect of the divergent possibilities. But what else is this source or basis of knowledge but the being of the Church, which itself can obviously be so diversely interpreted that whatever follows is quite different, as may be seen at every point in the debate between the Church and heresies ? To clarify the Evangelical understanding of those apparently or genuinely identical formal presuppositions is thus the inner necessity of dogmatic prolegomena now resting upon us.

Heretical trends and even whole heretical churches such as e.g., the Marcionite, Donatist and Arian, were known, of course, both in the early and mediaeval Church. It must still be said, however, that only since the Reformation has heresy become a generally and fundamentally experienced problem. If there was nothing new formally, it was something quite new materially that the Evangelical Church of a Luther or Calvin should see heresy in the Papacy and Roman Catholicism of the 16th and 17th centuries, and *vice versa*. It was then for the first time that the Church learned what is meant by divergent faith. That is why there have had to be all types of dogmatic prolegomena from that day forward. We find the first traces of them in the preambles on the Scripture principle which begin to appear especially in the Reformed confessions, first in the *Conf. Tetrapol.*, 1530, and then in most of those which follow. With the new material knowledge of Jesus Christ, which brought about the Reformation, especially in relation to the interconnexion of the forgiveness of sins and the Christian life, there was linked from the very first, comprehended in the doctrine of the sole normativeness of Holy Scripture, a new formal theology which inevitably demanded explicit and independent expression in face of the contradiction which confronted the matter itself and in face of the fact that this contradiction was that of divergent faith rather than of unbelief. The growing need in this respect may be gauged by the development of introductory discussions of the Scripture principle even in the different editions of the *Loci* of Melanchthon. As the first example of radically exhaustive prolegomena in our sense we shall have to claim the first ten chapters of the 1559 edition of Calvin's *Institutio*. Basic formal definitions in repudiation of the Evangelical Scripture principle were no less necessary for the opposing dogmatics of Roman Catholicism. We find the first visible step in this direction in the definitions of the dignity of Church tradition alongside or even in preference to Holy Scripture at the head of the rulings of the Council of Trent. And it is consistent and understandable that since the Vatican decree the prolegomena of Roman Catholic dogmatics should circle around the concept of the teaching office of the Church, unified in the Papacy, as the true source of revelation and of the corresponding " Catholic faith." The task of giving such an account of the formal presuppositions became even more urgent, and dogmatic prolegomena acquired even more evident importance and comprehensiveness, when pietistic and rationalistic Modernism became a third partner in the debate, particularly active and triumphant on the Evangelical side, yet not without interrelationships on the Roman Catholic. Even though this has neither been expelled from the Evangelical Churches nor undertaken to form its own Church, we must differentiate ourselves from it no less than from Roman Catholicism. The faith which is in conflict with doubt of the truth, with the question of the existence of God, is very different from the faith which asks whether the God whose existence is no problem is gracious or whether man must despair of himself. The first is Modernistic faith, the second Evangelical, and the two can recognise one another only in respect of identical formal pre-suppositions. They are one in Christ, and yet they are not one. Modernistic faith has felt this no less than Evangelical or Roman Catholic faith. For this reason, when it began to develop its own dogmatics, it found its own approach to the matter as it thought it should understand it in the distinctive 18th and 19th century doctrine of " religion." The significance of Schleiermacher consists above all in the fact that in his doctrine of Christian piety as the being of the Church he gave this heresy a formal foundation which not merely brought to culmination the preceding era but also proved prophetic for that which was to follow. He is not the inaugurator but the great and mature classical exponent of Modernism whom the latter must never allow itself to be prevented from following if it has a true understanding of itself.

2. THE POSSIBILITY OF DOGMATIC PROLEGOMENA

How are dogmatic prolegomena possible as a preliminary under-standing of the way of knowledge to be pursued ? Such an understanding obviously presupposes a place from which this way is visible and intelligible. What is this place ?

The answer proposed to theology since the days of the Enlightment and with a new urgency in our own time, the answer of Modernistic dogmatics, is that the Church and faith are to be understood as links in a greater nexus of being. Hence dogmatics is to be understood as a link in a greater nexus of scientific problems, from the general structural laws of which its own specific conditions of knowledge are to be deduced and its own specific scientific character known. This nexus of problems, however, is that of an ontology, and since Descartes this necessarily means that of a comprehensively explicated self-understanding of human existence which may also at a specific point become the pre-understanding of an existence in the Church or in faith, and therefore the pre-understanding and criterion of theological knowledge.

It was Idealistic philosophy which once led Schleiermacher and De Wette to understand human existence as a sum of capacities or tendencies or activities of human self-consciousness, and within this to discover at the central point, in the form of feeling or direct self-consciousness, an original disposition or basis for the piety which is to find historical actualisation, and therewith the noetic principle of Christian dogmatics as the self-explanation of this specific historically actual piety. The understanding of existence here presupposed was, of course, far too naive both formally and materially in relation to the real problems of human existence. This modern ontology, better instructed theoretically by Kierkegaard and practically by world war and revolution, interprets human existence not

merely secondarily but from the very outset as history, and materially not so much
as capacity but rather as " being projected into nothingness " (M. Heidegger,
Was ist Metaphysik ?, 1929, p. 20). And it was understandable that a theology
which was itself seeking a more essential understanding of the New Testament
should attempt to interpret existence according to this understanding as prior to
faith, i.e., that it should try to find in it the ontologically existential possibility
of the existential event of faith, and by means of its analysis attain to a prior
understanding of Christian utterance, Christian theology and above all exegesis
(R. Bultmann, *Der Begriff der Offenbarung im N.T.*, 1929 ; " Die Geschicht-
lichkeit des Daseins und der Glaube," *Z.Th.K.*, 1930, p. 339 f.). The methodological relationship of Bultmann's conception to that of Schleiermacher and
De Wette should not be overlooked. " That theology should begin with a definition of existence, or man . . . is at root a piece of Liberalism. One might have
thought that the attempt to speak of believing man apart from God had shown
itself to be impracticable " (Heinrich Barth, " Philosophie, Theologie und
Existenzproblem," *Z.d.Z.*, 1932, p. 113 f.). Cf. on this point the extolling of
Bultmann by G. Wobbermin (*Richtlinien evangel. Theologie*, 1929, p. 102, 110 n.,
116, 143).

Dogmatic prolegomena on the basis of this conception obviously
consist first in the demonstration that in a general ontology or anthropology there is actually a place for this ontic factor, for the being
of the Church or faith, and that human existence is practicable also as
believing existence. They then consist in the concrete historical reminder that this particular ontic factor is in fact present as an event
and is thus the object of ontic science. They finally consist in the
establishment of the rules suggested by this ontological-ontic foundation for this science, and therefore for the criticism and correction of
Christian utterance.

1. Anthropological possibility, 2. historico-psychological reality and 3. method
do in fact constitute the schema which is actually followed in the introductions
to Schleiermacher's *Der christliche Glaube* (§ 3–10, § 11–19, § 20–31) and De
Wette's *Lehrbuch der christlichen Dogmatik*, 1831 (§ 1–27, § 28–45, § 46–61), and
which would have to be followed by the introduction to a dogmatics in the sense
of Bultmann.

The statements of such prolegomena do not in this case aim to be
themselves statements of dogmatic knowledge. Hence the prefix *pro*
in the word prolegomena has here the force of " prior."

In the words of Schleiermacher, " the statements made at this point cannot
themselves be dogmatic too " (*Der. ch. Gl.*, § 1, 1).

The statements of such prolegomena have instead the character, in
part of statements borrowed from metaphysics, anthropology (Schleiermacher's ethics), religious philosophy and religious history, and in part
of purely methodological discussions. What dogmatic knowledge is, is
thus in fact affirmed *praenumerando* quite apart from dogmatics, and
might be affirmed even by those who have no mind to concern themselves any further with the subject.

The possibility of this solution stands or falls with the answer to the question whether there really is a nexus of being superior to the being of the Church and consequently a nexus of scientific problems superior to dogmatics. Is there in fact an existential potentiality which is different from the actuality of revelation and in the light of which the latter is to be understood ? Is there, as possibility, something generally human of which this specific human phenomenon may be regarded as an actualisation ? Is there an existentially ontological *prius* to this ontically existential factor ? If this presupposition is granted, then prolegomena of this kind are possible. This presupposition, however, does not have a neutral but a highly theological character. If there is involved a statement of what dogmatics is from outside dogmatics, this is correct only to the extent that the statement is made outside a specific dogmatics, namely, Reformation and Evangelical, or indeed Roman Catholic, dogmatics, but for this reason all the more definitely within Modernistic dogmatics. The assertion of an existentially ontological *prius* to ontically existential faith, or the definition of faith as a mode of the historical being of human existence, is a cardinal proposition of the faith which understands the being of the Church and itself decisively as a definition of the reality of man, of piety.

Schleiermacher's assertion that his introduction is not itself dogmatics is quite untenable. Even his disciple A. Schweizer has seen and stated that in it we do not have " merely an introductory account but the very basis of the doctrine of faith," and in relation to the task of dogmatic prolegomena he has thus declared that " a particular part of the doctrine of the faith itself must be advanced as the foundation in which the Christian consciousness of faith takes account of itself quite apart from the differentiation of the different elements residing in it " (*Die christliche Glaubenslehre*, 2nd ed., 1877, Vol. I, p. 92 f.). The assertion of Schleiermacher is to be judged in the light of the definitions of the Church which he gives a little later, namely, that it is " a fellowship which arises and can continue only by free human actions," and " a fellowship in relation to piety " (*D. ch. Gl.*, § 2, 2 ; § 3, 1). These definitions, which are decisive for all that follows and which obviously characterise Modernism, have their origin in English Congregationalism (cf. e.g., *Arts.* 20, 23 and 24 of the *Platform of the Savoy Declaration*, 1658). They and they alone could authorise Schleiermacher to commence his basic work of introduction with statements borrowed from ethics. And of themselves they are sufficient to characterise these borrowed statements as dogmatics, i.e., dogmatically heretical statements.

We regard this Modernist faith as also Christian to the extent that the being of the Church implies in fact a determination of human reality. But we cannot regard it as Christian to the extent that it interprets the possibility of this reality as a human possibility, to the extent that it fails to recognise that this determination of human reality derives and is to be considered only from outside all human possibilities, i.e., from the acting God Himself, to the extent that it seeks to interpret its history, not in terms of itself, but in terms of a general capacity or of the general historicity of human existence. If this faith falls, so does this interpretation of faith, so too the pre-supposition of an anthropological *prius* of faith, and so finally the possibility of prolegomena of this kind.

Heinrich Barth (*op. cit.*, p. 105) understands by " existence " the " concrete decision for a possibility which finds actualisation in this decision." But as distinct from M. Heidegger and R. Bultmann he says that it is " referred to something beyond itself " (p. 117), namely, to " the criterion which transcends it " (p. 108), which " for its part has the significance of existence " (p. 109), and which is identical with the " idea " of existence (p. 110). This " existence in limitation," H. Barth thinks, " might be called an ' analogy ' of the knowledge of God, to borrow the old Scholastic term." The theatre of the dialectic of existence interpreted in this way is history, and in such sort that " each historical phase represents something unique which cannot be repeated," Something unique of this kind thus meets us in that element of history which the theologian under-stands as " the history of revelation, in which the truth of existence, and there-fore the meaning and possibility of response to it, shine out in an absolutely unique way never previously known " (p. 118 f.). The interrelation of philosophy and theology is thus to be defined as follows : " The philosophy of existence starts with existence in general ; since it uses only the existence already before it as its point of contact, it can have no confidence that further thought will give it a clear picture of the ' new existence ' of biblical man. It is thus reasonable, and grounded in the nature of the problem of existence, that it should leave the further work of reflection to a special science, i.e., theology." What " constitutes this as a special science is the positive factor of a certain historical element. To this extent theology is a ' positive ' science " (p. 121). " Theology has as its theme the believing existence of biblical man and the self-understanding of his certainty of existence as stated in the message of Scripture. Theology must devote its reflection to this historical factor in a distinctive sense " (p. 122). " The possibility of a sifting and clarifying conception of the existential insights which there confront us " is what takes form specifically in the attempt at dogmatics (p. 122 f.). Now undoubtedly we have here a spirited and impressive effort to overcome the anthropological narrowness of Heidegger's philosophy of existence on the ground and with the weapons of this philosophy itself. We are given a philosophical scheme in which there is no place for an anthropological *prius* of faith and therefore for the patronising and conditioning of theology which are not overcome in Heidegger or Bultmann. Three points are to be noted in H. Barth's understanding. 1. The juxtaposition of the general and the particular does not imply a rationalistic attempt to master the particular, i.e., the problem of special historical reality, by subsuming it under a general concept. 2. The truth of existence which shines forth in the history of revelation is not to be regarded as identical with the general truth of existence, with which existential philosophy as such is concerned, but rather as the light which shines forth here and not elsewhere. The philosophical or general concept of existence does not offer knowledge of God, but only an analogy to such knowledge. Thus philosophy neither can nor does seek to integrate or subordinate theology to its own nexus of problems, but simply attempts to display its own attitude to dogmatics, which it may well do on the basis of that transcendent understanding. 3. Only in retrospect from revealed truth, i.e., by way of recapitulation and not anticipation, does the philosophical concept of existence seek to be an analogy to the know-ledge of God. In no sense, therefore, can it be accepted as an instrument of the knowledge of God. It is only to be wished that this self-interpretation of the

" critical philosophy of existence " could have been brought into the public debate in a far more unmistakeable form than is the case in the essay quoted (cf., e.g., the definition of theology given on p. 122 or the description of theology as one such unique factor on p. 119). It is also to be wished that towards this end the use of such loaded categories as the general and the particular, positive and historical, might have been abandoned. Again, it must be left to philosophy to assume responsibility for the assertion that in that transcendent knowledge of human existence we have an " analogy " to the knowledge of God, since this assertion cannot possibly be a theological statement. For it is hard to see what theological foundation could be found for it. A sharp warning should thus be given to the theologian that this new use of the " old Scholastic term " cannot give any philosophical certainty to his work, so that he must not be enticed by any fresh possibility of natural theology. Even the " critical philosophy of existence " cannot give rise to any dogmatic prolegomena. If the assertion of analogy is really to be regarded as recapitulatory rather than anticipatory, then this warning is also to be found in the meaning of this philosophy itself.

In distinction from the conception already contested, Roman Catholic dogmatics describes the place from which it ascertains its way of knowledge as the self-originating and self-grounded reality of divine revelation and the corresponding supernatural faith. Here, then, dogmatic prolegomena consist in the assertion that in the form of Holy Scripture, Church tradition, and the living teaching apostolate of the Church infallibly representing and interpreting both, there is to be found the objective principle of knowledge, and in the form of the *fides catholica*, which accepts revelation as proposed by the Church, there is to be found the subjective principle.

On this point, cf., e.g., M. J. Scheeben, *Handbuch der kathol. Dogmatik*, Vol, I, 1874 ; B. Bartmann, *Lehrbuch der Dogmatik*, 7th imp., Vol, I, 1928. How fluid even this conception can be in detail may be seen from the fact that on the one side J. Kuhn's *Einleitung in die katholische Dogmatik*, written in 1846 in debate with Idealism like the work of J. A. Möhler, can consist almost exclusively in a doctrine of faith, whereas on the other side the introduction to F. Diekamp's *Katholische Dogmatik*, Vol. I, 6th imp., 1930, can consist no less exclusively in a doctrine of the sources of dogmatics, i.e., of the objective principle of knowledge.

It is self-evident that these assertions are already statements of faith and therefore in their scientific form dogmatic statements. But we can regard these statements, too, only as those of another faith and an alien dogmatics. Their presupposition is that the being of the Church, Jesus Christ, is no longer the free Lord of its existence, but that He is incorporated into the existence of the Church, and is thus ultimately restricted and conditioned by certain concrete forms of the human understanding of His revelation and of the faith which grasps it. Again, there can be no mistaking the common Christian character of this faith to the extent that the concept of the acting God, of that which is radically beyond all human possibilities, is taken seriously as the source of dogmatic knowledge, at least in intention. But again our fellowship with this faith is broken by the way in which grace here becomes nature, the action of God immediately disappears and is taken up into the action of the recipient of grace, that which is beyond all human possibilities changes at once into that which is enclosed within the reality of the Church, and the personal act of divine address becomes a constantly available relationship. Roman Catholic faith believes this transformation. It can recognise itself and God's revelation in this constantly available relationship between God and man, in this revealedness. It affirms an *analogia entis*, the presence of a divine likeness of the creature even in the fallen world, and consequently the possibility of applying the secular " There is " to God and the things of God as the presupposition, again ontological, of that change or transformation, of that depriving of revelation and faith of their character as decision by evasion and neutralisation.

Inhorresco in quantum dissimilis ei sum ; inardesco in quantum similis ei sum (Augustine, *Conf.*, XI, 9, 11). *Id quod in Deo perfecte est, in rebus aliis per quandam deficientem participationem invenitur. . . . Et sic creatura habet quod Dei est ; unde et Deo recte similis dicitur* (Thomas Aquinas, *S. c. gent.*, cc I, c. 29). Cf. also *Conc. Later.*, IV, 1215, *De trin., etc., c.* 2 in Denzinger's *Enchiridion*, No. 432 towards the end, and the relevant comments of E. Przywara, *Religionsphilosophie kath. Theol.*, 1926, p, 22 f. and *passim.*

If this faith is not ours ; if we know nothing of such a change and its presupposition ; if we can as little say : " There is revelation," as we can : " There is faith," then we cannot possibly adopt the standpoint which yields this particular dogmatic knowledge.

The only possibility of a conception of dogmatic knowledge remaining to us on the basis of Evangelical faith is to be marked off on the one hand by the rejection of an existential ontological possibility of the being of the Church and on the other hand by the rejection of the presupposition of a constantly available absorption of the being of the Church into a creaturely form, into a " There is." On the one side we have to say that the being of the Church is *actus purus*, i.e., a divine action which is self-originating and which is to be understood only in terms of itself and not therefore in terms of a prior anthropology. And on the other side we have also to say that the being of the Church is *actus purus*, but with the accent now on *actus*, i.e., a free action and not a constantly available connexion, grace being the event of personal address and not a transmitted material condition. On both sides we can only ask how it may be otherwise if the being of the Church is identical with Jesus Christ. If this is true, then the place from which the way of dogmatic knowledge is to be seen and understood can be neither a prior anthropological possibility nor a subsequent ecclesiastical reality, but only the present moment of the speaking and hearing of Jesus Christ Himself, the divine creation of light in our hearts.

λάμπειν ἐν ταῖς καρδίαις ἡμῶν (2 Cor. 4⁶, compared by Paul with the " Let there be light " of Gen. 1³).

In the light of the fact that Jesus Christ is the being of the Church, the free personal decision may be expected concerning what is the proper content of Christian utterance and therefore concerning what should be the way to its knowledge, i.e., to the knowledge of dogma. Like the attempt to know dogma, any understanding of the orientation of this attempt can only be a particular form of the expectation of the decision of the Lord of the Church based upon and prepared by His promise.

Now this means that we find confirmation of the insight which is self-evident in the sphere of Roman Catholic dogmatics and which cannot finally be avoided in Modernist dogmatics, namely, that prolegomena to dogmatics are possible only as part of dogmatics itself. The prefix *pro* in prolegomena is to be understood loosely to signify the first part of dogmatics rather than that which is prior to it.

In order to give an account of the way of knowledge pursued in dogmatics, we cannot take up a position which is somewhere apart from this way or above the work of dogmatics. Such a place apart or above could only be an ontology or anthropology as the basic science of the human possibilities among which consideration is somewhere given to that of faith and the Church. But any supposed reality of the Church in which the decision of the Lord of the Church is already anticipated can only be viewed as such a place apart or above. In both cases, i.e., in both Modernist and Roman Catholic prolegomena, it can be known and said in advance, before actually embarking on dogmatics, what will be the proper way of knowledge. Evangelical dogmatics cannot proceed along these lines. It can only venture to embark on its way, and then on this way, admittedly perhaps as its first task, yet genuinely on this way, concern itself with the knowledge of the correctness of this way. It knows that there can be no entering the self-enclosed circle of this concern from without, whether from a general human possibility or an ecclesiastical reality. It realises that all its knowledge, even its knowledge of the correctness of its knowledge, can only be an event, and cannot therefore be guaranteed as correct knowledge from any place apart from or above this event. In no circumstances, therefore, can it understand the account which is to be rendered in prolegomena as an attempt to secure such a guarantee. This account can be given only within, even if at the beginning of, the dogmatic work which is not guaranteed from that point apart or above.

We perceive the possible point of departure for such an account in the fact that the Christian Church ventures to talk of God, or to regard what it says as talk about God. This fact itself, quite apart from the possible or actual contents of what is said, is obviously a part of talk about God. It says of God that the Church speaks of Him. This statement, however it is meant and however it may be explained, is as little self-evident and as much in need of explanation as all the other material statements which the Church may venture to make about God. Like them, it needs to be criticised and corrected. It must be the subject of enquiry with what right the Church comes to say this, and in what sense it does so. This right and sense are obviously identical with the norm by which what it says is to be measured, i.e., with the norm of the remaining content of its utterance concerning God. The knowledge of this right and sense is identical with the knowledge of the correctness of its insights, of the right way which it must take in the criticism and correction of its insights. If there should be specific reflection concerning this way as such—and we have seen that there should—then it must consist in the question, itself dogmatic, as to the true content of the presupposed statement concerning the talk about God which takes place in the Church. This statement has a true content when it is related to a prior Word of God Himself spoken to the Church which speaks about God. Only when and to the extent that such a Word of God is spoken by God Himself to the Church is there any right or sense in speaking about God in the Church. Only when there is such a Word of God is there a criterion, namely, this Word itself, of the correctness of such speech and therefore of the correct criticism and correction of such speech, i.e., of dogmatics. In the prolegomena to dogmatics, therefore, we ask concerning the Word of God as the criterion of dogmatics. In so doing, and therefore already on the way, we give an account of the way which we tread.

Basically, the theme of dogmatic prolegomena as understood in this sense is obviously none other than that which the older Protestant theology, in its resistance to Roman Catholicism and then to incipient Modernism, treated under the title *De scriptura sacra*. We shall see that the cardinal statement of the doctrine of the Word of God which we shall try to develop in what follows is indeed materially the same as the assertion of the authority and normativeness of Holy Scripture as the witness to divine revelation and the presupposition of Church proclamation. But in the modern situation, both as regards Roman Catholicism and also Modernism, what falls to be said about Holy Scripture as the criterion of dogmatics needs a comprehensive elucidation of context. Hence we shall attempt a doctrine of the Word of God and not merely of Holy Scripture, i.e., a doctrine of Holy Scripture in the context of an embracing doctrine of the Word of God. Even the older dogmaticians in their development of the *locus De scriptura sacra* could not in fact avoid decisive references to the contents of Christian utterance concerning God. That is, they could not avoid anticipating material dogmas, e.g., the doctrine of reconciliation, the Holy Spirit, faith, or the Church. We, too, must anticipate in this way, and we must do so to an even greater extent if we are to achieve true clarity. The most striking anticipation of this kind will consist in the fact that we shall treat of the whole doctrine of the Trinity and the essentials of Christology in this connexion, namely, as constituent parts of our answer to the question of the Word of God. We cannot pose the question of formal dogma without immediately entering at these central points upon material dogma. Indeed, what is thought to be formal dogma is itself highly material in fact. The only point is that here at the beginning of the whole work it is not to be estimated solely according to its material significance, but specifically according to its formal significance as the foundation of dogmatic knowledge as such.

CHAPTER I

THE WORD OF GOD AS THE CRITERION OF DOGMATICS

CHAPTER I

THE WORD OF GOD AS THE CRITERION OF DOGMATICS

§ 3

CHURCH PROCLAMATION AS THE MATERIAL OF DOGMATICS

Talk about God in the Church seeks to be proclamation to the extent that in the form of preaching and sacrament it is directed to man with the claim and expectation that in accordance with its commission it has to speak to him the Word of God to be heard in faith. Inasmuch as it is a human word in spite of this claim and expectation, it is the material of dogmatics, i.e., of the investigation of its responsibility as measured by the Word of God which it seeks to proclaim.

1. TALK ABOUT GOD AND CHURCH PROCLAMATION

Not all human talk is talk about God. It could be and should be. There is no reason in principle why it should not be. God is the Lord from whom and to whom we exist. Even the realities and truths distinct from Him and us which usually form the concrete occasion and subject of human speech exist from Him and to Him. Hence there is no genuinely profane speech. In the last resort, there is only talk about God. Yet serious reflection on human talk about God must take as its starting-point the fact that this is not at all the case, that it is quite impossible to interpret human talk as such as talk about God. We do not know man, i.e., ourselves, as man in his original estate and therefore as the man of the kingdom of glory. Of this man it might well be said that all his talk is talk about God. But we do not know ourselves as this man. We know ourselves only as the man to whom mercy is shown as one who is fallen, lost and condemned. We know ourselves only as man in the kingdom of grace, of the present age between the time of creation and that of redemption. We stand under the sign of a decision constantly taken between the secularity and the sanctification of our existence, between sin and grace, between a being as man which forgets God, which is absolutely neutral in relation to

47

Him and therefore absolutely hostile, and one which in His revelation is awakened by faith to being in the Church, to the appropriation of His promise. This cleavage continually applies, however, to human speech as well. It is not identical with the distinction between secular and religious utterance. Religious utterance is, of course, externally marked off from secular by the fact that God is its more or less explicit theme. It is also marked off internally by the intention expressly or tacitly orientated to this subject, by the more or less sincere purpose, directly or indirectly to speak about God. But the cleavage still takes place intrinsically within secular existence. Neither the subject nor the intention makes human speech sanctified talk about God, just as conversely it does not have to be secular because it does not have this subject or intention. This distinction, like the distinction between a believing and religious and an unbelieving and worldly attitude, is only a symptom, and not even an unequivocal symptom, of the true and final distinction between secular and sanctified existence. Nevertheless, it is a necessary symptom. The ongoing event of the final distinction, the event in which God Himself acts, casts its shadow before in the event of this provisional distinction in which man is at work.

It cannot, therefore, be generally correct to characterise this provisional distinction as the " human cleavage between sacramental daemonism and secular exorcism " (Paul Tillich, *Relig. Verwirklichung*, 1930, p. 64), To be sure, it is not co-extensive with the divine distinction, and to this extent it can be character-ised in such terms. But as a symptom of the divine distinction it can be a pointer to its reality, and it is not, therefore, exhaustively defined in this way. Again, it does not rest on careful discussion if it is stated generally that from God's standpoint the historical Church has no advantage over historical society, that revelation is addressed equally to society and the Church, and that the " invisible community " can be equally proclaimed and actualised " from the religious and the cultural angles " (P. Tillich, *Kirche und Kultur*, 1924, p. 10 f., 16 f., 19). Certainly, God is not bound to the historical Church. He is free and able to raise up children to Abraham from the stones. But this does not alter the fact that the antithesis between the Church and society can be a symptom of the divine distinction, and a pointer to its truth, not in the abstract equality but in the concrete inequality of the two sides. Finally, it is wrong to interpret this anti-thesis in general as basically non-essential (*op. cit.*, p. 9) and thus to make it the subject of a general protest from the standpoint of " the far side of being " (*Rel. Verwirklichung*, p. 46). For our standpoint is neither the time of creation nor that of redemption, and therefore it is not that of a far side of being. It is the present between the times, the time of the *regnum gratiae*, in which the symptom of this human cleavage, for all its ambiguous relativity and its provisional character, can always be highly essential as a pointer to the divine distinction.

The event in which God acts consists wholly in the fact that men are visibly awakened, separated and gathered by God to being in the visible Church. A visible distinction which arises within the secular sphere between religious and profane is now, not intrinsically but in this event of divine election, confirmed and maintained and therefore characterised as a genuine indication of the antithesis of judgment and grace in which, even though men do not act towards others, God Himself acts towards men. Only in faith, of course, is this event visible as such ; only in faith is being in the Church visible as divine election and sanctification. What is visible in itself is simply an event within the secular sphere. Its significance can be missed, but it cannot actually be taken away from it again.

" He thus shows with certainty that the preaching of the Gospel is not an eternal, lasting, static doctrine, but like a moving shower of rain which strikes what it strikes and misses what it misses. Nor does it return nor halt, but is followed by the sunshine and warmth which lick it up, etc. Hence our experience that in no place in the world has the Gospel remained pure and simple beyond a man's memory, but has stood and increased so long as those have remained who brought it, and its light has then gone out when they themselves passed on, being succeeded at once by schismatics and false teachers " (Luther, *Fasten-postille*, 1525, *W.A.*, 17^{II}, p. 178, l. 28).

The one who is awakened and gathered to being in the Church has every cause for the full assurance of faith, but none at all for certainty or over-confidence.

Why not ? Τὸ φῶς ἐν τῇ σκοτίᾳ φαίνει καὶ ἡ σκοτία αὐτὸ οὐ κατέλαβεν (Jn. 1^5). So it is with us.

Yet even though it is infinitely threatened in this way as seen from without, the being of man in the Church *ubi et quando visum est Deo* is a true and concrete event, a visible being in the visible Church. In the same sense there is human talk which, as talk about God, is truly and concretely distinguished from other human talk, not in itself and as such, but in virtue of the divine confirmation and preservation, yet in virtue of the divine confirmation and preservation of that which truly and and concretely distinguishes it from other human talk. If the being of the Church, Jesus Christ as the acting person of God, sanctifies the being of man in the visible sphere of human occurrence as being in the Church, then He also sanctifies its talk as talk about God taking place in the Church.

Not all talk in the Church's worship seeks to be proclamation. It does not seek to be such when it is talk addressed by man to God. The Church's prayers and hymns and confessions of faith obviously are what they purport to be only to the extent that so far as possible they cease to attempt the impossible task of proclaiming something to God or the unworthy one of incidentally proclaiming something to man. They are the response to God of the praise, confession and thanksgiving of those to whom proclamation concerning Him has come. They are the sacrifice the bringing of which can have before God only the meaning of a confirmation of what He has done to man, and in respect of which man can obviously have no intentions in relation to others who may also be present.

We think of Luther's demand in his sermon at the dedication of the Castle Church at Torgau in 1544, " that nothing else should take place therein than that our dear Lord Himself should speak with us through His holy Word, and we again speak with Him through prayer and praise. . . ." (*W.A.*, 49, p. 588, l. 15 ; cf. p. 592, l. 17 ; p. 594, l. 26). " Thirdly, that when we have heard God's Word we should bring before God our common holy smoke or incense, i.e., that we should together call upon Him and pray to Him " (p. 599, l. 25).

But there are also other elements in the life of the Church in which what we say about God is addressed to our fellow-men but which cannot seek to be proclamation. To this group belongs a function which from the very first has in some form been recognised to be an integral element in the life of the Church, namely, the expression of helpful solidarity in face of the external needs of human society. This, too, is part of man's response to God. When and because it is the response of real man, necessarily in terms of Mt. 5[14] it is a shining light to people among whom alone man is real man. If God exists for man, as the Church's prayer, praise and confession declare in answer to the proclamation heard, then this man as the man for whom God exists must also exist for his fellow-men with whom alone he is real man. Yet the special utterance about God which consists in the action of this man is primarily and properly directed to God and not to men. It can neither try to enter into quite superfluous competition with society's necessary efforts at self-help in its straits, nor can it seek, as the demonstration of distinctively Christian action, to proclaim how God helps. " That they may see your good works, and glorify your Father which is in heaven," that they may be a commentary on the proclamation of God's help, is, of course, freely promised, but cannot be its set intention. Like prayer, praise and confession, especially in cases like Francis of Assisi and Bodelschwingh, it has always been spontaneous, unpremeditated, and in the final and best sense unpractical talk about God. Then and in this way its light has shone out.

This was surely overlooked in H. Bär's work, *Weniger Predigt* !, 1930, in which it is recommended that to-day we should not make preaching so much as service in moral and social reform our mode of proclamation.

If the social work of the Church as such were to try to be proclamation, it could only become propaganda, and not very worthy propaganda at that. Genuine Christian love must always start back at the thought of pretending to be a proclamation of the love of Christ with its only too human action.

Again, the Church's education of youth cannot as such seek to be proclamation.

In this respect G. Bohne's book, *Das Wort Gottes und der Unterricht*, 1929, seems to me to lack a certain necessary sobriety. Similarly, T. Heckel in his *Zur Methodik des evangelischen Religionsunterrichts*, 1928, surely goes too far when on p. 33 he claims the evangelical teacher as " witness, priest and herald."

In this field talk about God, as a preparation or a kind of technical sub-structure for the understanding of proclamation, means quite simply instruction or teaching about what the Church thus far, up to the appearance of the new generation of those called to it, has recognised and confessed as the right faith. It is the making known of the most important elements in the tradition with which proclamation must to-day be linked. To be sure, the education of youth will necessarily have to pass over at a definite point, though one which it is not so easy to define outwardly, into the divine service of youth. Yet this must never in any circumstances be to the detriment of what it has to effect as compared with this. The education of youth has to teach and not to convert, not to bring to a decision, and to this extent not to proclaim.

Finally, according to our understanding of the matter, neither can theology as such claim to be proclamation. It, too, is talk about God to men. Proclamation, however, is its presupposition, its material and its practical goal, not its content or task. Theology reflects upon proclamation. It confronts it as a court of criticism. It is Church instruction of youth on a higher grade and with the special purpose of testing the coherence of modern proclamation by the original and dominant being of the Church, and of giving directions for its correct and relevant continuation. Here too, and in every branch of theology, there will unavoidably be invasions of the sphere of proclamation, and they will often be highly appropriate as reminders of the theme. But here, too, the exceptions prove the rule, namely, that theology as such is not proclamation, but science, instruction and investigation. In a rather wider sense, we may thus reckon the Church's instruction of youth and theology among the elements in the Church's life in which man answers the proclamation heard, in which he attempts to take up a position in relation to it. All the functions here enumerated have this in common, that they have as a presupposition the proclamation which has already taken place or is to take place.

The talk about God to be found in the Church, however, is meant to be proclamation when it is directed to men with the definitive claim and expectation that it has to declare the Word of God to them. We at once see that the concept " talk about God " is set here in quite a new light, and indeed acquires a content which threatens to burst it wide open. All that we have hitherto touched on as the talk about God which takes place in the Church has it in common with this particular talk, that, whether it is addressed exclusively to God Himself or also to men, it is unequivocally talk about God which has

God as its theme.   In the Church's proclamation, however, this unequivocal nature of the concept rather than the concept itself is shattered.   Proclamation, too, implies speaking about God.   But here, in what is said about God, there lies concealed as the meaning and purpose of the action the intention to speak the Word of God Himself.

Παραλαβόντες λόγον ἀκοῆς παρ' ἡμῶν τοῦ θεοῦ ἐδέξασθε οὐ λόγον ἀνθρώπων ἀλλὰ καθὼς ἀληθῶς ἐστιν λόγον θεοῦ (1 Thess. 2¹³).   Ὡς ἐκ θεοῦ κατέναντι θεοῦ ἐν Χριστῷ λαλοῦμεν (2 Cor. 2¹⁷).   Εἴ τις λαλεῖ ὡς λόγια τοῦ θεοῦ (1 Pet. 4¹¹).   *Praedicatio verbi Dei est verbum Dei (Conf. Helv. post.,* 1562, *Art.* I, 2.   According to the translation : " Therefore when even to-day the Word of God is proclaimed in the churches by duly called preachers, we believe that the Word of God is proclaimed and accepted by the faithful ").   *Idem verbum est, quod et homo praedicat et Spiritus sanctus cordi inscribit : Una proprie vocatio, sed cuius causa et medium duplex, organicum : homo verbum extus praedicans principale : Spiritus sanctus intus illud cordi inscribens* (H. Heidegger, *Corp. Theol.,* 1700, XXI, 22, quoted from H. Heppe, *Die Dogmatik der ev.-ref. Kirche,* 1861, p. 379).

Proclamation is human speech in and by which God Himself speaks like a king through the mouth of his herald, and which is meant to be heard and accepted as speech in and by which God Himself speaks, and therefore heard and accepted in faith as divine decision concerning life and death, as divine judgment and pardon, eternal Law and eternal Gospel both together.

Where human talk about God is proclamation, it raises this claim and lives in the atmosphere of this expectation.   By what right ? Certainly not by that of the logical form or material content, of the religious profundity or personal power, which might pertain to this human talk about God in itself.   In and with all that it is in itself, it can only serve God's own Word.   Nor does God's own Word cease to be itself when it allows itself to be served by human utterance.   But as it allows itself to be served by it, it is itself this human utterance, and as this human utterance serves it, it is itself God's own Word.

For a proper explanation of this " is " we should have to refer even at this early stage to the christological doctrine of the two natures.

If, then, human talk about God aims to be proclamation, this can only mean that it wills to serve the Word of God and thus to point to its prior utterance by God Himself.   It cannot assume that it is the Word of God, that God sanctifies the human pointer to be His own witness.   The human will in question can only be the will to accept a task.   It is a decisive part of the insight of all true prophecy that man as such has no possibility of uttering the Word of God.   What human utterance concerning God aims to be when it is intended as proclamation is not grace, but service of grace or means of grace.   If the will in question were man's will to reach out beyond himself, to put himself with his word about God in the place of God, it would be blasphemous rebellion. But there can no question of this in its claim and expectation. What is at issue is that the Church has a commission in relation to service of the Word of God, and that there must always be within it, therefore, the will to accept this commission. Thus proclamation is not asked concerning its formal or material perfection, since even the highest possible perfection would not make human utterance proclamation, nor could the least imposing prevent it from being proclamation. It is simply asked whether it is service, whether it is commissioned.

We might also say that it is asked whether it is διακονία τοῦ λόγου (Act. 6⁴), *ministerium verbi divini. Potes facere, quicquid infra te est : Quicquid autem* toucheth *dei cultum, nihil fac, nihil loquere, nisi certus sis habere dei verbum et opus . . . quando autem verbum Dei* runneth, *tum opera omnia bona sunt* (Luther, *Pred. a. 2. Advent*, 1523, *W.A.*, 11, p. 209, l. 22). " Tarry, beloved, until God bid thee, until thou hast certainty and boldness of heart. Yea, wert thou wiser and cleverer than Solomon and Daniel, thou shouldest flee as from hell from speaking a single word, except thou shouldest be bidden and called thereto. If God need thee, He will surely call thee. If He call thee not, beloved, let not thy skill tear open thy belly. Thou thinkest foolishly of the good and piety . . . thou wouldest achieve. Believe me, none will do any good by preaching except he who is bidden and forced to preach without his own will or desire. For we have but one Master, our Lord Jesus Christ, who alone teacheth and bringeth forth fruit through His servants, whom He hath called thereto. But whoso teacheth uncalled, teacheth not without harm, both to himself and the hearers, for that Christ is not with him " (*Festpostille*, 1527, *W.A.*, 17�II, p. 258, l. 38).

The will which does not say No but Yes, not so much to the venture of authoritative talk about God as to this commission that is to be accepted, is the will for proclamation in the Church. Its inner problem, insoluble because answered only in the divine predestination and in faith, is that of decision whether in this respect it is an obedient will.

But what is the function of proclamation in the Church among and alongside its other functions ? We have seen that not all the talk about God that is to be found in the Church is meant to be proclamation. Obviously, however, this does not mean that it might not still be so, and be so indeed to a much higher degree than that which seeks to be such. Real proclamation of the Word of God cannot be conditioned by our intention to speak the Word of God. Why should not praise and active love, instruction and theology, sometimes and perhaps much more genuinely be proclamation ? Given the validity of the *ubi et quando visum est Deo*, as this ought to be valid for us, obviously it is fundamentally impossible to say that it cannot. Nor is it a trivial truth, but a trivial question, whether the sacrificial part of public worship is not in fact much more genuinely proclamation than the other part which in claim and expectation is dedicated to proclamation, and whether the existence of a Bodelschwingh has not been proclamation to a far higher degree than the deliberate proclamation of a

C.D.—C*

thousand preaching parsons. The same question should also be raised, of course, in relation to Church instruction and theology. We must also bear it in mind that there can be nothing to prevent God from turning even such utterance concerning Him into proclamation of His Word to us which, in its character as sanctified utterance within the Church, is at first partially or even totally concealed from us. If the Church is visible, this need not imply that we actually see it in its full compass, that the dimensions of its sphere might not be very different from what we think we know them to be. God may suddenly be pleased to have Abraham blessed by Melchizedek, or Israel blessed by Balaam or helped by Cyrus. Moreover, it could hardly be denied that God can speak His Word to man quite otherwise than through the talk about Himself that is to be found in the Church as known or as yet to be discovered, and therefore quite otherwise than through proclamation. He can establish the Church anew and directly when and where and how it pleases Him.

Modus vocationis opposite consideratus in externum et internum distinguitur. Ille foris per verbi et sacramentorum administrationem, hic intus per operationem Spiritus sancti peragitur. Non semper Deus utrumque vocationis modum ad hominum conversionem sibi possibilem adhibet, sed quosdam interno tantum Spiritus sancti lumine ac numine absque externo verbi sui ministerio ad se vocat. Qui vocationis modus per se quidem est ad salutem sufficiens, sed rarus admodum, extraordinarius, nobisque incognitus (*Syn. pur. Theol.*, Leiden, 1624, *Disp.*, 30, 32–33). This doctrine is to be confused neither with the doctrine of the *ideae Dei potentia semper inexistentes* represented by A. Heidan (*Corp. Th. chr.*, 1686, Loc, I, p. 8 f.) under the influence of Descartes, nor with the Quaker doctrine of the *lumen internum* attacked, e.g., by Hollaz (*Ex. Th. acr.*, 1707, I, 1, 9). It, too, has faith in view, but it emphasises that God is not to be thought of as tied to the way of *vocatio ordinaria*, of proclamation, as the basis of faith.

Hence it can never be the case that the Word of God is confined to the proclamation of the existing Church, or to the proclamation of the Church as known to us, or to the talk about God in this known Church which specially claims to be proclamation. Church proclamation itself, in fact, regards itself only as service of the Word of God, as a means of grace in God's free hand. Hence it cannot be master of the Word, nor try to regard the Word as confined within its own borders. Nevertheless, even when we have calmly recognised as such all the divine possibilities which may be reasonably expected at this point, and even when we are as open as possible in our expectation of their realisation at any time, we have still to remember that the question what God can do is a very different one from that of the commission laid on us by the promise given to the Church.

Non pas que Dieu soit attaché à telles aides ou moyens inferieurs, mais pource qu'il luy plaist nous entretenir soubz telle charge et bride (*Conf. Gall.*, 1559, *art.* 35). The distinctiveness of the teaching of Paul Tillich, which ultimately makes it irrelevant as a contribution to the work of theology, seems to me to lie in the confusion of these two questions. If the first presupposition of thought is that we suppose we can think and speak about the Church equally well, if not better, from outside than from inside, without recognising the binding nature of its commission as those who are also bound by it, then to be sure the door is open for the " radicalism " which " on the basis of the unconditioned " can handle the Church and culture, the sacral sphere and the secular, sacrament and nature, Protestantism and proletariat, possession and exorcism, and indeed the symbol of the Word and all other symbols, with the same sovereignty, independence and consistency as we exercise towards things which are beneath us and not above us. But if " on the basis of the unconditioned " is supposed to mean the same thing as " on the basis of God," it cannot imply " on the basis of the infinite potentiality of God," but only " on the basis of the concrete behest of God," which cannot without violating the omnipotence of God either require of us the superior position of God nor allow us to choose our own possibility, but which, as a command that either finds or does not find concrete obedience, decides concerning our reality. The connexion of the Church with this command, and with this command alone, is the subject of theological reflection. A philosophy of culture may very well reflect upon other things, including an " unconditioned " or a " far side of being " discerned elsewhere than in the command. But it must not imagine than in so doing it has even touched the task of theology. In this sense we must apply to Tillich the continuation of the passage quoted from the *Conf. Gall.* : *En quoi nous détestons tous fantastiques qui voudroyent bien, entant qu'en eux est, anéantir le ministère et prédication de la parole de Dieu et de ses Sacrements.*

If the question what God can do forces theology to be humble, the question what is commanded of us forces it to concrete obedience. God may speak to us through Russian Communism, a flute concerto, a blossoming shrub, or a dead dog. We do well to listen to Him if He really does. But, unless we regard ourselves as the prophets and founders of a new Church, we cannot say that we are commissioned to pass on what we have heard as independent proclamation. God may speak to us through a pagan or an atheist, and thus give us to understand that the boundary between the Church and the secular world can still take at any time a different course from that which we think we discern. Yet this does not mean, unless we are prophets, that we ourselves have to proclaim the pagan or atheistic thing which we have heard. Finally, we may truly and rightly think that we have heard the Word of God in the worship and active love and youth education and theology of the Church known to us. This does not mean, however, that we have received a commission to pursue these things as proclamation. However it may stand with the undoubted possibilities of God outside the Church or in a new Church ; however it may stand with the greater sphere, perhaps unknown to us, of the visible Church, or even with the real, if involuntary, proclamation by other elements of Church life within the Church perceived by us, there can be no doubt that, together with the commission which it may seek to obey by listening and responding in these other functions, the Church known to us has a special commission of proclamation, and therefore not merely of listening and response but decisively of talk about God both to men and for them, and that it neglects this commission if it seeks to proclaim what it has no commission to do or where it has no commission to do so.

But what is this specially commissioned proclamation of the Church which it must accept as a commission to and for men ? Our initial answer is purely descriptive.

1. This proclamation is preaching, i.e., the attempt by someone called thereto in the Church, in the form of an exposition of some portion of the biblical witness to revelation, to express in his own words and to make intelligible to the men of his own generation the promise of the revelation, reconciliation and vocation of God as they are to be expected here and now.

It might be instructive to compare this with the definition given by Karl Fezer (*Das Wort Gottes und die Predigt*, 1925, p. 77 ; cf. the review by Eduard Thurneysen, Theol. Bl., 1925, p. 197 f.) : " Preaching is man's attempt by free speech to co-operate in securing that the God who grants us His fellowship in the Word of Scripture should be corporately present to a group of other men by the Holy Spirit." (I hear that the formula has taken a different form in the oral instruction given by Fezer. I do not quote it for polemical reasons, but with a view to indicating the problems to be considered at this point.)

2. This proclamation is the sacrament, i.e., the symbolical act which is carried through in the Church as directed by the biblical witness of revelation in accompaniment and confirmation of preaching and which is designed as such to attest the event of divine revelation, reconciliation and vocation which does not merely fulfil but underlies the promise.

Cf. the unusually clear and exhaustive definition of the term " sacrament " in the *Heidelberg Catechism*, 1563, *Qu.* 66 : " What are the sacraments ?—They are visible, sacred signs and seals appointed by God, so that through the use of the same He may the better give us to understand the promise of the Gospel, and seal the same, namely, that for the sake of the one sacrifice of Christ accomplished on the cross He graciously grants us remission of sins and eternal life."

This is what the talk about God that is to be found in the Church seeks to be when it is meant to be proclamation and is thus directed to men with the claim and expectation that it has to declare to them the Word of God. It can and should aim to be proclamation as preaching and sacrament because the Church has a commission to make such proclamation.

In attempting to interpret what we have described in this way, our primary task must be to make it clear that, when man cannot regard himself as the one who gives the commission but only as the one who is commissioned, there are only two ways of establishing the factuality and meaning of a commission. Either the order must be repeated as it is thought to have been received and heard, or a fact must be created by the mere attempt to obey it. In both cases the answer given to those who ask concerning its basis is indirect. In both cases it can thus be regarded only as most unsatisfactory. In both cases the answer constitutes indeed a counter-question, and it is left to the enquirer whether, in the handing on of what has been heard as an order or in the attempt to obey the order, he perceives or recognises the will of the one who has given the commission, the meaning of his will, and therefore the existence of a true and meaningful commission. If, then, we ask why the Church's talk about God seeks to be proclamation in the specific form of preaching and sacrament, or to what extent it thinks it has its particular commission to proclaim in this action, we can only give a twofold and either way a very simple answer. First, we can only reply that we learn from the biblical witness to revelation that Jesus Christ has given His Church not only the commandment of faith and love and hope, nor merely the commandment to call upon His name in concert and to show brotherly love, etc., but also the commission of proclamation, and indeed of proclamation by preaching and sacrament. Does He expect of His own only that they should take up their cross and follow Him ? Does He desire as witness of this following only those other functions of His Church ? Or does He not rather will these two things as He also and specifically and supremely wills that God's own Word should be proclaimed in and through His Church ? And if so, is not the saying in Mt. 28[19f.] : " Make disciples of all nations, baptising them—teaching them," a genuine summary of what we are told by the biblical documents with regard to this will of His, and has it not therefore to stand as His command to us ? But secondly we cannot prove the existence and content of this order by referring to the convincing excellence of our obedience to it, as though the former could speak for itself in the latter. For again the question whether our act is obedience to this command is not decided by the person commissioned but by the Giver of the commission. Our talk about God may intend to be proclamation in terms of our commission. It may intend to be preaching and sacrament according to the will and command of the Lord of the Church. But we shall not find comfort in our obedience or in the uprightness of our intention to obey. We shall find it only in the actual command that we have heard—a command which must in fact speak for itself if it is to be recognisable to others as such. Once again, then, we can only ask, timidly and reluctantly enough, whether, in spite of all the concurrent disobedience, the Lord's command may not also speak, and speak for itself, in what the Church does.

Hence it is only subsequently, *a posteriori*, exegetically and not in the sense of demonstrating the Church's commission, that we may rightly consider whether even the thought of God's Word being revealed outside the known existing Church is possible for one who has not previously come to be acquainted with real proclamation within the Church ; whether we can appeal to real parallel experiences, such as having heard the Word of God through Communism or some other reality that is thought to have existential application to us, unless we have brought a criterion to this hearing, and applied it either well or badly, on the basis of previous experience of the reality of the Word of God reaching us somehow as commissioned proclamation ; above all— and this is the real point in the present context—whether the life of the Church would not lack its decisive centre, the reference point of all its other functions, without this function, the function of proclamation. We have seen indeed that all these other elements are in some sense an answer to the Word of God heard. Certainly preaching and sacrament may also be put in the same category. They, too, are an answer to what man has heard. And the other elements can undoubtedly be proclamation too, and have actually been so again and again. But just as the answering elements, as we have seen, cannot try to be proclamation as such, so there must stand opposed to them an element which, while it may also be interpreted, of course, as an answer, nevertheless not only can be and time and again is proclamation as distinct from them, but also seeks to be this, and does so because it ought to do so. In this element the proclamation presupposed in the others has its proper place and distinctive position. To be sure this centre, this point of reference to which all the Church's life, including the elements of proclamation, is orientated, can only be the Word of God Himself, and proclamation will as little try to push into the place of this Word as this would be fitting for any other of the Church's functions. The question arises, however, whether the Word of God does not want representatives within the realm of man's willingness to obey, whether it does not demand a specific function in the Church, whether the Church's proclamation is not thereby made at least as much of a task as the Church's responding to God's Word, as this might take place in worship and Church nurture, in instruction and theology. Whether the answer to this question is yes is not a matter to be inferred ; it is decided by the commission which must be the source of all real proclamation.

Let us assume that this commission has been issued and accepted ; the next thing to be made clear will be that proclamation consists significantly and precisely in preaching and sacrament. That which in the form of proclamation should confront listening and answering in the Church as a representation of God's Word demands in some sense a setting apart, a special, imperious calling of the man who is to function here. Furthermore, what this man can try to say as God's Word in the discharge of preaching cannot be God's own Word as such but only the repetition of His promise, repetition of the promise : " Lo, I am

with you alway ! " (Mt. 28²⁰). Proclamation must mean announcement
—announcement as distinct from the real " I am with you " as future
fulfilment. Again, if this announcement is to be the legitimate repetition of not just any promise, but of the promise given to the Church by
God Himself, then it cannot be arbitrary religious discourse. It must
be homily, i.e., discourse which as the exposition of Scripture is controlled and guided. But if it is to be real repetition of this promise, it
cannot consist in the mere reading of Scripture or in repeating and
paraphrasing the actual wording of the biblical witness. This can be
only its presupposition. The concrete encounter of God and man to-day,
whose actuality, of course, can be created only by the Word of God
Himself, must find a counterpart in the human event of proclamation,
i.e., the person called must be ready to make the promise given to the
Church intelligible in his own words to the men of his own time.
Calling, promise, exposition of Scripture, actuality—these are the
decisive definitions of the concept of preaching. If proclamation is by
commission preaching—the fact that it is so need not be proved since
it cannot be proved—then these concepts are a supplementary explanation of the meaning of preaching. Obviously, however, proclamation
would suffer from a palpable weakness if understood solely as preaching.
Preaching is human speech in the form of words thought and expressed
by men. The promise as merely preached is thus a human work both
on the preacher's lips and in the hearer's ear. At best it is an
" existential " decision first made by the preacher and then to be
made by the hearer. Were it no more than this, how could it be a
pointer to the very Word of God ? Does not man's word spoken and
received, the more earnestly it is spoken and received, necessarily
imply as such a total eclipse of the Word of God which it seeks to
serve ? The promise given to the Church and attested in Holy
Scripture is itself obviously no such work of man, in contrast to the
promise preached. It is the Word as the enacted divine event, as the
accomplished divine action of judging and reconciling grace in which a
decision is made about man prior to all his own decisions, from which
alone his own decisions can be characterised as decisions of faith, from
which alone, then, what the preacher and his hearer may do in human
fashion can become a pointer to God's own Word. If this event is not
also proclaimed, how far is the promise given to the Church really
proclaimed, how far is the Church's proclamation, not a *ministerium
verbi divini*, but an insuperable obstacle placed in the path of God's
own Word ? Yet how is this event to be proclaimed too ? How can it
come about that proclamation proclaims not only truth but truth as
actuality, i.e., as God's work, and thereby for the first time unequivocally grace as grace ? How is this to happen inasmuch as
proclamation must be unambiguously identical with preaching ? We

are faced here with the fundamental difficulty in the task of preaching beside which one may with a good conscience describe all others as child's play. From this standpoint it is easy enough to understand that in practice little importance is attached in the Church to the claim and expectation that preaching should speak the Word of God. It is easy to understand that on the one hand Roman Catholic preaching seems to be largely content with the level of higher instruction in religion and morals while on the other hand typical Neo-Protestant preaching does not claim to be more than the most authentic and lively possible expression of the personal piety of the speaker concerned. We shall have to say more about these two aberrations. In face of the difficulty which is at the root of both, and in answer to the question how God's Word can be proclaimed as God's work, we cannot have recourse at once to what is, of course, the very true and valid reference to God Himself, to the Holy Spirit, who will confirm as His own work the work of the faith which is proclaimed in words of human thought and expression on the lips of the preacher and in the ears of the hearer, thus turning the preached promise into the event of the real promise that is given to the Church. This reference to the native power of God's own Word in and in spite of the darkness of the human word that serves it is, of course, the Alpha and Omega, the *ultima ratio*, apart from which not only the concept of preaching but also that of Church proclamation generally is quite impossible. The only question is whether, in the concept of the proclamation enjoined on the Church, this reference is not represented by a second element which is not identical with preaching as such and in which proclamation might be precisely what it cannot be as preaching alone, namely, the proclamation of reality, of the promise as God's work, of the grace of the faith preached and received, of the decision taken before and beyond all our decisions, which distinguishes human speaking and hearing as worship of God in spirit and in truth. Naturally, this second element in proclamation can also be no more than human talk about God. It can seek to be no more than preaching to the degree that it, too, can only announce, i.e., announce the future revelation, reconciliation and calling, and thus be repetition of the promise, a means of grace. Nor can it seek to be independent proclamation alongside preaching. It can only seek to be its confirmation, as the seal beneath a letter confirms its authenticity but adds nothing to its contents, making no statement except under the letter and in a sense standing apart. It must be co-ordinated with preaching in the sense that, as preaching represents the promise as such, it represents the character of the promise as event and grace in contrast to all man's work on the level of human occurrence. To represent this basis of the promise it must not consist in further words ; it has to be action. But to be proclamation, it cannot be arbitrarily selected action any more than preaching can. It has to be the action demanded and controlled by the biblical witness. Again, like preaching, it cannot seek to replace the Word of God itself. As preaching is a strictly representative word, so it can be only a strictly representative action. Like preaching it can only be a serving of God's Word. What in either case is more than representation, service and symbol, is the event whose subject is not the Church but God Himself. And the object which it has to represent must be the presupposition of preaching which preaching as such, as word in human thought and expression, cannot represent, for which the human word as such cannot be the symbol, namely, revelation, reconciliation and calling, which the Church can only believe, hope and proclaim that it has before it when it has it behind it as the act of divine grace, which it can only truly expect when it already owes its origin to it (as enacted once and for all in the epiphany of Jesus Christ). Promise in the form of an adjunct to preaching, action in distinction from mere word, conformity to Scripture, representative symbolical connexion with the " once-for-all " of revelation—these are the decisive definitions of the concept of sacrament. We have not postulated this concept either, but exegeted it on the presupposition that its content is a reality in the life of the Church on the basis of God's commission, and that to this extent it is before us as a text which can be exegeted. There can be as little question of a free establishing of the necessity of sacrament as there can of a necessity of preaching or of proclamation generally. Hence in retrospect of what has been said and in answer to the question of its final proof we should not omit to point away from the exegesis and back to the actual text before us.

In conclusion, however, this exegesis of the terms proclamation, preaching and sacrament requires an express declaration : As has been done, Evangelical dogmatics exegetes these concepts.

We may ignore at this point the fact that it is specifically Evangelical-Reformed dogmatics which has done this in detail.

As regards the main concept of proclamation this exegesis stands first in antithesis to Modernist dogmatics. This, too, is acquainted with the function specified but it is not aware of its essential distinctiveness as compared with other functions in the Church—a distinctiveness which accrues to it when it rests on a commission to and for men, when as man's talk about God it has to serve God's own Word spoken from an ineffaceable antithesis to all humanity. Modernist dogmatics is finally unaware of the fact that in relation to God man has constantly to let something be said to him, has constantly to listen to something, which he constantly does not know and which in no circumstances and in no sense can he say to himself. Modernist dogmatics hears man answer when no one has called him. It hears him speak with himself. For it, therefore, proclamation is a necessary expression of the life of the human community known as the " Church," an expression in which one man, in the name and for the spiritual advancement of a number of others, drawing from a treasure common to him and to them, offers, for the enrichment of this treasure, an interpretation of his own past and present as a witness to the reality alive in this group of men.

Even Schleiermacher's *Christian Faith* is not without a section on ministry of God's Word (§ 133 f.). But we are told at once that the " divine Word " is simply " the spirit in all men," i.e., in all those united in the Church (§ 134, 3). Thus ministry of God's Word is the " act of the community as such " (§ 135, 2), or, concretely, the " relation of the active toward the receptive " (§ 133, 1), or the " influence of the stronger on the weaker " (§ 113, 2) through the medium of self-impartation, i.e., a " self-display with a stimulating effect, in which the emotion of the displayer, taken up by imitation, becomes in the receptively stimulated person who takes it up a power which calls forth the same emotion " (§ 133, 1). It embraces the " whole Christian life " and only needs special " management " for the sake of good order and preservation of the common consciousness (§ 134, 3 ; 135). We are only at the other, realistic end of the same path which Schleiermacher entered upon idealistically when, a century later, P. Tillich argues that " a new sacramental situation " will have to be " created " to save Protestantism (*Relig. Verwirkl.*, 1930, p. 166) by our " successfully reaching the depths of our own undivided, pre-objective being " (*op. cit.*, p. 154) and thus gaining an understanding of the fact that there is a mastery over natural things and situations, and hence over the Word among other things, that this is experienced in the " historical destiny " of reciprocal apprehending and being apprehended, and that in virtue of it these things can become the vehicles of " sacramental mastery " for believers (p. 176). If by " sacramental situation " Tillich means the same as what we call proclamation, and if the way to this " sacramental situation," i.e., the historical destiny by which it is created, is really the relation between a deepened understanding of self and a deepened understanding of the world, and *vice versa*, then we are forced to conjecture that here too man is finally conceived of as conversing only with himself. And indeed " religious symbols are created in the process of religious history " (p. 206). " One has a right to say that, e.g., Christ and Buddha are symbols in so far as the unconditionally transcendent can be viewed in them " (p. 104). " God as Object is a representation of what is ultimately intended in the religious act " (p. 103). " The unconditionally transcendent goes beyond any positing of an essence, even a supreme essence. In so far as such is posited, it is also abrogated again in the religious act. This abrogation, the atheism immanent in the religious act, is the depth of the religious act " (p. 102). " The truth of a symbol rests upon its inner necessity for the symbol-creating consciousness " (p. 103). " At the point where—apart from all material connexions—the spiritual expresses itself, it expresses itself religiously " (p. 94).

On this view the ideas of speech, word, proclamation and preaching, which in themselves might all still point to the juxtaposition of God and man, must obviously disappear in the general concept of operation or movement or into the notion of a general dynamic or even meaning which embraces God and man, which is in some way the vehicle of the existence of each and all of us, and which somehow—this is where proclamation is needed—is to be articulated by us. But then Logos in its isolation as word spoken back and forth necessarily becomes one symbol among many others. " I cannot possibly rate the word so highly," i.e., as an expression of that dynamic or meaning. The question now becomes in all seriousness : Why do I choose precisely these symbols, talk about God and this form of it, namely, actual exposition of the Bible, along with these two or seven sacraments ? Are these really the truest symbols when my spiritual nature should and would express itself ? Might there not be truer ones than these ?

That it should be said of the Word of God!—" in the choice (!) of this symbol lies the spiritual character of the self-impartation of transcendent being. . . . But it is quite wrong to equate the Word as a symbol of the self-impartation of transcendent being with the Word as the physical medium of the self-comprehension and self-impartation of the human spirit, and in this way to mix up God's Word and the word of Scripture or the word of preaching " (P. Tillich, *Rel. Verwirkl.*, 1930, p. 48 f. ; cf. p. 60). " Word is not only present when it is spoken and conceived but Word is also present when it is made present and actualised in powerful symbols. *Verbum* is more than *oratio*. Protestantism has largely forgotten this. *Verbum*, the Word of revelation, may (!) be in everything in which spirit expresses itself, even in the silent symbols of art, even in the works of society and law. And therefore a church must be able to speak in all these forms. They must all become symbols for the Word of revelation. And that means that nothing less than the whole life of society in every aspect is ordained to be symbolically powerful for God " (*Kirche u. Kultur*, 1924, p. 19 f.). Which of the various expressions that one might choose has the most " symbolical power " to-day ? This is now the solemn question of the Berneuchener, and a " fountain " which is to be set up in the church " with running water as an allegory of God's creative life-stream " (*Berneuchener Buch*, 1926, p. 112), coloured window-panes as symbols of the " light from uncreated light," and various cheerful things of a similar nature, now have a chance of entering into not wholly purposeless rivalry with preaching, which has become less relevant ever since, long ago now, the organ was raised (by Julius Smend) to the dignity of a " second pulpit " that must proclaim to us in other tongues, above all in sacred tones, the element of the transcendent and ineffable in religion " (quoted according to Herbert Birtner, " Die Probleme der Orgelbewegung," *Theol. Rundschau*, 1932, p. 66). For the sigh has become general and can no longer be ignored : " Preaching, pedestalled (!) on the person of the preacher, stands now too much in the foreground " (O. Dibelius, *Das Jahrhundert der Kirche*, 5th edn. 1928, p. 252). Therefore : " Less preaching ! More action and more of other forms of proclamation ! " " The competition of other intellectual performances " has now become far too great. " More and more persons to-day have inadequate time to prepare their sermons." " Inspiration is needed in poets and in religious speakers. But few mortals can be inspired to order." Perhaps even Jesus would have been " increasingly dissatisfied with speaking had He been tied down to public work and public speaking for decades instead of a single year " (! !) (H. Bär, *Weniger Predigt* !, 1930, p. 8 f., 12 f.). And so on !

And over and above all this the ultimate question may and must arise : Why proclamation at all ? Why symbols at all ? Why not better be silent ? Why not, as the truest word we can utter, renounce all special talk about God, all use of symbols whatsoever ?

" Undoubtedly the supreme aim of a theological work would be to discover the point at which reality itself speaks unsymbolically both of itself and also of the unconditioned, to discover the point at which reality itself without a symbol becomes a symbol, at which the antithesis between reality and symbol is removed." Would it not be the most powerful expression of what is in us if we were to omit all expression in favour of " immediate talk about things so far as they impinge on us unconditionally, so far as they stand in the transcendent " (P. Tillich, *Rel. Verwirkl.*, p. 208) ?

What needs to be said in criticism of this teaching is said clearly enough by the teaching itself. Understanding of the concept of proclamation along these lines can end only with its dissolution. Proclamation as self-exposition must in the long run turn out to be a superfluous and impossible undertaking. To a large degree it has obviously turned out this way already. The distinction between such proclamation and the other functions of the Church cannot be shown to be essential. But if it is not, do not these other functions also become inessential as answers (answers to what ?) ? What is the Church, what is it meant to be, if it has no centre, if man is not really addressed in it ? Can the truth of its being really be that man is alone in and with his world ? Is it not plain that there is here a fateful confusion between the man of the present, the man of the *regnum gratiae*, and the man of eternal glory, who, as we saw at the outset, neither needs nor will need any special talk about God, and consequently any being addressed by God, and consequently any Church ? If we are not this man, whence does the Modernist doctrine get its legal ground ?

All that Evangelical faith cannot understand about this alien belief on the left may be summed up in the questions of Rom. 10[14] : Πῶς οὖν ἐπικαλέσονται εἰς ὅν οὐκ ἐπίστευσαν ; πῶς δὲ πιστεύσωσιν οὗ οὐκ ἤκουσαν ; πῶς δὲ ἀκούσωσιν χωρὶς κηρύσσοντος ; πῶς δὲ κηρύξωσιν ἐὰν μὴ ἀποσταλῶσιν ; . . . ἄρα ἡ πίστις ἐξ ἀκοῆς, ἡ δὲ ἀκοὴ διὰ ῥήματος Χριστοῦ.

The other no less serious difference that requires treatment here separates us from Roman Catholic dogmatics. In the first place, but only in the first place, it does not concern the main concept of proclamation but the mutual relations of the concepts of preaching and sacrament. The Roman Catholic Church is expressly and consciously the church of the sacrament. Its dogmatics cannot emphasise strongly enough that the Church lives by and in this means of grace.

The sacraments are the *canales gratiae*, the *vasa medicinae* against sin and death, the *fundamenta et cardines vitae christianae*, the river which flows out of Eden according to Gen. 2[10], the seven pillars on which wisdom has built her house according to Prov. 9[1], the bond of peace of Eph. 4[16] (H. Hurter, S.J., *Theol. dogm. compend.*, 12th edn. 1908, Vol. III, p, 214). " The Church's work in performing them is the truest revelation and the outer confirmation of its mysterious life ; they are the essential content of the Church's cultus and therefore the most excellent means of preserving the visible Church in unity and making it recognisable and distinguishable. Reception of them is the most essential mark of the Church's fellowship, their administration the most excellent and sublime activity of its priests. . . ." They are " the most concentrated expression and the inmost kernel of the Church's faith and life " (Scheeben-Atzberger, *Handb. d. kath. Dogm.*, Vol. IV, 1903, p. 463). Cf. also Bartmann, *Lehrb. d. Dogm.*, 7th edn., Vol. 2, 1929, p. 207.

But one might ask quite seriously whether the superlatives we have just heard do not always say too little when one realises that in this dogmatics preaching is not only assigned less importance, but virtually no importance at all compared to the sacrament which is received and celebrated so zealously. Nor is it merely that Roman Catholicism overemphasises the sacrament in the same way as Protestantism does oral preaching.

This schematism becomes pure nonsense when Klaus Harms (in his 95 theses of 1817) advances the exaggerated view that the Roman Church inclines to cling to the sacrament and build its life around this, that the Reformed Church does the same with the Word, but that the Lutheran Church " more splendidly than either " honours both sacrament and Word (briefly reproduced by Max Geiger, *Unsere Taufe*, 1931, p. 4). For one thing, Lutheran Protestantism, if it stays to any degree at all in Luther's footsteps, cannot wish to take middle ground and to break solidarity with Reformed Protestantism in respect of the greater emphasis on preaching and its higher ranking as compared with the sacrament. Again, for all the greater emphasis on preaching and its higher ranking, the importance which is assigned to the sacrament in the practice of the Reformed Church, and the care with which the problem of the sacrament has been and is treated in Reformed dogmatics, cannot possibly be regarded as parallel to what happens to preaching in Roman Catholic dogmatics. One would have to say the same even about Modernist dogmatics. Neither Schleiermacher's nor Troeltsch's estimation of the sacraments—judge them materially as one may—can be compared with what happens to preaching on principle and without exception, so far as I can see, in Roman Catholic dogmatics.

The fate of preaching here is quite simple : *Silentium altissimum.* Roman Catholic dogmaticians pass on from the treatise on grace or from that on the Church to the treatise on the sacraments. They develop the doctrine of the sacrament of the priestly *ordo*. They consistently speak of the teaching office of the Church as though preaching did not even exist as an indispensable means of grace that claims serious attention. The only points of interest in preaching, and naturally these have only passing interest, are legal questions like those about primary and secondary bearers of legitimate Church doctrine, the necessity of a special *missio canonica* for preaching, etc.

Even in the articles on the " teaching office " in Josef Braun, *Handlexikon d. kath. Dogm.*, 1926, p. 185 f., there is complete silence about preaching, proclamation, etc. Cf. *C. jur. can. c.* 1327/28.

It should be noted that in practical writings Roman Catholic theology can incidentally find lofty and what seem to be dogmatically relevant things to say about preaching.

Through "Word and sacrament" the priest builds up the mystical body of the Lord, the Church. "Through this word of preaching and in it Christ lives on mystically, edifies, extends, enlightens, comforts and blesses His Church continually, pursues His work of redemption through every century, feeds our souls on the bread of truth, just as He incorporates the whole man into Himself through the eucharistic bread. And preaching has no other task than to translate this Word of God into human speech, to expound and apply it." It works by itself becoming God's Word (Franz Hettinger, *Timotheus. Briefe an einen jungen Theologen*, 3rd ed. 1909, p. 45, 48). One would like to know whether such statements are to be regarded as merely *pia opinio* (or perhaps *propositio temeraria ?*) of an individual—or why, if not, they find no parallels in the manuals of Roman Catholic dogmatics. There is a homiletics by the same author under the title *Aphorismen über Predigt und Prediger*, 1888, but here again we seek in vain any dogmatic basis for the necessity of preaching.

The occasional affirmation does not alter in the slightest the fact that Roman Catholic dogmatics itself, and the standard dogmatic utterances of the teaching office, which are neither of them wont to be sparing in words on matters of importance to them, shroud themselves in almost complete obscurity on this point.

The strongest plea for preaching in Denzinger's collection (No. 426) is a concessive statement in the *professio fidei Waldensibus praescripta* of 1208. Here preaching is actually described as *valde necessaria et laudabilis*. There is also a comparatively noteworthy estimation of preaching in the *Praefatio* to the *Catech. Roman.* of 1566. But this seems to coincide very closely with the contemporary need for active measures against Protestantism (Qu. 5–7) and the dogmatic content in this text is not very considerable, at least in regard to the connection between preaching, faith and grace.

Again, the fact that a weekly Sunday sermon is prescribed for the Roman Catholic parish priest, and that the Roman Catholic Church has produced more than one outstanding preacher both past and present, cannot alter in the least the way in which this function is obviously forced into a backwater even in its exercise, as shown externally by the ruling that the Mass may be complete without it.

The liturgical place of preaching is in the so-called pre-Mass (the ancient *missa catechumenorum*). To-day the (Latin) reading of the Gospel constitutes the organic centre of this. Pius Bihlmeyer O.S.B. makes the following notes at the passage in question (*Das vollständige römische Messbuch*, 3rd edn., 1930, p. 533) : " Now Christ speaks to us through His Word or through His miracles and redemptive acts. The same loving, wonder-working Saviour will appear Himself at the holy sacrifice, to accomplish mysteriously in us (!) what according to the Gospel narrative He has wrought in others (!). In this faith and hope we listen to the Gospel. . . . To the Gospel there is often (!) appended by ancient usage (!) a sermon in which the holy words of God are more closely explained and expounded as the rule for our lives." Note that the approach to this action is constituted by 1, the *Introitus* with the *Kyrie*, 2. the christological *Gloria*, 3. an *Oratio* for the day in question, 4. the reading of the Epistle, 5. the *Graduale* with or without the Tractus and Sequence, 6. the beautiful prayers : *Munda cor meum ac labia mea, omnipotens Deus, qui labia Isaiae prophetae calculo mundasti ignito : ita me tua grata miseratione dignare mundare, ut sanctum Evangelium tuum digne valeam nuntiare. Per Jesum Christum Dominum nostrum. Amen. Jube, Domine, bene-dicere. Dominus sit in corde meo et in labiis meis : ut digne et competenter annuntiem Evangelium suum. Amen.* And upon that reading with or without sermon there then follows (obviously saying more than Bihlmeyer) : *Per evangelica dicta deleantur nostra delicta,* and then in conclusion the Niceno-Constantinopolitan Creed. One cannot avoid the impression that this mighty structure stands in no relation to the poverty of its centre to-day (e.g., is it worthwhile to appeal to Is. 6 for the sake of a mere lesson ?). Is there not absent the very thing to which everything seems to point, namely, the sermon as the true and necessary *annuntiatio* (beyond the mere lesson) ? Even the present-day Benedictine reform of the liturgy does not seem to counteract at all the liturgically anomalous and non-necessary status of the sermon.

Inwardly the incidental place of the sermon is shown by the fact that it hardly seems to want to rise in principle above the level of apologetic instruction and moral exhortation. It does not appear in the main to claim the character of true proclamation which is equal in seriousness to the celebration of the sacrament.

Cf. the words quoted from Bihlmeyer. As regards the content of preaching *C. jur. can. c.*1347, 1 reads as follows : *In sacris concionibus exponenda inprimis sunt, quae fideles credere et facere ad salutem oportet.*

In sharp distinction from the sacrament, preaching is not a constitutive element in the Roman Catholic concept of the priesthood.

Except in case of special dispensation, every priest has to celebrate his Mass daily, but according to *Trid. Sess.* XXIII *De sacr. ordinis, can.* 1, a man may be a priest without ever preaching.

This is something that cannot possibly be said of the position of the sacraments in the theory and practice of the Evangelical Churches except perhaps for certain sects.

If we are to understand this peculiar situation on the Roman Catholic side and then the meaning and significance of the opposing Evangelical thesis, we have to realise above all else that Roman Catholicism—not unlike Modernism in this respect—sees something quite different from proclamation take place at that centre of the Church's life which we have described as proclamation. Proclamation must mean repetition of the divine promise. On the basis of the Word which God has spoken to His Church attention is drawn in His Church, through men, to the Word which He wishes to speak to His Church. The presence of God is thus the grace of God, i.e., His unfathomably free act at a given time in which He recognises the attention drawn and therewith fulfils the promise in a twofold sense : by making the repetition effected by men a true one, and by corresponding to the proclaimed promise by a real new coming of His Word. The grace of this twofold fulfilment meets man, then, quite simply in his hearing of the promise and his obedience to it. It meets him only in faith. This is how the Reformers understood that event at the heart of the

Church's life. They understood it in terms of proclamation, i.e., of the *promissio* repeated by man's act, because they thought they could understand the presence of the holy God among unholy men only as the grace of the strictly personal free Word of God which reaches its goal in the equally personal free hearing of men, the hearing of faith, which for its part, too, can be understood only as grace. This presupposition is missing in Roman Catholic dogmatics. It, too, describes the event at the heart of the Church's life as grace. But it understands by grace, not the connexion between the Word and faith, but the connexion between a divine being as cause and a divine-creaturely being as effect. With due reservations one might even say that it understands it as a physical, not a historical, event. It sees the presence of Jesus Christ in His Church, the mystical unity of the Head with the whole body, in the fact that under certain conditions there flows forth from Jesus Christ a steady and unbroken stream or influence of divine-human being on His people.

At this particular point one can scarcely fail to see the inner connexion between the Roman Catholic view and the Modernist view. The assertion of fellowship between God and man in the form of an operation beyond the juxtaposition of the divine and human persons, beyond the act of divine and human decision, is at least common to both even if one has to remember that this synthetic operation is regarded as man's work on the side of Modernism and as God's on that of Roman Catholicism. But of what importance here (and not only here) is the distinction between " anthropocentric " and " theocentric " theology ? Both agree in the unwillingness to recognise the ultimate necessity of proclamation.

Proclamation obviously cannot be the term for this event. Grace here neither is (and remains) God's free and personal Word nor is (and remains) hearing faith. It neither has to be just Word from God nor faith in man. Man neither needs to listen to a Word of God already spoken nor to wait for a Word of God yet to be spoken. Faith neither has to grasp the promise made as made by God nor to wait for a fulfilment still to come. Blessedness is not seen in this grasping and waiting nor judgment discerned in a situation other than this grasping and waiting. All this can obviously be regarded only as partly inadequate, partly superfluous, and partly distorted if both from the standpoint of the divine Giver and also from that of the human recipient grace is an operation, an influence, an action and passion which takes place, not essentially and ultimately between person and person, but materially between God as author on the one hand and the ground of being in the human person on the other.

Protestant polemics is urgently recommended not to use the word " magical " in this connexion. The authentic Roman Catholic view of this material process cannot be brought under any meaningful definition of the term " magic " Cf. on this whole subject Damasus Winzen O.S.B. " Die Sakramentenlehre der Kirche in ihrem Verhältnis zur dialektischen Theologie," *Catholica*, 1932, p. 19 f.

We are faced with a basic decision at this point. For the man who can interpret an operation or influence of an impersonal kind as the grace of Jesus Christ, the rest follows self-evidently. On this view the sacrament has to become the one and all. As act in distinction from spoken Word it is well adapted, if influence be the thing that takes place between God and man in the Church, to be the medium and channel of this influence.

Naturally the significance of the sacrament has then to be described as a *causare, continere et conferre gratiam* (*Conc. Florent.* 1438 *Decr. pro. Arm.* Denzinger No. 695) and its power as effective *ex opere operato*, i.e., independently of divine decision and human faith—*Si quis dixerit, non dari gratiam per hujus modi sacramenta semper et omnibus, quantum est ex parte Dei, etiam si rite ea suscipiant, sed aliquando et aliquibus :* A.S. (*Trid. Sess.* VII *Can. de sacr. in genere can.* 7) *S.q.d., per ipsa novae legis sacramenta ex opere operato non conferre gratiam, sed solam fidem divinae promissionis ad gratiam consequendam sufficere :* A.S. (*ib. can.* 8).

And naturally preaching has to be forced into that particular backwater. It is in fact unnecessary here. It can continue alongside what is essential only as its preliminary and ancillary exposition and inculcation.

Certainly the Roman Catholic Church knows and stresses the fact (e.g., *Cat. Rom., Praef. qu.* 2) that *fides* comes *ex auditu* (Rom. 10[17]). But it regards the faith which comes from hearing the Word only as preparatory to receiving righteousness before God. *Disponuntur autem ad ipsam justitiam dum excitati divina gratia et adiuti, fidem ex auditu concipientes, libere moventur in Deum, credentes, vera esse, quae divinitus revelata et promissa sunt* (*Trid. Sess.* VI, *cap.* 6).

It cannot be a means of true sanctifying grace, *gratia gratum faciens*, only a means of preparatory grace.

If in the doctrine of what is called " actual " grace dogmaticians do talk about hearing too at a certain point, what is portrayed from this standpoint is only the very preliminary grace of *illustratio intellectus* (M. J. Scheeben, *Handb. der kath. Dogm.* Vol. 3, 1882, new edn. 1925, p. 666 ; B. Bartmann, *Lehrb. der Dogm.*, 7th edn., Vol. 2, 1929, p. 15).

Any other view would in fact mean reviving the partly inadequate, partly superfluous and partly distorted situation which inevitably arises when it is a matter of the Word and hearing it. But Roman Catholic dogmatics does not want to see and understand the event at the heart of the Church's life in this problematic way. For it, then, preaching can have a place only on the extreme margin of the Church's action. In Roman Catholic practice it cannot seek to be more than instruction and exhortation. When the grace of Jesus Christ can be understood as a *causare gratiam ex opere operato*, all is in order, and this is the only possible order.

The Reformers, however, did not see themselves as in a position to construe the grace of Jesus Christ in this way. They thought it should be understood, not as cause and effect, but as Word and faith. For this reason, they regarded the representative event at the centre of the Church's life as proclamation, as an act concerned with speaking and hearing, indicative of the fact that what is at issue in the thing proclaimed too is not a material connexion but a personal encounter. In this light they had to regulate the mutual relations of preaching and sacrament in a very definite way. To be sure, they could not and would not assign to the sacrament the place which falls to preaching according to Roman Catholic dogmatics. Proclamation of the basis of the promise which has been laid once and for all, and therefore proclamation in the form of symbolic action, had to be and to remain essential for them. But this proclamation presupposes that the other, namely, repetition of the biblical promise, is taking place. The former must exist for the sake of the latter, and therefore the sacrament for the sake of preaching, not *vice versa*. Hence not the sacrament alone nor preaching alone, nor yet, to speak meticulously, preaching and the sacrament in double track, but preaching with the sacrament, with the visible act that confirms human speech as God's act, is the constitutive element, the perspicuous centre of the Church's life. Understood *a parte potiori*, but only *a parte potiori*, the Evangelical Churches, Lutheran as well as Reformed, can and must be termed the churches of preaching.

" To achieve such faith God has instituted preaching, given the Gospel and sacraments " (Conf. Aug. art. 5). " Then the Word brings Christ to the folk and makes Him known in their hearts, a thing they never knew from the sacraments. Therefore 'tis a hard thing for our times that people are all for holding masses and hasten only to found masses, and unfortunately the foremost thing for which masses are instituted is left out, that is, preaching " (Luther, *Ausleg. deutsch d. Vaterunsers*, 1519, *W.A.*, Vol. 2, p. 112, l. 15). " Now to do away with this misuse, the first thing to know is that the Christian community should never come together, except there God's very Word be preached and prayer made. . . . Therefore where God's Word is not preached, 'tis better people should neither sing nor read, nor come together. . . . 'Tis better to leave out all, save the Word. And nought is better pursued than the Word. For all Scripture showeth that the same should be in full swing among Christians, and Christ also saith Himself, Lk. 10[42] ' One thing is needful.' For that Mary should sit at Christ's feet and hear His Word daily is the best part to choose, and is never taken away. It is an eternal saying that all else must pass away, however much there is for Martha to do " (*Von Ordnung Gottesdiensts*, 1523, *W.A.*, 12, p. 35, l. 19 and p. 37, l. 29). *Primum vero et summum omnium, in quo omnia pendent alia, est docere verbum Dei. Nam verbo docemus, verbo consecramus, verbo ligamus et solvimus, verbo baptisamus, verbo sacrificamus, per verbum de omnibus iudicamus, ut cuicunque verbum cesserimus, huic plane nihil negare possumus, quod ad sacerdotem pertinet* (*De instit. ministris Ecclesiae*, 1523, *W.A.* 12, p. 180, l. 5). ". . . Where the preaching chair lies and snores, so that it does not wake up nor expound the words, one may well sing and read in it, but without any understanding " (*E.A.* 1, 229 between 1530–34). " Therefore we should know that God hath so ordained that none should come to knowledge of Christ or acquire forgiveness through Him or receive the Holy Ghost without external public means, but hath put such treasure in the oral word or preaching office, and will not establish it in a corner or secretly in the heart, but will have it cried aloud and imparted openly among the people, as Christ enjoined : ' Go ye into all the world and preach the Gospel to every creature ' " (*Sermon on Matt.* 9[1f.], *W.A.* 29, p. 579, l. 25). *Est itaque Benedicere : praedicare et docere verbum Evangelii confiteri Christum et cognitionem ipsius propagare in alios.* Et hoc sacerdotale officium est et juge sacrificium Ecclesiae in novo Testamento, quae benedictionem illam distribuit praedicando, administrando sacramenta, absolvendo, consolando et tractando verbum gratiae (*Comm. on Gal.* 3[9], 1535, *W.A.* 40[I], p. 387, l. 21). *Ecclesia nihil facere debet, quam recte et pure docere Evangelium atque ita generare liberos* (*on Gal.* 4[27], p. 664, l. 27). " For the very greatest, holiest, most needful, highest service of God, which God has demanded in the first and second commandment as the greatest, is to preach God's Word, for the preacher's office is the highest office in the churches, where then the service of God is omitted, how can there be knowledge of God, the teaching of Christ, or the Gospel ? " (Melanchthon, *Apologie*, *C.R.* 28, 220). Calvin called preaching (*doctrina*) the *anima ecclesiae* (*Instit.* IV, 12, 1, cf. *Suppl. Exhort.* 1543, *C.R.* 6, 459), or the *mater ex qua nos Deus generat* (*Comm. Gal.* 4[24], *C.R.* 50, 237), and in his great letter to the Duke of Somerset (Oct. 1548, *C.R.* 13, 70 f.) he expressly declared that mere readings are no substitute for *prédication vive* and that the possibility of excesses on the preacher's part, which at all events, have to be reckoned with, should not be an obstacle : *Tous les dangers quon peult craindre ne doibvent empescher que l'Esprit de Dieu nayt sa liberte et son cours en ceulx ausquelz il a distribue de ses graces pour edifier l'Eglise.* For : . . . *de dire que nous puissions avoir dévotion, soit à prière, soit à cérémonie sans y rien entendre c'est une grand moquerie : combien qu'il se dict communement. Ce n'est pas une chose morte ne brutifve, que bonne affection envers Dieu : mais est un mouvement vif, procedant du sainct Esprit quand le coeur est droictement touché, et l'entendement illuminé . . . il n'y a nulle edification : sinon où il y a doctrine* (*Forme des Prières* 1542, *Epistre au Lecteur*, *C.R.*, 165 f.). In face of this one can only describe it as theological thoughtlessness and caprice that certain 19th-century Lutherans (Klaus Harms, Vilmar, Löhe), more or less plainly discrediting preaching, thought they could again proclaim the " altar " and the " sacrament of the altar " as the centre of the Church's action. In contrast, listen to the verdict of the un-objectionably Lutheran Hermann Bezzel : " How are Word and sacrament related to one another ? . . . The Word has been the first and will remain the first. We do not read : Heaven and earth shall pass away but my sacraments shall not pass away ; we read : But my words shall not pass away. And just because it is easy for overevaluation of the sacraments to enter in among us, since one expects a magical effect from them, it is essential that one consider the sober Evangelical concept as between them. The Word is the primary thing. The Word existed before the sacrament was. The Word stands alone, the sacrament cannot stand alone. The Word is God's original essence, the sacrament is first aroused by our need. The Word will remain after our need, the sacrament will disappear after our need. This presupposed, I must say that the Word is the audible sacrament and the sacrament is the visible Word. The Word was before the sacrament and exists without the sacrament and will also still exist after-wards " (Johannes Rupprecht, *Hermann Bezzel als Theologe*, 1925, p. 369).

2. DOGMATICS AND CHURCH PROCLAMATION

The claim with which church proclamation steps forward and the expectation with which it is surrounded should not mislead us ; it is always and always will be man's word. It is also something more than this and quite different. When and where it pleases God, it is God's own Word. Upon the promise of this divine good-pleasure it is ventured in obedience. On this promise depend the claim and the expectation. But proclamation both as preaching and sacrament does not cease to be representation, human service.

" Therefore we also confess that the servants of the Church are God's fellow-workers, as St. Paul calls them . . . yet with this addition and understanding that in all this we ascribe all effect and power to the Lord God alone, to whom servants render this service ; for 'tis sure that this power and effect never should or could be attached to any creature, but to God, who imparts it of His own free will to whom He will " (*Conf. Helv. prior* 1536, *art.* 15).

To the degree that it is this, it is not an unassailable action whose authenticity is assured. Like all human action it is exposed to the question of its responsibility. This question can, of course, be put in such a way that it must be dismissed. For instance, Church proclamation, as regards its content, cannot let itself be questioned as to whether it is in harmony with the distinctive features and interests of a race, people, nation, or state. It cannot let itself be questioned as to its agreement with the demands of this or that scientific or aesthetic culture. It cannot let itself be questioned as to whether it is contributing what is needed to maintain or perhaps even to overthrow this or that form of society or economy. A proclamation which accepts responsibilities along these or similar lines spells treachery to the Church and to Christ Himself. It only gets its due if sooner or later its mouth is stopped by some refined or brutal ungodliness. Far better no proclamation at all than this kind. Just because of its real responsibility Church proclamation must be unconditionally free in every other area. Its real responsibility arises out of its intention to be proclamation of the Word of God. The very claim with which it steps forward and the expectation with which it is surrounded also point towards the critical authority by which it must let itself be questioned and in terms of which its legitimacy must always be decided. And because in proclamation the centre of the Church's life is at issue to the degree that it seeks to be the representation of the divine summons to which all other elements in the life of the Church must answer, we have to state that with and in proclamation the Church itself is generally questioned by that critical authority regarding the authenticity of its existence as the Church.

Est autem ecclesia congregatio sanctorum, in qua Evangelium recte docetur et recte administrantur sacramenta (*Conf. Aug. art.* 7). Thus *docere Evangelium* and *administrare sacramenta* take place on the assumption of a *puritas* and *rectitudo* which is presupposed and sought in this action, of a norm that decides as to the rightness of the action. And this *rectitudo* of teaching and sacrament also decides whether the Church really is here and now the Church, the *ecclesia*, the *congregatio sanctorum*.

Thus it is precisely in terms of its origin and basis, of the being of the Church, that Church proclamation, and with it the Church itself, is assailed and called in question. No other attack that may arise can even remotely harass the Church in the same way as this one. To the degree that it is really harassed here it can and should be of good courage in face of all other assaults. But the harassment in this question will always have two aspects, the one relating to the past and the other to the future. What was it that sought to be Christian proclamation yesterday ? And what will it be that steps forward anew to-morrow with this claim and surrounded with this expectation ? Between the yesterday and the to-morrow, applying to both, attacking yesterday's effort in retrospect and to-morrow's in advance, censuring the one in order to correct the other, there arises the question of the responsibility which is our present concern. Because it is God's service that Church proclamation seeks to be, it is God Himself and God alone who asks here and to whom response must be made here. But for this very reason and in this very way the Church is seriously and concretely burdened with this responsibility. As it can and should evade all other responsibilities, this becomes a burning one. If it does not, if the Church with its proclamation can feel secure before God, then the other responsibilities will become burning ones, and it can and must happen that all the opposition to Church proclamation from the standpoint of the state, society, culture and the like, though not intrinsically justifiable, will be legitimate in relation to the Church, and will become very necessary criticism of the Church in its whole failure to be the Church.

The *Ad fontes* ! of the Humanists at the beginning of the 16th century was in itself simply a matter of a historicism which is easily seen through theologically and is definitely to be rejected. The discovery of the free creative individual which invaded every sphere with increasing force from the middle of the same century was intrinsically no more than a bit of reviving paganism. The rationality with which the 18th century thought it could master the problems of life better than the Church was sufficiently sharply distinct to be an obvious theological aberration. The eudaemonistic rationalist ideas in which modern Socialism had its origins and from which it derives its spiritual outlook even to this day can certainly have no place in the Church's proclamation. The new Humanism which is preached in America to-day, and which has some prospects of becoming the world-view of the immediate future, betrays already by its utter fatuousness that it is in a very inferior position *vis-à-vis* the Church. Nor can one see in the Asiatic crudities of Bolshevic ideology a rival which inwardly is even remotely a match for the Church's proclamation. But this is all true, and can still be true to-day, only if by " Church " we everywhere mean the Church which is conscious of its own responsibility regarding its proclamation, which is sorely pressed by it and seriously concerned about it. For an unconcerned and self-assured Church which is not assailed at its own centre, these opponents are all serious opponents.

The Church should fear God and not fear the world. But only if and as it fears God need it cease to fear the world. If it does not fear God, then it is not helped at all but genuinely endangered if it fears the world, listens to its opposition, considers its attitude, and accepts all kinds of responsibilities towards it, no matter how necessary and justified may be the criticism it receives from this quarter.

It was the prophetic thinker and preacher Hermann Kutter (1863–1931) who in the last generation, with a force unequalled by any of his contemporaries, represented the insight that the sphere of God's power is greater than the sphere of the Church, and that from time to time it has pleased and pleases God to visit His Church with warning and comfort precisely in the figures and events of secular world history. Especially in his older books *Sie müssen* (1903), *Gerechtigkeit* (1905) and *Wir Pfarrer* (1907) Kutter says this with particular reference to the Social Democracy of the era before the First World War. What Kutter meant, not as a programme, but as an actual scanning and interpretation of the signs of the times, was first developed by Leonhard Ragaz into the theory that the Church must take up a position towards Socialism as a pioneer manifestation of the Kingdom of God, and hence into a true system of religious Socialism. After the war P. Tillich, an incomparably more bloodless and abstract thinker than Kutter or Ragaz, replaced this Socialism by secular culture in general, and established and defended this secularism against the Church as a systematic principle, tricking it out with the insignia of prophetic significance. In relation to all this our comment in the present context is as follows. If we grant that there is truth in it, that the modern world, and perhaps Socialism in particular, has something decisive to say to the Church, then, if the most necessary criticism is not to be the most hopeless temptation, the only result of the encounter must be that the Church, recognising God's voice in this alien voice from without, lets itself be called to itself thereby, lets itself be reminded of the burden of its particular ministry with all its promise. Even the greatest and humblest and most open readiness of the Church to be told something by the world might mean that now for the first time it is not really thinking of taking its own responsibility more seriously but letting its energies be dissipated afresh, fondly imagining that it has only been wanting in relevance, openness and activity, and that, e.g., a sense of social need, a capacity for radical social insights and aims, and a will for social action can be a substitute for the required concentration on its own business which it has hitherto neglected. If there is really a prophetic view and interpretation of the opposition which the Church needs directly or indirectly from the world, if it is really God's " diction " which the Church thinks it sees in this " contradiction," then in any circumstances what is has to glean from it can only be a demand for this conscientious concentration on its own business, for renewed uneasiness about its faithfulness to its commission, and not an invitation to the scattered assumption of alien responsibilities. It is not just an adequate outcome of this encounter between the Church and the world, but the only possible outcome for it, that the Church should take more seriously than before the simple question : What is meant by *pure docere Evangelium, recte administrare sacramenta* ? In distinction from that of Ragaz and Tillich, Kutter's teaching pointed in this direction. More cannot be said even of him in this connexion. It might have been a salutary prophetic concentration and impatience, but it might also have been a backward looking rather than forward looking philosophy of immediacy that caused him to see in all theology only an attempt to theorise and secularise the divine rather than to live steadfastly in it. Of Ragaz one may say, without getting to closer grips with him, that he has never wrestled carefully or profoundly with the attempt to take seriously the Church's encounter with Socialism along these lines, and that he is not perhaps in a position to understand it with detachment. For all the respect we cannot withhold from him, he can hardly expect his fevered attacks (latterly in the work edited by Georg Wünsch, *Reich Gottes, Marxismus, Nationalsozialismus,* 1931, pp. 1–65) to make any serious impression on us. But Tillich has on the one side remained too incorrigible a historian of thought, too much an heir of liberal theological resentment against the Church (and, as it would seem, increasingly so), while on the other side he has let himself be too moulded and set systematically by the pseudo-eschatological " situation " of the immediate post-war years, for his protests against " the final supra-naturalistic stage of the dialectical movement in Barth's dogmatics " (*Rel. Verwirkl.*, 1930, p. 20) to arouse my interest. Both Ragaz (*op. cit.*, p. 53) and Tillich (*op. cit.*, p, 21) regard their own activity as dynamic and mine as static. . . . What am I to say to that ?

Now according to the teaching of the parable of the talents the fear of God which the Church needs cannot be inactive, nor can its awareness of the responsibility of its proclamation be a theoretical proviso. God's assault demands something corresponding on man's side, i.e., man's reflection and investigation. Did the Church's proclamation measure up to its responsibility yesterday ? Will it do so to-morrow ? If the question of the Church is really put by God, then it must meet the Church, press it, and stimulate it in the sphere of human possibilities. The prayer that must be the ultimate answer to this attack has to be accompanied by work as a penultimate answer : critical, corrective, investigative work at Church proclamation in the light of the divine verdict to which it appeals as that which it seeks to be. In that which the Church can and should do here there can be no question at all of its coming forward with its own verdict side by side with the divine verdict, or of its thinking it can carry out this divine verdict. It would not be taking seriously the judgment of God in which it stands if it thought it could carry it out even on itself with any act of its own.

The delimitation necessary here is obvious. Roman Catholic dogmatics speaks of an infallibility of the Church, of the teaching office of the Church specifically, and very specifically of the Pope, *in definienda doctrina de fide vel moribus* (*Conc. Vatic.* I, *sess.* IV, *Constit. dogm. de Eccl. Christi cap.* 4). This permits and commands it to treat the *doctrina (propositio) ecclesiae* (cf. Bartmann, *Lehrbuch der Dogm.* 7th edn. Vol. I, 1928, p. 33 f.) as an *infallibilis et divina regula* (Thomas Aquinas, *S. Theol.* 11¹, *qu.* 6, *art.* 3). But can one equate *doctrina ecclesiae* and *divina regula* ? Does not this imply that the Church is to judge itself with divine judgment ? We can only repeat here the question already put : On this presupposition how far will serious work be done on Church proclamation ? On this presupposition how far can concern for it be distinguished from the expository transmission of findings definitively known from of old ? And, if this question is not settled, how far is a serious challenge to Church proclamation as a human work recognised ? Or if it is not to be recognised, with what right and with what spirit ?

The Church can neither question its proclamation absolutely nor correct it absolutely. It can only exert itself to see how far it is questioned and how far it ought to be corrected. On its human work it can only do again a human work of criticising and correcting. And because this is so, it will be far from thinking that it either wants or is able to rid itself of the attack on its proclamation, the uneasiness which God Himself has prepared for it. This work of criticising and correcting its proclamation can be undertaken by the Church in the right sense only if it realises that the uneasiness prepared for it cannot be removed, and its success, if it is well done, will always be that of making it much more clearly aware of the uneasiness prepared for it. But this human work is obviously enjoined upon it with proclamation itself. Church proclamation has to be accompanied and confronted by Church theology, especially dogmatics. In distinction from all scattered answers to irrelevant questions, theology, and especially dogmatics, is the concentrated care and concern of the Church for its own most proper responsibility. In making its proclamation the raw material of dogmatics, it does the one thing it really needs apart from proclamation itself and the prayer that it may be right, the one and only thing it can do as the Church in relation to the obvious centre of its life. For how should not this be the one thing needful when it is not just a matter of right answers to the divine call as with its other functions (and this is certainly to be taken seriously too), but also of the correct representation of the divine call itself, and therefore of the service of God in the supreme sense of the term? And how should not serious reflection on the background of biblical exegesis and with reference to the practice of preaching be the only thing that has to be done, and can in fact be done, about this one thing (always apart from prayer)?

How disastrously the Church must misunderstand itself if, on whatever pretext, it can dream of being able to undertake and achieve anything serious in what are undoubtedly the important fields of liturgical reform or social work or Christian education or the ordering of its relation to state and society or ecumenical understanding, without at the same time doing what is necessary and possible with reference to the obvious centre of its life, as though it were self-evident, as though we could confidently count on it, that *evangelium pure docetur et recte administrantur sacramenta*! as though we could confidently leave this to God and in the meantime busy ourselves with the periphery of the Church circle, which has perhaps been rotating for long enough around a false centre! as though we could put ourselves in God's hands without a care in the world for what happens at this decisive point! Again, how disastrously the Church must misunderstand itself if it can imagine that theology is the business of a few theoreticians who are specially appointed for the purpose, to whom the rest, as hearty practical men, may sometimes listen with half an ear, though for their own part they boast of living " quite untheologically " for the demands of the day (" love "). As though these practical men were not continually preaching and speaking and writing, and were not genuinely questioned as to the rightness of their activity in this regard! As though there were anything more practical than giving this question its head, which means doing the work of theology and dogmatics! Again, how disastrously the Church must misunderstand itself if it can imagine that theological reflection is a matter for quiet situations and periods that suit and invite contemplation, a kind of peace-time luxury for which we are not only permitted but even commanded to find no time should things become really serious and exciting! As though there could be any more urgent task for a Church under assault from without than that of consolidating itself within, which means doing theological work! As though the venture of proclamation did not mean that the Church permanently finds itself in an emergency! As though theology could be done properly without reference to this constant emergency! Let there be no mistake. Because of these distorted ideas about theology, and dogmatics in particular, there arises and persists in the life of the Church a lasting and growing deficit for which we cannot expect those particularly active in this function to supply the needed balance. The whole Church must seriously want a serious theology if it is to have a serious theology.

We must now consider the relation between dogmatics and proclamation from the other side. When we call Church proclamation the raw material of dogmatics, what is meant is that Church proclamation is at all events man's talk about God as well. And precisely as man's talk it is the concrete problem of dogmatics, the *factum* and *faciendum* to which dogmatics relates as a science. Starting with the question how the Church talked about God yesterday, dogmatics asks how this should be done to-morrow. The question is aimed first and directly at those entrusted with the task of proclamation and then indirectly, though not on that account with any less weight, at the Church in general, which as a totality bears corporate responsibility for the proper discharge of this function as of all others. Only as a matter of order, but not in principle, and hence not without the possibility of exceptions, is the function of preaching and administering the sacraments linked to the class of theologians according to the Evangelical concept. This means, however, that in matters of the dogmatic question there can be no dispensation in principle for non-theologians either.

The luxury of " quite untheological " thought and talk which has no part in the dogmatic question, a luxury in which theologians of all people are also prone to indulge very gladly and not without being vain of their freedom, can strictly be achieved only by secretly leaving the Church either temporarily or permanently. The freedom claimed when men think they can and should theologise " quite untheologically " is the freedom to prattle heretically or in a way that makes for heresy. There is no room in the Church for this freedom.

The possibility of the dogmatic question, of dogmatic criticism and correction, arises out of the claim with which talk about God steps forth in the Church and out of the expectation with which it is surrounded there. One would have to deny this claim and this expectation, and therewith the Church itself, if one were seriously to disavow any interest in face of the dogmatic question. What is said about God in the Church seeks, as proclamation, to be God's Word. It is measured by its own specific criterion in dogmatics. In the raw material of dogmatics we first have a set of words which usually constitute the

C.D.—D

material of proclamation more or less constantly and emphatically in the Church and irrespective of its divisions. Here as elsewhere these words acquire their meanings through the associations and connexions in which they are used. In virtue of these meanings, talk about God becomes in every age specific and distinctive talk. It is in a plenitude of such specific usages that it exists at any given time for dogmatics, and in general the dogmatic question will be whether and how far this talk, i.e., the sense in which the words are employed in it, is adapted or not to its purpose of serving God's Word. Yesterday's proclamation, with criticism of which dogmatics methodologically begins, is in principle, then, the sum of earlier efforts at Church proclamation as variously determined by the meanings attached to these words. In fact it is only a very small fraction of the whole which, when dogmatic work is done, can be assumed to be known and thus made the object of investigation. Even within this known fraction there may be again only a few elements which stand out representatively from the rest and with which this work can concern itself. Finally it might be neither pertinent nor profitable for dogmatics to try to relate itself to Church preaching as delivered yesterday, the day before, or before that. Genuinely to promote the self-examination of the Church in respect of this central function it will rather turn to that form of yesterday's proclamation in which the latter is already tested, criticised and corrected, i.e., the results of the history of dogmatics. In earlier dogmatics the Church has already stated authoritatively how far it thought it could regard as proclamation the talk about God found within it when this was measured by the standard of the Word of God. The result is—and we must see this as a necessity without sentimentalities—that dogmatics is at the decisive point a debate of dogmaticians among themselves ; by dogmaticians, of course, we do not mean only dogmatic teachers and authors, but simply and generally all those both to-day and yesterday who are concerned about the dogmatic question. The essentially " gymnastic " character of dogmatics is shown already by these restrictions regarding the presupposed *factum*. As a critical survey of the past dogmatics can work only through examples and not comprehensively or exhaustively. But the same character is also revealed in relation to the sought after *faciendum*. Here again we have a set of words which constitute the material of all Christian proclamation. But now, so far as this is thought to be necessary, and on the basis of earlier criticism, these words are to be put in different associations and connexions, and they are thus to be used in new and, it is hoped, better senses. But as this correction of talk about God can deal with only a portion of what was said previously, so only a portion of what will be said about God in the Church to-morrow can be directly corrected, and even this portion can be regarded as only primarily and provisionally corrected. The self-examination of the Church in respect of its proclamation will have to continue to-morrow with the proclamation itself. On this side too, then, dogmatic work cannot claim more than a gymnastic character. It is *pars pro toto*. As may be stated already, it cannot aim to be a system of Christian truth. Apart from all else, this would mean that it could criticise the totality of the past proclamation of the Church and definitively set forth the totality of its corrected proclamation. But it cannot do this. In relation to to-morrow, too, it can only take examples, and it can only take certain examples, pending better instruction, and in no sense conclusively. In dogmatics criticism and correction of talk about God can be practised only on a specific section of the whole world of past and future Church proclamation. We have to learn, and in dogmatics, too, this can be done only for the needs of the next day. In this regard dogmatics shows plainly that its business is that of the school, whose instruction cannot anticipate in any sense the reality of life, but only give the most immediate and most necessary guidance for meeting this reality. Church proclamation is the raw material of dogmatics. But it would be a fatal confusion to try to reverse this and say that dogmatics is the raw material of proclamation.

It is a familiar and perhaps unavoidable beginner's mistake of students and assistants, when preaching, to think that they can and should confidently take the content of their preaching from their treasured college notebooks and text-books of dogmatics. On the other hand, older preachers are usually far too confident in removing themselves from the jurisdiction of this critical authority.

One cannot and should not expect to hear the content of proclamation from dogmatics. This content must be found each time in the middle space between the particular text in the context of the whole Bible and the particular situation of the changing moment. Dogmatics can only be a guide to the right mastery and the right adaptability, to the right boldness and the right caution, for the given moment when this space has to be found. It can only be a guide to orientation between the two poles of saying what has to be said in all circumstances and not saying what must not be said in any circumstances. In short, it can only be a guide to the act of choosing between various possibilities which is characteristic of this human action (as human action) in the same way as it is of all other human action. It can only be a guide from the standpoint that what is at issue in this action is proclamation of the Word of God, and that in this sense it must be given a form commensurate with human knowledge and conscience at its very best.

The direct connexion between theology, i.e., dogmatics, and the task of Church proclamation has been expressly stated already in Augustine : *ut non solum legendo alios . . . sed et aliis ipsi aperiendo proficiant* (*De doctr. chr.* Prol. 1, cf. I, 1). For the instruction of Church teachers the Reformation period yields not only Luther's *Larger Catechism* of 1529 but also the *Berne Synod* of 1532 and the *Catechismus Romanus* of 1566. That the aim of dogmatics is to make the theologian *aptum reddere ad instituendum hominem ad salutem* is notably asserted in older Protestantism by the Lutherans J. Gerhard (*Loci theol.* 1610, *Prooem.* 26 and 31), Quenstedt (*Theol. did. pol.* 1685, P.I, *cap.* 1, *sect.* 2, *qu.* 2, *ekth.* 15), Baier (*Comp. Theol. pos.* 1686, *Prol.* 1, 1) and Buddaeus (*Instit. theol. dogm.* 1724, I, 1, 28). Moreover, as is well known, it is none other than Schleiermacher who exalts the practical task of Church guidance to the status of a constitutive principle for theological science (*Kurze Darstellung*, 1830, § 1–13). He is vigorously followed by Vilmar of Marburg : " According as dogmatics removes itself from the sphere of the Church, it no longer serves salvation but panders to the intellectual vanity of the individual. Dogmatics has to realise that as a subject of preparation for spiritual office it stands in the relation of a school to real life, and to it, too, it is said : *Non scholae sed vitae discimus.* The life of the Church stands above dogmatics." We find in Vilmar the expression which characterises the view set forth here, namely, that dogmatics " properly contains *gymnasmata* for the Church office and its holders " (*Dogmatik*, I. Teil. 1874, p. 59). Sound words against the idea that dogmatics has to provide the practising theologian with material for his sermons and catechisings are to be found in Schleiermacher's pupil August Twesten (*Vorlesungen über die Dogm. d. ev. -luth. Kirche*, Vol. I, 1838, p. 82 f.) : Dogmatics does not yield him direct profit but the indirect and for that very reason all the more important profit that it impresses on all his activity the " character of a loftier circumspection." " But as concerns his teaching vocation, quite apart from its beneficent influence on the depth and breadth of his religious thinking, it accustoms him to a criticism which does not apply only to the form, as is usually the case, but also to the Christian content of his discourses and their relation to the highest tasks of practical theology in general " (*op. cit.*, p, 85). Finally the understanding of dogmatics in terms of a school and its relation to the " conduct of Christian instruction " is also a feature in the theological work of Albrecht Ritschl (*Unterricht i. d. christl. Rel.* 3rd edn., 1886, § 87 ; *Rechtfertigung und Versöhnung*, Vol. II, 4th edn., 1900, p. 3 and 13).

In all this what we are to understand by " proclamation of the Word of God " is primarily and decisively preaching and the sacraments, though with regard to the latter, which as *verba visibilia* in actions belong to a special order, the thing which counts is simply the oral proclamation which accompanies them, the doctrine of the sacraments which is significant for the particular meaning of their administration. We have seen, however, that the task but not the reality of proclamation may be reduced and restricted to these two categories of preaching and sacrament. The other, sacrificial and generally responsive elements in the Church's life may also be proclamation. And to the degree that in these other functions of the Church there is talk about God by men, they, too, are subject to the question how far this talk is correct. That the *factum* and *faciendum* of the Church's education of youth must come in the sphere of dogmatics follows at once from the ineluctability with which it must continually move on from teaching to proclamation. Even in theology itself the exegete on the one side and the practical theologian on the other cannot evade the dogmatic question. The exegete cannot do so because his exposition of the Bible, however faithful to the text, is invariably a tissue of biblical material with a wrapping of imported personal associations and consequently of possible meanings, so that if this exposition is to be advanced as authentic proclamation in the Church it cannot avoid the query as to the legitimacy of the imported element. Again, the dogmatic question has to be put to the practical theologian too, because even the most external question regarding the conduct of worship to-day can be given very different answers according to the insight into what is proper proclamation and what is not. Furthermore the prayers and praises of the Church cannot be regarded as of no dogmatic importance at all; the liturgy and hymnal must be taken seriously from the standpoint that their substance consists of human words and can thus be effective as proclamation, perhaps as very distorted proclamation.

It is a strange thing that when there are revisions of books of order and hymn-books in the Evangelical churches every possible authority is usually consulted as a standard but not dogmatic science. The results naturally correspond.

Again in social work, which is much to the fore to-day, there is a variety of talk as well as action, and much of this talk claims to be proclamation. But things will be very different when theological reflection stands behind it and when it does not. We have stated too that the possibility has to be taken into account that God may also speak from outside the Church as we now know it or as it really is, and to this extent the attention of dogmatics must not let itself be limited by the walls of the Church. It will always be a venture, a departure from its true line, when dogmatics thinks it should devote itself to this proclamation of God's Word outside the Church, or when, conversely, it thinks it should also speak to the world and not to the known visible Church, which is its normal office.

It would make no sense to try to lay this down as a rule. Dogmatics is not by nature a general *gnosis* of God and the world.

The individual dogmatician assumes the responsibility of the prophet when he does this. One cannot deny that he may sometimes have to do it. But the normal and central *factum* on which dogmatics focuses will always be quite simply the Church's Sunday sermon of yesterday and to-morrow. The Church stands or falls with this function enjoined upon it. It has every cause to take dogmatic work very seriously as the criticism and correction of this its decisive function.

In accordance with this statement of the problem we have now to interpret or correct what has been said about the raw material of dogmatics in both ancient and more recent times. In all kinds of variations, Roman Catholics and Protestants, ancients and moderns, have presented, as the raw material of dogmatics, God and the things of

God, or man in his relation to God, or God's revelation in Christ, or the Christian faith, or more recently the Christian principle, or the nature of Christianity, in short, the theme of Christian discourse, the subject-matter of Christianity.

Now obviously one cannot object to this in so far as Christian discourse is naturally the raw material of dogmatics as discourse about the subject-matter of Christianity, and so the subject-matter itself is indirectly the raw material too. But it is worth while not to lose sight of the indirectness with which alone this can happen. The three aspects which follow should be noted.

1. The necessity of dogmatics is different from that of Church proclamation. Proclamation is required as the execution of God's command to the Church. Dogmatics is required because proclamation is a fallible human work. These are two different things. The relation of proclamation to the theme of Christianity is obviously primary, that of dogmatics secondary. The datum from which dogmatics begins is neither God nor revelation nor faith. This is the datum from which proclamation starts. Certainly dogmatics can and should be proclamation too, and to this extent it, too, starts from this datum. But it also has its own function which is not the same as that of proclamation. Hence its datum is different, namely, the questionable fact that in proclamation God, revelation and faith are talked about by men in human terms—questionable because it is by no means self-evident that this is done in truth and purity, and because the Church cannot shirk the responsibility that it ought to be done in truth and purity. Dogmatics serves preaching by raising this question. It tests the orthodoxy of the contemporary kerygma. Concrete dogma, indeed, is simply the kerygma tested, provisionally purified, and reduced to a correct formula by the Church. One should not expect more of dogmatics than it can achieve *qua* dogmatics. And we should not take exception to much in dogmatics that is peculiar to it *qua* dogmatics.

An example is the *rabies theologorum*, which Melanchthon was so glad he would no longer encounter in heaven.

Dogmatics does not seek to give a positive, stimulating and edifying presentation. It does not even try to give an instructive exposition in the same sense as preaching. It deals with God, revelation and faith only in respect of their reflection in proclamation. Even as presentation it is also investigation and polemic, criticism and correction.

Its task is ἐπικόψαι τὰς τῆς πλάνης ὁδούς, ἵνα μίαν ὁδὸν βασιλικὴν ὁδεύσωμεν (Cyril of Jerusalem, *Catech.*, 16, 5). " The Church's definitions of doctrine are only the railings which guard against falling into the abyss on both sides ; they are like the buoys which mark off the proper channel " (F. A. Philippi, *Kirchl. Glaubenslehre*, 1854 f., Vol. 2, p. 150).

We shall spare ourselves many unnecessary disappointments over both the form and also the results of dogmatics if we keep this soberly in view.

2. Dogmatics serves Church proclamation. Its relation to this should be seen as parallel to what was called *pistis* and *gnosis* in the early Church and what has been called *credere* and *intelligere* since Augustine, *pistis* or *credere* being understood as the simple reproduction and propagation of the content of the message in a way which unreflectingly corresponds to what has been heard, *gnosis* or *intelligere* as the scientific investigation of this correspondence. But in this juxtaposition we must insist upon three provisos which were not always observed in the early Church and non-observance of which can lead us into error even to-day.

(*a*) As compared with proclamation dogmatics involves a different mode and function but in no sense a higher stage of faith or the knowledge of faith.

It was clearly one of the results of the struggle with ancient Gnosticism that the Church rejected an aristocracy of scientific theologians in its midst. But the idea is a natural one, and in practice it can always be a temptation.

We must be very clear that the simplest proclamation of the Gospel can be proclamation of the truth in the most unlimited sense and can validly communicate the truth to the most unsophisticated hearer if God so will. Dogmatics is not the technique of certain people who are better placed spiritually. It is not the privilege of an esoteric Christianity whereby the truth is enjoyed in a better form than that in which God has it proclaimed to all people in the Church. Striving to improve what man does here, the dogmatician is not better in faith or knowledge than any other member of the Church with respect to what God does here.

(*b*) As compared with Church proclamation dogmatics does not have access to a higher or better source of knowledge which is to be sought in the fact that only here does Christian thought begin, or that thought is here more exact, comprehensive and profound than in simple preaching. It is not true that the attempt to think in human terms about God, revelation and faith first began in dogmatics. This attempt is already made in proclamation itself inasmuch as it is undoubtedly human speech, and also in listening to proclamation inasmuch as this is human listening. Nor is there any reason why it should not and could not be undertaken here too in the form of exact, comprehensive and profound thought.

Paul Althaus writes : " Theology means performing the act of faith in the sphere of thought. Faith is to overcome the world. Theology is the struggle to overcome the world of spirits and of thoughts. Theologians thereby practise

deliberation . . . as a service to the whole community and therefore, as it were, in
representative thinking " (*Evangelium und Leben*, 1927, p. 26 f.). In spite of and
in face of this definition are we not ascribing too much to theology if we make the
goal of its " struggle " something that is promised only to faith as such (which may
also be the faith of a " layman ") ?

And certainly the introduction of critical reflection which distinguishes dogmatics from proclamation does not mean that a higher
norm of knowledge is substituted for the norm of proclamation.
Naturally there is the constant threat here that some philosophy will
rush in and then raise the claim *in concreto* that it represents this higher
source of knowledge. For where can this critically reflective thought
find its style and norm except in human reason and therefore *in
concreto* in a philosophy ? Here, then, we always need the insight that
critically reflective thought, even though it be that of human reason,
and no matter what philosophical tints it has, must still be set in
relation to the theme of the Church's proclamation, and its execution
must be governed, not by its human origin and nature, but by its
divine object.

The *credo ut intelligam* of Anselm (*Prosl.*, 1) certainly does not imply transition
from faith to another genus but an αἰχμαλωτίζειν πᾶν νόημα εἰς τὴν ὑπακοὴν τοῦ
Χριστοῦ (2 Cor. 10⁵).

In practice it is not in our power to check that incursion of philosophy into dogmatics. Nor is it in our power actually to give to
critically reflective human thought that relation to the divine object
and control by it. But it is in our power to keep before us the need
for that relation and control and hence to refuse to philosophy that
right of usurpation and to give the final word, not to the immanent
orders of critically reflective thought, not to the demands of the need
of human thought, but only to the requirement of the object here in
question. We can at least realise that only on one side should dogmatics
be unconditionally open and obedient, and that it has this side in
common, not with any philosophy, but with the Church's proclamation.

(c) As compared with Church proclamation, then, dogmatics
cannot wish to be an end in itself. The situation is not that God,
revelation and faith are given to proclamation and then independently
and in some way differently to dogmatics too. They are all given to the
Church, and they are not given for contemplation but for proclamation,
and only to this extent are they also given to dogmatics as the presupposition of its testing of the human work of proclamation. They
are given to the Church, namely, as its being, as the principle of life
which creates and establishes it, and for that very reason not as a mere
existent which might become the object of independent theory,

gnosis, or speculation remote from its action, but as the divine activity with which the Church itself must actively come to terms. This human activity of the Church, however, is primarily proclamation, and the aim of dogmatics cannot be more than its correct performance. It has place and justification as a critical theory, gnosis or speculation only to the extent that it serves this purpose.

In the debate between Thomas Aquinas and Duns Scotus as to whether theology is a *scientia speculativa* or *practica* older Protestant dogmatics with increasing definiteness came down on the side of Duns Scotus. The process, to which we shall return, is equivocal. It certainly had its origin on the one side in the rising religionism of the day and its lack of concern for God's objectivity. Yet on the other side it arose out of a healthy revulsion against an abstract and basically unchurchly contemplation and discussion of God, against the pure self-incurving theological speculation which achieved classical form in the celebrated writings of Pseudo-Dionysius, which exerted a powerful influence on the monastic scholarship of the Middle Ages and indeed on the Protestant orthodox themselves, and which may still be found to-day in certain sections of Roman Catholic dogmatics. It is in recognition of the danger which threatens Roman Catholic dogmatics from this angle that B. Bartmann in his manual appends to many (though by no means all) of his *loci* a final special section under the title " practical values " (namely, of this specific dogmatic theme), though after all the problem can hardly be solved as easily as that. Speaking of the practical character of theology could mean an acknowledgement that the Church is not an academy and that there is also no academic corner within it. *Semper cogitandum est, Filium Dei non ob eam causam prodidisse ex arcana sede aeterni Patris, et revelasse doctrinam coelestem, ut seminaria spargeret disputationum, quibus ostendandi ingenii causa luderetur, sed potius ut homines de vera Dei agnitione et omnibus iis quae ad aeternam salutem consequendam necessaria sunt, erudirentur* (M. Chemnitz, *Loci theol. ed.* 1590, *Hypomnemata* 9).

In sum, since dogmatics does not imply a higher possibility of Christian life, since it may not advance an independent source of knowledge and since it cannot claim as theory an autonomous role and significance, therefore the subject-matter of Christianity does not exist for it in any other way than as it is found in Christian proclamation.

3. The theme of Church proclamation or subject-matter of Christianity demands dogmatics to the extent that its proclamation is a responsible act and to the extent that dogmatics is the effort to meet this responsibility towards the theme of proclamation. Yet it is by no means the case that in dogmatics the Church becomes as it were the lord and judge of the subject-matter, so that the current results of dogmatics are to be accepted as a law imposed as it were on God, revelation and faith. Dogmatics has to investigate and say at each given point how we may best speak of God, revelation and faith to the extent that human talk about these things is to count as Church proclamation. It should not think that it can lay down what God, revelation and faith are in themselves. In both its investigations and its conclusions it must keep in view that God is in heaven and it on

earth, and that God, His revelation and faith always live their own free life over against all human talk, including that of the best dogmatics. Even if we have again weighed everything and corrected everything and formulated everything better, as is our duty to the subject-matter of Christianity in respect of human talk about it, and even if our findings have been given the status of Church confession and dogma, we have still to say : We are unprofitable servants, and in no sense are we to imagine that we have become in the very least masters of the subject.

In the well-known introductory words to the so-called Athanasian Creed dogmatics, or dogma, comes forward with the following claim : *quicunque vult salvus esse, ante omnia opus est, ut teneat catholicam fidem, quam nisi quisque integram inviolatamque servaverit, absque dubio in aeternum peribit.* This is going too far. Such fixing of saving faith by a human and to that extent disputable theologoumenon has nothing whatever to do with the binding and loosing on earth which according to the Gospel (Mt. 16^19 ; 18^18) corresponds to being bound and loosed in heaven, for the judicial force which in the Gospel is ascribed to the act of obedience to apostolic proclamation is now transferred to a formula abstracted from this act, to a sequence of words as such, which in distinction from the act of obedience is an instrument whereby man masters God, revelation and faith. We ask to what degree this mastery does not take place in the Roman Catholic understanding of dogmatics and dogma. Nevertheless, since dogma on this view is only partly known and proclaimed, since dogmatics, then, cannot be complete, and since on the other hand distinction is made between an explicit and an implicit *fides catholica*, Roman Catholicism, too, acknowledges that revelation and saving faith live their own life as distinct from the law of faith, a life which is richer on the one side though more restricted on the other. From the opposite angle the theology of Wilhelm Herrmann also calls for consideration here. No feature in it is more distinctive than his unwearying battle against the idea of a dogmatic law imposed on faith. This is what gave Herrmann's life work a pronouncedly anti-Catholic impress. What was he fighting for in this battle ? The independent life of the subject-matter of Christianity against all human pinning-down, against every attempt to make the " on earth " into an " in heaven," against all intellectual righteousness of works ? Or simply the human right of a Romantic anti-intellectualism, individualism, and fanaticism for truth ? One must admit that the latter is the answer in the foreground, the former the answer in the background. If with a certain exegetical daring one can include the former, then Herrmann's protest may be regarded as a necessary one against the *Quicunque vult salvus esse*. In so far as the latter is the answer, Protestantism is well advised not to identify itself with Herrmann.

We are also not to understand the task of dogmatics in relation to proclamation as though it had to offer God, revelation and faith to this as the content of preaching. We have seen already that what dogmatics has to give does not consist of contents but of guidelines, directions, insights, principles and limits for correct speech by human estimate. It can be called doctrinal law in this sense. But its presupposition is that preaching acquires its content elsewhere. For that reason it cannot be lord and judge here either. It can and should give counsel in all seriousness but it neither can nor should seek to give orders in the Church.

Here we may apply 2 Cor. 1²⁴ : οὐχ ὅτι κυριεύομεν ὑμῶν τῆς πίστεως, ἀλλὰ συνεργοί ἐσμεν τῆς χαρᾶς ὑμῶν.

Like the subject-matter of Christianity, Church proclamation must also remain free in the last resort, free to receive the command which it must always receive afresh from that free life of the subject-matter of Christianity. Church proclamation and not dogmatics is immediate to God in the Church. Proclamation is essential, dogmatics is needed only for the sake of it. Dogmatics lives by it to the extent that it lives only in the Church. In proclamation, and in God, revelation and faith only to the degree that these are its objects, dogmatics is to seek its material.

What Ambrose (*De fide ad Grat.*, 1, 5, 42) wrote against a heretical theology really applies to all theology : *Non in dialectica complacuit Deo salvum facere populum suum. Regnum enim Dei in simplicitate fidei est, non in contentione sermonis.*

THE WORD OF GOD IN ITS THREEFOLD FORM

The presupposition which makes proclamation proclamation and therewith makes the Church the Church is the Word of God. This attests itself in Holy Scripture in the word of the prophets and apostles to whom it was originally and once and for all spoken by God's revelation.

1. THE WORD OF GOD PREACHED

We have to speak about the presupposition which makes proclamation proclamation and therewith makes the Church the Church. Proclamation must ever and again become proclamation. From being an action which, coming forward with the corresponding claim and surrounded with the corresponding expectation, wants to be and should be proclamation, it must become an action which is proclamation. And because the event of real proclamation is the function of the Church's life which governs all others, we have to say that in this event the Church itself must ever and again become the Church. Proclamation and the Church are, of course, simply and visibly there just as the bread and wine of Communion are simply and visibly there and the distributing, eating and drinking of the bread and wine in Communion take place simply and visibly. They are not simply and visibly there, however, as that which they want to be and should be, as theologically relevant entities, as realities of revelation and faith. They have ever and again to come into being as this.

The connexion with the Lord's Supper is not to be regarded as just incidental. What applies to proclamation and the Church generally cannot be better illustrated than by the sacrament. Calvin says of the tree of life in Paradise and of Noah's rainbow : *Non quod arbor praestaret illis immortalitatem . . . aut arcus coercendis aquis foret efficax . . . sed quia notam a verbo Dei insculptam habebant, ut documenta essent testamentorum eius ac sigilla. Et antea quidem arbor erat arbor, arcus arcus ; ubi inscripta fuerunt verbo Dei, indita est nova forma, ut inciperent esse quod prius non erant (Instit.* IV, 14, 18). And H. Bullinger says of the earthly elements in the sacrament : *Verbo Dei fiunt, quae antea non fuerunt, sacramenta. Consecrantur enim verbo et sanctificata esse ostenduntur ab eo qui instituit.* For this reason and to this degree they are not called mere water, bread and wine but, without any change of nature, the bath of regeneration and the body and blood of the Lord *(Conf. Helvet. post.*, 1562, art. 19 in K. Müller, p. 207, l. 11 f. and 34 f.). It would be very out of place to recoil from terms like *fieri* and *nova forma* as used here by Reformed authors just because they bring to light a problem which cannot be easily dismissed, namely, that of the Roman

Catholic doctrine of change. In the sacrament and in preaching and in the whole life of the Church it is always true that the existence of the earthly body acquires a new form from the heavenly Head, that it becomes the actuality of revelation and faith. Again, it would be very out of place to regard it as a nominalistic softening of this becoming when, e.g., Bullinger so plainly rejects the doctrine of transubstantiation here and so firmly regards the new designation of the elements as just a designation. This designation is not an arbitrarily imported meaning but the *nota a verbo Dei insculpta.* We only show our failure to understand what it means that the earthly reality acquires this new *nota* by the Word of God if we regard this view of the new becoming as less realistic than that expressed in the Roman Catholic doctrine of transubstantiation or the Lutheran doctrine of consubstantiation.

The presupposition of this event is the Word of God. Between this central concept of our prolegomena and dogmatics generally on the one side and the concept of proclamation on the other there are four decisive connexions whose mutual relation may be compared to that of four concentric circles. These we must now analyse.

1. The Word of God is the commission upon whose givenness proclamation must rest if it is to be real proclamation. The necessity of proclamation does not find an objective foundation in the fact that certain circumstances and scales of value immanent in the existence of man and things crave to be known and declared. The answer to this craving is not proclamation but fundamentally secular science, and there can be no question but that all the circumstances and scales of value which might be regarded as possible objects of Church proclamation belong to the sphere of secular science and stand in no need of proclamation by preaching and sacrament. Again, the necessity of proclamation does not find a subjective basis in the fact that certain personal convictions of certain men call for this particular articulation. For in so far as these convictions are capable of rational presentation, the persons concerned should be referred again to the way of scientific exposition, and in so far as they are wholly or predominantly irrational they should be referred to the possibility of musical, poetic or artistic expression. In relation to all such objective or subjective motives, and the more so the more seriousness and worth they claim, one might well ask whether, quite apart from any scientific or artistic presentation, they might not be brought to primary expression in a practical moral and political attitude appropriate to them. However that may be, in presupposing such motives we lose all insight into the necessity of proclamation. Naturally such motives too will necessarily come into play, as everywhere, so also in the Church, even when it is a matter of proclamation. To speak even more plainly, these are the human motives of all alleged proclamation, and we cannot intrinsically have any others. It is not the case that we are able to reach above them and grasp and establish something higher, a motive which will be the necessary basis and actualisation of alleged proclamation. What more

could we establish than circumstances and scales of value on the one side and convictions on the other ? The fact that we are unable to indicate or establish a higher motive than these, and hence a real necessity of Church proclamation, and hence proclamation as real proclamation, is the very thing we acknowledge and confirm when we describe the commission to which it may be traced back as the Word of God. Certainly in so doing we are by implication speaking objectively of a circumstance and scale of values and subjectively of a personal conviction. This human motivation is the medium above which we can as little rise as we can cast off our shadows. But it is also the medium above which we will not want to rise because it is the place where we are to expect the divine commission. God's Word means in this context God's positive command : *God's* positive command, and hence a motive which acts according to its own absolutely superior principle even though present and at work within the whole un-avoidable world of human motivations ; God's *positive command*, and hence a motive which in its divinity is not present and at work in the way that circumstances and scales of value are over us and con-victions in us, i.e., which we are not able to establish because we cannot grasp at it, but rather which is present and at work when and where it wills to be present and to be at work. No proclamation does not also rest on those human motives which are there and which have to be established. But no proclamation is real proclamation to the degree that over and above all this it does not rest on the commission which we cannot in any way take to ourselves, which we cannot in any way take for granted, which we can only receive and have in the act of receiving, which comes upon us and the whole world of our motivations absolutely from without, which lifts us up and controls us as a command that goes forth in a way we cannot foresee, and to which, as stated earlier, we can only take up an attitude by repeating it as we think we have heard it and by trying to conform to it as well or badly as we can. Real proclamation, then, means the Word of God preached and the Word of God preached means in this first and outermost circle man's talk about God on the basis of God's own direction, which fundamentally transcends all human causation, which cannot, then, be put on a human basis, but which simply takes place, and has to be acknowledged, as a fact.

" So say ye now : ' whom God hath sent.' That is, God's Word is not named unless it is sent. That is, let none think that God's Word cometh to earth of man's device. If it is to be God's Word, it must be sent. Otherwise it is impossible that Holy Writ could be understood or expounded by any arbitrary device. It availeth not that one should speak and he is not called, for God's Word cometh alone because He sendeth it. Where not, the whole world cannot utter what could redeem from sins and comfort the consciences. If He had not sent the Word and the office, we had nought. Therefore we should neither utter nor hear aught

save only God's Word. If it is invented by man's choice and device, avoid it.
It cometh not except it be sent from heaven. And let him that hath dealings
with monks ask whether their thing is God's Word. Then wilt thou hear them
allege it is done of good intent to honour God. Hence 'tis service of God and God's
Word. But there is more to it than good intent to do God service and pay for
sins. From thy heart floweth the device, the opinion. But say thou whether
God hath sent it from heaven, also whether He hath commanded it. Yea, is it
done to God's honour ? The wickeder it is, and a double blasphemy, that thou
calledst that God's Word and service of God which thou thyself hast invented.
Thus hath the Pope led the world astray under the name and title of the Church.
But without God's sending cometh no Word into the world. Hath it grown out
of my heart, cling I to Chrysostom, Augustine and Ambrose, 'tis not then God's
Word. For there is a vast difference 'twixt the Word that is sent from heaven
and that which of my own choice and device I invent. Holy Writ, so it be grown
on earth, thus saith John : He that is of the earth speaketh earthly things. Thus
we must learn to set our blessedness soundly on the power of God's Word and
not on our own device or opinion " (Luther, *Ausl. des* 3. *und* 4. *Kap. Joh.*,
1538 f., *W.A.*, 47, p. 193, l. 10).

2. The Word of God is the theme which must be given to proclamation as such if it is to be real proclamation. Proclamation is asked how
far it is proclamation of something, objective proclamation, proclamation of a real theme. Again we must assert that in so far as this theme
belongs to the sphere of objects of human apprehension and thought,
to the sphere of objects of external or internal contemplation, it is hard
to see to what extent it should be proclaimed by preaching and
sacrament. Would not scientific, artistic, or even ethico-political
presentation and publication be incomparably more appropriate to
themes of this class ? Again we must admit, of course, that we have no
objects but those of outer and inner perception. This must be said even
of the object of proclamation. If we have it as an object at all, it is
as an object of outer or inner perception, of experience and thought.
If we did not have it thus, we should not have it at all. But to the
extent that we only have it thus, we do not have it as a possible object of
proclamation. Metaphysics or psychology could then take charge of it,
and indeed would have to do so. But these are the very sciences that
cannot take charge of a theme that is worth proclaiming. In calling
the object or theme of proclamation God's Word we mean that it is
not merely or even primarily the object of human perception. It must
become the object of human perception to be capable of being proclaimed. But to the extent that it is really proclaimed it is not at all the
object of human perception. It is proclaimed to the degree that it
presents and places itself as an object over against us and the whole
world of all our objects, certainly in the unavoidable medium of
perceptual objectivity, but in this medium as the object which can
never in any sense be our possession, to which we can never point back
as to a datum, which is a presupposition in the sense and only in the
sense that it sets itself where we cannot possibly set it. We have it as

it gives itself to us if we have it. In this way, in contrast to all the objects of metaphysics or psychology, it is the object of proclamation. Between this object and preaching and sacrament as the means to present and impart it there should be an inner connexion. Preaching and sacrament are, as we have seen, the promise of future revelation on the basis of the revelation that has already occurred. How, then, can one speak of this object except in the form of this promise, which is quite distinct from that of science, art, or politics? Real proclamation, then, means God's Word preached, and in this second circle God's Word preached means human talk about God on the basis of the self-objectification of God which is not just there, which cannot be predicted, which does not fit into any plan, which is real only in the freedom of His grace, and in virtue of which He wills at specific times to be the object of this talk, and is so according to His good-pleasure.

There are some excellent delimitations on this point in H. M. Müller, *Glaube und Erfahrung bei Luther*, 1929 : " The concrete, contingent givenness of faith, and to that extent the gift itself, is still something that can only be declared in the proclamation of the Gospel ; it remains declaration " (p. 95). " Preaching as impartation of the promise is precisely not the transmission of revelation ; it is an indication of the occurrence of revelation " (p. 119, cf. also p. 41, 149, 150, 162, 196, etc.).

3. The Word of God is the judgment in virtue of which alone proclamation can be real proclamation. Proclamation is also asked whether it is true. What is to decide this ? What is the criterion here ? One usually judges the truth of human speech by the nature of its theme on the one side and by the situation and concern of the speaker on the other. Naturally this may and must apply to Church proclamation too. It lies within the realm of human speech. The one who proclaims must submit to the question : What do you know of the thing you speak of ? And : What is your concern in speaking of it ? He has to let his work be judged by these questions. The only point is that what he says is not affected as proclamation by such judgments. What is assessed by them is its scientific or ethico-political or aesthetic character. Intrinsically proclamation as it takes place in preaching and sacrament presupposes that neither the nature of its object nor the situation or concern of the speaker is or can be so clear to any man as to put him in a position to pronounce on its truth. If there is to be any assessment at all of Church proclamation as such it must be from another angle. It is this fundamentally different aspect of the judgment to be made on Church proclamation that we have in view and describe when we acknowledge it to be the Word of God. We are not denying thereby that proclamation is subject to other criteria too. We are simply affirming that in fact we only know these other criteria in judging it here and now, that we are in no position to pronounce upon

its truth in any other way. But here and now we have 1. to recollect that, even though it is not known to anyone, a different criterion from these others has given itself to be known and 2. to expect that this criterion which we do not know now, or know only from this recollection, will give itself to be known again. This criterion which is recollected and expected, though not at our disposal in our own or any present, is the Word of God. We cannot " handle " this criterion. It is the criterion which handles itself and is in no other hands. We can handle the other criteria in recollection and expectation of this criterion. But its judgment alone is absolutely binding and inviolable. Proclamation becomes real proclamation when it is endorsed by this judgment. Real proclamation, therefore, is the Word of God preached, and in this third inner circle the Word of God preached means human talk about God which by God's own judgment, that cannot be anticipated and never passes under our control, is true with reference both to the proclaimed object and also to the proclaiming subject, so that it is talk which has to be listened to and which rightly demands obedience.

4. Finally—and only here do we make the decisive point—the Word of God is the event itself in which proclamation becomes real proclamation. It is not just the commission that man must have received. It is not just the theme or object that must enter the field in contrast to human talk. It is not just the judgment by which it must be confirmed as true. From all these angles the actualisation of proclamation might still be understood as an external and accidental characterisation, as a kind of clothing or enlightening of an event which as such is ultimately still the event of the willing and doing of proclaiming man. And then, of course, one misunderstands the significance of the " garment " or " light " in question, what it means that proclamation becomes real as God commands, God comes on the scene, God judges. But in this case who will not constantly misunderstand? Understanding of the subject in this statement has to render quite impossible all nominalistic misunderstandings regarding the predicate. But it lies deeply in the nature of the case that the nominalistic misunderstanding cannot be rooted out unequivocally and definitively. It is the miracle of revelation and faith when the misunderstanding does not constantly recur, when proclamation is for us not just human willing and doing characterised in some way but also and primarily and decisively God's own act, when human talk about God is for us not just that, but also and primarily and decisively God's own speech. It is this miracle that in the fourth and innermost circle of our deliberations we have not so much to explain as rather to evaluate as this specific miracle. " Not only—but also and primarily and decisively " is how the formula must run. The " not only—but also " means first that human talk, with its motives and themes and the judgments among which it stands

as human talk, is there even while God's Word is there. The miracle of real proclamation does not consist in the fact that the willing and doing of proclaiming man with all its conditioning and in all its problems is set aside, that in some way a disappearance takes place and a gap arises in the reality of nature, and that in some way there steps into this gap naked divine reality scarcely concealed by a mere remaining appearance of human reality.

The decisive principle in the Roman Catholic doctrine of change is that through priestly consecration there takes place a *conversio totius substantiae panis in substantiam corporis Christi Domini nostri et totius substantiae vini in substantiam sanguinis eius* (*Trid. sess.* XIII, *Decr. de ss. Euch. cap.*, 4), and this in such a way that only the *accidentia* of bread and wine remain *sine subjecto* (*ib. can.* 2 and *Conc. Constantiense* 1415 *Errores Joannis Wicleff* 2, Denz., No. 582).

The willing and doing of proclaiming man, however, is not in any sense set aside in real proclamation. As Christ became true man and remains true man to all eternity, real proclamation becomes an event on the level of all other human events. It can be seen and heard on this level, and its being seen and heard thus is no mere appearance but must take place in full essentiality. Without the ambivalence, the liability to misunderstanding and the vulnerability with which this takes place, with which it is itself one event among many others, it could not be real proclamation. But as Christ is not just true man, so it is not just the willing and doing of proclaiming man. It is also and indeed it is primarily and decisively the divine willing and doing. Precisely for this reason the human element is not set aside. What seems to be the burning question of the nature of the co-existence and co-operation of the two factors is a highly irrelevant question. God and the human element are not two co-existing and co-operating factors. The human element is what God created. Only in the state of disobedience is it a factor standing over against God. In the state of obedience it is service of God. Between God and true service of God there can be no rivalry. Service of God does not have to be removed in order that God Himself may be honoured in it. Where God is truly served, there—with no removal of the human element, with the full and essential presence and operation of the human element in all its humanity—the willing and doing of God is not just present as a first or second co-operating factor ; it is present as the first and decisive thing as befits God the Creator and Lord. Without depriving the human element of its freedom, its earthly substance, its humanity, without obliterating the human subject, or making its activity a purely mechanical event, God is the subject from whom human action must receive its new and true name : not just a title tacked on ; no, the name which belongs to it as essentially and primarily as possible in the full supremacy of the will of its Creator and

Lord. Where Church proclamation takes place according to this will of God, where it rests on the divine commission, where God Himself gives Himself to it as its theme, where it is true according to His judgment, where, in short, it is service of God, there on the one hand its character as an event that can be seen and heard on earth is not set aside.

Bread remains bread and wine wine, to put it in eucharistic terms. The realism of sacramental consecration does not imply destruction of the signs' own existence.

On the other hand, through the new robe of righteousness thrown over it, even in its earthly character it becomes a new event, the event of God's own speaking in the sphere of earthly events, the event of the authoritative vicariate of Jesus Christ. Real proclamation as this new event, in which the event of human talk is not set aside by God but exalted, is the Word of God. Again, then, real proclamation means the Word of God preached. Only now is it clear that " preached " belongs to the predicate, and to what degree. The Word of God preached means in this fourth and innermost circle man's talk about God in which and through which God speaks about Himself.

Adolf Harnack in a fine essay (" *Christus praesens—Vicarius Christi,*" *Sitz.- Berichte der preuss. Akad. d. Wiss.*, 1927, p. 415 f.) has shown how there could be and was a movement from the concept " Word of God " through the " adoption of the Church into the main theological equations " (God, Christ, Spirit, etc.) to the doctrine of the infallibility of the papacy. In fact we are confronted here not merely by the problem of the Roman Catholic doctrine of transubstantiation but also by the problem of the Roman Catholic view of all that may be summed up under the concept of ecclesiastical *potestas*. In itself it might well be wholly in line with our concept of the Word of God preached when Gregory of Nyssa (in actual analogy to the new qualification of the elements in the sacraments) says of the priest that up to yesterday he was simply one of many, one of the people, but now in virtue of his consecration as a priest he has become a καθηγεμών, πρόεδρος, διδάσκαλος εὐσεβείας, μυστηρίων λανθανόντων μυσταγωγός (*Or. in diem luminum*) ; or when Ambrose explains to baptismal candidates with reference to the Christian priest : *Vidisti illic levitam, vidisti summum sacerdotem. Noli considerari corporum figuras, sed mysteriorum gratiam . . . Quid tradiderit considera* (*De myst.*, 2, 6). *Non merita personarum considere, sed officia sacerdotum* (*ib.*, 5, 27) ; or when Augustine with special regard to the Christian preacher insists : *Boni fideles non quemlibet hominum, sed ipsum Dominum obedienter audiunt*—the *locus superior sedis ecclesiasticae* from which the speaker speaks, even though he be personally the very reverse of good, forces him of itself to say what is good (*De doctr. christ.*, IV, 27) ; or when he describes the earthly utterance of God's voice as follows, *quod creaturae motus expressit eam, serviens aeternae voluntati tuae ipse temporalis* (*Conf.*, XI, 6, 8) ; or when he says of the *doctrina de superiore loco in conspectu omnium personante* that it is always entails the decision concerning the hearers that *et qui faciunt audiant ad praemium et qui non faciunt audiant ad judicium* (*De civ. Dei*, II, 28). This absolute singling out of the function of Church proclamation is intrinsically something which is common in the Reformers too : " Now I and any man that speaketh Christ's Word may freely boast that his mouth is Christ's mouth. I am sure my word is not mine but Christ's Word and so my mouth must also be His whose Word it speaketh " (Luther, *Eine treue Vermahnung*, 1522, *W.A.*, 8, p. 263, l. 13). " Hereby all men on earth are subject to the preaching office, as the apostles and their successors lead on God's behalf, so that they must be submissive to the same and follow it if they would have God's grace and be saved " (*Pred. über Joh.* 16⁵¹·, 1533, *E.A.*, 3, p. 434). " That is a power against which emperor and king are naught, that an apostle, yea every disciple of Christ, may pronounce a judgment on the whole world that sin should go. And such judgment should be so powerful and certain as if Christ Himself had uttered it. . . ." (*Predigt über Joh.* 20¹⁹⁻³¹, 1533, *W.A.*, 52, p. 269, l. 18). 'Tis a right excellent thing that every honest pastor's and preacher's mouth is Christ's mouth and his word and forgiveness Christ's Word and forgiveness. If thou hast sin and dost confess the same and believest in Christ, the pastor and preacher shall forgive thee that same sin in Christ's name, and the words he saith to thee on God's behalf thou shalt receive, as if Christ Himself had said them to thee. We rightly call the pastor's or preacher's word God's Word. For his office is not his but God's, and the word he preacheth is not his but God's " (Sermon on the same text, 1534, *E.A.*, 3, p. 376). " On the last day God will say to me : Hast thou also preached that ? and I shall then say, Yea, then God shall say to thee, Hast thou also heard that ? and thou shalt say, Yea, and He saith further, Why then hast thou not believed ? and thou then sayest, Oh, I held it for a word of man since some poor chaplain or village parson said it. So then shall that same word which sticketh in thine heart accuse thee and be thine accuser and judge at the last day. For it is God's Word, 'tis God Himself thou hast heard, as Christ saith, ' He that heareth you heareth me,' and I have satisfied mine office for the judgment and before God when I have shown thee thy sins and iniquities and chastised thee for them, and am clean of thy blood. See thou then to it how thou standest " (*Ausl. des dritten und vierten Kap. Joh.*, *W.A.*, 47, p. 120, l. 28). " Hence might I be glad and say, God who hath created heaven and earth, who is the divine majesty, hath spoken with me. How ? Through my brother man. He doth it to us for good, namely, for love and friendship. But when a man seeth a preacher he thinketh, This is a poor wretched man, and none considereth that beneath lieth the divine majesty. An angel might make heaven full of fire that lightning and thunder should strike and heaven and earth become black and everything collapse. Why then wilt thou not hear God who maketh Himself like a weak man and hideth Himself and holdeth Himself like the dear apostles ? Therefore it is not a preacher's word but God's Word. Since it is God's Word thou shouldest start back thereat or be glad " (*ib.*, p. 213, l. 26). " If thou hear me who am a preacher, and hear and believe me none otherwise than another man, thou art condemned with me. . . . Therefore thou shouldest not hear me as a man that preacheth man's word. If thou hearest me thus, 'twere much better thou heardest me not at all. Thus too thy pastor shouldest thou not hear as a man that speaketh and preacheth man's word, but shouldest hear him as Him that speaketh the Word out of the mouths of babes and sucklings. . . ." (Sermon delivered in Merseburg, 1545, *W.A.*, 51, p. 15, l. 30, 36). *Repraesentant Christi personam propter vocationem ecclesiae, non repraesentant proprias personas ut testatur Christus : qui vos audit, me audit. Cum verbum Christi, cum sacramenta porrigunt, Christi vice et loco porrigunt* (Melanchthon, *Apol. De ecclesia*, *C.R.*, 27, 529). Calvin, too declares most emphatically that God is certainly not bound to the human word about Him and can draw His own to Himself by some direct way. Nevertheless it has obviously pleased Him to let us ripen into the manhood of Christ *educatione ecclesiae* and thus, without ceasing Himself and alone to rule in the Church, without abdicating His rights and honour to a man, to avail Himself of man's word as a *vicaria opera*. It may thus be said of Christian preaching : *Deus ipse in medium prodit, et quatenus huius ordinis autor est, vult se praesentem in sua institutione agnosci.* This is a proof that man can actually become God's temple. It is also a decisive test of our humility before God that we learn to render obedience to His Word not as one spoken directly from heaven but just as it meets us on the lips of a *homuncio quispiam ex pulvere emersus* who is in no connexion better than ourselves. Finally it is the strongest bond of the mutual love in which God wants to bind us together that in preaching He sets His Word on the lips of a fellow-man and thereby forbids us to try to satisfy ourselves (Sermon on Lk. 1¹⁶ᶠ·, *C.R.*, 46, 39 ; *Instit.*, IV, 1, 5 and 3, 1 ; cf. E. Brunner, *Gott und Mensch*, 1930, p. 65). The relation between the order that in preaching *homines* are to be instructed *per homines* and Christian *charitas* is already an insight of Augustine's (*De doctr. christ., Prol.*, 6).

In the light of this concept of the Word of God preached, the familiar singling out of the bishop's office as first espoused especially by Ignatius of Antioch, then by Irenaeus, Tertullian and Cyprian, cannot be called intrinsically impossible. One can neither estimate the Roman Catholic position correctly nor take up the correct Evangelical position if (with Harnack, *op. cit.*, p. 446) one takes offence already at the idea of vicariate or succession. One would have to deny *Christus praesens* to deny in principle the *vicarius Christi*. The difference between Roman Catholic dogmatics and ourselves, which, of course, we must always keep in view, cannot refer to the fact of this vicariate or succession, but only to its manner. The three questions which follow are decisive in this regard. 1. How does a man become *vicarius Christi* and *successor Petri* ? According to Roman Catholic teaching he does so through his place at the bottom of a list of bishops that goes back without a break to an apostle, finally to Peter, and last of all to Christ as the Founder of the Church. We ask how the secular, historico-juridical fact of such a list can come to vouch for the regularity of ecclesiastical office. What does this documentary succession have to do with real, i.e., spiritual succession ? 2. How does this vicariate or succession arise ? According to Roman Catholic teaching it consists in a character which by ordination a bishop or priest receives for life in addition to his humanity. We ask how there can be a character for life if ordination can relate only to the official acts of the person ordained and even in respect of these acts cannot try to mean more than the proclamation of a promise ? 3. In what consists this vicariate or succession ? According to Roman Catholic teaching it consists in the permanent authority of the teaching office to establish and proclaim irreformable definitions in matters of faith and morals. We ask how far the exercise of this permanent authority of a human court to speak irreformably can still be understood as service of God. How far does one have here only a representation and not rather a supplanting of Christ ? To summarise all three questions : Is not vicariate in the Roman Catholic sense one in which only the accidents of vicariate are retained while in substance it is simply the rule of Christ equated with that of the Church ? We realise that this whole doctrine is a genuinely significant attempt to come to terms with the problem of real proclamation. But does not this solution mean that proclamation is dehumanised through the ideas of historical succession, *character indelebilis* and the possibility of irreformable definitions, i.e., that it is set in a sphere in which it can only in appearance imply human action that is vulnerable, responsible, surpassable, and consequently serviceable ? It is a consistent but still an incomprehensible fact that on the day of his consecration Innocent III simply preached about himself (Harnack, *op. cit.*, p. 441). Roman Catholic dogmatics is naturally aware of the lordship of Christ as a lordship not only in His Church but also over His Church. But where can this lordship of Christ over His Church take concrete shape in this system, where can it come into proper play, when all its power has already been fully transferred to the Church, when its power is simply present in the Church ? And if it has no play of its own, is it distinguished in any way but name only from the power that is exercised in the Church by men without break, hindrance, or limit ? Certainly a Roman Catholic could approve of Luther's interpretation of the metaphor of the Good Shepherd in Jn. 10 : " Thus He refers the right shepherd's office, which is to help the rule of consciences and souls, to His own person alone, when He who alone hath done and accomplished it, the work of our redemption, who hath laid down His body and life for His sheep and founded the office, plies and upholds it, that through it He brings them to Himself and rules and sustains them. And thus the whole preaching of the Gospel is included where and when and by whom it is preached, who after Christ are also called shepherds, not on account of their own persons (for such can no one be save Christ Himself), but because they are in the office that is proper to Christ alone, and He exercises it through them and works in the same " (*Crucigers Sommerpostille*, 1543, *W.A.*, 21, p. 323, l. 3). But on the question as to what " person " means here there is an inexorable parting of the ways. According to the Evangelical view one can no longer speak of an action of Christ's person in and over the Church when human authorities in the Church are deprived of their humanity in the way described and when Christ's own decisions are swallowed up in the decisions of these authorities. What can become, as shown, the endowment, quality, power and dignity of other persons ceases to this degree to be itself active person. Personal presence implies the possibility of absence as well. A personal gift implies the possibility of its refusal. This limitation of the power of the Church by the person of Christ is needed to prove that the Church is the true Church which serves Christ and which thus has a share in the benefits of His lordship, presence and gifts. But this limitation is ruled out by the doctrines of historical succession, indelible character, and the possibility of irreformable definitions. Hence we must reject these doctrines. In the sermon just quoted Luther continues : " Therefore 'tis thus also in this spiritual rule of consciences, where Christ doth not Himself through His shepherd's office guard, lead and guide, no other preaching helpeth or availeth aught, no matter if it be otherwise good and right. For it cannot stand in straits against the devil when he opens wide hell's vengeance through fear of sins and eternal death. For if it comes to that the poor sheep standeth alone and forsaken, all by itself ; and its act, directed by the doctrine of the law and our works, hath neither help nor stay more with which to comfort itself and find rescue " (*ib.*, p. 324, l. 17). Then in a later sermon on the same text he says more belligerently : " That such preaching be used aright and be good and profitable, they must not enter into the sheepfold themselves like the others, nor imagine themselves to be shepherds, but only doorkeepers and servants of the true Shepherd Christ, who keep the sheep in watch and ward that naught strange break in on them. And they make way for the Shepherd and give place to Him who Himself leadeth them out and in to pasture. Therefore let such office be ordered not to point to self but to open up to the Shepherd that the sheep may hear Him and be pastured by Him " (*ib.*, p. 501, l. 8). In the Confession of the Synod of Strassburg in 1533 (cf. *Reformierte Kirchenzeitung*, 1931, No. 27, p. 211) Article 6 reads : " Faith cometh from hearing. Yet neither is he that planteth aught nor he that watereth, but God who giveth the increase is all. Hence injury is done to the divine grace and work if to the words and acts of evangelical preaching and sacraments they would ascribe some power to cleanse us from sins, which power they have in themselves be they but preached and administered by men, while those to whom they impart the Word and sacrament may believe as they like. . . ." And again Calvin has finely said what needs to be said about the Evangelical view of the relation (excluding any *opus operatum*) between God and man in the ecclesiastical office :

Et certe quum nobis constet Dei negotium hic nos et curare et agere, ipsum sibi operique suo minime defuturum confidimus. Caeterum qualiscunque exitus erit, nunquam nos coepisse, aut huc usque progressos esse poenitebit. Nobis Spiritus sanctus doctrinae nostrae fidelis est ac certus testis. Scimus, inquam, esse aeternam Dei veritatem quam praedicamus. Ministerium nostrum ut mundo sit salutare, optamus quidem, sicut par est : verum ut id consequamur, Dei est praestare, non nostrum (Suppl. Exhort., 1543, C.R., 6, 534). But we can also sum up our objection to the Roman Catholic doctrine in the direction given to the preacher by the greatest Catholic theologian, Augustine : Oret, ut Dominus sermonem bonum det in os eius (De doctr. chr., IV, 15). What does it mean if this oret is taken not merely as an ascetic and homiletic suggestion but more seriously in its material content, much more strictly than it need be even according to Augustine's own view ? Must we really pray for the sermo bonus ? Can we only pray for it ? Is Christ's action, real proclamation, the Word of God preached, tied to the ecclesiastical office and consequently to a human act, or conversely, as one might conclude from this oret, are the office and act tied to the action of Christ, to the actualising of proclamation by God, to the Word of God preached ? From the standpoint of our theses this question is the puzzling cleft which has cut right across the Church during the last 400 years.

2. THE WORD OF GOD WRITTEN

We have said that Church proclamation must be ventured in recollection of past revelation and in expectation of coming revelation. The basis of expectation is obviously identical here with the object of recollection. Hoping for what we cannot see, what we cannot assume to be present, we speak of an actualised proclamation, of a Word of God preached in the Church, on the basis that God's Word has already been spoken, that revelation has already taken place. We speak in recollection.

What is the meaning of this recollection of past revelation ? Recollection of God's enacted revelation might mean the actualisation of a revelation of God originally immanent in the existence of every man, i.e., of man's own original awareness of God. In this case recollection of God's enacted revelation would be identical with the discovery and fresh appropriation of a long hidden, forgotten and unused part, and indeed the most central and significant part, of the timeless essential constitution of man himself, namely, his relation to the eternal or absolute.

Augustine, following Plato's doctrine of anamnesis, understood memoria along these lines. Unde adest nisi ex memoria ? Nam et cum ab alio commoniti recognoscimus, inde adest. Non enim quasi novum credimus, sed recordantes approbamus hoc esse quod dictum est. Si autem penitus aboleatur ex anima, nec admoniti reminiscimur. Neque enim omni modo adhuc obliti sumus, quod vel iam oblitos nos esse meminimus (Conf., X, 19, 28). According to Augustine God is what we all seek as we all seek a vita beata. How is it that we want to be happy, that we love this vita beata ? We obviously know it already. Nimirum habemus eam nescio quomodo. . . . Neque enim amaremus eam nisi nossemus (ib., 28, 29). Knowledge of God, therefore, can only be a confirmation of this that is already known before about God : *Neque enim aliquid de te inveni, quod non meminissem ex quo didici te. Nam ex quo didici te, non sum oblitus tui. Ubi enim inveni veritatem, ibi inveni Deum meum ipsam veritatem, quam, ex quo didici, non sum oblitus (ib.*, 24, 35). Much later we find a very similar line of argument when it is a matter of introducing Cartesianism into theology. What is the use of instruction or teaching, thought A. Heidan (*Corp. theol. christ.*, 1686, *Loc.* I, p. 9), *nisi ex nobis ideam Dei formare possimus.* The *idea Dei* does not come to us from without (*aliunde*). It is *potentia nobis semper inexistens.* Along these lines, as Augustine already brought out quite clearly, recollection means inwardness, man's return from the distractions of the outside world and re-entry into himself to find God there. *Sero te amavi, pulchritudo tam antiqua et tam nova !* *Sero te amavi !* *Et ecce intus eras et ego foris et ibi te quaerebam . . . mecum eras et tecum non eram (Conf.*, X, 27, 38).

Is the recollection of God's revelation on which the venture of Church proclamation is ventured this kind of recollection ? One cannot prove *a priori* that this is impossible. Why could it not have pleased God to be immanent to His Church as the foundation which was hidden for a time, but which steadily endured because it had been timelessly laid, so that standing on it need be only a matter of profound self-reflection ? Why should not God have let the Church be grounded upon itself as the Church, so that it could continually ground itself upon itself by continually returning to itself as such, this being recollection of God's past revelation ? Why not ?

The Neo-Platonist and the Catholic churchman could obviously exist quite well in personal union in Augustine. Why should not both have been right ?

The concept of the divine freedom or potency provides no reason why this should be impossible. The real reason is that God did not make this specific use of His freedom or potency. The reason is thus a fact which points in a very different direction.

Here, too, we must begin exegetically, conscious that what we pursue is Evangelical and Reformation exegesis of the reality of the Church. The Church is not alone in relation to God's Word. It is not referred to itself or consequently to self-reflection. It has not the confidence to appeal to itself as the source of the divine Word in support of the venture of proclamation. It does not seek in the hidden depths of its own existence the commission, the object, the judgment and the event in recollection of which it is validated in its proclamation and believes it is summoned to proclamation. The return to its own being on the basis of which alone it may actually venture its proclamation does indeed mean for it a return to its own being, but to its self-transcendent being, to Jesus Christ as the heavenly Head to whom it, the earthly body, is attached as such, but in relation to whom it is also distinct as such, who has the Church within Himself but whom the Church does not have within itself, between whom and it there is no reversible or alternating relation, just as the relation between master and servant is not reversible. He is immanent in it only as He is transcendent to it. This is the fact which makes the recollection of God's past revelation different from reflection on its own timeless ground of being. It has pleased God to be its God in another way than that of pure immanence.

But this fact must be described more precisely. The distinction of the Head from the body and the superiority of the Head over the body find concrete expression in the fact that proclamation in the Church is confronted by a factor which is very like it as a phenomenon, which is temporal as it is, and yet which is different from it and in order superior to it. This factor is Holy Scripture. Holy Scripture is the concrete form of the reason why the recollection on the basis of which we expect God's revelation cannot be recollection of a timeless being of the Church. It is the bolt which in fact shuts out Platonic *anamnesis* here. It does so in the first instance simply because it is there and tells us what is the past revelation of God that we have to recollect. It does so in the first instance simply by the fact that it is the Canon.

Κανών means rod, then ruler, standard, model, assigned district. In the ecclesiastical vocabulary of the first three hundred years it was used for that which stands fast as normative, i.e., apostolic, in the Church, the *regula fidei*, i.e., the norm of faith, or the Church's doctrine of faith. From this (only apparently) wider concept of the κανών τῆς ἀληθείας or τῆς πίστεως there then develops from the 4th century onwards the more specialised idea of the Canon of Holy Scripture, i.e., the list of biblical books which are recognised as normative, because apostolic.

With its acknowledgment of the presence of the Canon the Church expresses the fact that it is not left to itself in its proclamation, that the commission on the ground of which it proclaims, the object which it proclaims, the judgment under which its proclamation stands and the event of real proclamation must all come from elsewhere, from without, and very concretely from without, in all the externality of the concrete Canon as a categorical imperative which is also historical, which speaks in time. And with its acknowledgement that this Canon is in fact identical with the Bible of the Old and New Testaments, with the word of the prophets and apostles, it expresses the truth that this reference of its proclamation to something that is concretely external is not a general principle, nor a mere determination of form whose content might be this or might be quite different, but that this reference is wholly determined in content, that it is a received direction and effected connexion, that this part of past history consisting of specific texts constitutes the working instructions or marching orders by which not just the Church's proclamation but the very Church itself stands or falls, which are not in any circumstances, not even hypothetically, to be lost to view, and which are not in any circumstances, not even hypothetically, to be regarded as replaced by others, if proclamation and the Church itself are not to be lost to view.

For a better understanding one should note first what we have called the similarity as phenomena between Church proclamation and this second entity which confronts it in the Church, namely, the Canon of Holy Scripture. This consists in the fact that in Holy Scripture, too, the writing is obviously not primary, but secondary. It is itself the deposit of what was once proclamation by human lips. In its form as Scripture, however, it does not seek to be a historical monument but rather a Church document, written proclamation. The two entities may thus be set initially under a single genus, Scripture as the commencement and present-day preaching as the continuation of one and the same event, Jeremiah and Paul at the beginning and the modern preacher of the Gospel at the end of one and the same series.

Luther had a good grasp of this relationship. On the one hand : " The Gospel simply means a preaching and crying out loud of God's grace and mercy merited and won by the Lord Christ with His death. And it is properly not what stands in books or is made up of letters, but rather an oral preaching and lively word and a voice that rings out in the whole world and is publicly cried out loud that it may be everywhere heard " (*Ep. S. Petri gepredigt unnd ausgelegt*, 1523, *W.A.*, 12, p. 259, l. 8). On the other hand : " For we have John Baptist's word and spirit, and we parsons and preachers are in our time what John Baptist was in his time. We let John Baptist's finger point and his voice sound : ' Behold, the Lamb of God that taketh away the sin of the world ' ; we deliver John Baptist's sermon, point to Christ and say : This is the one true Saviour whom you should worship and to whom you should cleave. Such preaching must endure to the last day, even though it abide not in all places, all the time, alike, yet must it abide " (Sermon on Mt. 11[2f.], *E.A.*, 1, p. 159).

In this similarity as phenomena, however, there is also to be found between Holy Scripture and present-day proclamation a dissimilarity in order, namely the supremacy, the absolutely constitutive significance of the former for the latter, the determination of the reality of present-day proclamation by its foundation upon Holy Scripture and its relation to this, the basic singling out of the written word of the prophets and apostles over all the later words of men which have been spoken and are to be spoken to-day in the Church. If what we have said is true, if the Church is not alone in respect of its proclamation but finds itself in a concrete confrontation in which it is mindful of the past revelation of God, and if the concrete form of its opposite is really the biblical word of the prophets and apostles, then obviously the latter must have fundamental distinction in relation to it. If the vicariate of Church proclamation is authentic, i.e., if the Church in its proclamation does not find its basis secretly in itself but in the Other who is its Lord without the Church ever becoming His lord, then the concrete form of vicariate must be succession.

This concept from the Roman Catholic definition of the ecclesiastical office is also one which intrinsically need not give rise to any objection. The series God, Christ, apostle, bishop, community as it begins to appear in Church writings at the beginning of the 2nd century (e.g., Clement of Rome *ad Cor.*, 42 and 44) becomes a criterion which is applied almost formally by Irenaeus : Where there is *traditio* or *successio apostolorum*, there is the Church (e.g., *C. o. haer.*, III, 2, 2 ; 3, 1 ; 4, 1 ; IV, 26, 2, 5 ; 33, 8 ; V, 20), and it is used in fighting heretics from the standpoint of the question of their relation to the apostolic origin of the Church : *Edant ergo origines ecclesiarum suarum, evolvant ordinem episcoporum suorum ita per successionem ab initio decurrentem, ut primus ille episcopus aliquem ex apostolis . . . habuerit auctorem et antecessorem . . . exhibent quos ab apostolis in episcopatum constitutos apostolici seminis traduces habeant* (Tertullian, *De praescr. haer.*, 32). In itself all this can have its proper place as an expression of awareness of the concreteness of the form in which Christ and His Church are combined and yet contrasted. Apostolicity is in fact one of the decisive notes of the true Church (*credo unam sanctam catholicam et apostolicam ecclesiam*). In virtue of its direct relation to the transcendent character of what is Christian it is also the decisive mark of true Church proclamation. The Evangelical Church says and confesses the same with its Scripture principle : " Now when He says, Ye also shall bear witness, for ye have been with me from the beginning, He thereby specially depicts the apostles for all preachers and confirms their preaching so that all the world should be bound to their word, and believe the same without any contradiction and be certain that all they preach and teach is right doctrine and the Holy Ghost's preaching which they have heard and received from Him. As I Jn. 1 adduces such witness and says : ' That which we have heard, that which we have seen with our eyes, that which we have beheld . . . of the Word of life, that declare we unto you.' Such witness have no preachers on earth save the apostles only, for the others are hereby commanded that they should all follow in the apostles' footsteps, abide by the same doctrine and preach nothing more nor otherwise. And moreover the right sign is shown by which one may know and test such preaching of the Holy Ghost, for He saith : ' The Holy Ghost shall testify of me ' " etc. (Luther, *Crucigers Sommerpostille, W.A.*, 21, p. 426, l. 2). Here again, then, the difference between the Evangelical view and the Roman Catholic view is not in respect of the That but the How. And even in respect of the How no objection in principle can be raised on our part against the concentration of the apostolate in Peter or the possibility of a primacy in the Church which might be that of the Roman community. The protest of Protestantism in this question of succession is directed solely and simply against the fact that the *Tu es Petrus*, etc., is mechanically transferred over Peter's head to every succeeding Roman bishop as a second, third and hundredth Peter, as if the succession and tradition of the Peter of Mt. 16, to whom flesh and blood had not revealed such things, could be related to any succession but a spiritual one, or as if, being spiritual, it could be tied to the secular circumstance of a list of bishops of this kind. " The visibility and the related stability of the Church demand, then, an ecclesiastical ordination which begins with Christ, the starting-point, and continues in unbroken sequence, so that, as the apostles were sent by the Saviour, they in turn appointed bishops, these again gave themselves successors, and so on to our own day. By this succession of bishops which began with the Saviour and has continued without a break it may be pre-eminently seen as by a sign which is the true Church founded by Him " (J. A. Möhler, *Symbolik*, 3rd edn., 1834, p. 396). It is to this that we can only say No. *Est enim ecclesia coetus non alligatus ad ordinariam successionem, sed ad verbum Dei. Ibi renascitur ecclesia, ubi Deus restituit doctrinam et dat Spiritum sanctum* (Melanchthon, *De ecclesia et de auctoritate verbi Dei*, 1539, *C.R.*, 22, 598). And the reason for the protest is that in these circumstances apostolicity necessarily ceases to be a divine gift and human task and becomes an assured human possession, that it is " pre-eminently " understood in a mechanically historical and legal way, that it can no longer be a norm which confronts the Church with direction and judgment, that in contrast it falls completely under the *judicium ecclesiae*, the control of the second or third or hundredth Peter.   Spiritual succession obviously presupposes that the *successor* is spiritually but not mechanically identical with the *antecessor*, so that the *antecessor* still has elbow-room of his own as distinct from the *successor*.   Such elbow-room, however, is not given to Peter in the Roman Catholic system.   Here the *antecessor* is taken up and absorbed in the *successor*.   What constitutes the apostolicity of proclamation here is the watch at Peter's grave.   On this presupposition neither Peter, the apostolate, nor the Holy Spirit is any longer a free power in the Church and over against the Church. On this presupposition the Church is again left to itself and referred to itself and its self-reflection.   This is why we cannot endorse the Roman Catholic doctrine of succession.   Nor especially can we endorse the form in which it is presented and espoused by Friedrich Heiler, *Im Ringen um die Kirche*, 1931, p. 479 (cf. esp. the " four grounds " p. 506 f.) ; theologically this form can only be called dilettante whether from the Roman Catholic or the Evangelical standpoint.

The apostolic succession of the Church must mean that it is guided by the Canon, that is, by the prophetic and apostolic word as the necessary rule of every word that is valid in the Church. It must mean that the Church enters into the succession of the prophets and apostles in their office of proclamation, and does so in such a way that their proclamation freely and independently precedes, while that of the Church is related to it, is ventured in obedience on the basis of it, is measured by it, and replaces it only as and to the extent that it conforms to it. It must mean that the Church always admits the free power of their proclamation over it. As far as the idea of a living succession is concerned everything depends on the *antecessor* being regarded as alive and having free power over against the *successor*. But if, as here, the *antecessor* has long since died, this can happen only if his proclamation has been fixed in writing and if it is acknowledged that he still has life and free power over the Church to-day in this written word of his. On the written nature of the Canon, on its character as *scriptura sacra*, hangs his autonomy and independence, and consequently his free power over against the Church and the living nature of the succession. Naturally it might also have pleased God to give His Church the Canon in the form of an unwritten prophetic and apostolic tradition propagating itself from spirit to spirit and mouth to mouth.

In this case it might be legitimate and it might make sense that the grave of Peter should be the central shrine of the Church. Canon might be the event of tradition, i.e., " the distinctive Christian meaning present in the Church and propagating itself by Church education . . . the living word continually alive in the hearts of believers " (J. A. Möhler, *Symbolik*, 3rd edn., 1834, p. 371).

Now one cannot wish to contest the fact that there is something of this kind in the Church apart from the real Canon. But one must also say that if it had pleased God to make this unwritten spiritual-oral tradition the Canon of His Church, the Canon would be as little distinguishable from the life of the Church as the blood of our fathers coursing through our veins is distinguishable from our own blood. In other words, the Church would again be left alone and referred to itself, to its own vitality. Whatever there may be of such spiritual-oral tradition in the Church, since it does not have written form it obviously cannot have the character of an authority irremovably confronting the Church. In unwritten tradition the Church is not addressed ; it is engaged in dialogue with itself.

The saying of Papias : οὐ γὰρ τὰ ἐκ τῶν βιβλίων τοσοῦτόν με ὠφελεῖν ὑπελάμβανον ὅσον τὰ παρὰ ζώσης φωνῆς καὶ μενούσης (Euseb, *H.E.*, III, 39, 4), is an indication of the change which came already at the beginning of the 2nd century and which was so disastrous in its effects. Living quality was now no longer sought and found in the written word of the apostles themselves but in the " voice " of those contemporaries who had known the apostles and preference was given to this " living and lasting voice " over the books, i.e., the apostolic writings. We are at the end of the same development—the living quality has now completely passed from *antecessor* to *successor*—when Karl Adam (*Das Wesen des Katholizismus*, 4th edn., 1927, p. 162) can speak of the " dead word " of the Bible in contrast to the " vitality " of Church tradition. But are we on another path, and not still in the middle of the same one, when Lessing refuses to suspend " no less than all eternity " " on a spider's thread," i.e., the word of the first witnesses (*Eine Duplik, Lessings Theol. Schr.*, ed. C. Gross, II, 2, p. 34) ? For here again the *regula fidei* is not identical with Scripture (*Nötige Antwort, ib.*, II, 2, p. 215 f.). Only the enduring miracle of religion and not Scripture is the decisive proof of Christianity (*Eine Duplik, ib.*, II, 2, p. 33). " It must surely be possible that everything written by the apostles should be lost again and the religion taught by them would still persist " (*Fragm. eines Unbekannten, ib.*, II, 1, p. 262). Really ? his opponent M. Goeze asked and Lessing answered defiantly : " God preserve me from thinking so poorly of Christ's teaching as to dare to answer this question with an outright negative. No, I will not utter this negative even though an angel from heaven dictated it to me. Even less when a mere Lutheran parson wants to put it on my lips " (*Axiomata, ib.*, II, 2, p. 118). With more right than the first words of John's Gospel, so Lessing thought, the Testament of John : " Little children, love one another," ought to be there in golden letters for all to read in the most visible place in all churches (*Das Test. Joh., ib.*, II, 2, p. 19). " It is, of course, apocryphal, this testament, but no less divine for that " (*Über den Beweis . . ., ib.*, II, 2, p. 14). Who does not feel reminded by this last statement that with Holy Scripture the Council of Trent too *nec non traditiones ipsas, tum ad fidem, tum ad mores pertinentes, tanquam vel oretenus a Christo vel a Spiritu sancto dictatas et continua successione in Ecclesia catholica conservatas, pari pietatis affectu et reverentia suscipit et veneratur* (*Trid. sess. IV Recipiuntur libri. . . .*). Was Lessing guilty of catholicising or was the Council of Trent guilty of modernising (which began, of course, with Papias) ? How are these two trends related to one another ? One thing is certain ; they agree in their effect, the granting of relative independence to the Church *vis-à-vis* the Canon of Holy Scripture, i.e., relative devaluation of this Canon.

If, then, apart from the undeniable vitality of the Church itself there stands confronting it a concrete authority with its own vitality, an authority whose pronouncement is not the Church's dialogue with itself but an address to the Church, and which can have *vis-à-vis* the Church the position of a free power and therefore of a criterion, then obviously in its writtenness as " Bible " it must be distinguished from and given precedence over the purely spiritual and oral life of ecclesiastical tradition. It is true that this real, biblical Canon is constantly exposed to absorption into the life, thought and utterance of the Church inasmuch as it continually seeks to be understood afresh and hence expounded and interpreted. Exegesis is always a combination of taking and giving, of reading out and reading in. Thus exegesis, without which the norm cannot assert itself as a norm, entails the constant danger that the Bible will be taken prisoner by the Church, that its own life will be absorbed into the life of the Church, that its free power will be transformed into the authority of the Church, in short, that it will lose its character as a norm magisterially confronting the Church. All exegesis can become predominantly interposition rather than exposition and to that degree it can fall back into the Church's dialogue with itself. Nor will one banish the danger, but only conjure it up properly and make it acute, by making correct exposition dependent on the judgment of a definitive and decisive teaching office in the Church or on the judgment of a historico-critical scholarship which comports itself with equal infallibility. If we assume that one or other of these authorities is worthy of the Church's highest confidence, then either way the Church goes astray in respect of the Bible by thinking that in one way or the other it can and should control correct exposition, and thereby set up a norm over the norm, and thereby capture the true norm for itself. The exegesis of the Bible should rather be left open on all sides, not for the sake of free thought, as Liberalism would demand, but for the sake of a free Bible. Here as everywhere the defence against possible violence to the text must be left to the text itself, which in fact has always succeeded in doing something a purely spiritual and oral tradition cannot do, namely, maintaining its own life against the encroachments of individual or total periods and tendencies in the Church, victoriously asserting this life in ever new developments, and thus creating recognition for itself as a norm.

" Inward truth," in spite of Lessing's protest (*Axiomata, op. cit.,* II, 2, p. 127), is " a wax nose that any knave can mould as he will to suit his own face," and if Counter-Reformation polemics did apply the same excellent metaphor to the Bible (*scriptura est tanquam nasus cereus ; quia flecti potest hinc inde,* quoted by Calvin, *Articuli Fac. Paris. cum Antidoto,* 1544, C.R., 7, 31), this simply proves to us how right it is to demand free exegesis for the sake of a free Bible.

Already as a text the canonical text has the character of a free power. All the Church need do is just this : After any exegesis propounded in it, even the very best, it has to realise afresh the distinction between text and commentary and to let the text speak again without let or hindrance, so that it will experience the lordship of this free power and find in the Bible the partner or counterpart which the Church must find in it if it is to take the living *successio apostolorum* seriously.

Now we must also ask, of course, how it comes about that the prophetic and apostolic word in particular takes up this normative position over against the Church and its proclamation. We have tried to make it clear that it must be a written word, a text, to be a true Canon as distinct from the Church's own life. But obviously the fact that it is written does not alone make it the norm. There are other texts about which much the same might be said regarding their exegesis or the free power residing within them. And finally a large part of the non-canonical tradition is also present as text, e.g., in so far as it has been given fixed form in dogma. What is it that makes the Bible of the Old and New Testaments the Canon ? Why must the Church's recollection of God's past revelation always have the Bible as its concrete object ? It is no evasion of this question, which we are always right to raise afresh, if in the first instance we reply at once that the Bible constitutes itself the Canon. It is the Canon because it imposed itself upon the Church as such, and continually does so. The Church's recollection of God's past revelation has the Bible specifically as its object because in fact this object and no other is the promise of future divine revelation which can make proclamation a duty for the Church and which can give it joy and courage for this duty. If we thought we could say why this is so, we should again be acting as if we had in our hands a measure by which we could measure the Bible and on this basis assign it its distinctive position. Our ultimate and decisive wisdom would then be once again the wisdom of a self-dialogue, even if a self-dialogue about the Bible. No, the Bible is the Canon just because it is so. It is so by imposing itself as such. And if we can only register this event (as such) as the reality in which the Church is the Church, nevertheless, when this is done, it is not impossible afterwards, exegetically, to state in what this self-imposing consists and how far it sets a limit to the wisdom of our dialogue with ourselves. At this point we should already refer in advance to the content of Holy Scripture. The prophetic and apostolic word is the word, witness, proclamation and preaching of Jesus Christ. The promise given to the Church in this Word is the promise of God's mercy which is uttered in the person of Him who is very God and very Man and which takes up our cause when we could not help ourselves at all because of our enmity against God. The promise of this Word is thus

Immanuel, God with us—with us who have brought ourselves, and continually bring ourselves again, into the dire straits of not being able to be with God. Holy Scripture is the word of men who yearned, waited and hoped for this Immanuel and who finally saw, heard and handled it in Jesus Christ. Holy Scripture declares, attests and proclaims it. And by its declaration, attestation and proclamation it promises that it applies to us also and to us specifically. The man who so hears their word that he grasps and accepts its promise, believes. And this grasping and accepting of the promise : Immanuel with us sinners, in the word of the prophets and apostles, this is the faith of the Church. In this faith it recollects the past revelation of God and in this faith it expects the future revelation that has yet to come. It recollects the incarnation of the eternal Word and the reconciliation accomplished in Him, and it expects the future of Jesus Christ and its own redemption from the power of evil. Thus Scripture imposes itself in virtue of this its content. In distinction from all other scripture the Scripture with this content—really this !—is Holy Scripture. When the Church heard this word—and it heard it only in the prophets and apostles and nowhere else—it heard a magisterial and ultimate word which it could not ever again confuse or place on a level with any other word. The Scripture with this content sets a natural limit for recollection in the form of self-dialogue. If " Immanuel, with us sinners " is true, then our own deepest ground of being, whatever we think concerning it, cannot be the past revelation of God, and the return to ourselves, however significant it may be in other ways, has nothing whatever to do with the return to God's revelation. The Scripture with this content must confront the life of the Church, which can be life only in this relation, as an entity full of its own vitality and free power, as a criterion which cannot be dissolved into the historical life of the Church. Finally, the Scripture with this content must always become again and again the thing we started with, the object of authentic recollection in which the Church with its proclamation looks and moves forward to the future. " I believe, therefore do I speak " (Ps. 116[10]). Hearing this word with faith in its promise demands proclamation and makes it possible.

The great historical example of this discovery of the Canon that is given to the Church in the Bible in virtue of its content is the early period of the Reformation. What took place in Wittenberg and Zürich in the twenties of the 16th century and in Geneva in the thirties is like a book of illustrations of what has just been said. The Church perceives again that it does not have Christ with His gifts in itself ; it must be found by His Word which comes to it from without (" Salvation has come to us of grace and pure goodness. . . ."). But it perceives this because His Word, and in this He Himself, has already found it, because it is no longer left to itself, because He has already come on the scene to comfort and to judge as its partner and counterpart in the biblical word, because, concretely, the Old and New Testaments have already spoken to it and already forced themselves on it as the " canon of truth." Its proclamation is again placed under the necessity of becoming a succession, an obedient following of the prophetic and apostolic word. Hence the Bible is now important to it again as a book, in its supremacy and freedom over against the Church itself, above everything, even its own exegesis of the book, and in its singularity, which consists in and is established by the fact that it is the book of Christ, of the promise of grace, which is not to be heard anywhere else and which puts an end to the distress and pride of the man who stands on himself and takes counsel with himself. And because this book is there as the Canon, it must be preached, as in that age it was preached, with a volume and intensity that surprises us to-day. Because it is there as the Canon, with the Bible and in the Bible and through the Bible the Church discovers in a completely new way what Church proclamation really is.

All that remains now is to add a final word. Presupposing that we are right about the fact described, that by Holy Scripture the Church is summoned and directed to its proclamation and empowered for it, this implies that Holy Scripture, too, is the Word of God. It is so in exactly the same sense in which we have said this of the event of real proclamation. Recollection of God's past revelation, discovery of the Canon, faith in the promise of the prophetic and apostolic word, or better, the self-imposing of the Bible in virtue of its content, and therefore the existence of real apostolic succession, is also an event, and is to be understood only as an event. In this event the Bible is God's Word. That is to say, in this event the human prophetic and apostolic word is a representative of God's Word in the same way as the word of the modern preacher is to be in the event of real proclamation : a human word which has God's commission to us behind it, a human word to which God has given Himself as object, a human word which is recognised and accepted by God as good, a human word in which God's own address to us is an event. The fact that God's own address becomes an event in the human word of the Bible is, however, God's affair and not ours. This is what we mean when we call the Bible God's Word. We confess and acknowledge therewith that the recollection of God's past revelation, without which the enterprise of Church proclamation would be impossible, is just as much God's grace and gift as is the actualisation our own proclamation needs. It is not in our own power to make this recollection, not even in the form of our grasping at the Bible. Only when and as the Bible grasps at us, when we are thus reminded, is this recollection achieved. If this takes place, if the Bible speaks to us thus of the promise, if the prophets and apostles tell us what they have to tell us, if their word imposes itself on us and if the Church in its confrontation with the Bible thus becomes again and again what it is, all this is God's decision and not ours, all this is grace and not our work. The Bible is God's Word to the extent that God causes it to be His Word, to the extent that He speaks through it. In this second equation no less than the first (namely, that Church proclamation is God's Word) we cannot abstract from the free action of God in and by which He causes it to be true to us and for us here and now that the biblical word of man is His own Word. The statement that the Bible is God's Word is a confession of faith, a statement of the faith which hears God Himself speak through the biblical word of man. To be sure it is a statement which, when venturing it in faith, we accept as true even apart from our faith and beyond all our faith and even in face of our lack of faith. We do not accept it as a description of our experience of the Bible. We accept it as a description of God's action in the Bible, whatever may be the experiences we have or do not have in this connexion. But this is precisely the faith which in this way sees and reaches beyond itself and all related or unrelated experiences to God's action, namely, to the fact that God's action on man has become an event, and not therefore that man has grasped at the Bible but that the Bible has grasped at man. The Bible, then, becomes God's Word in this event, and in the statement that the Bible is God's Word the little word " is " refers to its being in this becoming. It does not become God's Word because we accord it faith but in the fact that it becomes revelation to us. But the fact that it becomes revelation to us beyond all our faith, that it is God's Word even in spite of our lack of faith, is something we can accept and confess as true to us and for us only in faith, in faith as opposed to unbelief, in the faith in which we look away from our faith and unbelief to the act of God, but in faith and not in unbelief, and therefore precisely not in abstraction from the act of God in virtue of which the Bible must become again and again His Word to us.

In the struggle against Calvinists, Schwenckfeldians, Quakers, etc., Lutheran orthodoxy developed a doctrine of the *efficacia Verbi divini etiam ante et extra usum.* The Word of God preached and written has its own divine power no matter what may be its effect on those who hear or read. In the Bible and preaching there takes place a divine *actus purus* no matter how it stands with the *actus secundus* in the hearts of men (Quenstedt, *Theol. did. pol.*, 1685, I, *cap.* 4, *sect.* 2, *qu.* 16 ; Hollaz, *Ex. theol. acroam.*, 1707, III, 2, 1, *qu.* 4). Now in so far as the concern of this doctrine is to prove the truth of the statement of faith that the Bible and preaching are God's Word in its full compass as independent of subjective experience and superior to it, we must certainly concur. But the doctrine was trying to do more than this, and here we cannot accept it. Quenstedt even denied that the Bible is an *instrumentum* which requires *novo motu et elevatione nova ad effectum novum ultra propriam suam naturalem virtutem producendum.* The Bible and preaching are rather *media* in which *summa vis et efficacia* intrinsically and permanently reside (*ib., ekth.* 7). The Bible, so Hollaz thinks, is God's saving Word in the same way as the sun gives warmth even behind clouds, or as a seed of grain has force even in the unfruitful earth, or as the hand of a sleeping man is a living hand. Hollaz also declares in blunt terms that the Word of God is not an *actio* but a *vis*, a *potentia*, which as such has *efficacia* even *extra usum*, in other words a *vis hyperphysica analoga efficaciae physicae i.e. vera et realis.* As though the theological criterion of truth and reality could and should be the analogy to the physical ! A force comparable to sunshine or the thrust of a seed certainly needs no *nova elevatio*. It is there as natural forces are there. But is God's Word there in that way ? If it is really Word ? And if it is the Word of the God who is person ? One surely has to choose between the terms Word of God and *vis hyperphysica*, and in Evangelical theology there should not really be any doubt about the choice.

3. THE WORD OF GOD REVEALED

The Bible is the concrete means by which the Church recollects God's past revelation, is called to expectation of His future revelation, and is thus summoned and guided to proclamation and empowered for it. The Bible, then, is not in itself and as such God's past revelation, just as Church proclamation is not in itself and as such the expected future revelation. The Bible, speaking to us and heard by us as God's Word, bears witness to past revelation. Proclamation, speaking to us and heard by us as God's Word, promises future revelation. The Bible is God's Word as it really bears witness to revelation, and proclamation is God's Word as it really promises revelation. The promise in proclamation, however, rests on the attestation in the Bible. The hope of future revelation rests on faith in that which has taken place once and for all. Thus the decisive relation of the Church to revelation is its attestation by the Bible. Its attestation ! Once again, the Bible is not in itself and as such God's past revelation. As it is God's Word it bears witness to God's past revelation, and it is God's past revelation in the form of attestation. When the Canon, the staff which commands and sets moving and points the way, is moved by a living stretched-out hand, just as the water was moved in the Pool of Bethesda that it might thereby becomes a means of healing, then it bears witness, and by this act of witness it establishes the relation of the Church to revelation, and therewith establishes the Church itself as the true Church, and therewith its proclamation as true proclamation. By its witness ! Witnessing means pointing in a specific direction beyond the self and on to another. Witnessing is thus service to this other in which the witness vouches for the truth of the other, the service which consists in referring to this other. This service is constitutive for the concept of the prophet and also for that of the apostle ; the time has not yet come to speak of the difference between them.

When Paul writes of himself in 1 Cor. 9[16] : ἐὰν γὰρ εὐαγγελίζωμαι, οὐκ ἔστιν μοι καύχημα· ἀνάγκη γάρ μοι ἐπίκειται· οὐαὶ γὰρ μοί ἐστιν ἐὰν μὴ εὐαγγελίσωμαι, he is hereby describing (cf., e.g., Jer. 20[7f.]) the situation that is common to both the prophet and the apostle.

Standing in this service, the biblical witnesses point beyond themselves. If we understand them as witnesses, and only as such do

we authentically understand them, i.e., as they understand themselves,
then their self, which in its inner and outer determination and movement
constitutes as it were the matter of their service, must be decisively
understood by us from the standpoint of its form as a reference away
from themselves. They do not speak and write for their own sakes, nor
for the sake of their deepest inner possession or need ; they speak and
write, as ordered, about that other. They do not try to push themselves, not even as the champions or advocates of the cause they
represent ; beyond all immanent teleology they are forced to speak and
write about that other. They do not want to offer and commend themselves to the Church, and especially not their own particular experience
of God and relationship to God, but through themselves that other. And
not even " through themselves " in the sense that man himself must be
a more or less perfect organ for the revelation of objective facts and
values or subjective stimulations (as is true enough in the achievements
of science, politics and art), but through themselves in such a way that
what makes man a witness is solely and exclusively that other, the
thing attested, which constrains and limits the perfect or imperfect
human organ from without.

At this point we cannot reflect assiduously enough " on the difference between
an apostle and a genius " (Kierkegaard, 1847). The model of the biblical witness
in his unity of form is John the Baptist, who stands so notably at midpoint
between the Old Testament and the New, between the prophets and the apostles :
Ἐγένετο ἄνθρωπος, ἀπεσταλμένος παρὰ θεοῦ, ὄνομα αὐτῷ Ἰωάννης. οὗτος ἦλθεν
εἰς μαρτυρίαν, ἵνα μαρτυρήσῃ περὶ τοῦ φωτός, ἵνα πάντες πιστεύσωσιν δι' αὐτοῦ.
οὐκ ἦν ἐκεῖνος τὸ φῶς, ἀλλ' ἵνα μαρτυρήσῃ περὶ τοῦ φωτός (Jn. 1⁶ᶠ·, cf. 3²⁷ᶠ·). In
this connexion one might recall John the Baptist in Grünewald's Crucifixion,
especially his prodigious index finger. Could anyone point away from himself
more impressively and completely (illum oportet crescere me autem minui) ? And
could anyone point more impressively and realistically than here to what is
indicated ? This is what the Fourth Evangelist wanted to say about this John,
and therefore about another John, and therefore quite unmistakably about every
" John."

Why and in what respect does the biblical witness have authority ?
Because and in the fact that he claims no authority for himself, that
his witness amounts to letting that other itself be its own authority.
We thus do the Bible poor and unwelcome honour if we equate it
directly with this other, with revelation itself.

This may happen when we seek and think we find revelation in the heroic
religious personality of the biblical witness. But it may also happen in the form
of a general, uniform and permanent inspiredness of the Bible, which we shall
have to speak about later. In the work already mentioned (Der Begriff des
Auserwählten, ed. T. Haecker, 1917, p. 314), Kierkegaard very rightly says that
mistaking an apostle for a genius is to be seen not only on the side of heterodoxy
but also on that of hyperorthodoxy, and on that of thoughtlessness in general.
We should not in fact forget that the historical view of the Bible with its cult of

heroes and the doctrine of mechanical inspiration are both products of the same age and spirit. A common feature is that they both represent means whereby Renaissance man tried to control the Bible and also tried to set up obstacles to stop it controlling him, as indeed it ought to do.

The direct identification between revelation and the Bible which is in fact at issue is not one that we can presuppose or anticipate. It takes place as an event when and where the biblical word becomes God's Word, i.e., when and where the biblical word comes into play as a word of witness, when and where John's finger does not point in vain but really indicates, when and where we are enabled by means of his word to see and hear what he saw and heard. Thus in the event of God's Word revelation and the Bible are indeed one, and literally so.

" For this preaching means : ' Fear not, for unto you is born this day the Saviour, which is Christ the Lord.' Men's words which have grown up in the hearts of men are not like that. For the wisest folk on earth know naught thereof. But this preaching rang down from heaven, of which same, God be praised for ever, we are become partakers. For 'tis all the same if thou hearest or readest this preaching as if thou hadst heard it from the angel himself. For the shepherds too saw not the angels, they saw but the light and the glory. But the words of the angels they heard, which we still hear in preaching, may still be read in the Book, if we will but open our eyes and our ears and learn and use aright such preaching " (Luther, *Predigt von der Engel Lobgesang*, 1544, *W.A.*, 52, p. 50, l. 13).

But for this very reason one needs to see that they are not always the same and also to what extent they are not always the same, to what extent their union is really an event. Purely formally, the revelation to which the biblical witnesses direct their gaze as they look and point away from themselves is to be distinguished from the word of the witnesses in exactly the same way as an event itself is to be distinguished from even the best and most faithful account of it. But this distinction is trifling compared with the fact, for which there is no analogy, that in revelation our concern is with the coming Jesus Christ and finally, when the time was fulfilled, the Jesus Christ who has come. Literally, and this time really directly, we are thus concerned with God's own Word spoken by God Himself. What we have in the Bible are in any case human attempts to repeat and reproduce this Word of God in human words and thoughts and in specific human situations, e.g., with reference to the complications of the political position of Israel as a buffer between Egypt and Babylon, or with reference to the errors and confusions in the Christian Church at Corinth between A.D. 50 and 60. On the one hand *Deus dixit*, on the other *Paulus dixit*. These are two different things. And precisely because they are not two things but become one and the same thing in the event of the Word of God, we must maintain that it is by no means self-evident or intrinsically one that revelation should be understood primarily as the superior principle and the Bible primarily as the subordinate principle.

As early as the epistles of Ignatius of Antioch (e.g., *Ad Magn.*, 13, 2) a model is found for the hierarchical church-bishop relation in the apostle-Christ relation. Augustine in his first homily on John's Gospel compares the biblical witnesses to the hills from which help comes according to Ps. 121 : Yet not from the hills themselves but from the Lord who made heaven and earth and who is over these hills. For : *Audeo dicere fratres mei, forsitan nec ipse Joannes dixit ut est, sed et ipse ut potuit ; quia de Deo homo dixit : Et quidem inspiratus a Deo sed tamen homo. Quia inspiratus, dixit aliquid ; si non inspiratus esset, dixisset nihil : Quia vero homo inspiratus, non totum quod est dixit, sed quod potuit homo dixit.* One has to distinguish, says Augustine in another passage, between what *veritas incommutabilis per se ipsam ineffabiliter loquitur rationalis creaturae mentibus* and its expression *per mutabilem creaturam* by means of spiritual images and a physical voice (*De civ. Dei*, XVI, 6, 1). Anselm distinguishes in the same way between the directly (*sine humana doctrina*) enacted divine sowing in the hearts of the prophets and apostles and the increase from the resultant harvest with which we now work (*De concordia qu.*, III, 6). Holy Scripture is *super solidam veritatem . . . velut super firmum fundamentum fundata* (*Cur Deus homo ?* II, 19) ; it is not, then, just identical with it. Luther speaks of the same direct revelation when he distinguishes between the prophets on the one side and the wise men and scribes on the other : " They are prophets which preach out of the mere inspiration of the Holy Ghost, which have not drawn it from Scripture or through men, as Moses and Amos were. And these are the highest and best which are wise and know how to make others wise, and to set out and expound Scripture ; such were almost all the patriarchs before and with Moses, and after him many too, especially the apostles, who were laymen and sorely unlettered folk as Luke saith in Ac. 5, ' ignorant of Scripture ' " (*Kirchenpostille*, 1522, *W.A.*, 10[I], p. 271, l. 21). On the other hand wise men and scribes already presuppose the existence of prophetic Scripture. Even Calvin, who approximated revelation and Scripture much more closely than Augustine did, says in the very passage which is most frequently quoted, and with a plain reservation, that Holy Scripture has with believers the authority appropriate to it, *ubi statuunt e coelo fluxisse, acsi vivae ipsae Dei voces illic exaudirentur* (*Instit.*, I, 7, 1), and in the decisive passage his formulation of the doctrine of Scripture is that *summa Scripturae probatio passim a Dei loquentis persona sumitur* (*ib.*, 7, 4). Even in the orthodoxy of the following age with its fatal slide into the doctrine of inspiredness, recollection of a conscious distinction lives on in the most varied ways. According to Bullinger (*Comp. rel. christ.*, 1598, p. 5, quoted according to A. Schweizer, *Glaubensl. d. ev. ref. Kirche*, Vol. I, 1844, p. 200) we must say : *Literae, verba caro sunt, sententiae vero Dei.* According to W. Musculus (*Loci comm.*, 1564, p. 73, Schweizer, *op. cit.*, p. 199) Holy Scripture is called holy *quoniam de sacris rebus loquuntur.* According to Peter Martyr (*Loci comm.*, 1580, p. 13, Schweizer, *op. cit.*, p. 200) Holy Scripture is an *expressio quaedam sapientiae Dei.* According to J. Gerhard (*Loci theol.*, 1610, Prooem. 18) the *verbum externum Dei* goes forth one way *per inspirationem* and another way *per sermonem externum*, i.e., through angels, men, or human writings. In the *Syn. pur. Theol. Leid.*, 1624, *Disp.* 1, 8 we read : *Sacrae Theologiae revelatio a Deo prophetis et Apostolis facta, est immediata, quae autem per hos Ecclesiae Dei manifestata est, mediata est.* And frequently along the lines and even in the words of this very distinction the period of high orthodoxy (e.g., B. Bucan, *Instit. Theol.*, 1605, *Loc.* 4, 16), both Reformed (e.g., F. Turrettini, *Instit. theol. elenct.*, 1679, *Loc.*, 2, *qu.* 2, 5 f.) and Lutheran (Quenstedt, *Theol. did. pol.*, 1686, I, *cap.* 4, *sect.* 2, *qu.* 3, *ekth.* 3 and

I, 7, 1, *thes.* 1, *n.* 2 ; Baier, *Comp. theol. pos.*, 1686, *Prol.* 2, 1 ; Hollaz, *Ex theol. acroam.*, 1707, *Prol.* 3, *qu.* 2), for all its concentration on Scripture as such, could still find a place for discussion of revelation itself as this is to be distinguished from Scripture because it alone is what establishes it as inspired Scripture.

Revelation engenders the Scripture which attests it : as the commission or burden laid on the prophets and apostles, as the object which introduces itself in distinction from them, as both the judge and the guarantor of the truth of what they say, and as the event of inspiration in which they become speakers and writers of the Word of God. Because revelation engenders the Bible that attests it, because Jesus Christ has called the Old and New Testaments into existence, because Holy Scripture is the record of a unique hearing of a unique call and a unique obedience to a unique command, therefore it could become the Canon, and again and again it can become the " living " Canon, the publisher of revelation, the summons and command of God, God's Word to us. If in the prophets and apostles the Church has a concrete counterpart by which it is reminded of God's past revelation, set in expectation of future revelation, and thus summoned to proclamation and empowered for it, this takes place because it really has in them the publishers of past revelation. But the prophets and apostles did not appoint themselves the publishers of revelation, nor are they ever this intrinsically or as a matter of course. What makes them this is the occurrence of God's revelation itself apart from their own existence. The occurrence, and so we must call this thing that happened to them : *Deus dixit.* What has engendered Scripture and what Scripture for its part attests has happened truly and definitively, once and once-for-all. We have already discussed in outline what it was that happened : God was with us, with us His enemies, with us who were visited and smitten by His wrath. God was with us in all the reality and fulness with which He does what He does. He was with us as one of us. His Word became flesh of our flesh, blood of our blood. His glory was seen here in the depths of our situation, and the full depths of our situation were disclosed for the first time when illumined then and there by the Lord's glory, when in His Word He came down to the lowest parts of the earth (Eph. 4[9]), in order that there and in that way He might rob death of its power and bring life and immortality to light (2 Tim. 1[10]). This happened, and this is what the Old Testament as a word of prophecy and the New Testament as a word of fulfilment both proclaim as having happened, as having happened conclusively, totally, and sufficiently. This makes the biblical witnesses remarkable figures like John who cannot be brought under any morphology of genius. This is why it is true of them, though in different ways : " The zeal of thine house hath eaten me up " (Ps. 69[9]). This is why, although they seek no authority, even with their fallible human word they can continually claim and enjoy the most unheard-of authority. This came upon them, and through them it constantly seeks to come afresh upon the Church and to be cried aloud as absolutely the most urgent thing that any age and any man in any age and any man in any respect can and must hear : This " God with us " has happened. It has happened in human history and as a part of human history. Yet it has not happened as other parts of this history usually happen. It does not need to be continued or completed. It does not point beyond itself or merely strive after a distant goal. It is incapable of any exegesis or of even the slightest addition or subtraction. Its form cannot be changed. It has happened as self-moved being in the stream of becoming. It has happened as completed event, fulfilled time, in the sea of the incomplete and changeable and self-changing.

A bit of apocryphal Christian legend from the 2nd century might be mentioned here because for all its historical foolishness it shows very clearly what fulfilled time would look like if we were able to view it. In the so-called *Protevangelium of James*, chap. 18, Joseph, the foster-parent of Jesus, tells us what he is supposed to have experienced in the environs of Bethlehem on the night of the Lord's nativity : " But I, Joseph, went about and went not about. And I looked up at the vault of heaven and saw it stand still, and I looked up into the air and saw it fixed, and I saw the birds of heaven immovable, and I looked on the ground and saw a dish standing there and labourers lying down and their hands in the dish, and the chewers chewed not, and those on the point of lifting out brought nothing up, and those who wanted to bring to their mouths brought nothing to their mouths, but all faces were directed upwards, and lo, sheep were being driven and remained standing, and the shepherd raised his hand to smite them and his hand stayed up, and I looked at the water in the river and saw the mouths of the goats held down to it and they did not drink ; and suddenly everything resumed its course " (*NT Apokryph*, ed. E. Hennecke, 2nd edn., 1924, p. 91). If in its perfect divine actuality fulfilled time is to be the one and only truly moved and moving time, then it does indeed mean suspension, the total relativising of all other time and of its apparently moved and moving content.

This fulfilled time which is identical with Jesus Christ, this absolute event in relation to which every other event is not yet event or has ceased to be so, this " It is finished," this *Deus dixit* for which there are no analogies, is the revelation attested in the Bible. To understand the Bible from beginning to end, from verse to verse, is to understand how everything in it relates to this as its invisible-visible centre. But since this is so we have to say that we are in no position to understand the Bible ourselves. It can only be that the Bible gives itself to be understood by us, so that we come to hear the Bible as God's Word. To hear the Bible as God's Word means, therefore, that then and there, in the undoubtedly very modest, changing, perhaps increasing but possibly also decreasing compass in which it is true at any given time for an individual, we hear the human words of the Bible as the bearers of this eternal Word, based on this centre and having it in view again in everything they say. When the Bible itself is revelation in this way, it establishes the Church and makes its proclamation necessary and possible. The unity of revelation guarantees the unity of the biblical witness in and in spite of all its multiplicity and even contradictoriness. The unity of the Bible guarantees the unity of the Church in and in spite of the difference in the proportion of faith in which the Bible becomes revelation to this man and that man and to this man and that man to-day and to-morrow. On this basis the unity of the Church guarantees the unity of proclamation.

According to all that has been said revelation is originally and directly what the Bible and Church proclamation are derivatively and indirectly, i.e., God's Word. We have said of Church proclamation that it must continually become God's Word. And we have said the same of the Bible : It must continually become God's Word. The reference of this " continually," of course, is not to human experience, as though our reaction to this event or our attitude to it could be constitutive for its reality and content. The reference is to the freedom of God's Word. *Ubi et quando visum est Deo*, not intrinsically but in virtue of the divine decision taken ever and anon in the Bible and proclamation as the free God uses them, the Bible and proclamation are God's Word. But this cannot be said about revelation. When we speak about revelation we are confronted by the divine act itself and as such, which we have already had to bear in mind as the basis and boundary, the presupposition and proviso, of what had to be said about the Bible and proclamation. For (1) proclamation is real proclamation, i.e., the promise of future revelation, only as the repetition of the biblical witness to past revelation, and (2) the Bible is real witness, i.e., the factual recollection of past revelation, only in its relation to this past revelation attested in it. This being so, the freedom of God's grace is the basis and boundary, the presupposition and proviso, of the statements according to which the Bible and proclamation are the Word of God. The decisive content of these statements, the positive thing they state and the evident negations by which this is surrounded, the relation in which the statements are true, is their relation to revelation. But revelation is simply the freedom of God's grace. It is naturally not the principle of this freedom. This principle is only the obviously necessary product of human reflection on this freedom. It is rather the event in which the free God causes His free grace to rule and work. In this event of God's grace proclamation and the Bible are " held " in the three senses of the term : (1) " held up on high," singled out, made visible and familiar, to the degree that the Bible seeks to bear witness to this event and proclamation seeks to repeat this attestation, to the degree that in the Bible and proclamation this event

is what is really meant in the human talk; (2) " held in place,"
relativised, limited, to the degree that this event is also the boundary
of what proclamation and the Bible can try to accomplish in and of
themselves, the boundary which we obviously cannot think is set aside
by what men wanted and want to say; and (3) " held in store,"
preserved, secured, to the degree that this event is the confirmation
and ratification, the fulfilment of what proclamation and the Bible
achieve in and of themselves, the presence of what is meant in the
human word of the Bible and proclamation. Precisely in view of
revelation, or on the basis of it, one may thus say of proclamation and
the Bible that they are God's Word, that they continually become
God's Word. But for this very reason one cannot say the same of
revelation. One has to say the exact opposite, namely, that revelation
becomes God's Word, i.e., in the Bible and proclamation, because it is
this Word in itself. It is this that " holds " the Bible and proclamation
in that threefold sense. Revelation is itself the divine decision which
is taken in the Bible and proclamation, which makes use of them,
which thus confirms, ratifies and fulfils them. It is itself the Word of
God which the Bible and proclamation are as they become it.

ὅν γὰρ ἀπέστειλεν ὁ θεὸς τὰ ῥήματα τοῦ θεοῦ λαλεῖ· οὐ γὰρ ἐκ μέτρου δίδωσιν τὸ πνεῦμα.
ὁ πατὴρ ἀγαπᾷ τὸν υἱόν, καὶ πάντα δέδωκεν ἐν τῇ χειρὶ αὐτοῦ. ὁ πιστεύων εἰς τὸν υἱὸν ἔχει
ζωὴν αἰώνιον· ὁ δὲ ἀπειθῶν τῷ υἱῷ οὐκ ὄψεται ζωήν, ἀλλ' ἡ ὀργὴ τοῦ θεοῦ μένει ἐπ'
αὐτόν (Jn. 3³⁴⁻³⁶).

It does not stand, therefore, under any condition—one can say this
only of our knowledge of revelation—but is itself the condition. Of
it one may say, not *ubi et quando*, but *illic et tunc visum est Deo*. The
reference here is not to a possibility still to be realised but to the
reality of the Word of God as the basis of all possible self-
realisations. *Ubi et quando* can and must be said because ultimately
or primarily we have to say *illic et tunc*. Because there is a moving
hand there is also a moved and moving Canon and a commissioned,
objective, true and actual proclamation in obedience to this Canon.
When we say " Word of God revealed," then in distinction from the
" written " and " preached " of the two other forms of the Word of
God, " revealed " does not belong to the predicate. It is simply a
paraphrase, a second designation of the subject. If " written " and
" preached " denote the twofold concrete relation in which the Word
of God is spoken to us, revelation denotes the Word of God itself in the
act of its being spoken in time. Above this act there is nothing other or
higher on which it might be based or from which it might be derived
unless it was from the transcendence of the eternal Word of God that it
came forth in revelation. It is the condition which conditions all
things without itself being conditioned. This is what we are saying when
we call it revelation. Revelation, *revelatio*, ἀποκάλυψις, means the

unveiling of what is veiled. If this is meant strictly and properly, then all that is distinct from revelation is concealment, the hiddenness of the veiled.

The revealed Word of God is the mystery not made known to the aeons but veiled, Rom. 16²⁵ ; Col. 1²⁶ ; Eph. 3⁹. But this means that no other reason is to be sought or suggested for its disclosure than the actual disclosing itself. It is in the νῦν qualified by ἀποκάλυψις or φανέρωσις that the witness of revelation speaks as such. In this alone can it be understood as unveiled. The final word on the qualification is simply a reference to the will of God : κατ' ἐπιταγὴν τοῦ αἰωνίου θεοῦ (Rom. 16²⁵), οἶς ἠθέλησεν ὁ θεὸς γνωρίσαι . . . (Col. 1²⁶). " Christian faith and Christian life stand in the one little word revelation by God, for where this is not present, no heart can ever be rightly aware of this mystery, which was hidden from the world. Now God revealeth it only to His eternally elected saints, to whom He will have it made known, otherwise it is hidden from everyone and remaineth a proper mystery. What good can the free or enslaved and captive will say or do about that ? How will it come in its own might to this light and mystery ? If the almighty strong God hide it from it, by no preparation or good work will it ever reach thereto. No creature can come to this knowledge. Christ alone revealeth it to it in the heart. There all merit falleth to the ground, all the powers and abilities of reason, and count for nought with God. Christ alone must give it " (Luther, Sermon on Mt. 11²⁵⁻³⁰, 1527, *W.A.*, 23, p. 689, l. 4).

All revelation, then, must be thought of as revealing, i.e., as conditioned by the act of revelation. The event in which revelation occurs must be seen in connexion with what has happened once and for all in this act. All fulfilled time must be seen as filled with the fulness of this time. Revelation itself, however, is not referred to anything other, higher, or earlier. Revelation as such is not relative. Revelation in fact does not differ from the person of Jesus Christ nor from the reconciliation accomplished in Him. To say revelation is to say " The Word became flesh." To be sure, one can say something quite different by revelation, something purely formal, and relative as such. But to say this is not to say what the Bible means by the word or what Church proclamation is referring to when it refers to the Bible or what must be called revelation in Christian dogmatics if this is to take itself seriously as such. When in the word revelation we say " The Word was made flesh and dwelt among us," then we are saying something which can have only an intertrinitarian basis in the will of the Father and the sending of the Son and the Holy Spirit, in the eternal decree of the triune God, so that it can be established only as knowledge of God from God, of light in light. The same applies if instead of Jesus Christ we say concretely " God with us." It is true that in the term revelation we might have something relative rather than this absolute in view, but the Bible is thinking only of this absolute, and in the knowledge of this absolute the Church with the help of the Bible recalls past revelation, and a dogmatics that works in the sphere of the Church and not in a vacuum has also to cling to it. But to say " God with us " is to say something which has no basis or possibility outside itself, which can in no sense be explained in terms of man and man's situation, but only as knowledge of God from God, as free and unmerited grace. As the Bible bears witness to God's revelation and as Church proclamation takes up this witness in obedience, both renounce any foundation apart from that which God has given once and for all by speaking. The Bible and proclamation both appeal to this fact that has been given here and now. They cannot reproduce it as a given fact. They cannot bring it on the scene themselves. They can only attest and proclaim it. To bring it about that the *Deus dixit* is present with the Church in its various times and situations is not in the power of the Bible or proclamation. The *Deus dixit* is true—now the *ubi et quando* must come into force again— where it *is* true, i.e., where and when God, in speaking once and for all, wills according to His eternal counsel that it be true, where and when God by His activating, ratifying and fulfilling of the word of the Bible and preaching lets it become true. This being and becoming true of revelation consists, then, in the fact that the Church really recollects past revelation, and in faith receives, grasps and really proclaims the biblical witness of it as the real promise of future revelation, future revelation here being simply that which has taken place once and for all but it now directed to us too, just as the Christ who comes again is no other than the Christ who has come, but this Christ as the One who now comes also to us. The " God with us " becomes actual for us *hic et nunc* as the promise received and grasped in faith because it is *illic et tunc* a divine act. It is thus that which is true in and for itself, and it becomes true for us as recollection and also as promise, as recollection of Christ come in the flesh and as hope of Christ coming again in glory. It is Jesus Christ Himself who here speaks for Himself and needs no witness apart from His Holy Spirit and the faith that rejoices in His promise received and grasped. This independent and unsurpassable origin of the Word of God that comes to us is what we have in view when we speak of its third form, or materially we should rather say its first form, i.e., its form as the Word of God revealed.

4. THE UNITY OF THE WORD OF GOD

We have been speaking of three different forms of the Word of God and not of three different Words of God. In this threefold form and not otherwise—but also as the one Word only in this threefold form— the Word of God is given to us and we must try to understand it conceptually. It is one and the same whether we understand it as revelation, Bible, or proclamation. There is no distinction of degree or value between the three forms. For to the extent that proclamation really rests on recollection of the revelation attested in the Bible and is thus obedient repetition of the biblical witness, it is no less the Word of God than the Bible. And to the extent that the Bible really attests revelation it is no less the Word of God than revelation itself. As the Bible and proclamation become God's Word in virtue of the actuality of revelation they are God's Word : the one Word of God within which there can be neither a more nor a less. Nor should we ever try to understand the three forms of God's Word in isolation. The first, revelation, is the form that underlies the other two. But it is the very one that never meets us anywhere in abstract form. We know it only indirectly, from Scripture and proclamation. The direct Word of God meets us only in this twofold mediacy. But Scripture too, to become God's Word for us, must be proclaimed in the Church. So, to give a survey of the whole, the following brief schedule of mutual relations may be drawn up.

The revealed Word of God we know only from the Scripture adopted by Church proclamation or the proclamation of the Church based on Scripture.

The written Word of God we know only through the revelation which fulfils proclamation or through the proclamation fulfilled by revelation.

The preached Word of God we know only through the revelation attested in Scripture or the Scripture which attests revelation.

There is only one analogy to this doctrine of the Word of God. Or, more accurately, the doctrine of the Word of God is itself the only analogy to the doctrine which will be our fundamental concern as we develop the concept of revelation. This is the doctrine of the triunity of God. In the fact that we can substitute for revelation, Scripture and proclamation the names of the divine persons Father, Son and Holy Spirit and *vice versa*, that in the one case as in the other we shall encounter the same basic determinations and mutual relationships, and that the decisive difficulty and also the decisive clarity is the same in both—in all this one may see specific support for the inner necessity and correctness of our present exposition of the Word of God.

The doctrine of the three forms of the Word of God in the sketch attempted here is not new. We have seen in detail how revelation, Scripture and proclamation have from the very first stamped themselves on Christian thought as special forms of God's Word. Some passages in Luther are especially relevant here. Already in the *Dictata super Psalterium* (1513–16) Luther says (on Ps. 45[1]) : *Quod verbum Dei triplici modo dicitur* : 1. There is a speaking by God *per verbum externum et linguam ad aures hominum*, whose model Luther sees in the word of the Old Testament patriarchs and prophets under the veil of the mere letter. 2. There is a Word of God which He now speaks through His Spirit to His saints on earth, namely, in His Son, this being a *verbum consummans et abbreviatum* compared to the prophetic Word, but still wrapped in manifold veils. 3. There is a Word that God the Father speaks in Himself and to the saints in eternal glory. So we shall hear it one day, *cum nobis verbum suum ipse sine ullo medio revelabit. Unico et simplicissimo verbo suo* will He then satisfy us, and the Spirit Himself will then be the one sacrament in place of all signs (*W.A.*, 3, p. 262, l. 5). That scant justice is done here to the first form, *the verbum externum* of preaching, and that its significance is not understood, may be seen already from the fact that Luther saw no way to carry out the Trinitarian articulation which he obviously had in mind in relation to the second and third forms, because he could not very well relate to the Holy Spirit what he then regarded as a *verbum externum*. How he conceived of the advance from the first to the second form is also not clear in detail. Furthermore the separation between the Word that the Father speaks *in se ipso* in the third form and *in filio* in the second should not be made in the way it is. On the whole, however, the three forms, up to and including the eschatologically characterised third form, are very accurately perceived and described. There is an interesting variation on the theme in the already quoted sermon on Mt. 23[34f.] (*Kirchenpostille*, 1522, *W.A.*, 10[I], p. 272, l. 17), which refers to " the three ways in which the truth may be revealed : Scripture, word, thought ; Scripture by books, word by the mouth, thought by the heart. One cannot conceive the doctrine in any way save heart, mouth, and Scripture." The last form here, called thought, is simply our " revelation " in virtue of which Scripture and preaching reach man and touch his heart. More important is a passage in a sermon on the wise men (from the same *Kirchenpostille* of 1522). This surprises us especially by the completely new and one might almost say exaggerated value that the *verbum externum* or proclamation now has in Luther. " The oral and public sermon . . . the voice or word cried forth by the mouth " is now for him the light referred to in 2 Cor. 4[6] ; 2 Pet. 1[19]. " Now Scripture is not understood until the light ariseth." Scripture here is primarily the prophetic word to be found in the Old Testament. At first Luther simply contrasts the New Testament with this as living, i.e., oral proclamation whose task is to open up the prophetic word which is closed in its written form. " For through the Gospel the prophets are opened up, therefore the star must first rise and be seen. For in the New Testament preaching should be done publicly with a living voice and should bring forth to speech and hearing what was hitherto hidden in letters and secret guise. For the New Testament is nought other than an opening and revealing of the Old Testament, as is shown in Rev. 5, where the Lamb of God openeth the book with seven seals. We also see in the apostles how all their preaching was nought but bringing forth Scripture and building thereon." And now Luther has the astonishing continuation : " Therefore even Christ Himself wrote not down His teaching, as Moses did his, but did it orally and gave no command to write it. The apostles, too, wrote little, and not all of them that. . . . Even those who did write no more than point us to the ancient Scripture, as the angel pointed the shepherds to the manger and the swaddling clothes. And the star pointed the magi to Bethlehem. Therefore 'tis not like the New Testament to write books about Christian doctrine, but without books there should be in all places good, learned, spiritual, diligent preachers who draw the living word out of ancient writ and unceasingly din it into the people as the apostles did. For ere they wrote they first had preached to the people and converted them by the living voice, which was their proper apostolic and New Testament work. This is likewise the right star which sheweth Christ's birth and the angelic message telling of the swaddling bands and the crib. But man's need to write books is a great injury and it is a violation of the Spirit that the need hath compelled it and is not the way of the New Testament. . . ." New Testament Scripture as an adjunct or interpretation of the Old Testament is regarded as a defensive measure against corruption in the Church. " There finally had to be resort to that, and need was that some sheep should be saved from the wolves : so men began to write, and yet through writing, so far as possible, to bring Christ's little sheep into Scripture, and they prepared thereby that the sheep should be able to pasture themselves and guard themselves against the wolves when their shepherds would not pasture them or turned wolves." But it would have been better if other books had not been written in the Church. And the star of Bethlehem, the star of the wise men, should be in every case " the lively preaching and simple revelation of Christ as the same is hid and promised in Scripture ; therefore he that seeth the star knoweth assuredly the King of the Jews, the newborn Christ ; for the Gospel teacheth nought but Christ, and Scripture likewise hath nought but Christ. But whoso knoweth not Christ may hear the Gospel or hold the book right in his hands, but understanding of it he hath not yet, for to have the Gospel without understanding is to have no Gospel. And to have Scripture without the knowledge of Christ is to have no Scripture, and is none other than to let this star shine and yet not perceive it " (*W.A.*, 10^I, pp. 625–28). This exaggerated thought is by no means an isolated one in Luther at this period. For him the Old and the New Testament are related as the written word on the one side and the word preached on the other. " Thus the books of Moses and the prophets are also Gospel, since they have preached and described beforehand the same thing about Christ as the apostles have preached and written after. Yet there is a difference between them. For if both are written on paper as regards the letter, the Gospel or the New Testament should not really be written but put in the living voice, which then soundeth forth and is heard everywhere in the world. That it is also written is surplus. But the Old Testament is put only in writing and is thus called ' a letter,' and so the apostles call it ' writ,' for it hath pointed only to the coming Christ. But the Gospel is a living sermon about Christ already come " (*Ep. S. Petri.*, 1523, *W.A.*, 12, p. 275, l. 5 ; cf. also 259, 8 ; 556, 9). It need hardly be shown, of course, that in other passages Luther attached supreme importance to the written New Testament, that he did not treat it as a necessary evil, and that it is thus quite wrong to hold him systematically to this distinction. But one may still learn from the distinction how he viewed the relation between Scripture and preaching generally. Both have the same theme and content, and this in such a way that preaching takes it first from Scripture and can thus be no other than scriptural exposition, but also in such a way that it always draws from Scripture in the form of living proclamation and has thus to become God's Word to us. Allegorising on Lk. 2^{12} at the same period, Luther summed up his view as follows : " Christ is completely wrapped in Scripture as the body in the swaddling clothes. Preaching is the crib in which he lies and is set, and from it we get food and provender " (Sermon on Lk. 2, 1523, *W.A.*, 12, p. 418, l. 24). Protestant orthodoxy, which at the peak of its development had no liking for talk about the distinction between the forms of the Word of God and the fluidity of their mutual relations, emphasised the more zealously something which is equally true and instructive in itself, namely, their unity. With reference to the unity of the Word of God to the biblical witnesses and through them : *hae distinctiones non faciunt essentialem aliquam differentiam inter verbum Dei hominibus communicatum, sed tantum distinctos communicationis et revelationis modos exprimunt* (J. Gerhard, *Loci theol.*, 1610, *Prooem.* 18), *Distinctio Verbi in ἄγραφον et ἔγγραφον non est divisio generis in species . . . quasi alius esset Verbum non scriptum a scripto ; sed est distinctio subjecti in sua accidentia, quia eidem Verbo accidit, ut fuerit non scriptum olim et nunc sit scriptum* (F. Turrettini, *Instit. theol. el.*, 1679, *Loc.* 2, *qu.* 2. 4). *Nec vero aliud est verbum Dei quod a Deo vel quod inspiratum viris Dei, quam quod in scriptura traditur, aut praedicatur, vel mente humana reconditur* (Hollaz, *Ex. theol. acrom.*, 1707, III, 2, 1). All this is true. Yet in the statements of this period of transition one misses painfully the Reformers' insight into the dynamics of the mutual relationships of the three forms. Its absence comes to light in the theory of inspiration, which implies a freezing, as if were, of the relation between Scripture and revelation. But it may be seen especially in the fact that the theologians of this period hardly seem to have any more a true and essential awareness of the third form of the Word of God, proclamation. Preaching is called " God's Word " in them too, but the real connecting point between revelation and Scripture in the present is increasingly something far different from the act of Church proclamation ; it is the knowledge, faith, sanctification and blessedness of the individual. But this means that the unity of revelation and Scripture, however stiff the objectivity in which it is arrayed, takes on more and more the aspect, not of God's dealings with His Church, but rather of a private divine institution for so many private persons, preaching and the sacraments being adequate instruments of this as the so-called *media salutis*. Forgetting that the correlate of revelation and Scripture is not in the first instance the saving or amending of the individual but (on the same level as revelation and Scripture) proclamation as the service of God, the Church forgot nothing less than itself. From being a place for the service of God, through which as such men are also helped, it now made itself a place for the finest service of men in which God will finally have to figure as the supremely objective and supremely miraculous means, yet only as a means. Boasting of the objectivity with which the Word of God was invested, especially in its biblical form, was only the expression of a bad conscience. It helped to conceal the fact that the men of this age no longer knew what they were really saying when they said " Word of God," that they no longer knew that they were talking about the present-day action, not of man in his relation to God, but of God in His relation to man, and therefore about the Church. When they no longer knew this, was it surprising that the rising Modernism of the new age discovered that the goal of the finest service of man could be reached by a simpler and less miraculous way than that which orthodoxy still espoused with great external but not so great internal fidelity ? Was it surprising if the objectivity which orthodoxy still claimed for revelation and Scripture, and theoretically for preaching and the sacraments too, struck one bright mind and thousands of bright minds and even pious hearts as more and more a superfluous idol which it could only seem to them a good work, well-pleasing to God, to smash in pieces ? The catastrophic crash of orthodoxy in the 18th century, the consequences of which we still have to carry to this day, is no more puzzling than the collapse of a house whose foundations are giving way. Responsibility for the disaster must be borne, not by the philosophy of the world which had become critical, but by the theology of the Church which had become too uncritical, which no longer understood itself at the centre. For all our great respect for the work done by orthodoxy, and for all our understanding of the ultimate intentions of this work, our task to-day must be the different one of re-adopting Luther's concepts and taking proclamation seriously again as the work of the Church in and through which God is to be served and not man, and God is to speak. On that basis we must then try to understand once again in what sense first the Bible, and even before that revelation, is really the Word of God. It was here that forgetfulness set in before the disaster of the 18th century. It is here obviously that new reflection must begin. Hence the direct object of dogmatics to-day must be Church proclamation.

§ 5

THE NATURE OF THE WORD OF GOD

The Word of God in all its three forms is God's speech to man. For this reason it occurs, applies and works in God's act on man. But as such it occurs in God's way which differs from all other occurrence, i.e., in the mystery of God.

1. THE QUESTION OF THE NATURE OF THE WORD OF GOD

At this point we have to deviate in two ways especially from the first edition of this book. We refer first to the discussions in the original § 5, 1. There, after establishing the concept of the Word of God in its threefold form by means of an analysis of Church proclamation, we made a transition from a phenomenological treatment to an existential treatment, i.e., from thinking in terms of an outward observer to thinking in terms of an existential participant. Objection was rightly raised against this section from various quarters (cf. F. Gogarten, "Karl Barths Dogmatik," *Theol. Rundschau*, 1929, p. 70 f. ; T. Siegfried, *Das Wort und die Existenz*, I, 1930, p. 35 f., 250 f.). It might be asked whether the concepts of phenomenological and existential thought are properly specified and distinguished in this way. It might also be asked whether existential thinking is more than a particular form of phenomenological thinking or whether there is not even some point where the two coincide. It might thus be asked whether the idea of transition from the one to the other is not in any case impossible. But these are philosophical rather than theological questions. The objection that I have since made against myself is that these concepts, whatever their content and mutual relation may be, cannot in any way constitute or signify decisive turning-points on the way of dogmatic thought as seemed there to be presupposed. No matter how philosophers may or may not reach an understanding on these matters, they will do so as philosophers and not as theologians. That is, they will not do so out of any responsible regard for the theme of theology. Hence theology cannot learn anything from them and ought not to do so, unless it is ready to let them intrude a philosophical theme instead of its own, as has always happened when it has accepted material instruction from any philosophy. Now at this point in the first edition it was not my purpose to take up a philosophical theme in this way. When I spoke of " transition " this was meant to be much more innocuous and incidental than it has been taken to be. It is obvious that in dogmatics as in any science, while we do not have to use a specifically philosophical or any other vocabulary, we may do so when it lends itself to the incidental illustration or bringing into focus of what is said with theological intent, when the meaning and purpose of the linguistic borrowing is fixed with relative certainty by the context, and when there is comparatively little danger of the misunderstanding that theological statements are being supported by a reference to philosophical statements, or that a philosophical theme is being substituted for the theological. In the section at issue, however, this misunderstanding was relatively close, and it arose immediately. To my horror T. Siegfried (*op. cit.,*

p. 36) interpreted the passage as follows : " On this foundation (i.e., the existential thinking introduced) he proposes to build his dogmatics." This was not really my intention. But I ought to have had the better judgment to see that to drag in those concepts at that point in relation to what I wanted to say there was a superfluous and dangerous game : superfluous because it was not in any case followed by any attempt to prove the doctrine of the Word of God by showing it to be posited by existential thinking or by advancing an existential philosophy as its background and justification ; and dangerous because all that does follow on the basis of the passage can be regarded as a kind of grounding of theology in existentialist philosophy, though in obscure combination with the intentions of Roman Catholic and older Protestant theology. Moreover, there could and can be no way of developing seriously what I then understood by that transition. It would be quite fatal if in all that has been said thus far we have not been thinking and speaking as participators in these things at the level of existence. But if this has not been so thus far, it is not in our power to make a transition and to undertake to think and speak as participants now. On the other hand, neither before nor after can we ever fail, when thinking and speaking of these things, to regard them from without, however much we might participate in them. Again, it should be said of this contemplation from without that it is not in our power to regard the things of which we speak here exclusively from without. No matter how we analyse and relate philosophically the two approaches which I tried to distinguish there, they are more or less intrinsic to all human thought and speech. And a theological train of thought as such cannot be rendered correct or incorrect, important or unimportant, by reason of this " more or less." No serious theological decision is taken in the actual transitions from more to less and *vice versa* as they can naturally take place in theological trains of thought too. This leads us to the second point. In the first edition the doctrine of the Word of God is developed at this juncture as follows. In §§ 5 and 6 two analyses are given of man's situation first as preacher and then as hearer of the Word of God. In § 7 there is then an analysis of the distinctive knowledge of the Word of God generally. In the last sub-sections of the three sections there are then annexed to the three analyses as their ostensible results three more precise definitions of the Word of God which together represent what is here to be developed as the doctrine of the nature of the Word of God. That arrangement in the first edition had three faults. 1. The more precise definitions of the Word of God, being scattered over three sections and appearing almost in the form of appendices, were by this external placing isolated from the readers' attention in a way that was fatal to a proper understanding of the whole. It might easily happen, and did in fact happen, that these conclusions to §§ 5–7 could be regarded as a mere response to the analyses which might easily have been omitted, since the analyses themselves constituted the true and to some extent provocative part of the sections. 2. I did not succeed (and happily could not succeed) in making these conclusions on the concept of the Word of God, as I had proposed, illuminating and credible as results of the three analyses. There were certain associations of thought between the analyses and the more precise definitions, but fundamentally and comprehensively the latter are grounded elsewhere, they are not necessary at this point, and therefore they cannot be as impressive or catch attention in the same way as the actual analyses. 3. The (necessarily) unsuccessful attempt to deduce the doctrine of the Word of God from an analysis of the concrete situation of the preacher or hearer, or the man who knows God's Word generally, involved following a " false tendency " in the same sense and the same direction as the introduction and use of the concepts of phenomenological and existential thought already criticised. In fact the more precise definitions were not at all deduced from the analyses. But I proceeded as though they could and should be. An anthropology, albeit a

Church anthropology, was thus being advanced as the supposed basis on which we know decisive statements about God's Word. In this regard, along with the general declaration that from now on, and especially in §§ 5-7, we should be concerned with existential thinking, I was paying homage to false gods, even if only after the manner of the *libellatici* of the Decian persecution. If there is one thing the Word of God certainly is not, it is not a predicate of man, even of the man who receives it, and therefore not of the man who speaks, hears and knows it in the sphere of the Church. But it has to be this if the more precise definitions of its nature are really deduced from an analysis of the concrete situation of this man, as was my intention and claim there, even if it did not actually happen.

F. Gogarten in the review of the first edition already quoted had in the main two objections to its contents : 1. that it has no " true anthropology " (p. 66) and 2. that in some parts at least " it now speaks of a God isolated in and for Himself over against man and now of man isolated in and for himself over against God " (p. 72) instead of speaking always about both God and man in their inter-connexion (cf. also " The Problem of a Theological Anthropology " in *Z.d.Z.*, 1929, p. 493 f.). A special response will be made to the second objection in the course of this section. As regards the first, I have already stated my position in the preceding self-criticism and it remains only to make this explicit in relation to Gogarten. I might sum up all that has been said against myself by expressing regret to-day that five years ago I was at least on the way to a " true anthropology." Gogarten ought really to have acknowledged this from his own stand-point. The fact that he could not, but spoke of a lack of true anthropology in spite of my obvious tendency in this direction, is very comforting to me to-day, since it proves that the damage has not been so great as it might well have been. For I can only regard it as doing great harm to do what happily Gogarten has not found me doing but would like me to have done, namely, setting up a " true anthropology " as " the central task " and " real problem of theology " (*Z.d.Z.*, 1929, p. 505), as " the hardest bit of work " that theologians have to do to-day (*Theol. Rundschau*, 1929, p. 67), and that means, of course, as the source and criterion of all further theological propositions. Gogarten finds two bases for the concern behind his demand for a true anthropology. The first is historical (*Z.d.Z.*, 1929, p. 502 f.). As a result of his modern knowledge of nature and the world man has been externally pushed out of the central position that was so obviously his in the Middle Ages and he has thus been led to a discovery and inner awareness of himself and his historicity. The " humanising of life " was what bound Luther already to the humanists of his age and especially to the Renaissance, and for all the reservations we have to make Schleiermacher's theology is to be estimated as the first great attempt to make this feature of Lutheran teaching the feature of a theology planned and executed on a big scale. Since the thinking of the new age is more strongly affected by the problem of man himself, anthropology must be regarded as the real problem of a modern theology. Now let us assume that the historical background of this analysis of our age is right—though perhaps not all Lutherans would be pleased by this sketch— and let us also assume that the analysis itself is materially right—though this was probably more true before the First World War than in our own time, which has become much more realistic again and in which it can hardly be said of a large and especially a younger group of our contemporaries that the " humanising of life " is a significant concept in their life-consciousness. Even if we assume all this, however, the question always remains whether in face of the alleged anthropologising of the modern (or once modern) life-consciousness it is wise to follow in the steps of Schleiermacher and to orientate oneself to his life-consciousness even though under another sign. Theology has all too often tried to seek out and conquer the consciousness of an age on its own ground. We have protested already against theology allowing adversaries to dictate its action, since this can only mean conceding to them half or more than half of what should not be conceded, namely, the Church's lack of independence of life and thought over against the world and the primacy of the questions the world has to put to the Church over the questions the Church has to put to itself. Might it not be to-day that a theology which refuses even in method to make common cause with the aforesaid " humanising of life " will be more relevant—if this is the point —than one which admits at the very outset that it can speak only a second word, a word on the situation (the situation outside the Church) ? Gogarten's second concern seems to emanate from Christology. " Must not thought start out," he says (*Theol. Rundschau*, 1929, p. 73), " from the man God became ? Can there be any other starting-point than the God who is not isolated *vis-à-vis* man, and does not that mean that thought must start out from man ? " I could understand this if he had said " to man " instead of " from man." In fact theological statements are distinguished from those of metaphysics or morality to the degree that in conformity with the Immanuel that is the content of revelation, they take the reality and truth of which they purport to speak and make it intelligible as reality and truth from God to man. But is it really a consequence of Christology, of the incarnation of the Word, that *post Christum* thought can and even should start out from man—and for Gogarten this does not mean from Jesus, from the one God-man, but from that other man who has ceased to be isolated *vis-à-vis* God and yet is not identical with the God-man ? Is it really a consequence that this must be the very centre of theology ? Does the man who is no longer isolated from God, apart from the one God-man, really exist in such a way that he can and should be the starting-point of thought ? At any rate the older Lutheran dogmaticians did not draw this deduction even though their Christology might have suggested it. The first to do so was Schleiermacher, and then, with malicious intent, Feuerbach. Hence this second strictly theological concern of Gogarten's seems to me not merely unconvincing but materially dubious.—Yet I must still regard the anthropology which Gogarten fails to find in me as harmful because with it I see no way of avoiding the danger of a fresh betrayal of theology to some philosophy and therewith the loss of theology's real theme. I am not unaware that Gogarten (expressly in the essay in *Z.d.Z.* and also inferentially in the review in *Theol. Rundschau*, e.g., p. 68, 73) has declared quite clearly that the theme of his " true anthropology " is " man who cannot be thought of apart from the God who has united Himself with man in revelation," so that its content can be derived only from the Gospel itself or from the context of theology as a whole (*Z.d.Z.*, 1929, p. 494 f.). Gogarten's purpose here seems to be along the lines of what I called " Church anthropology " in my draft of 1927. But what I presented there, namely, an analysis of the self-understanding of the man who preaches and hears God's Word and knows it in this concrete situation, did not seem to satisfy Gogarten as being true anthropology ; indeed, he regarded it as so inadequate that he could not even recognise or praise what ought to have been from his standpoint my good intentions in this direction. Why was he not satisfied ? At the time Gogarten wrote that my undervaluation of anthropology was " very closely " connected with my failure to supply " a basic investigation of the question of the scientific nature of theology, i.e., the question of the relationship between theology and philosophy and all that this involves " (*Theol. Rundschau*, 1929, p. 66 f.). May one not assume—and does not his declaration of solidarity with Bultmann in this regard support the assumption—that Gogarten's own high estimate of anthropology is " very closely " connected with this investigation ? But if it is the purpose of anthropology to clarify the relation between theology and philosophy—and in Bultmann's proximity this certainly means to derive the possibility of theology from the relation perceived—then the question arises how one can take seriously the theological independence of the anthropology desired by Gogarten or its derivation from the Gospel and the Gospel alone. The decisive statements in Gogarten's programme are to the effect that there is a circle between the doctrine of man on the one side and the doctrine of God on the other : " There is no understanding of man without understanding of God, but . . . again I cannot understand this God without already understanding man " (*Z.d.Z.*, 1929, p. 496). If in the last clause Gogarten had written " also " instead of " already " no objection could be taken. The thought would then be that understanding man presupposes understanding God and understanding God always includes understanding man also. But this does not seem to be Gogarten's thought. It is indeed hard to see how one could move on from this to the primacy of anthropology, the elucidating of the relation between theology and philosophy, and the establishing of the scientific nature of theology. And Gogarten does in fact write " already." This " already " seems to give the understanding of man priority over the understanding of God, a priority which for its part seems unthinkable unless one presupposes a " pre-understanding " with regard to man, as Bultmann actually does. But such a pre-understanding, by means of which one can as it were leap into the aforementioned circle of the understanding of God and man in their mutual relationship, seems again not to be in harmony with Gogarten's unequivocal declaration that man may not be regarded primarily as one " who also exists outside revelation, who may thus be thought of without thinking also of God's revelation " (*op. cit.*, p. 497). God's revelation ! What does Gogarten mean by this in this context ? He interprets the expression in the same passage by adding : (the revelation) " in which God has bound Himself to man from creation as his God and Lord," and even more clearly a little later : " the revelation which is the creation and preservation of man from the beginning of the world " (*op. cit.*, p. 498). And this sets us a final puzzle. What are we to understand by the revelation which takes place from creation or which is man's creation and preservation ? It might mean (along the lines of *Qu.* 19 of the *Heidelberg Catechism*) the Gospel which has constantly been published to man since creation. But why should Gogarten lay explanatory stress on this in the present context ? And how can one deduce the primacy of anthropology, for which Gogarten is arguing, from the fact that the one Gospel is the Gospel for all ages from the foundation of the world ? The only other possibility is to assume, as the second formula suggests, that " from creation " means the revelation of God which is given in and with creation and preservation and which is present and known to us as such (i.e., apart from God's second revelation as distinct from creation) in the orders of the reality of our creatureliness, of our creaturely existence. The connexion and relationship between God and man on which Gogarten would erect his anthropology is in this case posited in the relation between God as Creator and man as creature. If this is so, then at a stroke everything is clear. On the one hand Gogarten can rightly say that his concern is solely and exclusively with the man who is to be found only in revelation, and on the other hand he can also quite rightly give to the understanding of man (with his " already ") priority over the understanding of God, i.e., the God who is to be understood in terms of His revelation in the Gospel. But there still remains the slight linguistic difficulty that Gogarten frequently speaks of the man who is to be understood in the light of the " Gospel " (and not just revelation). Gospel here, however, is this revelation which is given with creation and which precedes the proclaimed revelation, or perhaps it is the confirmation of this revelation of creation implicitly given in the Gospel. If this is so, then the primacy of anthropology, Bultmann's pre-understanding, the remarkable " already " and the even more remarkable " from man," not to forget finally the possibility of elucidating the relation of philosophy and theology and of establishing the scientific nature of theology, are all assured. If revelation in this context means a manifestation of God which precedes revelation in the more precise and proper sense, and which is posited with our creaturely existence as such, then an analysis of this creaturely existence, i.e., of God's manifestation in it as the " pre-understanding " of proper, special revelation, must really be the first step of theological reflection with which we leap into the circle of the understanding of God and the understanding of man from an outer and enclosing circle. In this case we cannot understand God, namely, the God of proclaimed revelation, "without already (i.e., first) understanding man," namely, the man to whom God is originally manifest as his Creator. Primarily, i.e., in the leap into the inner circle, our thought must start out " from man," i.e., from this man who is bound to God by the fact that he is created. And this man, who in the outer circle of his creatureliness is already bound in this way to God, can really be regarded as the common theme or as it were the turntable between philosophy and theology, and anthropology can be used to elucidate the relation between these two sciences or to establish theology as a science. If the revelation from creation to which Gogarten refers means this, then I can at least see some sense in the " true anthropology " which he does not find in me but so obviously represents himself. But I fail to see what difference there is between this intrinsically coherent scheme and everyday natural theology. To analyse man in the light of a divine revelation from creation as the *introitus* to the inner circle of true theology grounded in a *revelatio specialis* has always been the nature and purpose of all natural theology. And this is the urgent twofold question which confronts me : After all that has been said, to what extent can one say that the nature and purpose of Gogarten's " true anthropology " is not identical with the nature and purpose of all natural theology ? And : How can it be that Friedrich Gogarten of all men really wants to be understood in this way ? How can this be reconciled with the sharp declarations which Gogarten has made against natural theology even and precisely in this context (p. 495 f.) ? What are we to take seriously in Gogarten : his anthropological programme or his energetic renunciation of natural theology ? Or how far are we to take both seriously ? How is the one related to the other and *vice versa* ? However that may be, I can only say that I am unable to supply what he misses in me because I fail to see how anything other than a new (or rather the old) natural theology can result therefrom. But natural theology in the sense described is an enterprise that is possible only in the realm of Roman Catholicism, since this presupposes that God's manifestation in our creatureliness, the creation of man which is also the revelation of God, is in some place and in some sense, e.g., as confirmed by the Gospel. directly discernible by us. This direct discernment of the original relation of God to man, the discernment of the creation of man which is also the revelation of God, has, however, been taken from us by the fall, at least according to Reformation ideas of the extent of sin, and it is restored to us only in the Gospel, in *revelatio specialis*. But this means that it is restored to us in such a way that, while we must certainly understand God's Word in revelation, Scripture and proclamation to be God's Word to man, to man as God's creature, we cannot view it in such a way that propositions may be taken from it which, isolated from the giving of God's Word in revelation, Scripture and proclamation, can be known as general truths by man, i.e., by the man who now understands himself as God's creature on the basis of the Word of God heard, so that they for their part can then be made—and this is the decisive point—the presupposition of an understanding of God's Word or the basis of theology. There is, of course, a theological anthropology, but this will consist neither in an explication and application of christological statements such as Gogarten had perhaps originally in view nor in an analysis that can now be made again of the created state of pre-fallen man, which is also God's revelation. It will consist simply in a depiction first of the original *status integritatis* which is indicated in the Word of God itself and manifested in Jesus Christ and then of the *status corruptionis* which now obtains. This depiction certainly cannot serve to explain how there are any possibilities of moving from man to God. Its content is rather the isolation of man from God, concerning which there is as little chance of reaching agreement with any philosopher as there is in relation to any other locus of dogmatics. It is thus quite impossible to use it in the way Gogarten does to introduce his " true anthropology." The circle between the understanding of God and man of which Gogarten speaks so impressively, the circle in which man's relationship to God is known, is thus in truth only a single circle, and it is a tightly closed circle. Gogarten, too, speaks of only one circle, and a tightly closed one at that. But it is not clear to me that it remains either. If it is only one, tightly closed circle, then it is impossible even in terms of the concept of creation to leap into it from without, i.e., to advance a common platform on which to agree with the philosopher, be it Grisebach or Heidegger, as to how far movement is possible at all in this circle even as seen from without. For we do not even know we are created merely from being created but only from the Word of God, from which we cannot deduce any independent, generally true insights that are different from God's Word and hence lead up to it. Knowledge in this circle is irreversible. Movement in it is not automatically from above to below and below to above. It cannot be replaced by the religio-psychological circle of Wobbermin. We cannot according to our own caprice try now to understand man on the basis of understanding God and now to understand God on the basis of understanding man. Even on the basis of understanding man in the light of God, understanding God is always a new thing in itself. Or rather it is an understanding grounded in God's Word and not in the preceding understanding of man. " From man " can only mean from man of the lost *status integritatis* and hence from man of the present *status corruptionis*. Thus to understand God from man is either an impossibility or something one can do only in the form of Christology and not of anthropology (not even a Christology translated into anthropology). There is a way from Christology to anthropology, but there is no way from anthropology to Christology. On the basis of all these considerations I must not only decline Gogarten's invitation to improve my dogmatics by introducing a true anthropology. I must also eliminate all that might seem to be a concession in that direction in my draft of five years ago.

In the first place it must no longer seem as if the doctrine of the Word of God is either based upon or subsequently supported by the fact that it is a result of existential thought. And then secondly there must not even be the appearance of an anthropology serving as the basis of the understanding of God's Word. §§ 5–6 of the first edition, which dealt with man as the preacher and hearer of God's Word, may be dropped out altogether, partly because its essential content is already anticipated by §§ 3–4 of the new edition, partly because it belongs to the question of the knowledge of the Word of God, and partly because its real home is in homiletics rather than dogmatics. The fact that God's Word is His Word to man, and the extent to which this is so, will be shown in our discussion of the epistemological question, i.e., the question as to the truth of God's Word. But the answer to the question : What is the Word of God ?, the doctrine of its nature, must no longer seem to be governed by this enquiry. It must not arise in the proximity of a " true anthropology." It must be developed before this and independently.

We have spoken of the forms of the Word of God. Obviously form is always the form of a nature. But can one also speak of a nature of the Word of God ? Can one answer the very natural and popular question, also found not infrequently on the lips of theologians : What is the Word of God ? Confronted by this question as to the nature of the Word of God we find ourselves in the same difficulty as we shall be later on in dogmatics when we face the question of God's nature. God and His Word are not given to us in the same way as natural and historical entities. What God and His Word are, we can never establish by looking back and therewith by anticipating. This is something God Himself must constantly tell us afresh. But there is no human knowing that corresponds to this divine telling. In this divine telling there is an encounter and fellowship between His nature and man but not an assuming of God's nature into man's knowing, only a fresh divine telling. In this divine telling knowledge of God and His Word is actualised with the God with us. Only thus, i.e., in faith in God's Word, can we say who God is : He is the one God, Father, Son and Holy Spirit. And only thus, i.e., having regard to the reality of the Church in whose sphere we think, can we say what God's Word is that we recollect and expect here, the one Word of God : proclamation, Scripture and revelation. But of course, as in faith we who know *who* God is can and must say *how* He is, how there is on the basis of the doctrine of the Trinity a doctrine of attributes in which is manifested the nature of God that is hidden from us, that cannot be anticipated or repeated in any human word, that cannot be adequately rendered in any human word, so, as we know *what* God's Word is, namely, as we know its three forms, we can also say *how* it is, in what sequence of determinations it is this Word, God's Word, spoken to us in these three forms. Thus we can certainly say what God's Word is, but we must say it indirectly. We must remember the forms in which it is real for us and learn from these forms *how* it is. This How is the attainable human reflection of the unattainable divine What. Our concern here must be with this reflection.

2. THE WORD OF GOD AS THE SPEECH OF GOD

Church proclamation is talk, speech. So is Holy Scripture. So is even revelation in itself and as such. If we stay with God's Word in the three forms in which it is actually heard in the Church, if we do not go outside the Church and think of things God might have willed and done but has not done and so not willed in the Church, we have no reason not to take the concept of God's Word primarily in its literal sense. God's Word means that God speaks. Speaking is not a " symbol " (as P. Tillich, *Rel. Verwirkl.*, 1930, p. 48 thinks). It is not a designation and description which on the basis of his own assessment of its symbolic force man has chosen for something very different from and quite alien to this expression. For all its human inadequacy, for all the brokenness with which alone human statements can correspond to the nature of the Word of God, this statement does correspond to the possibility which God has chosen and actualised at all events in His Church. We are not absolutising the human possibilities of the intellect. We might well be of the opinion that it would have been finer and better if God had not spoken and did not speak with such " intellectualism," and that it would be more appropriate to God if God's Word meant all kinds of other things apart from the fact that God speaks. But is this private opinion of ours so important, resting as it does on a philosophy ? If perhaps not, then let us simply stick to the fact, and not try to think beyond it, that in this form in which the Church knows God's Word—the one and only form which necessarily, because imperiously, affects us—in this form God's Word means that " God speaks," and all else that is to be said about it must be regarded as exegesis and not as a restriction or negation of this statement. We shall have to regard God's speech as also God's act, and God's act as also God's mystery. But as only God's act is really God's mystery (and not any other mystery), so only God's speech is really God's act (and not any other act). Hence the concepts of act and mystery, exegetically necessary though they be, cannot point us away from the concept of speech. Being explanations, they can only point us back repeatedly to this as the original text. If they are true exegesis, then in their own way, of course, they say no less than everything, no less than the one and total thing, that has to be said here, like the original text itself. What the Word of God is can be said very well and without danger by the concepts of act and mystery too if our purpose in using them, unlike that of Faust who was merely seeking the proper symbol, is not to give a translation of Logos differing from that of speech but rather to explain the only possible translation in terms of the concept of speech. We shall first attempt without exegesis to understand the text itself in the only translation possible. What does it imply for the concept of the Word of God if the Word of God means originally and irrevocably that God speaks ?

1. It implies first of all the spiritual nature of the Word of God as distinct from naturalness, corporeality, or any physical event. We hasten to add that there is no Word of God without a physical event. The fact that preaching and sacrament belong to it is also a reminder of this. So, too, is the letter of Holy Scripture. So finally and supremely is the corporeality of the man Jesus Christ. But all this does not justify us in saying that the Word of God is equally and in the same sense both spiritual and also natural or physical. There is here in all forms of the Word of God an upper and lower aspect, a first and second, which in all its relativity is not to be effaced or reversed. The

Word of God is also natural and physical because without this it would not be the Word of God that is directed to us men as spiritual-natural beings, really to us as we really are. This is why the sacrament must stand alongside preaching. This is why preaching itself is also a physical event. This is why the letter of Scripture is the very reverse of a *pudendum* or *negligendum*. This is why the Church (though its relation of subordination is clearly shown therein) is called the body of Christ. The Word of God is also natural and physical because in the creaturely realm in which it comes to us men as Word there is nothing spiritual that is not also natural and physical. Nevertheless, the fact that the Word of God binds itself not only to the spirituality but also to the corporeality of the creature should not prevent us from seeing that it is in no sense neutrally above or in both, and that above all it is not primarily or pre-eminently nature.

At this point we should not let ourselves be disconcerted by the current wave of realism and antispiritualism. Reference is often made to the statement of F. C. Oetinger that corporeality is the end of all the ways of God. This was a sound if exaggerated expression of very necessary opposition to the flight of the Enlightenment spirit from nature, but it is not really suited for conversion into a dogma. And if Erich Przywara (*Stimmen der Zeit*, 1929, p. 231 f.) once levelled against me the criticism that I have a notable penchant for the two terms Word and Spirit, that I betray therewith a concealed spiritualism, and hence the ultimate immanence of what is supposed to be my very transcendent concept of God, whereas God is not bound to one realm of creation more than the other but is free in relation to both, the question arises whether, without prejudice to His freedom, God has not within creation bound Himself to spirit differently and more fully and closely than He has to nature ; whether the uniform anthropology of the Bible, which is really not to be changed, does not teach that man is to be considered first and especially with reference to the invisible quality of life breathed into him by God ; whether it is a mere accident that speaking about God is commanded hundreds of times in the Bible but setting up images of God is forbidden and barred *expressis verbis* ; whether it is just accidental that the terms Word and Spirit play this special role even in relation to God in both the Old and New Testament ; whether words from the other sphere of creation might be used just as well as *Logos* and *Pneuma* in the doctrine of the Trinity. It is an excellent thing that we are ready to hear again, as most of those immediately before us were not, what the New Testament has to say about the bodily resurrection of Christ and also about the resurrection of our own bodies. It is an excellent thing that we are being reminded again of a long neglected New Testament truth by the favourite doctrine of Eastern orthodoxy, namely, that eschatological redemption includes within it in the most comprehensive sense the cosmos, the creature, as well. But it would not be a good thing to try to overlook the fact that in the Old and New Testaments, while man is certainly addressed as a natural being, he is addressed as this particular natural being, the natural being characterised by spirit, or, as we might simply say, that he is *addressed*, that address and not a natural event, or address even in a natural event, is the way in which God visits him. A certain relative " canonisation of spirit against nature " (Przywara)—more ought not to be asserted—we surely find it impossible not to assert for all our recognition of the realistic concern.

The Word of God is primarily spiritual and then, in this form, in this spirituality, for the sake of it and without prejudice to it, it is also a physical and natural event. This particularly is what is meant when in accordance with the three forms in which we hear this Word we call it the speech of God. Speech, including God's speech, is the form in which reason communicates with reason and person with person. To be sure it is the divine reason communicating with the human reason and the divine person with the human person. The utter inconceivability of this event is obvious. But reason with reason, person with person, is primarily analogous to what happens in the spiritual realm of creation, not the natural and physical realm. The Word of God—and at this point we should not evade a term so much tabooed to-day—is a rational and not an irrational event.

The reminder of supposedly " deeper " layers of anthropological being beyond the rational rests on a philosophical construction and a philosophcal value-judgment on which philosophers themselves must find agreement. Our only comment on this is that according to what we know of it in the Church the encounter of God and man takes place primarily, pre-eminently and characteristically in this sphere of *ratio*, no matter how " deep " or less " deep " this may be by philosophical evaluation. ". . . the king of whom the psalm speaketh here, although of course He hath His kingdom on earth, yet so ruleth the spiritual world and pointeth to the heavenly that, though we see not His kingdom as a wordly realm, nevertheless we hear it. But how ? ' Out of the mouths of babes and sucklings thou hast ordained strength.' And Christ's kingdom is a kingdom of hearing, not a kingdom of seeing. For the eyes lead and guide us not thither where we find Christ and get to know Him, but the ears must do this. . . ." (Luther, *Sermon delivered in Merseburg,* 1545, *W.A.,* 51, p. 11, l. 25). " As when thou seest and hearest a preacher preach the Word of God by which at Christ's command he proclaimeth repentance and remission of sins, thou seest there no plough or barrow but seest and hearest that the preacher taketh up only the tongue and the word. . . . Hence also when we see the holy sacraments extend . . . deliverance and liberation from sins and death, that thou shouldest no longer be holden fast in the devil's kingdom, thou seest not but only hearest what is announced and granted to thee with the tongue of the preacher by the word " (*ib.*, p. 12, l. 9).

Speaking stands in correlation to hearing, understanding and obeying. Whatever problems may arise with regard to these terms through the fact that our concern here is with God's speaking, and hence with the hearing, understanding and obeying correlative to this speaking—it is faith that hears, understands and obeys God's speech— we must certainly not leave the level of these concepts of speaking, hearing, understanding and obeying if we are not to set ourselves at some other place than where God's Word is heard.

Whatever " the holy " of Rudolf Otto may be, it certainly cannot be understood as the Word of God, for it is the numinous, and the numinous is the irrational, and the irrational can no longer be differentiated from an absolutised natural force. But everything depends on this differentiation if we are to understand the concept of the Word of God.

The Word of God has natural force too. But primarily and pre-eminently and decisively it has the simple spiritual power of truth. What we are saying here about God's Word does not apply equally to every word. Of no other word can it be said that this word has decisively the power of truth. For every other word *physis* means a limit at which the impotence of its spirituality is also unmasked. Every other word lacks either truth or reality or both. Typical of every other word is a uncertain oscillation between a spasmodic idealism and an equally spasmodic realism. The naturalness and spirituality of every other word are those of fallen man. Only in God's Word do we find the normal order of the natural and the spiritual. But in God's Word we do find it, and we should not allow the aberrations of human spirituality in its flight from nature to lead us into an attempt to level up or even reverse the order. In theological and ministerial utterance we have to be clear, then, what it means to employ naturalistic terms. In view of the language of the Bible itself we cannot lay an absolute embargo on talking about life, light, fire, source, river, or storm, about irruptions, shatterings, overpowerings and experiences. But one must remember in so doing that in the Bible, to be precise, all this takes place within that definite order, so that in naturalistic speech the Word of God is not denoted in its primary sense, and while it certainly is also what is said, it certainly is not this in the first instance. One has thus to remember how easily there is here in either hearer or speaker a slipping into the natural sphere where it is no longer a matter of speech and answer, of perception and decision, but only of movement, pressure and impact, where it is no longer a matter of truth but only of reality. To be sure, this is always a concern too, and for this reason naturalism is not to be banished even from theological utterance. But this is not the first or proper concern in the Word of God. The moment, then, it becomes the only thing that matters in what we say, then by human judgment, by what we know about the Word of God through the Word of God itself, there can be no service of God in theology or proclamation. Awareness of the fact that the Word of God is primarily spiritual is an admonition to concentrate on the spiritual sphere and to beware of straying into the natural sphere.

2. God's Word means that God speaks. This implies secondly its personal quality. God's Word is not a thing to be described nor a term to be defined. It is neither a matter nor an idea. It is not " a truth," not even the very highest truth. It is *the* truth as it is God's speaking person, *Dei loquentis persona*. It is not an objective reality. It is *the* objective reality, in that it is also subjective, the subjective that is God. God's Word means the speaking God. Certainly God's Word is not just the formal possibility of divine speech. It is the fulfilled reality. It always has a very specific objective content. God always

speaks a *concretissimum*. But this divine *concretissimum* cannot as such be either anticipated or repeated. What God speaks is never known or true anywhere in abstraction from God Himself. It is known and true in and through the fact that He Himself says it, that He is present in person in and with what is said by Him.

Non satis est habere donum, nisi sit et donator presens, sicut petivit et Moses exo. 33 : " *Si non tu ipse precedas nos, ne educas nos de loco ipso* " etc. (Luther, Romans, 1515–1516, Fi. Schol., 140, 15). *A Deo enim vivo disceditur dum a verbo eius disceditur, quod est vivum et omnia vivificans, imo Deus ipse* (*Hebrews*, 1513, Fi. Schol., 42, 2). According to another saying of Luther Christ's Word is Christ's mouth : " That it ever proceedeth out of Christ's mouth from one mouth to another, and yet remaineth Christ's mouth " (*Sermon on John* 14²³ᶠ· *Cruc. Sommerpostille*, 1543, W.A., 21, p. 469, l. 3).

The underlying and basic third form of the Word of God, which we have tried to pin down in the concept of revelation, is what has forced us constantly to keep this proviso in mind in our analysis of the concepts of proclamation and Scripture. Understanding the Word of God not as proclamation and Scripture alone but as God's revelation in proclamation and Scripture, we must understand it in its identity with God Himself. God's revelation is Jesus Christ, the Son of God.

In the vocabulary of Trinitarian doctrine God's Son cannot be differentiated from God's Word. If Jn. 1¹ᶠ· reads : Ἐν ἀρχῇ ἦν ὁ λόγος, καὶ ὁ λόγος ἦν πρὸς τὸν θεόν, καὶ θεὸς ἦν ὁ λόγος. οὗτος ἦν ἐν ἀρχῇ πρὸς τὸν θεόν, the fourth statement is only a meaningless repetition of the second unless the οὗτος, though to be filled out in the first instance by λόγος, does not also in this emphatic use point forward beyond what immediately follows to the proper name mentioned for the first time only in v. 18, namely, Ἰησοῦς Χριστός, with whose bearer the Logos in the prologue of this Gospel is to be regarded as identical. And in Rev. 19¹²·¹³ the returning Christ, the rider on the white horse, is described as the wearer of a tiara ἔχων ὄνομα γεγραμμένον ὃ οὐδεὶς οἶδεν εἰ μὴ αὐτός, i.e., whose wording is obviously known to anyone who sees it but whose meaning—the being to which the name points—is known only to Himself. Καὶ κέκληται τὸ ὄνομα αὐτοῦ (the wording of this name) : ὁ λόγος τοῦ θεοῦ. Here again, then, what the Word of God is cannot be stated directly. It is the name of revelation, i.e., of the Revealer. He is the Word of God. From Him alone it may and will be experienced what the Word of God is. Of ourselves we can only say how it is, i.e., how He is.

The equation of God's Word and God's Son makes it radically impossible to say anything doctrinaire in understanding the Word of God. In this equation, and in it alone, a real and effective barrier is set up against what is made of proclamation according to the Roman Catholic view and of Holy Scripture according to the later form of older Protestantism, namely, a fixed sum of revealed propositions which can be systematised like the sections of a corpus of law. The only system in Holy Scripture and proclamation is revelation, i.e., Jesus Christ. Now the converse is also true, of course, namely that God's Son is God's Word. Thus God does reveal Himself in statements, through the medium of speech, and indeed of human speech.   His word is always this or that word spoken by the prophets and apostles and proclaimed in the Church. The personal character of God's Word is not, then, to be played off against its verbal or spiritual character.   It is not at all true that this second aspect under which we must understand it implies its irrationality and thus cancels out the first aspect under which we must understand it.

This is obviously the view of P. Tillich, in whom we find the following rather naive polemic : " But it is quite wrong to equate the Word as a symbol for the self-impartation of beyond being with the word as a physical medium of self-understanding and self-impartation on the part of the human spirit, and in this way to confound God's Word and the word of Scripture or the word of preaching. In reply to this one may simply (!) point out that for Christian theology Jesus Christ is the Word, not His words but His being, which finds expression equally in His words and also in His action and passion " (*Rel. Verwirkl.*, 1930, p. 49). On this one may comment that the words, action and passion of Jesus Christ and His being certainly cannot be separated from one another in such a way that the words, action and passion are only an expression of His being, as though His being stood behind the words, action and passion.   The being of this person is identical with His speech, action and passion.   But this being of Jesus Christ is not directly present to us.   It must be present to us and can be present to us only indirectly, namely, through the proclaiming of the Word first by Holy Scripture and then also by the Church.   If the being of Jesus Christ is present to us, this occurs altogether in such a way that it is equated with the word as a physical medium of self-understanding and self-impartation on the part of the human spirit, the word of Scripture and the word of preaching becoming the Word of God.   " For where My Word is, there also am I " (Luther, *Sermon on Mt.* 22, 1544, *W.A.*, 52, p. 509, l. 26) ". . . God could not otherwise send forth Christ into the world, He had to fashion Him into the Word and so spread Him abroad and bear Him to every man.   Otherwise Christ would have remained for Himself alone and unknown to us, and thus He would have died for Himself alone.   But because the Word beareth Christ to us, so it beareth us to Him who hath overcome death, sin and the devil " (*Sermon on Jn.* 8[46-59], 1525, *W.A.*, 17[II], p. 234, l. 11).

The personalising of the concept of the Word of God, which we cannot avoid when we remember that Jesus Christ is the Word of God, does not mean its deverbalising.   But it (naturally) means awareness of the fact that it is person rather than thing or object even if and in so far as it is word, word of Scripture and word of preaching.   To be person means to be subject, not merely in the logical sense, but also in the ethical sense : to be free subject, a subject which is free even in respect of the specific limitations connected with its individuality, able to control its own existence and nature both as particular form and also as living development, and also able to select new possibilities of existence and nature.   If we consider what this implies, it will not occur to us to see in this personalising of the concept of God's Word a case of anthropomorphism.   The doubtful thing is not whether God is person, but whether we are.   Can we find among us even one man whom

2. The Word of God as the Speech of God

we can call this in the full and proper sense of the term ? But God is real person, really free subject. And if it is true that this brings us up against His inconceivability, because we cannot think through this thought to a finish, it is also true that on hearing His Word we should not refuse to think this initial thought, to see Him as person precisely in His Word. What we are saying is that not just anything, not a θεῖον, but He Himself comes to us in His Word. Precisely in His Word God is person. But this then means concretely that He is Lord of the wording of His Word. He is not bound to it but it to Him. He has free control over the wording of Holy Scripture. He can use it or not use it. He can use it in this way or in that way. He can choose a new wording beyond that of Holy Scripture. What Holy Scripture proclaims as His Word can be proclaimed in a new wording as His Word so long as it is He Himself who speaks in this wording. Furthermore, the personal character of God's Word means, not its deverbalising, but the posing of an absolute barrier against reducing its wording to a human system or using its wording to establish and construct a human system. It would not be God's faithfulness but His unfaithfulness to us if He allowed us to use His Word in this way. This would mean His allowing us to gain control over His Word, to fit it in with our own designs, and thus to shut up ourselves against Him to our own ruin. God's faithfulness to His Church consists in His availing Himself of His freedom to come to us Himself in His Word and in His reserving to Himself the freedom to do this again and again.

3. God's Word means that God speaks. But this implies thirdly what one might call the purposive character of the Word of God. This might also be called its relatedness or pertinence, its character as address. In its form neither as proclamation, Holy Scripture, nor revelation do we know God's Word as an entity that exists or could exist merely in and for itself. We know it only as a Word that is directed to us and applies to us. The fact that it is this is not, of course, self-evident. It is not something one might deduce from a general concept of speech. It is so in fact, but it might not be. In the intertrinitarian life of God the eternal generation of the Son or Logos is, of course, the expression of God's love, of His will not to be alone. But it does not follow from this that God could not be God without speaking to us. We undoubtedly understand God's love for man, or in the first instance for any reality distinct from Himself, only when we understand it as free and unmerited love not resting on any need. God would be no less God if He had created no world and no man. The existence of the world and our own existence are in no sense vital to God, not even as the object of His love. The eternal generation of the Son by the Father tells us first and supremely that God is not at all lonely even without the world and us. His love has its object in

Himself. And so one cannot say that our existence as that of the recipients of God's Word is constitutive for the concept of the Word. It could be no less what it is even without us. God could satisfy His love in Himself. For He is already an object to Himself and He is an object truly worthy of His love. God did not need to speak to us. What He says by Himself and to Himself from eternity to eternity would really be said just as well and even better without our being there, as speech which for us would be eternal silence. Only when we are clear about this can we estimate what it means that God has actually, though not necessarily, created a world and us, that His love actually, though not necessarily, applies to us, that His Word has actually, though not necessarily, been spoken to us. The purposiveness we find in proclamation, the Bible and revelation is thus a free and actual purposiveness by no means essential to God Himself. We evaluate this purposiveness correctly only if we understand it as the reality of the love of the God who does not need us but who does not will to be without us, who has directed His regard specifically on us.

In this connexion it is appropriate and necessary for once to consider not what God has actually done but what He might have done, since it is only in this antithesis that we can really understand what He has done. In this light one can also see how dubious it is to set the doctrine of the Word of God in the framework of an anthropology. In that case the freedom of the divine purpose for man can be asserted only at a later stage, while it is really denied by the starting-point.

Hearing man, as the object of the purpose of the speaking God, is thus included in the concept of the Word of God as a factual necessity, but he is not essential to it. He is not, as I most astonishingly stated on p. 111 of the first edition, " co-posited " in it in the way Schleiermacher's God is in the feeling of absolute dependence. If he is co-posited in it with factual necessity, this is God's free grace. If we think that in this sense we must see in purposiveness or relation to us a third quality of the Word of God, and if we go on to investigate the content of this purpose, the implication of this relatedness or pertinence of God's Word for its understanding, we must remember that wherever and whenever God speaks to man its content is a *concretissimum*. God always has something specific to say to each man, something that applies to him and to him alone. The real content of God's speech or the real will of the speaking person of God is not in any sense, then, to be construed and reproduced by us as a general truth. As readers of Scripture and hearers of proclamation we can and must, of course, work with certain general conceptual materials, apparently repeating or anticipating what God has said to this or that man or will say to this or that man. There is obviously no other way in which we can remind ourselves or others of the Word of God that came then and will one day come again. We may do this in words of our own coining or in Scripture quotations. But in so doing we have always to bear in mind that these materials are our own work and are not to be confused with the concrete fulness of the Word of God itself which we recall and for which we wait, but only point to it. What God said and what God will say is always quite different from what we can and must say to ourselves and others about its content. Not only the word of preaching heard as God's Word but even the word of Scripture through which God speaks to us becomes in fact quite different when it passes from God's lips to our ears and our lips. It becomes the Word of God recollected and expected by us in faith, and the Word which was spoken and will be spoken again by God stands over against it afresh in strict sovereignty. But even in this strict sovereignty in which its true content remains inconceivable to us, it retains its purposiveness, it is the Word that comes to us, that is aimed at us, and as such it is a definite Word determined not by us but by God Himself as the One who aims it at us. We are not anticipating its actual content but simply noting the aspects under which we shall have to consider its actual content if we make the following points in relation to its purposiveness, in relation to the fact that it is an address to us.

(1) First, the Word of God as directed to us is a Word which we do not say to ourselves and which we could not in any circumstances say to ourselves. Every human word, including that of proclamation and even the Bible, we could and can perhaps say to ourselves as such. Encounter with the human word as such is never genuine, irrevocable encounter, nor can it be. Encounter with the Word of God is genuine, irrevocable encounter, i.e., encounter that can never be dissolved in union. The Word of God always tells us something fresh that we had never heard before from anyone. The rock of a Thou which never becomes an I is thrown in our path here. This otherness which is yet related to us and made known to us, though only in this way, stamps it fundamentally and comprehensively as the Word of God, the Word of the Lord, compared to which all other words, however profound or new or arresting, are not words of the Lord. Whatever God may say to us will at all events be said in this way ; it will be said as the Word of the Lord.

(2) Secondly, the Word of God as this Word of the Lord directed to us is the Word which aims at us and smites us in our existence. No human word has the competence to aim at us in our existence and no human word has the power to smite us in our existence. The only word that may aim at us in our existence and can smite us in our existence is one which questions and answers us in just the same way as death might question and answer us at the end of our existence. But death is dumb. It neither questions nor answers. It is only the end. It is

C.D.—F

not really a thing outside and above our existence which can aim at our existence and smite it. The Word of God is the Word of the Lord because it comes from the point outside and above us from which death itself would not speak to us even if it could speak at all. The Word of God applies to us as no human word as such can do, and as death does not do, because this Word is the Word of our Creator, of the One who encompasses our existence and the end of our existence, by whom it is affirmed and negated, because everything has come into being and is preserved by this Word, and without it would not exist. He who makes Himself heard here is the One to whom we belong. Whatever He may say, it will be said in this relation of the Creator to His creature.

(3) Thirdly, the Word of God as the Word of the Creator directed to us is the Word which has obviously become necessary and is necessary as a renewal of the original relation between us and Him. The fact that God speaks to us, that He reveals Himself to us, i.e., that He turns to us in a wholly new way, that as the Unknown He makes Himself known—even after creating us and although we belong to Him—all this implies on the one side a criticism of the reality of the present relation between Him and us and on the other side a declaration on His part to uphold and re-establish the relation in and spite of this criticism of His. Neither of these could be the content of a human word. Only the One who has instituted the relation can confirm and renew it when it is disrupted or destroyed. Only God can pronounce the verdict and give the promise and raise the claim which all lie equally in the concept of revelation. Under this third aspect of its purposiveness the Word of God is the Word of reconciliation, i.e., the Word of the Reconciler, of the God who effects a new creation, who sets up His covenant with us afresh in judgment and grace. Whatever God may say to us, it will at all events be said in this relationship of renewal.

(4) Fourthly and finally the Word of God as the Word of reconciliation directed to us is the Word by which God announces Himself to man, i.e., by which He promises Himself as the content of man's future, as the One who meets him on his way through time as the end of all time, as the hidden Lord of all times. His presence by the Word is His presence as the coming One, coming for the fulfilment and consummation of the relation established between Him and us in creation and renewed and confirmed in reconciliation. Again this final Word cannot be a word of man. Human words are never final words. They are never the promise of a specific and definitive coming of the Other. It is proper to God's Word and to God's Word alone to be also the full and authentic presence of the Speaker even if this be as the coming One. God's Word is the Word of our Redeemer, i.e., of the Lord who will be Lord as He was and is, who in His relation to us keeps faith both with Himself and us. In this way He is Lord indeed, the Lord of all lords. And whatever

God may say to us, it will at all events be said always in this final, consummating, eschatological relation too.

Again, what God says to us specifically remains His secret which will be disclosed in the event of His actual speaking. The concrete fulness of what He has said and will say specifically to men is and remains in truth His own business. We can only cling to the fact—but we must cling to it—that when He spoke it was, and when He will speak it will be, the Word of the Lord, the Word of our Creator, our Reconciler, our Redeemer. Understanding it as directed and applying to us, we are well advised to keep what we think and say about it open in at least these four directions, to be ready and vigilant from these four standpoints.

3. THE SPEECH OF GOD AS THE ACT OF GOD

When God speaks, there is no point in looking about for a related act. The fear that talk might be " only " talk is, of course, only too apposite in relation to human speech. When man speaks, then his misery, the rift between truth and reality in which he lives, is plainly exposed, and the more so the better and more beautifully and truly he speaks. When man speaks, he involuntarily tries to protect himself against being unmasked in this way, perhaps by making it known through tone and gesture that he is not just talking but engaged in action too, perhaps in content by speaking as practically as possible, i.e., by talking as much as he can about his own deeds or those of others, whether past or future. The fear that he is just talking, the question of the related act, will arise all the same and will undoubtedly apply to him in some respect. When God speaks, however, the fear is groundless. The man who has heard God speak and might still ask about the related act is simply showing that he has not really heard God speak. We can hear Christian sermons and ask what really happens as they take place. What does actually correspond to all these words? This is a question well worth putting. We can even hear Holy Scripture and simply hear words, human words, which we either understand or do not understand but along with which there is for us no corresponding event. But if so, then neither in proclamation nor Holy Scripture has it been the Word of God that we have heard. If it had been the Word of God, not for a moment could we have looked about for God's acts. The Word of God itself would then have been the act. The Word of God does not need to be supplemented by an act. The Word of God is itself the act of God. It is act to a degree that everything else that we usually call act, event, practice, life, etc., and that we usually miss and demand as a supplement to man's word, can only seem to be very questionable as real act in comparison with it. The Word of God makes history in the supreme sense.

" For he spake, and it was done ; he commanded, and it stood fast," Ps. 33⁹. When God's Word comes to the prophets of the Old Testament, this is denoted by the verb *hayah* (happen), cf. Jer. 1. We may recall all the direct connexions between Word and creation, Word and calling, Word and remission of sins, Word and miracle, Word and blessing, Word and punishment, etc., in both the Old Testament and the New. But even when the connexion is indirect, e.g., when the prophets speak of future events or the apostles speak in retrospect of the acts of Jesus, these are not just references to remote events but an immediate introduction, through the Word, of things understood to have happened already or to be still happening. " Look at the creation of all creatures. ' In the beginning God created heaven and earth.' How ? By His Word, as Moses writeth : ' God said, Let there be light, and there was light.' ' God said, Let there be a firmament between the waters ' etc., ' and it was so ' ; ' God said, Let the waters under the heaven be gathered into places apart, that dry land may appear, and it was so.' The speaking doth it. When this Speaker saith something that He will have, it must be so. So then of naught, solely by His speaking, God hath created heaven and earth and all creatures. How then should He not be able by His Word and sacrament to do what He willeth, especially as His Word standeth fast and beareth witness thereto ? " (Luther, *Sermon on the Sunday Cantate on* 1 *Cor.* 15, 1544, *W.A.*, 49, p. 405, l. 33). " And so . . . we should hold His Word glorious and lofty as an almighty power. For whoso hath it hath all and can do all. Again, whoso hath it not, him naught else can or shall guard against sin, death and devil. For what our dear Lord Christ doth here with the nobleman's son, saving him from death by His almighty word and keeping him alive, that will He do for us all by His Word if we will but accept it. . . ." (*Sermon on Jn.* 4⁴⁷⁻⁵⁹, *W.A.*, 52, p. 515, l. 4). " 'Tis for Christ but the matter of a little word, and it is forthwith yea. And so God ruleth His Christian Church, yea He so ruleth the whole world, that for Him 'tis no heavy task, but He effecteth all by a word. Thus should we learn to hold God's Word in honour and to believe the same. The same Word we have in the preaching of the Gospel, in baptism, in the sacrament, in absolution. . . . If we believe the Word it will happen to us as it happened to this nobleman, namely, that we obtain what is promised us in the Word " (*Sermon on Jn.* 4⁴⁷·⁵⁴, 1534, *E.A.*, 5, p. 215).

The distinction between word and act is that mere word is the mere self-expression of a person, while act is the resultant relative alteration in the world around. Mere word is passive, act is an active participation in history. But this kind of distinction does not apply to the Word of God. As mere Word it is act. As mere Word it is the divine person, the person of the Lord of history, whose self-expression is as such an alteration, and indeed an absolute alteration of the world, whose *passio* in history is as such *actio*. What God does when He speaks, in exactly the same way as what He says, cannot, of course, be generally defined either by way of anticipation or by that of reproduction. We can refer only to the *concretissima* of the acts which are attested in the Bible and which are also to be expected from God in the future.

It always was and always will be the special thing ὅσα ἡτοίμασεν ὁ θεὸς τοῖς ἀγαπῶσιν αὐτόν (1 Cor. 2⁹).

What we can and should consider is what it implies that God's speaking, and therefore the Word of God in all its forms, is in fact the act of God.

1. The fact that God's Word is God's act means first its contingent contemporaneity. What is meant by this is as follows. The time of the direct, original speech of God Himself in His revelation, the time of Jesus Christ (which was also and already that of Abraham according to Jn. 8[56]), the time of that which the prophets and apostles heard so that they could bear witness to it—that is one time. But the time of this witness, the time of prophecy and the apostolate, the time of Peter on whom Christ builds His Church, the time of the rise of the Canon as a concrete counterpart in which the Church receives its norm for all times—this is another time. And the specific time of the Church itself, the time of derivative proclamation related to the words of the prophets and apostles and regulated by them—this is yet another time. These are different times distinguished not only by the difference in periods and contents, not only by the remoteness of centuries and the disparity in the men of different centuries and millennia, but distinguished by the different attitude of God to men. Jesus Christ was no less true man than the prophets and apostles. But in virtue of His unity with God He stood absolutely over against them as a master over against his slaves. As men, even religious men, the biblical witnesses were not singled out in principle from later Church teachers or from us or even from the teachers and leaders of other religions. Yet in their office as witnesses they were and are in an absolutely once-for-all and unique position compared to all the rest of us. Again, even though our human existence may be closely compared in principle with that of Christ and the apostles, yet in virtue of our relation to Scripture, and through Scripture to revelation, and also through the intervening experience of the Church in which we have an advantage over the prophets and apostles, or which does at least distinguish us from them, our own situation in the Church is a third and very distinctive situation. It is this difference of order, of first and second, of higher and lower, that makes the times of the Word of God so different. Three times there is a saying of the Word of God through human lips. But only twice, in the biblical witnesses and us, is there first a letting of it be said to us, and only once, in our case, an indirect letting of it be said to us mediated through the Bible. The different position in God's order differentiates these three times as human times are not differentiated elsewhere, as they are differentiated only here, as only the times of God's Word are differentiated. One can, of course, dissolve the difference in time by ignoring the differentiation of the times in God's order, by viewing and presenting them, not as times of God's Word but only immanently, i.e., by taking into account only the difference of the

periods and their human contents as such. Estimating the difference along these lines need then be no obstacle to a direct insight into the continuity and unity of the times, to an insight into our contemporaneity with Christ and all His saints. Indeed, it rather facilitates and establishes this insight by teaching us to see and understand the man of the past, be he Jeremiah or Jesus or Paul, or Luther, as a fellow-man, to criticise him as such, but also to respect and love him, in short, to treat him as companion of one and the same time.

This is the way that recent Protestant theology, after overcoming the great crisis of the non-historical thinking of the Enlightenment, has now taken in all its typical representatives. The revelation of God in history is something they think they have discovered afresh and for the first time properly in emancipation from the rigid antitheses of the older Church and theology. So far as I can see and understand the matter, the epoch-making name in this regard is that of Lessing. The " ugly, wide ditch " (between the Bible and us), of which he said in a well-known passage (*Der Beweis des Geistes und der Kraft, Theol. Schr.*, ed. Gross, II, 2, p. 13) that for all his good intentions he could not jump across it, was not, and for the author of the *Laokoon* could not be, the general problem of a historical understanding that leaps over the gap of the centuries and their different forms of human life. Lessing could make this jump. So could Herder and Schleiermacher after him, and others up to A. Ritschl and Harnack, Lagarde and Troeltsch, always with increased excellence and skill. Similarly we should not trivialise Lessing's other famous dictum that " the accidental truths of history can never be proof of the necessary truths of reason " (*op. cit.*, p. 12), as though the truth of history were simply the specific concrete empirical truth of a historical datum as such and the truth of reason were the timeless truth of mathematical and philosophical axioms. The religious philosophy of Kant still moves within this antithesis of the singular and the general, the empirical and the rational. But this is not true of Lessing, who is the more modern in this regard. Lessing is well acquainted with a proof of Christianity through history. But it must be " the proof of spirit and of power." That is, history does not prove any truth for us so long as it is the " contingent truth of history " merely reported to us by others and not truth " felt " and " experienced " by ourselves. It becomes the " necessary truth of reason," i.e., truth that is necessary and real for us, when and to the extent that it is thus felt and experienced by us, experienced in the way " the paralytic experiences the beneficent shock of the electric spark." (" Religion is not true because the evangelists and apostles taught it ; they taught it because it is true. By its inner truth, scriptural traditions must be explained, and all the traditions in the world cannot give it inner truth if it does not have it," *Fragm. eines Ungen., op. cit.*, II, 1, p. 261 ; *Axiomata, op. cit.*, II, 2, p. 122 ; according to K. Aner, *Die Theologie der Lessingzeit*, 1929, p. 148 f., the apologetic use of experience may be found already in the sermons of Abbot J. F. W. Jerusalem from 1745). And Lessing obviously regards this inner truth as something quite accessible to us and apprehensible by us. We can judge its presence in virtue of our own feeling and experience. This is why he appeals from Luther's writings to Luther's spirit (*Anti-Göze, op. cit.*, II, 2, p. 140), from the letter of the Bible to the spirit of the Bible (*Axiomata, op. cit.*, II, 2, p. 112), from the reported miracles to the " ever continuing miracle of religion itself " (*Eine Duplik, op. cit.*, II, 2, p. 33), and finally from the Christian religion to the religion of Christ (*Die Rel. Christi, op. cit.*, II, 3, p. 448 f.). " No one in Hamburg will ever again wish to dispute with me the utter difference between gross and net " (*Axiomata*, *op. cit.*, II, 2, p. 108). " Historical words are the vehicle of the prophetic word " (*op. cit.*, p. 112). This was Lessing's obstacle, and this was the way he overcame the obstacle. His problem was the lack of contemporaneity between Christ, the apostles, and us. This lack was one of order, and, as he rightly saw, it could not be overcome. He thus abandoned it for an immanent lack of contemporaneity that could be overcome by way of immanence. From now on all the more lively thinkers, in contrast to the Enlightenment and Kant, found no further difficulty or stumbling block in interpreting revelation as history and history as revelation.

But if we abandon the distinction of the three times in terms of order, then no matter how loudly or sincerely we may talk about revelation and its concreteness and historicity, and no matter how illuminating or practical may be the shape we give everything, we have really abandoned the concept of the Word of God itself. When we are able to eliminate our non-contemporaneity with Christ and the apostles by putting ourselves on the same soil as them or putting them on the same soil as us, so that, sharing the same prophetic Spirit and having the measure of inner truth in our own feeling, we can discuss with them the gross and net value of their words ; when contemporaneity, therefore, rests on the hypothesis of a merely quantitative difference between them and us, then the concept of the Word of God is humanised in such a way that it is no wonder people prefer to use it comparatively rarely and in quotation marks ; the surprising thing is that they have not preferred to drop it completely and unequivocally. Distinctions immanent in history, no matter how seriously they are taken as such, cannot justify a serious use of the concept of God's Word. For fundamentally the appreciation of these distinctions does not mean that we let something be said to us. There can be no serious saying of the Word of God in the realm of these distinctions. Within these distinctions there is only a togetherness with Christ and the apostles. For all our respect for the greatness and vitality of history, it is we the living who have right on our side and who thus finally fix and manipulate the norm and the conditions of this togetherness. The present Church, however historically it may feel and think, speaks the last word as the heir and interpreter of history. Not having God's Word in the serious sense of the term, it stands alone and is referred back to itself. If, however, we insist that the concept of God's Word means that the Church is not alone and is not referred back to itself, then we must accept the fact that the distinction of the times is one of order, and in no case can the contemporaneity of modern proclamation with Scripture and revelation be understood as one that we can bring about by eliminating the distinction, by incorporating Scripture and revelation into the life of humanity. It can be understood only as an expression of the fact that God's Word is itself God's act. It thus has nothing directly to do with the general problem of historical understanding. Of course there is always some historical understanding when the Word of God is manifest to us in its contemporaneity. But this historical understanding as such does not mean hearing and does not establish proclamation of God's Word. When God's Word is heard and proclaimed, something takes place that for all our hermeneutical skill cannot be brought about by hermeneutical skill.

The biblical witnesses had also a specific relation of historical understanding to Jesus Christ (ἐγνώκαμεν κατὰ σάρκα Χριστόν, 2 Cor. 5[16]). But in this relation it did not come about through the immanent power of this relation that they saw in Jesus Christ the Son of God.

> They did not do so, then, by the power of Lessing's feeling and experiencing : σάρξ καὶ αἷμα οὐκ ἀπεκάλυψέν σοι (Mt. 16[17]). Those who receive the light that has come into the world, those who see the kingdom of God, do not do so in virtue of their earthly birth (Jn. 1[13] ; 3[3f.]). The Father has hidden the secret of the Son from the wise and prudent, i.e., from the judgment of an inner truth already known to man (Mt. 11[25]).

In the Old and New Testaments this recognition is rather traced back to election, revelation, calling, separation, new birth—concepts which as it were shatter the immanence of the historical relation from within inasmuch as God is the Subject of the action denoted by them, inasmuch as it is God's good-pleasure (εὐδοκία, Mt. 11[26] ; Gal. 1[15] ; Eph. 1[9]) that as a purely external truth first creates and posits the inner truth as such in the free action denoted by these terms, quite apart from all the undeniable historical relations, in these relations but not through them. These concepts are not to be regarded as later explanations of an event that is properly and intrinsically immanent. They do not explain ; they state how things are in the first instance. The immanent explanations of the terms are really the later interpretation. In the sense of the biblical authors one can only understand the concepts as terms for God's free acts, or else they are not understood at all. They tell us that without elimination of the distinction the time of Christ by God's free act becomes contemporaneous with the time of the prophets and apostles.

> The prophets prophesy of Christ and the apostles proclaim Him, neither as reporters, but both as witnesses who speak not only about Christ but also in Christ, not because they have experienced Christ as one might experience Plato, but because it pleased God ἀποκαλύψαι τὸν υἱὸν αὐτοῦ ἐν ἐμοί (Gal. 1[15]).

The Word of Scripture in its very different time and with its very different temporal content as compared with the Word of revelation is now put in its proper position. It is called the Word of the prophets and apostles, and as such, as witness of Christ and in subordination to the Word of Christ, it also speaks the Word of Christ.

The same step from one time to another, which can be understood only as God's act, is taken again when the proclamation of the Church becomes real proclamation, i.e., God's Word, by reason of the fact that

Holy Scripture comes to articulation in it, and the Word of Christ in Holy Scripture. Here again there is and has to be a specific relation of historical understanding with all the relevant components from philological analysis to the art of sympathetic identification. Proclamation is possible only in this relation of understanding, just as there could be prophecy and apostolate only in a specific relation of understanding. But in this relation proclamation of the Word of God does not come about through the individual or corporate components of the relation, e.g., through philological perspicacity or the most talented or refined identification. It comes about solely and simply through the power of the biblical Word itself, which now makes a place for itself in a very different time, and becomes the content of this place, as Paul steps forth in proclamation, not as a religious personality, but as an apostle of Jesus Christ, so that Jesus Himself is present in him. As the Word of God is this act, then in this step from revelation to Scripture and then to the proclamation of the Church, in a full and strict differentiation of the times, it is one, it is contemporaneous— Ἰησοῦς Χριστὸς ἐχθὲς καὶ σήμερον ὁ αὐτός (Heb. 13[8]).

We spoke of " contingent " contemporaneity to emphasise the fact that it has the character of an act, an event. Indeed, one might speak of a twofold contingency to the extent that in the relation between revelation and Holy Scripture and then again in the relation between Holy Scripture and proclamation there is always a contingent *illic et tunc* from the standpoint of the speaking God and a contingent *hic et nunc* from the standpoint of hearing man. We have spoken of a step from the one to the other in both relations. This step must not be volatilised into the general truth of a fixed or continuous relation between the three forms. It is really a step which has actuality only as this or that specific step, as a contingent act. The problem of God's Word is that this specific revelation of God is granted to this specific man to-day through the proclamation of this other specific man by means of this specific biblical text, so that a specific *illic et tunc* becomes a specific *hic et nunc*. The problem of the Word of God is always, then, a wholly specific, once-for-all and distinctive problem, and regarding this problem one can only say that it is solved by the Word of God itself as the Word of God spoken by the mouth of God is contemporaneous *illic et tunc* and also (i.e., as spoken *illic et tunc*) *hic et nunc*.

2. The fact that God's Word is God's act implies secondly its power to rule. God's speech is His action in relation to those to whom He speaks. But His action is divine. It is the action of the Lord. It is thus His ruling action. When and where Jesus Christ becomes contemporaneous through Scripture and proclamation, when and where the " God with us " is said to us by God Himself, we come under a lordship. The concepts election, revelation, separation, calling, and

C.D.—F*

new birth which we touched on earlier all denote a promise, a judgment, a claim on man by which God binds man to Himself. Gospel and Law as the concrete content of God's Word imply always a seizure of man. No matter what God's Word says to man *in concretissimo*, it always tells him that he is not his own but God's. If in the light of its origin in revelation, in Jesus Christ, we understand the Word of God as the epitome of God's grace, grace means simply that man is no longer left to himself but is given into the hand of God.

The Gospel or the Word of the cross is the δύναμις θεοῦ to believers, or to them that are saved, we read in Rom. 1¹⁶ and 1 Cor. 1¹⁸. The Word of God is called " living " in 1 Pet. 1²³ and " quick and powerful " in Heb. 4¹². And Mt. 4⁴ says of man that he lives παντὶ ῥήματι ἐκπορευομένῳ διὰ στόματος θεοῦ.

If a man knew nothing of this power that both sustains and stimulates, both protects and punishes, both pacifies and disturbs, if he merely heard about it without knowing it as a power, he would only give evidence that he knew nothing of the Word of God. We are acquainted with the Word of God to the degree that we are acquainted with this power. We speak of God's Word when we speak in recollection and expectation of this power, and when we do so in such a way that we realise that this power of the Word of God is not one power among others, not even among other divine powers, but the one unique divine power which comes home to us, to which we are referred, in face of which we stand in decision between the obedience we owe it and the unfathomable inconceivability of disobedience, and consequently in the decision between bliss and perdition. The Holy Spirit, at least according to the Western understanding of the divine Triunity, cannot be separated from the Word, and His power is not a power different from that of the Word but the power that lives in and by the Word. Nor do we know anything about God's power in the creation and governance of the world except through the Word revealed, written and proclaimed. And when we know it through this Word we cannot possibly separate it from the power of the Word.

Ἐδόθη μοι πᾶσα ἐξουσία ἐν οὐρανῷ καὶ ἐπὶ γῆς (Mt. 28¹⁸). Τὰ πάντα δι' αὐτοῦ καὶ εἰς αὐτὸν ἔκτισται · καὶ αὐτός ἐστιν πρὸ πάντων καὶ τὰ πάντα ἐν αὐτῷ συνέστηκεν (Col. 1¹⁷).

Where God has once spoken and is heard, i.e., in the Church, there is no escaping this power, no getting past it, no acknowledgment of divine powers that are not summed up in this power, that are not related to the manner of this power and active in its mode.

Καὶ αὐτός ἐστιν ἡ κεφαλὴ τοῦ σώματος, τῆς ἐκκλησίας (Col. 1¹⁸, cf. Eph. 1²²f.). This is said of Christ. But Christ is the Word of God, contemporary in prophecy and the apostolate and contemporary in the proclamation of His Church. If He is contemporary here, if He makes that step, then we are necessarily faced with the recognition of the sovereignty of God's Word in the Church which characterises the Reformation view of God and the Church. " The holy Christian Church whose sole Head is Christ is born of the Word of God, is incorporated in the same, and heareth not the voice of a stranger " (Zwingli, *Berne Theses* of 1528, *Art.* 1). " God's Word is a flowret, that is, the longer the dearer. . . . That is, whoso once graspeth God's Word aright, loveth it so dearly that he always desireth it more and more. . . ." (Luther, *Sermon on Lk.* 5^{1-11}, 1534, *E.A.*, 4, p. 342) ". . . our preaching is this, that whoso heareth this preaching about Christ and believeth in Him, hath everlasting life. The Word of God is sent from heaven to be heard, that even if thou wert burnt to ashes, thou wouldst yet know the outcome " (*Exposition of Jn.* 3–4, 1538 f., *W.A.*, 47, p. 188, l. 28). " For 'tis certain we all have salvation through God's Word alone. What should we know else of God, the Lord Christ and His sacrifice, and the Holy Ghost ? " (*Sermon on Mk.* 7^{31-37}, 1544, *W.A.*, 52, p. 451, l. 39). " For God hath given us no other staircase and shewn us no other way up which we can go to heaven save His dear Word, the holy Gospel. Whoso heareth the same gladly, marketh it diligently and sheweth desire and love thereto, is helped " (*ib.*, p, 452, l. 16). " For God will not reveal Himself in thy heart without the Word. Wouldst thou see and know Him, it must befall solely through the Word and the outward sacraments " (*ib.*, p. 453, l. 31). " How doth the Father train us ? Through Christ. How through Christ ? By the Word. Thus he attracteth and charmeth thee ; so an thy need driveth thee, go blithely to it, and boldly bring forth thine ill hap ; but ever bring the Word withal " (*Sermon on Jn.* 8^{46-59}, *E.A.*, 11, p. 130). " For the soul of man can be preserved by nought save the Word of God, that is its food and pasture, and so much as it availeth itself thereof, dependeth and believeth thereon, so far it is counselled and helped " (*Sermon on Lk.* 11, 1527, *W.A.*, 17^{II}, p. 280, l. 30). According to Luther there corresponds to the ascension and session of Christ at God's right hand the *regnum Christi* in the world, which is to be understood as a *doctrinale regnum* equivalent to the *ministerium Verbi* (*Enarr. ub. Cap.* 53 *Esaiae*, 1544, *E.A.*, *Exeg. Op. lat.*, 23, p. 448 f.). " For through the Word He shall rule and not otherwise " (*Passion*, 5th *Sermon*, 1534, *E.A.*, 3, p. 268). " That is the New Testament and kingdom of Christ that cometh home with as little might, and yet with almighty power and might which none can withstand. It appeareth to be foolish that Christ doth set up the New Testament in this wise " (*Sermon on Acts* 2^{1-13}, 1534, *E.A.*, 4, p. 86). " Yet there all is petty and naught to look at, both matter and instruments. The matter and preaching are petty ; the instruments, i.e., the apostles and disciples whom Christ useth as tools for this preaching are much pettier. Yet through this petty preaching and these worthless tools goeth the New Testament and kingdom of Christ " (*ib.*, p. 87). " This preaching is not come from men, but Christ Himself hath brought it and put it thereafter into the hearts of the apostles and their successors, that they grasped it, and into their mouths, that they spake and preached it. That is His kingdom, therefore ruleth He so that all His power standeth and resteth on the Word of God, and the Word then becometh so mighty that it createth all that is needed by man, and bringeth all good things that men may have. For it is the power of God that can and may save all those believe therein, as St. Paul saith in Rom. 1 " (*Sermon on Jn.* $10^{12ff.}$, 1523, *W.A.*, 12, p. 530, l. 24). " But He keepeth specially before Him two members, ears and tongue ; for the kingdom of God is founded upon the Word which one cannot grasp or conceive without these two members, ears and tongue, and ruleth alone through the Word and faith in the hearts of men. The ears grasp the Word and the heart believeth it : but the tongue uttereth or confesseth it as the heart believeth. So if we do away with the tongue and ears, there remaineth no marked difference betwixt the kingdom of Christ and the world " (*Sermon on Mk.* 7^{31-37}, *E.A.*, 13, p. 308). ". . . *la parole de Dieu seule doit estre suffisante pour nostre foy. Si on demande sur quoy nostre foy est fondee et comment elle vient à sa perfection c'est par la parole de Dieu* (Calvin, *Sermon on Gal.* 1^11t., *C.R.*, 51, 361. *Iterum hic memoria repetere convenit, qualis sit regni Christi natura. Ut enim ipse aureo diademata ornatus non est, vel instructus terrenis armis ; ita non dominatur in mundo armorum potentia, nec sibi autoritatem conciliat pomparum splendore, vel terrore et metu populum suum cogit : sed evangelii doctrina regium eius insigne est, quo sub obsequium suum colligit fideles. Proinde ubicunque annunciatur pure evangelii doctrina, illic Christum regnare certum est : ubi vero reiicitur, simul etiam aboleri eius imperium (Comm. on Is.* 11⁴, *C.R.*, 36, 240). *Car Dieu regne, quand il conduit tout par sa providence : mais cependant nous n'apercevons rien de son empire, quand nous luy sommes rebelles, que tout va pesle mesle et que sa parole n'est point escoutee, laquelle est le sceptre royal par lequel il domine sur nous : que son Esprit ne domine point pour nous conduire en son obéissance, et pour nous ranger tellement à luy, qu'il vive plustost en nous, que nous ne vivions à nos appetits, et selon nostre naturel. Dieu donc ne regne point en ceste facon sinon quand l'Evangile nous est presché et que nostre Seigneur Jesus Christ, qui a este constitué son lieutenant, nous gouverne tant par sa parole que par son S. Esprit. . . . Or il est bien certain que . . . Dieu estant Createur de tout le monde, n'a iamais quitté son authorite. If faut donc que sa puissance ait son estendue par tout : mais c'est d'une facon qui nous est cachée et incompréhensible, quand Dieu gouverne, et que sa parole cependant n'est point preschee . . . puis de là nous pouvons recueillir combien la doctrine de l'Evangile nous doit estre precieuse et amiable, veu que par icelle Dieu nous prend sous sa charge et nous recognoist et advoue pour son peuple . . . qu'il veut habiter au milieu de nous (Sermon on Mt.* 3², *C.R.*, 46, 490 f.).

Recognition of the power of God's Word to rule has the following implication. We are speaking of God's Word. Therefore we have to speak of its power, its might, its effects, the changes it brings about. Because the Word of God makes history, as Word it is also act.

" Is not my word like as a fire ? saith the Lord ; and like a hammer that breaketh the rock in pieces ? " (Jer. 23²⁹). " For as the rain cometh down, and the snow from heaven, and returneth not thither, but watereth the earth, and maketh it bring forth and bud, that it may give seed to the sower and bread to the eater : So shall my word be that goeth forth out of my mouth ; it shall not return unto me void, but it shall accomplish that which I please, and it shall prosper in the thing whereto I sent it " (Is. 55¹⁰f.). Cf. in the New Testament the basic connexion between καλεῖν, κλῆσις, ἐκκλησία, κλητός and the totality of that which ἐν Χριστῷ becomes radically different for man and in man.

The promise of the Word of God is not as such an empty pledge which always stands, as it were, confronting man. It is the transposing of man into the wholly new state of one who has accepted and appropriated the promise, so that irrespective of his attitude to it he no longer lives without this promise but with it. The claim of the Word of God is not as such a wish or command which remains outside the hearer without impinging on his existence. It is the claiming and commandeering of man. Whatever may be his attitude to God's claim, man as a hearer of His Word now finds himself in the sphere of the divine claim ; he is claimed by God. Again, the judgment of the Word of God is not a mere aspect under which man himself remains untouched, just as the same man may seem to be a giant from the standpoint of the ant or a dwarf from the standpoint of the elephant without in fact being any different either way. The judgment of God as such creates not only a new light and therewith a new situation, but also with the new situation a new man who did not exist before but who exists now, being identical with the man who has heard the Word. Again, that would not be the blessing of God's Word which as *benedictio* was not immediately and as such seen and understood to be *beneficium* as well, a real placing under God's good-pleasure and protection.

We find all this expressed in the strongest imaginable way in Jas. 1[18], where (cf. also 1 Pet. 1[23]) there is reference to the fact that the Christian is begotten of the λόγος ἀληθείας. Then v. 21 goes on logically to speak of a λόγος ἔμφυτος, i.e., a λόγος which, so to speak, belongs to man himself, without which man would no longer be himself.

And because the word at issue is the Word of God, we must add explicitly that its efficacy, its power to change, is not just relative as in the case of other powers. It is not uncertain. It is not conditioned or restricted by the behaviour of other factors, e.g., man. All this may be true of what it effects in man, of what may be seen of its operation in the life of man. But it is not true of its operation in itself and as such. The power of the Word of God in itself and as such is absolute power.

" All flesh is as grass, and all the glory of man as the flower of grass. The grass withereth, and the flower thereof falleth away τὸ δὲ ῥῆμα κυρίου μένει εἰς τὸν αἰῶνα (1 Pet. 1[24f.]). The Word of God is not only the λόγος ζῶν ; it is also the λόγος μένων. It is an incorruptible seed, v. 23 : ὁ λόγος τοῦ θεοῦ ἐν ὑμῖν μένει is said in 1 Jn. 2[14] to the " young men," i.e., to those not yet proved (cf. the anointing that abideth in v. 27).

All this must be said of the Word of God because the Word of God is Jesus Christ and because its efficacy is not distinct from the lordship of Jesus Christ. He who hears God's Word is drawn thereby into the sphere of the real power of this lordship. There applies to him and for him everything the Word of God says as promise, claim, judgment and blessing. Preaching does not put it into effect ; preaching declares and confirms that it is in effect. It is proclamation of the Word of God when it proclaims it as something that is already in effect.

This is also and especially true of preaching among both coloured and white heathen. If this were not based on the axiomatic presupposition that its hearers are already set aside as heathen, that they are already drawn into Christ's sphere of power even as God's Word is proclaimed to them, in what way would this be any better than propaganda, in what sense would it be " mission," i.e., sending, in what way would it be the proclamation of the Word of God that takes place in faith ? Though we may have all conceivable and even very accurate ideas as to the convictions and circumstances of the hearers, nevertheless, when we preach to them in faith in the promise of the presence and efficacy of the Word of God and the Gospel, only one thing concerns us in relation to them : " Thou hast borne all sin."

Nor is it faith that puts in effect all that the Word of God tells us. Faith too, and faith especially, is faith in Jesus Christ. It is thus the recognition and confirmation that God's Word was already in effect even before we believed and quite apart from our believing. Faith particularly—and this is the element of truth in the older Lutheran doctrine of the *efficacia verbi extra usum*—lives by the power which is power before faith and without faith. It lives by the power which gives faith itself its object, and in virtue of this object its very existence. Baptism was instituted for this reason, as a sign of this true and supreme power of God's Word. As a real act on man, as an act of sovereign disposition, it proclaims for its part that man belongs to the sphere of Christ's lordship prior to all his experiences and decisions. Even before he can take up an attitude to God, God has taken up an attitude to him. Whatever attitude he may adopt, it will be done within and on the ground of the attitude that God has adopted to him. If he believes, this will be just a confirmation of the fact that he has God's promise and is claimed, judged and blessed by God. If he does not believe, this again will not be a possibility he can freely choose. He will sin against God's Word. He will not show himself to be free, but unfree. He will not choose, but will be rejected. He will grasp, not a possibility, but an impossibility. In a Word, in his very unbelief he will be measured by the Word of God and smitten by its power. The preceding attitude of God to him will make his unbelief unbelief, his sin sin. Only in the sphere of grace is there faith and unbelief, righteousness and sin. Only through the power of God's Word are there the two categories, those who are saved and those who are lost.

Ἰδοὺ οὗτος κεῖται εἰς πτῶσιν καὶ ἀνάστασιν πολλῶν ἐν τῷ Ἰσραήλ (Lk. 2[34]). The stone laid in Sion becomes a stumbling-block and rock of offence to some, " and whosoever believeth on him shall not be ashamed " (Rom. 9[33]). And Paul calls his preaching of the Gospel a Χριστοῦ εὐωδία τῷ θεῷ ἐν τοῖς σωζομένοις καὶ ἐν τοῖς ἀπολλομένοις, οἷς μὲν ὀσμὴ ἐκ θανάτου εἰς θάνατον, οἷς δὲ ὀσμὴ ἐκ ζωῆς εἰς ζωήν (2 Cor. 2[15f.]).

This whole consideration should not be restricted to the relation of the Word of God to the isolated individual as such. All that has been said applies *mutatis mutandis* to the relation of the Word of God to the human cosmos in general, or, concretely, to the relation of Church and history or Church and society. It is not the case that God has somewhere and somehow revealed Himself, that somewhere there is a Bible and somewhere a Church with its preaching and sacraments—but history and society stand apart from all this, unaffected, sovereign, following their own laws, and the Church must come as it were from outside, from a God who has remained alien to this cosmos, to represent and champion its cause, or the cause of its God, to this cosmos by attack or defence. It is not at all true that the Church is outside with God and the world is inside without God. Things can be seen thus only if the Bible and the Church are seen apart from the revelation that constitutes them or if the revelation itself is understood, with Schleiermacher, only as the distinctive beginning of the religion that is our own. But this is not recollecting the Word of God that has come and expecting the Word of God that will come. If by revelation we understand this Word of God, and if the Bible and the Church are understood in the light of this recollection and expectation, then as a totality, too, the world of men standing over against the Word of God must be considered as subject to a decisive alteration. But in this case the world cannot be held to its ungodliness by the Church ; it cannot be taken seriously in its ungodliness. So long and so far as the Church holds it to this, it simply shows that it does not believe seriously in the Word of God. If it did, it would have to reckon concretely with its power. It is not, of course, that man is claimed for God on the basis of a relic of his relationship and commitment to God by creation, as though the fall had not been so radical in its consequences. It is not a question of natural theology but very much indeed of supernatural theology. But such a theology, bearing in mind the power of God's Word, will have to claim the world, history, and society as the world, history and society in the midst of which Christ was born and died and rose again. Not in the light of nature but in the light of grace, there is no self-enclosed and protected secular sphere, but only one which is called in question by God's Word, by the Gospel, by God's claim, judgment and blessing, and which is only provisionally and restrictedly abandoned to its own legalism and its own gods. What the Word says stands whatever the world's attitude to it and whether it redound to it for salvation or perdition.

'Ἐγένετο ἡ βασιλεία τοῦ κόσμου τοῦ κυρίου ἡμῶν καὶ τοῦ Χριστοῦ αὐτοῦ καὶ βασιλεύσει εἰς τοὺς αἰῶνας τῶν αἰώνων (Rev. 11¹⁵). Just because it is eschatological this ἐγένετο must be taken very literally and seriously. Christ does not have to become but already is βασιλεὺς βασιλέων καὶ κύριος τῶν κυρίων (Rev. 19¹⁶ ; cf. Phil. 2⁹ᶠ· ; Col. 2¹⁵ ; Eph. 1²¹).

The world, then, cannot evolve into agreement with God's Word on its own initiative nor can the Church achieve this by its work in and on the world. The Church is the Church as it believes and proclaims that prior to all secular developments and prior to all its own work the decisive word has in fact been spoken already regarding both itself and also the world. The world no longer exists in isolation or neutrality *vis-à-vis* revelation, the Bible, and proclamation. Whether it believes or not, whether it develops in this way or that, whether the Church exerts greater influence or less, whether it consists of millions of confessors and proclaimers or whether only two or three are gathered together in Christ's name—whatever becomes of the Church and the world the only thing that can matter is the event that follows the decisive word already spoken.

Sermo enim Dei venit mutaturus orbem, quoties venit (Luther, *De servo arb.*, 1525, *W.A.*, 18, p. 626, l. 26).

If the Church believes what it says it believes, then it is the place where the victory of Jesus Christ is not the last word to be heard and passed on but the first. For this reason and in this sense it is the place of revelation, of mercy and of peace, the hill of Zion to which the heathen, wittingly and willingly or not, are on the way. The Church which is this place will have something to say to the world and will be taken seriously by the world. In relation to what has been said here it is as well to remember that the power at issue is the power of the Word, the power rule, the power of God. All this distinguishes it from other powers, its efficacy from any other efficacy, its effect from any other effect. Precisely here it should not be forgotten that the Word of God is and remains the speech of God, and its power, which is not to be confused with any other power, is thus the power of truth. The fact that the truth, which is directly associated with grace in Jn. $1^{14f'}$, is also power is something we can state without reservation in the present context.

3. The fact that the Word of God is the act of God means thirdly that it is decision. This is what distinguishes an act from a mere event. Considered in itself a mere event is an occurrence subject to some higher necessity. It is occasioned by a cause. Beside it all the other events in whose nexus it occurs help to condition it. It is a cause because it is caused and as other things cause and are caused along with it. This is true of events in nature and also of those in the individual and corporate life of man. It is a mere hypothesis to call an event a deed, a decision, an act of free choice. At all events this predicate is not intrinsic to the concept of event. This must be remembered when the concept of the Word of God is connected with that of history. No doubt this must be done. According to all that we have said about the contingent contemporaneity of the Word of God and its power of rule, the Word of God is also historical, temporal event. But if it were only event, its character as act or decision would be as hypothetical as is the case with all the other things we usually allege to be such. The Word of God is not to be understood as history first and then and as such as decision too. It is to be understood primarily and basically as decision and then and as such as history too. If we think in terms of an act that might be interpreted equally well or even

better as a mere event, an act which takes place out of a higher necessity and which is conditioned by other acts on the right hand and the left, we are thinking of the ambivalent thing that is usually called an act in the human sphere ; we are not thinking of the Word of God. If we let ourselves be blinded by the circumstance that the Word of God is also, of course, a human act in Jesus Christ, in the Bible and in proclamation, and conclude from this that it is only a human act and is thus implicated in the unavoidable dialectic of human act and mere event, if we see it in the half-light of this dialectic, then *eo ipso* we are not thinking of the Word of God. The Word of God is first understood as decision or it is not understood at all. We might also say quite simply : as divine act. As divine act, even though it is a human act too, it is distinguished from all human acts by the fact that it is not affected by the *sic et non* of that dialectic. It is also human act, and as such it is also event, but as act and event it is free, as free as God Himself, for indeed God Himself is in the act. God is the Lord. There is no one and nothing above Him and no one and nothing beside Him, either on the right hand or the left, to condition Him or to be in a nexus with Him. God is *a se*. This is unreservedly true of His Word too. But God's aseity is not empty freedom. In God all potentiality is included in His actuality and therefore all freedom in His decision. Decision means choice, exercised freedom. We understand the Word of God very badly in isolation from the unconditional freedom in which it is spoken, but we also understand it very badly if we regard it as a mere possibility rather than freedom exercised, a decision made, a choice taking place. A choice taking place : In the humanity of Christ, in the Bible and in proclamation the Word of God is also a human act and it is thus a temporal event. But it is by choice that the Word of God is identical with the humanity of Christ, Holy Scripture, and proclamation, and is thus a temporal event. Both together, the choice and the event, make the Word of God the act of God as distinct from all other acts. The fact that the Word of God is the act of God and is thus a choice that takes place, a decision that is made, a freedom that is exercised, has the following concrete implications.

(*a*) The Word of God is not a reality in the way that a phenomenon is real if it is commensurate with our sense perceptions and our understanding. Nor is it a reality in the same way as the so-called laws of nature, which in a transformed perspective are also the laws of the spiritual world. Nor is it a reality in the sense of the axioms of mathematics and physics in so far as there are such. Nor is it a reality like the reality that I am I and not thou, or thou art thou and not I, or yesterday is not to-day and will never be to-morrow. It is not a reality in the sense that the structure of the so-called character and so-called destiny of each of us, down to the tiniest details, is probably a

cosmically (yes, cosmically !) predetermined reality which may perhaps
be read on our palms, or perhaps in our features, or our handwriting,
or the conjunction of the stars at our birth. In short, it is not a
reality in the same way as the totality of what we otherwise call
reality is real, even although it has a share in this reality and meets
us precisely in this reality. It is not reality in this way because unlike
all other reality it is not universally, i.e., always and everywhere
present, and hence it is not universally, i.e., always and everywhere
ascertainable. One cannot even say that at least it might be thus
present and ascertainable *mutatis mutandis*. The distinctive thing here
is the absence of this " might," of the potentiality in virtue of which
many comparable entities could be adduced. It is quite impossible to
say that the Word of God " might " be universally present and
ascertainable. This " might " always characterises a created reality
distinct from God in His aseity and actuality. The Word of God is
uncreated reality, identical with God Himself. Hence it is not
universally present and ascertainable, not even potentially. Never in
any circumstances can it be universally present and ascertainable.
Always in all circumstances the Word of God is reality in our reality
suo modo, sua libertate, sua misericordia. Consequently it is present and
ascertainable only contingently—again *suo modo*.

This is why there are times when a revelation from Yahweh is rare according
to 1 Sam. 3[1]. This is why we find such remarkable prophecies as Am. 8[11] :
" Behold, the days come, saith the Lord God, that I will send a famine and thirst
in the land, so that all its inhabitants mourn, not a famine of bread, nor a thirst
for water, but of hearing the words of the Lord, so that they shall wander from
sea to sea, and from the north even to the east, they shall run to and fro to
seek the word of the Lord, and shall not find it," and Mic. 3[6] : " Therefore night
shall be unto you, that ye shall not have a vision ; and it shall be dark unto you,
that ye shall not divine ; and the sun shall go down over the prophets, and the
day shall be dark over them. Then shall the seers be ashamed, and the diviners
confounded : yea, they shall all cover their lips ; for there is no answer of God."
For the prophets and others singled out by Yahweh, as for all Israel and the
individual Israelite throughout the Old Testament (not excepting even Ps. 119
and the later canonical literature generally), the concept of the word or law or
command or direction or order or claim of Yahweh thus implies an event that it
is to be expected and besought from Yahweh and revealed by Him, not one that
takes place by immanent necessity, and especially not a higher state of affairs
that is universally present and ascertainable. And for the same reason the
being of the true light in the world is described in the New Testament as an
ἔρχεσθαι εἰς τὸν κόσμον (Jn. 1[9]), as an ἀποκαλύπτεσθαι or φανεροῦσθαι. We again
have in mind here the connexion between revelation and the divine εὐδοκία. Ὅπου
θέλει πνεῖ (Jn. 3[8]) applies indeed to God's Word as well as God's Spirit. All this
plainly means that the Word of God is decision.

It is real, and can be understood as real, if and when it gives itself,
and gives itself to be understood. The question : What is God's Word ?
is utterly hopeless if it is the question as to the category in which God's

Word is to be put or the syllogism by which it might be proved. Questions of category and syllogism obviously presuppose that the Word of God is one of the realities that are universally present and ascertainable and therefore created. All concepts tending in this direction, even that of a supreme being, an *ens perfectissimum* or an unconditioned, even that of the breaking through and knowledge of such a supreme being, are not as such—as general concepts—the concept of the Word of God. As general concepts, they suppress the essential point that the Word of God is a reality only in its own decision. The fact that the Word of God is decision means that there is no concept of the Word of God apart from the name of God, which we love and fear and worship because it is identical with the Bearer of the name.

(*b*) Because the Word of God, unlike created realities, is not universally present and ascertainable, and cannot possibly be universally present and ascertainable, therefore, as decision, it always implies choice in relation to man. The Word of God is an act of God which takes place *specialissime*, in this way and not another, to this or that particular man.

" Before I formed thee in the belly I knew thee ; and before thou camest forth out of the womb I sanctified thee, and I ordained thee a prophet unto the nations " (Jer. 1⁵, cf. Is. 49¹). This is, of course, the concept of prophetic election, to which the only thing to correspond generally in the Old Testament is the election of Israel among the nations, which in Deutero-Isaiah is remarkably enough associated with the election of the individual prophet and Servant of the Lord. But in the New Testament the terms ἐκλέγεσθαι, ἐκλογή, ἐκλεκτός, undoubtedly in correspondence with καλεῖν etc., are also used of individual believers as such, and this in such a way that ἐκλέγεσθαι or προορίζειν is the presupposition of καλεῖν (Rom. 8³⁰), whereas not every καλεῖν has a corresponding ἐκλέγεσθαι.

This choice takes place as the Word is spoken and received : the choice of grace to faith and its righteousness or the choice of gracelessness to unbelief and its sin. The *vocatio* can take place *efficaciter*, *efficacissime*, and yet the *electio* effected therein may be *rejectio*, i.e., the Word may be spoken and received and yet the choice which takes place therein may be the choice of gracelessness.

Πολλοὶ γάρ εἰσιν κλητοί, ὀλίγοι δὲ ἐκλεκτοί (Mt. 22¹⁴). This critical relationship between κλῆσις and ἐκλογή is undoubtedly in view when Mt. 24⁴⁰f· and Lk. 17³⁴f· refer to the two who are together in the field, or sleeping in one bed, or grinding at one mill, and it has then to be said of them : ὁ εἷς παραλημφθήσεται, καὶ ὁ ἕτερος ἀφεθήσεται. We also recall the parable of the four different soils where the seed is expressly called the Word of God and the general exposition in Mk. 4¹¹ says specifically : " Unto you it is given to know the mystery of the kingdom of God ; but unto them that are without, all these things are done in parables, ἵνα βλέποντες βλέπωσιν καὶ μὴ ἴδωσιν, καὶ ἀκούοντες ἀκούωσιν καὶ μὴ συνιῶσιν, μήποτε ἐπιστρέψωσιν καὶ ἀφεθῇ αὐτοῖς.

Under the heading of the power of God's Word to rule, we have referred already to the twofold possibility of its operation. The inner ground of this twofold possibility is that it is decision and therefore choice. Do we have to know an inner reason for the choice, a vindication of God for the freedom He takes and enjoys, when speaking to man, now to accept and now to reject him, to illumine one with His light and to blind the other with the same light, to treat the one as Peter and the other as Judas ? By way of justification one need say no more than in the case of the general dogma of predestination disclosed here, namely, that the decision taken in the Word is God's decision and therefore it is a just and good decision. It is a decision to which the hidden reality of the relation existing between Jesus Christ and Peter or Jesus Christ and Judas certainly corresponds exactly, but the main point is that it is intrinsically justified as a divine decision. It is a fact that we may hear the Word of God and hear it again, and we may hear it correctly, accepting its promise as promise, obeying its claim as claim, submitting to its judgment, receiving its blessing, finding in it—in it and not in ourselves—the substance on which we feed and by which we live, or we may not hear it correctly, but only seem to accept, obey, submit and receive, so that we have to go on living without it as our sustenance. We may know the one or the other or both. But what we must know is that it is the Word of truth itself that decides as to the " correctly " or " not correctly," i.e., that we receive either grace or judgment as they come from God, and therefore come by right.

(c) As divine decision the Word of God works on and in a decision of the man to whom it is spoken. What does the revelation attested in Holy Scripture and proclaimed in preaching and sacrament say to me ? What is revealed to me in it ? " God with us " is how we stated generally the content of God's Word. But when this " God with us " is said to me and heard by me, without ceasing to be the content of the Word, without changing as such, as the living and inalterable content of the Word it must now reach its goal in my variously fashioned and conditioned situation over against it, in the qualification effected in me by the Word that God speaks to me. This new qualification of mine is the decision as to my faith or unbelief, my obedience or disobedience, i.e., the divine decision as to whether my act is faith or unbelief, obedience or disobedience, correct or incorrect hearing. This decision arises only in face of the Word of God spoken to me, only as the reply to it.

It is not a specific instance among the possibilities of human decision in general. Hence it cannot be pre-understood within the sphere of a general anthropology. Even the most radical crisis in which man may find himself as he views himself from the standpoint of general anthropology has nothing whatever to do with this crisis. For even in the most radical of general human crises man also discovers himself as the one who can select his own possibility. Decision does not come upon him ; he himself makes a decision. And this individual behaviour of his is the true and primary revelation of God. (Cf. on this H. E. Eisenhuth, *Das Irrationale als philosophisches Problem*, 1931, especially the closing section pp. 260–67, which perhaps follows through to the end, i.e., reduces *ad absurdum*, a theological use of the philosophy of M. Heidegger.) From this standpoint there can be neither faith nor unbelief, neither obedience nor disobedience, nor decision between them. The very possibility of faith or unbelief, obedience or disobedience, in relation to God's Word can be dealt with only in the framework of a theological anthropology.

As God's Word itself is revelation, i.e., a new word for me, so the situation in which it sets me as it is spoken to me is an absolutely new situation which cannot be seen or understood in advance, which cannot be compared with any other, which is grounded in the Word of God and in this alone. It is, of course, a situation of decision. But this is not the decision of my own particular resolve and choice (though there is a place for these too). It is a decision of being judged and accepted. And because the particular judgment and acceptance are God's, it is a decision of my particular reality, of the particular meaning of my resolve and choice. Just because the Word of God means " God with us," just because it is the Word of the Lord, of our Creator, Reconciler and Redeemer, it obviously pronounces our judgment to us. In it, it is decided who we are. We are what we are on the basis of this judgment, what we are as its hearers, i.e., we are believers or unbelievers, obedient or disobedient. Previously and *per se* we are neither the one nor the other. Previously and *per se* we do not even have the possibility of being either the one or the other. Faith and unbelief, obedience and disobedience, are possible only to the extent that, as our act, they are our particular reply to the judgment of God pronounced to us in His Word. In faith and obedience my resolve and choice is truly good before God. Whatever else may have to be said about me, I exist in correspondence to God's Word. I have received and accepted His grace. In unbelief and disobedience my own resolve and choice, whatever else may have to be said about me, is truly bad before God. I exist in contradiction to God's Word. I have not accepted His grace. Either way it is I—this is really my own supremely responsible decision. But it is not in my decision that it acquires the character of being a good choice on the one hand or a bad one on the other. The implication of this decision of mine taken with my own free will, namely, the step either to the right hand or to the left, the choice to believe and obey or the refusal to do either—this qualification of my decision is the truth within it of the divine decision concerning me. In speaking to me God has chosen me, as the man I am, to be the man I am. The new quality I acquire through the Word of God is my true and essential quality. I cannot give myself this true and essential quality. Only

God can judge me. I am wholly and altogether the man I am in virtue of the divine decision. In virtue of the divine decision I am a believer or an unbeliever in my own decision. In this decision whereby it is decided who I am in my own decision and whereby it is decided what my own decision really means—in this realisation of my reality, this bringing of our works to light (Jn. 3[20f.]; Eph. 5[12f.]), the Word of God is consummated as the act of God. It is always the act of the inscrutable judgment of God.

4. THE SPEECH OF GOD AS THE MYSTERY OF GOD

In order to refer everything that has been said from the standpoint of " speech-act " to the truly decisive point, that in everything our concern is with God's speech and God's act, we must now speak of the Word of God in a third series of attributes. In what has been said already we have constantly sought to set forth delimitations along these lines. But when we consider all the concepts : spiritual, personal and purposive character, contemporaneity, power to rule and decision, the question can continually arise whether we might not be speaking of some other logos, whether we are really speaking of God's Logos. Or there might be a continual temptation to think and speak of the Logos of God as thus described in the same way as we think and speak of some other spiritual factor that may be hard to grasp but can in fact be grasped, namely, in such a way that we think we know it—and the harder the work, the better and surer the knowledge—that we think we perceive its structure and understand its operation, so that in thought and speech at least we are its master, as well or as badly as man may become the master of any object of thought or speech.

At this point I should introduce a word of caution which can, of course, be given only a basis in experience, which can be understood only in terms of experience, and which it is thus easy to disregard. Continually raising it in relation to myself, I raise it to some degree in respect of all my older and younger theological contemporaries, especially in so far as they are engaged in what is called " systematic " theology. Serious theological work is an ideal on the lips of all of us. It seems that not only the Bible but also the fathers of Protestantism and the early Church are again speaking to us with greater emphasis. The great concepts of God, Word, Spirit, revelation, faith, church and sacrament, etc., have again come into our field of vision. We see again that great tasks are posed here for theology. Many of us already know how to speak of these things very cleverly, clearly and definitely. In many places theological dialogue has been initiated in a surprisingly intensive way. One can only rejoice at being a theologian in this time of ours. But it may be feared that we are all on the point of becoming much too positive. I am not thinking of the questionable and partisan meaning of the word, which is now obsolete, though something of the pathos of the earlier " positive " theology certainly lives on, or has come to life again, in what I am calling positive here. I am thinking rather of a certain assurance of voice, speech

and attitude with which, it seems, we think we can work on the new or older
field, a certain confidence with which we think we can take those great concepts
on our lips and analyse them and interrelate them constructively or in other ways,
a certain sprightliness with which we speak about the things denoted by them as
though we were speaking about them because we know how to speak about
them with comparatively so little freedom from restriction.   And this assurance,
confidence and sprightliness are perhaps all the greater because we are clever
enough to include an element of uncertainty or comforted despair or even a line
of death or the like in our more or less spiritual calculations.   Is it clear to our
generation in life as well as thought that the serious element in serious theological
work is grounded in the fact that its object is never in any circumstances at our
command, at the command of even the profoundest biblical or Reformation
vision or knowledge, at the command of even the most delicate and careful
construction ?   Absolutely any theological possibility can as such be pure
threshing of straw and waste of energy, pure comedy and tragedy, pure deception
and self-deception.   Even the most zealous amassing of theological treasures is
certainly mere folly without that being " rich toward God " (Lk. 12^{21}) which
none can manufacture for himself and none maintain.   A theology which is sure
in faith, i.e., sure of its object, can as little be without awareness of this danger
as clockwork without a pendulum.   And this awareness needs to be perceptible.
It needs to make theological thinking and utterance fruitful and full of content in
a proper sense.   To what extent may it be seen in the theological production of
our day ?   To what extent is that assurance, confidence and sprightliness, that
leaven of the positive and of positive theologians, compatible with this awareness ?   To what extent is our theological dialogue no real discourse ?   *C'est le
ton qui fait la musique.*   One cannot discuss tone in general, nor yet the tone
which can make discussion real discourse, and especially not with those to whom
we think ourselves closest at this point.   I fancy I can hear already the lamenta-
tion and the jeering and the " certainly—but " with which these lines will be
received.   Nevertheless, must it not be said again and again : Beware of this
leaven?

It would obviously confirm our question, and we should really be
speaking of another logos than the Logos of God, if we thought that in
face of this question we could and should prove that we have not
deceived ourselves, that we have really been speaking of the Logos of
God.   Thinking we can prove this in some sense, we should really
betray the cause, or rather betray the fact that we have confused this
cause with some other.   For if anything at all serious was intended in
what we said previously, we must accept the fact that only the Logos of
God Himself can provide the proof that we are really talking about Him
when we are allegedly doing so.   And we should have succumbed
already to the afore-mentioned temptation if we were to look about for
some means to ward it off, to secure ourselves against it, and to make
ourselves immune to temptation.   For it would be a highly refined
way of becoming master of God's Word to think we could put ourselves
in a position in which we have securely adopted the right attitude to it,
that of servant and not master.   Would not this be the loftiest triumph
of human certainty ?   But would it not be a confirmation of the
question and a fall into the temptation ?   For what would it imply if we

had made, or were in process of making, that delimitation of the divine from the human ? If we could do this, we should have said, or should be saying, what the Word of God is. The goal of all yearning in theology is to be able to do this, but this is the goal of an illegitimate yearning. The object of all pride in theology is to think one can really do this, but undoubtedly this is the object of an unhealthy pride. For according to all that we can know of the how of the Word of God, one thing is ruled out. It cannot be an entity which we can demarcate from other entities and thereby objectify, even though we do it with supreme humility and discretion. Certainly it is delimited from all other entities ; it is objective and *sui generis*. God's speech is different from all other speech and God's action is different from all other action. But do we not deny this very distinction if we think we can possess and apply a measure of this distinction ? Is it not a property of the other entities which are not identical with God's Word that we can more or less clearly distinguish them from one another and objectify them ? Is not this a sign that we can perceive and understand and ultimately master and control them, because finally we are on the same plane as they are ? Would the Word of God be *sui generis* if we could describe *suum genus* and allot it a fixed place as very much the " wholly other " ? Is not the Word of God *sui generis*, God's Word, just because we cannot do this, because it does it itself and it alone ? This is why even in the delimitations already prescribed we cannot, as it were, give the Word of God its own sphere in the world which is known to us and which is to be conceptually classified by us. All our delimitations can only seek to be signals or alarms to draw attention to the fact that God's Word is and remains God's, not bound and not to be attached to this thesis or to that antithesis. A sketch of the concept such as the philosopher would like has not emerged and should not do so. Only God conceives of Himself, even in His Word. Our concept of God and His Word can only be an indication of the limits of our conceiving, an indication which must not be allowed to condense into a negative proof. This cannot be our concern even now when we must give added sharpness to the decisive point that the Word of God is God's Word. We can sharpen this here only by remembering again and explicitly our own limits, only by making it even clearer to ourselves that we cannot utter even a wretched syllable about the how of God's Word unless the Word of God is spoken to us as God's Word, which means spoken to us in such a way that all we think and say about its how has its substance not in itself but outside itself in the Word of God, so that what we think and say about this how can never become the secret system of a what. It is for this reason and in this sense that we finally speak of the Word of God as the mystery of God. The issue is not an ultimate " assuring " but always a penultimate " de-assuring " of theology, or, as one might put it, a theological warning against theology, a warning against the idea that its propositions or principles are certain in themselves like the supposed axioms of the mathematicians and physicists, and are not rather related to their theme and content, which alone are certain, which they cannot master, by which they must be mastered if they are not to be mere soap-bubbles.

In using the term mystery to sum up what we have to say here we have in view the meaning of the word " mystery " in the New Testament. Mystery does not just denote the hiddenness of God but His revelation in a hidden, i.e., a non-apparent way which intimates indirectly rather than directly. Mystery is the concealment of God in which He meets us precisely when He unveils Himself to us, because He will not and cannot unveil Himself except by veiling Himself. Mystery thus denotes the divine givenness of the Word of God which also fixes our own limits and by which it distinguishes itself from everything that is given otherwise. Distinguishes itself ? This means that we cannot establish its distinction. Otherwise it would not be a mystery. It distinguishes itself by giving itself to us in this way and this alone ; not in such a way that we can arrive at a triumphant distinction, but in such a way that there is reserved for it the right to distinguish itself.

1. The speech of God is and remains the mystery of God supremely in its secularity. When God speaks to man, this event never demarcates itself from other events in such a way that it might not be interpreted at once as part of these other events. The Church is also in fact a sociological entity with definite historical and structural features. Preaching is also in fact an address. The sacrament is also in fact a symbol in compromising proximity to all other possible symbols. The Bible is also in fact the historical record of a Near Eastern tribal religion and its Hellenistic offshoot. Jesus Christ is also in fact the Rabbi of Nazareth who is hard to know historically and whose work, when He is known, might seem to be a little commonplace compared to more than one of the other founders of religions and even compared to some of the later representatives of His own religion. Nor should we forget that theology also, in so far as it uses human speech, is in fact a philosophy or a conglomerate of all kinds of philosophies. Even the biblical miracles do not break through this wall of secularity. From the moment they took place they were interpreted otherwise than as proofs of God's Word, and obviously they can always be interpreted in a very different way. The veil is thick. We do not have the Word of God otherwise than in the mystery of its secularity.

This means, however, that we have it in a form which as such is not the Word of God and which as such does not even give evidence that it is the form of the Word of God. In other words the self-presentation of God in His Word is not direct, nor is it indirect in the way in which a man's face seen in a mirror can be called an indirect self-presentation of this man,

When Paul speaks of a βλέπειν δι' ἐσόπτρου in 1 Cor. 13¹² the addition ἐν αἰνίγματι should be noted. He is pointing out that we have here a twofold indirectness of vision. First the Word of God meets us in a form that is to be distinguished from its content, and secondly the form as such is an enigma, a concealing of the Word of God. The relevant concept here is that of paradox. A paradox is a communication which is not only made by a δόξα, a phenomenon, but which must be understood, if it is to be understood at all, παρὰ τὴν δόξαν, i.e., in antithesis to what the phenomenon itself seems to be saying. Just because the Word of God alone fulfils the concept of paradox in full rigour, whereas in all other conceivable paradoxes the antithesis between communication and form is such that it can be dissolved from a superior point of vantage, it is to be recommended that theology make more sparing use of the term now that it has played its part, and also caused all manner of confusion.

The self-presentation of God in His Word is not comparable with any other self-presentation, for every other self-presentation that meets us is either direct communication or, if indirect, it is characterised by a certain similarity and correspondence between matter and form, a feature which makes it possible, as when a face is seen in a mirror, to dissolve the indirect into direct communication or knowledge. This is the very thing that is ruled out in the case of God's Word. Its form is not a suitable but an unsuitable medium for God's self-presentation. It does not correspond to the matter but contradicts it. It does not unveil it but veils it. The secularity of the Word of God does not imply only that it meets us in the garment of creaturely reality. Because this creaturely reality is that of fallen man and because the Word of God meets us in this reality, we have to say that its form is not that of a pure nature which as such stands in immediate contrast with the distorted nature of its environment. Even our knowledge of the Word of God is not through a reason that has somehow remained pure and that can thus pierce the mystery of God in creaturely reality. It is wholly through our fallen reason. The place where God's Word is revealed is objectively and subjectively the cosmos in which sin reigns. The form of God's Word, then, is in fact the form of the cosmos which stands in contradiction to God. It has as little ability to reveal God to us as we have to see God in it. If God's Word is revealed in it, it is revealed " through it," of course, but in such a way that this " through it " means " in spite if it." The secularity proper to God's Word is not in itself and as such transparent or capable of being the translucent garment or mirror of God's Word. And in face of it there can never be any question of getting behind it by any effort or skill and of perceiving that the secularity is precisely that of God's Word. What can be brought to light by interpretation or exegesis of this part of the world will always be itself a hidden part of the world, since it is in our own interpretation and exegesis that we try to find aid, and this part in turn will need fresh interpretation and exegesis, will ultimately resist all solution, and will thus be a contradiction of God's Word and not a

---

complement of God's Word and therefore its simple reflection. The real interpretation of its form can only be that which God's Word gives itself.

The passage which we can hardly take too seriously in this connexion is 1 Cor. 1¹⁸-2¹⁰. What Paul preaches is ὁ λόγος ὁ τοῦ σταυροῦ, Χριστὸς ἐσταυρωμένος, which is indeed the power and wisdom of God, by which God turns the wisdom of the world into folly, but which as such, from the world's standpoint, can only be μωρία, which stamps its proclaimers and hearers as foolish, weak and lowly, as nothings (μὴ ὄντα), which as σοφία ἐν μυστηρίῳ ἡ ἀποκεκρυμμένη can enlighten only by divine election, by the ἀπόδειξις πνεύματος καὶ δυνάμεως, by ἀποκάλυψις, " that no flesh should glory in his presence, " that your faith should not stand in the wisdom of men but in the power of God." What God has prepared for those that love Him, no eye has seen, nor ear heard, nor has it entered the heart of any man. It is the Spirit given by God that knows it, no one and nothing else. *Quia mirandum est, idcirco non creditur. Qualia enim decet esse opera divina, nisi super omnem admirationem ? Nos quoque ipsi miramur, sed quia credimus. . . . Nam si Deus et sapiens et potens . . . merito in adversariis sapientiae potentiaeque id est in stultitia et impossibilitate materias operationis suae instituit ; quoniam virtus omnis ex his causam accipit a quibus provocatur* (Tertullian, *De bapt.*, 2). At issue is the insight which in the Heidelberg Disputation of 1518 (*W.A.*, 1, p. 362 f.) Luther opposes as a *theologia crucis* to a *theologia gloriae*, i.e., a direct or only relatively indirect desire for knowledge of God. W. von Loewenich (*Luthers Theologia crucis*, 1929, p. 7 and 12) has rightly concluded that we do not have here merely a special chapter in theology but a special form of theology, and not just a principle of the younger Luther but a principle of his whole theology. *I am adhuc agimus cum Deo velato, in hac enim vita non possumus cum Deo agere facie ad faciem. Universa autem creatura est facies et larva Dei. Sed hic requiritur sapientia quae discernat Deum a larva. Hanc sapientiam mundus non habet, ideo non potest discernere Deum a larva* (*Comm. on Gal.* 2⁶, 1535, *W.A.*, 40¹, p. 174, l. 12). At a pinch a Roman Catholic theologian brought up on Plato or Aristotle might have said the same in an application of the doctrine of the *analogia entis*. (There is thus no point in following K. Heim and his disciples, who out of such statements about the character of all creation as *larva Dei* concoct a new and particularly profound conception of the world on Luther's part.) The core of Luther's idea is that the *larva Dei*, the indirectness of His self-communication, is twofold, one due to the creatureliness and another due to the sinfulness of the creature : *ut ergo fidei locus sit, opus est, ut omnia quae creduntur, abscondantur. Non autem remotius absconduntur, quam sub contrario obiectu, sensu, experientia. Sic Deus dum vivificat, facit illud occidendo ; dum iustificat, facit illud reos faciendo ; dum in coelum vehit, facit id ad infernum ducendo* (*De serv. arb.*, 1525, *W.A.*, 18, p. 633, l. 7). " The Word I hear, and I see Paul, who is a poor man. But this salvation, grace, life and peace, these I see not ; but rather their counterparts I must see daily, sin, terror, ill-luck, suffering and death ; that it seemeth there are no men so abandoned by God as Christians, so they hear this Word " (*Sermon on Ac.* 13²⁶ᶠ·, *E.A.*, 8, p. 191). And even more pointedly : *Nam fides ita dicit : Ego credo tibi Deo loquenti. Quid loquitur Deus? Impossibilia, mendatia, stulta, infirma, absurda, abominanda, haeretica et diabolica, si rationem consulas* (on *Gal.* 3⁶, 1525, *W.A.*, 40¹, p. 361, l. 14). And finally with almost unheard-of sharpness : " Therefore must God's faithfulness and truth even become first a great lie ere it become the truth. For to the world 'tis a heresy. So seemeth it ever to ourselves as if God would leave us and not keep His Word and in our heart He looketh to become a liar. And in fine God cannot be God, He must first become a devil, and we cannot come up to heaven, we must first go down to hell, we cannot become God's children, we must first become the devil's children. For all that God saith and doth, the devil must have said and done " (*Ps.* 117 *expounded*, 1530, *W.A.*, 31¹, p. 249, l. 21).

Thus in all applications of the proposition that proclamation, Scripture or revelation is God's Word we must have regard to the fact that this is true only in this twofold indirectness. In the speaking and receiving of God's Word what is involved is not just an act of God generally, and not just an act of God in creaturely reality as such, but an act of God in the reality which contradicts God, which conceals Him, and in which His revelation is not just His act but His miraculous act, the tearing of an untearably thick veil, i.e., His mystery.

This means that we are not to frame Church proclamation in such a way that within the cosmos it seems to be a necessary element in culture, education, national development, social progress, etc. We are not to try to show that the Bible is a credible and commendable book from various human standpoints, as was usually done in the age of orthodoxy and the Enlightenment (unfortunately even Calvin did something of the same incidentally in *Instit.*, I, 8), and as has been attempted with all the tools of historical thinking from the days of Herder. Above all, we should on principle spare revelation itself, i.e., Jesus Christ, all our direct or relatively indirect desire to prove its superiority over all other religions (cf. K. Holl, " Urchristentum und Religionsgeschichte," 1925, in *Ges. Aufsätze zur Kirchengesch.*, II, p. 1 f.). In the long run a purely historical treatment of Christianity will always prove to be theologically more fruitful here than these attempts at penetration which purport to be historical but which ultimately rest on a confusion of categories.

One is not to think of the secularity of the Word of God as a kind of fatal accident or an inconvenience which will some day be set aside either totally or at least in part. This secularity, this twofold indirectness, is in fact an authentic and inalienable attribute of the Word of God itself. Revelation means the incarnation of the Word of God. But incarnation means entry into this secularity. We are in this world and are through and through secular. If God did not speak to us in secular form, He would not speak to us at all. To evade the secularity of His Word is to evade Christ. Even though it dawns on us for the first time what is meant by the fact that we are flesh and therefore not God, that we have no organ or capacity for God, that we are in enmity against Him and powerless to be obedient to Him, nevertheless, what seems in the first instance an absurd obstacle that God Himself has put in the way is in fact His real way to us, and consequently a necessary way and a good way. It is not as though we could see why it can and must be so. We are not above God or ourselves. Hence the only sentence we can pronounce on the necessity and goodness of the relation in which God has set Himself to us is one that seeks to reproduce the actuality of this relation. But we have nothing else to reproduce, and therefore we must repeat the fact that just as surely as God enters into relation with us through His Word, so surely His Word must be as it is, i.e., secular, a Word spoken in twofold indirectness. It is not, then, that God was concealed from us by some unfortunate disturbance and that He revealed Himself by removing the concealment. If this were so, the attempts of man to help God by forcing his own way into the mystery would be understandable and excusable if not actually necessary. The truth is, however, that God veils Himself and that in so doing—this is why we must not try to intrude into the mystery—He unveils Himself. It is good for us that God acts as He does and it could only be fatal for us if He did not, if He were manifest to us in the way we think right, directly and without veil, without secularity or only in the innocuous secularity that can be pierced by the *analogia entis*. It would not be love and mercy but the end of us and all things if the Word were spoken to us thus. The fact that it is spoken as it is, revealing in its concealment, is a decisive indication of the truth that it has really come to us instead of our having to go to it, an attempt in which we could only fail. In its very secularity it is thus in every respect a Word of grace.

Among other places in a powerful passage at the beginning of his *Commentary on Galatians* (*W.A.*, 40¹, p. 75 ff.) Luther has made it clear that this must distinguish us from the papacy, Turks, Jews, and all *justitiarii, ut abstineamus a speculatione Maiestatis*, which can only be harmful to both body and soul ; *scrutator enim Maiestatis opprimitur a gloria*. To want to know God directly means righteousness by works, and righteousness by works means the fall of Lucifer and despair. We, on the contrary, must cleave to the true and actual Christ as He lies in the crib and in the Virgin's lap. Calvin spoke similarly : *Quand donc nous n'aurions sinon la maiesté de Dieu qui se présentera devant nos yeux, elle sera pour nous effrayer et n'y pourrons pas avoir aucun acces à cause que nous sommes creatures fragiles, et mesmes qu'il n'y en nous que peché : nous campons ici sur la terre : mais nous sommes dignes d'estre engloutis iusques au profond d'enfer* (*Sermon on Gal.* 1³ᵗ·, *C.R.*, 50, 289). *Magnifions la bonte de nostre Dieu, veu qu'il luy plaist d'avoir regard à nous et à nostre rudesse, et qu'il est content que sa gloire nous soit cachée, afin que nous n'en soyons point abysmez. Car . . . nous ne la pouvons porter estans ainsi fragiles que nous sommes* (*Sermon on Deut.* 5⁴ᵗ·, *C.R.*, 26, 248). " Yea, if one feel it as actually 'tis in truth, man must straightway from that hour die. For man being flesh and blood cannot understand it, in life man's heart is much too strait to conceive of such. . . . (Luther, *Sermon on Mk.* 16¹⁻⁸, *Sommerpost.*, 1526, *W.A.*, 10¹, 2, p. 216, l. 19). " It is forbidden, I must not see, feel, know or see it, but only hear it, and with faith cleave to it, and stand on the mere Word of God. And it is with us as with one that hath dizziness in his head should he climb a high tower or come on to a bridge under which deep water floweth, so that he must be blinded and be led blindly and hang a cloak about his head, and be led and borne, else he falleth from the tower and breaketh his neck, or falleth into the water and drowneth. So, if we are to be saved, we must follow our guide, and then we are safe. We, too, must shut our eyes tight and follow our leader, the divine Word, and say : I will let myself be wound in swaddling clothes and a cloak be wrapped about my head, and let myself be led to that which I believe and see not, and will live and die thereon. Otherwise we shall not feel it even if we tear ourselves to pieces therefor. Many have troubled themselves sorely and would fain know where our dwelling or lodging is when we die, whither we are going, and many great people have become mad that they wot not where one goes on leaving this life, and have therefore coined this saying :

> I live and know not how long,
> I die and know not when,
> I go and know not whither,
> A wonder 'tis I'm glad.

And 'tis true a non-Christian cannot know, but a Christian must judge otherwise thereof, he hath a trusty conductor, he followeth his leader and guide, Christ, who telleth what a man should do, and saith : Hear what we speak, for we know what to say, our words are truth, trust me, give thyself over and lay thee in my cloak that I have wound about thy head, I will carry thee over. If thou doest thus, thou wilt not be misled by Him. But thou dost say, I know not whither I go, I feel nought, grope for and grasp nought. That is true, but thou must rely on God's Word and trust God who will uphold thee so that if thou fallest from the tower thou wilt not break thy neck in twain or if thou shyest from the ship and art like to drown. But there is nought there to see, we know not where the ladder or the steps are or the cord on which the ladder hangs, we can see no way that leadeth to heaven. But in Christ the way to heaven is alone prepared for us, which is reserved for us through the divine Word, otherwise thou treadest upon air and so fallest. . . . This then is the difference between a Christian and a pagan, that a godless man and a pagan departeth like a cow, seeing, judging and feeling all things according to the old birth as what he feels and grasps. But a Christian followeth not as he seeth, but followeth what he seeth not nor feeleth, and abideth by the witness of Christ, heareth what Christ saith, whom he followeth right on into the darkness. Thus we stay fast in the bag and are wound in His cloak and He leadeth us where Himself is and in Christ we walk up to heaven that maketh him blessed " (*Exposition of Jn.* 3–4, *W.A.*, 47, p. 33, l. 38). " Lo, 'tis this whereon St. John insisteth strongly in his Gospel, that we should simply let go of fair and lofty thoughts whereby reason and clever folk go about and seek God in majesty outside Christ. He is ready in Christ to lie in the cradle and in His mother's lap and to hang on the cross ; they would mount up to heaven and find out how He sits and rules the world. These are vain and fearful thoughts when not guided aright. For they are all bound to this one spot where we should not grope or peer further. Wouldest thou seize and grasp all that God is and doth and hath in mind, then seek it nowhere save where He hath put and laid it. Thou hearest that in the saying, ' All that is thine is mine,' etc. Thus a Christian ought to know not to seek or find God otherwise save in the Virgin's lap and on the cross or as and where Christ sheweth Himself in His Word " (*Sermon on Jn.* 16²⁰, 1528–29, *W.A.*, 28, p. 135, l. 38).

In direct connexion with these thoughts of Luther and Calvin we must now come back again to F. Gogarten. In the first edition of this book, apart from the absence of a " true anthropology," he has objected especially to the fact that in some parts at least " it now speaks of a God isolated in and for Himself over against man and now of a man isolated in and for himself over against God " (*Theol. Rundschau*, 1929, p. 72). This may be seen in the use of the terms " objective " and " subjective " in relation to God and man, and in the distinction between an " eternal history of God " and God's revelation as history or man addressed by God, between a " God in Himself " and a " God for us." But it is a mistake, he thinks, to presuppose that in theology we should start our thinking

" with the past incarnation of the Word." I can scarcely be wrong in assuming that in this attack Gogarten had in view Luther's polemic against *speculatio Maiestatis*, of which a few instances have just been given. True he does not actually accuse me of overlooking this warning of the Reformers. He rather quotes a series of passages from my own book in which I contradict myself by erasing the distinction. He even believes that the erasure of the distinction is my own true opinion and that I then contradict it by making the distinction. He claims " to see that Barth gets very close to these things. But in getting close to them, he already leaves them again " (p. 73). Gogarten advances two explanations for this error of mine. He suggests first that it is the result of working with untested and unpurified concepts instead of first reducing them to order in a true anthropology. These unpurified concepts progressively introduced alien problems into my thinking and thus spoiled the first draft (p. 78 f.). But at the close of his essay Gogarten makes the rather different point that it is clear to him that in the very thing to which he has to take exception there is to be noted the " true theological concern " of the book, namely, the effort to put the stress on " God Himself " in all dogmatic questions, an intention in which he is in full agreement with me (p. 79 f.). In reply, let me admit that he is right when he says that I make the alleged distinction only to abandon it again, or *vice versa* that I come very close to things (Gogarten obviously means the clear and definitive erasure of the distinction) and then leave them again. As regards " unpurified concepts," I again concede the fact, but can only repeat that I reject the whole enterprise of an anticipatory purifying of concepts in an anthropology of theologically dubious character, and that for my own part I can expect results only from a purifying which takes place in the process of the dogmatic enquiry and exposition itself. As for the " theological concern " which Gogarten sees at work even in my alleged error, and in which he associates himself with me in spite of my error, it would have been instructive if he had stated to what degree he thinks the error is based not merely on certain mishaps with unpurified concepts, for which perhaps only formal regrets are in order, but upon certain material ineluctabilities. Does he perhaps think that what he censures cannot be avoided if thought is to start theologically, and not philosophically, with " the past incarnation of the Word " ? On this basis theological thought is distinguished from philosophical thought by the fact that it does not regard the incarnation of the Word as the truth of a state, e.g., the truth of the unity of subject and object, of the man-relatedness of God or the God-relatedness of man, which is then an underlying principle of dogmatics that has to be exegeted—this is something Luther and the older Lutheran dogmaticians never did in spite of their rejection of *speculatio Maiestatis*—but regards it rather as the truth of a divine act. But if it is understood as an act, then the *terminus a quo* (" God in Himself ") and the *terminus ad quem* (" man in himself ") must be differentiated and then interrelated in the description of the act as such. What would " God for us " mean if it were not said against the background of " God in Himself " ? To erase the distinction, i.e., in order to speak about this particular matter, there has also to be differentiation in this matter. If we are not prepared to say the latter here, we can obviously say nothing when we say the former. We recall what was said under the second sub-section about the purposiveness or pertinence of the Word of God. We tried to emphasise there that we properly understand God's love for us only when we regard it as unmerited and free, and similarly the Word of God is properly understood only as a word which has truth and glory in itself and not just as spoken to us. It would be no less God's eternal Word if it were not spoken to us, and what constitutes the mercy of its revelation, of its being spoken to us, is that it is spoken to us in virtue of the freedom in which God could be " God in Himself " and yet He does not will to be so and in fact is not so, but wills to be and actually is " God for us." This freedom of God, without which one cannot understand His Word as grace, seems to me to be obscured if in too triumphant a victory over what is called Greek thought we abandon altogether the distinction between objective and subjective in the Word of God, as Gogarten obviously wishes to do.

At this stage I must recall another critical review of my book in which I am censured from the very opposite side. In *Stimmen der Zeit* (Nov. 1928, p. 105) Erich Przywara S.J. wrote that there is a sinister reduction running through my whole work. I am affirming the whole world of Christian revelation only to the extent that it is the one manifestation of the process of revelation as Kierkegaard conceived of it, namely, as God's address to man. With me the Trinity supposedly dissolves into that of revealer, revealing and being revealed, the incarnation is only a concretion of this process of revelation, and grace is simply the subjective possibility of revelation. All the fulness of the divine life is thus reduced to the one address, and in the last resort the final pantheistic correlation-theology of Protestant Liberalism is simply reversed in me. The " from below upwards " is changed into a " from above downwards." God is not now reduced to the nature of man but—and this obviously seems to be much worse in Przywara's opinion—man is exalted to the nature of God to the degree that the nature of God Himself is called the " address of revelation " . . . Now this is certainly not a correct estimation of my intentions nor of what I actually said. But the fact that a clever and slightly malicious eye like that of Przywara could see and interpret me in this way I regard as a warning not to go further in the direction desired by Gogarten. If we do not wish to be understood as Przywara (however wrongly) understands me here, we have to be very clear that we are not engaged in cor-relation-theology, i.e., in a theology in which God swings up or down in His relation to us, either from below upwards so that God becomes a predicate of man, or from above downwards so that man becomes a requisite in God's nature. In the thinking necessary in correlating God and man we must not think away the free basis that this correlation has in God, as Wobbermin and his disciple R. Winckler so obviously do, and as Bultmann in my view can hardly avoid doing. If we are not to do this, then it is not just good sense but absolutely essential that along with all older theology we make a deliberate and sharp distinction between the Trinity of God as we may know it in the Word of God revealed, written and proclaimed, and God's immanent Trinity, i.e., between " God in Himself " and " God for us," between the " eternal history of God " and His temporal acts. In so doing we must always bear in mind that the " God for us " does not arise as a matter of course out of the " God in Himself," that it is not true as a state of God which we can fix and assert on the basis of the concept of man participating in His revelation, but that it is true as an act of God, as a step which God takes towards man and by which man becomes the man that partic-ipates in His revelation. This becoming on man's part is conditioned from without, by God, whereas God in making the step by which the whole correlation is first fashioned is not conditioned from without, by man. For this reason—and we agree with Gogarten here—theology cannot speak of man in himself, in isolation from God. But as in the strict doctrine of the Trinity as the presupposition of Christology, it must speak of God in Himself, in isolation from man. We know ourselves only as those addressed by God's Word, but precisely as those addressed by God's Word we must know God as the One who addresses us in freedom, as the Lord, who does not exist only as He addresses us, but exists as the One who establishes and ratifies this relation and correlation, who is also God before it, in Himself, in His eternal history. If this principle, this recollection of the immanent objective God-ness of God in Himself in distinction from His God-ness for us, is already *speculatio Maiestatis*, then Luther himself engages in *speculatio*

Maiestatis when he compares the Word that was in the beginning, that was with God and was God (Jn. 1¹), to the way in which love or anger, even without being expressed or declared, can absolutely fill a man and constitute the entire nature of this man, and then continues : " According to this metaphor God in His majesty and nature is also pregnant with a word or utterance which God hath with Him in His divine nature and which is His heart's thought, which same is as complete and great and perfect as God Himself, none seeth, heareth nor conceiveth this utterance save God alone. He hath an invisible and inconceivable utterance which hath been word for all angels and for all creatures, for afterwards hath He through this utterance and word given their nature to all creatures ; in utterance, word and thought God is indeed burning, He thinking nought else therefor " (*Exposition of Jn.* 1–2, 1537–38, *W.A.*, 46, p. 545, 1. 6). But what connexion is there between this and the *speculatio Maiestatis* which Luther attacks in the *Commentary on Galatians* and elsewhere ? The attack is not on recognising and understanding the incarnate Word in all seriousness as God's Word. It is not on acknowledging its invisible majesty. It is not on the distinction between what we can see and feel and grasp by reason and what we must believe on the presupposition of this whole visible aspect. It is an attack on the attempt to evade the necessity of believing by trying to get a direct or only relatively indirect knowledge of God apart from the secularity and the resultant mystery of the incarnate Word. When Luther points to the crib of Bethlehem and the cross of Golgotha, he is not saying that direct knowledge of God is possible and actual here in this very secular phenomenon as such. He is not saying that there is no need here to distinguish between what we see and hear and apprehend and what we have to believe, between the true humanity and the true deity, between the *terminus ad quem* and the *terminus a quo*. What he is pointing to is the total secularity, i.e., the hiddenness of the Word, and therewith the sole reality of indirect knowledge, and therewith that distinction whose elimination can only be thought of as in process and never as completed, and therewith the immanent Trinity, the eternal essence and the eternal counsels of God. Here in the *humanitas Christi* we are to seek and find everything. We seek and find this, but we seek and find ; we do not see and have directly. And now conversely I fail to see how, if we take the course indicated by Gogarten and make a direct identification of " God in Himself " and " God for us," we can avoid trespassing into what Luther has repudiated as *speculatio Maiestatis*, into a denial of the indirectness of our knowledge of the Word of God. If we really say indirectness and do not mean an innocuous indirectness of low potency that can easily be changed into directness in virtue of the *analogia entis*, but the true, emphatic and indissoluble indirectness of the revelation and knowledge of God in the flesh, in the offence of the cradle and the cross, then we must make the second statement in order to make the first, the only first that comes into consideration here. Are we taking the secularity and hiddenness of God's Word seriously if we think we can say the one thing in one word instead of two ? Naturally I am not claiming that Gogarten thinks this or that he wants to deny the indirectness of our knowledge of the Word of God. But I am again faced by a riddle : Since he obviously thinks the one and does not want to deny the other, what does he really have in mind and what is he really after in his criticism ? Has he broken with the conceptions of A. Ritschl, of which his criticism uneasily reminds me, in the way that one ought to break with these conceptions, i.e., with those of Enlightenment theology ? Be that as it may, Gogarten has not, strictly speaking, referred to actual mistakes of material importance in my presentation, but only to a source of possible material mishaps. In contrast, I learn from Przywara's review from the opposite corner how seriously advance in the direction desired by Gogarten would endanger material understanding in the very point which I regard as crucial. In this respect, then, it is unavoidable that I should speak even more sharply along the lines that Gogarten does not approve, or that I should preserve an even more eloquent silence, unable in either case to yield a single inch.

2. The speech of God is and remains the mystery of God in its one-sidedness. I have in mind here the relation of veiling and unveiling occasioned by the secularity of the Word. That God's Word is one-sided means that when spoken to us and received by us it does not meet us partly veiled and partly unveiled, but either veiled or unveiled, yet without being different in itself, without being spoken and received any the less truly either way. Its veiling can change for us absolutely into its unveiling and its unveiling can change absolutely into its veiling. Absolutely, for it is always unalterably the same in itself, always the one or the other for us. We can only grasp the other in the one, i.e., we can grasp the other only as we grasp the one ; we can grasp it only in faith. We are set in the greatest clarity in relation to the one, in such clarity that we have very distinct and in themselves clear thoughts regarding what is said to us, and we can react thereto with the whole outer and inner attitude of our lives, with joy, gratitude, confidence, zeal, seriousness, terror, confusion, anxiety, remorse. But this reaction is really reaction to the Word of God only when our clarity, our thought, our attitude, has a very definite limit in the other, the limit set by the very Word spoken to us, which will not let itself be made a whole, a synthesis or a system whether in theory or in practice, the limit beyond which the Word is a mystery, and really becomes a mystery again, for all the clarity with which it is spoken to us and received by us. To receive the Word of God does not mean on either side to be able to see and know and state the relation between the two sides, to be able to say why and how far the veiled Word now means unveiling or the unveiled Word means veiling. If we could know and state this, the Word of God would obviously cease to be a mystery, and would just be a paradox like others, a paradox behind whose supposed mystery one can more or less easily penetrate. The speech of God is and remains a mystery to the extent that its totality as such, and hence with all the weight and seriousness of God's Word, is always manifest to us only on one side and always remains hidden on the other side. Hidden, and not simply withheld : In what is manifest to us the hidden side is always contained, but as a hidden side, so that we can grasp and have it only as such, i.e., only in faith. In virtue of this one-sidedness what God says to us remains what it is. His ways remain higher than our ways and His thoughts higher than our thoughts (Is. 55[8f.]), not just in quantity but in manner and possibility. What remains hidden in what is made manifest to us remains in God's own hand. It is still to be sought and found there, with Him. It cannot be translated into our own insight

or the corresponding attitude. For the point of God's speech is not to occasion specific thoughts or a specific attitude but through the clarity which God gives us, and which induces both these in us, to bind us to Himself. This happens, however, as we are constantly set before our limit, i.e., before His mystery.

We must examine this more closely. When by the miraculous act of God His Word is spoken to us and received by us in its secularity, this may mean that we really hear the " God with us " that is spoken to us but we hear it only in the secular form in which it is said to us. But it may also mean that we do indeed hear it in its secular form but really hear it thus. From God's standpoint this is one and the same thing, but for us it is not the same ; it is two things, or one only in faith. The one time God unveils Himself in His Word, but also veils Himself therewith. The other time He veils Himself, but also unveils Himself therewith. In both instances it is a matter of hearing the full and true Word of God, the unveiling of God in His veiling or the veiling of God in His unveiling. The secular form without the divine content is not the Word of God and the divine content without the secular form is also not the Word of God. We can neither stop at the secular form as such nor can we fly off beyond this and try to enjoy the divine content alone. The one would be realistic theology, the other idealistic theology, and both bad theology. In both cases, however, we hear only in faith the full and true Word of God. Erasure of the distinction and indeed of the antithesis of form and content we cannot achieve. The coincidence of the two is clear to God but is not discernible by us. What is discernible by us is always form without content or content without form. Our thinking can be realistic or idealistic but it cannot be Christian. Obviously the concept of synthesis would be the least Christian of all, for it would mean no more and no less than trying to do God's miraculous act ourselves. In faith and in the thinking of faith there can be no thought of synthesis. Faith means recognising that synthesis cannot be attained and committing it to God and seeking and finding it in Him. Finding it in God, we acknowledge that we cannot find it ourselves, whether by achieving it in a specific attitude or by thinking it out systematically. Committing it to God and seeking it in God, we really do find it ; we hear the full and true Word of God, whether it be the divine content in its secular form or in the secular form the divine content. To hear the full and true Word of God does not mean perceiving the unity of veiling and unveiling, of form and content, and thus achieving Christian thought by the detour of faith. No, the thinking of faith will always be quite honestly a realistic or idealistic thinking, i.e., a thinking that in and of itself is most unchristian. As such, and without becoming any different in itself and as such, the thinking of faith is justified and sanctified thinking. But justification and sanctification in faith mean justification and sanctification by the object of faith, by God, though the believer, and therefore his thinking, do not cease to be less needy on this account. And since we cannot give ourselves faith, we ourselves cannot fashion this justification and sanctification of our thinking, nor can we make our thinking Christian, nor even affirm that it is so in ourselves or others. We can only believe this as God's grace even in face of the fact that our thinking either on the one side or the other is confronted by a wall which we can neither overthrow nor make transparent, namely, in face of the fact that considered in and of itself our thinking is irrefutably non-christian. Hence believing means either hearing the divine content of God's Word even though nothing but the secular form is discernible by us or it means hearing the secular form of God's Word even though only its divine content is discernible by us.

At this point we may certainly recall the notable relation between the concepts " Father " and " Son " in their application to God as such and His incarnate Word as such in the Gospel of John. Both concepts are used there in such a way that the content of the one is presupposed to be discernible and then there follows the declaration that from knowledge of the content of the one there can and must and will be knowledge of the content of the other. Thus " that which the Father giveth me " (6³⁷), or " whom the Father draweth " (6⁴⁴) or " to whom it hath been given of the Father " (6⁴⁵) or " whoso is given to the Son by the Father " (10²⁹), this man comes to me, the Son. Or on the other hand " he that honoureth not the Son, honoureth not the Father " (5²³), or " if any man serve me, him will the Father honour " (12²⁶), or " no man cometh unto the Father but by me " (14⁶), or " he that hath seen me has seen the Father " (14⁹), or " that the Father may be glorified in the Son " (14¹³). Then in almost direct contrast : " I honour my Father " (8⁴⁹), and : " My Father that honoureth me " (8⁵⁴). The statement that " I and the Father are one " (10³⁰), or ". . . that they may be one even as we are" (the Father and the Son, 17¹¹), obviously does no more than underline the fact that in John believing is equally both coming from the known Father to the unknown Son and also coming from the known Son to the unknown Father. There can hardly be anything contrary to the sense of John if in this context we substitute for Father and Son the concepts of form and content in their distinction and unity.

Invariably, then, faith is acknowledgment of our limit and acknowledgment of the mystery of God's Word, acknowledgment of the fact that our hearing is bound to God Himself, who now leads us through form to content and now from content back to form, and either way to Himself, not giving Himself in either case into our hands but keeping us in His hands.

It might seem surprising that the movement of faith, or rather the movement of God's Word which faith can only follow, is described so explicitly and totally as twofold. This is not done in the interests of a scheme but because the matter described leaves us no option. It is especially true that what is at issue in faith is to pierce, or to see to be pierced, the concealment in which God speaks to us in proclamation, in the Bible and in Christ Himself, and thus to see and hear that the very concealment of God is his true and real revealing.

We have in mind here the familiar and remarkable sermon of Luther on the story of the Syro-Phoenician woman in Mt. 15[21f.] : " Believing steadfastly in the proclamation of Christ that she has heard (in ' such good crying abroad '), the woman comes to Him, but lo, He takes another tack as though He would cause her faith and good confidence to fail and falsify the report of Him, so that she might well think, Is this the kindly, friendly man ? or are these the good words that I have heard tell of Him, wheron I have relied ? It must be untrue. He is thine enemy and favoureth thee not. Surely He might speak a word and say to me, I will not. But He is as silent as a stock. Lo, this is a hard blow if God show Himself so stern and angry, and hide His grace so high and deep. . . . Now what doth the woman thereupon ? She putteth from her eyes such unkind and hard bearing in Christ, is not deceived by all that, taketh it not to heart, but abideth downright and firm in her confidence, holding on to the good report that she had heard and conceived of Him, and leaveth not off. So must we also do, and learn to cling fast to the Word alone, though God range Himself towards all creatures other than the Word saith of Him. But oh, how sad that is for nature and reason that they must strip themselves bare and let go all they feel and lean alone on the mere Word although they feel the opposite. God help us in straits and dying to such courage and faith. Even the intercession of Jesus' disciples leadeth but to the answer, ' I am not sent but to the lost sheep of the house of Israel.' Here must all saints and all intercession halt. Yea, here must the heart let even the Word go, when its feeling is to cling to it. But what doth the woman ? She leaveth not off, cleaveth to the Word even though it be torn from His heart as it were by force, taketh no heed of such a stern answer, still trusteth firmly that His kindness yet lurketh beneath and will not yet judge that Christ is ungracious or might be. That is what it means to hold fast. And once more her own ' Help me, Lord ' leadeth but to the reply, ' It is not meet to take the children's bread and cast it to the dogs.' What will she say here ? He answereth her ill that she is one of the damned and lost that should not be reckoned with the elect. That is a right unanswerable reply that none can deal with. Yet she leaveth not off, but even agreeth with His judgment and granteth she is a dog, nor desireth more than a dog, namely, to eat the crumbs that fall from the master's table. Is not that a masterpiece ? She taketh Christ at His own words. He likeneth her to a dog ; that she granteth, and asketh no more than that He let her be a dog as Himself judgeth ; what then ? He was fairly taken. To a dog one indeed leaveth the crumbs beneath the table, that is its right. Therefore He openeth right up and yieldeth to her will, that she is not now a dog but even a child of Israel . . . here thou seest, though Christ take a seeming hard stand, yet giveth He no final judgment that He should say nay, but all His answers sound like nay, yet are not nay but swing in suspense. For He saith not, I will not hear her, but is quite silent, and replieth not yet a nay. Likewise He saith not that she is not of the house of Israel, but that Himself was sent to the house of Israel only. He thus leaveth it to hang and swing in suspense 'twixt yea and nay. So he saith not, Thou art a dog and shalt not be given the children's bread, but, it is not meet etc. He thus leaveth it again in suspense whether she be a dog or no. Yet all three sayings ring a bit stronger to nay than yea, but there is still more in them than nay. In sooth simple yea is in them, but very deeply and secretly, and what appeareth is simple nay. Thereby is indicated how our heart standeth in trial. According as it feeleth, so taketh Christ here His stand. Its thought really is that simple nay is there, yet 'tis not true. Therefore must it turn from such feeling and grasp and hold the deep and secret yea beneath and above the nay with firm faith in God's Word, as the woman doth, and concede God the rightness of His judgment on us. So have we won and captured Him in His own words, as when we feel in conscience God chideth us for sinners and judgeth us unworthy of the kingdom of heaven, then we feel hell and bethink us eternally lost. Whoso then learn here from this woman and capture God in His own judgment and say, Yea, Lord, 'tis true, I am a sinner and not worthy of Thy grace, yet Thou hast promised pardon to sinners and art not come to call the righteous, but, as St. Paul also saith, to save sinners, lo, so must God by His own judgment have mercy upon us " (*Fasten-postille*, 1525, *W.A.*, 17^{II}, pp. 201–4).

But conversely in the unveiling of God there is to be seen and acknowledged His veiling, i.e., the close relation between the content and the form, the glory and the humility, the goodness and the severity of the Word of God. Only in the consummation when faith ceases altogether can we imagine man no longer needing but relieved of this reverse movement of faith, this recollection of the secularity of the Word of God. Even the faith that breaks through or is led through the visible to the invisible, the No to the Yes, is after all regarded as human experience, action and thought, the faith of the man who even and precisely in his triumph stands in need of correction and completion, and indeed of a wholly new relation to God. He must therefore retrace the way already traversed. Freed by the Word, he must be taken captive again by the same Word. He must be placed again before God, which means before the God who is concealed in His concealment. What could experience of God's unveiling be but *superbia* if it were content therewith ? And what could thought about this experience be but *theologia gloriae, speculatio Maiestatis*, if it were to stop there ? Roman Catholic and Protestant *theologia gloriae* has constantly appealed to this experience, to triumphant faith, and has failed to see that in abandoning the indirectness of the knowledge of God it has immediately abandoned true faith and the real Word of God as well. In fact faith and the Word of God are no less needed for this return from finding to seeking, from being inside to being outside, from having to asking, from the triumph of experience and thought to honest and complete spiritual poverty. It is indeed no less hard and inconceivable for the victor that he too and he specifically should see and confess that he is beaten than it is for the beaten man to know that as such he is the victor.

An important difference between faith and mysticism is that the mystic as such denies this reversal ; in ecstasy before unveiled Deity he ceases to be aware of the veiling ; he regards proclamation, Bible and Christ in their secularity as mere symbols of the Godhead now unveiled to him, which have now become dispensable and which he can basically discard ; henceforth he sees his future only in ever fuller unveilings which lead him more and more into the depths or the heights. In contrast, the triumphant believer returns immediately as such to proclamation, the Bible, and Christ in their secularity ; he sits down again, as it were, in the lowest room ; he seeks his future only (and genuinely so) in the God who is totally concealed (not already revealed but totally concealed) from him as from every other sinner. It is in this very going and going back again that the believer as such, because both goings are at the command of the God who calls, has apart from all else an assurance that the mystic as such can never have.

Human experience and thought as such, if they were to follow their own bias, would proceed in a straight line from despair to even deeper despair, from solemnity to even greater solemnity (there is also a negative *theologia gloriae*), or from triumph to even higher triumph, from joy to even greater joy. To faith, however, this straight line movement is forbidden by the Word of God which calls us from despair to triumph, from solemnity to joy, but also from triumph to despair and from joy to solemnity. This is the *theologia crucis*. So, in this discipline by His Word, which never leaves us alone whether in our humility or our pride, God is faithful to Himself and to us, always, then, in an unequivocal one-sided advance or retreat in which the other side remains unsaid and everything depends on our hearing it either way as said by God. How necessary it is to be clear about this two-fold movement of the Word of God and the faith that follows it may be seen finally from the fact that one has only to extend the lines a little on both sides to move from the concepts of veiling and unveiling, or form and content, to other opposing concepts, namely, Law and Gospel, demand and promise, or in another direction letter and spirit, or in yet another God's wrath and judgment and God's grace. The Word of God in its veiling, its form, is the claiming of man by God. The Word of God in its unveiling, its content, is God's turning to man. The Word of God is one. In the claim there takes place the turning, and the turning does not take place without the claim. When man is truly and seriously put under the Law he comes to the Gospel, and when he comes to the Gospel by revelation and faith, he is truly and seriously put under the Law. God's wrath and judgment is only the hard shell, the *opus alienum* of divine grace, but the man who knows grace, the *opus Dei proprium*, he and he alone knows what is God's wrath and judgment. The letter of proclamation and the Bible is the bearer of the Spirit, but it is the Spirit that constantly brings us back to the letter. When we consider these pregnant concepts that develop out of the veiledness or unveiledness of God's Word, we shall not want to say—we could do so only by a hopeless weakening of all these serious concepts—that we simultaneously experience their content in its truth and that we can systematically interrelate them. One of them is always true in experience and thought, and we must always believe the other that we do not see.

In Ex. 19–20 we find the story of the concluding of the covenant between Yahweh and Israel at Sinai. The nature of the covenant is indicated by the reminder of the help Israel has thus far received from its God and by the promise : " Ye shall be my peculiar treasure among all peoples." But this is not the crucial content of this chapter. The important thing is on the one hand (Ex. 19) the astonishingly direct and impressive warning in all circumstances to keep away from the place where this gracious and friendly God manifests Himself in order to avoid instant death, along with the description of the terrible event of His manifestation which is experienced at close quarters only by the one man Moses, and then on the other hand (Ex. 20) the account of the conditions that Yahweh imposes on Israel, i.e., the commandments of the covenant, to whose strict observance the promise is tied. In the same Old Testament Canon Jer. 31[31f.] speaks again of a covenant of the same Yahweh with the same Israel. It is based on the presupposition that Israel broke the first covenant whose commandments it was supposed to keep. As if this did not signify the end of any possible covenant, as if God were unfaithful to Himself, a new covenant is now proclaimed. In it, too, there is to be a Law, but it is not now revealed from afar amid thunder and lightning. This Law—but what does Law mean in this case ?—is to be written in the hearts of the Israelites, so much so, so truly in their hearts, that all instruction in the knowledge of Yahweh from man to man will be superfluous. This new revelation of the Law, this completely new position of Israel close to Yahweh, this new covenant which is utterly inconceivable from the standpoint of the first, is to rest on the forgiveness of sins, " and I will be their God, and they shall be my people " (v. 33). Now if we are to listen to both Ex. 19–20 and Jer. 31, we obviously cannot listen to both at the same time. A historical analysis of the two texts will in its own way show us at once that a systematic conspectus of both is impossible. Hence we can only listen either to the one or the other at the one time. Nor can it be a matter of harmonising exegesis but solely a matter of faith to see the validity of each covenant in the other, of the new in the old and the old in the new. There is a similar relation in the Old Testament between predictions of salvation and predictions of disaster by the prophets. The prophets admittedly surprise us by the abrupt one-sidedness with which at one moment they relentlessly speak only of judgment to come and at another they speak unrestrainedly only of coming redemption. There was a time when Old Testament scholarship thought it impossible that one and the same prophet should have spoken one way in one passage and the other in another. We are more cautious to-day. We would say that prophecies of salvation and disaster in the absolute sense in which they occur were naturally impossible at the same time or in any inner connexion. There can thus be no system of prophetic utterance. It was either threat or promise. In this very one-sidedness it sought to be God's Word. To understand it there was and is needed what is called faith in the New Testament, namely, the perception either way of what is not said. In the New Testament itself we may recall the relation between the Synoptic tradition and the Johannine tradition in respect of the humanity and deity of Jesus Christ. Both speak of both, but with such varying interests and emphases that we can only misunderstand both if, as the historico-critical school once did, we try to measure the one by the other or (in what was once taken to be the positive method) we seek to balance the one by the other. That the Johannine view is actually directed against the Synoptic presentation is theologically a not too bad historical hypothesis favoured by many modern scholars. It is impossible to listen at one and the same time to the two statements that Jesus of Nazareth is the Son of God and that the Son of God is Jesus of Nazareth. One hears either the one or the other or one hears nothing. When the one is heard, the other can be heard only indirectly, in faith. I will adduce as a last example the relation between the cross or death of Christ and His resurrection in the preaching of Paul. Paul often used the two terms very close together, but they always point in very

different directions whether with reference to Christ Himself or with reference
to the reality of salvation for Christians. Paul undoubtedly has both in view
when he simply says Ἰησοῦς Χριστός or ἐν Χριστῷ, but it is worth noting that
he can really say both only by this name. But this name is not a system representing a unified experience or a unified thought ; it is the Word of God itself.
In it the cross and resurrection are one, but they are not one—either for Paul,
or his first readers, or us either—in what is said in explanation over and above
this name. We can listen only to the one or the other, realising what is said by
the one or the other, and then, in and in spite of the concealment, we can also in
faith hear the other in the one. These are just some of the great one-sidednesses
of the Bible written and received as God's Word. It is a characterisation of the
Bible as a whole when the Word of God is described (Heb. 4¹²) as " sharper
than a two-edged sword " (cf. also Rev. 1¹⁶) and when it is then said to pierce
asunder soul and spirit, joints and marrow, and to become judge of the thoughts
and intents of the heart, so that no creature can hide from it, but everything is
laid bare and held before its eyes.

As we must say already at this juncture, it is this external one-
sidedness of God's Word, resting on an inner one-sidedness not apparent
to us, that makes faith faith, that makes it the apprehended apprehension—moving from the depths to the heights and the heights to the
depths—of the ever invisible God who is beyond all experience and
thought. From the Word of God faith has not only its existence but
also this its nature.

'Ο λόγος Ἰησοῦ κεκτημένος ἀληθῶς, δύναται καὶ τῆς ἡσυχίας αὐτοῦ ἀκούειν, ἵνα τέλειος
ᾖ, ἵνα δι' ὧν λαλεῖ πράσσῃ καὶ δι' ὧν σιγᾷ γινώσκηται (Ignatius of Antioch, *ad
Eph.*, 2, 15). Luther calls the *fides Christi* a *res arduissima, quia translatio
et raptus est ab omnibus quae sentit intus et foris in ea quae nec intus nec foris
sentit scilicet invisibilem, altissimum, incomprehensibilem Deum (Hebr. Br.*, 1513,
Fi. Schol., 39, l. 3). *Non enim habent nomen neque speciem ea, quae fides intelligit.
Nam praesentium rerum prosperitas vel adversitas penitus subvertit omnem
hominem, qui fide non intelligit invisibilia. Hic enim intellectus ex fide venit,
iuxta illud ' Nisi credideritis, non intelligitis ' et est ingressus ille caliginis, in qua
absorbetur, quicquid sensus, ratio, mens intellectusque hominis comprehendere potest.
Coniungit enim fides animam cum invisibili, ineffabili, innominabili, aeterno,
incogitabili verbo Dei simulque separat ab omnibus visibilibus, et haec est Crux et
phase Domini (Oper. in Ps.*, 1519 f., *W.A.*, 5, p. 69, l. 24). More than once Luther
described the situation of the believing man as a *pendere* or *haerere* between heaven
and earth, drawn and held off on both sides, now held fast and now pushed away
(e.g., *Hebr. Br., Fi. Schol.*, p. 71, l. 11 ; *Lect. on Isa.*, 1527, *W.A.*, 25, p. 328,
l. 33). He did this classically in the words : " But to watch is to cling to the
eternal good and to see and long for the same. But therein he is alone and none
with him, for they are all asleep. And he saith, On the housetop, as though he
said, the world is a house, inside they are all asleep and locked up, but I am
outside the house, on the roof, not yet in heaven and not in the world, the world
I have under me and heaven above me, thus 'twixt the world's life and eternal
life swing I lonely in faith " (*Seven Pen. Pss.*, 1517, *W.A.*, 1, p. 199, l. 1). This
would all have to be termed madness if it did not have to be exactly thus and not
otherwise on the basis of the " one-sidedness " of the Word of God.

3. The speech of God is and remains the mystery of God in its
spirituality. With this statement, which must form the conclusion to

C.D.—G*

our exposition of the nature of God's Word, we expressly allude for the first time to the concept of the Holy Spirit. To say Holy Spirit in preaching or theology is always to say a final word. For when we do this, then whether we are aware of it or not, and it is best to be aware of it, we are always speaking of the event in which God's Word is not only revealed to man but also believed by him. We are always speaking of the way in which the Word of God is so said to this or that man that he must hear it, or of the way in which this or that man is so open and ready for the Word of God that he can hear it. To the extent that part of the nature of God's Word is that it may be perceived by man, we may say of it that it is spiritual, i.e., that where it is actual and where it is thus believed by man, it is itself finally and ultimately the ground of this event. The Bible and Church dogma and all older theology, whatever else they may say of this event when they come to speak of it, always refer to the Holy Spirit. All that has also to be said about man— and we have inevitably to speak about man here—all theological anthropology, i.e., all teaching about the man to whom God's Word is revealed and by whom it is received, must stand under this sign. The sign means that under this new aspect too, even when we take the concept of revelation (which is constitutive for that of Holy Scripture and Church proclamation) and try to grasp it from below as it were, in terms of ourselves, even then and then specifically it must be seen and said that God is the Lord in this event. The Lord of speech is also the Lord of our hearing. The Lord who gives the Word is also the Lord who gives faith. The Lord of our hearing, the Lord who gives faith, the Lord by whose act the openness and readiness of man for the Word are true and actual, not another God but the one God in this way, is the Holy Spirit. Quite apart from the place these things have in the actual Dogmatics, we shall return later in the Prolegomena to the whole aspect that opens up here and to the sign under which it is to be understood. For the moment we shall confine ourselves to the finding that even in reaching its goal in man, even in the event of human faith in the Word of God, the Word of God is God's miraculous act. We must believe in our faith no less than in the Word believed, i.e., even if we think we can and should regard our attitude to God's Word as positive, even if we thus confess our faith, we can regard it as positive only as it is made possible and actual by God, only as the miracle of the Holy Ghost and not as our own work.

Luther's well-known but insufficiently appreciated exposition of the Third Article is pertinent here : " I believe that of no reason or power of my own can I believe in Jesus Christ my Lord or come to Him ; but the Holy Ghost hath called me through the Gospel, illumined me by His gifts, hallowed and maintained me in the right faith, even as He calleth the whole of Christendom on earth, gathereth and sanctifieth it, and in Jesus Christ maintaineth it in the right faith. . . ." (*Smaller Catech.*, 1531, *W.A.*, 30[1], p. 367, l. 4).

Concretely this means that the hearing and receiving of the Word
of God by a man can be known by him and others only in faith. We are
saying the same thing when we say, in the Holy Spirit. Faith, of
course, is also a human experience. A specific human attitude corresponds to this experience, and this human attitude finds its expression,
too, in specific human thoughts. But whether or not this experience
is the experience, this attitude the attitude, and these thoughts the
thoughts of the faith that has heard the Word of God, is decided
spiritually, i.e., not by faith, but by the Word believed. Hence one
cannot lay down conditions which, if observed, guarantee hearing of the
Word. There is no method by which revelation can be made revelation
that is actually received, no method of scriptural exegesis which is
truly pneumatic, i.e., which articulates the witness to revelation in the
Bible and to that degree really introduces the Pneuma, and above all
no method of living, rousing proclamation that truly comes home to the
hearers in an ultimate sense. There is nothing of this kind because
God's Word is a mystery in the sense that it truly strikes us spiritually,
i.e., in all circumstances only through the Holy Spirit, in all its indirectness only directly from God. In its spirituality it is definitively
distinguished from any mere idea or hypostasis to which, if it is to be
discerned by us even as such, there must correspond with some
certainty, however small or hard to grasp, an experience, attitude or
concept on our side. One will seek in vain anything corresponding to
God's Word on our side even though one would be content with ever so
little and even though one would be ready to go to the ultimate depths
and outermost bounds of human existence to find it. Naturally the
Word of God is always actual in very specific human experiences,
attitudes and thoughts, but in its own power and dignity and not in
that of the human experiences, attitudes and thoughts, not, then, in
such a way that their existence can in any way guarantee the presence
of the Word of God, nor in such a way that they are necessarily and
unequivocally the signs of its reality.

As a modern instance of the way one can easily forget this spirituality of the
Word of God I adduce what P. Tillich tells the Church about its task of proclamation to-day. He thinks he should advise it above all to refrain from any direct
offering of the religious contents provided in the Bible and tradition. Instead the
following rules are to be observed : " First it must insist on a radical experience of
the borderline situation ; it must take from modern man the secret reservations
which prevent him from placing himself with unconditional resolution at the
frontier of his human existence. . . . Secondly, it must speak of the Yes that
comes to man in the borderline situation when taken with unconditional seriousness. . . . Thirdly, Protestantism must finally witness to the new being from which
alone it is possible to speak that word with authority, i.e., so to speak it that it
does not again become a ground of assurance " (*Rel. Verwirkl.*, 1930, p. 38 f.).
According to Tillich the task of Evangelical religious instruction is also " to bring
to light, in terms of the frontiers of the human, the situation of man in its secular

and religious expressions so far as these are known to the pupil and may be understood by him " (*Zeitschrift für den ev. Religionsunterricht*, 1931, p. 290). We ask : What is a " radical experience of the borderline situation " ? What is " unconditional resolution " ? How does one take from a man the reservations that prevent him from placing himself at this spot with resolution ? Does it go without saying that " in the borderline situation when taken with unconditional seriousness " a Yes comes to man, and what does it mean to speak about this Yes ? What is meant by speaking " in terms of the frontiers of the human " or indeed of the new being, i.e., speaking in such a way that the human word cannot become again a ground of assurance for the hearer ? Obviously Tillich thinks he can produce a new and better method with all this. A method for what ? One must give him credit that in what he says he has in view proclamation of the Word of God. But if so, are not all his proposals mere naiveties compared to which it is perhaps much more realistic to stick now as always to the direct proclamation of the contents of the Bible and tradition ? By means of the negations or delimitations of man which according to Tillich we can obviously carry out for ourselves we do not even remotely produce the Word of God for him or for ourselves. Precisely by proclaiming the contents of the Bible and tradition we bear witness to the fact that we are in no position at all to do so.

Naturally there can be no question of recommending as the true method the insight that no method is possible here at all. This insight is sound, but one can have and apply it just as well as any other without its having any bearing at all on the demonstration of the event of hearing the Word of God. It, too, is far from putting this handle in our hands. The search for the possibility of getting such a handle, the search for a receptacle of human experience, attitude and teaching which would be undoubtedly and unequivocally the receptacle of the divine content—this search is not one that should be pursued further and further into every new and hitherto unknown or even undreamed-of area of human reality, no matter whether it is a matter of new positions or merely of the possible limits of this or that or even all possible positions. The insight that is needed here is that this search is pointless.

H. M. Müller, in the book already quoted in which he follows E. Grisebach, introduces the concept of " experience " or " trial " into theological discussion in a new sense. But so far I am not clear how far this differs from a long sought and finally discovered frontier concept which is in no way adapted as such to denote unequivocally the real hearing of God's Word. The only proper thing to do here is to renounce altogether the search for a method of hearing God's Word, for an unequivocally correct description of its entry into man, into the realm of his experiences, attitudes and thoughts. " Since the Word of God is not in man's power either to speak or touch on fruitfully, but only in God's hand, therefore 'tis needful that we pray to Him to give us Himself the Holy Word through itself or through a man " (Luther, *German Exposition of the Lord's Prayer*, 1519, *W.A.*, 2, p. 108, l. 28). " No man can illumine another, but this word alone can lighten all of him, and preachers should just be forerunners and witnesses of this light to men, that all may believe in the light " (*Sermon on Jn.* 1^{1-14}, *Kirchenpostille*, 1522, *W.A.*, 10^I, p. 223, l. 3). " Therefore 'tis always a wondrous realm ; the word is there and no one aware that it is so active and achieveth such great things for them that believe in it ; it must itself be felt and tasted in the heart. Therefore we preachers can do no more than be our Lord Christ's mouth and

His tools by which He preacheth the Word bodily. He letteth the Word go forth publicly that every man may hear it. But that we may feel it inwardly in the heart is the work of faith and is a secret doing of Christ's where He seeth that it is to be done of His own divine foreknowledge and good-pleasure " (*Sermon on Jn.* 10$^{12f.}$, 1523, *W.A.*, 12, p. 531, l. 4). " Christian faith and Christian life stand in the one little word revealing by God, for where that is not to hand, no heart is ever right aware of this mystery that is hidden there from the world's standpoint. Now God alone revealeth it to His saints elect from eternity, to whom He will have it made known, otherwise it remaineth indeed hid from every man and a right mystery. What good will the free will or the slavish, captive will say or do about that ? How of its own power will it attain to this light and mystery ? If the almighty strong God hide it from it, 'twill ne'er arrive thereat by any preparation or good works. No creature can come to this knowledge. For Christ alone revealeth it to it in the heart itself. Thus falleth to the ground all merit, all powers and faculties of reason, and availeth naught for God. Christ alone must give it " (*Sermon on Mt.* 11$^{25-30}$, 1527, *W.A.*, 23, p. 689, l. 4).

Only on the assumption of this renunciation, which must be explicitly stated, shall we be able to speak of the knowability of God's Word in the next section. We shall have to speak there of the fact that it can be an object of human experience. But we cannot speak of it in such a way as to give an account of how this object and this knowledge can be delimited with clarity and certainty from other objects and knowledge of them. This would be the method of hearing God's Word, which is impossible as such because hearing God's Word is faith, and faith is the work of the Holy Spirit. Naturally the human experiences, attitudes and thoughts which are bound up with any confession of faith, including the Christian, lie as such in the realm of humanity and can be defined as such and delimited from others. But they do not lie in the realm of humanity to the degree that Christian faith is hearing the Word of God. As hearing of God's Word they can be attested in the realm of humanity only by appeal to proclamation by the Church, to Holy Scripture and to revelation in the form of interpretation of this threefold form of God's Word. But as hearing of God's Word they cannot be the subject of what might be called controversies within this realm. That is to say, as hearing of God's Word they cannot be justified and delimited alongside and over against whatever else is heard in this realm, and hence they cannot be domesticated within it.

The nature of the renunciation demanded here can be seen with perfect clarity from the three " inalienable verities " which Eduard Spranger, undoubtedly a chosen mouthpiece of modern German spirituality, ventures to suggest to theology " for fresh consideration " : 1. man's responsibility for the basis of his readiness to believe ; 2. controversy with the known autonomies of the so-called course of this world ; and 3. controversy with the existing multiplicity of religious convictions (" Der Kampf gegen den Idealismus," *Sitzungsberichte d. preuss. Akad. d. Wissenschaft*, 1931, XVII, p. 436). One might be surprised at the innocent way in which Spranger submits for " fresh consideration " what has been said profusely enough and adopted respectfully enough by Protestant theology for the last two hundred years. If he can be satisfied with the applause that even to this day his inalienable verities are sure to find in wide circles in the Church and theology, he must also allow us to evaluate them as excellent formulations of the very thing that any theology worthy of the name must in all circumstances and without reservation renounce. Here to-day, as in the past, our only reply can be one of the sharpest opposition : 1. As regards the basis of man's readiness to believe, theology has no responsibility outwards. The responsibility of theology is simply to make it clear that the readiness to believe, seen from outside, has its basis within itself and thus bears no responsibility in respect of its basis. 2. Theology cannot be in controversy with the autonomies of the course of this world because it is itself inside and not outside the course of this world, and because, like the Church in general, it has to attest but not to put into effect in this world God's own controversy with its autonomies. 3. Theology cannot be in controversy with the existing multiplicity of religious convictions because, though it does in fact find this multiplicity in the sphere of human experiences, attitudes and thoughts, it has no interest in controversy with it in this sphere, while it does not find it in the sphere of faith and therefore cannot be in controversy with it there. The question whether this reply to Spranger will enlighten and impress Spranger himself and his associates in philosophy and theology is relatively less important than the question whether there will always be a remnant in the Church which can only give this or a similar answer regarding the work that theology has to do.

If in respect of the event of hearing God's Word we do not point to a datum in man's existence, nor to the limit of all the data of human existence, nor finally to the possibility of a contingent experience, but only to faith, and that means to the Holy Spirit, we are simply confirming what was said at the beginning of the section, namely, that the question " What is the Word of God ? " can be answered only by indicating the How of God's Word in an interpretation of its threefold form. We thus ask : " How is the Word of God ? " and the answer is : It is on our lips and in our hearts as the mystery of the Spirit who is the Lord.

§ 6

THE KNOWABILITY OF THE WORD OF GOD

The reality of the Word of God in all its three forms is grounded only in itself. So, too, the knowledge of it by men can consist only in its acknowledgment, and this acknowledgment can become real only through itself and can become intelligible only in terms of itself.

1. THE QUESTION OF THE KNOWABILITY OF THE WORD OF GOD

Our way thus far has been briefly this. In § 3 we found in the concept of the Word of God the mandated content of Church proclamation and hence also the criterion of dogmatics as the scientific testing of Church proclamation. In § 4 we noted the three forms, namely, proclamation, Scripture and revelation, in which the entity denoted by the concept is actual. Finally in § 5, with these three forms in view, we asked concerning the nature of this entity and we learned to know it as three distinct but not different determinations, the speech of God, the act of God and the mystery of God. Before we now go on to give a provisional definition of the concept of dogmatics on the basis of these findings, we must first give an explicit answer to the question as to the knowability of the Word of God.

In the concept of Church proclamation and hence also in that of dogmatics it is obviously taken for granted that it is possible for man to hear and even speak, and hence also to know, the Word of God. In these concepts this is assumed, of course, not for human existence generally, but for a specific sphere of human existence, namely, the sphere of the Church. But even within the limits of this sphere as they are known to us or as they actually are in God's eyes, it is at any rate men who are summoned to hear God's Word and speak it. If the Church, and in it Church proclamation, and in the service of Church proclamation dogmatics, can make appeal to the truth, this must imply that men—not all men but certain men, and even these men not always and everywhere but in certain situations—may know the Word of God. If this were not so, the whole concept of the Word of God would have to be called a figment of the imagination, and Church proclamation, including dogmatics, would have to be called a pointless and meaningless activity, and therefore the Church would have to be called a place of self-deceptions without parallel. For even though there were in this case some unknown entity corresponding to the concept of the Word of God, if we really had no knowledge of it, the thing denoted by the concept would have no reality for us despite its unknown correlate, but would still be a figment of the imagination. In the concept of the Church as a place where the truth is spoken and heard, and in the concept of Church proclamation and dogmatics as a meaningful activity, it is presupposed that there can be knowledge of the Word of God by men.

By the knowledge of an object by men we understand confirmation of their acquaintance with its reality in respect of its existence and its nature. But confirmation of their acquaintance means that the reality of the object concerned, its existence and nature, being true in themselves, now become in some way, and with some degree of clarity and distinctness, true for men too. Their acquaintance with it, instead of being a contingent and outward determination of their own existence, now becomes a necessary and inward determination. Knowing, they are affected by the object known. They no longer exist without it, but with it. In so far as they think of it, with the same confidence with which they dare to think in general they must think of it as a true reality, as true in its existence and nature. Whatever else and however else they may think of it, they must begin by thinking of the truth of its reality. Face to face with this truth they can no longer withdraw into themselves in order to affirm, question or deny it thence. Its truth has come home to them, has become their own. And in the process they themselves have become the truth's. This event, this confirmation, in contrast to mere cognizance, we call knowledge. Cognizance becomes knowledge when man becomes a responsible witness to its content.

Knowledge of the Word of God in this sense is the presupposition of the Church. We may and must also reverse the statement and say that the Church is the presupposition of knowledge of the Word of God. Either way we are saying that the Word of God becomes knowable for men. In particular Church proclamation implies that God's Word can be heard by men and spoken by men themselves. If it were not knowable, if a self-confirming acquaintance with the Word of God were not possible, if it were not possible that its reality should affect men in such a way that they can no longer exist without it but only with it, that they can only think of its reality as true, that they can only start their existence with the truth of its existence and nature, if their freedom to retire into themselves in face of God's Word were infinite and inviolable—this would mean that any serious hearing and speaking of God's Word would be ruled out. Serious hearing and speaking rests on the possibility of knowledge. The presupposition of the Church is thus the possibility of this relation, the relation of knowledge between man and the Word of God. Or, conversely, the Church is the presupposition of the possibility of this relation of knowledge. On our path thus far we have tacitly counted on this presupposition, or one might also say that the question of its special nature and material correctness has already been implicitly raised and answered in the preceding section on the nature of the Word of God. But the question is important enough to demand independent and explicit treatment at this point. How can we men know the Word of God ? This is how we must formulate the question.

A few preliminary observations on this way of putting it will lead on directly to the matter itself.

1. We do not say : How do men know the Word of God ? This would mean asking about the reality of this knowledge. But after all that we have heard about its forms and nature, the reality of the knowledge of God can be the content of an answer that man must give to this question only in so far as this answer consists in the repetition of the biblical promise given to the Church and the reference to its coming fulfilment, and only in so far as the Word of God itself is added to this human repetition and reference and undertakes to give the real answer. In other words man's only answer to the question as put in this way is proclamation. But in order to be clear that this is so, our question must be : How can men know the Word of God ? We must ask about the possibility of this event. The very significance of the insight that the Word of God alone answers the question of real knowledge of the Word of God demands that we consider whether it can only be thus or whether it might be otherwise.

2. We do not say : How can all men know the Word of God ? or even : How can any man know the Word of God ? We have already recalled that it is not an issue of men universally or of man in general but very concretely and specifically of man in the Church. Where the Word of God is known and therefore can be known, it must have been spoken and it must have come as a divine call to specific men. God knows them, these men, who on specific occasions know God's Word as real hearers and proclaimers, who are thus able to know it, and who thereby constitute the Church as living human members in the body of Christ. Our concern is with the possibility of knowledge of these men.

3. Just because God knows them, we prefer not to say : How do Christians know the Word of God ? We might put it thus, but we should have to add : called and elect Christians, and this would be obscure, for the real issue is how men by knowing God's Word can become called and elect and therefore real Christians, hearers and proclaimers of the Word of God. God knows those who become this. But we know even

Christians only as men who as such put to us the question how it is possible that they should know the Word of God.

4. When we ask about the possibility of knowledge of the Word of God, we are presupposing that the concept of knowledge is known. But as above we shall deliberately have to take it so generally, with such philosophical and epistemological imprecision, that the possibility is left open of correction, restriction or reversal in the light of the object concerned. When knowledge was defined earlier as acquaintance with the reality of an object which is self-confirmed in the subject, this was meant to be only a sketch of the problem of knowledge and not an anticipatory interpretation. Any interpretation at this stage would mean philosophical and epistemological definition. But the problem of knowledge cannot be presupposed with such distinctness here even as a problem if we are not to incur the most serious risk of anticipating the answer in the presupposition in a very definite and perhaps most inappropriate way. What knowledge means as knowledge of God must in no case be introduced in a definitive form into investigation of this question.

As an example to the contrary I note a statement of F. Traub. In *Monats-schrift f. Past. Theol.*, 1928, p. 82 he brings against me the criticism that in my dogmatics no answer will be found to the question : " How can I succeed in affirming the Word of God, i.e., affirming it as the Word of God and as reality ? " Here " to be able to know the Word of God " is interpreted in advance as " to be able to succeed in affirming it." This is the premature introduction into the investigation of a philosophical and epistemological definition of the problem which in certain circumstances might be calculated to compromise in advance the treatment of this problem of knowledge. Who tells us that the constitutive act of knowledge of God's Word consists in our affirmation of it ? And above all who tells us that we can " succeed " in making such an affirmation ? The answer to the question as thus posed would obviously have to be the statement of a way or method by means of which this " success " can be achieved. Who tells us whether this question may be put at all and therefore whether any meaningful answer can be found at all ?

A result of the uniqueness of this object of knowledge might well be that the concept of its knowledge cannot be definitively measured by the concept of the knowledge of other objects or by a general concept of knowledge but that it can be defined at all only in terms of its own object.

2. THE WORD OF GOD AND MAN

How necessary is the reservation just made may be seen at once if we consider first what it means that it is man whom we are to understand here as the one who knows God's Word. It is part of the concept of the Church that this should be so. The Word of God which it hears

and proclaims, and which makes it the Church, is God's Word addressed
to men. Preaching and sacrament are addressed to men. The word of
the prophets and apostles is addressed to men. The revelation of God
Himself in Jesus Christ is addressed to men. The Word of God whose
three forms we have again denoted herewith is addressed to men. If it
is addressed to men, it obviously seeks to be known and therefore heard
by them, yet not only known and heard, but known in the sense already
generally established. Mediated by their acquaintance with it, it seeks
to confirm itself as a reality to them. It is addressed to them in order
that they may let it be spoken to them and that they may no longer be
what they are without it, but with it.

Consider here the connexion between grace (mercy) and truth in Ps. 89¹⁴· ²⁴ ;
98³ ; 117² and the way in which this connexion is taken up in Jn. 1¹⁴· ¹⁷. Consider the description of the Gospel as the λόγος τῆς ἀληθείας in 2 Cor. 6⁷ ; Eph.
1¹³ ; Col. 1⁵ ; 2 Tim. 2¹⁵ ; Jas. 1¹⁸. Consider finally the description of the
decisive thing in being a Christian as ἐπίγνωσις τῆς ἀληθείας in 1 Tim. 2³ ;
4³ ; 2 Tim. 2²⁵ ; 3⁷ ; Titus 1¹.

Primarily and originally the Word of God is undoubtedly the Word
that God speaks by and to Himself in eternal concealment. We shall
have to return to this great and inalienable truth when we develop the
concept of revelation in the context of the doctrine of the Trinity.
But undoubtedly, too, it is the Word that is spoken to men in revelation, Scripture and preaching. Hence we cannot speak or think of it
at all without remembering at once the man who hears and knows it.
The Word of God, Jesus Christ, as the being of the Church, sets us
ineluctably before the realisation that it was and will be men who are
intended and addressed and therefore characterised as recipients but
as also themselves bearers of this Word. The Word of God thus sets us
before the so-to-speak anthropological problem : How then can men be
this ? Before the " so-to-speak " anthropological problem, I said, and
I indicated thereby that it can be called this only with some reserve.
Or is this not so ? Shall we say unreservedly that the question of the
possibility of the knowledge of God's Word is a question of anthropology ? Shall we ask what man generally and as such, in addition to
all else he can do, can or cannot do in this regard ? Is there a general
truth about man which can be made generally perceptible and which
includes within it man's ability to know the Word of God ? We must
put this question because an almost invincible development in the
history of Protestant theology since the Reformation has led to an
impressive affirmative answer to this question in the whole wing of the
Church that we have called Modernist.

We have already mentioned incidentally the debates in Protestant orthodoxy
on the question whether theology is to be regarded with Thomas Aquinas as an
essentially theoretical science or with Duns Scotus as an essentially practical

science. With increasing deliberateness and universality decision was made in favour of the latter, and this meant that the object of theology was no longer, as with Chemnitz (*Loci. theol ed.*, 1592, *De usu et util. loc. theol.*, p. 12), the nature and will of God, or, as with Walaeus, *res divinae, nempe Deus ipse . . . et res omnes quae a Deo sunt* (*Loci comm.*, 1640, p. 5), but rather, as already with J. Gerhard (*Loci theol.*, 1610, *Prooem.* 28), *homo quatenus ad aeternam beatitudinem est perducendus*, or, as with Wendelin (*Theol. christ. lib.* II, 1639, *Prol.*, 1, 3), *vera religio, quae est ratio agnoscendi colendique Deum*, or, as with Burmann (*Syn. Theol.*, 1678, I, 2, 52), *vita hominis sive cultus ipsius erga Deum*, or, as with Mastricht (*Theol. theor. pract.*, 1698, I, 1, 26), *vita hominis formanda et dirigenda Deum versus.* One can interpret this development *in meliorem partem.* One of its most cautious proponents, F. Turrettini (*Instit. Theol. el.*, 1679, I, 5, 4), was well able to show that even so theology is still dealing with God, but *Deus quatenus revelatus est, Deus noster id est foederatus in Christo.* Along Reformation lines there was a desire to shun proximity to *nuda speculatio de Deo* (Quenstedt, *Theol. did. pol.*, 1685, I *cap.* 1, *sect.* 2, *qu.* 2, *font. sol.*, 7). There was already awareness that a " non-existential " theology is nothing : *theologia nisi ad praxin referatur ne theologia quidem est* (Burmann, *op. cit.*, I, 2, 51, cf. Cocceius, *S. theol.*, 1669, I, 8). It is true that H. Mulert (*Religion, Kirche, Theologie*, 1931, p. 28) and other modern authors claim that the orthodox regarded and pursued theology with rigid objectivism as *scientia de Deo et rebus divinis*, but this completely contradicts the tenor of the express declarations that are to be found in these theologians, even in the older ones who had not yet adopted the new fashion. From the very outset Protestant orthodoxy suffered from a surplus rather than a deficit in the regard it paid to the religious subject. Its aim at least —and this was the point of the turn to *scientia practica*—was to understand the Word of God altogether as a word addressed to man. The only trouble was that there was another meaning to the development as well. It is patent that what was also sought and attained with this development was that the object of theology, as scientific consciousness after the Renaissance was increasingly demanding, was transferred from a Beyond genuinely confronting the place of man to the sphere of man himself. Though it did not have to be, this object could now be thought of as one that is embraced and conditioned by the general truths of man. An attempt could thus be made to view it, or the possibility of it, within the sphere of man's self-understanding. The contemporary reconstruction of a *theologia naturalis* as the science of the *praeambula fidei* in the ancient Thomistic sense, the slow but noticeable withdrawal of the doubts the Reformers had had regarding the value of this enterprise, shows that were was interest in this incorporation from other angles too. In the 18th century, at any rate, it cannot be denied that deductions were drawn in this direction. We now find the definition that can still be made to-day, namely, that theology is the science of religion, by which is meant " academic knowledge of the doctrines and truths that give us the instruction necessary for our felicity and contentment concerning our relations to God, the duties which arise out of these relations, and the hopes that we may build on these relations " (G. J. Planck, *Einleitung in die theol. Wissenschaft*, 1794, Vol. I, p. 29). A Herder and a Schleiermacher could do better than this in understanding religion in its depth and power and autonomy. But the " we " which strikingly dominates Planck's statement remains, or indeed becomes, the cornerstone of their view too. It is the same Schleiermacher who for the first time fundamentally relates this newly discovered independent reality of religion to a corresponding possibility that can be generally demonstrated anthropologically, and who for the first time fundamentally undertakes to interpret Christianity itself, in the form of a concrete historical analysis of human existence, within the framework of a general doctrine of man :

1. the encounter of man with God is now to be understood as a human religious experience that can be established historically and psychologically ; 2. this experience is to be understood as the actualisation of a generally demonstrable religious capacity of man. For all the variety of types in individual interpretations, these are after Schleiermacher the two cardinal principles of the religious philosophy of the 19th and 20th centuries. The second of the two principles is naturally decisive. If we apply it to what we in our vocabulary call the doctrine of the Word of God it means that the real knowledge of the Word of God is the actualisation of a specific possibility of knowledge peculiar to man as such. If we accept this principle, then the answer to the question of possibility that now concerns us is to be sought in anthropology, and it is a secondary matter whether we follow the actual anthropology of Schleiermacher and his school or one more congenial to our age such as that of M. Heidegger. As it is, we are spared the choice, for we are not in any position to accept the principle on the basis of which we would have to make such a choice.

The consideration that forbids us to acquiesce in it is this. In the first place it is true (and partially at least this was the point in at least the early stages of the development) that the Word of God must be understood as an event in and to the reality of man.

There can be no objection in principle to describing this event as " experience " and even as " religious experience." The quarrel is not with the term nor with the true and important thing the term might finally denote, namely, the supremely real and determinative entry of the Word of God into the reality of man. But the term is burdened—this is why we avoid it—with the underlying idea that man generally is capable of religious experience or that this capability has the critical significance of a norm.

And in the second place it is true that a possibility or capability on man's part must correspond logically and materially to this event.

Even the concept of the religious *a priori*, which played so big a part in religious philosophy around 1910, would not have to be rejected absolutely or intrinsically if it were not for the unfortunate fact that on the basis of a right or wrong understanding of Kant it is understood as a capability or property grounded in man as such and as the corresponding freedom of control.

The question is whether this event ranks with the other events that might enter man's reality in such a way that to be able to enter it actually requires on man's part a potentiality which is brought by man as such, which consists in a disposition native to him as man, in an organ, in a positive or even a negative property that can be reached and discovered by self-reflection, by anthropological analysis of his existence, in short, in what philosophy of the Kantian type calls a faculty. It might also be that this event did not so much presuppose the corresponding possibility on man's part as bring it with it and confer it on man by being event, so that it is man's possibility without ceasing (as such) to be wholly and utterly the possibility proper to the Word of God and to it alone. We might also be dealing with a possibility of knowledge which can be made intelligible as a possibility of man, but, in contrast to all others, only in terms of the object of knowledge or the reality of knowledge and not at all in terms of the subject of knowledge, i.e., man as such. In the light of the nature of God's Word, and especially of what we said in § 5, 2.3. about its purposiveness or pertinence, its being aimed at man, its character as an address to man, we must decide against the first view and in favour of the second. From this standpoint, the same that concerns us here, we had to understand the Word of God as the act of God's free love and not as if the addressed and hearing man were in any way essential to the concept of the Word of God. That man is the recipient of God's Word is, to the extent that it is true, a fact, and it cannot be deduced from anything we might previously know about God's nature. Even less, of course, can it be deduced from anything we previously knew about the nature of man. God's Word is no longer grace, and grace itself is no longer grace, if we ascribe to man a predisposition towards this Word, a possibility of knowledge regarding it that is intrinsically and independently native to him. But the same results from what was said in the same passage about the content of the Word of God addressed to man. We then made the assertion that this content, whatever it might be *in concretissimo* for this man or that man, will always be an authentic and definitive encounter with the Lord of man, a revelation which man cannot achieve himself, the revelation of something new which can only be told him. It will also be the limitation of his existence by the absolute " out there " of his Creator, a limitation on the basis of which he can understand himself only as created out of nothing and upheld over nothing. It will also be a radical renewal and therewith an obviously radical criticism of the whole of his present existence, a renewal and a criticism on the basis of which he can understand himself only as a sinner living by grace and therefore as a lost sinner closed up against God on his side. Finally it will be the presence of God as the One who comes, the Future One in the strict sense, the eternal Lord and Redeemer of man, a presence on the basis of which he can understand himself only as hastening towards this future of the Lord and expecting Him. To be sure, it is not these formulae which describe the real content of the Word of God, but the content of the Word which God Himself speaks and which He does so always as these formulae indicate, the real content of the real Word of God, that tells man also that there can be no question of any ability to hear or understand or know on his part, of any capability that he the creature, the sinner, the one who waits, has to bring to this Word, but that the possibility of knowledge corresponding to the real Word of God has come to him, that it represents an inconceivable *novum* compared to all his ability and capability, and that it is to be understood as a pure fact, in exactly the same way as the real Word of God itself.

In 1 Cor. 2⁶ᶠ· we are told that the wisdom of God in Christ is a σοφία ἐν μυστηρίῳ unknown to the rulers of this world, not seen by any eye, not heard by any ear, having entered into no man's heart, accessible only to the πνεῦμα of God Himself and through the πνεῦμα of God Himself. It is not, then, accessible to the ψυχικὸς ἄνθρωπος who as such does not have the πνεῦμα and who cannot know what is accessible only to the πνεῦμα and through the πνεῦμα : οὐ δέχεται, οὐ δύναται γνῶναι. Man must receive (λαμβάνειν) not only the Word from Christ but also the πνεῦμα by which it is known, or he will not know it at all. Ἐδίδαξεν ἡμᾶς ὁ κύριος, ὅτι θεὸν εἰδέναι οὐδεὶς δύναται, μὴ οὐχὶ θεοῦ διδάξαντος, τουτέστιν ἄνευ θεοῦ μὴ γινώσκεσθαι τὸν θεόν (Irenaeus, *C.o.h.*, IV, 6, 4). " For what sort of a work is knowing ? It meaneth neither fasting, watching, mortification, nor aught a man may do or suffer with the body, but it lieth right within in the deepest foundation of the heart. In a word knowing is no work but precedeth all works. For works follow after and from knowledge. Work is what we do, but knowledge is of what we receive and take. Thus by the one little word ' knowing ' as by a mighty thunderclap is all doctrine smitten down which is founded on man's work, spiritual orders or divine service, as though thereby to be free from all sin, to reconcile God and to merit grace " (Luther, *Sermon on Jn.* 17³, 1528, *W.A.*, 28, p. 100, l. 21).

The Modernist view from which we must demarcate ourselves here goes back to the Renaissance and especially to the Renaissance philosopher Descartes with his proof of God from human self-certainty.

Among recent religious philosophers of this trend there have been some like G. Wobbermin (*System. Theologie*, Vol. 2, 1921, p. 455) and Heinrich Scholz (*Religionsphilosophie*, 2nd edn., 1922, p. 310) who have been open or incautious enough to appeal expressly to Descartes and to find fresh support in his train of thought.

" The I-experience establishes for man the surest certainty for reality that he can conceive of or that is possible for him at all. It is the presupposition . . . of all validation of reality with reference to the external world " (Wobbermin, *op. cit.*). One might ask whether this Cartesianism is really as impregnable as it usually purports to be even on the philosophical plane. But that is not our present concern and we must beware of opposing to it a philosophy more suited to our theological interest or of so wearying of Descartes that we throw ourselves into the arms of, e.g., Aristotle or Thomas. Suspicious of the other side too, we shall simply make the point that at any rate in theology one cannot think along Cartesian lines.

In his essay " Was hat die Rechtfertigungslehre dem modernen Menschen zu sagen ? " (1907 in *Ges. Aufsätze zur Kirchengeschichte*, Vol. 3, 1928, p. 559) Karl Holl once formulated as follows the fundamental principle that is " common to all men " and that constitutes " the plumb-line of their religion." " Nothing," he said, " is to be recognised as religiously valid but what can be found in the reality present to us and produced again out of our direct experience." This principle is in fact the principle of Cartesian thinking, which is quite impossible in theology. On the basis of this principle there is no knowledge of the Word of God. For we do not find the Word of God in the reality present to us. Rather— and this is something quite different—the Word of God finds us in the reality

present to us.   Again it cannot be produced again out of our direct experience.
Whenever we know it, we are rather begotten by it according to Jas. 1¹⁸.

The fact of God's Word does not receive its dignity and validity
in any respect or even to the slightest degree from a presupposition
that we bring to it.   Its truth for us, like its truth in itself, is grounded
absolutely in itself.   The procedure in theology, then, is to establish
self-certainty on the certainty of God, to measure it by the certainty of
God, and thus to begin with the certainty of God without waiting for
the validating of this beginning by self-certainty.   When that beginning
is made, but only when it is made, it is then, but only subsequently,
incidentally and relatively validated by the necessary self-certainty.
In other words, in the real knowledge of God's Word, in which alone
that beginning is made, there also lies the event that it is possible, that
that beginning can be made.   Again, we do not base this rejection of
the Cartesian way on a better philosophy.   It is not our concern here
whether there is such a philosophy.   In relation to this object, the
object of theology, we are content to say that one must affirm the
possibility of its knowledge by men in this way and no other.   Men can
know the Word of God because and in so far as God wills that they
know it, because and in so far as there is over against God's will only the
impotence of disobedience, and because and in so far as there is a
revelation of God's will in His Word in which the impotence of disobedience is set aside.   We shall return to the problem indicated here
in the third sub-section.   For the moment we are simply stating that
if one wants to call the problem of the knowability of the Word of God
an anthropological problem, the reference must be to a Church (or
theological) anthropology.   The question is not how man in general
and as such can know God's Word.   This question is pointless, for
vis-à-vis the Word of God there is no man in general and as such ;
the Word of God is what it is as it is concretely spoken to this or that
specific man.   The question is how these men to whom it is concretely
spoken can know it.   And our answer must be that they can do so when
the ability is given to them by the Word itself.   To this conclusion two
elucidations must be appended.

1. We have made a positive assertion, pronouncing a definite Yes
to the knowability of the Word of God.   This must be pointed out
already at this first stage in our deliberations because proponents of an
answer to the question on the basis of general anthropology usually
bring against all that has been said the objection that God's Word and
man are finally held apart or even " rent asunder " thereby.   In answer
we argue that others ought not so stubbornly to hear only the No in
what has been said.   To be sure, what has been said denies a connexion
between God and man, that is, a knowledge of God's Word by man, and

thus a knowability of God's Word by him, in the sense that a capability of man in abstraction from the Word of God can serve as the condition of this connexion. This condition, of course, cannot be met. The very man who knows the Word of God also knows that he can bring no capability of his own to this knowledge, but has first to receive all capability. But is it too much to expect that even modern theologians will not set their hearts on this impossible condition ? If one is alert, is it really possible to call the reference to the certainty of God that precedes all self-certainty an inadequate and unsatisfactory reference ? Is not the reference to this way, the way from certainty of God to self-certainty, the only positive thing, and yet also the absolutely certain and decisive thing, that can be said on this question ?

2. We have said something positive by the reference, of course, only to the extent that it was a reference, i.e., a reference to the event of the real knowledge of the Word of God. The power of this reference does not lie in itself ; it lies in that to which it refers. That to which it refers, that event, the factual priority of the certainty of God over all self-certainty, the fact of the knowledge of God's Word that does not presuppose its possibility in man, but, coming to man, brings the possibility with it—all this is something we can " presuppose " only as man can " presuppose " God. " Presupposition " in this case can only mean recollection of its promise and hope of its future, i.e., appeal to the biblical Word and expectation of its fulfilment. Our reference thus has just as much force as the promise is true and the future of the Lord is certain. Concretely it has just as much force as the text adduced (1 Cor. 2[6f.]) has truth and its content reality. In no respect, then, does the force of our reference lie in our hands. This applies not merely to the positive thing that we are trying to say but also and just as strongly to the associated negation. In other words, even the counter-thesis of theologians with Cartesian inclinations cannot be directly and strictly reduced *ad absurdum* and overturned. The power with which their mouth must be stopped is not under our control, and they themselves do not dispose of the power to let their mouths be stopped. Even knowledge of the impossibility of knowledge of the Word of God outside its reality is possible only on the presupposition of this real knowledge. There is no philosophy that can render faith or theology even this negative service. The positive reference to the possibility of knowledge that the Word of God brings with it can be rejected and therewith also the negative reference to its unknowability apart from the possibility of knowledge it brings with it. But when we make the twofold affirmation its power is not under our own control even with reference to ourselves. Our affirmation as such might be powerless because it is destitute of real knowledge of God's Word, because it is merely verbal and mental instead of being real over and above that,

If it is real, this does not lie in itself, not even in the seriousness and sincerity, nor the existential participation, with which we make it ; it lies in the real thing that is affirmed therewith. In short the binding nature of what we affirm and deny depends wholly and utterly on our own relevance to the matter as speakers and hearers. But our own relevance to the matter depends wholly and utterly, not on us, but on the matter itself. And this is so precisely because the matter, God's Word, is no mere thing ; it is the living, personal and free God. This elucidation must accompany us in all else that may have to be said on this question.

3. THE WORD OF GOD AND EXPERIENCE

What we have in view under this heading is the concrete application and execution of all that has been affirmed thus far. We have stated that knowledge of God's Word becomes possible for man in the event of the reality of God's Word. It " becomes possible for man "—this aspect of the thought is the one especially we must now interpret. We shall try to do it by means of the concept of experience.

H. M. Müller (*Glaube und Erfahrung bei Luther*, 1929), on the basis of certain passages in Luther, understands and considers experience in terms of the special experience of the trial of faith and the triumphant withstanding of the trial. Here we shall adopt a more general usage.

If knowledge of God's Word is possible, this must mean that an experience of God's Word is possible. We have defined knowledge as the confirmation of human acquaintance with an object whereby its truth becomes a determination of the existence of the man who has the knowledge. This determination of the existence of the man who has the knowledge we call experience. Man does not exist abstractly but concretely, i.e., in experiences, in determinations of his existence by objects, by things outside him and distinct from him. It is in past experience, i.e., as determined by the things that have thus far come to him from without in the way they have come, and then again in present experience, i.e., as he encounters specific external things in a specific way, that man is what he is, that he exists as man, and not otherwise. If knowledge of God's Word can become possible for men, this must mean that they can have experience of God's Word, that they can be what they are as determined by God's Word.

It should be stated explicitly that in this presentation we are adopting what might be rightly intended in the favourite 19th century formula of " religious consciousness." We cannot, of course, agree with 19th century thinkers when they say that " there is " or that " man has " a religious consciousness. But we might say that men can have a religious consciousness, or, in our own vocabulary, that the Word of God can become the ground and object of man's consciousness. Thus when Schleiermacher spoke of the Christian consciousness or of self-consciousness he had in view a " being affected " (to K. H. Sack, 9.4.1825, *Letters*, Vol. 4, p. 335) which is obviously very similar to our " being determined." If we prefer the concept of experience, it is because it expresses something more comprehensive.

By the experience of God's Word which is possible for men on the presupposition of its reality, we understand the determination of their existence as men by God's Word.

If there is such a determination of human existence by God's Word, the primary point to be made is that this is not to be confused with a determination man can give his own existence. Naturally experience of the Word of God always takes place in an act of human self-determination. But it is not experience of the Word of God as this act. No determination man can give himself is as such determination by God's Word. Nor is there any place here for the view that this experience is a kind of co-operation between divine determining and human self-determining. Again, the undeniable fact that this experience takes place in an act of human self-determination does not mean that man in this self-determining accomplishes as it were a greater or lesser part of the whole and then leaves the rest to God's determining. Finally, we must also reject a view that is often commended as a solution—it was that of Augustine and is a central dogma in the school of Holl— namely, that have here a simultaneity, interrelation and unity in tension between the divine and human determining : What is seen from the one side as grace is freedom when seen from the other side and *vice versa*. All these theories are to be rejected because they are in contradiction to the self-knowledge of man in real experience of God's Word as we know it from the biblical promise. If man lets himself be told by the Word of God that he has a Lord, that he is the creature of this Lord, that he is a lost sinner blessed by Him, that he awaits eternal redemption and is thus a stranger in this sphere of time, this specific content of the Word experienced by him will flatly prohibit him from ascribing the possibility of this experience to himself either wholly or in part or from dialectically equating the divine possibility actualised in this experience with a possibility of his own. These theories—and not least the third—do not emanate from the only competent witness in this matter, namely, the man who stands in the event of real knowledge of the Word of God as this man is presented to us by Holy Scripture. They emanate from an onlooker who is interested in the event but only from outside, who regards the two determinations that are obviously present here, the one by God and the other by man himself, as the kind of determinations that might be rivals of one another, and who thus, as one would rightly do with other competing determinations, attempts to understand them in their co-existence, to effect a synthesis between them, his main interest obviously being in some way to maintain the self-determination of man in face of the determination of man by God. But the external onlooker with this interest fails to see—and as an external onlooker with this interest he is bound to do so—that the co-existence of God and man as it occurs in the experience of God's Word is not a co-existence on the same level, so that it is completely impossible to see it from a higher vantage point and to view it in its possibility. He also overlooks the fact that there can be no point in trying to maintain man's self-determination in some way, even dialectically, over against the determination of man by God. Precisely as self-determination, it is subject to determination by God. Our very self-determination needs this determination by God in order to be experience of His Word. In this relation of total subjection and need *vis-à-vis* determination by God it cannot possibly replace this, as Pelagius wished, or co-operate with it, as the Semi-Pelagians wished, or be secretly identical with it, as Augustine wished. Such solutions may be generally possible when the reference is to other competing determinations of man or of an object, but here, where it is a matter of the determination of man by God and by himself, they are impossible.

It would be a similar misunderstanding on a spectator's part, however, if he were to try to understand the situation of man in the experience of God's Word as an elimination of his self-determination or as a state of partial or total receptivity or passivity.

Because it almost of necessity gives rise to this idea, we prefer not to adopt Schleiermacher's concept of " dependence " in this connexion.

Even though there seems to be in this a very high appreciation of the idea of the omnipotence of God and His Word, it involves a misconception of the nature of the encounter between God and man. If God is seriously involved in experience of the Word of God, then man is just as seriously involved too. The very man who stands in real knowledge of the Word of God also knows himself as existing in the act of his life, as existing in his self-determination. We do not have to pronounce here whether this can and must really be said of man in general to the extent that one has to regard him as not just a natural being but as essentially and primarily a historical being.

More recent philosophy of various schools says this, and in so doing it is perhaps living more on borrowings from theology than is good for it as philosophy.

However that may be, the man who really knows God's Word, as this man comes before us in the biblical promise, can understand himself only as one who exists in his act, in his self-determination. The Word of God comes as a summons to him and the hearing it finds in

him is the right hearing of obedience or the wrong hearing of disobedience. Whether it is finally the one or the other is not, of course, in
his hands. For that, for obedience or disobedience in his action, he
cannot resolve and determine himself. As he decides, as he resolves and
determines, he is rather in the secret judgment of the grace or dis-
favour of God, to whom alone his obedience or disobedience is manifest.
And this is the overlapping determination by God which befalls his
self-determination. Nevertheless, it does not alter the fact that his
hearing is self-determination, act, decision. That the co-existence of
God and man in man's experience of God's Word is not on the same
plane, that it cannot be viewed in the same way as that of two other
entities, that its possibility as co-existence cannot, then, be perceived,
is something that has thus to be taken seriously on this side too. For
the man who is concerned for God's omnipotence and wants to solve
the problem on this side might also be an outside spectator trying to see
and judge from a higher vantage point and for that reason having no
understanding of the matter at all. At this point we can only repeat the
two statements already formulated but with a shift of emphasis. Our
very self-determination here is subject to determination by God. Our
very self-determination needs determination by God in order to be
experience of His Word. If human self-determination were not as it
were the material which is subject and in need when we speak of the
determination of human existence by the Word of God, then how could
we speak of the determination of human existence or indeed of a
determination by God's Word in any sense ? If God's Word is not
spoken to animals, plants and stones but to men, and if determination
by God's Word is really a determination of human existence, in what,
then, will it consist if not in the fact that the self-determination in
which man is man finds its absolute superior in determination by God,
that as self-determination, and without in the least being affected or
even destroyed altogether as such, it receives a direction, is set under
a judgment and has impressed upon it a character, in short, it is
determined in the way that a self-determining being is by a word and
that man is by the Word of God. The fact that this happens to it, and
what happens to it, is not the work of human self-determination. But
conversely it is the work of human self-determination to which this
happens, no matter what else may happen to it therewith.

When this is clear, the way is open for a more precise explanation of
our statement that men can have experience of God's Word. This
statement must now mean that men in their self-determination can be
determined by God's Word : not just determined by any external
factor that comes upon them, though naturally this can be true as well,
but also determined by the Word of God. At this stage three points
should be relatively easy to perceive.

1. To define the anthropological locus at which experience of the Word of God is possible, it is not necessary to emphasise one or another among the various possibilities of human self-determining, as though this and this alone were the chosen vessel of this experience. Will, conscience and feeling have been mentioned as such places, and whole theological systems have been built on the one preference or the other.

The reason why some prefer one anthropological locus and others another has always been that each has thought or hoped he could best justify a specific synthesis of the relations between divine and human determination, whether indeterministic, dialectical or deterministic, in terms of the one anthropological locus or the other. The unreality which is then, of course, inevitable on the presupposition of the necessity or possibility of such a synthesis has usually avenged itself in the form of a very one-sided view of religious experience and then of the Word of God which is supposedly experienced in this way. Now we have seen that the synthesis in question is neither necessary nor possible. We have thus no need to justify such a synthesis anthropologically. We have no need to stress the will in emphasis on human freedom, or conscience as the place where man becomes one with God's will, or feeling in order to make clear man's absolute dependence on God's omnipotence.

We may quietly regard the will and conscience and feeling and all other possible anthropological centres as possibilities of human self-determination and then understand them in their totality as determined by the Word of God which affects the whole man.

2. There is also no compulsion to invest certain anthropological centres with the fundamental distrust and suspicion that is often found in the history of theology. I have in mind especially the extraordinary polemic which it has been the fashion in recent years to wage against the so-called " intellect " of man, his powers of thought and understanding, as the locus of possible religious experience of the Word of God.

Two directly opposite reasons have been and are advanced for the special incompetence of the intellect in matters of religious experience. In the eyes of one group its activity in this area is a fatal sign that man, instead of actively determining his life himself, is on the point of sinking into the indolent passivity of mere reflection and contemplation. In the eyes of the other group the activity of the intellect is the peak of an overbold self-determination which, as they see it, ought to be broken and indeed completely smashed in experience of the Word of God. On the one side, then, the intellect lacks the real power, on the other the real humility, and on both the real depth which one hopes to encounter at other anthropological centres, e.g., conscience or feeling, as distinct from the intellect. What shall we say in answer ? This surely, above all, that we, too, see no reason anthropologically to prefer the intellect especially. What man does when he uses this faculty, when he thinks and tries to understand, can in fact be indolence, hubris or both like any other human self-determination. But is not the same true of feeling, conscience, will, or anything else one might mention here ? Are they not all self-determination, and no less so ? Can they be less so seeing that the differences regarding the relation of spontaneity and receptivity which might call for consideration at this point drop seriously in importance *vis-à-vis* the comprehensive determination of the whole of human existence by God's Word ? Is it not an arbitrary pre-judgment that specifically in the act of thought man is man in a poorer sense than in his other self-actualisations ? Is this pre-judgment really a judgment of the Christian faith, as is so often alleged ? It is a well-known fact that only in retreat before modern agnosticism and not before has the Christian faith reached this extraordinary judgment. But this pre-judgment might imply a worse barricading of oneself against God's Word. We recall the fact established earlier that it is not just in the last resort, but primarily and predominantly, that God's Word is literally speech, i.e., an intellectual event. If this is so, then its being spoken to man must at least claim the intellect too, and experience of it must at least include also the intellect, and the claiming of the intellect. Does not the anti-intellectualism of modern theology involve on the one side a striving for sanctification which rests on self-delusion with reference to other anthropological possibilities and will necessarily end in disenchantment, and then on the other side a restriction of the possibility of experience of God's Word at the most decisive point, which might involve at once a complete denial of it ? We can in no sense regard this as a respectable proceeding. We regard it as a form of cramp from which one must be healed to be able to see what is really to be seen here.

The Word of God that determines human existence is strong enough to deal also with man as he determines himself in thought. The same may naturally be said, and for the same reason, when attempts are made on the other side to discredit or exclude feeling or conscience as the locus of possible experience of the Word of God. If we have to reject it as more than a suspicious tyranny when Christian experience is interpreted expressly and preferentially as the experience of feeling or conscience, we obviously cannot assent to any exclusion of these anthropological centres.

In this sphere especially Evangelical theology is always threatened by the temptation to elevate the necessities of ephemeral polemics into denials in principle which cannot be carried through as such. We must resist this temptation in every direction.

3. Nor is there any need here to claim, discover, or assert any unusual or hidden anthropological centres as the basis of the possibility of human experience of God's Word. The existence of such unusual centres, which are more fully considered and investigated to-day than in earlier times, and the possibility that many more exist than are considered and investigated to-day, can indeed scarcely be doubted. Thus there are conscious and sub-conscious possibilities, and there would seem also to be semi-occult and occult possibilities of the human soul. There is also an intuitive grasp of objects apart from discursive thought and in all kinds of combinations with it. It may be that apart from the possibility of aesthetic feeling and attitude there is also that of a specifically religious variety.

One result of philosophical enlightenment as to the nature and limits of theoretical reason in particular was that from the time of Schleiermacher's discovery of the special " province " proper to religion in the mind of man theologians turned with a certain interested preference to these subsidiary areas of psychology. On our own presuppositions we shall have to say that we can really take no special interest in exhibiting such supposedly special places of possible religious experience. The possibilities which call for consideration in these subsidiary fields, both the generally recognised and the doubtful ones, are also in any case possibilities of human self-determination. So far as they can be claimed at all as human possibilities, they are rational possibilities in the broadest sense of the term. Their hiddenness and strangeness certainly do not qualify them as points of entry for the determination of man by God's Word. Here again, to the extent that we have specific human acts at all, our concern is still with acts of human self-determination, and it always will be no matter what discoveries may be made here nor what interpretations may be found. We do not say this in order to rule out these special places of human experience of the Word of God but to set them alongside the other, better known anthropological centres in the totality of human existence which is our concern here as the object of determination by God's Word.

Why should not the subconscious, or intuition, or whatever else might be mentioned here, have its place, too, among the possibilities of human existence in its determination by God's Word ? But again, why should it have a special dignity alongside and among the other, better known possibilities ? What depth psychology may have to say to us here along various lines may remind us of the breadth with which the concept of human existence will in any case have to be construed. All the same, from even the deepest depths of depth psychology we will not receive or expect information on this openness of human existence to the Word of God.

To summarise, human existence means human self-determination. If experience of God's Word involves the determination of human existence and hence also of human self-determination by the Word of God, then by self-determination we are to understand the exercise of all the faculties in whose exercise man is man without basic emphasis upon and also without basic repudiation of any specific human possibility. In this context all such emphases and repudiations are to be resisted already on the score of method, since they are the results or presuppositions of a general philosophical anthropology by whose constructions, however right or wrong they may be in their own sphere, we cannot allow ourselves to be influenced here. From different angles the determination of human existence by God's Word can be understood just as much as a determination of feeling, will, or intellect, and psychologically it may actually be more the one than the other in a given case. The decisive point materially, however, is that it is a determination of the whole self-determining man.

This settled, we push on a step further to the question in what the experience of God's Word, i.e., the determination of the whole self-determining man by God's Word, might then consist. To this question, which is so crucial for the whole problem of this section, an answer is given in the introductory thesis when it speaks of acknowledgment. I am aware of no word relatively so appropriate as this one to the nature of the Word of God whose determinative operation is our present concern. And in relation to what we know or think we know of man, this word is precise enough to say the specific thing that needs to be said about him here and yet also general enough to say this specific thing with the comprehensiveness with which it must be said here. To develop the concept of acknowledgment we shall borrow the nine points of orientation on the nature of the Word of God that we stated and explained in § 5.

1. The word acknowledgment entails first the concept of knowledge. This must be so because the Word of God is primarily and predominantly speech, communication from person to person and reason to reason, spirit, a rational event, the Word of truth, because it is addressed to the human *ratio*, by which one is not to understand the intellect alone, yet at any rate the intellect also and not last of all. If this is so, experience of God's Word must correspond thereto as far as possible. The word acknowledgment is at least an indication of this.

2. But this word also expresses the fact that experience of God's Word involves a relation of man as person to another person, naturally the person of God. We can also speak, of course, of the acknowledgment of facts, and we find this here too. But the kind of fact one acknowledges is not a fact of nature—one does not acknowledge a landslip or a rainbow or the like. The acknowledged fact is a fact created and presented by a person or persons. The determination of man's existence by the Word of God is created thus ; it is determination by God's person. This is another reason why we call it acknowledgment.

3. Acknowledgment relates to a definite control (positive or negative) with respect to the one who acknowledges. It means not only subjection to a necessity, but adaptation to the meaningfulness of this necessity, approval of it, not just involvement in it but acceptance of it. Acknowledgment of God's Word relates to the purposiveness of God's Word, to its content as the Word of the Lord, the Word of man's Creator, Reconciler and Redeemer. It must consist in the fact that man approves this Word (even if in a very specific sense) and accepts its content (even if in a very specific sense) as truth valid for him. Acknowledgment of God's Word by man consists in avowal of and submission to the purposes of God declared in God's Word, in affirmation (naturally in a very specific way) of the " God with us " that the Word of God has to tell its hearers.

4. Acknowledgment of God's Word must also mean, of course, respect for the fact that takes place in God's Word. But this fact consists especially in its coming to us, in its contingent contemporaneity

C.D.—H

as revelation, Holy Scripture and Church proclamation. *Illic et tunc* becomes *hic et nunc.* Jesus Christ Himself lives in the message of His witnesses, lives in the proclamation of His Church on the basis of this message, strides forward as the Lord of grace and judgment to meet the existence of the hearer of the Word. Experience of God's Word, then, must at least be also experience of His presence, and because this presence does not rest on man's act of recollection but on God's making Himself present in the life of man, it is acknowledgment of His presence.

5. In the word acknowledgment, as we have already said, there lies the relation to a control, a necessity. We have to remember that the Word of God has power, power as word has power, the power of God's truth, the power of His promise, claim, judgment and blessing which are its content, but power. Acknowledgment of the Word of God by man is naturally, then, approval of the Word of God by man, yet not approval on the basis of persuasion between equals, but the kind of approval that arises on the basis of obedience, of submission between those who are utterly unequal. To have experience of God's Word is to yield to its supremacy. Whether it comes to us as Law or Gospel, as command or promise, it comes at any rate in such a way as to bend man, and indeed his conscience and will no less than his intellect and feeling. It does not break him ; it really bends him, brings him into conformity with itself.

6. Acknowledgment certainly means decision too. The coming of God's Word to man is the act of divine freedom and choice. It does not have to come to him. It comes according to God's good-pleasure, and it is again God's good-pleasure how it comes to him, whether for grace or judgment. In every case, then, experience of the Word of God is experience of the divine freedom and choice, and therefore it is itself decision, decision concerning man which is manifested as the characterising of man's decision as a decision for faith or unbelief, for obedience or disobedience. In the first instance, then, the conformity to God's Word to which we have just referred might mean either obedience or disobedience. Even in disobedience there is an acknowledgment of God's Word, though against man's will and to his perdition. Even in his disobedience man characterises himself as the man he is before God's Word. Even disobedience is in its own way a confirmation or approval of God's Word to the degree that it is disobedience against God's Word and to the degree that even in disobedience man's self-determination is a fulfilment of his determination by the Word of God. The same may naturally be said of the decision for obedience. Just because experience of God's Word is such decision, man can and must be summoned in the Church to ever new experience and therefore to decision.

7. There also lies in the concept of acknowledgment the fact that the

act denoted thereby means halting before an enigma, acquiescence in a situation which is not open but which is unexplained from the standpoint of him who does the acknowledging. In § 5 we spoke of the secularity of the Word of God, i.e., of the fact that it comes to us in a form which also means its concealment. Experience of God's Word, then, must also consist in the fact that we receive it in this form and this concealment, in this twofold indirectness. Our very acceptance of the Word, which will be especially important later, will participate in this twofold indirectness. It, too, will have a secular form, the form of all kinds of human acts, and this form will be its concealment, its ambivalence. Apart from this ambivalence, which is deeply rooted in the very nature of the matter, there is no experience of God's Word. It will always consist also in respect for, and acknowledgment of, the mystery of this Word.

8. Just because acknowledgment of the mystery of God in His Word is at issue, we must also stress the fact that the term acknowledgment denotes an act or movement on man's part, a movement which only as it is made is the acknowledgment required, so that it cannot be resolved into an attitude. What prevents the latter in experience of God's Word, and what makes this experience, where it is real, into a movement, is what we called in § 5 the one-sideness of the Word of God. We meant by this the fact that the total Word of God, whether veiled and unveiled, or unveiled and veiled, always encounters us, and that this is each time something specific for us, that it is one-sided for us, that now it encounters us in its veiling and now in its unveiling, that it is not manifest to us in the unity of the two, and yet that it always seeks to be heard by us as a complete Word of God. In view of this, acknowledgment of the Word of God necessarily means letting oneself be continually led, always making a step, always being in movement from the experience felt at one time or the thought grasped at one time to the opposite experience and thought, because hearing of God's Word always consists in also hearing the one in the other and the other in the one. In this movement which cannot be arrested by any synthesis a man acknowledges the mystery of the Word of God and he has Christian experience.

9. When acknowledgment takes place, there is a yielding of the man who acknowledges before the thing or person he acknowledges. He submits to the authority of the other. This is not in contradiction with the concept of self-determination but it does mean that the self-determination of man as such takes place at a specific point in a specific context. It has found its beginning and its basis in another higher determination. In the act of acknowledgment, the life of man, without ceasing to be the self-determining life of this man, has now its centre, its whence, the meaning of its attitude, and the criterion whether this

attitude really has the corresponding meaning—it has all this outside itself, in the thing or person acknowledged. So far as it has all this, it has it from the thing or person acknowledged. Thus acknowledgment as an attitude is in every respect the act of this man and yet from the standpoint of the meaning of the attitude it is not at all his act but a determination that has come upon him from the thing or person acknowledged by him and compelling his acknowledgment. First there is the thing or person acknowledged, and then in virtue of it, and in the last resort deriving wholly from it, there is acknowledgment. We are confronted here by what we called in § 5 the spirituality of the Word of God, i.e., the grounding not only of its being spoken but also of its being really heard by man in the Word itself, the appropriation of God's Word as a gift of the Holy Spirit, and therefore as the Word's own act on man. Therewith we are also brought up against the frontier of what we can say about experience of God's Word as such. The final thing to be said is that while the attitude of acknowledgment *vis-à-vis* God's Word is really an attitude of man, an act of his self-determination, nevertheless it is the act of that self-determination of man whose meaning and basis, whose final seriousness and true content, whose truth and reality, cannot be ascribed to man himself but only to his determination by the Word of God. It is the act of pure acknowledgment, one might also say, the act in which acknowledgment consists in the fact that it merely seeks to be the answer to a " recognition "— at this frontier even the meaning of the word must change—which has come to man from beyond all his own acts or powers, of which he himself is not the subject, but in whose free truth and reality he must be acknowledged if he is to acknowledge its truth and reality.

It is as well to see and say at once that by taking place as an experience this experience ceases to be an experience. In the concluding sub-section, in order to close the circle of the problem of man's possibility of knowledge of the Word of God, or rather to indicate the point where it must finally be left open, we shall have to introduce and discuss at this juncture the concept of the faith which corresponds to the Holy Spirit of the Word of God. But before we do that it will be worth our while to look back for a moment and to state explicitly that experience of God's Word is possible, but that in respect of its meaning and basis, its final seriousness and true content, its truth and reality, it is not experience but more than experience.

We preface this negative and amplifying statement by a positive one. In what has been said thus far we have not denied but affirmed the possibility of human experience of God's Word. We have characterised it as genuine experience by emphasising as strongly as possible its character as human self-determination. We have not protested against the introduction of feeling or conscience or especially the intellect into experience of the Word of God. We have not combatted the concept of experience and we have even accepted " religious consciousness " without demur. We have described this experience, not in the form of a psychological study, but in the form of a conclusion from our earlier understanding of the nature of the Word of God, by mentioning a series of acts which with the partial exception of the frontier instance at the end can all be claimed as fully human acts possible to man. We shall not object if the nine or eight points in which we have developed acknowledgment are regarded and described in some fashion as an attempt to depict—formally as the situation here demands—the religious experience or consciousness of the Christian.

I must emphasise this because to my regret I am continually hearing it said that I am putting revelation and faith up in the clouds so far as the believer is concerned and teaching a *fides quae creditur* " without regard for the *fides qua creditur*, the intimate personal conviction and experience of faith." " The intimate personal experience of faith is to be completely eliminated." The transmission of revelation is not thought of in such a way " that the nature of man is also to be taken into account in it " (cf. G. Wobbermin, *Richtlinien ev. Theol.*, 1929, p. 22, 104, 139, 141, etc.). Or again from E. Schaeder I continually hear the vague complaint (the last time in *Das Wort Gottes*, 1930, p. 37 f.) that I am in danger " of exaggerating in an untenable way the protest against the place and validity of the ego in faith and the theology of faith." In my work one is compelled as " believer and theologian " to do " the impossible, namely, to jump over one's own shadow." In me the necessary battle against idealism turns head over heels and even so pure distance between the Spirit of God and the human spirit or finite ego is not yet achieved (*op. cit.*, p. 41), etc. I do not doubt for a moment, and will return to this, that the difference between the view of Wobbermin and Schaeder (to mention these as spokesmen for many others) and the view presented here is as deep as it can possibly be within the Evangelical church, and I do not really have any thought of trying to commend myself to them by concessions. But it will clarify the issue in dispute if they and others will refrain from ascribing to me negations which I have never sponsored in this form, not even ten years ago. There cannot really be any dispute as to whether regard should be had to the " intimate personal experience of faith " or whether the nature of man should be " taken into account " or whether an exaggerated, i.e., an " absolute " protest should be made against the place and validity of the ego. What sense would there be here in even a relative negation and protest, let alone an exaggerated one ? Nevertheless, I believe that the quiet affirmative that one can and must make at this point has still to be followed by different statements from those which Wobbermin and Schaeder would like to see and which would be as crucial for them in the whole dispute as my own further statements are for me.

We can concede everything that is in fact to be conceded here. We can thus state, as we have done in due form, that experience of God's Word involves an authentic experience possible for man. But we must then go on to ask whether experience of God's Word is possible in such a way that by it the store of human possibilities is enriched by a further one; whether man has a possibility, an organ, a capability that he did not have before; or, conversely, whether the possibility of experience of God's Word, being given to man in virtue of its actuality, is so given to him that it becomes a possibility which is certainly extraordinary, which may even perhaps be called miraculous, but which is still a possibility independently proper to him, the possibility of the religious man (of the pardoned man as one can and must also say), yet still of man. Does there take place in the reality of this experience a kind of divine emanation towards man, or, from man's standpoint, a divine *influxus* whose outcome is the possibility in question ? Can one deduce from the possibility of the experience of God's Word that there are men who have this possibility, perhaps in the same way as others have artistic possibilities as distinct from many of their fellow-men ? Do these men exist in such a way that they can discover and recognise themselves as possessors of this possibility or be discovered and recognised as such by others ? Does experience of God's Word become real in such a way that its possibility may be advanced and presupposed as a predicate, as a specific characteristic of certain men, as the property of a human I or We which can be asserted directly, un-equivocally and unreservedly in relation to this I or We ?

This is obviously the deduction of, e.g., Schaeder from the general pre-supposition when he can speak of " a conjunction between the Word of God and the finite ego " (*op. cit.*, p. 41) which takes place and can be exhibited in faith, or of a " word-bound ego " (p. 45), or when " in the question of the Word of God " he wants to begin with the believing ego "—" what else can one do ? " (p. 43), or when he claims knowledge of " a word-mediated synthesis between the Spirit of God and the finite spirit " (p. 46), an " inmost synthesis of word, history, human ego, Spirit of God and faith " (p. 50), a " relationship of the Word of God to the strict presence of him who receives it " (p. 49), or when on one occasion he can even describe the Word of God as " having arisen out of the synthesis of divine self-offering or revelation and the human relationship of faith effected by this revelation " (p. 105), or when he feels no difficulty in remarking incidentally : " We shall make no headway in promoting God's Word " until we have met such and such conditions (p. 103), or when finally his doctrine of the Word of God culminates in the reference to certain " men of sensibility " who represent the decisive operation of the Word of God or the Church of the Word (p. 170). It is a valuable service that should be mentioned here, since it spares us saying any more, that Robert Winckler has not only explicitly described this theory as " parallel in its main outlines " to that of his teacher Wobbermin but has also called it a " platform " on which to-day " all non-dialectical theology may find itself united " (*Th. Lit. Z.*, 1931, p. 550 ; cf. also Torsten Bohlin, *Th. Lit. Z.*, 1931, p. 570).

We must try to realise above all what it would mean if this theory were correct. It would obviously mean that we might now assert an aptitude of man for God's Word, a possibility of fulfilling man's determination by God's Word by means of human self-determination. I say " might " because this is not in the first instance asserted by the champions of this theory, i.e., not as a general possibility nor as one proper to man from the very outset. Indeed, it can even be emphatically denied by them as a possibility in this sense. On the basis of this theory it can even be said very zealously that the possibility of this experience is given to man by God and by God alone.

What was expressly stated in the first edition of this book (p. 92 f.) must be repeated here. We do injustice to Schleiermacher (and his followers right up to our own day) if we foist upon them the intention which was, of course, that of Feuerbach, namely, that of making the human subject the creator of his determination by God, as though their theology were direct Cartesianism. I do not think I missed the significance of Schaeder's catchword " theocentric theology " in the polemic which I then conducted against him. Schaeder now sets store on the fact that he can understand as a " word-bound ego " the ego which on his view is to be questioned about the Word of God in theology. Now at that time I quoted sentences like the following from his earlier book : " The factors with which we deal in knowledge are all factors of consciousness or they are not there for us to deal with. The God with whom theology has to do is the God of our consciousness and no other. Or He is the divine spirit-content of our consciousness. . . . The present finite spirit or personal consciousness is investigated by theology respecting its possession of God or the divine Spirit and the conditions thereof. It is not easy to see how it could be otherwise. This I term the theocentric in theology. Naturally theology in selecting this term starts with man or the spiritual consciousness of man. What sensible man would not do this ? But in consciousness or on the basis of consciousness it seeks to grasp by the means of knowledge available the divine reality of the Spirit, the pneumatic element, the reality of God " (*Das Geistproblem der Theologie*, 1924, p. 2, 4). But already at that time I also cited and considered Schaeder's further statement : " We reach God only in the way He reaches us, i.e., only on the basis of His revelation to us, which at least ultimately and conclusively is achieved in our consciousness if it is to count as revelation " (*op. cit.*, p. 63). I also think I understood Schaeder then exactly as he has now interpreted himself (*Das Wort Gottes*, 1930, p. 43 f.), i.e., I presented as his meaning just what he has now added by way of interpretation. And it should be expressly emphasised that in Wobbermin, too, one can find statements like the following : " The way in question leads from God to man, not *vice versa* from man to God. Man, who is always entangled in sin and guilt, does not enter the way to God on his own. For sin and guilt lead him away from God. Only God can make a connexion between God and man, and bridge the chasm which is torn open, and continually torn open afresh, by the sin of man " (*Richtlinien ev. Theol.*, 1929, p. 102). Thus on the points that man is not apt for God's Word *a priori* and in general, that in experience of God's Word he does not act at all creatively, that the possibility of this experience is not to be regarded as one originally pertaining to him but rather as one accruing to him, there can be no quarrel with the representatives of this theory.

But what at first seems to hold good and is maintained on the basis of this theory, the action, creation or gift of God in the experience of His Word, suddenly ceases to apply at a specific point. And what at first seems not to hold good and is denied on the basis of this theory, the aptitude of man for this experience, suddenly comes into play at a specific point. The start is apparently not Cartesian but the subsequent course is plainly so. The reality of this experience, i.e., man's determination by the Word of God, is thought of in such a way that in it God hands something over to man in the sense that it really passes out of God's hand into the hands of man, or, from man's standpoint, in such a way that man receives something from God in the sense that it is really put in his hands. A conjunction or synthesis has taken place. Man's consciousness now has a divine content of spirit in the light of which it can be contemplated and investigated. The statement *homo capax verbi Dei* suddenly comes to life. There arises in the reality of this experience as something that is present and can be demonstrated and presupposed a new man, new not only in the sense that he is man addressed by the Word of God, new, then, not only in Christ—who could or would oppose that ?—but new in himself, changed in the immanent constitution of his humanity. Even if on the basis of his being addressed by the Word, this man now acquires autonomy and independent interest as a participant in the reality of the Word, so much so that if the introduction of the concept of mysticism is not quite indispensable it is at least obvious and desirable.

Cf. Schaeder, *Das Geistproblem*, p. 118 f. and more cautiously *Das Wort Gottes*, p. 54. I do not know whether to regard it as uncertainty in terminology or as material wavering when in his final statements Schaeder describes " faith-mysticism " primarily as the " active proximity of God," as the claiming, adoption and justification of man (*Das Wort Gottes*, p. 33 f., cf. also p. 47), but then goes further and says that it is not only that but also " a characteristic inner transformation of the ego or enrichment of its content " (*op. cit.*, p. 41). The decisive step is not the introduction of the concept of mysticism but the definition of it in this way, the assertion of the " conjunction " or " synthesis."

The man thus distinguished is not, then, man in general, nor does any possibility presupposed as such in man correspond to the content of divine Spirit. This man is the particular man usually called the religious man or the believing Christian man. And his possibility of being a bearer of the content of divine Spirit is the possibility he has received in the reality of experience of the Word of God. Nevertheless —and this is the point—it is a possibility which is proper to him, which has become proper to him, as this man, the religious man. In a depth of his being which is hidden, yet not completely hidden but penetrable, his existence or self-determination is identical with the fulfilment of his determination by God's Word. He does not stand only on the Word of God. While constantly appealing to the Word of God, he also stands on himself, on the conjunction or synthesis which is actual in him and therefore possible for him, on the *esse capax verbi Dei* imparted to him.

His " own personal experience of faith " now becomes, in the words of Wobbermin, the " opposite pole " to the Word and hence a " methodical aid " to knowledge of the Word, even though this be understood as a subordinate entity (*Richtlinien*, p. 140 f.).

And the reality of the experience of God's Word no longer rests on itself ; it has become an ellipse instead of a circle, and one of the poles, the one nearer us and opposite God, is the man who has the experience.

Is it not inevitable that the man who is thus characterised as the opposite subjective pole will find that he is nearer himself than the Word of God is, that the new epistemological order of man to God will come into force afresh, and that even with the double safeguard that the reference is to pardoned man and that the material order is the reverse (cf. Wobbermin, *Wort Gottes und ev. Glaube*, 1931, p. 9 and Robert Winckler, *Theol. Lit. Z.*, 1931, pp. 550–51) it will come into full force for the first time ? When a theology starts with the believing ego in the question of God's Word (Schaeder, *Das Wort Gottes*, p. 43), can it avoid making the believing ego, the known Christian believer, the criterion and standard of its statements about God's Word ? And can it be denied that the Cartesianism which has apparently been rejected is thereby brought back into theology as, so to say, an indirect Cartesianism, the Cartesianism of the believing Christian ? In this event has not the concept " theocentric theology " become a *lucus a non lucendo* ?

Thus in real experience of the Word of God man becomes an independent actualisation of this experience with his own independent interest. He thereby makes the experience possible. There are religious men into whose existence and nature the Word of God has entered and is present and whose existence and nature are therefore bound to become the depository and the first and decisive criterion and standard of knowledge of the Word of God. This thesis we must oppose.

Let it not be thought that this thesis and our opposition to it are just a theological quibble that might well be left unsettled. Behind Professors Wobbermin and Schaeder and their view of the independent being and possession of religious man with its independent interest there stands the *Ecclesiam habemus* of General Superintendents Dibelius and Schian, the " common sense " of practically the whole of our positive and liberal ministry, and the prevailing tendency in the pietistic community-movement, which at this point is intimately bound up with the prevailing tendency in the Church at large. Tell them what Wobbermin and Schaeder are also trying to tell them, that the material order with reference to experience of God's Word must run from God to man and not *vice versa*, and they will all applaud and agree with you to-day. Tell them further that for man generally, for man without faith or before faith, the epistemological order must also be from God to man, that without preceding revelation there can be no faith, and they will concede your point, not yet being affected themselves. But tell them that this epistemological order applies also and particularly to the religious man, that he also and particularly has no possibility, not even a received possibility, but can only receive the possibility of experience of God's Word, can use it only as it is conferred in the actuality of reception, tell them that this possibility is and remains God's possibility and does not pass out of His hands into any other hands, tell them this and at once bitter and irreconcilable controversy breaks out. When we tell them this, when we oppose to that thesis our counterthesis, which is separated from it only by a blade's breadth and yet by a chasm's depth, then an impressive majority among both the leaders and the led in the modern Evangelical Church is passionately against us. Now the

C.D.—H*

feeling on the other side that everything is at stake here for faith and love and hope, for thought and life, for the world and the Church—this feeling is in every respect ours too, and anyone who sees the issue will have this feeling, no matter what position he may adopt. Let everyone make his choice and let none continue to look around for new and tiresome attempts at mediation!

We must now develop the reason for our rejection of this indirect Christian Cartesianism and also our own thesis regarding the possibility of experience of God's Word.

To do this we must first summarise again the positive content of our train of thought thus far. We have stated that if there is any Church and Church proclamation in a serious sense, this implies that knowledge of the Word of God is possible for some men. The fact that this knowledge is possible for them necessarily means that experience of God's Word is possible for them, i.e., that it is possible that certain men may be determined by the Word of God in their existence, i.e., in the totality of their self-determination. It is possible, as we have said more precisely in the light of God's Word, that the relation of these men to the Word of God may be the relation of acknowledgment. In the possibility of acknowledgment of the Word of God there thus consists the possibility of experience and therefore of knowledge of the Word of God. At this point Cartesianism now encounters us a second time in the specific form of indirect Christian Cartesianism. This interprets the possibility as one which in the act of real acknowledgment (or experience or knowledge) of the Word of God, and in the form of an emanation from the Word of God spoken to man or an *influxus* into the man addressed by the Word of God, becomes man's own, a predicate of his existence, a content of his consciousness, his possession. We must now make a demarcation against this interpretation of the possibility in question.

To this end we return again to the beginning. We are dealing with the possibility of knowledge of God's Word. We are thus dealing with the possibility of confirmation of the acquaintance man has with God's Word. We are dealing with the fact that for men acquainted with God's Word through revelation, Scripture and proclamation, God's Word can and must become true in such a way that its truth becomes their own and they become responsible witnesses to its truth. We are dealing with the fact that the Church and Church proclamation can be there in truth among men and through men. As stated already at the beginning of the section, no small thing depends on this possibility. On our understanding of this possibility depends the way in which we understand the Church and Church proclamation, and as regards dogmatics the way in which we understand its particular ministry in the Church, the testing, criticising and correcting of Church proclamation. For the Word of God is the criterion of the Church, Church proclamation and dogmatics. When we ask where the possibility of knowledge of God's Word is to be sought, we are asking where the criterion is to be sought with which dogmatics works. It makes a great difference whether in answer to this question we say with indirect Christian Cartesianism that it is given by God to the religious man, the Christian believer, that it is handed over to him by God, that we are thus to seek it in him, in his own personal experience of faith as such, in his " word-bound ego," among the contents of his consciousness— whether we have to say all this or whether we are perhaps not to say it at all. Dogmatics will be very different, Church proclamation will be very different and finally the whole Church will be decisively different according to whether this must be said or not. The whole question of the relation of the Church to the truth will be put very differently according to whether the answer here is Yes or No, and so too will the relation of the truth to the Church. The presence of truth in the Church or its absence from it might depend on whether the Church goes the one way or the other at this point. Jesus Christ can and will confess in some way—and that a salutary and victorious way—even a Church with a bad dogmatics and a bad proclamation due to a wrong decision at this point. This can and should be said by way of comfort. But we neither can nor should be content with that. We must open our eyes as widely as possible at this cross-roads and only with the best possible conscience should we decide for the right hand or the left. We must be as sure of ourselves as men can possibly be when we seek the possibility of knowledge of God's Word either the one way or the other. And the question must now be : Can we be sure of ourselves if we seek this possibility in the religious man, the believing Christian ? Are we certain that in what we can find, affirm, consider and analyse in him as the possibility of such a man we can really find and affirm the possibility of knowledge of the Word of God ? Or, from the opposite angle, can we be sure that we can really find among the possibilities of such a man, and affirm in one of the possibilities of such a man, the possibility of knowledge that corresponds to real knowledge of the Word of God, this possibility on the understanding of which so much later depends ? Can we say with final human certainty that this is so ? Can we put our hand in the fire for it ? (We can only *ask* in relation to this decision, but at all events we *must* ask ; we must ask whether we can be responsible with ultimate human seriousness for ascribing the possibility of knowledge of the Word of God to the religious man as such.) And it is to the question as put in this way that our answer must be No. We could give an affirmative answer only with penultimate seriousness, only with a wavering conscience, only with semi-certainty.

We might well be responsible for saying Yes here if it were not a matter of the possibility of knowledge of the Word of God but only, e.g., the possibility of understanding Plato's wisdom and culture. Where else should we seek and find and study this if not in the representatives of this wisdom and culture, in the men gripped by its pathos and ethos? We might well take the responsibility of saying Yes at this point if it were not a question of the criterion of dogmatics but the principle of a philosophy or world-view, if it were not a question of the proclamation of the Church but of the message of a union of *illuminati* and men of profound insight, if it were not a question of the Church but of a society of stirred partisans seeking to stir others. If we were dealing with the possibility of human knowledge of things in man's sphere, it would in fact be natural and necessary to seek this possibility, whatever its objective content, in the appropriate experts, i.e., in ourselves if we are among them, or in others, or at all events in those involved. We might entertain with ultimate human certainty the expectation of really finding it there and getting orientation and instruction there.

But in the case of the possibility of knowledge of the Word of God the situation is quite different. To be sure, it, too, has its special bearers, its experts, its representatives. There are indeed men who have this possibility. We ourselves are perhaps among those who have it, namely, as the reflection or echo of its reality, in the act of the Word spoken to us, in the event of experiencing it. But if we regard ourselves or others among such men, and then affirm in ourselves or in them this possibility that has as it were been infused by God, do we not come up at once against an insuperable difficulty which proves to be the end of all, yes, *all* certainty in any such assertion? When we try to find the content of divine Spirit in the (pardoned) consciousness of man, are we not like the man who wanted to scoop out in a sieve the reflection of the beautiful silvery moon from a pond? What can or shall we find there to investigate? As the substance of human experience of God's Word, obviously that which we have designated and described as the act of acknowledgment of God's Word: a human process of a very characteristic and differentiated and at the same time comprehensive kind. Because this process is indeed present and may be lived, asserted and described, we speak of a possibility of human experience of the Word of God. In establishing this process in ourselves or others, we take this possibility into account. But does this mean that we really find this possibility in the process, that we reckon with the possibility, because we have found it in this process? Is it not the case that we do not see or grasp the possibility at all in this process as such, that what we do see and grasp is never more than the process itself, which might as such be something very different from that possibility? Is it a fact that the acknowledgment that takes place in us or others must really be acknowledgment of the Word of God, that it can refer only to this, the counterpart of the divine Word, that it is a faithful mirror of this counterpart, that we may deduce this counterpart from the human acknowledgment, that we may regard man as confronted with this counterpart ? Who tells us that ? Who guarantees it ? Who, when we have in view the ascertainable human possibility as such, can vouch for it that this is the possibility corresponding to the reality of the Word of God and not a completely different possibility ? For all the nine elements we assembled under the concept of acknowledgment (with the possible exception of the last, to which we ventured to apply the concept of experience only in part), cannot striking parallels be adduced among possibilities of a very different kind ? Can this acknowlegment of God's Word be differentiated even from the phenomenon of what are called " other religions " with any clear distinctiveness or individuality? To the degree that it has its reality in this human acknowledgment, does not Christianity undeniably belong to the sphere of general religious history in which there are no doubts hills and valleys but no heaven ? And does not the whole sphere of religious history itself lie in the comprehensive sphere of the general history of culture ? Is there even a single so-called religious phenomenon which cannot be more or less completely interpreted as the prototype or residuum of a thoroughly this-worldly attempt at civilisation, as a phenomenon of work in the broadest sense of the term ? And is culture anything but the life-act of man understood from the standpoint of work ? If we cling to what we can affirm and investigate as the human acknowledgment of God's Word, to what can be experienced in Christian experience, where shall we find there the criterion by which to distinguish this experience from others, the authentic from the inauthentic ? What is there here to stop us interpreting everything in terms of the religious, the cultural, the human generally, or finally indeed the biological ? With what certainty can one know and maintain that in what is seen to take place as an act of acknowledgment in the religious man there is really present the acknowledgment of the Word of God spoken to him and therefore the possibility of his experience or knowledge of it ? No, the certainty that dogmatics, Church proclamation and the Church itself need in relation to the possibility of knowledge of God's Word is not to be attained here. All that can be attained consists only of vague assertions in support of which one can hardly avoid having recourse to direct philosophical Cartesianism.

Schaeder's dictum is simply not true, that " every subjective explanation of these subjective phenomena of consciousness breaks down " (*Das Geistproblem d. Theol.*, 1924, p. 65). And when Wobbermin insists that " the ultimate supreme reality " which is the opposite pole of the " basic act of religion " shows itself to be secure against the suspicion of subjective illusion by the fact that this basic act, as I-related, enjoys " the primal reality of the whole certainty and validity of reality," namely, the I-consciousness (*Syst. Theol.*, Vol. 2, 1921, p. 456), this simply shows that even as a follower of indirect Cartesianism one is forced at the crucial point to take refuge in the original and direct form and to swear by the certainty of the self-certainty of man in general. In fact what happens to us when we point to what the Word of God itself does to and in and through us is exactly what happened to Aaron when he caused his rod to turn into a serpent before Pharaoh and his court : " Then Pharaoh also called the wise men and the sorcerers : now the magicians of Egypt, they also did in like manner with their enchantments. For they cast down every man his rod, and they became serpents " (Ex. 7[10f.]). The only thing is that we unfortunately cannot command the sequel : " But Aaron's rod swallowed up their rods."

It might be objected, of course, that in all this we have been looking only, so to speak, at the outward aspect of the act that we may experience, that we have been viewing it only, so to speak, as a phenomenon. It would have to be granted that it cannot be recognised as this specific act, and that certainty as to its authenticity cannot be reached, when it is viewed thus. But things are quite different, it might be argued, when we ask what the man engaged in the act knows about himself, whether for this man—and therefore universally in so far as this man is a normative witness to the matter in question—the act is not distinctively, unequivocally, visibly and perceptibly this act and not another, whether the possibility of experience or knowledge of God's Word that is sought is not, then, visibly and perceptibly distinct from all other acts and possibilities. Our reply is that in fact the apparently unavoidable relativising of the act might find its own limit in the limit of its external aspect, of its purely theoretical consideration, and that beyond this (on the basis of its inner aspect and hence in analysis of its existential character) new territory might open up, and there might also result a certain interpretation of the act with reference to its relation to the Word of God. How could we refuse, then, to entertain the proposal that the question be put in this broader or deeper form ? One thing, however, we must stipulate. The man engaged in this act, who is to be a witness here and whose self-understanding must decide, must be the man we know from the promise. Only this man can tell us about the possibility that corresponds to real experience of the Word of God. My self-understanding can be significant here only to the degree that I understand myself as confronted with the promise, i.e., with the Word of God as it encounters me in revelation, Scripture and proclamation, only to the degree that I see myself in the specific light that falls upon my existence from this. Analysis of my self-understanding here can only mean appealing to what the promise tells every man about himself, and to what only the promise can tell him decisively and effectively about himself. Asseverations about a personal situation, if this is what existential talk means, can be of no importance here. If on these conditions we accept the demand that the inner aspect of the apprehensible act of acknowledgment and therefore of Christian experience be given its say, then we are

simply saying that from this angle it is not the human act as such, not
what can be and is experienced as such, not what is really put in our
hands as such, not what can be achieved and established by man as
such, that absolutely distinguishes, characterises and qualifies this
specific act among and alongside man's other possibilities as the act in
which the determination of man by the Word of God takes place. To
be sure, the man who is really determined by God's Word will perform
this act. There is no real knowledge of the Word without performance
of this act. As man knows God's Word, all that we have said about this
act can be and is experienced. It becomes real and can be established
psychologically. There takes place an understanding, a personal
involvement, an acceptance, an assent, an approval, a making present
of remote times, an obedience, a decision, a halting before the mystery,
a stimulation by the inner life, a basing of man's whole life on this
mystery that is beyond himself. All this takes place and has to do so.

That man's encounter with God according to the Old and New Testaments
is the very opposite of a transcendental drama which man confronts almost as a
bored spectator, that the biblical concepts of renewal and sanctification, of faith,
knowledge and obedience, of repentance, love, humility, gratitude, etc., invariably
point also to a very concrete event and act that can be experienced and established psychologically, is something that admittedly no less a person than Luther
repeatedly emphasised. We may simply recall in this connexion some of the most
general passages in which the accent falls especially on the fact that this event
can be experienced : " The same peace hovers over all sense, reason and understanding. Hence thou must not think of it as though none could feel or experience
it ; for if we are to have peace with God, then we must first feel it in heart and
conscience, how else could our heart and mind be kept by it ? . . . (*Advents-
postille*, Phil. 4[4f.], 1522, *W.A.*, 10[12], p. 186, l. 15). " For if a man enter into the
illusion he has faith and yet never experiences it, he will rot and dry up, and nought
is found when it comes to the point it should be found " (*Sermon on Jn.* 4[10f.], 1532,
W.A., 36, p. 468, l. 29). " If then . . . ye have grasped the resurrection of Christ
with faith and have received power and comfort of the same, and are therefore
risen together with Him, that must prove itself in you such that it is felt and
traced in you as it hath begun to work in you, that it is not alone word but truth
and life. For to those that feel it not thus, Christ hath not yet arisen . . . (*Cruc.
Sommerpostille, Sermon on Col.* 3[1-7], *W.A.*, 21, p. 266, l. 20). ". . . take to thyself
the Word of God, go and listen to man's preaching, or read or write or even sing
it, so that thy sole concern and act is with it, then wilt thou feel somewhat,
that will not fail " (*Sermon on Lk.* 24[13ff.], 1523, *W.A.*, 12, p. 500, l. 10). ". . . the
call of the spirit in the heart must thou feel, for it is always also thy heart's call,
how shouldst thou not then feel it ? . . . If thou feelest not the call, take thought
and cease not to pray till God hear thee ; for thou art Cain and it standeth not
well with thee. . . ." (*Kirchenpostille*, 1522, *Sermon on Gal.* 4[1f.], *W.A.*, 10[1],
p. 372, l. 10 ; p. 373, l. 2). Cf. also Calvin : *Consequitur fidem a pio affectu nullo
modo est distrahendam* (*Instit.*, III, 2, 9). *Id autem* (assurance of faith) *fieri nequit,
quin eius* (God's goodness) *suavitatem vere sentiamus et experiamur in nobis ipsis*
(*ib.*, III, 2, 15).

But the fact that all this happens and must happen does not mean
in the least that the possibility of experience of God's Word is to be

seen and found in this event, that in it human self-determination becomes the opposite pole of the divine determination, that man becomes a " word-bound ego " in contemplation of which we must orientate ourselves in the question of the Word of God. The very man who is really engaged in this act will never even partially, not even in the tiniest part, see in this act as such something that makes possible what is the meaning, basis and end, the truth and reality of this act. No matter how authentic and good and strong he feels, he will not " feel " himself to be an " opposite pole," he will not think that as a " word-bound ego " he can leave his own sphere, he will not expect new experience, not even partially, in the form of self-experience. He will indeed be called by God in his whole existence ; " with all his heart and soul and mind and strength " he will be involved. But not for a moment or in any respect will he think that his being involved is even approximately an adequate counterpart to the promise and claim confronting him. Not for a moment or in any respect will he rely upon the fact that he is involved, or orientate himself by it, or take from it the standard for understanding the reality in which he stands : he will not want to reflect on it but will simply be in it. Not for a moment or in any respect will he want to come back to his involvement or cling to it or build upon it. The judgment of the divine Word is passed on his involvement even as it takes place. What acknowledgment of God's Word in our experience, what understanding, involvement, assent, obedience, etc., can even remotely deserve to be called real acknowledgment of God's Word ? What acknowledgment of God's Word in our experience is not unmasked and convicted by the Word of God even as it takes place, convicted not of its imperfection and inadequacy but of its total corruption and futility ?—for as surely as all else we do it is the work of the human heart whose inventions and endeavours are bad from youth up and can be helped only by forgiveness. In what acknowledgment of God's Word in our experience, then, can there be anything like a sure and necessary correspondence to the Word of God ? If there really is, then it is in virtue of the acknowledgment which man cannot achieve and therefore cannot assert, but which comes by grace upon his work that is corrupt and dead through sin, for Christ's sake and not for the sake of his inner disposition. How else can it be even in the religious man, the believing Christian ? He it is specifically who knows, who alone knows, that this is how it is and not otherwise. The saying *finitum non capax infiniti* cannot really prove what has to be proved at this point. If the real experience of the man addressed by God's Word is against this saying, then the saying must go, as every philosophical statement in theology that is in contradiction with this experience must go. As a philosophical saying it does not interest us in the slightest. We do not say *finitum* but *homo peccator non capax*, and we do not continue *infiniti* but *verbi Domini*. The real experience of the man addressed by God's Word is the very thing that decides and proves that what makes it possible lies beyond itself.

We think of Peter's ἐξελθε ἀπ᾽ ἐμοῦ ὅτι ἀνὴρ ἁμαρτωλός εἰμι (Lk. 5⁸) and of the saying of the father of the epileptic boy : πιστεύω · βοήθει μου τῇ ἀπιστίᾳ (Mk. 9²⁴). The same Luther who rates experience so highly can also say along this line : " Faith is such that it feeleth not but droppeth reason, shutteth the eyes and simply surrendereth to the Word, and followeth the same through death and life. But feeling goeth not beyond what can be grasped by reason and the senses, as what is heard, seen and felt, or known by the outward senses. Therefore feeling is counter to faith, faith to feeling. . . . Whoso then pursueth feeling, he is destroyed, but whoso counter to feeling dependeth heartily upon the Word, he will be brought through " (*Sommerpostille*, 1526, *Sermon on Mk*. 16¹ᵗ·, *W.A.*, 10¹² p. 222, l. 21 and p. 223, l. 34). " But an I believe God and be born anew, I close my eyes and grope not and let the soul's being wholly perish and exclaim, Ah, God, in thy hand standeth my soul. Thou hast preserved it in my life, and I have never known where Thou hast set it, therefore will I likewise not know what Thou wilt do with it now and henceforth, of this alone am I sure, it standeth in Thy hand, Thou wilt surely help it " (*Sommerpostille*, 1526, *Sermon on Jn.* 3¹⁻¹⁵, *W.A.*, 10¹², p. 301, l. 20). " The Word I speak thou hearest well, but thou knowest neither its beginning nor its end. Just as thou knowest not where the wind starteth or where it ceaseth, so also thou knowest not whence the Word cometh and whither it goeth. The bodily voice and the outward sound thou hearest well, but the power of the Word thou seest not, what it doeth, how the Spirit worketh with and by the Word. Therefore the Word must be believed against all sight and feeling of the understanding. If we would discuss much how it befalleth, 'tis all up " (*Sermon on Jn.* 3¹⁻¹⁵, 1532, *E.A.*, 4, p. 177). " And so not a Christian do I see. Nor can I myself say, This hour or in that place shall I become a Christian. In short 'tis not within sight or time or place, 'tis beyond grasp or feeling, it dependeth not on apparel or on this or that we see or feel, 'tis literally nought. Well, what concern of mine, if 'tis nought ? Yea, 'tis nought if thou quiz thy five senses thereon or take counsel with thy reason and wisdom. But thou must set aside sense and reason and consider 'tis somewhat other that maketh a Christian, whereof thou hearest no more than the breath and rustle. An thou hearest the voice, follow it and have faith in it, so shalt thou be born anew " (*Expos. of Jn* 3, 1538–40, *W.A.*, 47, p. 29, l. 22). This, too, is the place to recall a thought that Calvin was fond of expressing, namely, that the weakness and folly of all philosophical talk about the " supreme good " is that in it man is riveted to himself : *quum necesse sit extra nos exire*. The " supreme good " is *coniunctio cum Deo*. But this demands a *conformatio* of man with God. But this can take place only in a negation of man, in a full *quiescere ab operibus nostris*. And so : *hinc semper faciendum est exordium, quum de regula pie sancteque vivendi agitur, ut homo sibi quodammodo mortuus Deum patiatur vivere ; ferietur ab operibus propriis, ut locum Deo agenti concedat. Fateri enim necesse est, tunc recte demum constitutam esse vitam quum Deo subiecta est. Atqui propter ingenitam pravitatem hoc nunquam fit, donec a propriis operibus supersedemus. Talis inquam repugnantia est inter Dei gubernationem et nostros affectus, ut in nobis agere, nisi otiosis, nequeat* (*Comm. on Heb.* 4¹⁰, *C.R.*, 55, 48).

The " perishing of the being of the soul " or the " 'tis literally nought " of Luther and Calvin's *locum concedere Deo agenti*, the passivity and even death of man in face of the divine act, undoubtedly mean that a mystical vocabulary has already appeared. We should not object to it, for this vocabulary can hardly be avoided at this point. If experience of God's Word is such that it can have its basis and certainty only outside itself, then understanding of it as true and actual experience is in fact understanding of its own radical end and of the fact that there is here a real perishing and dying of man. This is the new land which opens up when one does not just consider Christian experience as a phenomenon but lets it speak for itself. If we want to call the thought of the far side of all experience that comes to light here a mystical one, it is not worth while contesting the word so long as it is clear—and this is not often clear in what is called mystical thinking—that this far side cannot be as it were a hinterland of the sphere of human acts, experiences and possessions, a hinterland which we have still to tread and occupy, a human act, or the content of a human act, which can now be established by new methods. The far side in which real experience seeks and finds its true basis, in relation to which it knows it is true and actual experience, in acknowledgment of which alone it is ready to consist, to consist without claim to a content or seriousness of its own, so to consist that it is ready to consist as acknowledgment from and to this alone—this far side is to be understood as a genuine and immutable far side which cannot be changed into this side, as the side of God the Lord, the Creator, the Reconciler and the Redeemer. Human self-determination as it takes places also and precisely in acknowledgment of God's Word, i.e., human experience of God's Word, will never be able to see, perceive or understand itself, if it is real, as determined by the Word of God. It will be this without seeing or understanding itself in this being. It will just be true from God that human existence is engaged here in acknowledgment of the Word of God. For it will be true that God has spoken and man has heard. A new, regenerate man will arise in the act of this acknowledgment as the man whom God has addressed and who hears God, unknown, of course, to himself and others, in a newness that cannot be ascertained, for what can be ascertained in him will always be the old, not possessing himself, for to the extent that he possesses himself he certainly does not possess this regenerate man. But it will be true that he is kept in the peace of God which passes all understanding. It will be true in absolute independence of all the criteria of truth that the secular or even the religious man has first to provide and apply critically before he very kindly resolves to let what is true be true. All this will be true in itself just as the Word of God is true in itself. Its truth will be nothing other (no opposite pole ! no subjective counterpart !) than the truth of God's Word itself. The possibility of knowledge of God's Word lies in God's Word and nowhere else. In the absolute sense its reality

can only take place, and it can do so only as a miracle before the eyes
of every man, secular and religious, Greek and Jew.

" It is only an appearance that the rainbow stands on the earth, in reality it
arches over the earth ; true, it stoops down to the earth, yet it does not stand on
our earth, but is only perceived from it. So it is with divine truth ; this needs
no human support, as the rainbow does not need the earth. True, it shines on
man and he receives it ; yet it is not dependent on man. It withdraws and man
remains in darkness ; it returns and man walks in light. But man is not its
assistant ; he cannot produce the light ; similarly he cannot store it " (Eduard
Böhl, *Dogmatik*, 1886, p. XXV). " Therefore when I die—but I die no more—
and someone finds my skull, let this skull preach to him and say : I have no
eyes, yet I behold Him ; I have no brain nor understanding, yet I comprehend
Him ; I have no lips, yet I kiss Him ; I have no tongue, yet I praise Him with
all who call upon His name. I am a hard skull, yet I am quite softened and
melted in His love ; I lie outside here in the churchyard, yet I am within in
Paradise. All suffering is forgotten. This His great love has done for us, since
for us He bore His cross and went forth to Golgotha " (H. F. Kohlbrügge,
Passionspredigten,[3] 1913, p. 173 f.). This is the voice of true Christian experience.

This miracle is faith, and in the fourth sub-section we shall say
what needs to be said about this in the present connexion.

Let us make here the final statement in the present train of thought.
We have put to Christian Cartesianism the question whether we can
be responsible for the thesis of the immanence of the possibility of
experience of God's Word in the consciousness with the final human
seriousness commensurate with its significance for dogmatics, Church
proclamation and the Church generally, whether we can put our hand
in the fire for it, whether, one might also ask, we can pledge ourselves
to champion and defend it as *articulus stantis et cadentis ecclesiae*. We
have seen that the act of acknowledging the Word of God, so far as its
immanence in the consciousness can be established from outside,
historico-psychologically, by observation of ourselves or others,
cannot even be characterised unequivocally as this act, let alone known
in its relation to the Word of God. All that can be established are human
possibilities in immovable proximity and indissoluble similarity to other
human possibilities. We have also seen that even the transition to
" existential " thinking does not help us here but proves definitively
that nothing is to be gained along these lines. For if this thinking is the
self-understanding of the man who has learned about himself from
God's Word, then this inward aspect of Christian experience will itself
bear witness that real acknowledgment of the Word of God does not rest
at all on a possibility imparted to man and thus integral to him or
immanent in him, but that it rests in God's Word itself, which man and
his possibilities can in no sense precede but only follow. And now we
for our part must advance the following positive conclusion. This
possibility, in distinction from others that slip through our fingers, the
possibility of human experience of the Word of God understood as

the possibility of this Word itself, is one that we can and must affirm with certainty, with final human seriousness. It can and must be championed and defended as *articulus stantis et cadentis ecclesiae*. We can and must actually put our hand in the fire for its character as a unique possibility. When we refer to this possibility in dogmatics, in Church proclamation and in the Church generally, we are in all circumstances building on the rock and not on the sand.

H. M. Müller (" Credo ut intelligam," *Theol. Bl.*, 1928, p. 167 f.) has brought against me the charge that in my dogmatics I merely confront the one " unheard of assurance " of Neo-Protestantism with another. Of course! is my only possible reply. The " assurance " of the Neo-Protestant thesis is not " unheard of " because it is assurance, but because it is not and cannot be what it purports to be. The assurance with which dogmatics, Church proclamation and the Church may refer to the possibility of human knowledge of God's Word cannot be great enough, and it is my opinion—and naturally not mine alone—that in relation to the unique and distinctive possibility at issue here, in relation to the self-certainty of the divine Word, it must even be an " unheard of " assurance.

It will be continually asked, of course, whether we know this possibility. Now it stands or falls with the real utterance of God's Word to us, which we cannot anticipate as such, which we can only have before us and expect as the event of God's grace. In this event the possibility of knowledge of God's Word comes into view for us, not otherwise and not before. But this means that it comes into view as it is actualised, as we have knowledge of God's Word, as our self-determination is determined by God. We know it when we can only affirm it because we ourselves are its actualisation in our entire existence. It may be asked whether we know it because this event, as it comes into view for us, stands in the freedom of God. Grace would not be grace if God could not give and also refuse us this reality and with it this possibility too. The knowability of the Word of God stands or falls, then, with the act of its real knowledge, which is not under our control. On this actualisation, then, there also depends whether we can know and affirm it. On it there also depends the assurance of this affirmation. It can only be the assurance of faith, the assurance of the man whom God in His free grace has not passed by but whom He has called to faith by His Word, and who, called by His Word, stands in faith. In faith man has and knows and affirms only this possibility of knowledge of God's Word, the possibility which lies in the Word of God itself, has come to him in the Word, and is present to him in the Word. Hence the assurance of his affirmation of this possibility can only be that of the Word of God itself. This means, however, that it cannot be self-assurance. He is not sure of himself but of the Word of God, and he is not sure of the Word of God in and of himself but in and of the Word. His assurance is his own assurance, but it has its seat outside

him in the Word of God, and it is his assurance in this way, as the
Word of God is present to him.

*Quare facile senties, si advertas, hunc affectum ex tuis viribus in te non esse :
impetrandus ergo per humilem et in seipso desperatum spiritum. Fabulae ergo sunt
opinatorum Scholasticorum, hominem esse incertum, in statu salutis sit nec ne.
Cave tu, ne aliquando sis incertus, sed certus, quod in te ipso perditus : laborandum
autem, ut certus et solidus sis in fide Christi pro peccatis tuis traditi* (Luther, *Comm.
on Gal.* 1⁴, *W.A.*, 2, p. 458, l. 26).

When the Word of God is present to us, this means that we are
turned away from ourselves and towards the Word of God, that we are
orientated to it. To stand in faith means to be called to new faith. The
presence of the Word and standing in faith mean, then, having the
Word and faith before one and expecting them, being directed anew
to the free actualisation of the grace experienced, clinging anew to the
promise, looking anew for the event in which the possibility of knowledge of God's Word comes into view for us.

ἐλάβομεν καὶ χάριν ἀντὶ χάριτος (Jn. 1¹⁶). The righteousness of God is revealed
ἐκ πίστεως εἰς πίστιν (Rom. 1¹⁷). This can and must also mean παρ᾽ ἐλπίδα ἐπ᾽
ἐλπίδι ἐπίστευσεν (Rom. 4¹⁸).

If a man, the Church, Church proclamation and dogmatics think
they can handle the Word and faith like capital at their disposal, they
simply prove thereby that they have neither the Word nor faith.
When we have them, we do not regard them as a possession but
strain after them, hungering and thirsting, and for that reason blessed.
The same is true of the possibility of knowledge of God's Word. When
we know it, we expect to know it. The assurance of its affirmation is
thus the assurance of its expectation—the expectation which rests on
its previous presence, on the apprehended promise, or, as we can
already say here, on received and believed baptism—but still the
expectation. When we maintain the possibility of knowledge of God's
Word, this means that we relate ourselves to the event of its actualisation. And this means again that we do not maintain it but confess it,
as we must confess faith when we believe and as we can only confess
the event of the grace of God. This event, grace, and in and with grace
faith, must come first. Confessing, relating ourselves to the grace
already proclaimed and received, we then affirm the possibility of
knowledge of God's Word that is given to man. Affirming this
possibility, then, we are asked in all earnestness how we get to that
point, whether we are not thereby presuming something one cannot
presume, whether we are not perhaps trying to build a tower without
counting the cost, whether we are not thinking and alleging we can be
something that we must first have received in order to be it in truth.
The Church, Church proclamation and dogmatics have to realise that

when they explicitly or implicitly affirm the possibility of knowledge of God's Word they stand in the crisis of this question, the question : Where do they come from ? Do they really come from the Word and faith and believed baptism ? And even if they do come from there, their affirming of this possibility can only be a self-relating to the new and future event of the actualisation of this possibility which is always included and taken up in its actualisation. It is from this that it seeks to make itself known and to give itself to us, and that when made known and given it wants to be sought and found afresh. The assurance of its affirmation is really the assurance of its expectation. The assurance of grace, of faith, of believed baptism, is the assurance of the faith that constantly looks ahead in new hope. It cannot be but that the assurance of this expectation is an assurance in the deepest jeopardy. In this expectation man must let go and surrender all the assurance he himself brings. He is thrown back completely on free grace, which might well be replaced by merited condemnation. Apart from its actualisation in God's Word it would then be all up with the possibility of knowing it, and what would then become of our cocksure affirmation of this possibility ? Thus the assurance of this expectation is as it were a trembling assurance. Its power lies in submission to grace or non-grace. Seen alone it has no foundation, no hold on God, and it is empty compared with other human assurances which do not have their seat so strictly outside man. It is more human, i.e., more unsure, than all other human assurances just because it is the assurance of expectation, of this expectation. And yet it is an " unheard of assurance " ? It is an assurance which one may quietly and confidently compare with the assurance that has its basis in the human self-consciousness, the assurance of the directly or indirectly Cartesian thesis about the knowability of the Word of God, and find it superior in every respect ? Yes indeed, for again it cannot be but that just because it is so profoundly jeopardised, just because it relates itself to the confirmation that we cannot achieve but can only hope for, just because it is included in the divine actualisation, and is thus withdrawn from our grasp, and is thus to be sought there alone and expected thence alone, for this reason and in this way it is an assurance with a metal that makes it superior to every other assurance : because and so far as it is confession of God's free grace, because and so far as it is surrender to grace and non-grace, i.e., an appeal to God Himself. But again it is all this only to the extent that it is assurance of grace already received, the grace of faith, the grace of baptism. If it is this assurance—the question is whether our assurance is this assurance and this depends on God—but if it is this assurance, then our affirmation of the knowability of God's Word is the knocking to which it shall be opened. It is then in the circle of promise and faith in which is no Yes and No but only Yes. Praying that it might be this boundless affirmation, it is even in its total humanity an affirmation of " unheard of " assurance.

" (Man) must not doubt or waver as to whether he is one of those to whom such grace and mercy are given, who have surely received them by baptism or sacrament. When he believeth this, then he must freely say of himself that he is holy, pious, righteous and God's child, certain of blessedness, and must not doubt therein at all, not because of himself or his merit or work, but of the pure mercy of God poured out upon him in Christ. The same he seeth to be as great as it is, so that he doubteth not that it maketh him holy and God's child. And when he doubteth it, he doeth his baptism and sacrament the highest dishonour and giveth the lie to God's Word and grace in the sacrament. For there should be no fear or doubt that he is pious and God's child by grace, but only fear and care how he may remain steadfast to the end, in which alone all fear and care stand ; for there all bliss is assured. But it is uncertain and a matter of concern whether he stand fast and maintain it, there one must walk in fear ; for such faith boasteth not of work or self but only of God, and His grace cannot and may not leave him so long as the boasting lasts. But how long it will last he wots not ; whether some temptation may drive him that the boasting ceaseth, and so grace ceaseth also. So Solomon means in Eccles. 9 : ' The righteous and their works are in the hands of God ' ; yet is it all set in future uncertainty, so that man knoweth not whether he is worthy of grace or the reverse. He saith not that it is uncertain in the present but in the future, hence that man knoweth not whether he will withstand the assaults of temptation " (Luther, *Kirchenpostille*, 1522, *Sermon on Gal.* 1⁴ᶠ·, *W.A.*, 10ᴵᴵ, p. 331, l. 17).

Because it is surrounded by this ultimate uncertainty, by the freedom of God, the assurance of our affirmation of the knowability of the Word of God cannot be great enough. Good care is taken that it will be limited enough in its appearance, and we really need not fear the absolutising so fearfully portrayed at this point by those who have no understanding.

4. THE WORD OF GOD AND FAITH

At the beginning of this section we said that we could investigate only the knowability and not the knowledge of God's Word, because the knowledge of God's Word is no other than the reality of the grace of God coming to man, whose How as a reality is as hidden from us as God Himself is, so that we can only relate ourselves to it with our questions and answers. God has revealed it and will always reveal it, and man may proclaim it. We cannot ask how that happens but only, assuming that it does, how it can happen, how we are to understand it that men become the subject or object of this event. Now this very question has led us back again, and for the first time in full truth, to the event itself. We have found that the possibility of the knowledge of God is absolutely grounded, implied and included in the event of its actualisation, and our Yes to this possibility is one long reference to this event. We cannot produce this event and so we cannot give a basis for our reference ; we could do so only by producing the event to which it points and letting it speak for itself. Hence we can only ask—and we certainly must ask—what the reference means in this context, how far, in what sense, with what special necessity we refer to that event as the place where the question of the knowability of the Word of God is decided. To the question so put the answer is that we refer to this event as the event of faith. Faith—we could no longer avoid the term at the end of our deliberations on experience in the third sub-section—is the making possible of knowledge of God's Word that takes place in actual knowledge of it. The event concerned can and must be understood under many other concepts. Following the general tradition of the Church and theology, we choose this particular term here because it does in fact denote both precisely and yet also comprehensively the element in this event which constitutes it the making possible of knowledge of the Word of God. If one asks about the reality of the knowledge of God, which is so inconceivable in its How, which can be revealed only by God, which can be proclaimed by man only in the service of God and in virtue of His presence ; if one asks what this reality is in so far as the knowability of God is included within it, the only possible answer which is both accurate and exhaustive is that this reality is faith.

We best make this clear to ourselves if we think of the use of the term πίστις in the New Testament. πίστις may signify, as one sees from Rom. 3³ and especially from the use of the adjective πιστός, the faithfulness of God, the reliability and trustworthiness of God and His Word, and therefore that attribute of God and His Word in virtue of which man attains to a knowledge of God from God, because God is πιστός. But already in Paul (Rom. 12⁶ ; Gal. 1²³ ; 3²²f. ; 1 Tim. 4¹⁻ ⁶), and then in Jude (v. 3, 6), πίστις also means the doctrine of faith, the Gospel revealed to man, and therefore the way on which knowledge of God is made possible from God by His making Himself known. Again and especially —think of the so-called *genetivus mysticus* πίστις Ἰησοῦ Χριστοῦ and of the many Pauline and Johannine passages to the same effect—πίστις denotes the state created by God's revelation in Christ, the being of Christians, their being ἐν Χριστῷ, by which they are put in a position to achieve for their part the knowledge of God or of Christ as the Kyrios, the reality of man in which this achievement is an event. In the πίστις Ἰησοῦ Χριστοῦ we see the divine decision made about man. Only then and on this basis does the word slip down, as it were, into the sphere of human actions ; now—and this includes most of the Synoptic references and a number from the Epistles too—πίστις is fairly frequently and clearly described as trust, as the attitude in men in which they honour and revere the worth of God, His readiness to help, His might, His truth as it encounters them in Christ, by their acknowledgement as such, by their submission thereto ; the possibility of knowing His Word which is offered by God in Christ is now actualised in them. Πιστεύειν is now the decision made by man's own attitude. Πίστις, as is known, can then be used in the further and more concrete sense of a Christian *charisma* or virtue beside which there are others, and beside these others it has

no particular prominence and may even (1 Cor. 13¹³) be of less account. Finally
πίστις, πιστεύειν, πιστός can simply denote what one might call the Christian
religion or adherence to it. In this respect it is a term for the historical phenomenon which can be seen very directly in the form of a specific community, a
specific cultus, a specific confession and a specific manner of life, and the relativity
and ambivalence of which can also be stressed in the very sharp way familiar to
us from the Epistle of James. At this point we seem to be far removed from the
very objective πίστις θεοῦ of Rom. 3¹³ and also from the very cryptic, important
and effective πίστις Ἰησοῦ Χριστοῦ. In reality, however, all these meanings of
the term stand under a common denominator. Invariably, no matter how
objective or subjective, how central or peripheral, how simple or manifold the
use of the term may be, from the mystery of God to what could be seen directly
on the streets of Corinth and Rome, πίστις is the real event which rests on the
will and Word of God and relates to the will and Word of God, in which is also
included at all events the fact that the proclamation of Christ confirms itself to
men, in which men, touched by its truth, themselves become its bearers, and in
which the knowledge of God becomes real. Πίστις says more than γνῶσις, but
in all circumstances it says γνῶσις too. Augustine rightly says : *Si tollatur
assensio, fides tollitur ; quia sine assensione nihil creditur* (*Enchir.*, 20). And
Thomas Aquinas has the correct definition : *fides cognitio quaedam est, in quantum
intellectus determinatur per fidem ad aliquod cognoscibile* (*S. theol.*, I, *qu.* 12, *art.* 13).
At the crucial point the same may be said of Bonaventura : *Fides non est aliud
nisi habitus, quo intellectus noster voluntarie captivatur in obsequium Christi* (*Sent.*,
III, *d.* 23, *a.* 1, *qu.* 1, quoted acc. to R. Seeberg, *Dogmengeschichte*, Vol. 3, 2.-3.
edn., 1913, p. 336). Along the same lines cf. Luther too : *fidem nihil aliud esse
quam veritatem cordis hoc est rectam cogitationem cordis de Deo* (*Comm. on Gal.* 3⁷,
1535, *W.A.*, 40¹, p. 376, l. 23). *Apprehenditur Christus . . . ratione seu intellectu
informato fide et illa apprehensio Christi per fidem proprie est speculativa vita*
(*ib. on Gal.* 3¹³, *W.A.*, 40¹, p. 447, l. 15). *Fides est in intellectu. . . . Fides dictat
et dirigit intellectum. . . . Est igitur fides doctrina seu notitia. . . . Fides habet obiectum
veritatem. . . . Primum omnium pius habere debet rectam opinionem et intellectum
fide informatum. . . . Fides igitur est Dialectica, quae concipit ideam omnium
credendorum* (*ib. on Gal.* 5⁵, *W.A.*, 40¹¹, p. 26, l. 11 f. and p. 28, l. 9 f.). And
Calvin : *Non in ignoratione, sed in cognitione sita est fides* (*Instit.*, III, 2, 2).
Fateor . . . generale fidei obiectum . . . esse Dei veritatem (*ib.*, III, 2, 30). But the
content of the term γνῶσις is so included in the term πίστις that it is patent how
God Himself or Christ is at once the object, meaning, empowering and measure
of the real knowledge of God and yet this does not cease to be a wholly concrete
act performed by men and experienced by men.

Thus it is in faith, as the possibility given in faith, that we have to
understand the knowability of the Word of God. In the event of faith
it is as it were born, it comes into view, and it is to be sought and found.

Of the event of faith according to the understanding of the New
Testament peculiar to the Evangelical Church, three things at least
must be said as important in the present context, and these will yield
three different definitions of the concept of the knowability of the
Word of God.

1. In faith as real experience the acknowledgment of God's Word
which we have understood to be the concrete form of its experience by
man is as it were put into effect by the Word of God known. In

however perfect or imperfect a form, human action understood as acknowledgment comes into play. In faith it is true, accepted and acknowledged acknowledgment, not because man himself has the power or he himself has been able to achieve this proper acknowledgment, but because what he can do and does is acknowledged by the acknowledged Word of God, not as self-determination but as the self-determination determined by God's Word. We insist that faith is experience, a concretely ascertainable temporal act of a specific man, the act of acknowledgment. But experience is not self-evidently real experience, experience of God's Word. Of no experience as such, however perfect its form, can this be said. Not, then, as experience is faith faith, i.e., real experience, even though it is certainly experience. Or, the act of acknowledgment is not as such acknowledgment of the Word of God. Nor is it this in virtue of any perfection with which it is performed. It is the Word, Christ, to whom faith refers because He presents Himself to it as its object, that makes faith faith, real experience. Let it be clearly understood: because He presents Himself to it as its object. For faith is not faith by the mere fact that it has or is a reference—it might well be in reality a pointless reference to an imagined object. It is faith by the fact that the Word of God is given to us as the object of this reference, as the object of acknowledgment, and therefore as the basis of real faith.

As regards the epistemological problem a particularly instructive document for the constitutive significance for faith of the object of faith is the first chapter of the *Proslogion* of Anselm of Canterbury. In the closest material relation to the famous proof for the existence of God immediately following, there is brought up here in the form of a prayer the problem whether God is present at all to the thinker who sets out to understand and explain the existence and nature of God. He needs Him to be the man who can see and understand Him aright, but beyond that to have Him at all as the discoverable object of his search. *Quando illuminabis oculos nostros et ostendes nobis faciem tuam ? . . . Nec quaerere te possum, nisi te doceas, nec invenire, nisi te ostendas.* And Anselm does not find himself at all in this presence which is so necessary to him in the twofold sense. God's face is hidden from him as if he himself were blind. The twofold encounter he needs on God's part does not take place. He does not have in mind here the philosophical incomprehensibility of God but specifically the mystery of God which can be regarded only as a punishment on sinful man. As a son of Adam he knows his exact situation in this respect. But he is not as it were rhetorically putting himself in the place of the heathen in speaking thus. No : *Tu me fecisti et refecisti et omnia mea bona tu mihi contulisti et nondum novi te.* It is altogether as a Christian, then, that he thinks he must say what he says. Again, it cannot be merely that this Christian is experiencing an accidental and passing relapse from faith to unbelief, for in the same breath he describes his concern as follows : *Desidero aliquatenus intelligere veritatem tuam, quam credit et amat cor meum.* Apart from this there is really no special need to recall that the whole thing occurs in the sphere of the Catholic Church and against the background of its unshakably acknowledged creed. " The archbishop (? not till thirty years later !) is not a bad Catholic " (H. M. Müller, *Theol. Bl.*, 1928, p. 169 f.). All this, and all that was said before, undoubtedly means that the unrest with which Anselm seeks the presence of God is not an absolute unrest. It is not the direct opposite of the peace of God. It is the relative unrest of man which has as such its definite place and play, and which has somewhere and somehow in the Church the counterpart of a rest that may be his own or may not be his rest at all, but that is at least superior to his unrest. Would not the desire for unrest which the prospect of this superior rest excludes, would not the assertion of an absolute unrest, be the most foolish of all the foolish self-apotheoses of man ? Can and should a destruction of man's possibility of knowing God such as seems to be assumed at least in this chapter of Anselm really be carried through with full consistency ? Can one persist in standing in crisis either in the Roman Catholic or the Evangelical Church, as H. M. Müller seems to demand of Anselm and theologians generally ? As though man could in fact stand in an absolute crisis on this side of the end of all things ! If there is true and honest human seeking in the Church, will it not show itself to be one on which, for all its perhaps hopeless despair, there does not still lie the reflection of having found, and there does not already lie the reflection of finding again ? But be that as it may, it is humanly not good, it has no basis in the text or in other texts of Anselm, and there is something extraordinarily foolish and unspiritual about it, when H. M. Müller dismisses this chapter of Anselm out of hand, assigning no importance to the question it raises, because it is raised only within the " system," and therefore it has its answer secretly within it. In so doing he suppresses at once the fact that the question in the chapter is at least an open one as a question, and that it is solved neither by appealing to the creed of the Church or the *credere* of the Christian thinker, nor dialectically, nor by pointing to an answer to prayer already received. Why in the world should it not have been as bitterly serious for Anselm as only an open question can be serious for a man, even and especially if he knows that with his question he is in the sphere of the Church and therefore of the answer that he has still to find but that is already given and will certainly come ? And above all H. M. Müller fails to see that if in Anselm this question does in fact stand in the reflection of the solution that has been achieved already and also comes afresh, and yet it is still a radically open question, then the reference to Anselm's Catholicism cannot really be enforced as the only possible interpretation. One might also say that it is far from being proved that the reference to Anselm's Catholicism necessarily implies an interpretation *in malam partem*. Why should not the remarkable coincidence of ultimate disquiet and ultimate peace that characterises this chapter in Anselm be viewed from the standpoint that Anselm prays as he asks and asks as he prays. Is it not more pertinent and respectful to keep to this fact ? Can one ignore this, or discredit it as bad Catholicism, because of a completely unprovable suspicion that there might be a " system " here ? Only if one assumes this—and the inhumanity and at the same time the unspirituality of H. M. Müller's exposition of the matter is that he does assume this—only then can one treat as lightly as he does the unrest of Anselm, which is not absolute but limited, of course, against the background of the doctrine of absolute unrest. If we take seriously the fact that Anselm prayed in this unrest and that he suffered this unrest in prayer, one will evaluate the chapter as in its own way a distinctive illustration of the truth that authentic, utterly certain and hidden faith is always in transition from expectation to fresh expectation. All faith's unrest is, in fact, set aside in prayer, but its prayer is its profound unrest. And both as prayer and also as unrest it is expectation, expectation of its object. It lives by its object, at rest or in unrest, having found, seeking, finding again and seeking anew. But this object is the free God who is hidden from man because he is a sinner, who has, of course, put man in the new state of faith in which He can be known by him, but who in this very state—it is indeed that of faith—wills to be sought and found anew and then anew again. For faith, He is and remains enclosed in objectivity, in the externality of the Word of God, in Jesus Christ. He must teach man to seek Him and He must show Himself to him in order that he may find Him. But it is by this external object that Christian faith lives.

Non ex visione credentis, sed a visione eius cui creditur results the *determinatio intellectus ad aliquod cognoscibile* (Thomas Aquinas, *S. Theol.*, I, *qu.* 12, *art.* 13, *ad.* 3). *Non enim fides assentit alicui nisi quia est a Deo revelatum (ib.*, II², *qu.* 1, *art.* 1). *Tolle verbum et nulla jam restabit fides* (Calvin, *Instit.*, III, 2, 6). *Quoties nos de fide loquimur, intelligi volumus obiectum scilicet misericordiam promissam. Fides non ideo iustificat, quia ipsa sit opus per sese dignum* (not because . . . in itself 'tis our work or ours), *sed tantum quia accipit misericordiam promissam* (Melanchthon, *Apology*, *art.* 4, *De justif.*, 55 f., cf. 86). *Non enim in sensum sed in promissionem recumbit fides* (C. Olevianus, *De subst. foed.*, 1585, p. 304, *cit.ap.* Heppe, *Dogmatik d. ev. ref. Kirche*, 1861, p. 388). *Non propter fidem quatenus est virtus vel opus nostrum justificamur* (M. Chemnitz, *Loci. theol.*, 1591, Vol. II, p. 255) *. . . sed propter objectum quod fides apprehendit Christum (ib.*, p. 252). *De fide non est statuendum ex sensu consolationis et gaudii spiritualis : quia quintus ille gradus sequitur fidem, non est de essentia fidei et Deus sensum illum pacis credentibus saepe subtrahit (ib.*, p. 252). *Ancoram fidei nostrae iactam esse in ipsum coelum et quidem ubi Christus pro nobis sacerdos (ib.*, p. 257). Then with delightful precision High Orthodoxy explains that *fides* is *justificans* not as a *qualitas inhaerens* nor as an *actio* of man but *ut est in praedicamento relationis*, as a relation (σχέσις) to its object ; and again not *per relationem* (through relating to itself) but *in relatione : quatenus sibi applicat et appropriat meritum Christi, cui unico dignitas illa competit.* Finally it may be said that the act of justifying faith (*fides quae justificat*), while it is, of course, correctly described by such terms as *notitia, assensus, fiducia*, is to be understood as justifying (as *fides qua justificat*) only to the extent that beyond what makes it an act it is a *nuda apprehensio seu fiducialis acceptatio bonorum foederalium et beneficiorum Messiae passiva, admissiva motuum Spiritus, requietoria in sanguine et meritis Christi* (Quenstedt, *Theol. did.-pol.*, 1685, III, *cap.* 8, *sect.* 2, *qu.* 6, *ekth.* 8–10).

In this context we must speak especially of Luther. There are two sayings of Luther, one of which is adduced time and again in the modern theological debate by Wobbermin, who obviously never grows tired of it (cf. *Richtl. ev. Theol.*, 1929, p. 124 f. ; *Wort Gottes und ev. Glaube*, 1931, p. 5), after having played, with its whole context, a very similar role the previous century in A. Ritschl (*Rechtf. u. Vers.*, 4th edn., Vol. I, p. 218 f. ; Vol. 3, p. 201 f.) ; it is to the effect that " faith and God belong together " and it stands at the beginning of the exposition of the First Commandment in the *Larger Catechism*. The other is in the Lectures on Romans and, as every reader of Wobbermin knows, it runs : *fides et promissio sunt relativa* (Wobbermin persistently writes *correlativa* for this, cf. *Richtl.*, p. 109, 125 and *Wort Gottes*, p. 5). The first saying occurs in the following passage : " What does it mean to have a God, or what is God ? Answer : A God is that by which one is to be supplied with all good and with which one should take refuge in all afflictions. Thus, to have a God is nought other than to trust and believe in Him from the heart, as I have often said, which thing alone, the trust and faith of the heart, maketh both God and false god. If the faith and trust is right, so also is thy God right, and again where the trust is false and wrong, there also the right God is not. For the two belong together, faith and God. Whereupon then (I say) thou hangest and confidest thy heart, that is really thy God " (*Deutscher Catechismus*, 1529, *W.A.*, 30¹, p. 132, l. 34). And the other : *fides et promissio sunt relativa ; idem cessante promissione cessat et fides et abolita promissione aufertur et fides et econtra (Gloss on Rom.* 4[14], *Fi.*, p. 40, l. 24). For the sake of completeness we will add two further sayings of Luther that tend in the same direction. The first is parallel to the passage from the *Larger Catechism* : " As thou turnest and wheelest, so God, too, turneth and wheeleth. Thinkest thou that He is wroth with thee, so He is wroth. Thinkest thou that He is unmerciful to thee, and wishful to thrust thee into hell, then so He is. As thou believest of God, so thou hast Him " (*Sermon on Jn.* 4[47l.], 1534, *E.A.*, 5, p. 224). " Therefore, as we believe, so it befalleth us. If we hold Him for our God, He will certainly not be our devil. But if we hold Him not for our God, He is certainly likewise not our God, but must be a consuming fire " (*ib.*, 5, p. 229). The other is a parallel to the gloss on Romans : " So ought Word and faith to stand splendidly together. For the one cannot exist without the other. Whoso hath faith and not the Word believeth like Turks and Jews. They have the faith that God is gracious and merciful. But the promise is lacking, for God will not be gracious apart from Christ. Thus, whoso hath the Word but not faith, there the Word accomplisheth naught. Thus Word and faith are given together in wedlock, and naught can cause them to part from one another " (*Hauspost.*, 1544, *Sermon on Mt.* 9[1t.], *W.A.*, 52, p. 498, l. 22). Wobbermin wants to show from these sayings that the relation between the Word of God and faith according to Luther is to be regarded as a relation of " connexion " or " correlation," as a " circular " relation, a relation of " reciprocity " or " two-poled relation " (*Richtl.*, p. 125, 140 f. ; *Wort Gottes*, p. 5 f., 14, 27, etc.). I do not wish to contest these descriptions, though they are too ambiguous for me to adopt. I would only say regarding Luther that he is simply stating that in a man's faith or erroneous faith or unbelief the decision is made what kind of a God he has, so that man always has the God he believes in. But this is not at all the same thing as saying that faith is as it were the human counterpart of the Word of God, that the relation between the Word of God and faith is the symmetrical one of two partners, one superior and the other subordinate but still two partners, and that this relation is just as basically grounded in faith as it is in the Word of God. To be sure, it is only in faith that one has the true God, and this God, as the God believed in, is that on which man sets his heart's trust. But it is not at all true that the fact that He is believed in, that the heart's trust, man's " interest " in Him as A. Ritschl puts it, makes Him the true God. As the object of faith or trust he might equally well be a false god. What makes Him the true God is that one believes in Him in true faith. And the fact that the faith in which the true God is believed in is true faith is not due in any way or in any sense to itself but to the fact that the true God has revealed Himself to it, i.e., it is due to the Word of God. In this concept the circular movement of reflection necessarily ends, and it does so in Luther, for he is denoting the point where the true and irreversible circular movement of Word and faith takes its beginning, which is not conditioned by an opposite pole. Wobbermin thinks the saying that " faith and God belong together " might be rendered by the different one that " faith and the Word of God belong together " (*Wort Gottes*, p. 5). This might be conceivable if we had only this saying to deal with. But in view of the content of the rest of the passage from the Catechism this translation is quite untenable. Obviously Luther neither intended to say nor could he say that the trust and faith of the heart constitute the Word of God, that when man's faith and trust are right God's Word is right. All that he says in the *Catechism* is that always and in every sense of the term " God " is for man that whereon he sets his supreme trust. There is thus no point in building one's understanding of Luther or one's whole theology on this popular preamble. Neither in the *Larger Catechism* nor elsewhere did Luther teach the God defined thus but only the true God of true faith, and in the question of this God he never referred to faith as such or its immanent correctness nor did he ever raise it to the rank of a counterpole or partner of God's Word. What we read is that " to believe aught without God's Word is no faith but a false delusion, for naught will ever come of it, just as if thou shouldst believe thou wouldst yet become the Roman Emperor. . . ." (*Hauspost.*, 1544, *Sermon on Jn.* 4[47f.], *W.A.*, 52, p. 518, l. 22). " Whoso then hath not nor knoweth God's Word can have no such confidence and must get this good comfort " (*Ib.*, *Sermon on Lk.* 5[1f.], *W.A.*, 52, p. 396, l. 7). " It is this, then, that I have said, that God will not suffer it that we rely on aught else or with the heart depend on what is not Christ in His Word, be it as holy or spiritual as it like. Faith hath no other ground on which it can stand " (*E.A.*, 11, 26). " In faith all things must be put out of sight save the Word of God. Whoso alloweth aught else to come into view but the Word itself is already lost. Faith dependeth on the pure Word alone, turneth not its eyes therefrom, regardeth naught else, neither its work nor merit. If the heart standeth not simply thus, it is already lost " (*Sermon on Jn.* 4[4f.], 1522, *W.A.*, 10[III], p. 423, l. 17). " This is the nature and property of faith, that it may suffer naught beside it by which man steers or turns save the simple Word of God or divine promise . . . faith letteth go all creatures, all visible things in the world, even itself, and dependeth on God's Word. Thus it must be, dear friend, faith relieth on naught, gropeth not after aught, what it is sure of that will it cling to " (*Festpost.*, 1527, *Sermon on Lk.* 1[26f.], *W.A.*, 17[II], p. 400, l. 14, 32). In faith there takes place a *speculatio qua Christus apprehenditur*, a *speculatio theologica fidelis et divina inspectio serpentis suspensi in palo hoc est Christi pendentis in cruce pro meis tuis et totius mundi peccatis* (*Comm. on Gal.* 3[13], *W.A.*, 40[I], p. 447, l. 18). It should also be noted that in the Romans gloss and the sermon on the marriage between the Word and faith the emphasis of Luther's expositions lies throughout on the thought that without the Word there can be no faith. The dialectical supplement that without faith one cannot have the Word is simply added in both passages but not developed. In sum, when Luther speaks of the Word and faith he is saying, of course, that where there is no faith the Word cannot be, or cannot be fruitful, but he is saying primarily, and this is the point, that where faith is, it does not have its ground and its truth and its measure in itself as a human act or experience, but even though it is a human act and experience it has these things in its object, in Christ, or God's Word. In my view terms like circular or reciprocal or correlative relation are very imprecise descriptions of what Luther meant to say and did say in this matter. In fact, what we learn from Luther about the Reformation insight into this matter is exactly the same as what we learn from Melanchthon.

In the light of this it should now be quite plain that the interpretation of faith as *fiducia*, trust, or confidence in the older Reformers and the whole of the older Protestant theology (*Est itaque fides non aliud, nisi fiducia misericordiae promissae* . . ., Melanchthon, *Loci*, 1521, *De justif. et fide*, IV ; cf. *Conf. Helv. post.*, 16 ; *Heidelb. Cat. qu.* 21) has nothing whatever to do with a shifting of the reality of faith from its object to the believing subject. The stressing of *fiducia* is designed to differentiate real faith from a mere *opinio historica*, from a neutral recollective knowledge and affirmation of biblical or ecclesiastical statements such as is possible apart from the reality of faith. The possibility of excluding the element of *notitia* or *assensus*, i.e., the element of knowledge from faith, of making faith a trust either devoid of intellectual form or indifferent to it, of viewing it as any kind of trust in any kind of object, of throwing doubt on the object of faith and transferring the reality of faith to the believing subject, was one of which we can say with complete certainty (in spite of what K. Aner seems to assume in RGG[2], Art. " Glaube, IV, dogmengeschichtlich ") that even in the early days of the Reformation none of the responsible leaders ever considered it seriously even for a single moment. For Older Protestantism faith is *fiducia*, and hence more than *notitia* and *assensus* in relation to the content of God's Word, to the degree that in faith man accepts the merciful Immanuel spoken by God's Word, i.e., applies to himself the mercy of which the Word speaks, takes comfort in it on the basis of the Word, relies upon it in the light of the Word, to the degree that the believer is a man who is comforted by the Word of God. To be sure, faith becomes faith only when it is *fiducia*. *Notitia* and *assensus* alone would not be faith, but only the *opinio historica* that the ungodly can have too. Nevertheless, how can faith be *fiducia* without also being, even as *fiducia*, *notitia* and *assensus*, *fiducia promissionis*, trust in the mercy of God which encounters us as *misericordia promissa*, i.e., in the objectivity of the Word, which has form and even a form of words, and therefore has also a form of knowledge, of acceptance of its truth, in the faith which receives it ? A few lines before his well-known definition of *fides* as *fiducia* Melanchthon himself has the definition : *Quid igitur fides ? Constanter assentiri omni verbo Dei.* He would certainly not have said with Wobbermin (who in *Wort Gottes*, p. 10 f. ; *Richtlinien*, p. 131 can even speak of a " radical rejection of *fides historica* ") that this *assentiri* is subordinate to *fiducia*, because for him there can be no question of a true and serious and theologically important subordination of *assensus* to *fiducia* in real faith, only of both to their object. Hence Melanchthon, as we have seen, said of faith understood as *fiducia* that it can be regarded as true justifying faith, not as *opus per sese dignum*, but only with reference to its *obiectum*. With reference to its object, however, faith is necessarily and in no way secondarily *notitia* and *assensus* too (Melanchthon seems not to distinguish the two in the *Loci* of 1559, *C.R.*, 21, p. 242 f.) ; it is knowledge, accepting as true the Word of the divine person in which it reposes its trust. The word *fiducia* itself shows clearly that this is so, and that it has to be so. With its psychological sense it also has a legal sense, and it is linguistically legitimate at least to refer to the latter for an understanding of the former. Legally *fiducia* means leaving a property in trust, or the contract arranging this transfer (e.g., a fictitious sale), or even the security given as a mortgage in such a case. *Fiducia* then, in a legal transaction by which a man provisionally and temporarily puts something of his own in the hands of another, is that which he retains in his own hand as a pledge establishing his legal claim both before and after the transaction. It may be simply belief in the integrity of the other person, or a contract guaranteeing his integrity, or a deposit guaranteeing the contract. *Fiducia* relates, therefore, to the reliability or *bona fides* of the other with whom what is mine, without ceasing to be mine, is now lodged. To have *fiducia* is thus to have reason to rely on his reliability. Without the reference to this object, to the *bona fides* of the other, there is no *fiducia*. I have it as I stand in this relation to him and in order to be able to stand in this relation to him, not otherwise. This is the *tertium comparationis* between the legal and the psychological and then the theological concept of *fiducia*. It should be noted that already in the New Testament it can be said incidentally of God : πίστιν παρασχὼν πᾶσιν ἀναστήσας αὐτὸν ἐκ νεκρῶν, i.e., in the resurrection of Jesus He gave a surety to all, and this surety is simply what they can now have in the form of faith (Ac. 17[31]). No less than *notitia* and *assensus*, *fiducia* denotes the objective reference of faith. But *fiducia*, the reliance on God's reliability that takes place in faith, denotes this objective reference in a specific way, and in virtue of the material content of faith expressed in the term *fiducia* the terms *notitia* and *assensus* with their reference to the divine opposite as such are needed to mark off its formal content. *Ultimus actus fidei nempe fiducia anima fidei justificantis est, sive perfectio eius formalis qua stante impossibile est hominem perire. Interim tamen praesupponit obiecti justifici cognitionem explicitam et assensum generalem . . . et specialem* (Quenstedt, *Theol. did.-pol.*, 1685, III, *cap.* 8, *sect.* 2, *qu.* 6, *ekth.* 7).

A word in closing might be said about two terms which have recently enjoyed a considerable vogue again (especially in Wobbermin), namely, *fides quae creditur* and *fides qua creditur.* This distinction originates with Augustine : *Aliud sunt ea, quae creduntur, aliud fides qua creduntur. Illa quippe in rebus sunt . . . haec autem in animo credentis est (De trin.,* XIII, 2, 5). Anselm of Canterbury then divides the element of *fides qua* by distinguishing between *credere id* and *credere in id, quod credi debet (Monol.,* 76–78). This *in id* also derives from Augustine (e.g., *Tract. in Ioann.,* 29, 6). Peter Lombard first adduces the first reference from Augustine and then (is this original ?) even uses a threefold formula for the *fides qua creditur* in relation to the second : *aliud est enim credere in Deum, aliud credere Deo, aliud credere Deum (Sent.,* III, 23 C. and D. ; cf. the marginal note of Luther on this, *W.A.,* 9, p. 90, l. 15). J. Gerhard then found the first Augustine passage in Peter Lombard and in relation to it he was probably the first to use the terms so familiar to us to-day, *fides quae creditur* and *fides qua creditur,* the first denoting the object of the second, the *materia circa quam,* the second the πεποίθησις et πληροφορία *in animo credentis (Loci theol.,* 1610 ; *Loc.* 16, 66). But Gerhard also found in Lombard the threefold formula for the *fides qua creditur,* and, believing it to be Augustinian, he regarded it as a confirmation of his own formula *fiducia, assensus, notitia (ib.,* 67). The *fides quae* and *qua* and the three terms in explanation of *fides qua* then became more or less the common stock in trade of Protestant Scholasticism. In J. Wollebius (*Chr. Theol. Compend.,* 1626, I, 26, 1 and 7) the two had already been adopted by Reformed dogmatics, though, e.g., M. Chemnitz on the Lutheran side and W. Bucan on the Reformed side do not yet seem to have taken them for granted as familiar formulae. Obviously the distinction between *fides quae* and *qua* can only have the significance of denoting the dialectic of the object-subject content of the term faith as it has met us already in the New Testament use of πίστις, the problem of faith and the object of faith as such. To the discussion of this problem the distinction itself makes no contribution, for, as the labours of Anselm and Lombard show, everything depends on defining what is meant by *fides qua.* We ourselves have been examining the decisive term *fiducia* and we have made the point necessary in the present context, namely, that *fiducia* itself—and with it *fides qua* generally, which is not for this reason mere *fiducia*—refers beyond itself to the object in relation to which it is *fiducia.* The realist Augustine, who seems to have been the first to speak of this *quae* and *qua,* certainly did not understand his *fides qua* any differently.

If this is how it stands with faith, then one may say of the knowability of the Word of God given in the event of faith that it is not a possibility which man for his part brings to real knowledge, nor is it a possibility which in real knowledge accrues to man from some source as an enrichment of his existence. But as faith has its absolute and unconditional beginning in God's Word independently of the inborn or acquired characteristics and possibilities of man, and as it, as faith, never in any respect lives from or by anything other than the Word, so it is in every respect with the knowability of the Word of God into which we are now enquiring. We cannot establish it if, as it were, we turn our backs on God's Word and contemplate ourselves, finding in ourselves an openness, a positive or at least a negative point of contact for God's Word. We can establish it only as we stand fast in faith and its knowledge, i.e., as we turn away from ourselves and turn our eyes or rather our ears to the Word of God. As we hear it, we have the possibility of hearing it. Hence we do not affirm our own possibility but its reality, which we cannot do except as we stand fast. In its reality we also have our own possibility, not to contemplate it, but only to use it. Contemplating it, we no longer hear, and we thus lose the reality and with it our own possibility that we want to contemplate. As the possibility which comes to us in the Word's reality it is our possibility, just as faith is our possibility as that which comes to us. It is really ours, the possibility of the entire creaturely and sinful man ; yet not in such a way that contemplating this man one can discover it or read it off somewhere in him or on him ; only in such a way that this creaturely, sinful man waits for the Word that comes to him and therewith for his faith, so that he believes already, he who, contemplating himself, will continually have to say that he cannot believe.

P. Althaus has a very fine and pertinent saying about this : " I do not know whether I believe, but I know in whom I believe " (*Grundriss d. Dogm.*, 1929, p. 19 ; cf. *Communio sanctorum*, 1929, p. 92 f.).

This is exactly how it is with the knowability of God's Word in faith. It is not an extraordinary art. Or should one rather say conversely that is it a highly extraordinary art ? Its practice does not presuppose any special endowment whether natural or supernatural. The believer is the same ungifted and idle or gifted and busy man he was as an unbeliever and may become again. He believes as the man he is, with the inventory corresponding to his condition. There is no question of an exalting or abasing of his existence ; what is at issue is the grace or judgment of God on his existence. Therefore there is nothing extraordinary here in so far as it is a matter of man and his knowledge as he is. It is all highly extraordinary, of course, in so far as the Word of God becomes the truth here to this man and his knowledge. But whether extraordinary or not it is at least a possibility given to us, a possibility given for use, not for putting in an inventory or catalogue, not for storing on ice or placing in a museum.

Even in its details the story of the " manna " in Ex. 16 is an illustration of what has to be said about faith in this connexion.

The possibility, then, is not one we can exhibit but only one to which we can point, like faith, or the Word of God itself, or the child born of the Virgin Mary in the manger at Bethlehem. The force and seriousness of this pointer must be the force and seriousness of God if we are really to point. Thus the first thing that must be said about the knowability of the Word of God as the possibility given to us in faith is that it arises and consists absolutely in the object of real knowledge.

2. If what happens in faith is that acknowledgment of God's Word,

as it can become a human act and experience, is, as it were, brought into force not by itself but by the Word of God acknowledged, so that it is real acknowledgment, we must now make the positive statement that in faith men have real experience of the Word of God, and no *finitum non capax infiniti*, no *peccator non capax verbi divini*, can now prevent us from taking this statement seriously with all that it involves. The statement refers, not to our human capacity, but to men on the assumption of their complete incapacity. The principle of the incapacity of the *finitum* or the *homo peccator* must be accepted. And what we say about the man who can have real experience of God's Word does not invalidate it. But it transcends and brackets it. Faith is not one of the various capacities of man, whether native or acquired. Capacity for the Word of God is not among these. The possibility of faith as it is given to man in the reality of faith can be understood only as one that is loaned to man by God, and loaned exclusively for use. The moment we regard it as a possibility which is in some sense man's own, the opposite statement regarding man's incapacity comes back into force. We do not understand it as a possibility which is in any sense man's own. But for this reason there can also be no objection from the standpoint of man's possibilities when we say that in faith there takes place a conformity of man to God. We do not say a deification but a conformity to God, i.e., an adapting of man to the Word of God. In faith, as he really receives God's Word, man becomes apt to receive it. If one were to deny this one could no longer describe and understand faith as the act and experience of man nor man as the subject of faith. But if we ascribe to man this aptness which is not his own but is loaned to him by God, which is not to be contemplated but simply used in faith, an aptness to receive the Word of God, then we cannot shrink from speaking of a conformity to God proper to him in faith. There can be no receiving of God's Word unless there is something common to the speaking God and hearing man in this event, a similarity for all the dissimilarity implied by the distinction between God and man, a point of contact between God and man, if we may now adopt this term too.

This point of contact is what theological anthropology on the basis of Gen. 1[27] calls the " image of God " in man. In this connexion we cannot possibly agree with E. Brunner (*Gott und Mensch*, 1930, p. 55 f.) when he takes this to refer to the humanity and personality which even sinful man retains from creation, for the humanity and personality of sinful man cannot possibly signify conformity to God, a point of contact for the Word of God. In this sense, as a possibility which is proper to man *qua* creature, the image of God is not just, as it is said, destroyed apart from a few relics ; it is totally annihilated. What remains of the image of God even in sinful man is *recta natura*, to which as such a *rectitudo* cannot be ascribed even *potentialiter*. No matter how it may be with his humanity and personality, man has completely lost the capacity for God. Hence we fail to see how there comes into view here any common basis of discussion for philosophical and theological anthropology, any occasion for the common exhibition of at least the possibility of enquiring about God. The image of God in man of which we must speak here and which forms the real point of contact for God's Word is the *rectitudo* which through Christ is raised up from real death and thus restored or created anew, and which is real as man's possibility for the Word of God. The reconciliation of man with God in Christ also includes, or already begins with, the restitution of the lost point of contact. Hence this point of contact is not real outside faith ; it is real only in faith. In faith man is created by the Word of God for the Word of God, existing in the Word of God and not in himself, not in virtue of his humanity and personality, not even on the basis of creation, for that which by creation was possible for man in relation to God has been lost by the fall. Hence one can only speak theologically and not both theologically and also philosophically of this point of contact, as of all else that is real in faith, i.e., through the grace of reconciliation.

" Conformity to God " was what we called the possibility of receiving God's Word. The concept of the *imago Dei* is to the same effect. But we have to realise that at this point we are only a hair's breadth from the Roman Catholic doctrine of the *analogia entis*. Even and precisely in this close proximity, however, our teaching must be very different. We do not construe the analogy, similarity, or conformity to God that is actually to be maintained here as an *analogia entis*, i.e., as an analogy that can be surveyed and perceived, as an analogy that can be understood in a synthesis from an onlooker's standpoint. Not a being which the creature has in common with the Creator for all their dissimilarity, but an act that is inaccessible to any mere theory, i.e., human decision, is in faith similar to the decision of God's grace for all its dissimilarity. Of more than an analogy or similarity we should not speak. And it must be emphasised, as the Roman Catholic doctrine of the *analogia entis* also emphasises for that matter, that this is a similarity in great dissimilarity. This helps us to understand why the previously mentioned theory of Augustine (and of the Holl school) about the secret identity of the divine and human decision is inadmissible. If secret identity existed here, one would not have to speak of similarity in dissimilarity but of equality in inequality, but then we would not be dealing with mere conformity to God but with a deification of man. Nevertheless, we cannot be dealing with less than conformity to God. In rejecting the Thomist *analogia entis* we affirm the other idea of Thomas in which, for that matter, one might discern the content of truth in even the so-called *analogia entis : quum igitur christiana fides hominem de Deo . . . instruit . . . fit in homine quaedam divinae sapientiae similitudo* (Thomas Aquinas, *S. c. gent.*, II, 2). Luther speaks similarly of the act of justification ; it happens in such a way that God *nos tales facit, quale est verbum suum, hoc est justum, verum, sapiens, etc. Et ita nos in verbum suum, non autem verbum suum in nos mutat. Facit autem tales tunc, quando nos verbum suum tale credimus esse scilicet justum verum. Tunc enim iam similis forma est in verbo et in credente, id est veritas et justitia (Schol. on Rom. 3*[4], *Fi.*, II, p. 65, l. 16). And elsewhere : *Necesse est sapientiam carnis mutari et suam formam relinquere ac formam verbi suscipere. Quod fit, dum per fidem se ipsam captivat et destruit, conformat se verbo, credens verbum esse verum, se vero falsam (ib., on Rom. 6*[14], *Fi.*, II, p. 160, l. 3). And again : *per fidem fit homo similis verbo Dei (Schol. on Heb. 3*[13], *Fi.*, II, p. 44, l. 4). And again in another passage : " As is the Word, so becometh also the soul by it, like as iron becometh glowing red like fire from union with fire " (*Freedom of a Christian Man*, 1520, *W.A.*, 7, p. 24, l. 33). With reference to the righteousness that man receives in faith, Luther could well say : *fides ita exaltat cor hominis et transfert de se ipso in Deum, ut unus spiritus fiat ex corde et Deo (Schol. on Heb. 7*[1], *Fi.*, II, p. 74, l. 9). With reference to the constancy and certainty of faith he could even say : *fide homo fit Deus* (*Comm. on Gal.* 2⁷, 1535, *W.A.*, 40ᴵ, p. 182, l. 15). With reference to the power of real faith : *Qualia diligimus, tales efficimur. Deum diligis, Deus es* (*Schol. on Rom.* 3¹², Fi. II, p. 78, l. 12). " God help us, what a boundless, rich and mighty thing is faith ! for it maketh man in all things a god, to whom naught is impossible. . . ." (*Kirchenpost.*, 1522, *Sermon on Lk.* 2²¹, *W.A.*, 10ᴵ, p. 518, l. 5). And with reference to the fact that in faith and only in faith does man honour God as God, he says even more boldly : *Ea* (*sc. fides*) *consummat divinitatem et, ut ita dicam, creatrix est divinatitis, non in substantia Dei, sed in nobis. Nam sine fide . . . nihil maiestatis et divinitatis habet Deus* (*Comm. on Gal.* 3⁶, *W.A.*, 40ᴵ, p. 360, l. 21). In the same sense Augustine had already been able to say that in man's *justificatio* in so far as it makes us God's children, a *deificatio* takes place, though he does not neglect to add the comment : *sed hoc gratiae est adoptantis non naturae generantis* (*Enarr. in Ps.* 49²). Neither in Augustine nor in Luther is there anything about a deification in faith in the sense of a changing of man's nature into the divine nature. What makes the expressions possible is the *apprehensio Christi* or *habitatio Christi in nobis* or *unio hominis cum Christo* that takes place in real faith according to the teaching of Gal. 2²⁰. In emphasising this more than mystical and more than speculative principle that faith means union with what is believed, i.e., with Jesus Christ, Calvin did not lag in the least behind Luther nor either of them behind an Augustine, Anselm, or Bernard of Clairvaux. Without this principle it is impossible to understand the Reformation doctrine of justification and faith. How it was distinguished from the idea of an essential deification of man in the Reformation period may be seen especially from Calvin's controversy with A. Osiander (*Instit.*, III, 11, 5 f.) ; there can be no question of a *mixtura Christi cum fidelibus*. It is *in medio tenebrarum* (Luther on Gal. 2¹⁶, *W.A.*, 40ᴵ, p. 229, l. 18), in full concealment, that there takes place this *unio*, this self-presentation of Christ or the Word of God or God Himself in the believer, this *inhabitatio totius sacrosanctae trinitatis* as was said later. In this relation man remains man with his possibilities and limitations, and Christ Himself and alone, or the Word, remains the object of faith and it is not an inpoured love or the like that is the *forma fidei* (Luther, *ib.*, 229, 28), i.e., that which distinguishes the believer from the unbeliever, that which makes his experience and act real faith and therefore a possibility that is given to him for use. But at any rate there is this distinction. Its complete concealment corresponds only to its complete reality as divine grace, a reality about which so much can be said without exaggeration.

In faith man is in conformity to God, i.e., capable of receiving God's Word, capable of so corresponding in his own decision to the decision God has made about him in the Word that the Word of God is now the Word heard by him and he himself is now the man addressed by this Word. One is not to seek this capability among the stock of his own possibilities. The statement about the indwelling of Christ that takes place in faith must not be turned into an anthropological statement. There must be no subtraction from the lostness of natural and sinful man, as whom the believer will for the first time really see himself. But this natural and sinful man that he is, and that in faith he must see himself to be, is dead in faith, in Christ, according to Rom. 6³ᶠ·, and I am alive in faith, a miracle to myself, another man, and as such capable of things of which I can only know myself to be absolutely incapable as a natural sinful man.

Part of this capability is that the Word of God is knowable to man in faith, that it can be spoken to him, and that he can hear it, that he can receive it as a word, and indeed as God's Word.

It can come about in faith that man has a ὑπόστασις ἐλπιζομένων, i.e., a confidence corresponding and open to the nature of the thing hoped for, an ἔλεγχος οὐ βλεπομένων, i.e., a proof of that which is invisible and inaccessible to him (Heb. 11¹). To the man who is righteous before God in faith it may be said : ἐγγύς σου τὸ ῥῆμα ἐστιν, ἐν τῷ στόματί σου καὶ ἐν τῇ καρδίᾳ σου (Rom. 10⁸). What Irenaeus once demands is now possible : ἵνα ἀεὶ μὲν ὁ θεὸς διδάσκῃ, ἄνθρωπος δὲ διὰ παντὸς μανθάνῃ παρὰ θεοῦ (C. o. h., II, 28, 3). This ability with reference to God's Word is the conformity of the believer to God and in particular it is the knowability of the Word of God which is the object of our present enquiry.

To the image of God in man which was lost in Adam but restored in Christ there also belongs the fact that man can hear God's Word. Only as the Word of God is really spoken in spite of his sin and to his sin, only in the grace with which God replies to sin, can this possibility revive. But in grace it does revive : not, then, as a natural capacity in man—it is grace after all that comes to sinners, to incapable men— but as a capacity of the incapable, as a miracle that cannot be inter- preted anthropologically, nevertheless as a real capacity which is already actualised in faith, regarding whose existence there is no further room for discussion, whose existence can only be stated, since in becoming an event it already showed itself to be a possibility even before any question about it could arise.

What no eye has seen, nor ear heard, what has not entered into the heart of man, God has already prepared for those who love him (1 Cor. 2⁹). There are men—God has vouchsafed that there should be such—who know God's gracious acts (2¹²), who search out the " deep things of God " (2¹⁰), who can discern what is spiritual spiritually (2¹³), men to whom one can speak about their acquaintance with the Word of God : δέξασθε τὸν ἔμφυτον λόγον (Jas. 1²¹), who can " stand " in faith (1 Cor. 16¹³).

As God's Word is spoken to man, it is in him and he is in the Word. The only proof of this mutual indwelling of the Word and man is a reference to the fact that as the Word of God is spoken to some other man it can be in him too, and he in it. The proof of faith consists in the proclamation of faith. The proof of the knowability of the Word consists in confessing it. In faith and confession the Word of God becomes a human thought and a human word, certainly in infinite dissimilarity and inadequacy, yet not in total alienation from its real prototype, but a true copy for all its human and sinful perversion, an unveiling of it even as its veiling. This does not imply an immanent transformation of human thought or human speech. It does not imply even a modest removal of the offence with which the Word is flesh here. Nor does it imply any diminution of the miracle of the mutual indwelling, any supernatural physics trying to make the incomprehensible comprehensible. Again, what must be said here cannot be meant as analysis of a present reality, for as such it evades our grasp and knowledge. In the strict sense it is meant only as recollection of the promise and as expectation of its future fulfilment. But in this sense the mutual indwelling and indeed the union of the divine and human logos in faith cannot be ignored or denied. This mutual indwelling or union is the knowability of the Word of God, the possibility of Church proclamation whether from the preacher's standpoint or the hearer's, and therefore the possibility of dogmatics too. As the Church provides the ministry of proclamation and as we pursue dogmatics, we confess that we believe this possibility. For all the menacing proximity of the *analogia entis*, mysticism and identity philosophy, and in spite of all the so-called dangers, we have every reason to speak out clearly on this point.

Uniatur tecum cogitatio mea, una et singularis sit tecum intentio mea ubi tecum a te misericorditer suscepta beata iam regnat substantia nostra (Anselm, *Medit.*, 1, 6). So, too, Luther : *In ipsa fide Christus adest. Fides ergo est cognitio quaedam vel tenebra, quae nihil videt et tamen in istis tenebris Christus fide apprehensus sedet sicut Deus in Sinai et in templo sedebat in medio tenebrarum* (*Comm. on Gal.* 2[16], *W.A.*, 40[I], p. 229, l. 15). " The statement of revelation that God speaks is identical with the statement that man hears " (E. Thurneysen, *Das Wort Gottes und die Kirche*, 1927, p. 222 ; Wobbermin's indignation at this sentence in *Wort Gottes u. ev. Glaube*, 1931, p. 27 is not very penetrating either actively or passively).

With our statement about man's conformity to God in faith and therefore in his possibility of knowing God's Word we are saying—and this is our second definition of the knowability of the Word of God— that when and where the Word of God is really known by men the manner of this knowing corresponds to that of the Word of God itself. If as our first definition of the knowability of the Word of God we construed it as a human possibility that becomes a possibility in face of the object that encounters man, in face of the Word of God itself, as a reflection of its own self-grounded possibility, we must now say that it becomes a possibility in the same way as the Word of God itself and in itself is possible. We have thus described what acknowledgment of God's Word by man is, not in the form of an analysis of man's consciousness of faith, but in the form of a postulate directed to man's consciousness of faith by the nature of the Word of God. We have to think of man in the event of real faith as, so to speak, opened up from above. From above, not from below ! What can be seen and grasped and analysed from below, as human experience and act, as the consciousness of faith, is not the fulfilment of this postulate. It is in itself a vacuum which might be filled in quite another way than by the Word of God. The true believer is the very man who will not hesitate to acknowledge that his consciousness of faith as such is human darkness.

Hence we cannot omit to investigate the consciousness of our known ego with reference to the content of God's Word. The opening up from above that takes place in the event of real faith remains just as hidden for us as the event itself or God Himself. But we must also say that it is as manifest to us as this event is manifest or God is manifest, i.e., in recollection of the promise and hope of its fulfilment. As we can and should believe the Word of God itself, as we are summoned to believe it, so we must believe our faith in the Word, our possibility of knowing it or its knowability for us, the presence of the *forma Dei* in the midst of human darkness, Christ's presence in the *tenebrae* of our heart. If the event of faith is the event of the presence of the believed Word in man, the union of man with it, then this must mean that the darkness of man —we can never see or understand it as anything else—can be light. Thus the possibility of man, inadequate in itself, can become the adequate divine possibility. In its fulfilment it is the adequate divine possibility. In affirming the knowability of God's Word as it is promised to us and as it takes place in the event of faith, we affirm the divine possibility. To the extent that we can affirm it only in its concealment, in the husk of the human possibility that meets us as darkness, we will not deny the dissimilarity between the divine possibility in itself and what it becomes in our hands. We can see the stick dipped in water only as a broken stick. But though we cannot see it, it is invisibly and yet in truth a completely unbroken stick. For all the dissimilarity, the possibility of grasping the promise in faith is not without similarity to the divine possibility of its actualisation : not in itself, not as a human possibility, but, according to our first definition, in terms of its object, as the possibility of grasping the promise. In virtue of this similarity our possibility of knowing God's Word is the possibility of a clear and certain knowledge, not equal but at least similar to the clarity and certainty with which God knows Himself in His Word. In virtue of this similarity the confession of faith, corresponding to the knowledge of God's Word, acquires the definiteness which distinguishes it basically from all human convictions, however profound or serious ; it acquires the final human seriousness which belongs only to confession, to the confession of faith. In virtue of this similarity the Church, Church proclamation and dogmatics are possible. The clarity and certainty of knowledge, the confession of faith and the Church rest on the fact that whenever and wherever the Word of God is really known it is known after the manner of the Word of God itself, in this similarity to what is believed and known.

Our reply to the Roman Catholic doctrine of the *analogia entis* is not, then, a denial of the concept of analogy. We say rather that the analogy in question is not an *analogia entis* but according to Rom. 12⁶ the ἀναλογία τῆς πίστεως, the likeness of the known in the knowing, of the object in thought, of the Word of

God in the word that is thought and spoken by man, as this differentiates true Christian prophecy in faith from all false prophecy. This *analogia fidei* is also the point of the remarkable passages in Paul in which man's knowledge of God is inverted into man's being known by God. Paul calls Christians γνόντες θεόν only to amend it once at: μᾶλλον δὲ γνωσθέντες ὑπὸ θεοῦ. It is obviously this γνωσθῆναι that distinguishes their γιγνώσκειν as Christians from their previous non-knowing of God as pagans (Gal. 4⁸ᶠ·). If here in the Christian community a man thinks he has known something, he has not known what must be known. One can never look back on the human, even the Christian act of knowledge as such as on a successful work corresponding to its object. The man who loves God οὗτος ἔγνωσται ὑπ' αὐτοῦ. Again it is the divine act of knowledge which takes place on man rather than through man that distinguishes those whose knowledge is grounded in love of God and therefore in true fellowship with Him, in the presence of God (1 Cor. 8²ᶠ·). But even in the Christian this being known, the divine possibility, remains distinct from the human possibility of knowing ; this cannot exhaust it ; there is only similarity, analogy. To see God " face to face " without dissimilarity must await the eternal consummation even in the case of Christians : τότε δὲ ἐπιγνώσομαι καθὼς καὶ (i.e., not just correspondingly, similarly, analogously, but exactly as) ἐπεγνώσθην (1 Cor. 13¹²). We find the same reversal in the words of Augustine : *Qui autem per Spiritum tuum vident ea* (*sc. opera Dei*) *tu vides in eis. Ergo cum vident quia bona sunt, tu vides quia bona sunt : et quaecumque propter te placent, tu in eis places et quae per Spiritum tuum placent nobis, tibi placent in nobis* (*Conf.*, XIII, 31, 46). One must also be sufficiently impartial not to overlook that which for all the dubious elements can still be taken *in bonam partem* in the words of the Hegelian P. Marheineke : " In the human spirit God is not manifest through this but through Himself, and hence manifest also to the human spirit. This, as reason, is annulled in Him. The hardest thing that science requires of every devotee is that pure substance show itself as subject, that he with his spirit should subject himself to the divine spirit and be patient under it. His true knowledge of the absolute is itself absolute " (*Grundlehren d. ch. Dogm. als Wissenschaft*, 1827, § 115). Precisely when we describe both the conformity of man to God that takes place in faith and also the point of contact for the Word of God posited in this conformity, not as an inborn or acquired property of man but only as the work of the actual grace of God, our only final word at this point can be that God acts on man in His Word. Because man's work in faith is that on which God's work is done, man can know the Word of God. He knows as he is known by God.

3. The last turn in our discussion of the concept of the *analogia fidei* has brought us already to the third and final thing which must be said in this connexion about faith and the knowability of the Word of God for man. If it is true that man really believes 1. that the object of faith is present to him and 2. that he himself is assimilated to the object, then we are led in conclusion to the third point that man exists as a believer wholly and utterly by this object. In believing he can think of himself as grounded, not in self but only in this object, as existing indeed only by this object. He has not created his own faith ; the Word has created it. He has not come to faith ; faith has come to him through the Word. He has not adopted faith ; faith has been granted to him through the Word. As a believer he cannot see himself as the acting subject of the work done here. It is his experience and act. He is not

at all a block or stone in faith but self-determining man. He does not sink into passive, apathetic contemplation in faith, and even if he did he would still do so as self-determining man. Whatever his state of soul, at least in thinking, willing and feeling he is himself and lives his own life. Nevertheless, the point is that in faith he must regard this in no sense diminished self-determination, himself in his own activity, in the living of his own life, as determined by the Word of God. In his freedom, in the full use of his freedom as a man, he must see himself as another man that he had no power to become, that he still has no power to become, that he is not free to become or to be (though he is free as he becomes and is), in short, that he can be only by being this man. Man acts as he believes, but the fact that he believes as he acts is God's act. Man is the subject of faith. Man believes, not God. But the fact that man is this subject in faith is bracketed as a predicate of the subject God, bracketed in the way that the Creator encloses the creature and the merciful God sinful man, i.e., in such a way that man remains subject, and yet man's I as such derives only from the Thou of the subject God.

The older theology was describing this when it called faith a gift of God, of the Holy Spirit. This could be meant and said with varying degrees of strictness. We must take it in a more incisive sense than it is stated and understood, e.g., in Augustine. Augustine, of course, taught very explicitly and impressively against the Pelagians that faith is grace. But his *Ut credamus Deus dedit* remained equivocal, for there was always the other saying : *fides in potestate est*, in which *potestas* meant the *facultas faciendi* (*De Spir. et lit.*, 31, 55), and the relation of the two is described thus : *Quid habeat et quid accipiat, Dei est ; accipere et habere utique accipientis est* (*ib.*, 34, 60). In one of his last writings against the Semi-Pelagians he certainly tried to correct this : *Habere fidem gratiae est fidelium*, but over against this there is still the other saying : *Posse habere fidem naturae est hominum* ; there is a general human *natura in qua nobis data est possibilitas habendi fidem* (*De praedest.*, 5, 10). Since it is hard to find any basis in man even for this *possibilitas habendi*, let alone a *habere*, it is better to say with Luther : *fidem esse . . . simpliciter donum Dei, qui ut creat ita conservat fidem in nobis* (*Comm. on Gal.* 1[12], 1535, *W.A.*, 40[I], p. 130, l. 13). " Here we must not regard reason or its work when we speak of faith and God's work. Here God worketh alone and reason is dead, blind, and compared to this work an unreasoning block, on which Scripture insists when it says, ' God is marvellous in his saints,' also Is. 55 : ' As heaven is high above the earth, so are my ways high above your ways ' " (*Fastenpost.*, 1525, *Sermon on Mt.* 8[1t.], *W.A.*, 17[II], p. 85, l. 10). " But they who gladly hear God's Word and to whom Christ hath said as here to the deaf, ' Ephphatha, ear, thou shalt stand open,' 'tis these are rightly holpen against the devil, for God hath given us no other stairs nor shown us any other way whereon we may go up to heaven save His dear Word, the holy gospel. Whoso gladly heareth the same, marketh it with diligence, and hath desire and love thereto, he receiveth help. This is a miraculous work which is still done daily in Christendom, that our ears which the devil hath stopped by sin are opened again by the Word, that we hear God's Word " (*Hauspost.*, 1544, *Sermon on Lk.* 18[9t.], *W.A.*, 52, p. 452, l. 14). " Like then as God giveth the Word, 'tis His and not our Word, so too giveth He faith in the Word. For both are God's work,

C.D.—I*

Word and faith " (*Hauspost.*, 1544, *Sermon on Mt.* 9[1t.], *W.A.*, 52, p. 501, l. 19).
" But that thou hearest and apprehendest such, is likewise not of thine own
power, but of God's grace, who maketh the gospel fruitful in thee, that thou
believest it. . . ." (*Adventpost.*, 1522, *Sermon on Mt.* 21[1t.], *W.A.*, 10[12], p. 30, l. 5).
" Where Christ sat not on the right hand of God nor daily poured forth of His
Spirit, Christian faith could not exist. For 'tis counter to all human reason and
the devil is hostile to it. Therefore, where the outpouring of the Holy Ghost
kept not continual guard, the devil would not let a single man abide by the
preaching of Pentecost and by faith in Christ " (*Sermon on Acts* 2[14t.], 1534, *E.A.*,
4, 105). It should be noted that Luther here is not dealing with a mere assent to
truth but with the living and direct relation to Christ that takes place in faith,
with the faith that lives in works. It is this that he traces back to and nails to
the fact that it is not a human work (as mere assent to truth might be) but
the gift of God. " There be some that hear and read the gospel and what is
said anent faith and they fall swiftly thereon and give the name of faith to what
they think. But they think no further than that faith is a thing that standeth
in their power to have or not to have, like any other natural human work ; therefore, when in their heart they effect a thought that saith, Verily the doctrine is
right and I believe it is so, at once they think faith is there. When they then see
and feel in themselves and in others that there is no change. . . . Lo, they then
fall away and cry and say, Ah, faith doeth it not alone. Why ? Ah, for this
reason that there are so many of them that believe and do nothing more than
before, they likewise find themselves no otherwise minded than before. These
are they whom Jude in his epistle (v. 8) calleth dreamers who deceive themselves
with their own dream. For what other is this thought of theirs that they call
faith than just a dream and a mere ghost of faith which they themselves of their
own power, without God's grace, have made in their hearts ? who become thereafter worse than they were before. . . . But the right faith whereof we speak
letteth not itself be made with our thoughts but 'tis a pure work of God in us
without any aid of ours. . . . Therefore, 'tis likewise a mighty, active, restless,
busy thing, which alike reneweth a man, beareth him elsewhere, and leadeth him
altogether into a new way and nature, such wise that 'tis impossible that the same
should not do good works without intermission " (*Sermon on Lk.* 16[1t.], *E.A.*,
13, 235, cf. *Hauspost.*, 1544, *Sermon on Jn.* 16[5t.], *W.A.*, 52, p. 292, l. 31).

The application to the problem of knowledge is self-evident.

We may now rejoin Augustine : *Non parva ex parte intelligit et scit Dominum,
qui intelligit et scit etiam hoc a Domino sibi dari, ut intelligat et sciat Dominum*
(*Conf.*, XVII, 4, 8). And Anselm : *Intellectus ex auditu gratia est* (*De concordia*,
Qu., III, 6).

The Word of God becomes knowable by making itself known. The
application of what has been said to the problem of knowledge consists
in stopping at this statement and not going a single step beyond it.
The possibility of knowing the Word of God is God's miracle on us
just as much as is the Word itself or its being spoken. Here again we
are not arguing for a passivity in man which sets aside or even limits
his freedom. Here again our concern is to realise that the mutual
indwelling or union of the divine and human possibility, of man's
knowing and his being known by God, is an event in the freedom of
man, and yet that it cannot in any sense be regarded as its product, as

the result of an intuition, of a conceivable or attainable deepening or enhancing of the life of the human soul. This may take place—and why should it not ?—but it does not have to take place. And in any case it is not the thing that brings about that union and therefore the knowability of the Word of God. Even the idea of a *sacrificium intellectus* is only a last desperate attempt to make the knowledge of God a work of man, to have a human possibility correspond to what is God's work alone. If we have understood that the knowability of God's Word is really an inalienable affirmation of faith, but that precisely as such it denotes the miracle of faith, the miracle that we can only recollect and hope for, then as a final necessity we must also understand that man must be set side and God Himself presented as the original subject, as the primary power, as the creator of the possibility of knowledge of God's Word. Christ does not remain outside. And it is true enough that man must open the door (Rev. 3^{20}). But the fact that this takes place is *quoad actum* and *quoad potentiam* the work of the Christ who stands outside. Hence it is also unconditionally true that the risen Christ passes through closed doors (Jn. 20$^{19f.}$).

THE WORD OF GOD, DOGMA AND DOGMATICS

Dogmatics is the critical question about dogma, i.e., about the Word of God in Church proclamation, or, concretely, about the agreement of the Church proclamation done and to be done by man with the revelation attested in Holy Scripture. Prolegomena to dogmatics as an understanding of its epistemological path must therefore consist in an exposition of the three forms of the Word of God as revealed, written, and preached.

1. THE PROBLEM OF DOGMATICS

In the three preceding sections we have described the criterion of dogmatics, its three forms, its nature and its knowability. What we had in view when in § 3 we called the Word of God the standard by which dogmatics must measure Church proclamation should now have become provisionally comprehensible in all its incomprehensibility. Provisionally, we shall have to say, for all that we have said thus far implies only a turning around and placing ourselves in the direction in which we must look to see the point from which the Church realises that its proclamation is perceived and judged and from which, therefore, it must make every effort to think about itself so that, fully aware of its responsibility, it may submit to the necessary self-examination in respect of its proclamation. In all that has been said thus far we have as it were only sketched the sphere of this criterion, trying to visualise its distinctiveness as compared with other objects of human and even Christian reflection and its difference from other intrinsically possible criteria. Although with constant regard to the concrete content of this criterion, we have put only the formal question and received the corresponding formal answers. More can and must be said about the Word of God than has been said thus far, though always in recollection of the promise made to the Church and in expectation of its fulfilment. The recollection to which the Church knows it is summoned relates to a wholly concrete content of the Word of God, and so, too, does the expectation inseparable from the recollection. This concrete content of the criterion of dogmatics has not yet been put in the centre of our attention or discussed independently. But this must be done. Only when we have understood it in the unity of form and content, only when it is clear that the form that has concerned us thus far is the form of a very concrete content, have we understood the Word of God in such a way that its application as the criterion of Church proclamation has meaning and authority. As yet, therefore, our doctrine of the Word of God is far from complete. Its most characteristic statements have still to be made. In one sense we cannot go further or expect to hear more. We have said that what is meant by the Word of God must have become comprehensible now in all its incomprehensibility. First, we accept and shall continue to accept the incomprehensibility of the fact that the Word of God is spoken to man. No consideration yet to be adduced, not even that which must and will be directed to its specific content, will ever help us to see how this reality comes to be. We have investigated its constitution and will investigate it further. We have been able to ask *a posteriori* concerning its possibilities, namely, those grounded in itself. How it came about and comes about as thus constituted, what is the possibility of its possibilities, must and will always remain incomprehensible to us. Secondly we accept and continue to accept the incomprehensibility of the nature of the Word of God in itself. For one thing, as what it is it is only the content of the specific event of its being spoken to this man or that. Then again, as what this man or that receives and accepts and can give an account of as God's Word in the event of faith, it is no longer what the Word of God that is spoken to him is in itself, but only his recollection of what is said to him and his expectation of what will be said to him afresh. Dogmatics cannot get round this twofold barrier even by turning its attention to the concrete content of the Word of God. With the whole Church it can know its concrete content only in recollection and expectation and therefore neither in its That nor (in the narrower sense) in its concrete What, neither with a proof lying outside itself nor as the *verbum concretissimum* that comes to specific men but is veiled from each man even as it is revealed to him. One should not expect anything superhuman from dogmatics ; its office cannot be to tear down the barriers of faith that are set for the Church. Part of its task is rather to make these barriers known as such, to say what can be said and therewith to warn against violations or illusions regarding things one cannot say. In this sense it should now be comprehensible what is meant by the two terms " God's Word " : provisionally comprehensible and comprehensible in all its incomprehensibility. To say " provisionally " is to indicate the possibility of further insights. To say " in all its incomprehensibility " is to imply that we shall still be moving within fixed limits even in all these further insights.

But before we can enter upon this further path, we must turn once again, instructed to some extent about the one thing needful, to the task of dogmatics as such. In § 1 we generally defined this as the Christian Church's task of self-examination regarding the content of its specific talk about God. Then in § 3 we said rather more precisely that it is a matter of investigating the " responsibility " of this talk, namely, of Church proclamation measured by the Word of God that it is seeking to proclaim. The primary result was a need to ask and say what is meant by this standard by which Church proclamation is to be measured and by means of which that self-examination is to be performed. Now that this has been done we move on to a third and even more precise definition of the dogmatic task. It should be noted that even this cannot be the last one. That can be reached only when we have examined the criterion according to its concrete content, or rather in the last stage of this examination itself. But in order to determine in which direction we must move we must now for a moment turn our attention afresh to the task as such for whose sake the question of the criterion has been put and is still to be put.

The task of dogmatics is the examination of Church proclamation in respect of its agreement with the Word of God, its congruity with what it is trying to proclaim. In the human form of the proclamation offered by the Church, the Word of God should, of course, be present too. This is the claim with which the Church advances its proclamation and also the expectation by which it is surrounded. Dogmatic work begins by taking this claim and expectation with full seriousness, by taking the Church at its word, so to speak, in respect of this claim and this expectation. In dogmatics the Church accepts what it is undertaking in its proclamation. It tests this undertaking by confronting it critically, by suspending the claim and expectation for a moment to the degree that it dissociates proclamation and the Word of God in thought, not in order to measure the Word of God by its proclamation, but in order to measure its proclamation by the Word of God. The Church does not cease to believe that God will confess it and its work, that He will put His Word in its proclamation and thus make its proclamation real proclamation. But the fact that it believes this means that it grasps God's promise. " It believes " does not mean " it thinks it possesses," but " it hopes it will be given." The reflection of faith, then, consists in the fact that the Church holds apart God's Word and its own and questions the latter in the light of the former. Faith knows that it is asked whether as a human work it is also obedience. To faith the judgment of God to which all human work is subject as such is no idle thought. It is a summons to judge itself regarding this work. The corresponding critical concern for Church proclamation is the task of dogmatics. But can it do justice to this task ? How and where may it see the Word of God as an entity distinct from Church proclamation so as to compare the latter with it and measure it by it ? Is there any possibility of this at all ? If there were no such possibility, we should be faced by a remarkable dilemma.

We might still scrutinise Church proclamation in many different ways. We might ask whether it is really commensurate with the Word of God that it purports to proclaim and indeed to be. Disturbed by its human imperfection, we might examine it in terms of this congruity and improve it accordingly. We might test it philosophically in terms of its epistemological, logical, cosmological and psychological content, or test its form historically, ethico-pedagogically, or politically. We might adjust it to the prevailing modern philosophy, or the most pressing practical needs and tasks, or the most eloquent forms of expression. There are many such criteria which one might advance in place of the absent criterion of the Word of God. It might be that Church proclamation would correspond to God's Word to the degree that it stands the test of one or other of these criteria or all of them together. Theology would then consist in administering these criteria and their relevance with the utmost possible strictness of application, always on the assumption that in this way justice is done to the inconceivable true criterion of theology, the Word of God.

The theology of Modernist Protestantism might be understood in this way and against this background. It too, gripped and impelled in its own way by concern for the Church, was trying to do justice to the task handed down by the Reformation and the older Church. It, too, was trying to promote concern for correct Church proclamation in accordance with the Word of God. It, too, desired and therefore had its dogmatics. But it had lost the proper criterion above and over against Church proclamation as the Reformation especially had put this in its hands. It still knew it, but it no longer regarded it as a criterion in its distinction from and superiority to the present action of the Church. It still took it into account, but it no longer understood its dignity, its character as a final court of appeal. It forgot to look to this and to this alone in the question as to the Word of God by which Church proclamation must be measured. In this question it constantly looked elsewhere. The empty place of the criterion of Reformation theology had to be occupied, and was occupied, in some other way. Even though one regards as heretical this newer theology which attained to leadership with Pietism and the Enlightenment, we must admit that it wanted to continue the critical function of theology. It still wanted to be the conscience of the proclaiming Church. It also saw that conscience must have a criterion. And if it no longer understood the criterion of Reformation theology as such, and therefore seized on other criteria, it did so with the idea of finding in these other criteria a full and equal replacement or substitute for what had been lost. It was out of good intentions rather than bad intentions that it became as philosophical, as moral, as secular, in short, as culturally Protestant as it became and continued to become in ever new forms throughout the 18th and 19th centuries and on into our own. The golden calf (Ex. 32), too, was not meant to represent a strange god but the God who had led Israel out of Egypt. Israel, too, acted out of piety in this matter, and Aaron met its wishes with the best of intentions. This is how we might regard the theology of Modernist Protestantism. It could see no further possibility of viewing the Word of God as an entity distinct from Church proclamation. But it could clearly see other entities distinct from Church proclamation and at least very normative. Their epitome was modern cultural awareness. It therefore set up this cultural awareness as a surrogate in the place of the Word of God which had now lost all concreteness for it and had volatilised into a mere idea. And it now judged according to this surrogate.

If we cannot make the distinction, if the Word of God is not for us a concrete entity distinct from Church proclamation, then we might be tempted to take this course—and it is not the only one available at this point. But if we do, we should be aware of the serious problems that arise on this path, and the question is whether they are surmountable.

1. How do we know what we obviously think we know on this path, namely, that the process of losing the Word of God as a concrete theological criterion, and therefore of losing a specifically theological relevance, is a good and necessary process whose results one can and should simply accept ?

2. How do we know whether the criteria newly selected to replace that which is lost are really commensurate with this undertaking, with Church proclamation, whether in applying them we are not causing confusion where there should be order and destroying where we ought to build ?

3. How do we know whether here, where perhaps only an absolutely given criterion ought to come into consideration, we are not decisively in error in the very fact that, however good our intentions, we even look around for criteria, choose them, and set them up as such ?

4. How do we know, finally, whether any other criterion can replace the Word of God that we can no longer grasp, whether we are not rather to accept the impossibility of seeing the Word of God concretely, whether it would not better to renounce all critical concern for Church proclamation, i.e., all theology ?

Naturally these questions will really harry and possibly force off that path only those who have not completely lost sight of the Word of God as a concrete independent criterion, so that for them the possibility of a comparison between this criterion and the others has not been totally cut off.

This stage has not been reached even in the age of theological Modernism. The very different approach of the first centuries of the Reformation churches has not ceased to have an unsettling effect. Its influence, of course, was often reduced to a minimum. If anything served to restrict it and hence to harden the Modernist position, it was the resistance which the official ecclesiastical authorities offered to theological Liberalism from the days of Wöllner's edict on religion, through the disastrous period of Frederick William IV and up to the time before the First World War. For this opposition was not based on better theology or on real perception of what Modernism could no longer see. In the main it rested on blind conservative instincts. Again, the opposition did not follow the only way that is possible in the Church, that of spiritual conquest. Instead, it took the form of political repression of what was then the new theology. The human brilliance which has enveloped theological Liberalism right up to the final phase characterised by such names as Harnack and Troeltsch, and the religious passion with which it could be presented at the same period in the theology of W. Herrmann, were the brilliance and passion of a martyrdom by which the Church authorities, powerless to oppose to it a superior word, continually vindicated it in its own eyes and in the eyes of the world. What an ecclesiastical orthodoxy that was so unsure of its cause as that of the 18th, 19th and 20th centuries could and did accomplish when faced by the great Modernist *Quid pro quo* was far from being a salutary unsettling of this new Protestantism by Reformation insights. And if to the very last Liberal theology was opposed by a " positive " theology of imposing power which did formally maintain the Reformation thesis with respect to the criterion of dogmatics, this ought to have steered clear of any alliance with the unspiritually conservative Church authorities ; it ought to have declined their political support ; it ought to have shown itself much more unequivocally to be what it meant to be, namely, a theology of revelation. But did the modern positive block in which the remnants of the former Erlangen and Leipzig schools regrouped in the first decade of the present century really have so much to reproach its Liberal opponents with as it made out ? In the last resort, where was the theological orthodoxy about which Liberal journals had so much to say ? How it had joined in the chase after new criteria ! How it had dabbled in apologetics ! How many of its members could waken up one morning with no particular transformation to find themselves tolerably authentic religious philosophers, religious historians or religious psychologists ! How in the field of exegesis in particular it even increased the confusion of approaches by a historicism which was not better because it was a traditionally inclined and supernatural historicism, which certainly had not the slightest influence on the opposition and which could not prevent the increasing and final obliteration of the frontiers between " positive " and " liberal " Old and New Testament scholars, always to the disadvantage of the so-called " positives " ! And how finally, when the great moment came (in 1914) in which a theology of revelation had to differentiate itself at least in some measure from a theology of culture within the relativity of all things human, it went along with it hand-in-hand in both ethos and ethics ! I make these points, which are not really my concern here, only because the complaint is continually made to-day (especially in the writings of E. Schaeder, though cf. also P. Althaus, " Die Theologie " in C. Schweitzer, *Das. relig. Deutschland der Gegenwart*, Vol. 2, 1930, p. 140) that it has now been largely forgotten that there has been a constant theological protest against cultural Protestantism for a long time. Certainly there was this protest. Indeed, it was there in Liberal theology itself. It had to be if theology was not going to sell out completely and retire. Liberal theology was not really as bad as it often made itself out to be. Under the pressure of the problem there were some note-worthy counter-movements even in its own ranks. To-day Wobbermin, e.g., in the Preface to *Richtlinien*, 1930, or *Wort Gottes*, 1931, p. 4, n. 2, is no less zealous than E. Schaeder in announcing that he was long ago " in the sharpest conflict not only against all psychologism but also against all historicism " (*op. cit.*, p. 6). But what point or value is there in contesting or maintaining priorities here ? If and to the degree that " it " was really said long ago by Positives and by Liberals themselves, it had then the effect and significance that it could have in the form in which it was said. The one thing that is certain is that the real power to unsettle did not come from the Church authorities or the theology of the period but from the simple fact that the Church lived on and its proclamation continued, that whether led or led astray, whether promoted or devastated by Modernist theology, it nevertheless continued through the 18th and 19th centuries and on into the 20th century. The Church lived on because the Bible was preserved for it, a Bible much relativised by history and psychology, a Bible misinterpreted by religious philosophy, a Bible whose right and claim to constitute the textual basis of Church proclamation were disputed, a Bible which was affirmed in fact rather than theoretically and in large measure even against theological theory, a Bible to which only relative commitment was felt, nevertheless the Bible, and with the Bible the problem, and with the problem a sense of dissatisfaction with the Neo-Protestant solution. It is in this way, by ongoing proclamation bound somehow—very much " somehow "—to the Bible, by the ongoing life of the Church in this its decisive function, that a challenge has always been maintained to the Modernist answer in this matter.

When in face of the possibility of replacing the Word of God by other criteria in dogmatics, we raise those four questions, when we say that there is no way of knowing what is thought to be known at all those points, when we thus state that that whole possibility of solution is unsound, we are appealing to the simple fact that Church proclamation, whether this be understood or not understood, whether it is inwardly reasoned out or merely a matter of tradition, is in fact confronted with the Bible. So long as this confrontation is not set aside, no one can truly say that the problem does not exist for him, that the possibility that the Word of God is the true and concretely independent criterion of Church proclamation has been completely banished from his field of vision.

From the book by Wilhelm Pauck, *Karl Barth, Prophet of a New Christianity ?*, 1931, p. 99, I take the following observation. " It is important to remember . . . that the difference between modern preaching in America and Protestant Europe is fundamental. The American sermon is seldom Biblical and expository. Its reference to the Scripture is in the majority of cases casual or superficial. It deals generally with ' religious ' topics. The European Protestant, however, follows the old tradition of preaching the ' Word ' whether he is affiliated with liberal or orthodox theology." If this is generally true as concerns America, then even the actual confrontation with the Bible which is presupposed here is no longer, or scarcely any longer, an event there. And if not, then naturally the problem based on this confrontation does not arise. In that case I may expect from the descendants of the Pilgrim Fathers neither interest nor understanding for what follows, nor indeed for the whole of this Dogmatics. But perhaps even in America there is at least a dim recollection that the preaching of the Church might stand in some sort of special connexion with the Bible. And even there it will surely happen some day that " religious " topics will become so stupid and stale that the dim recollection might become once again a clear recollection.

From the situation of the parson in the pulpit, who not only has to say something somehow, but has to say it in face of the open Bible and supposedly in accordance with the Bible and in exposition of the Bible, from this situation even the man outside the Church, the abjurer of faith, can at least gather this, that here there is at the very lowest the possibility of a protest against the introduction of other criteria of Church proclamation, or as we might also put it, of the assertion of the Bible as the criterion, as the concrete form of the Word of God. Or it might be that the Bible has already spoken or will speak to us again as the Word of God and that we have to think and judge in this matter, not as outsiders, but as those who stand on the Church's own ground. Considered as a human place of human willing and doing, the Church rests, not on the presupposition, but very definitely on the recollection and the expectation that God in fact has spoken and will speak the Word to us in the Bible. Can one stand in this recollection and expectation, and to that extent in the Church, without having to raise those four questions? And can the questions be answered except as follows?

1. If it is true that we no longer know concretely whether and how far the Word of God is the standard by which Church proclamation is to be measured, if the Word of God has really dissolved from a concrete counterpart into a mere idea, then we do not have to accept this as a historical fate in intellectual history, but it is a sign of the wrath of God, a trial of faith, a falling into the consequences of disobedience in which one cannot be a mere spectator of oneself, with which one cannot come to terms in the Church, but, realising that it is a matter of divine chastisement, one can only reply by crying to the hidden God that He will give again the standard that has been lost. This is in keeping with the recollection and expectation of faith. At any time faith can fall into unbelief and then theological relevance is indeed lost and the temptation arises to make a golden calf representing the God of Israel, the temptation as it were to settle down comfortably in unbelief and to fend for oneself. Faith overcomes this temptation. Faith does not make a virtue of the necessity. Even and precisely in the depths of unbelief faith hears the new summons to faith. In the trial regarding God's Word which did not indeed come only with the 18th century, faith may thus lose theological relevance, but it can lose it only to find it again.

2. In fact Church proclamation is not an undertaking which can come under other criteria than God's Word in respect of its content. What is undertaken in it is exempt from the claim to be judged by any philosophy or ethics or politics, if not in respect of its human motives and forms, at least in respect of its believed intention. The introduction of other criteria here can only mean that the undertaking itself has become a different one, that it ceases to be the Church's undertaking laid upon it by commission and accompanied by the divine promise. For the introduction of another criterion means renunciation of the believed intention of this undertaking. To the extent that another standard is really applied here and not the Word of God itself, only confusion and destruction can actually result, no matter how true or weighty the other standard may be in and for itself. For the decisive word about its proclamation the Church cannot listen to any other voice than the voice of its Lord. If it does not hear this, the darkness

of an utter lack of counsel or leadership would be ever so much better than the light of strange lights however bright.

3. It is indeed a decisive mistake to think that other criteria can be sought and chosen and set up in matters of Church proclamation. The criterion to which the Church knows it is subject is not one it has chosen and adopted ; it has been given to it. It is in force before and as proclamation is undertaken ; proclamation is undertaken on the basis of the fact that it is already in force. It may be regarded or not regarded, acknowledged or not acknowledged, but when it is regarded and acknowledged it can be regarded and acknowledged only in an act of obedience, only in a finding preceded by no human seeking. The choice of other criteria in place of God's Word betrays itself already as an act involving abandonment of the Church's ground, of its recollection and expectation and to that extent of its faith, by the very fact that it is a choice, an act of human perplexity and prudence, instead of an act of acknowledgment of God's prevenient goodness.

4. But if it is finally objected that there is not any real surrender of the one criterion of the Word of God, that the other criteria are merely brought in to represent this one (in view of its incomprehensibility), that theology is not giving up its task but simply assuming as it were an incognito by putting other standards alongside the one standard that is not thereby denied or replaced but merely given surrogates or a surrogate (always in view of its incomprehensibility), the answer is that these other criteria are to be rejected as irrelevant and injurious because they cannot serve vicariously as surrogates, because all vicariate is fundamentally impossible here. Philosophy, ethics, politics and anything else that might be suggested here may all have their own dignity and justification in their own spheres but they are the philosophy, ethics and politics of sinful and lost man whose word, however profound and true it may be, cannot be recognised as judge over the Word which is addressed in the name of God to these sinful and lost men, as judge, therefore, over Church proclamation. In seeking to judge himself here, man would not be judged. Trying to serve proclamation on this basis, dogmatics would not serve it with true and serious criticism and correction. Theology itself would be only one of the many forms of dialogue that man has with himself about himself when what it ought to do is to serve the discourse that God directs to man. The true problem of Church proclamation, the problem of the question how sinful man can be a messenger of the divine Word, would be ignored, for even the best-founded and most considered human judgment cannot help with this problem. If theology had no answer to this true problem of the Church, it might in fact be just as well abandoned.

The other possibility in the dilemma in which we would be placed if we did not know any concrete form of the Word of God as the supreme criterion of Church proclamation would consist in our having to start with the fact that the Church with its proclamation is indeed left to itself and cast back on its own resources. But, it might then be asked, would this really mean that it is without God's Word and therefore in no position to control, criticise and correct itself by God's Word ? May not and must not the juxtaposition of God's Word and Church proclamation be viewed as a relative one ? Have we not said ourselves that the reflection in which the Church makes this distinction is the reflection of faith, which, even as it makes the distinction, lays hold of the divine promise, Lo, I am with you alway ! and precisely in so doing abrogates the distinction again ? Might not the distinction amount to no more than a distinction within the reality of the Church itself, the distinction between the human and divine elements of its reality, which are both still to be regarded as elements of its reality ? Is the Word of God not given to it as the Church of Jesus Christ ? Is not, then, the absent concrete authority established and alive within itself ? Is not precisely this the glory of the Church, the presence of its Lord within it, that on the one hand it can and should proclaim the Word of God and on the other hand it can and should itself regulate, criticise and correct its action in this respect by means of the same Word of God ?

In this possibility we are primarily confronted again by the Roman Catholic view of the relation of the Bible to the teaching office, which we discussed already at an earlier stage. According to this view the Church has, of course, a lord and judge over its acts. It has, of course, the Word of God over it. But it has this over it as it has it in it, indistinguishable from itself. Though it puts tradition alongside the Bible, the Roman Catholic Church, too, has and reads and honours the Bible. But this is not the Bible in itself, the emancipated Bible, the Bible which confronts the Church as an authority. The fact that the Bible in its own concreteness is the Word of God, and that as such it is the supreme criterion of Church teaching, is not acknowledged here. What we have here is the Bible as it is authoritatively interpreted by the Church itself or by its teaching office, which is the living voice of Christ. What we have here is the Bible which belongs to the Church, which is understood aright and expounded aright and applied aright by its teaching office. This Bible is the Word of God by which all proclamation is to be measured. The *regula proxima fidei*, the nearest immediate plumbline of Catholic faith, is not, then, the verdict of the Bible but the verdict of the teaching office on the Bible. (Cf. Diekamp, *Kath. Dogm.*, Vol. 1, 1930, p. 63 f.) Even and especially in relation to the Bible the Church keeps in its own hand both proclamation and also the norm of its necessary criticism, i.e., the Bible correctly understood and applied, which is in fact the norm employed in this criticism. There is in fact only a relative difference between the two, and their synthesis can cause no surprise to the Church which in its head is both *norma normata* and *norma normans*, both *ecclesia audiens* and *ecclesia docens*, for at least in its head, i.e., its teaching office, it has oversight of both and full authority and power to effect the synthesis and therefore to pursue dogmatic criticism according its own free judgment. But in this possibility we are not merely confronted by the Roman Catholic view of the teaching office. For according to the teaching of Protestant Modernism as well we ultimately find the Church dependent on itself and left to its own devices. Here again this does not have to mean that the Church is necessarily without the Word of God and consequently without the criterion of its proclamation. Here again the Bible has not just been pushed aside in favour of philosophical, historical, political and other criteria. Here again the connexion of proclamation with the Bible and therefore a certain critical participation of the Bible in dogmatics remain. There even remain as a rule—and this largely serves to obscure the issue—strong traditional theoretical statements about the normativity and even the sole normativity of the Bible. " I am quite serious in bringing to full and unrestricted validity the principle of Luther that the Word of God alone has to set up articles of faith . . . that Holy Scripture alone must be accepted exclusively and unconditionally as the source of dogmatic work, all so-called subsidiary sources being sharply rejected." So Wobbermin! (*Chr. u. Wiss.*, 1932, p. 179). But here again the Church does not have the Bible over it as a concrete and supreme criterion. Here again it has the Bible over it only as it has it in it. To be sure, there is no infallible teaching office authoritatively representing the Bible's being in the Church and constituting with its interpretation of the Bible the *regula proxima fidei*. But the fact that the Church in its unity as *norma normata* and *norma normans* does have this specific representative in Roman Catholicism is not the essential point of this position even there. The essential point is rather the presupposed relativity of the difference between the Church and the Bible, or the insight into this relativity which is ascribed to the Church, its ascribed competence to determine for itself how far it will let itself be judged by the Bible, and therefore to be finally the judge in its own cause. Protestant Modernism does this without a teaching office. That this is so is perhaps seen most plainly in that one of its many schools in which, apart from Schleiermacher, its essence has in general been most clearly and consistently developed, namely, in theologians philosophically orientated to Hegel. When P. K. Marheineke ascribes quite unreservedly to the Christian community the " holy spirit of Jesus Christ " who " not only has knowledge in himself but is knowledge " (*Grundlehren der christl. Dogmatik*, 1827, § 15), when he can thus say of the Christian religion that " in it God is known humanly as He knows Himself. It is truth in and for itself " (§ 69), when in this Christian " spirit " he finds not only reason but also Church tradition and the Bible " abrogated in their aseity " (§ 113), and when he then expressly makes this " spirit " the normative expositor not only of tradition but also of the Bible (§ 112 and 588), the expositor who, being himself the spirit of the Bible, takes his own standpoint in this, and therefore in dogmatics as in Church tradition simply repeats what he already has and indeed himself is (§ 116), what does all this mean but that the Bible is retained as a stage which the self-movement of the Christian spirit must pass through but which has completely lost as such the character of a court that is independent of this self-movement and that really judges it ? What does all this mean but that the difference between the divine and the human word is already perceived and overcome in its relativity by the Christian thinker even as it discloses itself to him ? Does it make any basic difference if this Christian thinker is not the pope and does not have a pope over him to decide authoritatively the extent of this perceiving and overcoming ? Is not the nature of the basic view more clearly exposed, perhaps, if every man is called upon to be his own pope in virtue of the spirit that is alive within him as a member of the Christian community ? And when A. E. Biedermann sets dogmatics the task of logically developing our experiential knowledge of the Christian act of faith and thus gaining autonomously an understanding of its nature, of the Christian principle (*Christl. Dogm.*, 1869, § 92), when he thinks he sees this Christian principle in the " religious personality of Jesus," i.e., in the reciprocal relation between God and man which is in Jesus the fact of His religious self-consciousness " (§ 99), when he thus calls the Bible the place where " in the first instance " (alongside it, as in Marheineke, Church tradition, i.e., the historical development, calls for consideration on the same level) the Christian principle is to be communicated by historical science in the " original form of the Christian faith " (§ 140), what does all this mean but that the relation of dogmatics to the Bible is understood as a dialectical circle whose course is determined by the dogmatician himself ? He develops his experiential knowledge of the act of faith in just the same way as he controls (as historian) the Christian principle in so far as this meets him in the original biblical form of the Christian faith and in the development of the Church. There can be no confrontation by a ἕτερος νόμος on this theory in spite of its acceptance of a historical point of reference. The Church of the present, which always has the Word of God already within itself, is left in splendid isolation. And it is only a secondary question of no great significance whether this isolation is the more impressively symbolised by the Roman Catholic establishment of an authoritative teaching office or by the obvious lack of any such teaching office in Protestant Modernism. The Roman pope infallibly interpreting the Bible and the Neo-Protestant professor of theology who bears the Christian principle or the Christian spirit no less surely in himself than he rediscovers it in the Bible are figures which perhaps stand out equally effectively against the same background.

With regard to this second possibility, too, there is no direct proof of its impossibility. If we were to presume to attempt such a proof we should as it were confound ourselves ; we should ourselves prove *ipso facto*, not its impossibility, but in the closest accord with the adversary whom we are supposed to refute, its possibility. To prove that the juxtaposition of the Word of God and Church tradition is not just a relative one as maintained, that it is not a distinction within the Church of the present itself, that the Word of God in the Bible en-counters and continually confronts Church proclamation as a judicial authority, that the Bible as this supreme authority which addresses the Church is not at all the Bible that is already dogmatically and histori-cally interpreted by the pope or the professor but the Bible that is not yet interpreted, the free Bible, the Bible that remains free in face of all interpretation—to prove that we should obviously have to put ourselves in a place above proclamation and the Bible, we should have to share the opinion that it is for us to make this relation clear, to order it one way or the other, and that we can establish the supremacy of the Word of God in this relation. But then the Bible whose supremacy we could establish would obviously not be the free Bible which constitutes an effective court. It would obviously have become a Bible interpreted already in a particular way, a Bible made over to us and thus put as an instrument in our hands. To that degree, even though we could perhaps prove its supremacy, it would still be only an element in the Church of the present which we ourselves constitute. We shall thus be on our guard against attempting this kind of proof. It could only prove the opposite of what it is supposed to prove. At this point we can only point to a fact, and in view of this fact, with no more proof than before, lodge an objection. The fact is again the significance that the Bible actually has in the Church irrespective of all theories about its significance.

It has this even in the Roman Church in spite of the fatal doctrine of the teaching office, and it has it also in Protestant Modernism in spite of the equally fatal doctrine of the spirit of the Christian community or the Christian principle.

It has never wholly lost the significance of a relative court over against the consciousness and proclamation of the present-day Church, the significance, so to speak, of a second voice which the Church has always wished to hear alongside its own voice and in harmony with it. Some care and concern for this harmony, for establishing and maintaining it, has never completely vanished. But this means that in spite of the theory, or in a fulfilment of the theory that was better than the theory itself, the possibility always remained, not that the Church would rule the Bible but that the Bible would rule the Church, that the controlling relation which is theoretically ordered so completely in favour of the Church or of man in the Church, that the relation of " over " and " in " the Church, could be completely reversed in practice. There remained at least the possibility of resistance by the free Bible which perhaps cannot be wholly taken captive by any interpretation. Even the Bible which seemed to be assimilated to the Church was never so completely assimilated that there was utter failure to call to awareness from time to time at least the relative distance between it and ourselves, that a complete denial of even the formal—and perhaps in fact the purely formal—distance as such was hazarded. The Bible found a voice and finds a voice *in* the Church. Hence the possibility is not ruled out that it may also find a voice *over against* the Church. Certainly this fact and the implied possibility are only a sign. The sign may be overlooked. The story of the Bible in the Church may be viewed and interpreted in such a way that the pope and the professor have always done as they wanted with the Bible. But we do not have to view and interpret it thus. Even if we do view and interpret it thus, we have to concede that it might be viewed and interpreted otherwise—not perhaps that it can be, but at any rate that it might be. The sign as such, whether understood or not understood or however understood, cannot be refuted. Of course the sign as such is not an answer to the question whether the Bible is God's Word over the Church and to the Church. This question is the question of faith. How can it be answered by the existence of a sign ? One cannot even say more generally that the question of faith is at least raised by the presence of the sign. One can only say that the question of faith might be put by the sign. In face of the sign it might happen that man in the

Church is summoned to faith. It might happen that in the Bible whose voice still sounds in the Church man hears the Word of God, that he really hears the Word which cannot be held captive or bracketed by the Church, which cannot be integrated into the Church's own reality, which cannot by any interpretation be translated into a word of man, the Word which encounters the Church, with which the Church cannot sing a duet, but which it has simply to listen to as a full and unique solo. We cannot presuppose that this event, the event of faith, has happened. We can only relate to this event in so far as it is the content of the promise given to the Church or, as one might also say, of the command given to the Church. With reference to this event we cannot speak out of the present, the fulfilment, but only out of the recollection and the expectation. As this event takes place according to the promise, as the Church will be the Church of Jesus Christ, the Bible will be heard as God's Word. It is to this coming fulfilment of the promise received that we relate. The Word of God is the speech, the act, the mystery of God. It is not a demonstrable substance immanent in the Church and present within it apart from the event of its being spoken and heard. Thus the Church is not constantly or continuously the Church of Jesus Christ. It is this in the event of the Word of God being spoken to it and believed by it. Therefore the sign that is set up in the Church, the Bible speaking and being heard in some way, is a genuine sign, no less but also no more. If with reference to that event we could speak of a fulfilment that has already happened and is illuminating as such rather than of the promise and command of God, if we could speak of the present instead of the future, if we could argue from faith and with faith as though it were a present presupposition available to us, then the sign would cease to be a sign. Faith assumed to be present would dissolve the sign as such into a directly visible and perceptible datum. On the presupposition of that datum the Bible could then be understood directly as the Word of God. This datum with faith, or faith with this datum, would then constitute the proof of the Bible as God's Word. But by being adduced this proof would contradict what it is meant to prove.

It would lead us back exactly to where we began, namely, to the twofold construct of Roman Catholicism and Protestant Modernism. Nothing is more characteristic of either than the presupposition of the already enacted event of faith in the Word of God and therefore of an already present faith, a faith from and with which one can argue. By means of the presupposition the sign is there dissolved as a sign and therefore made possible as a proof, namely, the proof that the Word of God as an authority is not over the Church but in the Church, that it is an authority which properly and finally is integrated into the Church and subordinated to it.

The Word of God over the Church and to the Church will permit of no proof, not even and least of all this proof from the faith present in the Church. The conclusion that because I believe, and because for me as a believer the Bible is the Word of God, therefore and thus far it is God's Word, destroys the divinity of the Word of God, since it is no longer understood as the Word that stands over the Church and is directed to it. This conclusion involves *theologia gloriae*, which, in spite of its loud protestations to the contrary, does not in fact subject itself to God's Word. There is thus no question of this conclusion if the Bible is to be understood as the free and supreme criterion of Church proclamation. The reference with which this is done, the reference to the event of faith, or to God's Word being spoken and heard, does not claim to be a proof. The reference to this event does not mean that an argument is adduced, an argument operating with the ultimate force of the directly religious, an argument which puts us in a position to demonstrate the soundness of our position over against Roman Catholicism and Protestant Modernism, and to defend it by attack. We have to realise that the reference to this event might equally well be turned against ourselves, since we do not have the event in our own hands, since it is by nature a divine decision whose outcome we cannot anticipate. Whether the Bible will speak to us as God's Word, whether we will hear it, whether we will believe it as God's Word—we and those with whom we speak—is something we can neither appropriate to ourselves nor give to them. We cannot, then, presuppose it as something that has happened. We cannot argue from it and with it. What we might presuppose as our faith might even be God-forsaken unbelief and our arguing from it and with it might be powerless in the extreme. We can only point to the fact that in that event, in faith in God's Word in the Bible, a flat and irrefutable decision will be made against any view of the Bible as a court instituted and superintended by the Church, as a purely relative counter-authority to the Church proclamation of the day. Otherwise, if this decision were not made even as it takes place, it would not be this event. Now it is true, of course, that a direct pointer to this event does not achieve the reference now at issue. If we presumed to point to it directly, i.e., if we ourselves tried to come forward in the posture of Grünewald's John as witnesses to this event, we should be alleging what one ought never to think of alleging, namely, that we have its reality as it were behind us, that we are based upon it, that we can refute others by appealing to it. The word " pointer " would then be just another word for " presupposition." But we cannot speak either as prophets or as apostles. We cannot speak with the full assurance of the biblical witness : " We beheld his glory " (Jn. 1¹⁴). What we saw and what—we cannot say empowered us, but shall we simply say—caused us to give the pointer in question, the *ratio* of this pointer, is again very simply the Bible, not yet put out of the Church, not yet totally estranged from its proclamation, not yet divested of all its normativeness in relation to it, this fact, this sign, as we said before. We relate to the event of faith by relating to this sign. That to which we point is thus itself a pointer. Both Roman Catholics and Modernists can and must grant that neither they nor we have fashioned and set up this sign, this pointer. But we have all found it there. Among perhaps many other signs in the Church that point in the same direction, there is in the Church which believes itself to be the Church of Jesus Christ at least this sign too, the voice of Moses and the prophets, of the Evangelists and the apostles, not completely unnoticed and not completely suppressed. What they say is the direct pointer to the event of the Word of God and faith : " We beheld his glory," and : " We have believed and known " (Jn. 6⁶⁹). We cannot say this in the same way of ourselves. For again we are not witnesses in the same sense as the prophets and apostles. But it is before our eyes and ears that they said it of themselves and claimed thereby to have spoken, not just a human word, but God's Word in human words, the Word which God Himself speaks to man, the Word in which God acts on man, the Word in which God's mystery is manifest. This is the sign of the Bible set up among us. And we may pay to this sign, i.e., to this utterance of the prophets and apostles, to the claim they make, the same attention, good or bad, that we do to other facts. We are in a position, and indeed we are summoned, to pay attention to it as we live in the sphere of the Church. What takes place when we perhaps do this is an act of recollection. Nothing in itself is changed if we do except that the world of our spiritual images is increased by another image. *Notitia* has taken place ; we have formed an *opinio historica*. This does not make us prophets and apostles. It does not place us, then, in the reality of the Word and faith to which they bear witness. No development or enrichment of this image, no deepening of this recollection of ours, no systematic elucidation of its content, can bring us even a single step nearer the reality to which it points. Hence we do not refer to a method of actualisation that is placed in our hands or anyone else's hands along with the Bible when we for our part point to this sign, to this pointer that is given to us. Naturally we cannot do this pointing except as we already interpret the Bible, even if only very briefly, in a specific sense which is already our own. But this interpretation itself cannot make any other claim than that of drawing attention to the sign that has been set up as such. Interpretation itself can be only a pointer, not the discovery of the Holy Spirit or the Christian principle in the Bible, nor the mediation of the Word of God spoken in it. What may or may not take place over and above this indicating and being indicated, this recollection and *notitia*, the speech or silence of the Bible, the talking of the prophets and apostles *hic et nunc* and the readiness of the men of to-day to be talked to, the confirmation of the claim that this is God's Word, the decision taken, the event or non-event of faith—all this escapes our own view and grasp and that of every man. It is true by being true. It does not lie behind us but before us. Thus and only thus can we refer to it as to the decision against the relative validity and in favour of the absolute validity of the Bible as the Word of God, as the authentic and supreme criterion of Church proclamation and therefore of dogmatics as well. In making this reference we are acting as it were " irresponsibly." That is to say, we have not in any sense or in any way to answer for it that the Bible is really God's Word. Any desire to answer for it would be here a denial of what we would answer for. We can say no more than this, that the Bible can answer for itself in this matter. Just as we cannot say unequivocally, directly and generally that it does answer for itself, so we cannot say, nor can anyone say, that it cannot answer for itself. We say that it can, and in so doing we refer to the event of faith in which the decision is made that the Bible must speak and the Church must hear. If it is asked with what right we say this, we answer : By no right that we have and claim for ourselves, but by the right that proves itself to be such in the event of faith when it occurs. If we are asked why we do this, why we say No to the Roman Catholic and Modernist doctrine of the Word of God in the light of this possible self-responsibility of the Bible, our reply is that we as little know why we do this as we as we know why we got out of bed to-day with the right foot first rather than the left, and neither question finally applies to others in the same way. The fact is that we oppose the doctrine. If someone presses us and asks us whether it is an accident then that we make this objection, we would rather bite off our tongue than claim the Holy Spirit or our faith or our conscience or the like as that which grants us the required authorisation with people, and we shall answer that an accident comes from accidents. Thus it has perhaps befallen us that we should make and represent the opposition. Not because of me, but simply because there is this opposition, you have to deal with a modest fact and sign that makes no further claim. And if it is further said that this is then a secret appeal to a special grace, a Lutheran " I can do no other," a prophetic illumination, again we cheerfully reply : This opposition seeks to be nothing of all that, nothing special, no prophecy or apostolate, just a very earthly, harmless, ambivalent matter, devoid of all mystical splendour or mystery, just a little Protestantism, a sign to which we can give no signifying power, which may in fact be opposed or totally overlooked or misunderstood, and about whose unimportance among all the other signs in which the world and the Church are so rich we have no illusions. Is it a sign at all ? That we can neither will nor know. With no motive or claim at all we can only act accordingly, i.e., raise our opposition. But in so doing, seeing we face the task of dogmatics, we decide, of course, to accept the Bible as the absolute authority set up over against Church proclamation. This opposition, which is simply mounted factually and with no validating proof in the light of the biblical sign, decides the point that dogmatics cannot be " dogmatics " in the sense of the Roman Catholic Church, i.e., the development of the truths of revelation immanent in the Church, nor the " doctrine of faith " in the sense of Protestant Modernism, i.e., the exposition of the faith of the men united in the Church. This opposition implies that the possibility of seeing God's Word as an entity distinct from Church proclamation is given to us—as we have seen, actually as a possibility—in the fact that the Bible is read in the Church, and we refer to this fact when, not in Roman Catholic or Modernist but in Protestant fashion, i.e., in opposition, we take practical account of this possibility. Presupposing this opposition in the strictest sense, we imply thereby that dogmatics as the question of the Word of God in Church proclamation must be the critical question as to the agreement of Church proclamation, not with a norm of human truth or human value (the first possibility in our dilemma), nor with a standard of divine truth already known and proclaimed by the Church (the second possibility), but with the revelation attested in Holy Scripture. This is the specific point of the question of the Word of God which has to be put in dogmatics. In the light of § 4 we may also say that the task of dogmatics is to deal with the problem of the equation of the Word of God and the word of man in its form as Church proclamation with a view to the confirmation of this equation, and it does this by measuring Church proclamation as man's word by the second form of the Word of God, i.e., Holy Scripture, in so far as this itself is in turn witness to its third and original form, revelation.

Because and to the extent that dogmatics has this task, it is called dogmatics, *theologia dogmatica*. Our translation of this is not " the science of dogmas " but " the science of dogma." Dogma is the agreement of Church proclamation with the revelation attested in Holy Scripture. Dogmatics enquires into this agreement and therefore into dogma. This brings us into conflict with the Roman Catholic definition of the terms dogma and dogmatics. According to this view a dogma is a truth of revelation defined by the Church and dogmatics is the collection of these dogmas and commentary on them.

The word " dogma " (cf. for what follows A. Deneffe, S.J., " Wort und Begriff," *Scholastik*, 1931, p. 381 f. and 505 f.) meant primarily in the usage of pagan antiquity and also of the Greek Old and New Testaments an order, statute, or decree. Thus the law of the Medes and Persians according to which Daniel was put in the lions' den is a dogma according to Dan. 6[16]. The decree issued by Caesar Augustus in Lk. 2[1] is also a dogma. The statutes of the OT Law are dogmas according to Eph. 2[15] and Col. 2[14]. But a second meaning of the term in antiquity also calls for consideration. The philosophical or the more generally academic principle of an individual teacher, school, or movement is a dogma. It is in the second rather than the first sense that the word, almost always used in the plural, seems already in the 2nd century (first in Ignatius of Ant., *Ad Magn.*, 13, 1) to have passed into the usage of the Greek Church as a term for Christian truths. But Cyprian, Tertullian, Ambrose, Augustine, Leo the Great and Gregory the Great still did not know it or were not prepared to use it in this sense, and it is indeed rarely employed in this sense by Thomas Aquinas. Right up to our own time the very opposite sense has competed with it (cf. already Iren., *C. o. h.*, I, 31, 3 ; this is perhaps the only one Augustine knew). According to this view dogmas, distinguished as such by all kinds of uncomplimentary adjectives, are the false teachings of pagans or heretics. (Leo XIII can still speak of the *prava dogmata Socialistarum* in the Encyclical " Quod Apostolici " of Dec. 28, 1878.) From the 16th century, however, the term seems to have come into use with systematic emphasis in the second of the meanings given above (in the sense of *dogma fidei, dogma catholicum, dogma Ecclesiae*). At all events, it is only along these lines that there have been serious theological attempts to define the concept in the Roman Catholic Church. Deneffe (*op. cit.*, p. 531), in agreement with Diekamp and Bartmann, sums up the results in the proposition : Dogma is *veritas a Deo formaliter revelata et ab Ecclesia sive solemniter* (by *ex cathedra* decision or conciliar degree) *sive ordinarie* (by the fact that it has been generally taught in the Church without opposition) *definita*. (As against R. Seeberg, *Lehrbuch der Dogmengeschichte*, Vol. 1, 3rd edn., 1920, p. 1, we thus have to say that the Church's formal acknowledgment of the propositions in question does not exhaust the concept of Church dogma.) On the Roman Catholic view the systematic exposition of these revealed truths is then dogmatics. (Cf. Bartmann, *Lehrbuch d. Dogm.*, 7th edn., Vol. I, 1928, p. 2 ; Diekamp, *Kath. Dogm.*, 6th edn., Vol. I, 1930, p. 1). On the Evangelical side R. Rothe (*Zur Dogm.*, 1863, p. 14) understood the task of dogmatics in the same sense.

We may begin by stating that we recognise that there are dogmas in the sense of this definition, though naturally we shall have to explain more fully why we do this. In a later section of the Prolegomena we shall have to deal with dogmas, i.e., with the doctrinal propositions acknowledged and confessed by the Church and deposited in its symbols, with their relative authority and with their importance for dogmatics. At the same time—and this is our first objection to the Roman Catholic view of dogmas and dogmatics—we must deny that dogmas constitute the goal of dogmatic work or that dogmatics is called dogmatics on their account. For dogmas are not *veritates a Deo formaliter revelatae*. In dogmas it is the Church of the past that speaks. This is venerable. It deserves respects. It is normative. It speaks *non sine Deo*, as is fitting. Yet it is still the Church. In dogmas the Church defines, i.e., limits revealed truth, the Word of God. The Word of God thus becomes the word of man. It is not an insignificant word. Indeed, it is a supremely significant word. Yet it is still the word of man. The Word of God is above dogma as the heavens are above the earth.

The proximity of *dogmata ecclesiastica* to *dogmata haereticorum* should be enough to remind us of the basic vulnerability of the dogma defined by the Church and also to ward off the idea of an infallible dogma of this kind. It may also be pointed out that according to Roman Catholic teaching itself not all dogmas have yet been confessed or defined by the Church, that even if revealed truth is substantially closed there is still dogmatic progress (cf. Diekamp, *op. cit.*, p. 15), and that ultimately it is the material content (*sensus*) rather than the formula that is said to be the unchangeable and infallible truth in dogmatic formulations (Bartmann, *op. cit.*, p. 38). There is perhaps an admission of the human character of dogmas in this explanation. Nevertheless, it is always the Church itself that is the subject of the expected dogmatic progress, and the *sensus* which is to be distinguished from the formulae can only be the *sensus, quem tenuit ac tenet sancta mater Ecclesia* (*Conc. Vatic. I, Constit. dogm., De fide cath., cap.* 2). There can never be here any real disputing of dogmas, or of the Church which proclaims and elucidates them. There can never be any clear and serious distinction between dogmas and the Word of God.

In the identification of the Word of God and Church dogma as we find it in this definition of the term we can only see an example of the splendid isolation in which a church must find itself when it has seized the Word of God for itself, taken it under its own management, and lost the capability of listening to the voice of another. If in dogmatics this voice from without is to be heard as the criterion of what the Church says and does, then dogmatics cannot stop at the question of Church dogmas, nor can Church dogmas be the form in which it hears the voice from without. Otherwise dogmatics on this side too would just be a dialogue of the Church with itself, of the Church of to-day with the Church of yesterday and the day before. In the context of God's dialogue with the Church this dialogue of the Church with itself can also take on significance. As we shall still have to show in principle, there will also have to be in dogmatics this dialogue of the Church of to-day with the Church of yesterday and the day before. But if dogmatics tries to stop at this, it certainly cannot do justice to its task as the discharge of the Church's responsibility to the Word of God. Indeed, it has not even taken up this task at all. The dogma which dogmatics investigates cannot, then, be the *veritas ab Ecclesia definita*. The *veritas ab Ecclesia definita* is itself the question of dogma. It can and should guide dogmatics. But it cannot seek to be the dogma which is the goal of dogmatics.

Our second point must be that while the dogma which dogmatics investigates is not the truth of revelation, it aims at the truth of revelation. The same may be said of the dogmas of the Church, which we shall not be dealing with more specifically at this juncture. These are propositions which grasp and reproduce the truth of revelation only to the extent that they strive after it.

Even Thomas Aquinas follows a definition of the concept of the *articulus fidei*, and therefore of the individual, concrete Church dogma, which was given by Isidore of Seville : *Articulus est perceptio divinae veritatis tendens in ipsam* (*S. th.*, II,[2] *qu.* 1, *art.* 6).

The epitome of all possible propositions of this kind, that which all dogmas are saying in their striving after the truth of revelation, is the dogma which dogmatics investigates. When we call it the epitome of all propositions of this kind, we are saying already that it is not itself a proposition, that it is not proclaimed by any church. Dogma is what is intended in all possible propositions of this kind. It is the dogma for the sake of which the Church proclaims dogmas. Dogma is the essence of which dogmas and also dogmatic propositions, i.e., the propositions of dogmatic science, claim to be phenomena, the essence from which real dogmas and real dogmatic propositions may arise, i.e., when they are modelled on it. For the sake of dogma dogmatics must deal with dogmas. Dogmas call upon it to pay attention to dogma. They direct it, in the way that the Church can direct it, to the question of dogma. At a third and lowest stage dogmatics then builds its own scientifically dogmatic propositions. Dogmatic propositions, dogmas and dogma have this in common : They are not the truth of revelation. Dogma aims at the truth of revelation and dogmas and dogmatic propositions seek to do so (and do, with the proviso that by the grace of God they come to do so through watching and prayer). Dogma in the true and original sense as the epitome of all dogmas and dogmatic propositions is a concept of relation, and on the basis of it so, too, are dogmas and dogmatic propositions. The only difference in their case is that there is the proviso whether they are realised concepts of relation, i.e., concepts of a relation that is really present. What this relation is we know already ; we refer to the relation of the agreement of Church proclamation with the Bible as the Word of God. One may thus define dogma as Church proclamation to the degree that it really agrees with the Bible as the Word of God. To know dogma and to have dogma is to know and have the Word of God itself in a specific and specifically demonstrable form and manifestation of Church proclamation, for dogma is Church proclamation that is really in agreement with the Word of God. But a theology claiming to know and have dogma would be a *theologia gloriae*, which the dogmatics of the Church ought not to seek to be. What it is faced with is always actual Church proclamation in the whole humanity of its form and manifestation on the one hand and on the other hand the sign set up in the Church, the promise and command of the Bible. And the task it is set is to ask about the Word of God in the proclamation of the Church and therefore to ask about dogma, the necessary orientation of Church proclamation to the Bible as the Word of God. Every answer, every actualisation of this orientation and agreement, can only be one of two things, either the event of the Word of God itself which dogmatics can neither presuppose, postulate, nor effect, or one of the great illusions and prolepses of a dogmatics unaware of the fact there can be no presupposing, postulating or effecting of this event. Thus the real results of dogmatics, even though they have the form of the most positive statements, can themselves only be new questions, questions to and fro between what the Church seems to proclaim and the Bible seems to want proclaimed, questions which can be put only with the greatest modesty and a sense of supreme vulnerability if they are perhaps serious and significant questions. If questioning ceased, if dogma itself came on the scene instead of dogmas and dogmatic propositions, if the agreement of specific Church proclamation with the Word of God and therefore the Word of God itself in this specific Church proclamation could be demonstrated, then dogmatics would be at an end along with the *ecclesia militans*, and the kingdom of God would have dawned. The second possibility of the appearing of dogma or the Word of God itself can only be that of great illusions and prolepses.

To this extent one may call dogma an " eschatological concept," as I myself did in the first edition of this book (p. 112, 123).

The older Lutheran theology (e.g., Quenstedt, *Theol. did.-pol.*, 1685, I, *cap.* 1, *sect.* 1, *thes.* 3–14) made a pertinent distinction between the *theologia archetypos* which God has and indeed Himself is, and the *theologia ektypos* which apart from Christ according to his human nature and the angels men may also have. The *theologia hominum* which is possible for us is then divided again into the *theologia patriae* in eternal redemption and the *theologia viatorum* in present temporality. In this temporality there is also another distinction *ante* and *post lapsum*, and then *post lapsum* we have *theologia naturalis* and *theologia supranaturalis*, and in the latter there is *theologia immediatae* and *mediatae revelationis*, the former that of the prophets, apostles and Evangelists alone, the latter ours as we are directed to their writings. This theology of ours, the *theologia ektypos mediatae revelationis hominum viatorum post lapsum*, can then obviously be seen once again from two angles. On the one side it may be seen in the appropriate relation to its prototype, *theologia immediatae revelationis*, a relation which is hidden and future for us, which we cannot achieve, and which is thus the object of our enquiry. In this case and to this degree it is dogma. On the other side it may be seen in its performance as the concrete dogmatic work which is done by the Church and in the Church in time and at specific times, the enquiry into the relation which is laid upon us for the sake of Church proclamation. In this case and to this degree we are to understand by *theologia ektypos mediatae revelationis hominum viatorum post lapsum* Church dogma on the one hand and that which occupies us here, the scientific work of dogmatics, on the other.

We shall now have to put a third question to the Roman Catholic concept of dogma and dogmatics, namely, whether the fact that the term " dogma " was adopted into the Church's vocabulary in the sense of doctrinal proposition rather than that of " command " or " decree," which is more readily suggested by biblical usage, is not the symptom of a false development of very early origin. Assuming that Church dogma is to be equated with *veritas revelata*—that it aims at the truth of revelation we too admit—does it follow that *veritas revelata* is the truth of a doctrinal proposition ? Is the truth of revelation—we must press the question—like other truths in the sense that it may be established as ἀλήθεια, i.e., as the manifestation of something hidden, in human ideas, concepts and judgments, that it may be, as it were, conserved in this restricted and specialised form, that it can be had as truth apart from the event of its being manifested ? Such is obviously the case with the truth of a doctrinal proposition. But will the truth of revelation submit to such materialisation and depersonalisation ? Can one have it in abstraction from the person of Him who reveals it and from the revelatory act of this person in which it is given to other persons to perceive ? Can the possession of this truth take place otherwise than again in an act on the part of the person who perceives it, in a decision, i.e., in the adoption of a position ? If the truth of revelation is the truth of a doctrinal proposition, then obviously the answer is Yes.

The truth of a doctrinal proposition can be viewed neutrally as neutral truth. It may also happen, of course, that one agrees or disagrees. But it is no part of its nature to require decision. Nor is adoption of a position an essential part of encounter with it. The Roman Catholic definition of dogma as doctrinal proposition actually excludes this. That dogma as such is only doctrine and not also command is not clear in the usage of the fathers of the 2nd and 3rd centuries nor in Eusebius and Athanasius in the 4th century. But it is clear in Cyril of Jerusalem, Gregory of Nyssa and Cyril of Alexandria, in whom dogma as the doctrine of the faith and dogma as command are kept apart as two distinct entities (cf. Deneffe, *op. cit.*, pp. 508–13). One of the most prominent characteristics of Roman Catholic dogmatics results from the fact that it not only equates dogma with *veritas revelata* but also equates *veritas revelata* with the truth of a doctrinal proposition. We have already touched on this at an earlier point. Roman Catholic dogmatics is theory *qua* theory and for the sake of theory. To be sure, it is accepted theory. By nature, however, it is pure theory according to the prevailing Thomist conception. Theory *qua* theory means that the affirmation of the *veritas revelata* is the judgment of a thinker who as such is not forced into this judgment or its opposite. In itself, it is not primarily a demand for this judgment or the constraint to adopt a position. It is pure, neutral truth. It is true in itself in the established and developed form of the proposition and then it is true for us, whatever our attitude may be, in the form of perception and understanding of the proposition in question. Theory for the sake of theory means that the theory, contemplation of the *veritas revelata*, has its goal and end in itself. There does not have to be a corresponding act, and it certainly cannot be regarded as an act itself. The whole linking of dogmatics to Church proclamation as we presuppose it here is already contrary to Roman Catholicism for the simple reason that in Roman Catholic dogmatics the search for a dogmatic task outside dogmatics itself is just as impossible as is the search for the special task of mystics, angels, or the blessed in heaven in their vision of God. The task which awaits the Roman Catholic dogmatician can only be that of grasping and expounding in its integrated wealth the divinely ordered world of specific spiritual matters that God has revealed once and for all in the *veritates revelatae* (cf. on this E. Peterson, " Über die Forderung einer Theologie des Glaubens," *Z.d.Z.*, 1925, p. 282).

The very reserve with which one can confront the truth of a doctrinal proposition, the possibility of a purely theoretical attitude to it, and, in objective correspondence to this possibility, the idea of a purely material and impersonal presence of truth in the proposition—this is what makes the equation of *veritas revelata* and the doctrinal proposition suspect, and more than suspect, in our view.

We might ask for a moment—and it is instructive to do so—whether our suspicions would not also be roused if we pursued the second Roman Catholic equation in virtue of which Church dogma is identified as *veritas revelata*. Even on Roman Catholic soil would not the question arise whether *veritas revelata* and therefore Church dogma can be a truth detachable from the person of the God who speaks and who acts by speaking, a truth which does not as such force to decision, to action, a truth whose acceptance as such does not mean decision or service in a task lying outside itself ? In dealing with a neutral truth of this kind which allows him to be neutral too, is man really dealing with God ? Can a doctrinal proposition as such really be regarded as God's Word ? Even and especially on Roman Catholic soil, if dogma is equated with God's Word, will it not have to be understood primarily as command in accordance with the usage of the Bible which was at least possible in the fathers of the first centuries too ? Will it not have to be understood as a truth that we can have as truth only as it is spoken to us by God and only as encounter with it is impossible without decision for a specific attitude to what is spoken to us ? Will it not have to be understood as a dogma which is also a doctrinal proposition (there is no cause to rule out this meaning ; why should we ? Why should not a command too, and especially a command, be able to teach us ?), but a doctrinal proposition which can teach us and be a dogma only to the extent that it goes out from God as the " dogma " went out from Caesar Augustus, as a decree goes out, and comes to us in the act of obedience (or does not come to us, does not teach us, does not exist for us as a dogma, in the act of disobedience), i.e., comes to us or does not come to us as a command, goes out in a divine decision and comes to us in a human decision ? But we have to realise, of course, that we can enter the Roman Catholic sphere with this question or this proposal only to leave it again at once, or if we find a hearing in Roman Catholic territory with this question it will cease to be Roman Catholic territory. For is it not inevitable that this question or proposal will call in question at once the presupposed Roman Catholic equation between Church dogma and *veritas revelata* ?

According to the Roman Catholic view Church dogma must have primarily the character of a doctrinal proposition in order that it may be an object of contemplation and in order that its truth may escape being made problematical either by the position adopted towards it by men or by God Himself. In a way that its character as command could not do but would rather endanger, its character as doctrinal proposition is supposed to guarantee its objectivity, its intrinsic truth, and therefore its credibility as *veritas revelata*. Roman Catholic theology would rather accept the materialising and depersonalising of revealed truth that is entailed when dogma is understood as doctrinal proposition ; it would rather make a virtue of necessity and declare that its very materiality and impersonality, its very abstraction from all human and divine decision, the non-paradoxical disclosure which it expresses as a proposition, are the things that characterise and accredit dogma as the truth of revelation ; it would rather say this than abandon the equation. Roman Catholic theology stands or falls with the equation, with the presupposition that revealed truth is given to the Church in the form of dogmas (not in this form alone, but in this form too), that it has it and has to guard it as such, that it must be concerned theologically for its validation as such, for the credibility of its intrinsic truth. It has to make a virtue of the necessity. Or rather, the necessity is no real necessity for it. It not only accepts this ; as Roman Catholic theology it wills from the very first everything that the character of dogma as doctrinal proposition entails. Only in our view and not in that of Roman Catholic theology is what happened to the word " dogma " a false development. On its view it all had to turn out as it did. It would have to betray itself if it were to come back again to the question whether the sense of command or decree should not be proposed for " dogma " and whether this would not be of decisive significance for its understanding as doctrinal proposition. If our question or proposal in this regard is taken seriously, as seriously as we naturally intend it ; if the teaching of dogma is really to be understood as a command (and not the command, which is naturally not denied by Roman Catholic theology, as a doctrine for contemplation), then it will be immediately apparent that the dogma established by the Church itself cannot be this command but can only be a serious recollection of this command.

A command is what it is only in the act of the one who gives it and the one who obeys or disobeys it. One cannot give oneself a command in the way the Church gives itself Church dogmas. Nor can one have the truth of doctrine that can be received by a command in the way the Church has the truth of its dogmas. If *veritas revelata* is a command, it cannot be identical with Church dogma. Church dogma and *veritas revelata* necessarily part company. We must therefore withdraw, realising that there is no place for our concern on Roman Catholic soil.

Or rather we must say polemically that the impossibility of the Roman Catholic equation of the truth of revelation and Church dogma is betrayed for us by the fact that hereby the truth of revelation has to become what it has become in Roman Catholicism. The material and impersonal intrinsic truth ascribed to dogma, the contemplative objectivity which is the issue in Roman Catholic theology when it emphasises the sense of doctrinal proposition in the concept of dogma, this is for us the mark of a truth which is conditioned and limited not merely by the creatureliness of man but also by his sinfulness, a truth in comparison with which the truth of God in His revelation is quite different. By the very fact that as a proposition it can only be contemplated, that it is neutral and permits neutrality, that as a theory—and who can deny that Church dogma is this too ?—it bears witness itself to where it belongs, namely, to the Church, its talk, its testimonies, its proclamation, its dialogue with itself—all this with great distinction, for it is not our intention to disparage Church dogma on this its proper level—and yet still to the Church and not the Word in which God addresses the Church. We do not understand and we can never understand how the truth that is put in the hands of the Church as Church dogma can be the truth of God. What we think we know as the truth of God's Word from the witness of Holy Scripture is a very different truth, a sovereign truth.

Our recalling of the older use of dogma does not mean, then, that we want to equate Church dogma as command with the Word of God. To the extent that Church dogma is command—and in our view it should be pointed out that on the basis of the Old and New Testaments it would have been more natural to introduce the word into the Church's vocabulary chiefly in this sense—it is a human command, a command of sinners even if of sinners assembled in the Church, and as such a command which is surrounded and permeated by all the ambiguity and frailty and corruption of human commanding. Heaven is as high above Church dogma regarded as command as it is above Church dogma regarded as proposition, and we are not thinking of putting the Church in possession of God's Word by the detour of this second, or rather this first, meaning of the word. On the other hand, recollection of this first meaning of the word can shed significant light on our understanding of the concept of dogma about which dogmatics asks, on our understanding of the agreement of Church proclamation with the Word of God in Holy Scripture. Remembering this first meaning of the word, we shall have to understand the relation implicit in this concept of dogma as the relation between command and obedience and only then and in this way as also the relation between doctrine and instruction. The agreement of Church proclamation with the Word of God naturally means the truth of Church proclamation as well. But truth cannot be the last word about this agreement. For what truth is must be measured by what is higher here, what God's will is. His Word goes out to the Church of assembled sinners as the Word of the Lord whose knowledge must be worked out in the form of acknowledgment. In logical if not temporal priority it must first be believed and only then and in that way can it be known as truth. *Credo ut intelligam.*

The Roman Catholic Church itself has finely expressed this in the formula : *Credimus non propter intrinsecam rerum veritatem naturali rationis lumine perspectam, sed propter auctoritatem ipsius Dei revelantis, qui nec falli nec fallere potest* (*Conc. Vatic.* I, *Constit. dogm. de fide cath., cap.* 3). To be sure the *auctoritas* is also *veritas*, but what makes it credible is not that it is *veritas*, but that it is *auctoritas*.

It would be knowledge of real dogma if we knew a form of Church proclamation which was appropriate to the will of God, in which the command of God to the Church was fulfilled, in which the faith of the Church was co-extensive with the order of its Lord. Then and to that extent it would also be perfect truth in comparison with which all other truth that it might have otherwise than in fulfilling the divine command could not make it real dogma but would rather be shown to need the enquiry into dogma, since it would always be untruth when measured by it. Now seeing that knowledge of real dogma will never take place before the end of all things, this must be the point of our enquiry into dogma. It is not in the first instance the enquiry of a pupil who is anxious that his thoughts should agree with the superior thoughts of his teacher. It is primarily the question of a servant who has to ask whether his actions agree with his master's intentions and who undoubtedly in so doing will also learn something that he did not know before. When we call the dogma into which dogmatics enquires a concept of relation, we mean that it is the concept of a relation which exists between a demand and the decision corresponding to the demand. Dogma is the relation between the God who commands and the man who obeys His command, the relation which takes place in the event of this commanding and obeying. Hence it is not an *opus supererogationis*, a luxury, an academic game, when dogmatics is pursued in the Church. It is not at all the case that the Church carries on its proclamation properly, in good faith, and according to God's will, and then occasionally the question arises—and perhaps it is only the question of certain people with a particular intellectual interest—whether and how far this proclamation is true, and dogmatics comes into being to meet this need. It is not the case that in regard to the obedience of the Church in its proclamation everything is for the best and only a " thinking through " or explication of the faith is lacking, only the cry for a world-view, for the relating of this intrinsically excellent faith to knowledge, is unsatisfied, and along with all the other things the Church offers dogmatics must also be offered by someone somewhere to meet the demand of curiosity or the supposed need for credibility. No, the fact is that what is under debate in dogmatics is the Church's fundamental relation of obedience to its Lord in respect of its proclamation. It is not a matter of offering a little truth to those who feel especially uneasy on this score while in all else they are as satisfied as all the rest. It is a matter of the will of God whose acknowledgment or non-acknowledgment in the Church's proclamation is something that should truly unsettle the whole Church, the Church as such and in all its members. The Church stands or falls with the object of dogmatic enquiry. Hence it has to undertake this enquiry. It cannot pursue dogmatics or not pursue it. A dogmatics which it might not pursue, in whose enquiry it did not wholly participate as in the enquiry about its whole existence, a dogmatics which might let itself be crowded into the corner of religious intellectuals or the intellectually religious, could only be a poor, useless and tedious dogmatics which it would be better not to pursue at all. We pursue dogmatics because, constrained by the fact of the Bible, we cannot shake off the question of the obedience of Church proclamation. The question of its obedience includes that of its truth. But the question of its truth can be put only as the question

of its obedience. As the question of its obedience it is the question of
dogma.

2. DOGMATICS AS A SCIENCE

At an earlier point (§ 1, 1) we argued that when theology generally,
and with it dogmatics, understands and describes itself as a science, it
does not do so in principle, i.e., it does not raise the claim as one by
whose recognition it will stand or fall, but it raises it without being
able or even desiring to argue and justify it before an external tribunal.
It does not recognise the need to understand and legitimate itself
as a science at all. Nor does it recognise as normative for itself the
general concept of science that is authoritative to-day. Nor does it
recognise any obligation to oppose to this another concept which will
include and therefore justify itself. It understands and describes itself
as a science because it has no interest in *de facto* self-segregation from
the other human efforts at knowledge that bear this name, because it
must protest against a concept of science that would exclude its own
effort at knowledge, because it accepts a hidden but coming and
therefore real unity of all such human efforts, because, one might also
say, it affirms the Church as the hidden yet very real sphere of all such
efforts. What it means by science when it calls itself a science, it
defines in responsibility to the Church which it serves—and which the
other sciences can and should and ultimately and conclusively will
serve—in responsibility to its object and to the task imposed by this
object. For it realises for one thing that in its question about dogma,
i.e., about the agreement of Church proclamation with the Word of
God, it has to tread a defined path of knowledge, a path defined by this
particular problem. And then it realises, too, that it has to submit to
itself, i.e., everyone who has a share in it, an account regarding this path
of knowledge. In this twofold inner obligation to itself consists the
concrete significance of its claim to be a science, which it cannot prove
externally before the forum of a general concept of science. Its
scientific character consists in its orientation, in its conscious orientation,
in what must always be its conscious orientation, to the question of
dogma which is raised by the existence of the Church. When the
enquiry is pressed with this orientation, or, as we might also say, with
this objectivity, then dogmatics takes place as a science.

At this point we must make a relative distinction ; there is a
regular dogmatics and an irregular dogmatics.

By regular dogmatics we mean an enquiry into dogma which aims
at the completeness appropriate to the special task of the school, of
theological instruction. If it is to be a good school, the theological

school must offer training in independent enquiry into dogma. For this reason it must be as complete as possible. It must impress on the student how one question breaks up into many questions and how in every respect and from every possible standpoint all these many questions are in fact open and inter-related. Thus a regular or academic dogmatics must cover the whole field in respect of the range of concepts and themes that are significant for Church proclamation, in respect of the biblical witness in which this proclamation has its concrete criterion, in respect of orientation to the history of dogmas and dogmatics, i.e., to the concrete forms of Church proclamation existing thus far, in respect of real and possible difficulties and contradictions that one will find in every individual question, and finally in respect of the implicit and explicit distinctness of the path of knowledge. These are the demands which naturally arise if dogmatics is to be taught and if this instruction is to be planned guidance, i.e., guidance to independent dogmatic work, and not just the imparting of the specific results of the work of a specific teacher.

Origen's Περὶ ἀρχῶν, the great " Discourse " of Gregory of Nyssa, the *Catecheses* of Cyril of Jerusalem, Augustine's *Enchiridion* and the ῎Εκδοσις ἀκριβής τῆς ὀρθ. πίστ. of John of Damascus are dogmatic works in this sense in the early Church, while in the Middle Ages we have the writings of Anselm of Canterbury (as a whole and according to their intent), the *Sentences* of Peter Lombard, and naturally the *Summas* of the great Dominicans and Franciscans. The increasingly academic character which one unmistakably finds in the Scholastics as compared with the Fathers is repeated in the Evangelical world when one compares the regular dogmatic works of the Reformation period itself (Melanchthon's *Loci*, at least in the later editions, Zwingli's *Commentarius de vera et falsa religione* and especially Calvin's *Institutio*) with the orthodoxy of especially the 17th century, which was so very industrious and fruitful in producing both comprehensive text-books and compendious outlines, and which was opposed by a Roman Catholic theology by no means inferior in learning. A slow but clear decline began with the 18th century. Roman Catholic dogmatics recovered from this after the middle of the 19th century, chiefly by a common and deliberate return to Thomas Aquinas. Thanks to the achievement of Schleiermacher, and under his influence, e.g., in the works of A. Schweizer, A. E. Biedermann and J. A. Dorner, Evangelical dogmatics enjoyed a new golden age even before the Roman Catholic revival. But this incontestable formal rise of Evangelical dogmatics in the first half of the 19th century had too little inner necessity, was too little due to a fresh understanding of the matter of Evangelical theology, was too much impelled by a mere acceptance of the achievements of contemporary philosophy, and in this connexion was too much influenced by a wholesale surrender of the theme of Evangelical theology, to be able to stand the test. It was a tired age that thought it could see a gleam of hope in the theology of A. Ritschl, which in the event merely reached back over Idealism and Romanticism to the quintessence of the Enlightenment. The end of the spasmodic concentration that made the dogmatics of this school impressive for a time was simply an individualistic simplification and abridgement of all questions which has given a journalistic impress to modern Evangelical dogmatics even as compared with its own past in the age before Ritschl. To see what is meant one should compare, say, the

Glaubenslehre of Troeltsch, the leading figure of the post-Ritschlian period, with the dogmatics of A. E. Biedermann or the achievement of a follower of that age like H. Lüdemann, who is so worthy of respect in his own way. Let us be under no illusions ; this decline has not been arrested even to-day. In terms of academic exactitude, nothing we are producing now can stand comparison with the achievements of mediaeval and post-Reformation dogmatics, nor with Idealistic dogmatics, nor with Thomistic, let alone with the dogmatics of the Reformation. Would that we had even reached the point where we again regarded regular dogmatics as at least an admonitory ideal worth striving after !

It is part of the human reality of the Church that there has to be in it not just theology but also the theological school or the theology of the school (*theologia scholastica*), i.e., the theology which is practised not just for free intellectual exchange but also for instruction. It was a fateful theological error, for which Anabaptist spiritualism must share some blame, to think that this could be dispensed with. If we face the fact of the Church's humanity, we cannot release it from the task of pursuing academic theology and we must thus accept in principle the task of a regular dogmatics.

By irregular dogmatics, on the other hand, we mean the enquiry into dogma in which there is no primary thought of the task of the school and there is thus no primary concern for the completeness mentioned above. Dogmatics as free discussion of the problems that arise for Church proclamation from the standpoint of the question of dogma can and must be pursued in the Church outside the theological school and apart from its special task. Such free dogmatics existed before there was the regular dogmatics of the school, and it will always have its own necessity and possibility alongside this. It will differ from it by the fact that it does not cover the whole ground with the same consistency, whether in respect of Church proclamation itself, the decisive biblical witness, the history of dogma, detailed systematics, or strictness and clarity of method. Perhaps for specific historical reasons it will take up a specific theme and focus on it. Perhaps it will be relatively free in relation to the biblical basis or its choice of partners in discussion. Perhaps it will be more of an exposition of results, and will take the form of theses or aphorisms, and will observe only partially or not at all the distinction between dogmatics and proclamation. Perhaps it will leave much to be desired as regards the explicit or implicit distinctness of its path of knowledge. In one respect or another, or even in many or all respects, it will be, and will mean to be, a fragment, and it will have to be evaluated as such.

The dogmatic work that has come down to us from the early Church, even from the pens of its most significant and learned representatives, is not for the most part regular dogmatics but irregular dogmatics in the sense described. In distinction from Origen and John of Damascus, Athanasius wrote no true dogmatics. Luther in contrast to Melanchthon and Calvin was a typical irregular dogmatician. From the more recent and less classical past one might also recall men like J. G. Hamann, G. Mencken, H. F. Kohlbrügge, J. C. Blumhardt, and H. Kutter, whose work undoubtedly belongs formally to this category. From early times and on into our own day irregular dogmatics has been produced in dogmatic treatises, Bible commentaries, historical accounts, sermons, pamphlets and other forms of what is called devotional literature. Tacitly or even openly everyone does a little irregular dogmatics if he is interested in the problem of dogmatics but does not have the call or the desire or the time or the equipment to take part in regular dogmatics. On the whole it must be admitted that in spite of its name irregular dogmatics has been the rule, and regular dogmatics the exception, in every age of the Church. It should also be noted that regular dogmatics has always had its origin in irregular dogmatics, and could never have existed without its stimulus and co-operation.

If we keep clearly in view the complete difference between the two both materially and historically, we shall be on guard against overhasty estimation or disparagement of either the one or the other. In particular we shall refrain from immediately ascribing a scientific character to regular dogmatics and a non-scientific character to irregular dogmatics. If the scientific nature of dogmatics lies in its special objectivity, namely, in its orientation to the question of dogma, then there is no obvious reason why both regular and irregular dogmatics should not be either scientific or non-scientific.

It has happened, of course, and this was especially true in the age of orthodoxy, that the scientific character of academic dogmatics has had to be vindicated against free-lances. But it has also happened that the scientific character of dogmatics has had to be vindicated by free-lances against the dogmatics of the schools. Naturally it cannot be denied that the aversion to the dogmatics of the schools which may be found a little in every age has often rested on enthusiasm of some sort and not on solid Christian insight, that it has had little or nothing to do with the seriousness of the question of dogma, and that it is not, therefore, a sign of scientific concern. But it is also impossible to deny that the transition from irregular to regular dogmatics—when perhaps the school has ceased to be aware that it had to serve life, i.e., the Church—has often been accompanied by a decline in the seriousness, vitality and joyfulness of Christian insight, by a lameness in the enquiry into dogma, and therefore by a loss of the true scientific character of dogmatics.

At this point there must be openness and readiness on both sides. No general statement can be made, but it should be asked from time to time whether the aphoristic style of irregular dogmatics or the systematic style of regular dogmatics does more or less justice to the task of dogmatics. The call for the one or the other may become a necessity, just as it may also be necessary to confine either the one or the other to its proper limits.

What is to be attempted here is regular dogmatics. At no time, even and especially in times of greatest flux, can the Church do without this, and on every hand there are indications that especially for Protestantism to-day an orderly school dogmatics might be healthier than a further plethora of irregularities in which it has always been so dangerously rich, particularly in the modern period. The results of irregular dogmatics are more exposed than those of regular dogmatics to the danger of being purely accidental, for in form at least they nearly always tend to be strongly influenced by the person and biography of their authors. The seriousness of their significance for the Church must at all events be proved by the fact that they can be presented not merely as the results of irregular dogmatics, e.g., in the form of sermons or the tone of pamphlets, not merely as the expression of religious and perhaps even prophetic experiences and impressions, but also in the stricter form of deliberations that can be tested academically. Almost all the insights in our field have first seen the light in the form of aphorisms and in the tone of proclamation. Dogmatics, i.e., the criticism and correction of previous proclamation, usually has its origin in proclamation itself. But an insight that is tied to the form of aphorisms or the tone of proclamation, an insight that cannot be taught as well, is no true insight, and hence dogmatics must develop as regular dogmatics even if it cannot begin as such. Nothing that can claim to be truly of the Church need shrink from the sober light of " scholasticism." No matter how free and individual it may be in its first expression, if it seeks universal acceptance, it will be under constraint to set up a school and therefore to become the teaching of a school. Fear of scholasticism is the mark of a false prophet. The true prophet will be ready to submit his message to this test too.

The phenomenon of Luther's theology, which might be given a very different name, is instructive enough as regards the dangers to which irregular dogmatics is exposed. But it is a sign of its significance for the Church that it could survive being put in the school theology of Melanchthon and Calvin and their successors, and all that it possibly lost in the process should not prevent us from recognising that the process was a necessary one for the sake of the Church character of the Reformation.

Anyone who wants to pursue regular dogmatics will have, of course, special cause to remember that this way of doing the task cannot claim a monopoly, even or especially as regards scientific character. It is certainly as well to reflect that at any moment it is possible that the question of dogma may be put and answered much more seriously and fruitfully in the unassuming Bible class of an unknown country parson than in the most exact academic discussion imaginable. School dogmatics should not try to regard itself as better dogmatics, only as a necessary second form of dogmatics. And it should not disdain to listen time and again to the voice of free dogmatics.

It has had disastrous results that the dogmatics of the 19th century Protestant schools, which was much prouder at this point than that of the age of orthodoxy, did very largely disdain to listen in this way, and it was thus able simply to sleep through the existence of phenomena like Kohlbrügge and Blumhardt.

Whether or not regular or irregular dogmatics is scientific depends on the answer to the question how far they stick to their task and are not distracted by very different things. But their task consists in criticism and correction of Church proclamation regarding its agreement with the revelation attested in Holy Scripture. Three things may thus be demanded of a scientific dogmatics, whether regular or irregular.

1. It must devote itself to the problem of Church proclamation as such and not to problems of thought which might arise in proximity to certain concepts in Church proclamation but which have nothing to do with proclamation itself. A system of Christian truth can be the task of dogmatics only to the extent that we are dealing with Christian truth that is proclaimed and is to be proclaimed, so that the exposition of it is less a system than the report of an event. Dogmatics as gnosis without regard for the task of Church proclamation, dogmatics as self-motivated and self-grounded metaphysics is unscientific as dogmatics no matter how profound, erudite and logical it may seem to be. When and where the transition to this type of metaphysics takes place, it is, of course, impossible to say generally. It should be realised that the concepts of pure metaphysics can become the concepts of proclamation and *vice versa*, so that the range of legitimate subjects in dogmatics is variable *in concreto*.

It is a mistake one cannot respect when uneasy and limited scholars or those whose reading is fundamentally cursory think they should reject a theological exposition out of hand because it uses concepts that they find elsewhere in metaphysical usage. The legitimacy of such use must be decided by the context in which the concepts occur. But the context must also decide the legitimacy of all concepts, even those that seem to belong to proclamation. They, too, might become the concepts of a metaphysics that has nothing whatever to do with proclamation. And one may well ask whether this is not pre-eminently the case with Ritschl, from whom the anxious and others received their cue.

Nevertheless, this does not alter the fact that at this point a question is always put to dogmatics and a boundary drawn for it. Not all the statements of dogmatics are adapted to become directly statements of Church proclamation. To be precise, we must even say that no single statement in dogmatics is adapted to be a statement in proclamation. Dogmatics is preparation for Church proclamation. It formulates statements that have to be pondered before Church proclamation formulates its statements. But it is by this relation that the statements of dogmatics must be tested. They should never stand in the air (perhaps as statements constructed merely for the sake of logical or philosophical or moral completeness) in such a way as to be unintelligible as preparation for Church proclamation and intelligible only as pure gnosis. There are border-line cases (we shall meet them in the doctrine of God, the doctrine of creation and eschatology, least of all in the doctrine of reconciliation, but there too in Christology) which cannot be avoided, but which are to be handled with extra caution. Yet when we say that there are border-line cases we are admitting that there is a border. It is sometimes easier to find and sometimes harder, but it must always be borne in mind and it will never be crossed with impunity.

The question of being unscientific in this respect arises with regard to the parties in mediaeval and the older Protestant dogmatics in which it seems to have been more a matter of satisfying the formal need of the general scholar or teacher for completeness than of the consistency and exactitude of the scholar or teacher in the Church. But it arises even more in respect of certain enterprises in modern dogmatics which do not seem to be concerned with the Church's task as such but with all kinds of accommodations respecting its possibility in relation to this or that general view. What seem to have been the loftiest peaks of learning in our field, both ancient and modern, always seem to have been most exposed to the danger of being unscientific in the form of the ever-threatening transition to pure gnosis.

2. Scientific dogmatics must devote itself to the criticism and correction of Church proclamation and not just to a repetitive exposition of it. Dogmatics cannot just be a historical account of the classical expression of the faith proclaimed by this or that period in the Church's past. Nor can it just be the clarification and presentation of the faith as the dogmatician concerned personally thinks it should be proclaimed. Nor again can it be just the phenomenology of a cross-section of the common faith proclaimed in a given present.

The first of these was the task of dogmatics according to R. Rothe, the second was its task according to Schleiermacher and Hofmann, and the third was its task according to A. Schweizer. Against all these approaches one may make the objection that in them the Church is, as it were, seen from without, or it is its own spectator. But the true Church exists in the act of the hearing and proclaiming of God's Word by men. The only dogmatics to answer the question of this true Church is the one which examines the problematic nature of its own existence, which does not merely aim to say something, but by saying something aims to serve, to help.

Repetitive exposition according to the intentions of the theologians named will, of course, be indispensable for dogmatics at every step. But dogmatics cannot be only exposition. Its scientific character consists in unsettling rather than confirming Church proclamation as it meets it in its previous concretions and especially in its present-day concretion. It consists in putting it at variance with itself as is proper, in driving it outside and beyond itself. The historical account and the personal confession of faith in the name of contemporaries can only be means to this end. Dogmatics becomes unscientific when it becomes complacent. But it becomes complacent—even when pursued with lively feeling and great perspicacity—when it limits itself to the unfolding and display of a possession already to hand. It is not only what is called the " rigid " dogmatics of the old style (often the Roman Catholic style) that is to be called unscientific in this sense. The same can and must be said of the most fluid, mobile and pious modern dogmatics to the degree that its critical nerve is perhaps dead, to the degree that for the Church around it its significance is merely that of a pleasant certification that all is well and can go on as it has been. So long as the Church on earth is a Church of sinners and its proclamation is thus beset by the most serious problems, one can say very definitely that a dogmatics which takes this attitude and produces this result is wrong. The true Church is waiting for something far different from certification. Again we must say that the line between a purely historical dogmatics and one that is, as it ought to be, critical, is a line that cannot be fixed in general. In all seriousness a critical dogmatics too, and especially, will simply have to give historical accounts over wide stretches, and it is precisely in so doing that it will criticise and correct.

It is obvious that in some circumstances more can be done for dogmatics by adducing a single passage from the Bible or the Fathers than by the most penetrating dialectical discussion.

On the other hand a dogmatics that criticises and corrects at every step might end up as a mere historical record.

The *Glaubenslehren* of Schleiermacher and A. Schweizer contain a veritable wealth of criticism and correction and yet one might well ask whether all the criticism and correction do not finally end up, and are not meant to end up, as a grandiose certification, in remarkable harmony with the Roman Catholic conception of dogmatics.

Appearances may deceive on both sides and there is no firm guarantee against slipping into the forbidden opposite. Nevertheless, the question is put here too, and it must be answered by every dogmatics, whether dogmatics is a part of Church history or of information about the present-day Church, or whether it is itself a part of the Church's action. Only in the latter case is it a science in the sense of its commissioned task.

At the beginning of his work *Die Theologie der Tatsachen wider die Theologie der Rhetorik* (4th edn. 1876, p. 1) A. F. C. Vilmar tells of a certain teacher of dogmatics he heard in his youth who used to accompany and conclude certain sections of his discipline with the words : " *In futuram oblivionem*, gentlemen." Remarkably enough these sections included those on faith, justification, the person of Christ, the sacraments and the gifts of the Holy Spirit. But be that as it may, whatever can be taught and learned in dogmatics *in futuram oblivionem*, as the mere material of knowledge, whatever can be had in black and white and confidently carried home, has certainly nothing to do with science. Dogmatics is a science, not as the offering of all sorts of material, though it must be this too, but as the movement of this material or as this material in motion. So long and so far as this movement or state of movement has not started, dogmatic work itself has not begun.

3. Scientific dogmatics—and now we come to the decisive point—enquires into the agreement of Church proclamation with the revelation which is attested in Holy Scripture. This is what we called the meaning and point of dogma in the first sub-section. If the scientific nature of dogmatics consists in its specific objectivity, i.e., in its orientation to the question of dogma, then we have here the decisive test by which its scientific character has always to be proved. We have already seen that Church proclamation could and can be criticised and corrected from very different standpoints too. What might happen when this is done could even be science from these different standpoints. But it would certainly not be dogmatic science. The two aberrations mentioned above do not have to be fatal to dogmatics. Both a gnostic and also an uncritical dogmatics might incidentally at least do justice to the task of dogmatics. But this is ruled out in the case of the third error, namely, the confusion of the criterion of dogmatics with other criteria. Humanly speaking, and this is the only way we can speak, the result in this case can only be perversion. Dogmatic work stands or falls by whether the standard by which Church proclamation is measured is the revelation attested in Holy Scripture and not a philosophical, ethical, psychological or political theory. Now it is obvious that everyone who works at dogmatics works more or less with specific intellectual presuppositions. The only question is whether in addition to these he also knows the sign of the divine promise which is set up in the Church and whether he is able and willing, in a way that admits of no proof, to take this sign so seriously that in this context its direction takes absolute precedence over all the directions he might owe to the humanities. If and so far as this is so, his work is scientific, and if and so far as it is not so, his work is not scientific, no matter how scientific it may be considered from other angles. It is quite right—and we are not questioning this here but emphatically underlining it—that an education in the arts and a familiarity with the thinking of the philosopher, psychologist, historian, aesthetician, etc., should be demanded of the dogmatician or the theologian. The dogmatician, too, must think and speak in a particular age and should thus be a man of his age, which also means a man of the past that constitutes his age, i.e., an educated man. Nevertheless, the only element in education that makes him a dogmatician is the one which is not provided in all these other disciplines and which consists in indemonstrable and unassuming attention to the sign of Holy Scripture around which the Church gathers and continually becomes the Church. By this attention, and by nothing else, the theologian

becomes a theologian. It is not a question, then, of depreciating other disciplines. It is sheer nonsense to talk of criticising culture in this regard, for in the last resort attention to Holy Scripture might be called an element of culture or education. Nor is it a question of the barbarous demand that the problem of culture as such must be indifferent to the theologian. The problem of culture is the problem of being human, which undoubtedly exists for the theologian too, since theology is a specific activity of humanity. The problem of theology and dogmatics can also be seen as wholly set within the framework of the problem of culture. What is at issue is just the simple insight that this special problem, like all the other problems of culture, has its own set of laws which is not to be confused nor intermingled with any other.

Once when Luther wanted to show why theology like jurisprudence and medicine has and must have its own vocabulary, the *phrasis Spiritus sancti*, he formulated the issue in the statement: *Non debet ars artem impedire, sed unaquaeque debet retinere suum quasi cursum et uti suis terminis (Comm. on Gen. 1*[14]*, W.A., 42, p. 35, l. 35).* Why should we want it to be otherwise? Dogmatics is in fact an *ars* among other *artes* and can be taught and learned like them, but it is the art whose law points us to Holy Scripture as the decisive norm without whose validity and observance it becomes sheer bungling.

Certainly this problem is a very special and extremely distinctive problem. We must beware of trying to level it down or to deduce or prove the fact or extent that it can be viewed as set within the framework of the problem of culture generally. The man who argues that this is so and who knows what he is saying in so doing can only believe that we are dealing here with *the* problem of culture, with the framework of all cultural problems. He has to realise, then, that he must not only grant this problem its own laws but must also refrain from deriving these from a superior general law, though he must also refrain, of course, from trying to prove as a general necessity the superiority of this problem over all other problems, e.g., in the form of a theological philosophy of culture. He will know the nature of this problem well enough to realise that this is all forbidden. We cannot postulate of any man that for him, too, this problem is posed in the context of the problem of his humanity and indeed as the problem that dominates the context, just as we cannot postulate of any man that he knows he is in the Church when he does not know that he is. But when a man says he is stirred by this problem, and when he wants to take part in the work of dogmatics, we may postulate that he will observe the proper laws of this problem no matter how remarkable they may be, just as in any other field he would observe the relevant if possibly less remarkable laws of the field. We may postulate that he will conduct himself as an expert in the field and not as a bungler. Without any arrogant criticism of culture we may postulate that he will realise that in this sphere the criteria of other philosophies cannot play the role which they might perhaps be assigned in every other sphere.

If anyone resolutely refuses to accept this but insists on deriving the final standard in this field, too, from this or that logic, ontology, psychology, or sociology, his attention must be kindly called to the fact that all the rest of the land is open to him but he should desist from working here, where he can only cause confusion with these other final standards.

The time has come to lodge a protest in the name of purity and propriety against the corruption of theology which has now been in full swing so long and which has been brought about by trying to understand and treat it simply as a branch of the humanities in general. To give this protest inner justification more will be needed, of course, than phenomenological interest in the respecting of existing orders and categories or the jealousy of an intellectual trade unionism insisting on its special rights. The formal need for the autonomy of theology can and should be pointed out, but one should not forget that the seriousness of the reference stands or falls with the attention that is actually paid to the witness of Holy Scripture and not just with speaking about it. The truly effective summons to theological relevance can in fact be issued only by a wholly relevant theology and in the last resort it can indeed consist only in the work of this wholly relevant theology. Not the description but the existence of such a theology says what has really to be said here and can be heard as what has really to be heard here, namely, that at no time and in no situation and under no pretext can theology know any more urgent concern than always remaining true to itself and always becoming truer to itself as scriptural theology. Without the existence of such a theology it is futile and unprofitable to debate the question of correct theology even though the answer we propound be ever so powerful and impressive in theory. Only he who actually pursues this theology knows and can effectively advocate what is meant by purity and propriety here, not he who on some ground thinks he knows in general that in theology, as in all else, everything should be done with purity and propriety and that Scripture should thus be and become and remain the master in theology's house. A single attempt to think and speak on this presupposition in a concrete question is far more cogent that the most exact discussion of the fact that one should think and speak in this way, of why one should do so, and to what extent. At this point the question becomes an urgent one whether it has not more often been irregular dogmatics rather than regular dogmatics that has simply existed in this sense as true theology and thus done the decisive thing to establish the scientific character of dogmatics. But be that as it may, i.e., no matter how this third mark of the scientific character of dogmatics be established, it is beyond question that we have here the mark where the roads diverge most pitilessly and momentously to the right hand and the left. So fully is everything involved here that if the boundary between a dogmatics that is finally determined by Scripture and a dogmatics that is finally determined by other authorities could be generally traced all further discussion between the one side and the other would be cut off. One could only admit on both sides that under the same name we were engaged in matters that differed *toto coelo* and that we had nothing to learn from one another apart from a warning against what is absolutely forbidden, which would mean giving a share to the other side. Let us be under no illusions! The sword of this total separation does hang over both our opposition to Roman Catholicism and also our opposition to Protestant Modernism, and something of its threat will always be discernible in the necessary discussions with both. The only point is that in reality the course of this boundary cannot be traced in a general way but has always to be found in each individual case and in the last analysis it is indeed completely hidden from us.

Dogmatic work which truly sets itself under the criterion of Holy Scripture is finally and properly a matter of calling whose presence and continuation are outside human influence in just the same way as is the call to real proclamation of the Word of God. In relation to the possibility of this calling as it is suggested by the biblical promise itself this work may be the matter of a constantly renewed intention. Only to this extent can it be a programme as well. But no programmatic orientation to this decisive mark of scientific dogmatics can be a mechanical safeguard against slipping into a non-scientific or non-scriptural procedure. In fact there has never been, not even in the Reformation, an unequivocally scriptural dogmatics that has not been determined at all by other authorities. On the other hand one must admit that determination by Scripture, and therefore a truly scientific character, can be achieved in part in dogmatics, and by good fortune has been achieved, even when this basic insight, and therefore programmatic regard for this sign, have been more or less seriously lacking. This twofold truth explains why discussion with Roman Catholicism and Modernism has not been broken off but is always possible and necessary in practice, why, even when both sides can only view each other as heretics, they must still reckon with the presence of the sphere of the Church that embraces the heretic, so that for all the menace of the situation they cannot utterly separate from one another.

But once again and even here the fact that the boundary cannot be traced in a general way, that all concrete judgments will be provisional, that the actual course of the boundary will always be a matter for decision in which the first might become last and the last first—this fact cannot mean that the boundary is not drawn in specific instances. For here again the question is put to dogmatic work, and, as we must emphasise once again, it is put in such a way that the real answer, the actual meaning that a particular dogmatics has or has not when considered from this standpoint (however much or little we may know about it *in concreto*), means a verdict of life or death on its scientific character. We have every cause to be cautious in judging whether a given dogmatics has or has not as its standard the revelation of God attested in Holy Scripture. There can be no doubt that in every age men have been much too ready with both positive and negative judgments in the heat of the controversy. It is as well to realise that even when it seems that a verdict can and should be given in a specific case, we can only make, as it were, a judgment for the moment, for to-day, and tomorrow we must give another hearing to find out whether we have perhaps been deceived in some respect and ought thus to alter the judgment. Such judgments, even those that are well-founded, even those that the divided Church has solemnly laid down in its mutually opposed and mutually accusatory confessions, must always be regarded in principle merely as very sharply put questions and not as God's own judgments. But when all this is seen and said, it must also be seen and said that the sword of God's real judgment does hang over our heads— over our own heads as well as those of our heretical partners in the controversy—when we take up and pursue this work. The ultimate question cannot be whether we are doing regular or irregular dogmatics. Nor can it be whether we avoid the mistakes of a gnostic or uncritical dogmatics to which we referred earlier, though these mistakes must certainly be kept in view and avoided so far as possible. What finally counts is whether a dogmatics is scriptural. If it is not, then it will definitely be futile, for we shall definitely have to say regarding it that in it the Church is distracted, i.e., it is busy about other matters and is not doing justice to the scientific task set for it by the problematic nature of its proclamation.

3. THE PROBLEM OF DOGMATIC PROLEGOMENA

We have now reached the real goal of this section. Dogmatics, we have said, understands and describes itself as a science. This means that it consciously and explicitly treads its own very specific path of know-ledge as specifically defined by its object. But what this specific path is, is something on which agreement cannot be presupposed in the situation in which the Church has found itself for the last four hundred years. The path of Roman Catholicism and the path of Protestant Modernism differ from the path of the Evangelical Church. Evangelical dogmatics has to explain to itself why it thinks it should go its own distinctive way and what this way is. According to our deliberations in § 2 this is the task of the prolegomena to dogmatics. What we have done thus far in relation to this task is to define the criterion of dog-matics. But we have not yet spoken of the application of this criterion. This means—and to this extent we cannot break off at this point, but the greater part of the task is still ahead—that we have not yet spoken of the path of knowledge as such which must be taken in dogmatics. Definition of the criterion of dogmatics—and this was the purpose of the first chapter that is now drawing to a close—resulted from a consideration of the promise and task of proclamation given to the Church. We have seen that it is the promise and task of this proclamation to be God's Word to men. We first put and answered the formal questions where and how the Word of God is to be found, what it is, and how it may be known. We did all this on the presupposition that its promised and commissioned identity with Church proclamation is called in question by the fact that the latter is always the work of man. Church proclamation has to become what it is when seen from the standpoint of the promise and the task. From this " becoming what it is " there develops for the Church another task alongside that of proclamation, namely, that of dogmatics, i.e., the task of testing, criticising and correcting the actual proclamation of the Church at a given time. We then saw that God's Word concretely confronts Church proclamation in the form of Holy Scripture as the witness to God's revelation given to the Church. Church proclamation in agreement with Scripture is the fulfilment of the concept of dogma which dogmatics is concerned to know. Thus far we have not gone beyond this definition of the criterion of dogmatics. How are we now to go on to define its path of knowledge as such, to define the employment of this criterion ? The choice which must be made here cannot be an arbitrary one. It arises out of the matter itself, as we have already learned. If we were on the right track in bringing the problem of proclamation and the Word of God under the denominator of proclamation and Holy Scripture, we must now go back to that point in our enquiry where we have already encountered proclamation and Holy Scripture in their interrelationship. This encounter took place in § 4, which dealt with the three forms of the Word of God. In the relationship shown there between proclamation and the Word of God there is obviously implied the theme of our present enquiry, namely, the path of knowledge to a critical investigation of the agreement of proclamation with Holy Scripture. We were then dealing with proclamation and Holy Scripture as such, or rather as two forms of the Word of God. We had not yet taken up the question how the former is to be measured by the latter, how it is to be criticised and corrected by it. To answer this question, then, we must go back to that relationship. If the path of knowledge which we are now beginning to seek is to be plain, the following points that have not yet been clarified obviously demand clarification.

1. We must show how we are to understand it when we understand the Bible as the sign of the promise set up in the Church, namely, as the witness to God's revelation and to that extent as the Word of God by which proclamation is to be measured. We must show what it

means to have this sign as the Church and in the Church, and to hear and accept it as such. And we must show how men can come to the point of accepting this sign. In other words, we must offer an explicit doctrine of Holy Scripture.

2. We must also show how we are to understand the fact that man's word in Church proclamation can and should become God's Word in virtue of the promise. We must exhibit the norm to which man's word is to be subject in view of this promise. And we must describe the nature of a thinking that is ready to subject itself to this norm. In other words, in strict correspondence to the doctrine of Holy Scripture that needs to be set forth, we must attempt an equally explicit doctrine of Church proclamation. If we succeed in exhibiting the correspondence then we are obviously saying what needs to be said generally about the use of the criterion of dogmatics or the path of knowledge in dogmatics.

3. But investigation of this correspondence and the actual doctrines of Holy Scripture and Church proclamation would be left strangely in the air if finally and supremely the question of the Word of God itself and as such were not also raised again in a completely new way. The whole point of the correspondence between Holy Scripture and proclamation, and therefore the whole point of the path of knowledge in dogmatics, consists in the fact that in both Holy Scripture and Church dogmatics we are dealing with the Word of God. There is the distinction that in the one (in Holy Scripture) we have simply to find it so far as concerns the task of dogmatics while in the other (in proclamation), at least in connexion with the task of dogmatics, we have not so much to find it as to ask after it, to investigate proclamation with reference to it. Nevertheless in either case we are still dealing with the Word of God. If the correspondence is not just asserted but is to be understood as intrinsically meaningful, we cannot evade the question how this correspondence can arise, and what we mean when we speak of finding the Word of God in the Bible and of the question of the Word of God in proclamation. One can hardly leave it as a presupposed thesis that both of these come into consideration, and that dogmatics has to reckon with the problem of this identity. Certainly no external basis is needed for it, nor can any such be given. But an inner basis is both necessary and possible. And if there is really this correspondence between the Bible and proclamation, if a dogmatic path of knowledge is thus brought to light, this can hardly be seen as an accident or as the result of general didactic considerations. It must arise out of the matter itself, i.e., out of the fact that the Bible and proclamation are or can become God's Word. It must be shown how and how far the questions already put with reference to the Bible and proclamation are not spun out of the void, are not those of random

curiosity, do not spring from a logical schematism which can be applied
here as elsewhere, but necessarily result from the fact that both the
Bible and proclamation are or can become God's Word. It is for this
reason that the question of God's Word in itself and as such must be
raised again in a completely new way. In a completely new way ! The
fact that God's Word exists in three forms, that it is God's speech, God's
act and God's mystery, that it may be known by men, and how far,
does not need to be repeated explicitly. We shall refer in the future
to this definition of the criterion of dogmatics—and it will be of real
importance at every point—as to an insight that is for the moment
presupposed. There is, however, one point in our deliberations thus
far which in the interests of an answer to the question of the path of
knowledge needs new and very thorough clarification. We have spoken
in § 4 of three forms of the Word of God, proclamation, the Bible, and
then thirdly (although secretly first and decisively) revelation, the
whence of God's Word in the Bible and proclamation, the primary
form of the Word of God, in relation to which and by participation in
which the Bible and proclamation can also be God's Word. We have
called this God's Word in an absolute sense apart from any becoming,
the event of God's Word in whose power the Bible and proclamation
become God's Word. As the Word of God reveals itself, the Bible and
proclamation are the Word of God. Hence it is the concept of revelation which must give us the key to an understanding of the relations
between the two and from which we must also take the very questions
with which we approach the two. It alone can show us what it means
that preaching to-day and yesterday is measured by the Bible. But
we cannot enquire into revelation generally. We cannot enquire
into that which is common in all religions so that what the religion
of the Bible and Christian proclamation calls revelation must even
in its distinctiveness be integrated with it. By putting such general
questions we should show already that we were not asking about the
revelation of the Word of God and we could certainly not give any
answer to this question. And in any case what reason have we in
this context to ask generally about revelation or to ask about a
revelation in general ? We are asking about the revelation in terms
of which proclamation can and must be measured by the Bible and
to which the Bible and proclamation both relate in what is also,
then, a mutual relation. We have to do with the concrete concept
of revelation which the Bible attests to have taken place and proclamation promises will come, with the concrete bracket which
embraces a specific past, the epiphany of Jesus Christ, and what
is always a specific future, the moment when men will hear God's
Word, in the Scripture that is adopted by the proclamation of the
Church or in the proclamation of the Church which is set in motion

by Scripture. We are asking about the concrete present of God's Word between the times, a present that is as certain as it is inconceivable, as unique as it is ever new. Naturally the reality of revelation stands beyond the concept, even and precisely the concept derived from the Bible and proclamation. We cannot try to deal with the reality. Neither in proclamation nor in dogmatics can we produce the attested past and promised future as a present. Nor can we think that in any present that we can produce we are producing this past or this future. We are dealing with the concept of revelation, i.e., with the present of God's Word between the times. But we are still dealing with a concrete concept of revelation, with a concrete present of God's Word. We are dealing with the concept of the revelation of the God who according to Scripture and proclamation is the Father of Jesus Christ, is Jesus Christ Himself, and is the Spirit of this Father and this Son. Naturally one might also investigate the concept of completely different revelations and perhaps even a general concept of revelation. But in so doing one would abandon the task of dogmatics. For it is the concept of this God, and this concept alone, that interests dogmatics. From this concept and this concept alone can it expect light on the relation between the Bible and Church proclamation and guidance in criticism and correction of the latter. If we are not to make a transition to some other discipline which may well be good and necessary but is not dogmatics, then at this point where the relation between the Bible and Church proclamation is in question we can only investigate this concrete revelation.

But how can we perform this investigation ? Clearly only by first considering and analysing the fact of this revelation—obviously the revelation which is attested to have taken place in Scripture and is promised as coming in proclamation ; clearly only by analysing how the fact " God reveals Himself " is itself brought before us in the Bible and revelation ; clearly only by analysing it as required by the fact itself and by the way it makes itself known to us. Again it is from the fact itself that we are to learn how far it may be understood as intrinsically possible and as self-actualising. But analysis of this fact itself can only be a development of what has always played a distinctive role in dogmatics under the name of the doctrine of the Holy Trinity. The answer to the question of the inner possibility of this fact will be provided on the one hand by the basic propositions of Christology and on the other hand by the basic propositions regarding the work of the Holy Spirit. But we shall first investigate the concept of revelation in order to clarify the presuppositions of the doctrine of Holy Scripture and the doctrine of Church proclamation which are our practical concern. The concept of revelation will have to show us how far the Bible and proclamation are to be understood as God's

Word, what correspondence there is between them, and how the latter is to be measured by the former. Investigation of the concept of revelation belongs, therefore, to the beginning of the whole. In the further course of our prolegomena we shall have to have three chapters on revelation, Holy Scripture and the Church's proclamation in which we shall speak of them in such a way that the whole can be regarded as an exposition of the doctrine of the three forms of the Word of God intimated in § 4. The only point is that we shall no longer be concentrating on a demonstration of the forms but rather on their inner structure and mutual relations. We shall thus have to reverse the order. Previously we began with proclamation as the problematic factor in the whole nexus. Revelation must now form the starting-point and proclamation the goal.

CHAPTER II

THE REVELATION OF GOD

CHAPTER II

THE REVELATION OF GOD

PART I

THE TRIUNE GOD

§ 8

GOD IN HIS REVELATION

God's Word is God Himself in His revelation. For God reveals Himself as the Lord and according to Scripture this signifies for the concept of revelation that God Himself in unimpaired unity yet also in unimpaired distinction is Revealer, Revelation, and Revealedness.

1. THE PLACE OF THE DOCTRINE OF THE TRINITY IN DOGMATICS

If in order to clarify how Church proclamation is to be measured by Holy Scripture we first enquire into the prior concept of revelation, already in this enquiry itself we must keep to Holy Scripture as the witness of revelation. Perhaps more important than anything dogmatics can say with reference to the pre-eminent place of Scripture in the Church and over against the Church is the example which dogmatics itself must give in its own fundamental statements. It must try to do what is undoubtedly required of the Church in general, namely, to pay heed to Scripture, not to allow itself to take its problems from anything else but Scripture. The basic problem with which Scripture faces us in respect of revelation is that the revelation attested in it refuses to be understood as any sort of revelation alongside which there are or may be others. It insists absolutely on being understood in its uniqueness. But this means that it insists absolutely on being understood in terms of its object, God. It is the revelation of Him who is called Yahweh in the Old Testament and θεός or, concretely, κύριος in the New Testament. The question of the self-revealing God which thus forces itself upon us as the first question cannot, if we follow the witness of Scripture, be separated in any way from the

second question : How does it come about, how is it actual, that this
God reveals Himself ? Nor can it be separated from the third question :
What is the result ? What does this event do to the man to whom it
happens ? Conversely the second and third questions cannot possibly
be separated from the first. So impossible is any separation here that
the answer to any one of the questions, for all the autonomy and
distinctiveness it has and must continue to have as the answer to a
particular question, is essentially identical with the answer to the
other two. *God* reveals Himself. He reveals Himself *through Himself*.
He reveals *Himself*. If we really want to understand revelation in
terms of its subject, i.e., God, then the first thing we have to realise
is that this subject, God, the Revealer, is identical with His act in
revelation and also identical with its effect. It is from this fact,
which in the first instance we are merely indicating, that we learn
we must begin the doctrine of revelation with the doctrine of the
triune God.

In the first edition of this book (p. 127) I referred to these three questions
and then continued with the words : " Logically they are quite simply questions
about the subject, predicate and object of the short statement : ' God speaks,'
' *Deus dixit.*' " On various sides these words have been taken amiss. The serious
or mocking charge has been brought against me that here is a grammatical and
rationalistic proof of the Trinity, so that I am doing the very thing I attack
elsewhere, namely, deriving the mysteries of revelation from the data of a
generally discernible truth. Along these lines a doctrine of the Trinity might
equally well be constructed on the utterance of the revelation of any other god
or supposed god, or even on the statement : " I show myself " (so T. Siegfried,
Das Wort und die Existenz, 1928, p. 52). That is to say, words which I can still
repeat to-day in due form were then in fact used unguardedly and ambiguously.
Attentive and sympathetic readers could see even then, of course, how they were
intended. The words were obviously not meant to be a proof themselves. They
were simply meant to reduce a completed proof provisionally to a suitable
formula which would be as perspicuous as possible. Naturally it was not my
thought then, nor is it now, that the truth of the dogma of the Trinity can be
derived from the general truth of such a formula. Rather, it is from the truth
of the dogma of the Trinity that the truth of such a formula can perhaps be
derived in this specific application, namely, to the dogma of the Trinity. We
must say " perhaps," for the truth of the dogma of the Trinity does not stand
or fall with such a formula. I still fail to see why as a formula it is not a right
one for the questions demanded by the matter itself. All dogmatic formulations
are rational, and every dogmatic procedure is rational to the degree that in
it use is made of general concepts, i.e., of the human *ratio*. It can be called
rationalistic, however, only when we can show that the use is not controlled
by the question of dogma, i.e., by subordination to Scripture, but by something
else, most probably by the principles of some philosophy. If it is clearly understood that dogmatics generally and necessarily involves rational formulation,
a rational formulation which is, of course, related to a completed proof and which
takes account of Scripture, then no objection can be taken to logical and grammatical formulae as such, for we fail to see why these should be especially suspect
any more than certain legal formulae. The only thing is that we must ask
whether in a given case they are appropriate to the matter or not, which means,

concretely, whether it is an arbitrary anticipation, simplification or even com-
plication to say that what Holy Scripture tells us about the revelation that
it attests constrains us to enquire into the subject, predicate and object of the
short statement in question, or to say that our attention is drawn to the doctrine
of the Trinity by these three questions or the answer to them that we find in
Scripture, or to say that in these three questions there is opened up a way, not to
prove, but certainly to understand the doctrine of the Trinity. Whether a doctrine
of the Trinity might be derived from the statement " I show myself " is something we need not investigate here. But it might be asked especially whether
this can be regarded as obligatory and meaningful in the same way as the biblical
statement that " God speaks."

In practice the nature of the biblical answer to the question :
Who is God in His revelation ? is such as to answer at once the two
other questions : What is He doing ? and : What does He effect ?
and to answer them, not just incidentally, not just in such sort that
what we hear can be erased the next time these other questions are
put, but in such a way that in receiving the answer to the first question
we are bound to hear the answer to the others too, so that the first
answer is properly heard only when it is heard as given in the other
answers. Is this true in regard to other records of revelation too ?
Possibly so, possibly not ; that is not our concern here. It is certainly
true in the Holy Scriptures of the Christian Church. The first question
that must be answered is : Who is it that reveals Himself here ? Who
is God here ? and then we must ask what He does and thirdly what
He effects, accomplishes, creates and gives in His revelation. But if
the first question is intelligently put, when it is answered the second
and third questions will be answered as well, and only when answers
to the second and third questions are received is an answer to the
first question really received.

1. The Bible certainly tells us who the God is whom it attests as
self-revealing.

It names and describes Him as Elohim (perhaps Him that is to be feared),
Yahweh (we shall have to come back specifically to this most important name),
El Shaddai (perhaps the All-sufficient), the Lord and Protector of Israel, the Creator
of heaven and earth, the Ruler of the world and its history, the Holy and the
Merciful and in the New Testament as the Lord of the coming kingdom, the Father
in heaven, the Father of Jesus Christ, the Redeemer, the Spirit, love, etc.

2. But does anyone really hear and understand here without also
hearing and understanding what is said further about the That and
the How of the revelation of this God ? That this revelation happened
and how it happened is no accident in face of the fact that we are
referring specifically to the revelation of this God. In the That and
the How of this revelation He also and specifically shows Himself to
be this God. Indeed, this God will and can make Himself manifest
in no other way than in the That and the How of this revelation.
He is completely Himself in this That and How.

This is already true in the Old Testament in view of the fact that here it is on the figures of Moses and the prophets that the reported process of revelation concentrates (they are really not just instruments in God's hand but as such His representatives too, not just witnesses of revealed truth but delegates of the self-revealing God). But already in the Old Testament we must also point to the remarkable figure of the angel of Yahweh who in some places is identical with Yahweh in His acts. The same applies to an even greater extent in the New Testament, where revelation coincides with the manifestation of Jesus Christ. Thus it is in the event of revelation itself that we are now to seek and discern the Revealer.

3. But according to the direction of the whole Bible the question who God is in His revelation is to be answered thirdly with a reference to the men who receive the revelation, with a reference to what the Revealer wills and does with them, to what His revelation achieves in them, to what His being revealed thus signifies for them.

In the Bible revelation is always a history between God and certain men. Here one man is separated and led out into a foreign country like Abraham. There another is called and anointed to be a prophet, a priest, or a king. Here a whole nation is chosen, led, ruled, blessed, disciplined, rejected and adopted again. There faith and obedience are aroused, or there is complete hardening. There a Church is gathered in the light of this whole occurrence, and the kerygma and sacraments are instituted as signs of recollection and expectation, because man is now " in Christ," a future has been won, and along with it a present between the times.

All this, this revealedness of God attested in Scripture, is not just the effect of the Revealer and His revelation, an effect which is simply to be differentiated from these, as indeed it is. It is also the answer to the question : Who reveals Himself ? and to the second question : How does He reveal Himself ? Thus the man who asks about the God who reveals Himself according to the witness of the Bible must also pay heed to the self-revealing as such and to the men to whom this self-revealing applies.

The fact that in putting the first question we are led on at once to a second and a third is what first brings us close to the problem of the doctrine of the Trinity. Close, for we could not say that these considerations summon us to develop the doctrine of the Trinity. The one thing we now know is that the God who reveals Himself in the Bible must also be known in His revealing and His being revealed if He is to be known. These considerations become significant and indeed decisive in this context only when we go on to make the two statements that follow.

4. The question : Who is the self-revealing God ? always receives a full and unrestricted answer also in what we learn about God's self-revealing as such and about His being revealed among men. God Himself is not just Himself. He is also His self-revealing.

He comes as the angel to Abraham, He speaks through Moses and the prophets, He is in Christ. Revelation in the Bible is not a minus ; it is not another over against God. It is the same, the repetition of God. Revelation is indeed God's predicate, but in such a way that this predicate is in every way identical with God Himself.

Again He Himself is not just Himself but also what He creates and achieves in men.

For this reason the Word that the men of the Bible hear and pass on can be called the Word of God even though it is heard by their ears and shaped by their mouths and is indubitably their word. All gifts and graces and also all punishments and judgments in the Bible are significant not for what they are in themselves apart from revelation and apart from Him who reveals Himself but because they are His work on man, and in them He is either near men or far from them, either friend or foe.

Thus it is God Himself, it is the same God in unimpaired unity, who according to the biblical understanding of revelation is the revealing God and the event of revelation and its effect on man.

5. It does not seem possible, nor is any attempt made in the Bible, to dissolve the unity of the self-revealing God, His revelation and His being revealed into a union in which the barriers that separate the above three forms of His divine being in revelation are removed and they are reduced to a synthetic fourth and true reality.

Nowhere in the Bible are we left in any doubt about the fact that without prejudice to His revelation God as God is invisible, i.e., inaccessible to man as such, since in distinction from man He is and continues to be eternal and holy. If this God reveals Himself—and without prejudice to His invisibility He does reveal Himself, He does make Himself accessible to man—He is in revelation after a manner with which His first being can be identified indirectly but not directly, not simply, not by removal of the distinction. The angel of Yahweh in the Old Testament is obviously both identical and not identical with Yahweh Himself. It is quite impossible that the non-identity, too, should not be and remain visible. In the New Testament the names of Father and Son are similarly inexchangeable. But the same applies to the revealedness of God attested in the Bible. If God gives Himself to man, He is still someone other as Giver and as gift. So the names Christ and Spirit or Word and Spirit are inexchangeable.

Thus to the same God who in unimpaired unity is the Revealer, the revelation and the revealedness, there is also ascribed in unimpaired differentiation within Himself this threefold mode of being.

It is only—but very truly—by observing the unity and the differentiation of God in His biblically attested revelation that we are set before the problem of the doctrine of the Trinity.

So once again, and perhaps understandably as the subsequent formulation of something presented by the Bible, it may be said that we stand before the problem that in the statement that God speaks—not in the general statement but in that taken from the Bible—the subject, predicate and object are to be both equated and also differentiated. It is cheap to say that this can also be formulated of the equivalent general statement or of similar statements about some other god or even of the statement : " I show myself." We *can* do all kinds of things. But it is obviously not unimportant here that while we can do many things only theoretically we do not actually do them because there is neither cause nor need to do so. If any one wants to assert that even outside the biblical witness to revelation we are actually and not just potentially brought up against the problem of the doctrine of the Trinity, then if he is to present a substantial objection he must show—by taking it upon himself actually to develop the other doctrine of the Trinity in another dogmatics in another church— that there is cause and need to do what perhaps we only *can* do in relation to these other statements.

If, then, in understanding the concept of revelation it is right to ask first who God is, and if guided by the Bible we have to ask this in the way we have just done briefly, then, in accordance with the question thus disclosed, we have to pursue the answer already disclosed. That is to say, we must first address ourselves, naturally following again the answer just disclosed, i.e., Holy Scripture, to a development of the doctrine of the triune God.

In putting the doctrine of the Trinity at the head of all dogmatics we are adopting a very isolated position from the standpoint of dogmatic history.

Yet not wholly isolated, for in the Middle Ages Peter Lombard in his *Sentences* and Bonaventura in his *Breviloquium* took the same position.

Otherwise it neither has been nor is the custom to give this place to the doctrine of the Trinity. The reason for this strange circumstance can be sought only in the fact that with overwhelming unanimity it has obviously been thought that a certain formally very natural and illuminating scheme of questioning should be followed in which one can and should speak first of Holy Scripture (or in Roman Catholic dogmatics the authority of the teaching office, or in Modernist dogmatics the reality and truth of religion) as the *principium cognoscendi* (apart from the actual content of faith), and then that even in the doctrine of God itself one can and should deal first with God's existence, nature and attributes (again apart from the concrete givenness of what Christians call " God ").

Even Melanchthon and Calvin, and after them Protestant orthodoxy in both confessions, followed this pattern in a way that was strangely uncritical, and similarly none of the later movements in Roman Catholic and Protestant theology has led to the taking of a different path at this point.

The reason why we diverge from this custom is this. It is hard to see how in relation to Holy Scripture we can say what is distinctive for the holiness of this Scripture if first we do not make it clear (naturally from Holy Scripture itself) who the God is whose revelation makes Scripture holy. It is also hard to see how what is distinctive for this

God can be made clear if, as has constantly happened in Roman Catholic and Protestant dogmatics both old and new, the question who God is, which it is the business of the doctrine of the Trinity to answer, is held in reserve, and the first question to be treated is that of the That and the What of God, as though these could be defined otherwise than on the presupposition of the Who.

At this juncture Calvin himself might be quoted against the procedure adopted by him : *Quomodo enim immensam Dei essentiam ad suum modulum mens humana definiat . . . ? Imo vero, quomodo proprio ductu ad Dei usque substantiam excutiendam penetret . . . ? Quare Deo libenter permittamus sui cognitionem. Ipse enim demum unus, ut inquit Hilarius, idoneus sibi testis est, qui nisi per se cognitus non est. Permittemus autem si et talem concipiemus ipsum qualem se nobis patefacit : nec de ipso aliunde sciscitabimur quam ex eius verbo* (*Instit.*, I, 13, 21).

There is in fact a serious risk, in the doctrine of Scripture as well as the doctrine of God, that we may lose ourselves in considerations and be driven to conclusions which have nothing whatever to do with the supposed concrete theme of the two doctrines, if we begin by discarding the concreteness as it is manifest in the trinitarian form of the Christian doctrine of God. And the doctrine of the Trinity itself is threatened by the same danger, the danger of irrelevant speculation, if we state it only at a later stage and do not give it the first word as that which gives us information on the concrete and decisive question : Who is God ?

The common idea that one must follow the far too obvious and illuminating scheme : How do we know God ? Does God exist ? What is God ? and only last of all : Who is our God ? is in direct contradiction to the very important declarations that no one can then avoid making about the actual and comprehensive significance of the doctrine of the Trinity. What we are trying to bring to practical recognition by putting it first is something which has not been concealed in the history of dogmatics and which has often enough been stated very strongly, namely, that this is the point where the basic decision is made whether what is in every respect the very important term " God " is used in Church proclamation in a manner appropriate to the object which is also its norm. The doctrine of the Trinity is what basically distinguishes the Christian doctrine of God as Christian, and therefore what already distinguishes the Christian concept of revelation as Christian, in contrast to all other possible doctrines of God or concepts of revelation. Certainly the decision is repeated at every stage. But it is from this point that it is repeated. This is where it gains its momentum. It is on this basis that it becomes so serious, so simple and at the same time so complicated, as in the last resort it always actually is.

C.D.—L

If we do not know God in the way in which He reveals Himself as the One, namely, *distincte in tribus personis*, the inevitable result is that *nudum et inane duntaxat Dei nomen sine vero Deo in cerebro nostro volitat* (Calvin, *Instit.*, I, 13, 2). *Quia de Deo sentiendum est sicut se patefecit : Credimus, agnoscimus, confitemur et invocamus tres personas, Patrem, Filium et Spiritum sanctum. . . . De re summa et excellentissima cum modestia et timore agendum est et attentissimis ac devotis auribus audiendum, ubi quaeritur unitas trinitatis, Patris, Filii et Spiritus sancti. Quia nec periculosius alicubi erratur, nec laborosius quaeritur, nec fructuosius invenitur* (M. Chemnitz, *Loci*, 1591, I, p. 31). *Ignorato vel negato Trinitatis mysterio tota salutis* οἰκονομία *ignoratur vel negatur* (J. Gerhard, *Loci*, 1610, III, 1, 7). *Deus Deus esse non potest nisi tres habeat distinctos existendi modos sive personas* (B. Keckermann, *Systema S. S. Theol.*, 1611, p. 20, cited according to H. Heppe, *Dogm. d. ev.-ref. Kirche*, 1861, p. 86). *Qui non addunt mentionem trium personarum in descriptione Dei, eam nequaquam genuinam aut completam sistunt, quum sine iisdem nondum constet, quisnam sit verus Deus* (A. Calov, *Systema loc. theol.*, 1655 f., II, 182, cited according to H. Schmid, *Dogm. d. ev.-luth. Kirche*, 4th edn., 1858, p. 78). " So long as theism only distinguishes God and the world and never God from God, it is always caught in a relapse or transition to the pantheistic or some other denial of absolute being. There can be full protection against atheism, polytheism, pantheism or dualism only with the doctrine of the Trinity. . . . Faith in the eternal, holy love which God is can be achieved in both theory and practice only by knowledge of the perfect, eternal object of the divine self-knowledge and love, i.e., by the thought of the Father's love for the only-begotten Son. Finally the full quickening nature and impartation of God, which is neither a diminution nor a limitation of His being, can be safeguarded only by the trinitarian doctrine of the Spirit " (C. J. Nitzsch, *System d. christl. Lehre*, 6th edn., 1851, p. 188). " With the confession of God's triunity stands or falls the whole of Christianity, the whole of special revelation. This is the kernel of the Christian faith, the root of all dogmas, the substance of the new covenant. From this religious, Christian concern the development of the Church's doctrine of the Trinity has sprung. What was really at issue was not a metaphysical theorem or philosophical speculation but the very heart and essence of the Christian religion itself. So strongly was this felt that all who still set store by the name of Christian acknowledge and honour a positive Trinity. In every Christian confession and dogmatics the deepest question is this, how can God be one and yet also three. And precisely in proportion as this question is answered does Christian truth come either less or more into its own in all parts of Christian doctrine. In the doctrine of the Trinity beats the heart of the whole revelation of God for the redemption of mankind " (H. Bavinck, *Gereformeede Dogmatiek*, Vol. II, 4th edn., 1918, p. 346 f.). " The trinitarian name of God expresses the specifically Christian consciousness of God, and since the consciousness of God is the basis and content of all faith the trinitarian name of God is the Christian Gospel. For this reason baptism is in this name " (A. Schlatter, *Das. chr. Dogma*, 2nd edn., 1923, p. 354). Even Troeltsch found in the trinitarian formula, naturally according to his own understanding of it, " a brief expression of Christianity as the revelation of God given in Christ and effective in the Spirit . . . the abiding classical formula of Christianity in which the whole doctrine of the faith can be summed up " (*Glaubenslehre*, 1925, p. 124). Cf. also Joseph Braun, S.J., *Handlexikon der kathol. Dogmatik*, 1926, p. 55 : " The doctrine of the Holy Trinity is the basic dogma of Christianity."

If this or something similar must be said, it is hard to see why it should not find expression in the external and especially the internal position of the doctrine of the Trinity in dogmatics.

There is a group of modern dogmaticians who have met this need at least externally by constructing what they call special dogmatics according to the threefold division of Father, Son, and Holy Spirit : P. K. Marheineke, *Grundlehren der christl. Dogm. als Wiss.*, 1827 ; A. Schweizer, *Glaubenslehre d. ev.-ref. Kirche*, 1844 f. and *Christl. Glaubenslehre nach prot. Grundsätzen*, 2nd edn., 1877 ; H. Martensen, *Die chr. Dogm.*, 1856 ; T. Haering, *Der christl. Glaube*, 1906 ; M. Rade, *Glaubenslehre*, 1924 f. Now it is true that the need for this emphasis, and therefore the constitutive significance of the doctrine of the Trinity, is mostly not very clear from what the authors say about it in itself and as such. Thus in A. Schweizer it is obscured by the broadly developed natural theology in Part I, which is put in by force first. Nor do I know any among those mentioned in whose development of the doctrine, even though it serves as a framework for the whole, there is any evidence of a material decision that is significant for this whole. Nevertheless, the choice of this order, irrespective of the reasons for it, is unmistakably a factual confirmation of the presence and urgency of at least the problem of the Trinity. The same naturally applies to Schleiermacher too, who could put the doctrine of the Trinity outside the series of other dogmatic *Loci* and use it as a solemn conclusion to his whole dogmatics. Of course, the fact that Schleiermacher can use his doctrine of the Trinity only as the conclusion to his dogmatics and not equally well as its beginning shows that it does not have constitutive significance for him either, so that here again the fact is more important than the intention or the manner.

In giving this doctrine a place of prominence our concern cannot be merely that it have this place externally but rather that its content be decisive and controlling for the whole of dogmatics. The problem of the Trinity has met us in the question put to the Bible about revelation. When we ask : Who is the self-revealing God ? the Bible answers in such a way that we have to reflect on the triunity of God. The two other questions : What does this God do and what does He effect ? are also answered primarily, as we have seen, by new answers to the first question : Who is He ? The problem of the three answers to these questions—answers which are like and yet different, different and yet like—is the problem of the doctrine of the Trinity. In the first instance the problem of revelation stands or falls with this problem.

Apart from the indicated way by which we have reached it, two mutually related historical facts strengthen us in this conviction that discussion of the doctrine of the Trinity belongs directly to the context of discussion of revelation. The older Protestant orthodox, whether or not they knew what they were saying, could not emphasise enough the character of the Trinity as a mystery or indeed as *the* mystery of the faith. *Mysterium trinitatis neque lumine naturae inveniri, neque lumine gratiae, neque lumine gloriae potest comprehendi ab ulla creatura* (H. Alsted, *Theol. scholast.*, 1618, cited according to Heppe, *op. cit.*, p. 86 f.). *Sublimitas tanta est, ut ὑπὲρ νοῦν, ὑπὲρ λόγον καὶ ὑπὲρ πᾶσαν κατάληψιν :* *Quare ex ratione nec oppugnari nec expugnari, nec demonstrari, sive a priori, sive a posteriori potest aut debet* (J. F. König, *Theol. pos. acroam.*, 1664, I, § 78). For this reason, in harmony with the Fathers and the mediaeval Schoolmen, they never spoke so impressively as here about the need for revelation as the only source of the knowledge of this mystery that governs all mysteries. And this fits in exactly with the aversion that Modernist Protestantism has had for this very doctrine from the days of Servetus and other anti-Trinitarians of the age of the Reformation.

As Schleiermacher very rightly saw and stated, it is distinguished from all other Christian doctrines by the fact that it cannot be made comprehensible as the immediate utterance of Christian self-consciousness. " Or who would assert that the impression made by the divine element in Christ obliges us to think of such an eternal distinction (in the supreme being) as the basis of it (namely, the impression) ? " (*Der. chr. Glaube*, § 170, 2). The fact that this theology declares it has no access to the matter from the standpoint of what it understands by revelation we take to be a sign that this matter must be noted and discussed first when it is a question of real revelation.

2. THE ROOT OF THE DOCTRINE OF THE TRINITY

Thus far we have merely established the fact that in enquiring into what Holy Scripture attests as revelation we come up against the doctrine of the Trinity and thus have good reason to turn our attention to this first. We need to examine it at this stage in order to make it clear that the Christian concept of revelation already includes within it the problem of the doctrine of the Trinity, that we cannot analyse the concept without attempting as our first step to bring the doctrine of the Trinity to expression.

According to Scripture God's revelation is God's own direct speech which is not to be distinguished from the act of speaking and therefore is not to be distinguished from God Himself, from the divine I which confronts man in this act in which it says Thou to him. Revelation is *Dei loquentis persona*.

From the standpoint of the comprehensive concept of God's Word it must be said that here in God's revelation God's Word is identical with God Himself. Among the three forms of the Word of God this can be said unconditionally and with strictest propriety only of revelation. It can be said of Holy Scripture and Church proclamation as well, but not so unconditionally and directly. For if the same can and must be said of them too, we must certainly add that their identity with God is an indirect one. Without wanting to deny or even limit their character as God's Word we must bear in mind that the Word of God is mediated here, first through the human persons of the prophets and apostles who receive it and pass it on, and then through the human persons of its expositors and preachers, so that Holy Scripture and proclamation must always become God's Word in order to be it. If the Word of God is God Himself even in Holy Scripture and Church proclamation, it is because this is so in the revelation to which they bear witness. In understanding God's Word as the Word preached and written, we certainly do not understand it as God's Word to a lesser degree. But we understand the same Word of God in its relation to revelation. On the other hand, when we understand it as revealed, we understand it apart from such relations, or rather as the basis of the relations in which it is also the Word of God. We thus understand it as indistinguishable from the event in virtue of which it is the one Word of God in those relations, and therefore as indistinguishable from God's direct speech and hence from God Himself. It is this that—we do not say distinguishes, since there is no question of higher rank or value—but rather characterises revelation in comparison with Holy Scripture and Church proclamation (cf. on this § 4, 3 and 4).

According to Holy Scripture God's revelation is a ground which has no higher or deeper ground above or below it but is an absolute ground in itself, and therefore for man a court from which there can be no possible appeal to a higher court. Its reality and its truth do not rest on a superior reality and truth. They do not have to be actualised or validated as reality from this or any other point. They are not measured by the reality and truth found at this other point. They are not to be compared with any such nor judged and understood as reality and truth by reference to such. On the contrary, God's revelation has its reality and truth wholly and in every respect—both ontically and noetically—within itself. Only if one denies it can one ascribe to it another higher or deeper ground or try to understand and accept or reject it from the standpoint of this higher or deeper ground. Obviously even the acceptance of revelation from the standpoint of this different and supposedly higher ground, e.g., an acceptance of revelation in which man first sets his own conscience over it as judge, can only entail the denial of revelation. Revelation is not made real and true by anything else, whether in itself or for us. Both in itself and for us it is real and true through itself. This differentiates it even from the witness which the prophets and apostles and the witness which the expositors and preachers of Scripture bear to it, at any rate to the extent that this witness is considered *per se*. If we can also say that the witness both in itself and for us is grounded through itself, this is in virtue of the fact that this witness does not merely seek to relate itself to revelation but does actually relate itself to it, because revelation has become an event in it. This can happen. And it must happen if Scripture and proclamation are to be God's Word. They must become it. Revelation does not have to become it. The fulness of the original self-existent being of God's Word reposes and lives in it.

For this whole context cf. Eduard Thurneysen, " Offenbarung in Religionsgeschichte und Bibel," *Z.d.Z.*, 1928, p. 453 f. The Old and New Testaments are fully at one in the view that the divine oracles as they went forth to men according to their witness constitute a self-contained *novum* over against everything men can say to themselves or to one another. One can either obey or disobey, either believe or not believe, what is called revelation in the Bible—both are possible—but from no other standpoint can one get into a position to see whether it has really happened and its content is true. One cannot produce it oneself, as the priests of Baal wanted to do on Carmel in 1 K. 18. Nor can one control revelation, as was vainly attempted when Jesus was asked for signs. One can only stand within its self-closed circle, or rather one can only move within it or stay and move outside it—the enigmatic yet always uncannily close possibility of the *mysterium iniquitatis*, " concluded under unbelief " (Rom. 11³²). Jesus speaks ὡς ἐξουσίαν ἔχων, Mt. 7²⁹. What does this mean ? The verse goes on, Not as their scribes, i.e., obviously not like those who at best must refer to the higher court of a witness to revelation already present. This is why it is so important for the apostle Paul to have seen and heard the Lord Jesus Himself and not just to be acquainted with Him through the tradition. His apostolate stands or falls with this immediacy to revelation, i.e., with this immediacy of revelation itself. Equally self-grounded and ultimate in authority is what the New Testament especially introduces as the Spirit with His decisions in matters both great and small (down to the route of the apostles' journeys). The man who according to the Bible came to share God's revelation and became obedient to it had no motives or grounds for this, he was not instructed or persuaded, he followed neither his own reason or conscience nor the reason or conscience of other men— all this might also happen, but the Bible has little to say about it and it is not the important thing in this matter. He was simply confronted with this ἐξουσία and he bowed to it and not to anyone or anything else. He obeyed a command.

We may sum all this up in the statement that God reveals Himself as the Lord. This statement is to be regarded as an analytical judgment. The distinction between form and content cannot be applied to the biblical concept of revelation. When revelation is an event according to the Bible, there is no second question as to what its content might be. Nor could its content be equally well manifested in another event than this. Although, in keeping with God's riches, revelation is never the same but always new, nevertheless as such it is always in all circumstances the promulgation of the βασιλεία τοῦ θεοῦ, of the lordship of God. And how can the promulgation of this βασιλεία be made except through what we call revelation here ? To be Lord means being what God is in His revelation to man. To act as Lord means to act as God in His revelation acts on man. To acquire a Lord is to acquire what man does in God when he receives His revelation—revelation always understood here in the unconditional sense in which it encounters us in the witness of Scripture. All else we know as lordship can only be a copy, and is in reality a sad caricature of this lordship. Without revelation man does not know that there is a Lord, that he, man, has a Lord, and that God is this Lord. Through revelation he does know it. Revelation is the revelation of lordship and therewith it is the revelation of God. For the Godhead of God, what man does not know and God must reveal to him, and according to the witness of Scripture does reveal to him, is lordship. Lordship is present in revelation because its reality and truth are so fully self-grounded, because it does not need any other actualisation or validation than that of its actual occurrence, because it is revelation through itself and not in relation to something else, because it is that self-contained *novum*. Lordship means freedom.

The biblical concept of ἐξουσία which we have emphasised above obviously includes both.

Godhead in the Bible means freedom, ontic and noetic autonomy. In the decisions taken in this freedom of God the divinely good becomes event, and truth, righteousness, holiness, and mercy deserve to be called what their names declare because they are real in the freedom of God. It is thus, as One who is free, as the only One who is free, that God has lordship in the Bible. It is thus that He also reveals it. The self-sufficiency or immediacy so characteristic of the biblical revelation is the very thing that characterises it as God's revelation on the one side and as the revelation of lordship on the other. But all this becomes fully characteristic only when we note that what we have here is not an abstract revelation of lordship but a concrete revelation of the Lord, not Godhead (even Godhead understood as freedom) but God Himself, who in this freedom speaks as an I and addresses by a Thou. That this happens is revelation in the Bible and it is thus the revelation of His lordship. By the fact that He speaks as an I and addresses by a Thou God announces His kingdom and differentiates this intimation from all speculations about freedom, lordship, or Godhead such as man might perhaps engage in even without revelation. As freedom, lordship and Godhead are real and true in God Himself and only in God Himself, being inaccessible and unknown if God Himself, this I, does not speak and address by a Thou, so, in God Himself, they are the meaning of the event that the Bible calls revelation. That God reveals Himself as the Lord means that He reveals what only He can reveal, Himself. And so, as Himself, He has and exercises His freedom and lordship, He is God, He is the ground without grounds, with whose word and will man can only begin without asking Why, so that in and with this he may receive everything that deserves to be called true and good. It becomes and is true and good through the fact that we receive it from Him, that God, as Himself, is with us, with us as a man who says I and addresses us as Thou is with others, but with us as the One He is, as the Lord, as He who is free. According to the Bible God's being with us is the event of revelation.

The statement, understood thus, that God reveals Himself as the Lord, or what this statement is meant to describe, and therefore revelation itself as attested by Scripture, we call the root of the doctrine of the Trinity.

Generally and provisionally we mean by the doctrine of the Trinity the proposition that He whom the Christian Church calls God and proclaims as God, the God who has revealed Himself according to the witness of Scripture, is the same in unimpaired unity and yet also the same thrice in different ways in unimpaired distinction. Or, in the phraseology of the Church's dogma of the Trinity, the Father, the Son and the Holy Spirit in the biblical witness to revelation are the one God in the unity of their essence, and the one God in the biblical witness to revelation is the Father, the Son and the Holy Spirit in the distinction of His persons.

When we call the statement that God reveals Himself as the Lord, or the revelation denoted by this statement and attested by Scripture, the root of the doctrine of the Trinity, this implies two things.

First, and negatively, the statement or statements about God's Trinity cannot claim to be directly identical with the statement about revelation or with revelation itself. The doctrine of the Trinity is an analysis of this statement, i.e., of what it denotes. The doctrine of the Trinity is a work of the Church, a record of its understanding of the statement or of its object, a record of its knowledge of God or of its battle against error and on behalf of the objectivity of its proclamation, a record of its theology and to that degree of its faith, and only to that extent, only indirectly, a record of revelation. The text of the doctrine of the Trinity, whether we have in view one of its dogmatic formulations by the Church, or our own or some other theologico-dogmatic explication of the Church dogma, is not, then, identical with one part of the text of the biblical witness to revelation. The text of the doctrine of the Trinity is at every point related to texts in the biblical witness to revelation. It also contains certain concepts taken from this text. But it does this in the way an interpretation does. That is to say, it translates and exegetes the text. And this means, e.g., that it makes use of other concepts besides those in the original. The result is that it does not just repeat what is there. To explain what is there it sets something new over against what is there. We have in view this difference from revelation and Scripture, which the Church and theology must be aware of in their own work, when we call our statement about revelation—and already it, too, can be regarded only as an interpretation—merely the root of the doctrine of the Trinity.

Already in the early Church the doctrine of the Trinity was attacked on the ground that it is not biblical, that in the form in which it was formulated by the Church's theology it cannot be read anywhere in the Bible. This is especially true of the crucial terms " essence " and " person " which theology used. But it is also true of the word " Trinity " itself. Now this objection can be raised against every dogma and against theology in general and as such. It would also have to be raised against proclamation, which does not stop at the mere reading of Scripture but goes on to explain it too. Now explanation means repeating in different words what has been said already. The Fathers of the Church and the councils, and much later the Reformers in their battle against the new anti-Trinitarians, were naturally well aware that the doctrine of the Trinity is not in the Bible. But they rightly rejected the view that in relation to the legitimacy, i.e., the biblical character of a Church dogma or theology what counts is *ipsa etiam verba* (i.e., the words of Holy Scripture) *totidem syllabis et literis exprimere* (M. Chemnitz, *Loci*, edn. 1591, I, p. 34). This would be an *iniqua lex* for the Church, an arresting of all biblical exposition, whose very essence is *explicare quod Scripturis testatum consignatumque est* (Calvin, *Instit.*, I, 13, 3). *Si oporteret de Deo dici solum illa secundum vocem quae sacra scriptura de Deo tradit, sequeretur quod nunquam in alia lingua posset aliquis loqui de Deo, nisi in illa in qua prima tradita est scriptura veteris vel novi testamenti. Ad inveniendum autem nova nomina antiquam fidem de Deo significantia coegit necessitas disputandi cum haereticis* (Thomas Aquinas, *S. th.*, I, qu. 29, art. 3). Inaccurate explanations of the Bible, made in the speech of a later period, had to be countered in the speech of the same period. There thus arose in every age the task of dogma and dogmatics. This is what gives dogma and dogmatics their own special character as distinct from the Bible. But they are not necessarily on this account un-biblical or contrary to the Bible. As we must admit at once, they find themselves in the same dangerous sphere as the errors which they must repel. But this is no other sphere than that of the *ecclesia militans* which seeks to listen to the prophets and apostles but seeks to understand their word in the language of later periods, even to understand it aright even at the risk of misunderstanding. *Nec enim Deus frustra donum prophetiae dedit ecclesiae ad interpretandas scripturas, quod inutile sane foret, si rem scripturis traditam nefas esset aliis vocabulis exprimere* (F. Turrettini, *Instit. Theol. elenct.*, 1679, I, L. 3, qu. 23, 23). But even if this objection is to be resisted, we should take from it not merely this reminder of the risk of all theology but also with Calvin the insight that in doctrine as such we are always dealing with *impropria loquutio* as regards the object, that the explanation as such, in so far as it is different from the text, in so far as it must work with concepts alien to the text, might be gladly " buried " if a right understanding of the text could be assured in some other way. (*Utinam quidem sepulta essent, constaret modo haec inter omnes fides, Patrem et Filium et Spiritum esse unum Deum : nec tamen aut Filium esse Patrem, aut Spiritum Filium . . . ib.*, 5.) In contrast it is a confusion of categories as well as a wresting of the facts to think one can achieve this assurance : *Trinitatis dogma non est ecclesiae traditio tantum, sed doctrina in sacris literis expressa* (J. Wollebius, *Christ. Theol. Comp.*, 1626, L. I, cap. 2, can. 2, 1).

Secondly, and positively, to call revelation the root of the doctrine of the Trinity is also to say that the statement or statements about the Trinity of God purport to be indirectly, though not directly, identical with the statement about revelation. The newness or otherness with which they stand alongside the first statement (or its content) cannot mean that a first age, which we may call biblical, had faith without revelation or knowledge of the Triune God, that what it meant by the contrast and unity between Yahweh and the angel of Yahweh, between the Father, the Son and the Spirit, was in reality an im-perfectly clarified monotheism, a greatly disrupted polytheism or the like, and then there came a second age, let us say that of the early Church, which for various reasons thought it should give to the same faith a trinitarian formulation in the sense of the dogma, and that we now stand in a third age, the modern period, for which the Bible and the dogma are both records of the faith of past ages in face of

C.D.—L*

which we are free to express our own faith either in the same way or not. No, we regard the dogma—with what right and in what sense has still to be shown of course—as a necessary and relevant analysis of revelation, and we thus think that revelation itself is correctly interpreted by the dogma. The Bible can no more contain the dogma of the Trinity explicitly than it can contain other dogmas explicitly. For its witness, which was given in a specific historical situation or in many such, does indeed confront erring humanity generally as the witness to revelation, but it does not confront the specific errors of Church history as such. Its witness as the witness to revelation is not just the record of the faith of a given time. Even as it is this, it is also the authority by which faith must always let itself be measured, and can be measured, irrespective of the difference of times.

There is thus no meaningful way in which one could or can refute Arius or Pelagius, Tridentine Roman Catholicism or Servetus, Schleiermacher or Tillich, directly out of the Bible, as though their errors were already answered there *totidem syllabis et literis*, chapter and verse, as though the Word of God had there pronounced on all the specific concerns of different ages and had only to be looked up to produce the proper decision. For dogmatic decision in the specific concerns of different ages one can and must argue from a basis of Scripture that has to be discovered each time afresh if one is not to argue as arbitrarily and untheologically as the adversary would seem to do.

It thus follows that we cannot prove the truth of the dogma that is not as such in the Bible merely from the fact that it is a dogma, but rather from the fact that we can and must regard it as a good interpretation of the Bible. Later we shall have to show why it is that dogmas must be approached with some prejudgment in favour of their truth, with some very real respect for their relative, though not absolute, authority. But this includes rather than excludes the fact that dogmatics has to prove dogma, i.e., to indicate its basis, its root in revelation or in the biblical witness to revelation. If dogma had no such root, if it could be shown that its rise was mostly due to eisegesis rather than exegesis, if, then, it could not be understood as an analysis of revelation, it could not be recognised as dogma.

In this sense we cannot recognise as dogma a whole series of Roman Catholic dogmas, e.g., that of justification coincident with sanctification, or that of Mary, or that of purgatory, or that of the seven sacraments, or that of papal infallibility. As little, naturally, can we recognise as dogma the specific dogmas of Protestant Modernism such as that of the historical development of revelation or that of the continuity between God and man in religious experience. We fail to detect the " root " that these teachings would have to have in revelation or its biblical attestation to be able to be dogmas.

In calling revelation the root of the doctrine of the Trinity we are thus indicating that we do not confuse or equate the biblical witness to God in His revelation with the doctrine of the Trinity, but we do see an authentic and well-established connexion between the two. This obviously means that the doctrine of the Trinity has a wholly actual and not just a historical significance for us and for the dogmatics of our age, even though this is a very different age from that of Arius and Athanasius. In other words, it means that the criticism and correction of Church proclamation must be done to-day, as it was then, in the form of developing the doctrine of the Trinity. It means that the text of the doctrine of the Trinity—naturally in our own exposition, for to abandon exposition would be to abandon the text too—must become for us a commentary that we have to make use of in expounding the Bible and therefore in employing the dogmatic criterion.

But let us come to the point : The basis or root of the doctrine of the Trinity, if it has one and is thus legitimate dogma—and it does have one and is thus legitimate dogma—lies in revelation.

Qu. 25 of the Heidelberg Catechism runs as follows : " Since there is but one divine Being, why namest thou three, Father, Son and Holy Ghost ? " The question is taken almost word for word from the *Geneva Catechism* of 1545, where Calvin himself answers it as follows : *Quoniam in una Dei essentia Patrem intueri nos convenit . . . deinde Filium . . . postremo Spiritum sanctum* (K. Müller, *Bekenntnisschr. d. ref. Kirche*, 1903, p. 118, 25). What is meant by *Quoniam nos convenit* ? Calvin gives a clearer answer in the *Institutio* (I, 13, 2) : *nam ita se praedicat unicum esse, ut distincte in tribus personis considerandum proponat.* And the *Heidelberg* formulates its answer accordingly : " Because that God hath thus revealed Himself in His Word, that these three distinct persons are the one true eternal God." Therefore for this reason and to this extent *convenit*. We might object at this point that in appealing to revelation Calvin and his followers meant only that like much else the triunity of God is attested in Scripture. But the fact that the introduction of this particular doctrine is established in this singular way would still be very striking. And we may recall at this point the words already quoted from Calvin and others to the effect that for the older Protestants the doctrine of the Trinity was not just one article of faith among others but was the basic answer to the question : Who is God ? to which all the other articles are related. In answering this question with the doctrine of revelation as such, we are technically doing something that was not done in this way four hundred years ago. But materially we are not diverging from the intention of that age when we point out that revelation as such, namely, the revelation attested in the Bible, is the basis of the doctrine of the Trinity, or that the doctrine of the Trinity is the appropriate interpretation of this revelation as such.

We are not saying that the doctrine of the Trinity is merely the interpretation of revelation and not also an interpretation of the God who reveals Himself in revelation. This would be nonsensical, for revelation is the self-interpretation of this God. If we are dealing with His revelation, we are dealing with God Himself and not, as Modalists in all ages have thought, with an entity distinct from Him. And it is as an answer to the question of the God who reveals Himself in revelation that the doctrine of the Trinity interests us. This means that it is a constituent part, the decisive part, of the doctrine of God, which is not yet under discussion at this stage. We now anticipate the discussion of this part of the doctrine of God and will later construct whatever else must be developed in this connexion on this presupposition of God's triunity. In a dogmatics of the Christian Church we cannot speak correctly of God's nature and attributes unless it is presupposed that our reference is to God the Father, the Son, and the Holy Spirit. But the fact that the doctrine of the Trinity is the basic presupposition of the doctrine of God too is no obstacle to regarding it already as also and precisely the interpretation of revelation as such. Not as an exhaustive interpretation; to give that we should have to speak not only of the God who reveals Himself but also of the way He does it and the man to whom He does it, and we should thus stand in need of further anticipations from the area of specific doctrines; there are certain parts of christology and pneumatology that we should have to consider. What we do in fact gather from the doctrine of the Trinity is who the God is who reveals Himself, and this is why we present the doctrine here as an interpretation of revelation. We are not saying, then, that revelation is the basis of the Trinity, as though God were the triune God only in His revelation and only for the sake of His revelation. What we are saying is that revelation is the basis of the doctrine of the Trinity; the doctrine of the Trinity has no other basis apart from this. We arrive at the doctrine of the Trinity by no other way than that of an analysis of the concept of revelation. Conversely, if revelation is to be interpreted aright, it must be interpreted as the basis of the doctrine of the Trinity. The crucial question for the concept of revelation, that of the God who reveals Himself, cannot be answered apart from the answer to this question given in the doctrine of the Trinity. The doctrine of the Trinity is itself the answer that must be given here. When we say, then, that the doctrine of the Trinity is the interpretation of revelation or that revelation is the basis of the doctrine of the Trinity, we find revelation itself attested in Holy Scripture in such a way that in relation to this witness our understanding of revelation, or of the God who reveals Himself, must be the doctrine of the Trinity.

We do not have in view only those passages which in view of their wording one can or should with a high degree of probability regard as explicit references to the doctrine of the Trinity as this rightly arises and is already presented in revelation or in the biblical witness to it. We do not have in view, then, only the passages in which there is plain reference to a unity in trinity or trinity in unity of the self-revealing God.

In the Old Testament Is. 61¹ᶠ· might be adduced as one such explicit reference. This speaks in one breath both of the Lord Yahweh and also of a bearer of the message of salvation who is anointed by this Lord and on whom the Spirit of this Lord rests. In the New Testament we are naturally thinking in the first instance of the baptismal command in Mt. 28¹⁹. Here, no matter to what stratum of the tradition it may belong, the Father, Son and Holy Ghost are not just mentioned expressly and in distinction and even in what became later the classical order, but they are also comprehended in the concept of the divine " name " into which (or into the divine reality denoted by this name) the " nations " are to be baptised. Alongside this verse one might also place Rom. 1¹⁻⁴, where according to the author the Gospel is εὐαγγέλιον θεοῦ and according to content it treats of the υἱὸς θεοῦ, while the πνεῦμα ἁγιωσύνης is mentioned as the factor by which this Son of God was marked off as such in His resurrection and to that extent was instituted (ὁρισθείς) as such (for those to whom He is manifested and who believe in Him). At the climax of the same epistle we then find (11³⁶) the well-known saying : ἐξ αὐτοῦ καὶ δι' αὐτοῦ καὶ εἰς αὐτὸν τὰ πάντα, on which one should not put the many and serious exegetical and systematic stresses that Wobbermin does (esp. *Systemat. Theol.*, III, 1925, p. 392) since it is definitely not so much a statement about God as rather about the world and its relation to God. But for this reason the saying is the more illuminating for the connexions in which the divine αὐτός may be seen as three times the same and three times the same in different ways. Nor can the way in which the terms θεός, κύριος, πνεῦμα occur and are used in 2 Thess. 2¹³ be purely fortuitous. (On the other hand the passage 1 Jn. 5⁷ᶠ·, which was still highly valued in the age of orthodoxy, is in the original form of Spirit, water and blood an interesting testimony to the unity and distinction between Christ and the Spirit, but in the later form of Father, Son and Spirit, in which it enjoyed some publicity and renown, it cannot be used to ascertain New Testament teaching as such.) Alongside these four references we may then set a series of others in which the three appear more or less clearly in the same specific functions but in much varied sequence. Thus according to 1 Pet. 1² the election of the saints is grounded in the πρόγνωσις θεοῦ πατρός, worked out in the ἁγιασμὸς πνεύματος and directed εἰς ὑπακοὴν καὶ ῥαντισμὸν αἵματος Ἰησοῦ Χριστοῦ. Rev. 1⁴ tells us that the grace and peace wished for the seven churches come ἀπὸ ὁ ὢν καὶ ὁ ἦν καὶ ὁ ἐρχόμενος (note how the first and basic concept is here again paradoxically broken into a significant trinity) καὶ ἀπὸ τῶν ἑπτὰ πνευμάτων ἃ ἐνώπιον τοῦ θρόνου αὐτοῦ (the one Spirit is here obviously meant to be called too the specific Spirit of each of the seven churches) καὶ ἀπὸ Ἰησοῦ Χριστοῦ the faithful witness, etc. If in two instances Christ, though certainly important, stands in the third place, in two others He is first. This is so in 2 Cor. 13¹³, where the so-called apostolic blessing ascribes grace to Jesus Christ, love to the Father and κοινωνία to the Holy Ghost, and then in Mk. 1⁹ᶠ·, where it is on Jesus as the main subject of the baptism story that the Holy Spirit descends, whereupon a voice from heaven confirms His divine sonship. (Cf. on this F. Turrettini, *Instit. Theol. elenct.*, 1679, I, *Loc.* 3, *Qu.* 25, 7 : *Alius auditur, sed nec videtur, nec descendit. Alius non auditur, sed visibili specie descendit. Alius descendit et ascendit e flumine baptizatus in conspectu omnium.*) Again there are passages in which the Holy Spirit is named as the first and in the context the most notable member of the Trinity. Thus in Jud. 20–21 the Father and the κύριος Ἰησοῦς Χριστός follow the Holy Spirit and in 1 Cor. 12⁴ᶠ· and Eph. 4⁴ᶠ· the classical order of Father, Son, and Holy Ghost is reversed, and another special feature in these two passages is the stress on unity in the αὐτός or εἷς with which the three terms are introduced.

We have agreed that we need not expect to find the doctrine of the Trinity expressly in the Old Testament or the New. But in view of the presence of these explicit references we cannot deny that the problems that developed later in the doctrine of the Trinity are not alien to the Bible but are at least prefigured in it. And the explicit indication of the doctrine is given added weight by the fact that it is enveloped in a whole net of implicit references and especially by the fact that the whole theme of God's revelation as it is treated in the Old and New Testaments, with its focus on the New, cannot be discussed, let alone grasped, without encountering the prefiguration of these problems. This is what we have now to show.

God reveals Himself as the Lord ; in this statement we have summed up our understanding of the form and content of the biblical revelation. The question now is whether we must take this statement in a threefold sense without infringing the unity of its content or whether we must take it in its unified content without infringing its threefold sense. If this statement demands this understanding, not in any general signification but in relation to what the Bible calls revelation, then we see something that can only be conjectured as highly probable on the basis of the passages adduced, namely, that this statement is in fact the " root " of the doctrine of the Trinity, that the problems of the doctrine of the Trinity are in fact prefigured in revelation as it is attested in the Bible. And now we are no longer following the schema of subject, predicate, object (revealer, revelation, revealing), which was only designed to show to what extent we are in fact led by revelation itself to the problem of triunity. Or rather, we now dissolve this scheme—which still has and retains its significance —in the manner suited to the concrete form of revelation on the one side and the doctrine of the Trinity on the other. The question of revealer, revelation and being revealed corresponds to the logical and material order both of biblical revelation and also of the doctrine of the Trinity. We shall thus return to this order when the latter is developed. But we must now follow another order if we are to see how biblical revelation and the doctrine of the Trinity are interconnected, how the second could and did proceed out of the first. This is a historical question which has as such its own special form. But it is governed by the fact that biblical revelation has on the one side a specific historical centre and the doctrine of the Trinity has on the other side a specific historical occasion in biblical revelation. Historically considered and stated the three questions answered in the Bible, that of revealer, revelation and being revealed, do not have the same importance. The true theme of the biblical witness is the second of the concepts, God's action in His revelation, revelation in answer to the question what God does, and therefore the predicate in our statement. Within this theme the two other questions, materially no less important, are answered. Similarly the doctrine of the Trinity, when considered historically in its origin and development, is not equally interested in the Father, the Son and the Holy Ghost. Here too the theme is primarily the second person of the Trinity, God the Son, the deity of Christ.

In dogmatic history this is the insight which Harnack (*Lehrb. d. Dogmengesch.*, 4th edn., 1909, Vol. I, p. 90) formulated in the sentence : " Confession of the Father, the Son and the Spirit . . . is a development of the belief that Jesus is the Christ." O. Scheel (RGG[2] Art. " Dreieinigkeit," III) is in material agreement : " The history of the doctrine of the Trinity is primarily a history of the Logos concept in Christianity." This is the same insight as that which Irenaeus already developed in relation to the name of Christ and with appeal to Is. 61[1] : *In Christi enim nomine subauditur qui unxit et ipse qui unctus est et ipsa unctio in qua unctus est. Et unxit quidem Pater, unctus vero est Filius in Spiritu qui est unctio (C. o. h., III, 18, 3).*

Within this framework of the question of Christ's deity, but claiming equal weight both logically and materially, the other two questions then arose in the first instance as a necessary counterpart to the question of the Son, namely, the question of the Father on the one side and that of the Spirit of the Father and the Son on the other.

If this was so necessary and right, we should have to say that in the order in 2 Cor. 13[13], that of Christ, God, and Spirit, we have the most authentic form of the biblical witness in this matter. At any rate, the historical development of the doctrine of the Trinity out of the witness to revelation followed this route, and this is the route we must now take.

1. Revelation in the Bible means the self-unveiling, imparted to men, of the God who by nature cannot be unveiled to men. The element of self-unveiling in this definition may be described as the historical if not the logical or material centre of the biblical revelation. When the Bible speaks of revelation, it does so in the form of the record of a history or a series of histories. The content of this history or of each of these histories, however, is that self-unveiling of God. But as the record is given, our experience also is, of course, that the One who thus unveils Himself is the God who by nature cannot be unveiled to men, and that this self-unveiling is to specific men. Logically and materially this is just as important as the recorded self-unveiling. Historically the latter constitutes the centre. But what does self-unveiling mean here ? Since the One who unveils Himself is the God who by nature cannot be unveiled to men, self-unveiling means that God does what men themselves cannot do in any sense or in any way : He makes Himself present, known and significant to them as God. In the historical life of men He takes up a place, and a very specific place at that, and makes Himself the object of human contemplation, human experience, human thought and human speech. He makes Himself an authority and factor, a

concrete authority and historical factor, a significant and effective element of human life in time and in historical relations. He Himself, as God, exists for men exactly as other things or persons exist for them, as Esau did for Jacob, Mount Horeb or the ark of the covenant for Israel, John for Peter or Paul for his churches. He naturally does so in His own special form which cannot be mistaken for any other. But He does so truly and concretely, so that the men concerned can say without any speculation or metaphor : Immanuel, God with us ! so that without any fiction or self-deception they can say Thou to Him and pray to Him. This is what self-revelation is. This is what man cannot provide for himself, what only God can give him, what He does give him in His revelation. The concept of form is the concept we must single out from what has been said as the decisive one. No matter who or what else the self-revealing God may be, it is beyond dispute that in His revelation according to the biblical witness He takes form, and this taking form is His self-unveiling. It is not impossible nor is it too petty a thing for Him to be His own *alter ego* in His revelation, His *alter ego* to the extent that His self-unveiling, His taking form, obviously cannot be taken for granted but is an event, and an event that cannot be explained by or derived from either the will or act of man or the course of the world at large ; to the extent that He Himself must take a step towards this event ; to the extent that this step obviously means something new in God, a self-distinction of God from Himself, a being of God in a mode of being that is different from though not subordinate to His first and hidden mode of being as God, in a mode of being, of course, in which He can also exist for us. The God who reveals Himself here can reveal Himself. The very fact of revelation tells us that it is proper to Him to distinguish Himself from Himself, i.e., to be God in Himself and in concealment, and yet at the same time to be God a second time in a very different way, namely, in manifestation, i.e., in the form of something He Himself is not.

To be God a second time in a very different way—this may be seen in the Old Testament primarily in the fact that almost all the attributes that characterise the Yahweh of Israel, His righteousness with which He watches over His covenant with Israel, His goodness and faithfulness to His own, His glory and also His Word and Spirit, the wisdom of the later Old Testament, and the countenance which is anthropomorphically—or should we say not at all anthropomorphically—ascribed to Him, His arm, His hand, His right hand, all these are sometimes referred to as though they were not just in or of Yahweh but were Yahweh Himself a second time in another way. Revelation means that all these human, all too human concepts are not just that, are not just descriptions and representations of the reality of Yahweh ; they are themselves the reality of Yahweh. In these concepts, and therefore in the sphere, physical as well as intellectual, of men who are truly different from Himself, Yahweh has what we have called form. In them all Yahweh Himself is there ; He subsists ; He has objectivity for those to whom He is manifest. Religious science usually defines concepts used in this way as hypostases, i.e., realities of the one God which are both distinguishable and yet also indistinguishable from Him. And why should we not accept this definition ? Religious science for its part has obviously borrowed it from the history of Christian dogma. Now the fact is that in this series of hypostases there is one that stands out in a significant and, if appearances do not deceive, a comprehensive way as the epitome of what God is a second time in another way in His self-unveiling. This is the concept of the name of God. Knowledge, love, fear, trust, hope, praise, preaching, invocation are all related continually to this apparent sub-centre alongside Yahweh and yet even so they are unmistakably connected to Yahweh Himself. The righteous man thinks, speaks and acts in this name when he stands before Yahweh, under His protection and blessing. To this name of Yahweh, not to the One who dwells in Sinai or according to the later view in heaven, a house or temple is built in Jerusalem. Conversely this name is the court for whose sake Yahweh forgives and is gracious and guides and does not forsake Israel ; His name dwells indeed, as Yahweh chose, in Jerusalem. But the angel of Yahweh, who is frequently mentioned, also stands in the closest connexion to the name of Yahweh. What makes Him the angel of Yahweh according to Ex. 23[21], and what gives Him authority as such, is that " my name is in him." In His name is concentrated everything He is in His relation to His people, to the righteous, and from His name proceeds in some way everything that the people or the righteous can expect from Him as they stand in this relation. What does all this mean ? Not for the old Testament alone but for ancient thought generally, and perhaps for what is called primitive thought (though it is not really primitive), a man's name is not something that comes to him from without, something accidental and non-essential, a mere *nomen* in the sense of the mediaeval debates. At this point, and perhaps only at this point in distinction from the attributes mentioned earlier, the name is a being, belonging of course to another being, identical with it in a way one cannot explain, yet still a separate being, so that statements about the name and him who bears it can be differentiated from and yet can also replace one another " Where the name is, there is the bearer of the name ; where the name works, the bearer of it works " (Hans Schmidt, RGG[2], Art. " Namensglaube," I). When the Old Testament applies this realistic view of the name to Yahweh, this means on the one side that it distinguishes between Yahweh who dwells on Sinai or in heaven and Yahweh who dwells in Canaan, Shiloh, and later Jerusalem, between Yahweh in His hiddenness and Yahweh in His historical form in which, as the fact that His name is given shows, He is known in Israel and has dealings with Israel. " God's name is an expression for His personal essence as present in the sanctuary and people " (O. Procksch in G. Kittel, TWNT, Vol. I, Art. ἅγιος, p. 90 (TDNT, p. 91)). But it also means on the other side that the Old Testament does not pretend to knowledge of two or many gods. It knows only one God. The hidden Yahweh Himself is present in His name and all the predicates of the name are those of the hidden Yahweh Himself. Nevertheless, it knows the one God a first time and then a second time in a very different way. And for Israel or the righteous everything depends on knowing Him thus, this second time in a very different way. For the Yahweh who exists this second time in a very different way, the name of Yahweh, is the form in which Yahweh comes to Israel, has dealings with it, is manifest to it. Therefore the decisive act of revelation by which Israel is chosen as Israel and becomes the people of this God is the revelation of the name of God. It is significant enough that this revelation of the name (Ex. 3[13f.]) is in fact, in content, the refusal to give a name, for " I am that I am " can hardly mean more than that " I am He whose true name no one can utter." By its very wording the revealed name is intended to recall the hiddenness even of the revealed God. But under this name, which in itself and as such pronounces His mystery, God does reveal Himself to His people, i.e., He begins, as Ex. 3 instructively shows, to have dealings with Israel through the announcing by Moses of its deliverance out of Egypt. From this standpoint one must add to the concept of the name of God that of the covenant, which belongs to a very different plane, if one is to see fully what the form of God, and to that degree His being in concealment, signifies in the Old Testament. In covenant with this people—" I will be their God and they shall be my people " (Jer. 31[33])—the name of God is actualised, i.e., in the covenant with its divine promise and claim, with its record deposited in the Law, everything takes place that does take place through the name of Yahweh. In the language of our historians, " the thought of the covenant is the form in which is clothed Israel's consciousness of the relation with this God made in history and also of that which is divinely willed in this relation " (J. Hempel, RGG[2], Art. " Bund," II, A). To have knowledge of the name of Yahweh, and to that degree knowledge of Yahweh Himself, and to participate in His revelation, is to be a partner in the covenant made by Him. Yahweh is thus God a second time in a very different way in the fact that He elects a people, makes it His people and rules it as His people.

It is now relatively simple to see the fundamental concern in the New Testament. God a second time in a different way is obviously the point here too, but in a manner incomparably more direct, unequivocal and palpable. It is so much more direct that even the hypostases of the Old Testament are weak in comparison ; to use the well-known metaphor of Hebrews, they appear only as shadows. It is so much the more direct that especially the notable position and significance of the name of Yahweh may be regarded quite simply and yet at the same time quite meaningfully, as the Church has always maintained against Judaism even if only from this standpoint, as a prophecy of the fulfilment present here. Into the place, not of Yahweh on Sinai or in heaven, but of the name of the Lord which finally dwells very really in a house of stone in Jerusalem, there now comes the existence of the man Jesus of Nazareth. At one of the high points of the New Testament message He is called " my Lord and my God " (Jn. 20[28]). The remote but ever near and actual background is here again the God who has no historical form, the " Father in heaven." But the Jesus of the New Testament calls precisely this God not merely the Father who has sent Him but very emphatically my Father alongside whom He may place Himself, or knows that He is placed, as He lives as man among men, as He does the Father's will, i.e., as He reveals Him, the Father, from whom He is separated not by anything essential but simply by this form of His as man, i.e., by the possibility of being God in this form. Inalienably important as this background is, little as it can be thought away even for a single moment, the picture which the New Testament itself sets before us is that of the self-disclosure of this Father in which He is not the Father but the Son, the historical figure of this Man on His way from Bethlehem to Golgotha, the " name " of Jesus. Again, the concreteness and actuality of the self-unveiling of God for man, and the enigma of the self-distinction in God Himself which makes this self-unveiling possible, has not just increased quantitatively here in comparison with the Old Testament. Is not perhaps every purely speculative or figurative or fictitious understanding of the real objectification of God in His revelation ruled out for the first time here ? Is not the question of faith in revelation, of acceptance of the God with us, put for the first time here in such a way that it demands decision—here where in place of the invisible form of the name of the revealed God, which is real only in the sphere of human conception, there has now entered the unique, contingent, somatic, human existence of Jesus ? Has not the rejection of Jesus by the Jews

made it shatteringly clear that it was possible to accept the God of the Old
Testament in what seemed to be the most profound reverence and the most
zealous faith and yet in fact to deny Him to the extent that His form, now
become quite concrete, became an offence to the righteous ? Or what other
objection could Israel bring against Jesus apart from the divine self-unveiling
which now, not for the first time, but for the first time quite unequivocally,
encountered it, making, as it were, bodily contact with it ? In thinking that it
has to defend against Jesus as against a blasphemer the name of God dwelling
in the house of stone in Jerusalem, it denies this very name, and thus separates
itself from it and from its own Holy Scripture, which is one long witness to this
name as God's real presence and action in the human sphere. This presence
and action of God Israel declines. Why is it that the Lord's Prayer in the New
Testament begins in the style of the Old Testament : " Hallowed by thy name ! " ?
How else could it begin ? one might almost reply. This is the whole point with
Jesus. His concern is not with something new but with that which is first and
primal, with the God who wills to be God and to be known as God a second time
in a different way, the God of Abraham, Isaac and Jacob, the God who wills to
be revealed in His name and hallowed in His name. This is why, in explanation of the first petition, the Lord's Prayer continues at once : " Thy kingdom
come ! Thy will be done, as in heaven, so (N.B.) on earth ! " This καὶ ἐπὶ γῆς
was the self-unveiling, the form of God which Israel found attested in its Holy
Scripture on every page and which now, when it stood fulfilled before it, it
denied again just as the fathers in the desert had murmured against Moses
and later the prophets had been stoned, not out of irreligion, but in the protest of
the most refined and most ponderable religion against revelation, which will not
leave even or especially the righteous man alone but literally confronts him with
God. Thus the revelation in Jesus ends with His crucifixion by the most pious
men of their time, who even though they had Immanuel daily on their lips and
in their hearts did not want this Immanuel in its unconditionally enacted
fulfilment. But just because Immanuel had been unconditionally fulfilled in
Jesus the crucifixion of Jesus was bound to mean something different from the
stoning of even the greatest prophets, namely, the end of the history of Israel
as the special people of revelation, the destruction of the house of stone as the
dwelling of the name of the Lord, the free proclamation, not of a new Gospel
but of the one ancient Gospel to both Jews and Gentiles. As the Word became
Flesh : λόγος συντελῶν, bringing fully to light what revelation in the Old
Testament had always brought to light only in the form of a pointer, it had
also to become λόγος συντέμνων, the dissolution of this revelation and its written
testimony, not their contradiction, abolition, or destruction, but their dissolution
into itself, just as the early light of dawn disappears in the brightness of the
rising sun itself (Rom. 9²⁸) : Christ the τέλος of the Law (Rom. 10⁴). We see
here the theme of the great battle which Paul above all others fought at the
rise of the Church. It was not a battle against the Old Testament, but like
the battle of Jesus Christ Himself, to whom he simply wished to testify, it was
a battle for the Old Testament, i.e., for the one eternal covenant of God
with men sealed in time, for acknowledgment of the perfect self-unveiling of
God.

That God is capable of what the Bible ascribes to Him in its accounts
of what happened from the patriarchs by way of Moses and the
prophets to Golgotha and on to Easter and Pentecost ; that God can
be made manifest to men in the strictly real sense, as one may finally
see in the revelation in Jesus, i.e., that God can become unlike Himself

in such a way that He is not tied to His secret eternity and eternal secrecy but can and will and does in fact take temporal form as well ; the fact that God can and will and actually does do this we now understand as a confirmation of our first statement that God reveals Himself as the Lord. To all talk of other revelations apart from that attested in the Bible our primary question must be whether the reference there too is to an authentic assumption of form by the Godhead over against man, and not perhaps to mere appearances for which identity with the Godhead cannot be seriously claimed but only a certain participation in it. A second question must then be whether the lordship which is perhaps ascribed to the Godhead there too is also seen there in this intrinsic freedom of God, i.e., the freedom to be unlike Himself. When these questions cannot be answered in the affirmative, or to the extent that they cannot be answered thus with certainty, one should at least exercise great caution in inserting the biblical revelation into the series of other revelations. But be that as it may, the lordship discernible in the biblical revelation consists in the freedom of God to differentiate Himself from Himself, to become unlike Himself and yet to remain the same, to be indeed the one God like Himself and to exist as the one sole God in the fact that in this way that is so inconceivably profound He differentiates Himself from Himself, being not only God the Father but also—in this direction this is the comprehensive meaning of the whole of the biblical witness—God the Son. That He reveals Himself as the Son is what is primarily meant when we say that He reveals Himself as the Lord. This Sonship is God's lordship in His revelation.

2. Revelation in the Bible means the self-unveiling, imparted to men, of the God who by nature cannot be unveiled to men. We now emphasise the second part of the saying and in so doing we return to the subject of revelation. The revelation attested in the Bible is the revelation of the God who by nature cannot be unveiled to men. There are other things and even other gods that are inscrutable to man. That is, man does not in fact have any experience or concept of them. Yet he might very well have some experience or concept of them, so that their inscrutability is only factual. Some day it might be set aside by another fact, since it is not grounded in the nature of the matter or the god in question. But inscrutability, hiddenness, is of the very essence of Him who is called God in the Bible. As Creator, this God is different from the world, i.e., as the One He is, He does not belong to the sphere of what man as a creature can know directly. Nor can He be unveilable for man indirectly in the created world, for He is the Holy One to see whom, even indirectly, other eyes are needed than these eyes of ours which are corrupted by sin. And finally this God by His grace, i.e., by His self-unveiling, says to everyone to whom it is imparted that of himself he could not do what is there done to him and

for him. It is thus of the very nature of this God to be inscrutable to man. In saying this we naturally mean that in His revealed nature He is thus inscrutable. It is the *Deus revelatus* who is the *Deus absconditus*, the God to whom there is no path nor bridge, concerning whom we could not say nor have to say a single word if He did not of His own initiative meet us as the *Deus revelatus*. Only when we have grasped this as the meaning of the Bible do we see the full range of its statement that God reveals Himself, i.e., that He has assumed form for our sake. We cannot withdraw one iota from our previous interpretation of revelation, namely, that it consists in God having assumed form. To deny that is to deny revelation itself. But the fact that it is the God who by nature cannot be unveiled to man that reveals Himself there has distinct significance for our understanding of His self-unveiling. It necessarily means that even in the form He assumes when He reveals Himself God is free to reveal Himself or not to reveal Himself. In other words, we can regard His self-unveiling in every instance only as His act in which He reveals Himself to a man who is unable to unveil Him, showing Himself indeed in a specific form, but still unveiling Himself. Revelation always means revealing even in the form or means of revelation. The form as such, the means, does not take God's place. It is not the form, but God in the form, that reveals, speaks, comforts, works and aids. The fact that God takes form does not give rise to a medium, a third thing between God and man, a reality distinct from God that is as such the subject of revelation. This would imply that God would be unveilable for men, that God Himself would no longer need His revelation, or rather that God would be given up into the hands of man, who, God's form being given him, could more or less control God as he does other realities. The fact that God takes form means that God Himself controls not only man but also the form in which He encounters man. God's presence is always God's decision to be present. The divine Word is the divine speaking. The divine gift is the divine giving. God's self-unveiling remains an act of sovereign divine freedom. To one man it can be what the Word says and to another true divine concealment. To the same man it may be the former to-day and the latter to-morrow. In it God cannot be grasped by man or confiscated or put to work. To count on it is to count on God's free loving-kindness, not on a credit granted once and for all, not on an axiom to which one may have recourse once and for all, not on an experience one has had once and for all. If this were so, the revelation in question would not be that of the God who by nature cannot be unveiled to man. We should simply have one of those mysteries that one day unveil themselves to us and are mysteries no more. The mysteries of the world are of such a kind that some day they can cease to be mysteries. God is always a mystery. Revelation is

always revelation in the full sense of the word or it is not revelation, or
at any rate not what is called revelation in the Bible.

We have already noted the remarkable circumstance that the great revelation
of the name in Ex. 3 according to the most likely interpretation of the text
consists precisely in the refusal to give a name. "Wherefore askest thou after
my name, seeing it is wonderful ? " is also the answer of the angel of the Lord
to Manoah in Jud. 13¹⁸ cf. Gen. 32³⁰. In revelation there is no delivering up of God
to man such as a knowledge of His true name would imply. Revelation itself is to
be understood, and to continue to be understood, as the revelation of the free
loving-kindness of God. This reserve of Yahweh, His concealment even in His
revelation, is also indicated by the urgent warning in Ex. 3 : " Draw not nigh
hither ; put off they shoes from off thy feet, for the place whereon thou standest
is holy ground." Similarly and more generally the concept of God's holiness in
the Old Testament bears no relation to speculation about the transcendent God
but belongs strictly to His immanence, i.e., to His revelation, His name. In
the Old Testament everything is holy that is connected with what we call the
form of God in His revelation, with what in this connexion and because of it
demands another attitude from man than the profane world in whose sphere and
environment it may be seen and heard as the form of God, a discerning, reserved
and utterly reverent attitude, an attitude in which man has to set aside all self-
assertion or clumsy interference—one has only to think of the unfortunate
experiences that could be had by meddling with the ark of the covenant. Everything the Old Testament says about God's self-unveiling stands *eo ipso* under
what seems to be the very opposite sign as well : " Am I a God at hand, saith
the Lord, and not (also) a God afar off ? " (Jer. 23²³). In Mal. 3¹ the angel of
the covenant is Himself expressly called the Lord, though this does not prevent
Him from also being sent by the Lord. In Is. 6 the manifest God whose mere
train fills the temple is holy, while He Himself sits on a high and lofty throne,
incomprehensible to the prophet and the people, even as He turns to them with
His revelation. God is holy, and what is connected with Him is holy, because
and in so far as God, even in disclosing and imparting Himself, also draws and
establishes the boundary which separates man from Him and which man, therefore, may not cross. Holiness is the separation in which God is God and in which,
as God, He goes His own way even and precisely as He is " God with us." It is
the reserving of His gracious or non-gracious decision with which one must
always reckon in relation to Him and in virtue of which He must always be
sought afresh and always with the same humility. Holiness also has unquestionably the meaning of strange ; God comes to men, but not to be at home with
them. This God is not only a God of action, as the founding of the Sabbath
tells us with special beauty. He can not only work ; He can also rest from all
His works. Even as He enters the sphere of our existence, He still inhabits
and asserts the sphere which is proper to Him and to Him alone. In relation
to this God, as one may gather from the attitude of the prophets and especially
the psalmists, we are always dealing with the totality, and the history of His
acts is a history of ever renewed beginnings. Of course there is and ought to be
a tradition of revelation, an institutional cultus, but over against it in the
sharpest dialectic stands prophetism, always ready and armed thoroughly to
unsettle afresh everything that wants to settle down, and to set afresh before
the mystery of Yahweh everything that wants to clarify itself in human, in only
too human fashion. From this standpoint the sharpness of the prohibition of
images is to be seen as a ban not so much on the enjoyment of the senses as on
the pious obtrusiveness and cocksureness of the religion of Canaan. One cannot
stress enough that this concealment of God in the Old Testament is never a

matter of esoteric metaphysics, that it rather is and always continues to be supremely practical, because it is the concealment of the revealed and active God. But the very fact that this God can be seen and heard only as the active God, and never (or only *per nefas*) as comprised and enveloped in a medium, is guaranteed by His concealment, by His incomprehensibility.

This relation is not altered in the New Testament either. On the contrary, it is now supremely true that God conceals Himself in revealing Himself, that even and precisely in assuming form He remains free to become manifest or not to become manifest in this form. The form here is that of the *humanitas Christi*. And this brings us up against one of the hardest problems of Christology that will claim our attention more than once : Can the incarnation of the Word according to the biblical witnesses mean that the existence of the man Jesus of Nazareth was as it were in itself, in its own power and continuity, the revealing Word of God ? Is the *humanitas Christi* as such the revelation ? Does the divine sonship of Jesus Christ mean that God's revealing has now been transmitted as it were to the existence of the man Jesus of Nazareth, that this has thus become identical with it ? At this stage we can only reply that when this view has really been held, there has always been more of less clearly discernible the very thing which, as we have seen, the Old Testament tried to avoid with its concept of the holiness of the revealed God, namely, the possibility of having God disclose Himself through man, of allowing man to set himself on the same platform as God, to grasp Him there and thus to become His master. The " fairest Lord Jesus " of mysticism, the " Saviour " of Pietism, Jesus the teacher of wisdom and friend of man in the Enlightenment, Jesus the quintessence of enhanced humanity in Schleiermacher, Jesus the embodiment of the idea of religion in Hegel and his school, Jesus a religious personality according to Carlyle's picture in the theology of the end of the 19th century—all this looks at least very dubiously like a profane and sacrilegious intrusion in the Old Testament sense in which it is thought possible to come to terms, as it were, with the presence of God in Christ and to take control of it with the help of certain conceptions deriving from the humanity. From the fact that such attempts at secularisation were not made in the New Testament we may see that here even Christ's humanity stands under the caveat of God's holiness, i.e., that the power and continuity in which the man Jesus of Nazareth was in fact the revealed Word according to the witness of the Evangelists and apostles consisted here too in the power and continuity of the divine action in this form and not in the continuity of this form as such. As a matter of fact even Jesus did not become revelation to all who met Him but only to a few. Even these few could also deny and leave Him and one of them could be His betrayer. Revealing could obviously not be ascribed to His existence as such. His existence as such is indeed given up to death, and it is in this way, from death, from this frontier, since the Crucified was raised again, that He is manifested as the Son of God. Nor is His resurrection described as an operation proper to the *humanitas Christi* but rather as something done to it, as a being raised from the dead by God (frequently, cf. Gal. 1[1] ; Rom. 6[4] ; Eph. 1[20] expressly by God the Father). To use the language of a later age, the Godhead is not so immanent in Christ's humanity that it does not also remain transcendent to it, that its immanence ceases to be an event in the Old Testament sense, always a new thing, something that God actually brings into being in specific circumstances. In the comprehensive formula of Paul in 2 Cor. 5[19] : θεὸς ἦν ἐν Χριστῷ κόσμον καταλλάσσων ἑαυτῷ, one should not lay such stress on ἦν that its connexion with the verb καταλλάττειν is overlooked. This reconciling action of God is the *being* of God in Christ, but it is this reconciling *action* that is the being. The Son " glorifies " the Father, yet not without the Father glorifying Him, the Son (Jn. 17[1]). It is not any son that speaks here, but the Son of this

Father, who even as the Father of this Son remains the Father in heaven, the Father who sends the Son, to conclude with this Johannine description of the divine action.

And now we repeat that the God of the biblical revelation can also do what is ascribed to Him in this respect by the biblical witnesses. His revelation does not mean in the slightest a loss of His mystery. He assumes a form, yet not in such a way that any form will compass Him. Even as He gives Himself He remains free to give Himself afresh or to refuse Himself. This His new self-giving remains man's only hope. His " second time in a different way " does not really prevent Him from remaining the same. In all this we hear confirmation a second time, though obviously in a very different way from the first, that God reveals Himself as the Lord. And again we have also to ask whether in other instances in which men think they can speak of revelation the abiding mystery of the self-revealing God really belongs also to the concept of revelation, whether the lordship there ascribed to " God " can really exist in this freedom of God with regard to His own utterances, or whether in these cases revelation does not always consist in a secularisation of God and therefore in an empowering of man, so that " God " does not remain free at all but at best must become a partner and at worst a tool of the religious man. Even there one may also speak of " revelation," but it would be as well, we repeat, not to be in too big a hurry at least to link biblical revelation with the other variety. But that is merely by the way. What is beyond dispute is that the lordship of God discernible in the biblical revelation consists in this freedom of His, in His permanent freedom to unveil Himself or to veil Himself. God reveals Himself as the Father, that is to say, as the Father of the Son in whom He takes form for our sake. God the Father is God who always, even in taking form in the Son, does not take form, God as the free ground and the free power of His being God in the Son. It would not be revelation within the bounds of the biblical witness if God did not also reveal Himself thus, as the Father. That He does this is the other thing—really other, the same, yet not to be brought under a single denominator as the first—that is meant when we say that He reveals Himself as the Lord. God's fatherhood, too, is God's lordship in His revelation.

3. Revelation in the Bible means the self-unveiling, imparted to men, of the God who by nature cannot be unveiled. Our stress is now on the words " imparted to men." We have asked : Where does revelation come from ? We now ask : Where does it go to ? The revelation attested in the Bible does not just take place in the sphere of man, as might also be said of the theogonies and cosmogonies which are the theme of the witness in the records of, e.g., Babylonian religion. It is also aimed at man, not just mythical man, man in general, but always

a specific man occupying a very specific place, a specific historical place. Part of the concept of the biblically attested revelation is that it is a historical event. Historical does not mean historically demonstrable or historically demonstrated. Hence it does not mean what is usually called " historical " (*historisch*). We should be discarding again all that we have said earlier about the mystery in revelation if we were now to describe any of the events of revelation attested in the Bible as " historical " (*historisch*) ; i.e., apprehensible by a neutral observer or apprehended by such an observer. What a neutral observer could apprehend or may have apprehended of these events was the form of revelation which he did not and could not understand as such. It was an event that took place in the human sphere with all the possibilities of interpretation corresponding to this sphere. In no case was it revelation as such.

Millions in the ancient Orient may have heard the name of Yahweh or seen His temple on some occasion. But this " historical " element was not revelation. Thousands may have seen and heard the Rabbi of Nazareth. But this " historical " element was not revelation. The " historical " element in the resurrection of Christ, the empty tomb as an aspect of the event that might be established, was not revelation. This " historical " element, like all else that is " historical " on this level, is admittedly open to very trivial interpretations too.

As regards the question of the " historical " certainty of the revelation attested in the Bible we can only say that it is ignored in the Bible itself in a way that one can understand only on the premiss that this question is completely alien to it, i.e., obviously and utterly inappropriate to the object of its witness. The neutral observer who understood the events recorded in it as revelation would cease thereby to be a neutral observer. And for the non-neutral, for the man who hears and sees, for the believer, there is and always will be in the form of revelation its mystery too. That is, he has to realise that what can be established here " historically " (*historisch*) is very little or nothing at all or something quite different which is of no importance for the event of revelation. This cannot be what we have in view, then, when we say that the biblical revelation is by definition a historical event. What we mean by this is rather that the Bible always understands what it calls revelation as a concrete relation to concrete men. God in His incomprehensibility and God in the act of His revelation is not the formula of an abstract metaphysics of God, the world, or religion which is supposed to obtain at all times and in all places. It is rather the record of an event that has taken place once and for all, i.e., in a more or less exact and specific time and place. If the time and place are largely obscure for us " historically," if the individual data the Bible offers concerning them are subject to " historical " criticism, this is not surprising in the documents of a time and culture that had no knowledge at all of a " historical " question in our sense, quite apart from the fact that " historical " interest even in the sense that was possible in that age and culture could play no serious role in the composition of these documents, which were meant to be records of revelation. Nevertheless this does not alter the fact that the Bible by what it calls revelation always means a specific event at a specific time and place. Thus, even if according to the standards of modern historiography it does in certain instances, having no interest in this regard, commit " errors " in what it says about the time and place, the important thing is not the more or less " correct " content but the very fact of these statements. This fact that the Bible in both the Old Testament and the New does continually and with notable emphasis make chronological and topographical statements, that it thus wishes in each instance to ascribe a set place in time and space to the divine revelation which it records, that the recorded processes in which revelation comes to men are put in the setting of other events at the same time and in the same place, that ancient Egypt, Assyria and Babylon come into view on the horizon of the experiences of the people of Israel, that Cyrenius the governor of Syria cannot be left out of the Christmas story and Pontius Pilate has an authentic place in the Creed—all this signifies that when the Bible gives an account of revelation it means to narrate history, i.e., not to tell of a relation between God and man that exists generally in every time and place and that is always in process, but to tell of an event that takes place there and only there, then and only then, between God and certain very specific men. The divine self-unveiling which it records, with the holiness which it ascribes to God in this act, is not imparted to man but to such and such men in very definite situations. It is a very specific event and as such it is incomparable and cannot be repeated. To hear the Bible as the witness to God's revelation is in all cases to hear about this history through the Bible.

Hearing history such as that which is an event in the revelation attested in the Bible obviously cannot mean regarding such an event as possible, probable, or even actual on the basis of a general concept of historical (*geschichtlich*) truth. Even histories enacted between God and man do, of course, come under this general concept of history on their human side and therefore in relation to the statements on its temporal form which are so assiduously emphasised in the Bible. But they do not fall under this general concept on their divine side. Hence the " historical " (*historisch*) judgment which presupposes this general concept can in principle relate only to the temporal side. It can neither claim nor deny that at this point or that God has acted on men. To be able to claim or deny this it would have to abandon its presupposition, that general concept, and become a confession of faith or unbelief *vis-à-vis* the biblical witness. No genuinely " historical " verdict can be passed on the singular historicity of the history recorded in the biblical witness. But again—and this is less obvious—hearing a history such as that enacted in the revelation attested in the Bible cannot be dependent on the " historical " assessment of its temporal form. The judgment in virtue of which a biblical story may be regarded with some probability as history in the sense of the general concept of historical truth is not necessarily the judgment of faith *vis-à-vis* the biblical witness. For the judgment may be passed without any understanding of the story in its particularity, i.e., as history between God and man. Again, the opposite judgment need not be that of unbelief, for it may involve an understanding of the story in its particularity, i.e., as history between God and man. The question which decides hearing or non-hearing of the biblical history cannot be the question of its general historicity ; it can only be that of its special historicity.

Thus the judgment that a biblical story is to be regarded either as a whole or in part as saga or legend does not have to be an attack on the substance of the biblical witness. All that might be said is that according to the standards by which " historical " truth is usually measured elsewhere or generally, this story is one that to some degree eludes any sure declaration that it happened as the narrative says. Saga or legend can only denote the more or less intrusive part of the story-teller or story-tellers in the story told. There is no story in which we do not have to reckon with this aspect, and therefore with elements of saga or legend according to the general concept of " historical " truth. This applies also to the stories told in the Bible. Otherwise they would have to be without temporal form. Yet this fundamental uncertainty in general historicity, and therefore the positive judgment that here and there saga or legend is actually present, does not have to be an attack on the substance of the biblical testimony. For (1) this judgment can in any case concern and contest only the general historicity of a biblical record, (2) even in the clearest instance it is by nature only a judgment of probability, and (3) even saga or legend is in any case meant to be history and can thus be heard as a communication of history irrespective of the " historical " judgment. So long as this is so, the question of the particular historicity of the story at issue is at least not answered negatively.

The situation changes when the category of myth is introduced. The verdict that a biblical story is to be understood as a myth is necessarily an attack on the substance of the biblical witness. This is because " myth " does not intend to be history but only pretends to be such. Myth uses narrative form to expound what purports to be always and everywhere true. It is an exposition of certain basic relationships of human existence, found in every time and place, in their connexions to their own origins and conditions in the natural and historical cosmos, or in the deity. These are given narrative form on the assumption that man knows all these things and can present them thus or thus, that he controls them, that in the last resort they are his things. Myth (cf. for what follows Eduard Thurneysen, " Christus und die Kirche," *Z.d.Z.*, 1930, esp. p. 189 f.) does not impute any exclusive character to the event narrated by it—in other words : " What myth narrates as a fact may happen in any time or place. It is not a unique event but one that can be repeated. . . . But what can be repeated and can happen over and over again, even though it may be surprising, is a general possibility akin to natural occurrence. What happens in this way rests on nothing other than the assumption that the man to whom the revelation narrated in myth is imparted stands ultimately in an original and natural relation and connexion, hidden, of course, but present potentially at least everywhere, to the final ground of his existence, to his God. In the events narrated in myth this latent possibility becomes, so to speak, active. In ever new theophanies man experiences the ground of the world as present and himself as connected to it. But this means that there is here an ultimate identity between God and man. There is no thought of a profound and final distinction. What myth, then, recounts as a unique happening is not unique at all ; it is the unchanging, final, basic relation which, evoked by all kinds of wizardry and magic, is again lived through and experienced and will be continually lived through and experienced."

Joyous was it years ago—
So eagerly the spirit strives
To seek and come to know
How nature, in creating, lives.
And 'tis the eternally One
That is manifold revealed.
Small the great and great the small,
Each according to its kind ;
Ever changing, standing fast,
Near and far and far and near,
Forming thus and then transforming—
To marvel am I here.

(Goethe, *Parabase*, Jub. Edn., Vol. II, p. 246).

This is the birth of myth. (The only distinction between myth and speculation proper is that in speculation the narrative is stripped off again like a garment that has become too tight, so that what is presented as fact in myth is now elevated to the sphere of pure idea or concept, and the present and acknowledged wealth of the origins and relations of human existence is thus expressed in its " in and for itself." Myth is the preparatory form of speculation and speculation is the revealed essence of myth.) To be sure, one cannot prevent a historian from applying the category of myth to some of the events recorded in the Bible. One might ask, of course, whether the supposed myths have really been found in the text of the Bible and not somewhere behind the text, whether the context in which the passage concerned finds its point has not been dissolved, whether what it says in the context has not been ignored on the assumption that so-called " sources " of a special character and independent content underlie the biblical text, and whether certain parts of the biblical text have not been combined with parts of non-biblical texts which might perhaps be claimed as mythical. In a word, one might ask whether the verdict " myth " as applied to the biblical texts is not even from the purely " historical " standpoint a mistaken verdict because it can perhaps be made only when there is a failure to hear what the real biblical texts are trying to say and do say if we read them as we actually have them, in their narrower and broader context, as biblical texts. But even if this objection does not seem to make sense, the historian who resolves on this verdict must realise at least that if this verdict is possible for him he has as it were read the Bible outside the Christian Church, that he is not asking about revelation but about something else, perhaps myth or speculation, that perhaps he himself is quite unaware or forgetful of the fact that there is such a thing as revelation, that perhaps he himself is aware, or at this moment aware, of no more than man's general ability to control the origins and relations of his existence by fable or thought or some other means, because these are in fact his own things. It is really quite natural that an age whose thought, feeling and action are so highly mythical as the so-called modern period that culminates in the Enlightenment (including Idealism and Romanticism) should seek myth in the Bible too— and find it. Historicism is " the self-understanding of the spirit in so far as its own achievements in history are concerned " (E. Troeltsch, *Ges. Schriften*, Vol. III, 1922, p. 104). Good ! For the person who does not ask about revelation there is nothing left, of course, but to ask about myth, and the man who asks about myth because he must, because myth is his own last word, will not be restrained by the objection that even a historian might feel from seeking myth in the Bible too, and really finding it there, and perhaps, strictly speaking, finding a little of it in every part of the Bible. We can only declare that the interpretation of the Bible as the witness to revelation and the interpretation of the Bible as the witness to myth are mutually exclusive. The category of saga, the questioning of the general historicity of the biblical narratives, is not an attack on the substance of the Bible as witness, but the category of myth is, for myth does not just question but fundamentally denies the history as such, and therefore the special historicity of the biblical records, and revelation regarded as myth would not be a historical event but a supposed non-spatial and timeless truth, i.e., a creation of man.

The Bible lays such extraordinary stress on the historicity of the revelation recorded by it because by revelation it does not mean a creation of man. It says so emphatically that revelation was imparted to these men in these situations because it is describing it thereby as an impartation to men. This is what the use of the concept of myth rather than saga in relation to the Bible overlooks or denies. The revelations attested in the Bible do not purport to be manifestations of a universal or an idea which are special by nature but which can then be comfortably compared with the idea and understood and evaluated in their particularity.

Because this is not the case, the philosophy of religion of the Enlightenment from Lessing by way of Kant and Herder to Fichte and Hegel, with its intolerable distinction between the eternal content and the historical " vehicle," can only be described as the nadir of the modern misunderstanding of the Bible.

The revelation attested in the Bible purports to be a historical event. In this regard, if we bring in the concept of history in explanation, our only possible *tertium comparationis* can be the fact that in revelation as in history the reference is to a definite event which is different from every other event and which is thus incomparable and cannot be repeated. If with the Enlightenment we were to regard the event as again the mere exponent of some general occurrence, a special case under a rule, or the realisation of a general possibility ; if history were to be understood as a framework within which there might also be something like revelation, then at this point we should have to reject the concept of historicity no less emphatically than that of myth. In relation to revelation the term historical can only denote event as a fact over which there is no court by reference to which it may be regarded as a fact, as this particular fact. It is thus that revelation is imparted to man according to the Bible, and this is why the Bible lays such stress on chronology, topography and contemporary world history, i.e., on the contingency and uniqueness of the revelations recorded by it. In doing this it is simply saying that revelation comes vertically from heaven. It befalls man with the same contingency with which, living in this specific place at this specific time and in these specific circumstances he is this specific man at this specific stage of his inner and outer life, the only difference being that this historical contingency of his can still be surveyed and explained in all possible dimensions. The statement : *Individuum est ineffabile*, can indeed be made but characteristically it cannot be proved, whereas revelation is the *ineffabile* which encounters and reaches man and proves itself to be such. From this standpoint, then, we finally achieve full clarity regarding what was said in 1. and 2. about the unveiling and veiling of God in His revelation. These two relationships in which the Bible regards God as existing cannot be interpreted as the elements of a present and known truth and reality that must be established by a general necessity of thought. Otherwise, even if we were not ready to admit it, we should still be regarding the biblical revelation as a myth. The fact that the *Deus revelatus* is also the *Deus absconditus* and the *Deus absconditus* the *Deus revelatus*, that the Father glorifies the Son and the Son the Father, is not self-evident, i.e., intelligible *per se*, as the immanent dialectic of this or that sphere of human life, or perhaps a dialectic like the Hegelian In itself and For itself, is intelligible *per se*, i.e., resolvable into a third. If the goodness and holiness of God are neither experiences we can manufacture nor concepts we can form for ourselves but divine modes of being to which human experiences and concepts can at least respond, then their conjunction, their dialectic, in which both are only what they are, is certainly not a dialectic which we can know, i.e., achieve for ourselves, but one which we can only ascertain and acknowledge as actually taking place. And this actual occurrence, this being ascertained and acknowledged, is the historicity of revelation. By this concept we mean that in the Bible revelation is a matter of impartation, of God's being revealed, by which the existence of specific men in specific situations has been singled out in the sense that their experiences and concepts, even though they cannot grasp God in His unveiling and God in His veiling and God in the dialectic of unveiling and veiling, can at least follow Him and respond to Him.

The thing to note at this third point is the element of vocation in the biblical concept of revelation. We again find agreement between the Old Testament and the New in their view that man can in no wise produce revelation for himself. We have referred already to the priests of Baal on Carmel who in their attempts to invoke God show precisely how man has no access to Yahweh. The so-called false prophets of the Old Testament are obviously viewed in the same way as proclaimers of a self-snatched revelation which for that very reason is no revelation at all. Similarly in the New Testament (e.g., Mk. 10[17f.] ; Lk. 9[57f.]) those who want to win life or follow Jesus in their own strength are shown to be the very people who are unable to do it. On the other hand the promise given to Abraham is in the first instance for Abraham himself as well as Sarah (Gen. 17[17]) a matter of mirth, while Jacob-Israel (quite apart from other traits that are found objectionable to-day) is in Gen. 32[22f.] a fighter, and indeed a victorious fighter, against God, and the resistance to calling seen in a Moses, Isaiah, Jeremiah or Jonah seems to be of the very essence of the genuine prophet. The great New Testament example of this is naturally the calling of Saul to be Paul. And even in relation to Peter the view of the tradition is perhaps that his true calling is by the Risen Lord, i.e., after his denial of Jesus. To him in particular it is most emphatically said that flesh and blood have not revealed it (the divine sonship of Christ) to him. It would naturally be foolish to see in all this a kind of negative disposition of the men concerned towards revelation. In many callings this resistance is not especially stressed, though neither is there in any instance a preparation for the call. What the Bible is trying to say here is obviously that there is no disposition in man at all. Calling is a non-derivative fact, or derivative only from election. The prophets and apostles are not portrayed as heroes. They stand there in their utter humanity. Yet for all that they have as it were come from heaven as prophets and apostles. They are no less astonishing to themselves than to those around them. They are set in an office which cannot be explained by their existence and they bear a " burden " which they have not taken up themselves but which has been laid on their shoulders. In the New Testament the puzzle or the solution of the puzzle of this inconceivably factual presence of real men at God's revelation is expressed by the concept of πνεῦμα. As by unveiling we ultimately say no other than Easter, and as by veiling, with an unavoidable backward glance at the source of revelation, we say no other than Good Friday, so now, looking forward to the man to whom and for whom the revelation becomes event, to the threshold over which revelation crosses into history, we say no other than Pentecost, the outpouring of the Holy Ghost. The πνεῦμα is the miracle of the presence of real men at God's revelation. At Pentecost we are not dealing with anything other than the event of Good Friday and Easter. But here it is for real men, for such human men as the apostles according to the way they are depicted in the New Testament. The event of Good Friday and Easter can and does concern them, come home to them, call them. Not just Jesus Christ is there, but Jesus Christ in the Church of Jesus Christ, in faith in Jesus Christ. This is the specific feature of Pentecost and the Spirit in the New Testament. We had Pentecost in view when we called revelation an event that from man's standpoint has dropped down vertically from heaven. How else can we put it if we are to keep close to this text and perhaps to all the New Testament texts bearing on the " Spirit of God " or the " Spirit of Christ." The miracle that we cannot stress too strongly corresponds simply on the one side to the mystery of God from which revelation comes forth and by which it is always invested and then on the other side to the paradox that in revelation God really does come forth out of His mystery. This is how it is with God's being revealed.

Without God's being historically revealed in this way, revelation would not be revelation. God's being revealed makes it a link between God and man, an effective encounter between God and man. But it is God's own being revealed that makes it this. In this respect too, with reference to the goal, our statement that God reveals Himself as the Lord is confirmed. The fact that God can do what the biblical witnesses ascribe to him, namely, not just take form and not just remain free in this form, but also in this form and freedom of His become God to specific men, eternity in a moment, this is the third meaning of His lordship in His revelation. There is talk of revelation outside the Bible too, and we have no reason to say that this is absolutely impossible. But there is every reason to put the third question whether the concept of revelation presupposed in such talk takes into account this element of God's being revealed as an act of God Himself, this understanding of the appropriation of revelation as an absolute assignment irrespective of any disposition, or whether in these other places where people think they should accept the attestation of revelation the decisively important role is not played rather by perhaps the positive or perhaps (as in Buddhism) the negative disposition of man, whether what is called revelation here would not better be described as myth because the decisive point is really man's debate with himself. But we are not stressing these side-issues. Our positive concern is that in the biblical witness the lordship of God in this third sense is one of the decisive marks of revelation. God reveals Himself as the Spirit, not as any spirit, not as the basis of man's spiritual life which we can discover and awaken, but as the Spirit of the Father and the Son, and therefore the same one God, but the same one God in this way too, namely, in this unity, indeed, this self-disclosing unity, disclosing itself to men, of the Father and the Son. The fact that He does this ; this third thing which does not follow self-evidently from the first and the second, just as there is nothing at all self-evident in their being and being together either ; the fact that there is this being revealed of the Father and the Son, this is what we have in mind when we say that He reveals Himself as the Lord. The fact that according to Jn. 4²⁴ God is Spirit is also God's lordship in His revelation.

We look back and draw to a close. We have been asking about the root of the doctrine of the Trinity, its root in revelation, not in any revelation, not in a general concept of revelation, but in the concept of revelation taken from the Bible. We have been asking whether revelation must be understood as the ground of the doctrine of the Trinity, whether the doctrine of the Trinity must be understood as having grown out of this soil. And after a side-glance at the passages in the biblical witness which directly reflect the doctrine of the Trinity, we have enquired what revelation means in the Bible, asking, but asking concretely with reference to the biblical texts, whether the statement that God reveals Himself as the Lord really has a threefold meaning and yet a simple content in these texts. If we have been right to emphasise in the biblical witness to revelation the three elements of unveiling, veiling and impartation, or form, freedom and historicity, or Easter, Good Friday and Pentecost, or Son, Father and Spirit ; if we have rightly characterised these elements in detail ; if we have set them in a right relation to one another ; if our threefold conclusion that God reveals Himself as the Lord is not, then, an illicit move but a genuine finding ; if in this statement we have really said the same thing three times in three indissolubly different ways, then we may now conclude that revelation must indeed be understood as the root or ground of the doctrine of the Trinity. As its root or ground, we say. The doctrine of the Trinity has not yet encountered us directly. Even in the verses which sound trinitarian the characteristic elements of the doctrine itself are missing. Our concepts of unimpaired unity and unimpaired distinction, the concept of the one essence of God and of the three persons or modes of being (*Seinsweisen*) to be distinguished in this essence, and finally the polemical assertion, which we touched on only briefly, that God's triunity is to be found not merely in His revelation but, because in His revelation, in God Himself and in Himself too, so that the Trinity is to be understood as " immanent " and not just " economic "—none of this is directly biblical, i.e., explicitly stated in the Bible ; it is Church doctrine. We have established no more than that the biblical doctrine of revelation is implicitly, and in some passages explicitly, a pointer to the doctrine of the Trinity. In its basic outline it must be interpreted as also an outline of the doctrine of the Trinity. If the doctrine of the Trinity can be established and developed as such, we have to say that in respect of revelation there is a genuine and necessary connexion with the doctrine of the Trinity. The doctrine of the Trinity with its implications, distinctions and synopses is concerned with a problem that is really and very centrally posed by the biblical witness to revelation. It is in fact exegesis of this text. It is not, as we may now say already, an arbitrarily contrived speculation whose object lies elsewhere than in the Bible. Any child knows that it uses some of the philosophoumena of declining pagan antiquity. But according to our findings this cannot mean that it is a non-Church construct, i.e., one which was not necessary as such in the Church, one which did not arise in its day on the basis of Scripture, of the faith in God's revelation to which Scripture gave rise, a doctrine dealing merely with a theme of pagan antiquity. On the contrary, its statements may be regarded as indirectly, though not directly, identical with those of the biblical witness to revelation. It is Church exegesis, i.e., it exegetes this text, the witness to revelation which is accepted as such in the Church. When we come to expound it in detail as Church exegesis of this text, we must never cease to refer back to this biblical text itself with the question whether and how far we are on the right track in our treatment. The fact that it is Church exegesis, that the theses of the doctrine of the Trinity stand in relation to biblical revelation as directly as only an answer can stand in relation to a question, should be provisionally guaranteed by the proof which we have already offered.

3. *VESTIGIUM TRINITATIS*

Before we turn to the actual development of the doctrine of the Trinity in the final section, a critical discussion is required in respect of the findings we have reached thus far. We have asked about the root of the doctrine of the Trinity. In trying to analyse the biblical concept of revelation, we have arrived at the thesis that this analysis reduced to its simplest form, the threefold yet single lordship of God as Father, Son and Spirit, is the root of the doctrine of the Trinity. In other words the biblical concept of revelation is itself the root of the doctrine of the Trinity. The doctrine of the Trinity is simply a development of the knowledge that Jesus is the Christ or the Lord. When we say that the doctrine of the Trinity grows from this root we are saying critically and polemically that it does not stem from any other root. It is the fact that it does not stem from any other root which we must now consider specifically. The problem of the *vestigium trinitatis* which is posed by the history of the doctrine of the Trinity gives us cause to do this. This expression seems to come from Augustine and it means an analogue of the Trinity, of the trinitarian God of Christian revelation, in some creaturely reality distinct from Him, a creaturely reality which is not a form assumed by God in His revelation, but which quite apart from God's revelation manifests in its own structure by creation a certain similarity to the structure of the trinitarian concept of God, so that it may be regarded as an image of the trinitarian God Himself.

Augustine deals with the subject in, e.g., *Conf.* XIII, 11, 12 ; *De civ. Dei*, XI, 24 f., and especially *De trin.*, IX–XI. Instructive for a general understanding of the problem as the fathers and School-men saw it is *De trin.*, VI, 10 : *Oportet igitur, ut creatorem per ea quae facta sunt intellectum conspicientes, trinitatem intelligamus, cuius in creatura, quomodo dignum est, apparet vestigium. In illa enim trinitate summa origo est rerum omnium et perfectissima pulchritudo et beatissima delectatio. . . . Qui videt hoc vel ex parte, vel per speculum et in aenigmate, gaudeat cognoscens Deum et sicut Deum honoret et gratias agat : qui autem non videt, tendat per pietatem ad videndum.*

It must be sharply stressed that our concern here is (unfortunately) not with the distinction imparted to a creaturely reality in revelation, in virtue of which a man, an angel, a natural or historical event, human words or actions, and supremely, finally, yet also as the epitome of all the creatures thus distinguished, the *humanitas Christi*, becomes a divine organ or instrument or medium. We might, of course, call this, and we can certainly call the form that God assumes in His unveiling as the Son or Word, the *vestigium trinitatis*. But this is not what was meant in the development and use of the concept. The concern here was with an essential trinitarian disposition supposedly immanent in some created realities quite apart from their possible conscription by God's revelation. It was with a genuine *analogia entis*, with traces of the trinitarian Creator God in being as such, in its pure createdness. If it be acknowledged that there are *vestigia trinitatis* in

this second sense then the question obviously arises—and this is why
we must discuss the matter in the present context—whether we do
not have to assume a second root of the doctrine of the Trinity alongside the one we have indicated in the previous sub-section. The
vestigium trinitatis would patently have to be considered as a second
root of this kind if there is such a thing in the second sense of the term.
We should then have to ask whether the development of the doctrine
of the Trinity must not also, at least, be traced back to the insight
into these traces of the Trinity that are present and perceptible
in the created world quite apart from the biblical revelation. And if
this question be admitted, then the further question can hardly be
avoided : Which of the two roots of the doctrine of the Trinity that
both call for consideration is the true and primary root, and which is a
secondary " runner " ? But then we should also have to allow the
question whether the derivation of the doctrine of the Trinity from
the biblical revelation is not just the later confirmation of a knowledge
of God which can be won from His revelation in creation quite apart
from the biblical revelation. And then it is difficult to omit the final
question whether these *vestigia* on which the doctrine of the Trinity
is really based are in fact to be regarded as the *vestigia* of a Creator
God transcending the world and not as determinations of the cosmos
which must be viewed as strictly immanent and, because the cosmos
is man's cosmos, as determinations of man's existence ; whether we
should not then erase the concept of natural revelation as well as
biblical revelation and adjudge the doctrine of the Trinity to be a
bold attempt on man's part to understand the world and ultimately
himself, i.e., adjudge it to be a myth. The problem which is posed
when the presence and knowability of these *vestigia trinitatis* are
asserted is actually, then, of the greatest importance, not only for the
question of the root of the doctrine of the Trinity, but also for that of
revelation, of the grounding of theology in revelation alone, and finally
even for that of the meaning and possibility of theology as distinct from
mere cosmology or anthropology.

The question is whether these *vestigia trinitatis*, in virtue of the conclusions
that are to be drawn from their acknowledgment even if only in the form of the list
of questions mentioned, do not compel us to pass over first to the easy double track
of " revelation " and " primal revelation " (P. Althaus) and then very quickly
from this half-measure to the genuine Roman Catholic theology of the *analogia
entis*. And then would they not bring to our attention at the right moment the
fact that theology would do well to desist from the impossible attempt to understand itself as theology and to acquiesce in being the only thing it can be at root,
namely, part of man's understanding of the world and himself, in the development
of which the concept " God," like a superfluous x in the numerator and denominator, should now be cancelled out to simplify the counting on both sides, since
with or without the concept the only real concern is man, or, in this case, man's
own triunity. But the question can, of course, be put in a very different way : Do

we not have in this idea of the *vestigium trinitatis* an ancient Trojan horse which one day (for the sake of *pulchritudo* and *delectatio*, to echo Augustine) was unsuspectingly allowed entry into the theological Ilium, and in whose belly—so much more alert have certain experiences made us since Augustine's day—we can hear a threatening clank, so that we have every cause to execute a defensive movement—perhaps there is no more we can do here—by declaring, perhaps only very naively, that we do not want to have anything to do with it ?

To acquaint ourselves first with the *quaestio facti*, the question what can be and has been in mind concretely when there is reference to *vestigia trinitatis*, let us subdivide into phenomena from nature, from culture, from history, from religion, and from the life of the soul.

Since there can be no possibility of any kind of systematic completeness, we may give some typical examples from each of the five spheres. (For what follows cf. H. Bavinck, *Geref. Dogmatiek*, 1918, Vol. 2, p. 332 f.)

1. Nature. Anselm of Canterbury compares Father, Son and Spirit in the Trinity to the existence and mutual relation of spring, stream and lake, which as a united whole might be called the Nile. Not just the united whole, however, but the spring, stream and lake individually are also the Nile. Yet the spring is not the stream, the stream is not the lake, and the lake is not the spring, while on the other hand there are not three Niles but only one. The one whole Nile is spring, stream, and lake. It is just as difficult or impossible as in the case of the persons of the Trinity to say what the common concept is under which all three fall. But it is equally clear in this case that the spring does not derive from the stream or the lake, that the stream does not derive from the lake but the spring, and the lake derives from both the spring and the stream (*Ep. de incarn. verbi, c.* 13). Luther, in his Table Talk at least, seems to be fond of the principle that *in omnibus creaturis licet invenire et cernere trinitatem istam esse expressam,* and he illustrates it by examples from the sun, water, the stars, plants, etc. A concise account of one of these illustrations from natural phenomena is to the effect that " in all creatures there is and may be seen an intimation of the Holy Trinity. First their nature signifies the omnipotence of God the Father, then their figure and form signifies the wisdom of the Son and thirdly their usefulness and power is a sign of the Holy Ghost, and therefore that God is present in all creatures, even in the tiniest little leaf and poppy seedlet " (*W.A., Ti.,* 1, 395 f.). Let it suffice us to mention by way of example that weight, number and measure, or the solid, fluid and gaseous states, or the three dimensions of solids, or the primary colours of yellow, red and blue, or the harmony of the key-note, third and fifth, have all been brought into connexion with the Trinity.

2. Culture. Teachers, soldiers and producers in society, epic, lyric and drama in poetry, and the three basic disciplines of mediaeval scholarship are all supposed to be *vestigia trinitatis* in this sphere. Luther is again our spokesman : " The Father in divine things is *Grammatica*, for He giveth the Word and is the fountainhead from which, if one may so speak, floweth good, excellent, pure speech. The Son is *Dialectica* ; for He giveth the arrangement whereby a thing should be set in good order of succession so that conclusion and consecution be certain. But the Holy Ghost is *Rhetorica*, the orator, for He excellently sustaineth, bloweth, and impelleth, maketh quick and powerful, so that an impression is made and hearts are taken " (*W.A. Ti.,* 1, 564).

3. History. To this sphere belongs a doctrine which constantly recurs in Church history, that of the three kingdoms which are supposed to be seen in the Old Testament age, the New Testament age, and the age of the Christian Church, or, with an eschatological thrust and in combination with the three great apostolic

figures, (1) the Petrine age, the past, which is the kingdom of fear, i.e., of the Father, (2) the Pauline age, the present, which is the kingdom of truth, i.e., of the Son, and (3) the Johannine age, the future, which is the kingdom of love, i.e., of the Spirit. In this connexion the Holy Spirit became the special catch-word of all the so-called fanatical, or, better, the chiliastic parties in the Church ; one might almost say He became the specifically non-Church or anti-Church God, so that it could even happen that, e.g., Luther, meeting this one-sided appeal, sometimes felt he had to be equally one-sided in His appeal to the Word, and " spiritualistic " came to be a term specifically used in criticism of everything fanatical. Moeller van den Bruck (*Das dritte Reich*, 2nd edn., 1926, p. 13) has called the idea of the third kingdom " a cosmological concept " which " reaches beyond reality." " It is no accident that the ideas which arise already with the concept, being ideologically unmasked from the very outset . . . with the name of the third kingdom, are strangely nebulous, sentimental and vague, and completely other-worldly." Moeller v. d. Bruck, as is well-known, wanted " to rescue (the concept) from the world of illusion and relate it entirely to the political sphere." But even in this secularisation he retained something of the feeling of the early and mediaeval philosophy of the historical *vestigium trinitatis* as it lived on—to mention only a single name—in Joachim of Fiore.

4. Religion. The Middle Ages had already referred in this connexion to the subjective religious consciousness : *cogitatio, meditatio, contemplatio,* or *fides, ratio, contemplatio,* or the *via purgativa, illuminativa* and *intuitiva* of mysticism influenced by the Areopagite, whose nature and order reflected the Trinity. Alongside this one may set the statement of Wobbermin that Christian trinitarian monotheism brings the basic conviction of all religious belief to fruition in so far as the latter always includes three motifs that come to expression in the sense of religious dependence, the sense of religious security and the sense of religious longing (*Wesen und Wahrheit des Christentums,* 1925, p. 432). Yet it was not the modern age with its interest in the history of religion but rather the older theology, as is clear from J. Gerhard, *Loci,* 1610, *L.,* 3, 30, which was the first to note that the number three, especially in the Godhead, played an outstanding role in the objective phenomena of religion too, including non-Christian religion. We single out the fact that the ancient Babylonians had two triads of gods, a cosmic : Anu, Enlil and Ea (the gods of heaven, earth and water) and then a superior and sidereal triad : Shamash, Sin and Ishtar (sun, moon and the planet Venus). The ancient Egyptians also had the divine family of Osiris with his spouse Isis and their son Horus, and in a similar relationship the ancient Canan-ites, Syrians and Carthaginians knew a supreme God, then the *magna mater* later worshipped also under the name Cybele, and the Son of God known, e.g., as Attis or Adonis, while again, presumably in a similar relationship, ancient Etruscan Rome had the so-called Capitoline triad, *Jupiter optimus maximus, Juno regina* and *Minerva.* Later Brahmanism has the so-called Trimurti : the mystical unity of Brahma, who brings forth the world, Vishnu, who upholds it, and Siva (or Rudra), who destroys it. To this day the confession of a convert to Buddhism runs : " I take my refuge in Buddha, I take my refuge in Dhamma, I take my refuge in Sangha " (the " three jewels "), Buddha denoting personality, Dhamma teaching and Sangha the community of the founder of the religion.

5. The Human Soul. The reference here according to Augustine is to the three powers of the soul, *mens* the power of inward apprehension, *notitia* the power of outward apprehension, and *amor* the power to relate the one to the other and thus to complete apprehension. But the reference might also be to the three corresponding elements in the actual process of consciousness, *memoria,* i.e., the underlying act of subjective and objectiveness consciousness generally and intrinsically as pure form, *intellectus,* i.e., the consummation in thought of a

subjective or objective conception in a definite image, and *voluntas*, i.e., the affirmation of this image and also the return of the image to pure consciousness. Thus it is the same *vestigium* in different words and not another one when Augustine makes the distinction : *amans, id quod amatur, amor*. Let us hear Augustine himself in a particularly pregnant formulation of his thought : *sine ulla phantasiarum vel phantasmatum imaginatione ludificatoria mihi esse me, idque nosse et amare certissimum est. . . . Quid si falleris ? Si enim fallor, sum. Nam qui non est, utique nec falli potest. . . . Consequens est autem, ut etiam in eo quod me novi nosse, non fallor. Eaque duo cum amo . . . quiddam tertium . . . eis . . . adiungo (De civ. Dei*, XI, 26). What Augustine thought he saw in this structure of human consciousness was more the *imago Dei* or *trinitatis* than a mere *vestigium*. But this theory of the *vestigium* above all others made an impression and formed a school throughout the centuries. We find it in all sorts of modifications, e.g., in Anselm (*Monol.*, 67 and *passim*), Peter Lombard (*Sent.* I, *dist.*, 3), Thomas Aquinas (*S. theol.*, I, *qu.* 45, *art.* 7), Bonaventura (*Breviloq.*, II, *c.* 12), in the Reformation period Melanchthon (*Enarr. Symb. Nic.*, 1550, *C.R.*, 23, 235 ; *Loci*, 1559, *C.R.*, 21, 615, etc.), among the Reformed B. Keckermann (*Syst. S. S. Theol.*, 1611, p. 20 f.), in the Enlightenment Lessing's *Education of the Human Race*, § 73, in the 19th century A. Twesten (*Dogm. d. ev.-luth. Kirche*, Vol. 2, 1837, p. 194 f.), more recently none other than A. Schlatter : " Since we are in possession of our image, there constantly arises in us a kind of triunity ; to the person who knows there comes the one known, yet not in such a way that the two stand over against one another, but there appears at once the third, the person who knows himself in the one known " (*Das chr. Dogma*, 2nd edn., 1923, p. 24). Equally trinitarian for him is the order of our volition : " We have a direct volition, an elective volition, and the union of the two, the volition elected by us, which has within it the power to act " (*op. cit.*, p. 148). We need only refer to the relation which results from this to Schelling's triad of subject, object and subject-object and to Hegel's " in itself " of the subjective spirit as thesis. " for itself " of the objective spirit as antithesis, and " in and for itself " of the absolute spirit as synthesis. We may quietly state that these very climaxes of Idealist philosophy would be quite unthinkable except against the background of Christian dogmatics even if they were not just new variations on Augustine's proof of the Trinity. It is clear that the logico-grammatical scheme of subject, object and predicate would also belong to this context if it were our real key to the doctrine of the Trinity. And it is equally clear that the mediaeval construct of the religious consciousness, and that of Wobbermin too, must also be seen in this context as a variation on the general Augustinian argument from consciousness.

What are we to say to all this material ? What are we to make of it ? The first step is naturally to try to think of it in the sense in which it was originally intended, namely, as an interesting, edifying, instructive and helpful hint towards understanding the Christian doctrine, not to be overrated, not to be used as a proof in the strict sense, because we need to know and believe the Trinity already if we are really to perceive its *vestigia* as such in the microcosm and the macrocosm, but still to be valued as supplementary and non-obligatory illustrations of the Christian Credo which are to be received with gratitude.

Irenaeus already sounded the warning that we have not to understand *Deum ex factis, sed ea quae facta sunt, ex Deo (C. o. h.*, II, 25, 1). Augustine himself expressly added to his exhortation that man should learn to see the Trinity in himself the further admonition : *cum invenerit in his aliquid et dixerit, non iam se putet invenisse illud, quod supra ista est incommutabile (Conf.,* XIII, 11). Peter Lombard, too, obviously draws back : *Non enim per creaturarum contemplationem sufficiens notitia trinitatis potest haberi vel potuit sine doctrinae vel interioris inspirationis revelatione. . . . Adiuvamur tamen in fide invisibilium per ea quae facta sunt (Sent.,* I, *dist.* 3 F), and he refers expressly to the *dissimilitudines* which are to be found even in the Augustinian *similitudo. Trinitate posita, congruunt hujusmodi rationes ; non tamen ita, quod per has rationes sufficienter probetur trinitas personarum* (Thomas Aquinas, *S. th.,* I, *qu.* 32, *art.* 1). Similarly Luther's statements on the matter are certainly not to be regarded as a theological basis but simply as theological table-talk.

We need not regard the achievements of the older theology at this point as just an idle game, no matter how trifling much of what is adduced may undoubtedly seem to be.

The other impression we undeniably get from the whole material is that in varying degrees there must be " something in " the connexion between the Trinity and all the " trinities " to which reference is made here. Why should there not be something in it ? The only question is what. Theology and the Church, and even the Bible itself, speak no other language than that of this world which is shaped in form and content by the creaturely nature of the world and also conditioned by the limitations of humanity : the language in which man as he is, as sinful and corrupt man, wrestles with the world as it encounters him and as he sees and tries to understand it. The Bible, the Church and theology undoubtedly speak this language on the presupposition that there might be something in it, namely, that in this language God's revelation might be referred to, witness might be given, God's Word might be proclaimed, dogma might be formulated and declared. The only question is whether this possibility is to be understood as that of the language and consequently of the world or man, or whether it is to be regarded as a venture which is, as it were, ascribed to the language, and consequently to the world or man, from without, so that it is not really the possibility of the language, the world, or man, but the possibility of revelation, if in the form of concepts and ideas that exist elsewhere and independently, in correspondence with the created world and the capacity of man as he attempts an understanding of this world, we really come to speak of revelation and therefore of the Trinity, of the remission of sins and eternal life, i.e., of things for which man's speech as such has no aptitude whatever. Now it cannot be said that the discoverers of *vestigia trinitatis* have made this distinction. As we make it, we are brought back to a realisation that the true *vestigium trinitatis* is the form assumed by God in revelation. So far as I can see, this was not the view of the Fathers and Schoolmen when they spoke of the *vestigium trinitatis.*

But with the help of this distinction one can understand how they came on the one hand to affirm the idea of the apprehensibility of the *vestigium trinitatis* and on the other hand to bracket it again at once with the declaration that there can be true apprehension of it only on the presupposition of revelation, *trinitate posita*. They might actually have meant something very different from what they seemed to be saying. They were in search of language for the mystery of God which was known to them by revelation, which, as they constantly repeated, was known to them only by revelation, and which could be made known to all men only by revelation. In this search for language, the first materials they encountered apart from those offered by the Bible consisted, as is known, in a number of applicable abstract categories from the philosophy of the day.

Strictly speaking the term *trinitas* as such would have to be regarded as a *vestigium trinitatis* found in the field of logic. And F. Diekamp, *Kathol. Dogm.*, Vol. I, 6th edn., 1930, p. 260, rightly points out that the analogies adduced by the Fathers are in the long run only further expositions and multiplications of the biblical terms Father, Son, and Spirit, which are already analogical.

The dogma was then formulated in this biblico-philosophical language. But the mystery of revelation which still lived on in the formulated dogma made a further and even more urgent demand for language now that a correct understanding had been decided. And it was now found for the first time, not that the language could grasp the revelation, but that revelation, the very revelation correctly and normatively understood in the formulated dogma, could grasp the language, i.e., that on the basis of revelation enough elements could be found in the familiar language used by all to be able to speak about revelation, not exhaustively or appropriately or correctly, but still to some extent intelligibly and perspicuously, elements which could be employed with some prospect of success to denote certain factors and relations in what can be said about revelation. When men wanted to talk about the Father, Son, and Spirit, or *unitas in trinitate* and *trinitas in unitate*, they opened their eyes and ears and found they could and should venture to refer, with this end in view, to spring, stream and lake, or weight, number and measure, or *mens, notitia* and *amor*, not because these things were in and of themselves suitable for the purpose but because they were adapted to be appropriated or, as it were, commandeered as images of the Trinity, as ways of speaking about the Trinity, because men who knew God's revelation in Scripture thought they might be given the power to say what in and of themselves they naturally do not say and cannot say. There is " nothing in it " if we try to say that source, stream and lake or *esse, nosse* and *velle* are related to one another in the same way as Father, Son and Spirit. But there is " something in it " if we say that Father,

Son and Spirit are related in the same way as source, stream and lake. Men were sure of the Trinity but they were not sure of the language of the world in relation to the Trinity. Nevertheless, they had to speak about the Trinity in this language. They thus had to claim it for the Trinity, namely, for witness to the Trinity. What happened, then, was not that they tried to explain the Trinity by the world but on the contrary that they tried to explain the world by the Trinity in order to be able to speak about the Trinity in this world. It was not a matter of apologetics but of polemics, not of demonstrating the possibility of revelation in the world of human reason but of establishing the actual possibilities of the world of human reason as the scene of revelation. *Vestigia trinitatis in creatura*, they said, but perhaps what they really had in mind was *vestigia creaturae in trinitate*—naturally in the Trinity of self-revelation, in the Trinity inasmuch as it takes creaturely form. They did not believe that the Trinity is immanent in things and that things have the capability of reflecting the Trinity. On this side everything is admittedly incomplete and questionable and dependent on preceding revelation. But they did have confidence that the Trinity can reflect itself in things, and all the more or less felicitous discoveries of *vestigia* were an expression of this confidence, not of confidence in the capacity of reason for revelation but of confidence in the power of revelation over reason. In this sense one may say that the problem at issue is that of theological language, which even though it can only be the language of the world, must still believe at root, cost what it will, that contrary to the natural capabilities of this language it can and should speak of God's revelation in this language as theological language. Understood in this radical way—in so far as it may be understood thus—the doctrine of the *vestigia* is no playing with words.

But why does it so commonly, and, as we continually feel, so necessarily and legitimately make this impression on us, the impression that it is all table-talk which is not to be taken too seriously, and that fundamentally it is in some ways a dangerous profanation of holy things ? We can only answer that this is so because we can never be so clear about the purpose which may lawfully be pursued here that there is not at every moment the possibility of a reversal of the whole order just developed, polemics becoming apologetics, the attempt to fashion theological language becoming a surrender of theological language in favour of some alien speech, the assumed and asserted intelligibility of revelation becoming an original commensurability of reason with revelation, the synthetic " God into the world " becoming an analytic " God in the world," the claiming of the world by revelation becoming a claiming of revelation by the world, and the discovered intimation becoming a self-conceived proof. When there was no guarantee against this reversal—and to a large extent there was not—the idea of a second root of the doctrine of the Trinity was bound to take hold. It could now be believed that fundamentally the root and basis of the Trinity may be just as well found in human consciousness or other created orders as in Holy Scripture, and this was bound to give rise to the danger already indicated that interest would increasingly focus on the trinities in the world that are so much closer to men, and it would be increasingly supposed that the divine Trinity is to be found in them as such. Was it really found ? Was the Triune God who was supposedly to be found in the world first and then independently, really the One whom Holy Scripture calls God ? Or was He just an epitome, a supreme principle of the world and ultimately of man ? Though the proof given proved something, did it not fail to prove what it was meant to prove, and if this was not perceived, did it not really lead away from what it was meant to prove ? Was not the proof of the Trinity along these lines bound to lead logically to a denial of the trinitarian God of Holy Scripture because it proved and put in His place a God constituted *totaliter aliter* ?

Let us suppose that someone seriously wanted to prove the truth of the divine Trinity from its attestation in the history of religion. What would he or could he prove ? The two Babylonian triads and the Brahman Trimurti can be demonstrated only as formulations of a triply membered world principle. In the Egyptian, Canaanite and Etruscan triads it is no less plain that what is really intended and worshipped is the basic relation of the family. In the three jewels of Buddhism, the personality, teaching and community of Buddha, we obviously have, in so far as there is any reference to a divine Trinity, the deified historical process of the founding of religion. If all that is found here by way of a triadic Godhead deserves to be called God, then the history of religion offers a confirmation of the Christian Trinity ; but not otherwise. For what is left over when one deducts the question as to the nature which is described here as God's nature is really only the number three. And the reasons the history of religion provides for the divinity of this number (" it is perhaps sacred because primitive man was not yet acquainted with any higher number," RGG[2], Art. " Dreieinigkeit," I) can hardly be described as particularly illuminating. J. Gerhard (*op. cit.*) really said all that can be said on the value of the history of religion for this problem : *In verbis nobiscum consentiunt, in verborum istorum explicatione ac sensu dissentiunt.* We only step into the void if we try to plant our feet here.

Let us further suppose that someone wanted to base faith in the Triune God secondarily on the philosophy of history. It could easily be shown that the three-beat rhythm of history which is continually advanced is just the rhythm of wrestling with past, present and future in which active man always finds himself as he reflects on his action. One can certainly count on it that the third element which is decisive in every philosophy of history always denotes the precise point where the relevant philosopher himself stands or which he is striving to reach, the two not being so very different. If the dream he dreams from this standpoint is the wisdom of God, then this philosophy of history is a proof of the doctrine of the Trinity, but certainly not otherwise, for if it is not, the philosopher of history has proved nothing at all apart from his own vision and his own will.

Luther already drew attention to the threat in the Augustinian argument from consciousness. We have seen how cheerfully he engaged in all other possible arguments of this kind. The more admirable, then, is the instinct which stopped him using this one, in contrast to Melanchthon. He declared that the fatal *disputatio de libro arbitrio* must follow from the Augustinian doctrine, from the *imago dei* in man present in *memoria, intellectus* and *voluntas*. *Ita enim dicunt : Deus est liber, ergo cum homo ad imaginem Dei sit conditus, habet etiam liberam memoriam, mentem et voluntatem. . . . Ita nata est hinc periculosa sententia, qua pronuntiant Deum ita gubernare homines, ut eos proprio motu sinat agere (Comm. on Gen.* 1²⁶, *W.A.*, 42, 45, 25). The development of anthropological speculation by way of Descartes and Kant to Schelling and Hegel and finally and logically Feuerbach has clearly justified him. Certainly Augustine thought he was remote from the possibility of a reversal of this kind. But when B. Keckermann (*op. cit.*) could venture to say : *quam est necessarium, hominem esse rationalem, . . . tam est necessarium in Dei essentia tres esse personas,* the way was prepared for this reversal. Could it be avoided once this *quam . . . tam* was attempted ? Unquestionably the image of God in consciousness is primarily and intrinsically and as such the image of free man. He who sees in this image as such the image of God is saying thereby that he knows free man as God. If this free man is really God, the proof is successful. But if God is not free man, if He confronts free man in sovereignty, then obviously this most natural and profound and historically influential proof has failed in a very distinctive way.

And so it is with the rest of the material once we consider it in itself with the question whether and how far *vestigia trinitatis in creatura* are really present in it. That there are *vestigia trinitatis* is undeniable of course ; the only question is, of which trinity ? If it is the divine Trinity that really meets us in the three dimensions of space, or the three notes of the simple harmony, or the three primary colours, or even the spring, stream and lake, then, as was seen in ancient Babylonia and India, God is the mysteriously threefold law or nature of the known world, the mystery of the cosmos whose traces meet us in this triplicity of all or at any rate many things, and which is obviously very intimately related to the mystery of man and the mystery of man's religion. If this is God—and it might be—why should not the plenitude of trinities in nature and culture really prove the trinity of this God ? But only the trinity of this God. The question remains whether this God can really be claimed even as the Creator God and therefore whether he does not perhaps bear his name as " God " illegitimately.

Nor have we referred as yet to the profound incongruities, which even proponents of the doctrine have never denied, between the *vestigia* and the biblical and ecclesiastical doctrine of the Trinity. One will find that what are in fact the decisive theses in the doctrine, the indissoluble unity and the indestructible distinction of the three elements, cannot be sustained in relation to any of the *vestigia*. The proof which can be taken from them can never be more than the proof either of three divine beings alongside one another or of a single divine monad with no hypostatic self-differentiation, so that even if the presupposed divine being is worthy to be called God, the trinity of God in the sense of the Christian doctrine of God is the very thing that cannot be proved from these *vestigia*. Quenstedt is quite right : *nulla vera et plena similitudo trinitatis in creaturis reperitur (Theol. did. pol.,* 1685, P. I, *c.* 6, *sect.* 2, *qu.* 3, *font. sol.* 5). Lombard was saying the same thing when he referred to the *dissimilitudines* in the *similitudo,* and finally, in spite of everything, Augustine could also have said the same. And so, as the possibility of the doctrine has been half conceded— it has seldom been contested outright—the objection has always been brought

against it that it is much too easy, that the scorn of unbelievers has been evoked
by it, and that it has led the simple into error (cf. Thomas Aquinas, *S. theol.*, I,
qu. 32, *art.* 1 ; Calvin, *Instit.*, I, 13, 18 ; Quenstedt, *op. cit., font. sol.* 6), and in
fact, in spite of Augustine's authority and in opposition to it, the problem is
simply touched on by most of the older dogmaticians and then dropped again as
useless and dangerous. What can this objection and this attitude of distrust
mean in a matter that one neither can nor will deny altogether except that there
has been a sense of the alien character of what was supposed to be demonstrated
as " God " by means of the *vestigia*, and of the complete difference between this
" God " and the God of Abraham, Isaac and Jacob, the New Testament Father,
Son and Holy Ghost, who should be the theme of the doctrine of the Trinity.

This is the obvious reason for the impression of trifling and even
frivolity one obviously gets when pondering this theologoumenon no
matter how pleasing and credible it seems at first in the words of an
Anselm or a Luther. The moment it is taken seriously it leads plainly
and ineluctably into an ambivalent sphere in which in a trice, even
with the best will in the world, we are no longer speaking of the God
of whom we want to speak and whose traces we meant to find but of
some principle of the world or humanity, of some alien God. The
original intention was to speak of God's revelation. But what happened
was talk about the world and man, and this talk, understood as talk
about God's revelation, necessarily wound up by being talk against
God's revelation. The conqueror was conquered. This game cannot
yield serious results. Taken seriously it can be only a profanation of
holy things. This explains the feeling of frivolity we can hardly avoid
in its presence.

This does not mean, however, that the game can be forbidden in
principle or that the admittedly distinguished theologians who have
more or less seriously played it must be regarded out of hand as
heretical in this matter. We have tried to show with what good
intentions it might be played and we have also indicated its basis in
the problem of theological language. But even in relation to these
good intentions and the linguistic problem there is a lesson to be
learned here. There are obviously possibilities in language—and we
seem to have one of these here—with whose development the Church
and theology will be undertaking something which is not indeed forbidden in principle but which is certainly non-obligatory, outside the
scope of its commission and very dangerous to the extent that the
new translation, establishment and understanding of the theme which
is the task here comes precariously close to the adoption of a totally
different theme, to the extent that suddenly a μετάβασις εἰς ἄλλο
γένος might take place. The finders of the *vestigia trinitatis* had no
wish to postulate a second and different root of the doctrine of the
Trinity side by side with revelation. Far less did they wish to represent
this second root as the only true one or to deny the revelation of

the trinitarian God. But their action is deeply overshadowed by the question whether this is not precisely what they did. We are plainly dealing with that non-obligatory, uncommissioned and dangerous possibility whenever theological language, as here, thinks it must not just be the interpretation of revelation but also its illustration. Interpretation means saying *the same thing* in other words. Illustration means saying the same thing *in other words*. Where the line is to be drawn between the two cannot be stated generally. But there is a line, for revelation will submit only to interpretation and not to illustration. If we illustrate it we set a second thing alongside it and focus our attention on this. We no longer trust revelation in respect of its self-evidential force. What we say about it must be buttressed and strengthened and confirmed by something other than itself. This other thing at least shares the interest. Its power to illustrate revelation, and who knows but what we should say at once its power to prove it, now becomes a circumstance important in itself, and the same obviously applies also to the being and nature of this other thing, which has already acquired such weight as the illustration of revelation that, because it lies much closer to man than revelation, because it is in the last resort his own being and nature, it inevitably becomes a threat to his attention to revelation, a limitation of the seriousness with which he takes it. Is not even the desire to illustrate revelation, let alone the claim that illustration is essential, let alone the assertion that this or that is an illustration of revelation, already to be regarded as tantamount to a desertion of revelation ? Does it not imply that unbelief has already taken place ? Does not the transition from interpretation to illustration already stand as such under the interdict : Thou shalt not make unto thee any likeness ? Obviously this transition is one that should not take place in theological language. The point, then, is whether we do not perhaps have a typical example of it in the doctrine of the *vestigia*, an example which we are thus to reject as such. We may grant that no interpretation of revelation—not excepting the most careful dogmatics and even Church dogma itself—does not contain elements of illustration. We may grant that if, leaving the actual words of Scripture, we even open our mouths or take up our pens we shall depart from revelation in the direction of that non-obligatory, uncommissioned and dangerous possibility, i.e., in the present instance, in the direction of the *vestigia trinitatis*. Thus we have to realise that when in the previous subsection we sought to arrange the biblical concept of revelation under the aspects of veiling, unveiling and impartation we came remarkably close to the fatal Augustinian argument and in no sense safeguarded ourselves against the suspicion that we, too, might be using an illustration and playing a little game with a supposed *vestigium trinitatis* (that could perhaps be traced back to the little sentence " I show myself "). In this respect did not we, too, let ourselves be buttressed, strengthened and confirmed by something other than revelation, namely, by a possibility of logical construction ? In the last resort was it the Bible that spoke to us or only this possibility ? Did we find the root of the doctrine of the Trinity in revelation or ultimately only this other root ? We wanted to find the root of the doctrine in revelation, not another root. We did all kinds of things to make it clear that this and this alone was our concern. But if anyone were to bring against us the charge that the real issue for us too was the other root, we could never accuse him of malice, for even with the best will in the world we could not completely or unequivocally escape the appearance that this might be so. It is as well to be clear about all this. Here as elsewhere we are not as theologians to anticipate or to pronounce to ourselves the justification of our own acts. Nevertheless, this cannot alter in the least the validity of the command which is given to us as theologians on that boundary between interpretation and illustration which is always drawn for theological language if it is to be and to remain theological language. It does not alter in the least the need to take note of this boundary, the need to ask constantly where we are when we speak, on this side of it or on that. Decision regarding this is not really in our hands, just as it is not for us in the last analysis to decide whether the finders of *vestigia trinitatis* really crossed the boundary or not. But concern for this decision is certainly laid upon us and reflection and attentiveness are demanded. Theological language is not free to venture anything and everything. When we reflect on the crisis in which we always stand and which we can never escape, we will make distinctions in what we do. To derive the Trinity consciously and intentionally from the scheme of man's consciousness or from some other creaturely order instead of Scripture is not the same thing as to derive it from Scripture and at the same time to grasp at a scheme which admittedly bears no small resemblance to that of man's self-consciousness and other creaturely orders. True, there is only a relative difference. The difference does not justify us in doing the second and not the first. In the last resort, at the same risk as all the rest, including the finders of the ancient *vestigia trinitatis*, we can only try to point to the fact that the root of the doctrine of the Trinity lies in revelation, and that it can lie only in this if it is not to become at once the doctrine of another and alien god, of one of the gods, the man-gods, of this aeon, if it is not to be a myth. It is in the name of a pointer of this kind that we reject the doctrine of the *vestigia*. We cannot claim to be driving it from the field in the name and power of revelation. Revelation would not be revelation if any man were in a position to advance and to establish against others the claim that he specifically speaks of and from revelation. If we know what revelation is, even in deliberately speaking about it we shall be content to let revelation speak for itself. To show that this is what we are doing we shall finally confront the doctrine of the *vestigia* with a very simple and unassuming No, a No whose point is just that the boundary seems to us to be crossed in this doctrine, but a No whose power stands or falls with the fact that we relate it also and not least to ourselves, and in the last resort we delicately leave it unproved. Its only possible basis is that we are told no man can serve two masters. The master or lord who may be seen in the *vestigia* we can understand only as a different Lord from the one so called in the Bible.

There is of course, and with this we close, a true *vestigium trinitatis in creatura*, an illustration of revelation, but we have neither to discover it nor to bring it into force ourselves, As we have tried to understand it as the true and legitimate point of the *vestigia* doctrine, it consists in the form which God Himself in His revelation has assumed in our language, world, and humanity. What we hear when with our human ears and concepts we listen to God's revelation, what we perceive (and can perceive as men) in Scripture, what proclamation of the Word of God actually is in our lives—is the thrice single voice of the Father, the Son, and the Spirit. This is how God is present for us in His revelation. This is how He Himself obviously creates a *vestigium* of Himself and His triunity. We are not adding anything but simply saying the same thing when we point out that God is present for us in the threefold form of His Word, in His revelation, in Holy Scripture, and in proclamation.

In the light of this true *vestigium trinitatis*, if we are to apply what Luther said about *Grammatica, Dialectica* and *Rhetorica* in his table-talk, we may say that the theological encyclopaedia will consist, as in § 1, 1, of exegetical, dogmatic and practical theology.

This *vestigium* is plain and reliable. It is the *vestigium* of the God who deserves to be called God. It is really the *vestigium* of the triune God in the sense of the Church doctrine of the Trinity. But this *vestigium* is better described as *vestigium creaturae in trinitate* as noted earlier. In adhering to this, we shall not be accepting a second root alongside the first but just the one root of the doctrine of the Trinity.

§ 9

THE TRIUNITY OF GOD

The God who reveals Himself according to Scripture is One in three distinctive modes of being subsisting in their mutual relations : Father, Son, and Holy Spirit. It is thus that He is the Lord, i.e., the Thou who meets man's I and unites Himself to this I as the indissoluble Subject and thereby and therein reveals Himself to him as his God.

I. UNITY IN TRINITY

In order to achieve the necessary conceptual clarification of the question of the Subject of revelation we shall now address ourselves to the development of the Church doctrine of the Trinity.

The doctrine of the triunity of God, as this has been worked out and rightly maintained in the Church as an interpretation of biblical revelation regarding the question of the Subject of this revelation, does not entail—this above all must be emphasised and established—any abrogation or even questioning but rather the final and decisive confirmation of the insight that God is One.

The concept of the unity of God as such will claim our attention later in the doctrine of God. It concerns us here only in relation to the further insight that God's triunity does not imply any threat to but is rather the basis of the Christian concept of the unity of God.

In our demonstration of the root of the doctrine of the Trinity in the biblical revelation we began with and continually returned to the revealed name of Yahweh-Kyrios which embraces both the Old Testament and the New. The doctrine of the Trinity is not and does not seek to be anything but an explanatory confirmation of this name. This name is the name of a single being, of the one and only Willer and Doer whom the Bible calls God.

It is obvious that no difference can be or is made here by the distinction which is made in Holy Scripture itself between Yahweh dwelling on Sinai and Yahweh dwelling in Jerusalem, or in the New Testament the distinction between the Father and the Son, or the distinction manifested in the contrasts between Good Friday, Easter and Pentecost. The man who prays to the Father, who believes in the Son and who is moved by the Holy Ghost is a man whom the one Lord meets and unites to Himself. We quoted the Pauline passages 1 Cor. 12[4f.] ; Eph. 4[4f.] ; in these, however, one should note not only the distinction between θεός, κύριος, πνεῦμα but also the unity to which emphasis is given by the repetition of αὐτός or εἷς. The Church doctrine of the Trinity, too, not only does not seek to obscure the εἷς θεός but rather to set it in the light as such. From the very outset it opposes antitrinitarians as those who fail also and specifically to confess the one God. The presupposition and goal of the Church in this matter is the doctrine of the unity of God, of the divine μοναρχία, in which it sees τὸ σεμνότατον κήρυγμα τῆς ἐκκλησίας τοῦ θεοῦ (Pope Dionysius, *Ep. c. Tritheistas et Sabellianos a.* 260, Denz., No. 48).

The trinitarian baptismal formula could not be more wrongly understood than by understanding it as a formula of baptism into three divine names.

Tertullian *Adv. Prax.*, 26 spoke of the *singula nomina*. But the ὄνομα of Father, Son and Holy Ghost in Mt. 28¹⁹ is one and the same. *Ita huic sanctae trinitati unum naturale convenit nomen, ut in tribus personis non possit esse plurale* (*Conc. Toled.*, XI, *a.* 675, Denz., No. 287). Baptism is *in nomine*, not *in nominibus Patris, Filii et Spiritus sancti*, as is finely stressed in *Cat. Rom.*, II, 2, 10.

The faith which is confessed in this formula, and similarly the faith of the great three-membered confessions of the ancient Church, is not, then, a faith which has three objects.

Non habes illic : credo in maiorem et minorem et ultimum ; sed eadem vocis tuae cautione constringeris, ut similiter credas in Filium, sicut in Patrem credis, similiter in Spiritum sanctum credas, sicut credis in Filium (Ambrose, *De myst.*, 5, 28). *Quid sibi vult Christus, quum in nomine Patris et Filii et Spiritus sancti baptizari praecepit, nisi una fide in Patrem et Filium et Spiritum credendum esse ? Id vero quid aliud est, quam clare testari Patrem, Filium et Spiritum unum esse Deum* (Calvin, *Instit.*, I, 13, 16).

Three objects of faith would mean three gods. But the so-called " persons " in God are in no sense three gods.

Deus Pater, Deus Filius, Deus Spiritus sanctus. Et tamen non tres dii sunt, sed unus est Deus. Ita Dominus Pater, Dominus Filius, Dominus Spiritus sanctus et tamen non tres domini sed unus est Dominus (*Symb. Quicunque*).

We may unhesitatingly equate the lordship of God, to which we found the whole of the biblical concept to be related, with what the vocabulary of the early Church calls the essence of God, the *deitas* or *divinitas*, the divine οὐσία, *essentia, natura,* or *substantia*. The essence of God is the being of God as divine being. The essence of God is the Godhead of God.

The more explicit development of this concept must be reserved for the doctrine of God. At this point the definition of Quenstedt may suffice (*Theol. did.-pol.*, 1685, P. I, *c.* 6, *sect.* 1, *th.* 11). The essence of God is the *quidditas per quam Deus est, id quod est*. From the biblical standpoint, it is that which makes Yahweh-Kyrios, or wherein Yahweh-Kyrios is, the One He describes Himself to be by this name, the name of the Lord.

It may be said of this essence of God that its unity is not only not abrogated by the threeness of the " persons " but rather that its unity consists in the threeness of the " persons." Whatever else we may have to say about this threeness, in no case can it denote a threeness of essence. The triunity of God does not mean threefold deity either in the sense of a plurality of Gods or in the sense of the existence of a plurality of individuals or parts within the one Godhead.

The Church doctrine of the Trinity may be summed up in the equation *Deus est Trinitas*, but it is noted at once in relation to *Trinitas : non triplex sed trina* (*Conc. Tolet.*, IX, Denz., No. 278). *Quidquid est in Deo, est ipse Deus unus et solus* ; whatever one may have to say about the distinctions in God, they cannot denote a distinction of the divine being and existence (*essentia* and *esse* ; Bonaventura, *Breviloq.*, I, 4).

The name of Father, Son and Spirit means that God is the one God in threefold repetition, and this in such a way that the repetition itself is grounded in His Godhead, so that it implies no alteration in His Godhead, and yet in such a way also that He is the one God only in this repetition, so that His one Godhead stands or falls with the fact that He is God in this repetition, but for that very reason He is the one God in each repetition.

In relation to the name of Father, Son and Spirit we have to distinguish *alius—alius—alius* but not *aliud—aliud—aliud* as though we had here parts of a whole or individuals of a species (Fulgentius, *De fide ad Petrum, c.* 5). *Personas distinguimus, non deitatem separamus* (*Conc. Tolet.*, IX, Denz., No. 280). *Quibus est unum esse in deitatis natura, his est in personarum distinctione specialis proprietas* (*Conc. Tolet.*, XVI, *a.* 693, Denz., No. 296). The so-called " persons " are a *repetitio aeternitatis in aeternitate*, not then a threeness of eternity *extra se* but a threeness of eternity *in se*, so that *quotiescunque repetatur aeternitas in aeternitate, non est nisi una et eadem aeternitas* (Anselm, *Ep. de incarn.*, 15). *Simplicissimam Dei unitatem non impedit ista distinctio . . .* for *in unaquaque hypostasi tota intelligitur natura* (Calvin, *Instit.*, I, 13, 19). *Ipsa etenim Dei essentia est maxime unita individua ac singularis, idemque de tribus personis tamquam species de individuo nullo modo dici potest* (*Syn. pur. theol.*, Leiden, 1624, *Disp.*, 7, 12).

The idea we are excluding is that of a mere unity of kind or a mere collective unity, and the truth we are emphasising is that of the numerical unity of the essence of the " persons," when in the first instance we employ the concept of repetition to denote the " persons." It is as well to note at this early stage that what we to-day call the " personality " of God belongs to the one unique essence of God which the doctrine of the Trinity does not seek to triple but rather to recognise in its simplicity.

This concept, too, will have to be dealt with explicitly in the doctrine of God. The concept—not what it designates but the designation, the explicit statement that God is a He and not an It—was just as foreign to the Fathers as it was to the mediaeval and post-Reformation Scholastics. From our point of view, not theirs, they always spoke much too innocently and uncritically of the *deitas*, the *essentia divina*, etc. as though God were a neuter. The concept of the " personality " of God—which we are provisionally emphasising by defining God's essence as His lordship—is a product of the battle against modern naturalism and pantheism.

" Person " as used in the Church doctrine of the Trinity bears no direct relation to personality. The meaning of the doctrine is not, then, that there are three personalities in God. This would be the worst and most extreme expression of tritheism, against which we must be on guard at this stage. The doctrine of the personality of God is, of course, connected with that of the Trinity to the extent that, in a way yet to be shown, the trinitarian repetitions of the knowledge of the lordship of God radically prevent the divine He, or rather Thou, from becoming in any respect an It. But in it we are speaking not of three divine I's, but thrice of the one divine I. The concept of equality of essence or substance (ὁμοουσία, *consubstantialitas*) in the Father, Son and Spirit is thus at every point to be understood also and primarily in the sense of identity of substance. Identity of substance implies the equality of substance of " the persons."

The claim that the Church with its doctrine of the Trinity was defending the recognition of God's unity, and therefore monotheism, against the antitrinitarians may well seem paradoxical at first, for the concern of antitrinitarians in every age has apparently been to establish the right relation between the unique significance and power of the revelation in Christ and His Spirit on the one side and the principle of monotheism on the other. It might be asked whether perhaps all one can say is that in spite of the doctrine of the Trinity the Church wanted to retain and has in fact retained the unity of God as well ; that it has shaped the doctrine of the Trinity in such a way that it has attempted to do justice to Christian monotheism too, and succeeded in this attempt. But we must give an insistent No to this weaker understanding. Christian monotheism was and is also and precisely the point also and precisely in the Church doctrine of the Trinity as such. We have simply missed the point if we see here the competition between two different interests in the assertion of whose rights tensions and cleavages, etc., can easily arise. Certainly one can understand the antitrinitarian heresies from this standpoint. These all became heresies because they were answers to questions that had been wrongly put. In other words, they were attempts to reconcile falsely opposed concerns, i.e., to remove irrelevantly manufactured tensions. In contrast, the Church's line is already distinguished formally from the heretical line by the fact that what happens on it is intended and is to be understood from the very outset as responsibility to the one concern as well as the other, because in fact we do not have two concerns which are opposed to one another and then artificially reconciled. On this thin but steady line where the basic issue is not this or that principle but quite simply the interpretation of Scripture, the point from the very first and self-evidently is both the oneness of God and also the threeness of God, because our real concern is with revelation, in which the two are one. On the other hand all anti-trinitarianism feels it must confess the threeness on the basis of Scripture and the oneness on the basis of reason, that it must then combine them, which it naturally cannot do because it is prevented already by the difference in the sources from which and the sense in which it speaks of the two. Inevitably—and we must see this if we are to understand the sharpness with which the Church has fought it— all antitrinitarianism is forced into the dilemma of denying either the revelation of God or the unity of God. To the degree that it maintains the unity of God it has to call revelation in question as the act of the real presence of the real God. The unity of God in which there are no distinct persons makes it impossible for it to take revelation seriously as God's authentic presence when it is so manifestly different from the invisible God who is Spirit. On the other hand—and this must be our primary concern here—to the degree that it is ready to maintain revelation but without acknowledging the substantial equality of the Son and the Spirit with the Father in heaven, the unity of God is called in question. In its concept of revelation it will not in fact be able to avoid interposing between God and man a third thing which is not God, a hypostasis which is not divine—it does not want that—but semi-divine ; it cannot avoid making this the object of faith. In so far as it is not a denial of revelation, antitrinitarianism in any form is a cruder or subtler deifying of revelation.

When Arius and his followers wanted to see and honour in Christ the first and highest and most glorious creature of the one God, of which it may be said that ἦν ποτε ὅτε οὐκ ἦν καὶ οὐκ ἦν πρὶν γένηται, that it is created out of nothing like all other creatures, that as compared with the Father it is ἀλλότριος καὶ ἀνόμοιος, that as υἱὸς τοῦ θεοῦ κτιστός it is called God without really being so— they obviously did violence to the divine unity by the very adoration they thought they should pay this creature, and the more so the more seriously the adoration was intended. If Christ is not very God, what else can faith in Him be but superstition ? Similarly, when the Arian and non-Arian Pneumatomachi, e.g., Eunomius or Macedonius of Constantinople, regarded the Holy Spirit as a created and ministering spiritual power, was it not inevitable that all the earnest religious statements about this creaturely *pneuma* should represent it as a semi-divine authority alongside God and thus do very serious injury to the very monotheism this whole school was supposed to be serving ? Christ and the Holy Spirit are simply " the vital forces by which God created the willing and achieving of good in men " (K. Holl, " Urchr. u. Rel. Gesch.," 1925, *Ges. Aufs. z. KGesch.*, Vol. II, 1928, p. 27). It was precisely against this talk of " vital forces " that the monotheistic spearhead of the Church dogma of the Trinity was directed. Subordinationist Christology—we are thinking chiefly of Origen—will certainly let the Son and the Spirit share in the essence of the Father, but in graduation ; the idea of a hierarchy, a variable measure of divine substance, is introduced into the essence of God. One can only say that this solution, too, is incompatible with the unity of God. As for the Adoptionist Monarchians, an Artemon and then a Paul of Samosata, the same must be said in this respect of their human Christ, who is endowed with special divine power and finally exalted to divine dignity, as we have had to say about the Christ of Arius. And when we turn finally to the Modalist Monarchians, Noetus of Smyrna, Praxeas, especially Sabellius, and then Priscillian, in whose steps Schleiermacher and his school have walked in the modern period, we find that they did indeed assert the substantial equality of the trinitarian " persons " but only as manifestations behind which God's one true being is concealed as something other and higher, so that one may well ask whether revelation can be believed if in the background there is always the thought that we are not dealing with God as He is but only with a God as He appears to us. If the τρόπος ἀποκαλύψεως is really a different one from the τρόπος ὑπάρξεως and if the ὕπαρξις is the real being of God, then this means that God in His revelation is not really God. To take this unreal God seriously as God is diametrically opposed to monotheism even though it was and is the point of the distinction to protect this. The result is—and this gives rise to the questions we should put specifically to modern Sabellianism too—that belief in revelation necessarily becomes idolatry.

If revelation is to be taken seriously as God's presence, if there is to be a valid belief in revelation, then in no sense can Christ and the Spirit be subordinate hypostases. In the predicate and object of the concept revelation we must again have, and to no less a degree, the subject itself. Revelation and revealing must be equal to the revealer. Otherwise there is no room for them beside the revealer if this be the one God. The unity of God would render revelation and revealing impossible. Christ and the Spirit would not just be foreign to and totally unlike the Father, as Arius said in dangerous proximity to a denial of all revelation. They would have no more to do with Him than any other creatures. Only the substantial equality of Christ and the Spirit with the Father is compatible with monotheism.

In hac trinitate nihil prius aut posterius, nihil maius aut minus. Sed totae tres personae coaeternae sibi sunt et coaequales (Symb. Quicunque). Nullus alium aut praecedit aeternitate aut excedit magnitudine aut superat potestate (Conc. Florent. a. 1441, *Decr. pro Jacobitis*, Denz., No. 704).

2. TRINITY IN UNITY

As the doctrine of the *repetitio aeternitatis in aeternitate* the doctrine of the Trinity confirms the knowledge of the unity of God, but not any knowledge of any unity of any God.

As we now know, a kind of monotheism is represented not only by Judaism and Islam but in some form, whether in the background or as the culminating superstructure of its pantheon or pandemonium, by almost every religion right back to the animisms of the so-called nature religions of Africa. A kind of monotheism—this cannot be sufficiently emphasised—had also permeated for a long time the philosophy, the teachings of syncretistic cults, and especially the feeling for life of later antiquity in the West when Christianity arose and, e.g., Paul's epistle reached the Rome of the time. One need not expect that the dogma and dogmatics of the Church will simply confirm any monotheism or let itself be measured by any monotheism. The antitrinitarian heresies arose and will continually arise on this false presupposition.

At issue here is the revealed knowledge of the revealed unity of the revealed God—revealed according to the witness of the Old and the New Testaments. The unity of God confirmed in the doctrine of the Trinity is not to be confused with singularity or isolation.

> *Sustulit singularitatis ac solitudinis intelligentiam professio consortii* (Hilary, *De trin.*, 4).

Singularity and isolation are limitations necessarily connected with the concept of numerical unity in general. The numerical unity of the revealed God does not have these limitations. No logical necessity need prevent us from simply acknowledging and stating this.

> It is true of numerical concepts in the doctrine of the Trinity generally that *haec sancta trinitas, quae unus et verus est Deus, nec recedit a numero, nec capitur numero* (*Conc. Tolet.*, XI, Denz., No. 229). *In divinis significant (termini numerales) illa de quibus dicuntur*, they are to be understood metaphorically, they do not posit quantity in God, and in the last resort they merely imply negations. (Thomas Aquinas, *S. theol.*, I, qu. 30, art. 3). *Quid ista ibi significent, ipso de quo loquimur aperiente, insinuare curemus* (Peter Lombard, *Sent.*, I, dist. 24 A). Thus the number 1 implies the negation of all plurality of or in God. All further deductions from the use of the concept of number are to be rejected as irrelevant. We must be quite clear that the use of concepts of number and rational concepts generally in the doctrine of the Trinity (and not only the doctrine of the Trinity) in the early Church stands under the sign of Hilary's statement (*De trin.*, 4) : *Intelligentia dictorum ex causis est assumenda dicendi, quia non sermoni res, sed rei sermo subjectus est.* Without having this statement before us, we cannot understand the point here, and he who does not adopt this statement as his own methodological axiom is no theologian and never will be.

God is One, but not in such a way that as such He needs a Second and then a Third in order to be One, nor as though He were alone and had to do without a counterpart, and therefore again—this will be of decisive significance in the doctrine of creation and man and also in the doctrine of reconciliation—not as though He could not exist without the world and man, as though there were between Him and the world and man a necessary relation of reciprocity. In Himself these limits of what we otherwise regard as unity are already set aside. In Himself His unity is neither singularity nor isolation. Herewith, i.e., with the doctrine of the Trinity, we step on to the soil of Christian monotheism.

> Μὴ συμπαραφέρου τοῖς 'Ιουδαίοις πανούργως λέγουσι τὸ Εἷς θεὸς μόνος, ἀλλὰ μετὰ τοῦ εἰδέναι ὅτι εἷς θεὸς γίνωσκε ὅτι καὶ υἱός ἐστι τοῦ θεοῦ μονογενής (Cyril of Jerusalem, *Cat.*, 10, 2). *Confitemur : Non sic unum Deum, quasi solitarium* (*Fides Damasi a.* 380 ?, Denz., No. 15).

The concept of the revealed unity of the revealed God, then, does not exclude but rather includes a distinction (*distinctio* or *discretio*) or order (*dispositio* or *oeconomia*) in the essence of God. This distinction or order is the distinction or order of the three " persons," or, as we prefer to say, the three " modes (or ways) of being " in God.

At this point, not only we but without exception all who have studied this matter before us enter upon the most difficult section in the investigation. What is meant here by the commonly used word " person " ? Or, more generally, what is meant by what is distinguished or ordered in God as Father, Son and Spirit ? Under what common term are these three to be understood ? What are these three —apart from the fact that all together as well as each individually they are the one true God ? What is the common principle of their being, now as Father, now as Son, and now as Spirit ?

We have avoided the term " person " in the thesis at the head of the present section. It was never adequately clarified when first introduced into the Church's vocabulary, nor did the interpretation which it was later given and which prevailed in mediaeval and post-Reformation Scholasticism as a whole really bring this clarification, nor has the injection of the modern concept of personality into the debate achieved anything but fresh confusion. The situation would be hopeless if it were our task here to say what is really meant by " person " in the doctrine of the Trinity. Fortunately this is not our task. Yet the difficulties in which we are involved in relation to this classical concept are only a symptom of the general difficulty of the question itself, to which some answer must now be given.

The word *persona*, πρόσωπον, like *trinitas*, which is supposed to have been used first by Tertullian, originates with the controversy against the Sabellian heresy and is thus designed to denote the being in and for themselves of Father, Son and Spirit respectively. But did not *persona*, πρόσωπον, also mean " mask " ? Might not the term give new support to the Sabellian idea of three mere manifestations behind which stood a hidden fourth ? In view of this the Greek Church largely preferred to translate *persona* by ὑπόστασις rather than πρόσωπον. On the other hand ὑπόστασις necessarily suggested to the Westerners *substantia* in the sense of *natura* or *essentia*. and so they saw themselves threatened here by the proximity of tritheistic ideas. Finally, if the West clung to *persona* and the East to ὑπόστασις, neither party could be perfectly content with the other nor ultimately with itself.

It is something of a relief that a man of Augustine's standing openly declared (*De trin.*, V, 9, VII, 4) that to call what is meant " person " is simply a *necessitas* or *consuetudo loquendi*. A really suitable term for it just does not exist. The reference to the three divine persons certainly means something very different from a juxtaposition like that of three human persons, and for this reason, that a juxtaposition of human persons denotes a separateness of being (*diversitas essentiae*) which is completely excluded in God—in this way the possibility of the Greek objection to πρόσωπον is formally acknowledged. To the question : *quid tres ?* i.e., what is the *nomen generale* or general concept for Father, Son and Spirit, no real answer can be given, *quia excedit supereminentia divinitatis usitati eloquii facultatem. Verius enim cogitatur Deus quam dicitur et verius est, quam cogitatur.* (The more the distinction of persons is regarded as taking place in and grounded in the divine essence itself, the more inconceivable in fact becomes the inconceivability of this distinction ; this distinction participates in the inconceivability of the divine essence, which would not be the essence of the revealed God if it were conceivable, i.e., apprehensible in the categories of *usitatum eloquium.* Hence neither *persona* nor any other term can perform the service of making this distinction really conceivable. There is place here only for more or less fruitful and clarifying designations of the incomprehensible reality of God.) If, thinks Augustine, one still uses the expression *tres personae*, this is done *non ut illud diceretur, sed ne taceretur omnino. Non enim rei ineffabilis eminentia hoc vocabulo explicari valet* : not in order to say that the three in God are precisely *personae* but in order to say with the help of the term *personae* that there are three in God—and even the number 3 here cannot express more than the negation that Father, Son and Spirit as such are not 1. Following Augustine, Anselm of Canterbury spoke of the *ineffabilis pluralitas* (*Monol.*, 38) of the *tres nescio quid : licet enim possim dicere trinitatem propter Patrem et Filium et utriusque Spiritum, qui sunt tres, non tamen possum proferre uno nomine propter quid tres.* Anselm had against the term *persona* the soundly based objection that *omnes plures personae sic subsistunt separatim ab invicem, ut tot necesse sit esse substantias, quot sint personae.* This is true of human persons but it is not true of the divine persons. Hence he, too, will speak of *personae* only *indigentia nominis proprie convenientis* (*ib.*, 79).

Under the influence of Aristotle the Middle Ages then tried to establish a special systematic content for the concept of person. The point of contact for the deliberations initiated here was constituted by the definition of Boethius (early 6th century, *C. Eutych. et Nest.*, 3) : *Persona est naturae rationabilis individua substantia.* According to Thomas Aquinas (*S. theol.*, I, qu. 29, *art.* 1–2) a *substantia individua* (equivalent to *singulare in genere substantiae* or *substantia prima*) is an essence existing in and for itself, separate in its existence from others, unable to impart its existence to others, an individual essence. *Natura* denotes the general essence, the *essentia speciei*, the *substantia secunda*, to which such an individual essence belongs. *Natura rationabilis* or *rationalis* is thus rational nature (including God, angels and men on the mediaeval view) as opposed to *natura irrationalis*, irrational nature (including all other substances from animals downwards). *Persona*, then, is simply *substantia individua* (which can also be called *res naturae, subsistentia* or among the Greeks ὑπόστασις) to the degree that the individual essence in view belongs to rational nature. The definition of Boethius is thus to be translated in Thomas as follows : Person is the individual rational essence. Thomas argues that this concept can be applied to God (*ib.*, *art.* 3) on the ground that *persona* carries with it the mark of a dignity, that it even denotes indeed the *perfectissimum in tota natura*. This dignity or *perfectissimum* must be attributed to God in an eminent sense, *excellentiori modo*. Unfortunately Thomas did not say in what, according to his view, this dignity contained in the concept of person, this *perfectissimum* of the *persona*, consists. Is it the superiority of the rational individual essence over the irrational ? Is it the superiority of the individual rational essence over rational nature as such ? Or is it both ? Be that as it may, Thomas himself recognises the objection that the *principium individuationis*, which is also decisive for the concept of person, is a material that exists in individuation, a something with individual existence, a potentiality, even when the reference is to rational nature. But for Thomas too, and specifically, God is *immaterialis, actus purus*. Thomas has to admit, therefore, that when the concept of person is applied to God all that remains of the element of *individua substantia* is the attribute of the *incommunic-abilitas*, non-communicability, of the existence of the essence concerned to others, so that all that remains of the concept of the individual essence is what makes it an *individual* essence, and the fact that it is an individual *essence* has been set aside (*ib.*, *art.* 3, *ad.* 4). Thomas is also familiar, of course, with the even more important objection, raised already by Augustine and Anselm, that a plurality of persons necessarily involves a plurality of essences as well, and therefore, when applied to God, a plurality of divine essences, or at least a division of the one divine essence. He has thus to state, in a way which is materially correct but which is also a threat to his concept of person, that the *personae* of the Trinity are *res subsistentes* in (i.e., in the one) *divina natura*. Thomas cannot help conceding that the ὑπόστασις of the Greeks is in this respect nearer the facts than the Latin *persona* and that he avoids it only on account of the fatal translation *substantia*. But the *res subsistentes in divina natura* are also, according to him, nothing but *relationes*, intradivine relations (*ib.*, *qu.* 29, *art.* 4 ; *qu.* 30, *art.* 1). Glad as we are to follow him here, and glad as we are to agree with him methodologically when he appeals here to the uniqueness of the concept in its relation to what is meant, i.e., to what is divinely revealed—*aliud est quaerere de significatione huius nominis " persona " in communi et aliud de significatione personae divinae* (*ib.*, *qu.* 29, *art.* 4c)—we can hardly feel convinced that even a comparative aptness—there can be no question of any other—in the use of the concept of person has been explained by Thomas in such a way that we are forced to abandon the reservations in relation to it for which appeal can always be made to Augustine and Anselm. If Thomas has provided a true explanation, within the bounds of the possible, for what the three involve in triunity, he has done this, not in the form of an interpretation of the concept of person, but by means of the concept of relations.

Quite in line with Augustine and Anselm (and materially not in contradiction to Thomas) Calvin could criticise the concept of person in the words : *Les anciens docteurs ont usé de ce mot de personne et ont dit, qu'en Dieu il y'a trois personnes : Non point comme nous parlons en notre langage commun appelant trois hommes, trois personnes ou comme mesmes en la papauté ils prendront ceste audace de peindre trois marmousets* (mannikins) *et voilà la trinité. Mais*—is Calvin's further opinion —*ce mot de personnes en ceste matière est pour exprimer les propriétez lesquelles sont en l'essence de Dieu* (*Congrégation de la divinité de Christ, C.R.*, 47, 473). Later J. Gerhard (*Loci*, 1610 L. III, 62) also spoke of a *magnum imo infinitum discrimen* between the divine persons and the human ones known to us.

What is called " personality " in the conceptual vocabulary of the 19th century is distinguished from the patristic and mediaeval *persona* by the addition of the attribute of self-consciousness. This really complicates the whole issue. One was and is obviously confronted by the choice of either trying to work out the doctrine of the Trinity on the presupposition of the concept of person as thus accentuated or of clinging to the older concept which since this accentuation in usage has become completely obsolete and is now unintelligible outside monastic and a few other studies. The first possibility was chosen in the teaching of the Roman Catholic theologian Anton Günther, who was condemned by Pope Pius IX in 1857. On his view the individual persons of the Trinity are individual substances, three independently thinking and willing subjects, proceeding from one another and related to one another, and thus coming together in the unity of the absolute personality. Along the same lines on the Protestant side Richard Grützmacher (*Der dreieinige Gott—unser Gott*, 1910) ascribed a separate I-centre with a separate consciousness and will and content to Creator, Son and Spirit respectively. As he saw it, each of the three is also absolute personality, one with the others in the fact that the essence of all three is love and holiness, so that they are always experienced as working side by side and together. One can only say that it is hard not to think here of the *trois marmousets* rejected by Calvin and that it is thus hard not to describe this doctrine as tritheism. The definition offered by Melanchthon in more than one passage (e.g., *Exam. ordinand.*, 1559, *C.R.*, 23, 2) and often quoted later : *Persona est subsistens vivum, individuum, intelligens, incommunicabile, non sustentatum ab alio*, has a suspicious sound in this regard, especially if one sets alongside it the fact that he could also say in the plural : *tres vere subsistentes . . . distincti seu singulares intelligentes* (*Loci*, 1559, *C.R.*, 21, 613). *Vita* and *intelligentia* as features in the concept of person necessarily import at least an appearance of tritheism into the doctrine of the Trinity. And the attribute of individuality when it is related to Father, Son and Spirit as such instead of the one essence of God, the idea of a threefold individuality, is scarcely possible without tritheism. " In God, as there is one nature, so there is one knowledge, one self-consciousness " (F. Diekamp, *Kath. Dogmatik*[6], Vol. I, 1930, p. 271).

In face of the danger which threatened at this point almost all Neo-Protestant theology obviously thought it had to seek refuge in Sabellianism. It had on the one side a desire to apply the modern concept of personality to Father, Son and Spirit, but also a justifiable fear of doing this ontologically as Günther and Grützmacher had done. It thus limited itself to a purely phenomenological doctrine of the three persons, an economic Trinity of revelation, three persons in the sense that God Himself was still in the background as absolute personality. In relation to this view it has never been clear either in ancient or modern times how far the real reference was to a Quaternity rather than a Trinity, and the more seriously revelation is taken the greater is the risk of this. One can certainly see why Schleiermacher preferred to say nothing at all about the concept of the personality of God and why D. F. Strauss (*Die christl. Glaubenslehre*, Vol. I, 1840, § 33) and A. E. Biedermann (*Christl. Dogmatik*, 1869, §§ 618 and 715 f.) went to the length of eliminating it altogether, i.e., of banishing it from the realm of truth, in which God is nothing but absolute Spirit, and assigning it to the lower sphere of an inadequate religious idea. One may still ask, of course, whether the hypothesis of a threefold divine self-consciousness is not to be described also as polytheistic if the threefoldness is described " merely " as a matter of the economy of revelation or the religious idea. What does " merely " really mean here if man still lives in fact with God in the power of the economy of revelation or the religious idea, but at this very point the *trois marmousets* are nevertheless to be the final word ?

The second possibility has been adopted by Roman Catholic theology, whose doctrine of the Trinity even to this day speaks of the " persons " as though the modern concept of personality did not exist, as though the definition of Boethius still continued to be relevant and intelligible, and above all as though the meaning of the definition had been so elucidated in the Middle Ages that it is possible with its help to speak profitably of the trinitarian three.

In view of the history of the term person in the doctrine of the Trinity one may well ask whether dogmatics is wise to continue using it in this connexion. It belongs to another locus, to the doctrine of God proper, and to this as a derivation from the doctrine of the Trinity. For it follows from the trinitarian understanding of the God revealed in Scripture that this one God is to be understood not just as impersonal lordship, i.e., as power, but as the Lord, not just as absolute Spirit but as person, i.e., as an I existing in and for itself with its own thought and will. This is how He meets us in His revelation. This is how He is thrice God as Father, Son and Spirit. But is this really the concept which explains the threeness as such and which can thus be made the foundation of the doctrine of the Trinity as its hermeneutical principle ? The man who wants to retain it consistently will find that in addition to ancient ecclesiastical and academic usage about the only valid argument for its venerable position is that he does not have any other or better concept with which to replace it. Yet we must always ask seriously whether the argument of piety on the one side or the technical one on the other is weighty enough to cause the dogmatician to add to the thought of the Trinity, which is difficult in any case, the extra burden of an auxiliary thought which is itself so difficult and which can be used only with so many reservations. We have no cause to want to outlaw the concept of person or to put it out of circulation. But we can apply it only in the sense of a practical abbreviation and as a reminder of the historical continuity of the problem.

The truly material determinations of the principle of threeness in the unity of God were derived neither by Augustine, Thomas nor our Protestant Fathers from an analysis of the concept of person, but from a very different source in the course of their much too laborious analyses of this concept. We prefer to let this other source rank as the primary one even externally, and therefore by preference we do not use the term " person " but rather " mode (or way) of being," our intention being to express by this term, not absolutely, but relatively better and more simply and clearly the same thing as is meant by " person." The fact that God is God in a special way as Father, as Son, and as Spirit, this aspect—not that of the participation of Father, Son and Spirit in the divine essence which is identical in all and which does not, therefore, describe Father, Son and Spirit as such, nor that of the " rational nature " of Father, Son and Spirit, which can hardly be called threefold without tritheism—is usually stressed in analysis as the first and decisive element even by those who think that they must analyse the concept of person at this point. Hence we are not introducing a new concept but simply putting in the centre an auxiliary concept which has been used from the very beginning and with great emphasis in the analysis of the concept of person. The statement that God is One in three ways of being, Father, Son and Holy Ghost, means, therefore, that the one God, i.e. the one Lord, the one personal God, is what He is not just in one mode but—we appeal in support simply to the result of our analysis of the biblical concept of revelation—in the mode of the Father, in the mode of the Son, and in the mode of the Holy Ghost.

" Mode (or way) of being " (*Seinsweise*) is the literal translation of the concept τρόπος ὑπάρξεως or *modus entitativus* as, e.g., Quenstedt (*Theol. did.-pol.*, 1685,

P. I, *c.* 9, *sect.* 1, *th.* 8) put it in Latin. But the word ὑπόστασις understood in the sense in which, after initial hesitation and in face of the permanent doubts of the West, the Eastern Church finally accepted it in place of πρόσωπον, means *subsistentia* (not *substantia*), i.e., mode of existence or mode of being of an existent. It is perhaps in this sense that Heb. 1³ already called the Son χαρακτὴρ τῆς ὑποστάσεως θεοῦ, i.e., in His mode of being an " impress " or countertype of the mode of being of God the " Father." We have seen already that Thomas defines the divine persons as *res subsistentes in natura divina.* The term *res* would not be a happy one, for *res in natura* does not sound too well. But the term *subsistere* is one of the two serviceable elements in the older concept of " person." Similarly the main concept in Calvin's definition (*Instit.*, I, 13, 6) is to the same effect : *subsistentia in Dei essentia* (in the *Congrégation* quoted earlier he expressly declared that with the Greeks, and on account of the biblical basis in Heb. 1³, he would regard the words *substance* or *hypostase* as *plus convenable* in this matter). In the period that followed I. Wollebius (*Chr. Theol. comp.*, 1626, I, *c.* 2, *can.* 1, 4) said, e.g., that *persona* means *essentia Dei cum certo modo entis*, while *Syn. pur. Theol.*, Leiden, 1624, *Disp.*, 7, 10 speaks of *substantia divina peculiari quodam subsistendi modo* and F. Burmann (*Syn. Theol.*, 1678, I, *c.* 30, 13) of *essentia divina communis et modus subsistendi proprius.* We may also appeal at this point to more recent Roman Catholic authors. M. J. Scheeben (*Handb. d. Kath. Dogmatik*, Vol. I, 1874, new edn. 1925, p. 832) states expressly that the individuality of the divine persons is identical with the specific form in which each possesses the divine substance, being a modality of individuality that belongs essentially to the individuality of the divine substance itself. Again B. Bartmann (*Lehrb. d. Dogmatik*, 7th edn., Vol. I, 1928, p. 169) writes : " That whereby the three persons are distinguished from one another is not to be sought in the essentiality nor yet primarily in the person in itself, which is fully equal to the others and perfect and eternal, but in the different way of possessing the essentiality." It is what these theologians call *subsistentia, modus entis*, form or mode of possessing that we, by saying " mode (or way) of being " at the decisive point, are making the focus of attention, which in fact it has always been in the various analyses of the concept of person, although, as it seems to us, far too much obscured by the context.

What we have here are God's specific, different, and always very distinctive modes of being. This means that God's modes of being are not to be exchanged or confounded. In all three modes of being God is the one God both in Himself and in relation to the world and man. But this one God is God three times in different ways, so different that it is only in this threefold difference that He is God, so different that this difference, this being in these three modes of being, is absolutely essential to Him, so different, then, that this difference is irremovable. Nor can there be any possibility that one of the modes of being might just as well be the other, e.g., that the Father might just as well be the Son or the Son the Spirit, nor that two of them or all three might coalesce and dissolve into one. In this case the modes of being would not be essential to the divine being. Because the threeness is grounded in the one essence of the revealed God ; because in denying the threeness in the unity of God we should be referring at once to another God than the God revealed in Holy Scripture—for this very reason this threeness must be regarded as irremovable and the distinctiveness of the three modes of being must be regarded as ineffaceable.

We have seen that Thomas Aquinas found he could retain the element of *incommunicabilitas* as well as *subsistere* in his concept of person, i.e., it proved to be serviceable to the concept of person in the doctrine of the Trinity. Nor is it any accident that *Conf. Aug. Art.* 1 included precisely these two elements in its definition : Person in the context of the doctrine of the Trinity means (*quod*) *proprie subsistit.* The " *quod* " in this definition must in fact be put in brackets. What *proprie subsistit* is not the person as such but God in the three persons, God as thrice *proprie subsistens.* It is worth noting that F. Diekamp (*Kath. Dogmatik*, Vol. I, 6th edn., 1930, p. 352 f.), who works with the *res subsistentes* of Thomas, comes to the conclusion that absolute subsistence belongs only to the divine substance as such, and only relative subsistence to the persons as such. But this relative *subsistere* of the persons is a *proprie subsistere.* Similarly Calvin said that person means *subsistentia in Dei essentia quae . . . proprietate incommunicabili distinguitur* (*Instit.*, I, 13, 6). In *Conf. Aug. Art.* 1 Melanchthon added in explanation : *Non pars aut qualitas in alio,* and in the *Loci : Non sustentata ab alio.* Extending Melanchthon's explanation Quenstedt (*op. cit., th.* 12) strengthened the *incommunicabilis* by paraphrasing: *per se ultimato et immediata subsistens.* If one notes and stresses the fact that the distinctiveness in question can actually be denoted only by adverbs (*proprie*, etc.) or ablatives (*proprietate*) qualifying the verb *subsistere*, while the subject of this *subsistere*, and therefore of the *proprie subsistere* too, cannot strictly speaking be a *res* or *substantia* different from the one essence of God but only this one essence of God itself, then the concept of " mode of being," strengthened and elucidated now by the adjective as " distinctive mode of being," will be the more clearly unpeeled as the core of what dogmatics has had to retain of the older concept of person. Certainly there is more to be said about the Father, Son and Spirit than is said in the formula " distinctive mode of being." We are dealing with God's modes of being, with God's threefold otherness. Calvin's definition is right when he says that *persona* means *natura divina cum hoc quod subest sua unicuique proprietas* (*Instit.*, I, 13, 19). But from this and indeed from all the earlier definitions quoted we see that the " more " here—what Father, Son and Spirit are as " more " than " distinctive modes of being "—is the *natura divina*, the one undifferentiated divine essence with which Father, Son and Spirit are, of course, identical. If we now ask about the element that is non-identical, that distinguishes and is distinguished, the element that makes the Father the Father, the Son the Son and the Spirit the Spirit, the *quod subest sua unicuique proprietas*—and we must obviously ask about this when we seek to investigate the threeness in the oneness—we shall have to be content with the less expressive formula, " distinctive mode of being." We also describe the one divine essence thereby, but we describe it thereby (and to be exact only thereby) as the one divine essence which is not just one but also one in three.

For this reason Father, Son and Spirit are not to be understood as three divine attributes, as three parts of the divine property, as three departments of the divine essence and operation. The threeness of the one God as we have met it in our analysis of the concept of revelation, the threeness of revealer, revelation and being revealed, the threeness of God's holiness, mercy and love, the threeness of the God of Good Friday, Easter and Whitsunday, the threeness of God the Creator, God the Reconciler and God the Redeemer—all this can and should, as we shall soon show, draw our attention and serve as a pointer to the problem of threeness in God. By separating the three elements, we have not yet reached in these three elements as such the concept of the three really distinctive modes of being in God. For whether it be a matter of the inner property or the outer form of God's essence, all that is to be said can and must finally be said in the same way of Father, Son and Spirit. No attribute, no act of God is not in the same way the attribute or act of the Father, the Son and the Spirit. The knowledge of God's revelation means, of course, the knowledge of specific and different qualities which cannot be reduced to a common denominator and which will then make clear to us God's being as Father, Son and Spirit. But because it is of the essence of the revealed God to have these attributes, in His essence they, too, are indistinguishably one, and they cannot, therefore, be distributed ontologically to Father, Son and Spirit. In the revelation attested in the Bible God always meets us, as we have seen, in varying action, in one of His modes of being, or, more accurately, as distinguished or characterised in one of His modes of being. But this relatively distinct revelation of the three modes of being does not imply a corresponding distinction within themselves. On the contrary, we shall have to say that as surely as the relatively different revelation of the three modes of being points to a corresponding difference in themselves, so surely it also and specifically points to their unity in this distinction.

Thus we might envisage the essence of the Father by means of the concept of eternity, but how could we do this without at once and in the very same way understanding the Son and the Spirit in terms of the same concept ? With Paul and Luther we can see in Christ the revelation of God's righteousness, but obviously we then have to regard the Father and Spirit as well in the same way. We can find in the Spirit the epitome of the divine life, but this necessarily means that we understand the same life as the life of the Father and the Son. In the story of the baptism of Jesus—I am here following Luther's exposition in *Von den letzten Worten Davids*, 1543, *W.A.*, 54, 59, 12—we shall call the One who appeared in the form of a dove the Holy Spirit and not the Father or the Son, we shall call the voice that came from heaven the voice of the Father and not the voice of the Son or the Spirit, and we shall call the man baptised in the Jordan the incarnate Son and not the incarnate Father or the incarnate Spirit ; nevertheless, we shall not forget nor deny that everything, the voice from heaven, the incarnate One, and the gift from above, are all the work of the one God, Father, Son and Spirit. *Opera trinitatis ad extra sunt indivisa.*

The difference in ways of being, the *alius—alius—alius*, which is the theme of our present enquiry, cannot have its basis here. But if not here, where ? The only possible answer which can be given, and which has in fact been given from the very beginning, confirms us in thinking that we have done well to put in the centre of our whole investigation the concept of mode of being rather than that of person. This answer is that the distinguishable fact of the three divine modes of being is to be understood in terms of their distinctive relations and indeed their distinctive genetic relations to one another. Father, Son and Spirit are distinguished from one another by the fact that without inequality of essence or dignity, without increase or diminution of deity, they stand in dissimilar relations of origin to one another. If we have rejected the possibility of deriving the difference in the three modes of being from the material differences in the thought of God contained in the concept of revelation, because in the last resort there can be no question of any such differences, we can and must say now that formal distinctions in the three modes of being—that which makes them *modes* of being—can indeed be derived from the concept of revelation. These are the distinctions in their relation to one another. The Why of these distinctions can no more be explained, of course, than the Why of revelation. But it is possible to state and describe the That of revelation, as we have tried to do, and one cannot do this—as we could not—without encountering, in and with the material distinctions that are not our present concern, certain formal distinctions in the three modes of being which prove to be also ir-removable distinctions as distinctions of the one essence of God the Lord.

Quite rightly reference has been made here first and foremost to the New Testament names of Father, Son and Spirit. If these three names are really in their threeness the one name of the one God, then it follows that in this one God there is primarily at least—let us put it cautiously, something like fatherhood and sonship, and therefore something like begetting and being begotten, and then a third thing common to both, which is not a being begotten, nor a proceeding merely from the begetter, but, to put it generally, a bringing forth which originates in concert in both begetter and begotten. But then, applying our ternary of revealer, revelation and being revealed, we can also say quite confidently that there is a source, an authorship, a ground of revelation, a revealer of himself just as distinct from revelation itself as revelation implies absolutely something new in relation to the mystery of the revealer which is set aside in revelation as such. As a second in distinction from the first there is thus revelation itself as the event of making manifest what was previously hidden. And as the result of the first two there is then a third, a being revealed, the reality which is the purpose of the revealer and therefore at the same time the point or goal of the revelation. More briefly, it is only because there is a veiling of God that there can be an unveiling, and only as there is a veiling and unveiling of God that there can be a self-impartation of God.

We might say further that the fact that God is the Creator is the presupposition of the fact that He can be the Reconciler and the fact that the Creator is the Reconciler is the ground of the fact that He can be the Redeemer. Or, the fact that God can be merciful to us in Christ is grounded in His holiness, and thus the love of God for us is grounded in His holiness and mercy. To clarify these relations of origin in the God of revelation Calvin was fond of the terms *principium* (namely, *principium agendi*), *sapientia* (namely, *dispensatio in rebus agendi*), *virtus* (i.e., *efficacia actionis*) (*Instit.*, I, 13, 18, cf. *Cat. Genev.* 1545, in K. Müller, p. 118, 1. 25).

Now the real modes of being in God cannot be derived, of course, from the material distinctions in these or similar conceptual ternaries. For everything that is materially distinct here must be viewed as being even in its distinctness sublimated again in the unity of the divine essence. But they can be derived from the regularly recurring relations of the three concepts to one another as these occur most simply between the concepts of Father, Son and Spirit. The threeness in God's oneness is grounded in these relations. This threeness consists in the fact that in the essence or act in which God is God there is first a pure origin and then two different issues, the first of which is to be attributed solely to the origin and the second and different one to both the origin and also the first issue. According to Scripture God is manifest and is God in the very mode or way that He is in those relations to Himself. He brings forth Himself and in two distinctive ways He is brought forth by Himself. He possesses Himself as Father, i.e., pure Giver, as Son, i.e., Receiver and Giver, and as Spirit, i.e., pure Receiver. He is the beginning without which there is no middle and no end, the middle which can be only on the basis of the beginning and without which there is no end, and the end which is based wholly and utterly on the beginning. He is the speaker without whom there is no word or meaning, the word which is the word of the speaker and the bearer of his meaning, and the meaning which is the meaning of both the speaker and his word. But let us stay clear of the zone of *vestigia trinitatis* on which we are already trespassing. The fact that the *alius—alius—alius* which can be illustrated by these other ternaries does not signify an *aliud—aliud—aliud* ; that the One and the Same can be this and that in the truly opposing determinations of these original relations without ceasing to be the One and the same ; and that each of these relations as such can also be the One in whom these relations occur—for this there are no analogies. This is the unique divine trinity in the unique divine unity.

Our reference in what has just been said is to the concept which is known in dogmatic history as the doctrine of relations. It seems to have been familiar already to Tertullian : *Ita connexus Patris in Filio et Filii in Paracleto tres efficit cohaerentes, alterum ex altero* (*Adv. Prax.*, 25). The Cappadocians (e.g., Gregory Naz.. *Orat.*, 29, 16) were the first to speak expressly of σχέσις, relation or connexion, as the element that constitutes the persons in God. In the West the doctrine was then plainly represented by Augustine. *His enim appellationibus* (Father, Son and Spirit) *hoc significatur quo ad se invicem referuntur* (*Ep.*, 238, 2, 14) . . . *quae relative dicuntur ad invicem* (*De trin.*, VIII, *prooem.* 1). *Non quisque eorum ad se ipsum, sed ad invicem atque ad alterutrum ita dicuntur* (*ib.*, V, 6). In the Middle Ages Anselm (*De proc. Spir.*, 2) coined the formula : *In divinis omnia sunt unum, ubi non obviat relationis oppositio*, and this was given the status of a dogma at the Council of Florence, 1441 (*Decr. pro Jacob.*, Denz., No. 703). In another passage Anselm stated it as follows : *Proprium est unius esse ex altero et proprium est alterius alterum esse ex illo* (*Monol.*, 38, cf. also 61 and *Ep. de incarn.*, 3). Thomas Aquinas then introduced the concept of relation into his concept of person and defined the trinitarian *persona* as *relatio ut res subsistens in natura divina* (*S. theol.*, I, *qu.* 30, *art.* 1 c, cf. *qu.* 40, *art.* 1–2). Similarly Calvin's definition, which we now quote in full, is as follows : *personam voco subsistentiam in Dei essentia, quae ad alios relata, proprietate incommunicabili distinguitur.* Luther very rightly expounded the whole doctrine of triunity in terms of the doctrine of relations : " The Father is my and thy God and Creator, who hath made thee and me, the selfsame work that thou and I are, the Son hath also made, and is as much thy and my God and Creator as the Father. Thus the Holy Ghost hath also made the same work that I and thou are, and is my and thy God and Creator as much as the Father and the Son. Yet there are not three Gods or Creators but one single God and Creator of the twain of us. Here by this faith I guard myself against the heresy of Arius and his like, that I divide not the single divine essence into three Gods or Creators, but in true Christian faith retain no more than the one God and Creator of all creatures. Again, if I now pass beyond and outside creation or the creature into the inward, incomprehensible essence of the divine nature, I find, as Scripture teacheth me (for reason is naught here), that the Father is a different person from the Son in the one undivided eternal Godhead. His distinction is that He is the Father and hath not divinity from the Son nor from any one. The Son is a distinct person from the Father in one and the same fatherly Godhead. His distinction is that He is the Son and hath divinity not from Himself nor from any one but only from the Father as eternally born of the Father. The Holy Ghost is a distinct person from the Father and the Son in one and the same Godhead. His distinction is that He is the Holy Ghost that proceedeth eternally from the Father and the Son together, and He hath Godhead neither from Himself nor from any one, but from both the Father and the Son together, and all this from eternity to eternity. With this faith I here guard myself against the heresy of Sabellius and his like, against Jews, Mahomet, and all that are wiser than God Himself, and mix not the persons into one person, but in true Christian faith retain three distinct persons in the one divine, eternal essence, all three of which, to us and creatures, are one God, Creator and Worker of all things " (*Von den letzten Worten Davids*, 1543, *W.A.*, 54, 58, 4). In contrast, it is characteristic of the tritheistic weakness of Melanchthon's concept of person that, to the detriment also of the Lutheran orthodoxy that followed him, he did not at least incorporate the concept of relation in his definition but usually introduced it, if at all, only by way of later explanation.

The relations in God in virtue of which He is three in one essence are thus His fatherhood (*paternitas*) in virtue of which God the Father is the Father of the Son, His sonship (*filiatio*) in virtue of which God the Son is the Son of the Father, and His spirit-hood (*processio, spiratio passiva*) in virtue of which God the Spirit is the Spirit of the Father and the Son. The fourth logically possible and actual relation, the active relation of the Father and the Son to the Spirit, cannot constitute a fourth hypostasis because there is no relative " opposition "

C.D.—N

between it and the first and second hypostases, because it is indeed already included in the first and second hypostases, because *spirare* is part of the full concept of the Father and the Son. *Spiratio convenit et personae Patris et personae Filii, utpote nullam habens oppositionem relationem nec ad paternitatem nec ad filiationem* (Thomas Aquinas, *S. theol.*, I, qu. 30, art. 2c ; cf. J. Pohle, *Lehrb. d. Dogmatik*, Vol. I, 1902, p. 329 ; B. Bartmann, *op. cit.*, p. 211). These three relations are the divine persons as such, explains Thomas (*paternitas est persona Patris, filiatio persona Filii, processio persona Spiritus sancti procedentis, ib., art.* 2, *ad.* 1). All modern Roman Catholic dogmatics agrees with him in this. The thing denoted by the concept person, explains M. J. Scheeben (*op. cit.*, p. 834), even though formally the term has no relative signification, is a subsisting relation or substance in a specific relation. " The divine persons in themselves are nothing but subsistent relations " (J. Pohle, *op. cit.*, p. 328). " The trinitarian persons do not have their own subject of inherence, but exist as *relationes subsistentes* " (B. Bartmann, *op. cit.*, p. 211). A divine person is " an intradivine relationship in so far as it subsists for itself and is completely incommunicable " (F. Diekamp, *op. cit.*, p. 350). " The relations . . . are . . . that which makes the individual persons these persons " (J. Braun, *Handlexikon d. kath. Dogm.*, 1926, p. 228). In relation to all this both in Thomas' own explanation and more especially in those of his modern pupils we may well ask :

1. What has become of the definition of the persons as *res subsistentes in natura divina* (*S. theol.*, I, qu. 30, *art.* 1c) ? Why are Roman Catholic dogmaticians silent about this ? Why do they speak only of the reality of the relations as such ? They are, of course, right ; no other course is possible. The duplication (or quadruplication) of subject expressed in the *res* and *natura* must be abandoned as at least misleading.

2. If we hold Scheeben to his explanation that the name " person " in itself does not express relativity in God any more than in creatures, that formally it has no relative signification, and yet that relativity is the very thing that is to be expressed here, why should we cling to the concept of person which invariably obscures everything ? " The terminology has been fixed by ecclesiastical and theological usage in such a way that it can no longer be discarded " (J. Pohle, *op. cit.*, p. 25).

The relevance of this argument is not apparent. It is obvious for one thing that the ancient concept of person, which is the only possible one here, has now become obsolete. It is also obvious that the only possible definition of the matter in question is not a definition of this ancient concept of person. Thus at the point where earlier dogmatics and even modern Roman Catholic dogmatics speak of persons we prefer to call the Father, Son and Spirit in God the three distinctive modes of being of the one God subsisting in their relationships one with another.

This, then, is the repetition in God, the *repetitio aeternitatis in aeternitate*, by which the unity of the revealed God is differentiated from everything else that may be called unity. We shall postpone our survey of the individual concepts that have come to light here, especially *paternitas*, *filiatio* and *processio*, until they come up for discussion in their respective contexts. Our present task is to answer the general question of the trinity in unity, Augustine's : *quid tres* ?

It is as well to realise that even when an answer has been given this question is still put again and again. There have been constant attempts to answer it. We, too, have now made such an attempt.

We wished to give a relatively better answer than those which have been traditionally given in terms of the concept of person. But the fact that in the last analysis we could only group the familiar elements in the older concept of person (more intelligibly, we hope) around the concept of mode of being, may serve as a reminder that our answer cannot claim to be an absolutely better answer. The great central difficulties which have always beset the doctrine of the Trinity at this point apply to us too. We, too, are unable to say how an essence can produce itself and then be in a twofold way its own product. We, too, are unable to say how an essence's relation of origin can also be the essence itself and indeed how three such relations can be the essence and yet not be the same as each other but indissolubly distinct from one another. We, too, are unable to say how an essence's relation of origin can also be its permanent mode of being and, moreover, how the same essence, standing in two different and opposed relations of origin, can subsist simultaneously and with equal truth and reality in the two different corresponding modes of being. We, too, are unable to say how in this case 3 can really be 1 and 1 can really be 3. We, too, can only state that in this case it all has to be thus, and we can state it only in interpretation of the revelation attested in the Bible and with reference to this object. None of the terms used, whether it be essence or mode of being or relation of origin, whether it be the numeral 1 or the numeral 3, can adequately say what we ought to say and are trying to say in using it. If we pay attention only to what the terms as such can say in their immanent possibility of meaning; if we are unwilling or unable to accept the indication they are supposed to give, we shall only cause ourselves endless vexation. And who is not constantly faced by the question whether these terms are really an indication to him or whether, by clinging to their immanent possibility of meaning, he is not caused endless vexation? The axiom *non sermoni res, sed rei sermo subiectus est*, without adopting which we cannot really be theologians, is not really a self-evident axiom and never will be. The fact that this is so is obvious here too and here especially. The truth is that all the concepts which we have tried to use here have some value in relation to what we have to say, but that they then cease to have any value or their only value is that in their valuelessness, and with other valueless things of the same type, they point beyond themselves to the problem as it is set before us by Scripture. When we have said what that is : Father, Son and Spirit, we must then go on to say that we have said nothing. *Tres nescio quid* was the final answer that Anselm, too, found that he could and should give to Augustine's question. But the danger incurred here in relation to all concepts as such also arises in relation to the object. The inadequacy of all concepts not only implies the menacing proximity of a philosophical criticism based on the immanent possibilities of meaning of these concepts—this can be borne, because in the long run it is incompetent as such. What it also implies is the menacing proximity of theological error. We, too, are unable to avoid the fact that every step of ours in this field is exposed to danger, whether the threat comes from the tritheistic heresy or the modalist heresy, or whether there be on either side suspicion of the opposite error. We, too, are unable to take a middle course in such a way that every misunderstanding is ruled out and our orthodoxy is unequivocally assured. We, too, can in this respect return only a relatively satisfactory answer to Augustine's question. On all sides good care is thus taken to see that the *mysterium trinitatis* remains a mystery. There can be no question of rationalising because rationalising is neither theologically nor philosophically possible here. That is to say, as philosophers we cannot give a full interpretation of the object with an apparatus of concepts already elucidated—for we always come up against the fact that from the standpoint of the object the decisive act of interpretation is an elucidation of the conceptual apparatus which is so radically ill-suited to this object. Again, as theologians we cannot really safeguard ourselves by means of this conceptual apparatus against the two opposing errors that threaten us here, for we always come up against the fact that in contrast to a theological language which uses this apparatus and is thus insecure, the truth creates the necessary safeguard for itself. Theology means rational wrestling with the mystery. But all rational wrestling with this mystery, the more serious it is, can lead only to its fresh and authentic interpretation and manifestation as a mystery. For this reason it is worth our while to engage in this rational wrestling with it. If we are not prepared for this we shall not even know what we are saying when we say that what is at issue here is God's mystery.

3. TRIUNITY

In the doctrine of the Trinity our concern is with unity in trinity and trinity in unity. We cannot advance beyond these two obviously one-sided and inadequate formulations. They are both one-sided and inadequate because a slight overemphasis on the unity is unavoidable in the first and a slight overemphasis on the trinity is unavoidable in the second. The term " triunity " is to be regarded as a conflation of the two formulae or rather as an indication of the conflation of the two to which we cannot attain and for which, then, we have no formula, but which we can know only as the incomprehensible truth of the object itself.

" Triunity," we say. The common German word for Trinity (" Dreifaltig-keit "), as Luther once said, is " right bad German." It has an " odd sound." Luther was obviously objecting to the tritheistic ring reminiscent of the fatal *triplicitas*. He suggested instead a " Gedritt " in God (*Sermon on Lk.* 9²⁸ᶠ·, 1538, *W.A.*, 6, 230). But " triunity " (" Dreieinigkeit ") is to be preferred because better than *trinitas* or τρίας, and certainly better than " Dreifaltigkeit " or even " Gedritt," it gives expression to both the decisive numerals, and its stress on the unity indicates that we are concerned here, not just about unity, but about the unity of a being one which is always also a becoming one. For this reason " Dreieinigkeit " is also to be preferred to " Dreieinheit."*

In practice, however, this concept of " triunity " can never be more than the dialectical union and distinction in the mutual relation between the two formulae that are one-sided and inadequate in them-selves. We see on the one side how for those who hear and see revelation in the Bible the Father, Son and Spirit, or however we name the three elements in the biblical revelation, come together in the knowledge and concept of the one God. And we see on the other side how for them the source and goal of this knowledge and concept are never a sterile one but are rather the three, whatever we call them. In practice the concept of triunity is the movement of these two thoughts.

Ex uno omnia, per substantiae scilicet unitatem, et nihilominus custodiatur oikonomiae sacramentum, quae unitatem in trinitatem disponit, tres dirigens Patrem et Filium et Spiritum—tres autem non statu, sed gradu, nec substantia sed forma, nec potestate sed specie—unius autem substantiae et unius status et unius potestatis, quia unus Deus, ex quo et gradus isti et formae et species in nomine Patris et Filii et Spiritus Sancti deputantur (Tertullian, *Adv. Prax.*, 2). Calvin often (e.g., *Instit.*, I, 13, 17) referred to a saying of Gregory Nazianzus (*Orat.* 40, 41) which does in fact state very well this dialectic in the knowledge of the triune God : οὐ φθάνω τὸ ἓν νοῆσαι καὶ τοῖς τρισὶ περιλάμπωμαι· οὐ φθάνω τὰ τρία διελεῖν καὶ εἰς τὸ ἓν ἀναφέρομαι. (*Non possum unum cogitare quin trium fulgore mox circum-fundar : nec tria possum discernere quin subito ad unum referar.*) Similarly Gregory Naz. (*Orat.*, 31, 14) developed the thought that we can only think of God's act and will and essence as one, but then, remembering their distinct origins, we know three as the object of worship, even if we do not worship three alongside one another. The trinitarian dialectic is also very well presented in the " Preface on the All-Holiest Trinity " in the *Missale Romanum : Domine sancte, Pater omnipotens, aeterne Deus ! Qui cum unigenito Filio tuo et Spiritu Sancto unus es Deus, unus es Dominus : non in unius singularitate personae, sed in unius trinitate substantiae. Quod enim de tua gloria, revelante te, credimus, hoc de Filio tuo, hoc de Spiritu sancto, sine differentia discretionis sentimus. Ut in confessione verae sempiternaeque Deitatis et in personis proprietas et in essentia unitas et in maiestate adoretur aequalitas.* It should be noted that in the three-membered conclusion to this passage *maiestas* counterbalances the *personae* and *essentia* in God, and *aequalitas* (obviously equivalent to ὁμοουσία) the *proprietas* and *unitas*, so that some effort is made to give a place of its own to the third thing to which the trinitarian dialectic points.

---

* Editors' note. Since it is hardly possible to reproduce the nuance of *Dreieinigkeit* in recognisable English (cf. the " Three-in-Oneness " of the first edition), the term " triunity " is adopted here to render *Dreieinigkeit* rather than *Dreieinheit*.

The triunity of God obviously implies, then, the unity of Father, Son and Spirit among themselves. God's essence is indeed one, and even the different relations of origin do not entail separations. They rather imply—for where there is difference there is also fellowship —a definite participation of each mode of being in the other modes of being, and indeed, since the modes of being are in fact identical with the relations of origin, a complete participation of each mode of being in the other modes of being. Just as in revelation, according to the biblical witness, the one God may be known only in the Three and the Three only as the one God, so none of the Three may be known without the other Two but each of the Three only with the other Two.

It need not be specially proved that when the trinitarian distinction is in view in the Old Testament or the New the particular stress on one of God's modes of being never implies its separation from the others. What is always stated implicitly or explicitly—think of the express statements about the Father and the Son in John (e.g., Jn. 10³⁰, ³⁸ ; 14¹⁰, ¹¹ ; 17¹¹) or the relation of Christ and the Spirit in Paul—is not, of course, the identity of the one mode of being with the others but the co-presence of the others in the one.

Since John of Damascus (*Ekdosis*, I, 8 and 14) this insight has found expression in theology in the doctrine of the perichoresis (*circumincessio*, passing into one another) of the divine persons. This states that the divine modes of being mutually condition and permeate one another so completely that one is always in the other two and the other two in the one. Sometimes this has been grounded more in the unity of the divine essence and sometimes more in the relations of origin as such. Both approaches are right and both are ultimately saying the same thing. *Nec enim Pater absque Filio cognoscitur, nec sine Patre Filius invenitur. Relatio quippe ipsa vocabuli personalis personas separari vetat, quas etiam, dum non simul nominat, simul insinuat. Nemo autem audire potest unumquodque istorum nominum, in quo non intelligere cogatur et alterum* (*Conc. Tolet.*, XI, Denz., No. 281). *Propter unitatem naturalem totus Pater in Filio et Spiritu sancto est, totus quoque Spiritus sanctus in Patre et Filio est. Nullus horum extra quemlibet ipsorum est* (Fulgentius, *De fide ad Petr.*, 1). *Est et enim totus Pater in Filio et communi Spiritu et Filius in Patre et eodem Spiritu et idem Spiritus in Patre et Filio . . . Tanta igitur . . . aequalitate sese complectuntur et sunt in se invicem, ut eorum nullus alium excedere aut sine eo esse probetur* (Anselm, *Monol.*, 59 ; cf. also Peter Lomb., *Sent.* I, *dist*, 19 E ; Thomas Aquinas, *S. theol.*, I, qu. 45, *art.* 5). On the basis of this doctrine the inner life of God would appear to be a kind of uninterrupted cycle of the three modes of being, and we are glad to be reminded of the inappropriateness of the figure resulting from the literal meaning of περιχώρησις by the fact that instead of a temporal sequence the Latin Church adopted a spatial juxtaposition and thus preferred to speak in terms of *circuminsessio* (dwelling in one another, *immanentia, inexistentia*) rather than *circumincessio*. In one way or the other this theologoumenon, which is not so far from the necessary biblical basis of genuine dogmatics as might at first sight appear, implies both a confirmation of the distinction in the modes of being, for none would be what it is (not even the Father) without its co-existence with the others, and also a relativisation of this distinction, for none exists as a special individual, but all three " in-exist " or exist only in concert as modes of being of the one God and Lord who posits Himself from eternity to eternity. Not unjustly, therefore, J. Pohle (*Lehrb. d. Dogm.*, Vol. I, 1902, p. 355) called the doctrine of perichoresis " the final sum of the two factors under discussion," namely, the doctrine of *unitas in trinitate* and *trinitas in unitate*. It must in fact be regarded as an important form of the dialectic needed to work out the concept of " triunity."

To the unity of Father, Son and Spirit among themselves corresponds their unity *ad extra*. God's essence and work are not twofold but one. God's work is His essence in its relation to the reality which is distinct from Him and which is to be created or is created by Him. The work of God is the essence of God as the essence of Him who (N.B. in a free decision grounded in His essence but not constrained by His essence) is revealer, revelation and being revealed, or Creator, Reconciler and Redeemer. In this work of His, God is revealed to us. All we can know of God according to the witness of Scripture are His acts. All we can say of God, all the attributes we can assign to God, relate to these acts of His ; not, then, to His essence as such. Though the work of God is the essence of God, it is necessary and important to distinguish His essence as such from His work, remembering that this work is grace, a free divine decision, and also remembering that we can know about God only because and to the extent that He gives Himself to us to be known. God's work is, of course, the work of the whole essence of God. God gives Himself entirely to man in His revelation, but not in such a way as to make Himself man's prisoner. He remains free in His working, in giving Himself.

This freedom of His is the basis of the distinction of the essence of God as such from His essence as the One who works and reveals Himself. On this freedom rests the incomprehensibility of God, the inadequacy of all knowledge of the revealed God. The triunity of God, too, is revealed to us only in God's work. This is why the triunity of God is incomprehensible to us. This is why all our knowledge of the triunity is inadequate. The comprehensibility with which it is presented to us, primarily in Scripture and secondarily in the Church doctrine of the Trinity, is a creaturely comprehensibility. It is absolutely and not just relatively different from the comprehensibility with which it exists for God Himself. It rests on the free grace of revelation alone that this comprehensibility in this absolute difference from its object is nevertheless not without truth. In this sense the triunity of God as we know it from God's work is truth. In a bridging of the gulf (from God's side) between divine and human comprehensibility it comes to pass that in the sphere and within the limits of human comprehensibility there is a true knowledge of God's essence generally and hence also of the triunity. In this sphere and within these limits revelation occurs. Otherwise how could it be revelation where this sphere is merely our sphere ? How else could we perceive the triunity except in this sphere and within these limits ? Only revelation as God's step towards us is, of course, the guarantee of its truth. As we cannot make the step across the abyss, so we cannot be the guarantee. We can only let it be guaranteed for us. And we should not be surprised at the incomprehensibility in which it still remains for us as it becomes comprehensible to us. We should not confuse our comprehension and its allotted and appropriate truth with the truth of the triunity from which by God's grace it comes to our comprehension as this takes place in us with the appropriate and allotted truth. It is thus legitimate for us to differentiate the three modes of being of the one God on the basis of the revelation which takes place in the sphere and within the limits of human comprehensibility.

The revelation of God attested in Scripture forces us to make this differentiation. Scripture itself continually speaks in terms of these differentiations and it does so with great seriousness, i.e., in such a way that we are in no position to remove them without exegetical wresting. It shows us God in His work as revealer, revelation and being revealed, or as Creator, Reconciler and Redeemer, or as holiness, mercy and goodness. In these distinctions we can and should perceive the distinctions in the divine modes of being in the truth allotted and appropriate to us. The limit of our comprehension lies in the fact that even as we comprehend these distinctions we do not comprehend the distinctions in the divine modes of being as such. These do not consist in distinctions in God's acts and attributes. If we were to assume this we should be assuming three gods or a tripartite essence of God. God's work would then be a remarkable combination of three divine truths or powers or even individuals. Hence we must believe already that even though the distinctions in God's work take place in the sphere and within the limits of our comprehensibility, here also and especially they do not signify the last word in the hidden essence of God, and the distinctions in God Himself cannot rest in these distinctions.

But why should they not draw our attention to the incomprehensible distinctions in God Himself, to the distinctions which rest on the various ways in which God posits Himself and is His own origin in the hiddenness of His Godhead ? Why should not the comprehensible distinctions in God's revelation, provisional though they are, confront us with the problem of His incomprehensible and eternal distinctions ? One must say at least that they can be regarded as fit and proper to give us this hint. There is an analogy—we recall our exposition of the doctrine of relations in this regard—between the terms Father, Son and Spirit along with the other formulations of this triad in revelation on the one side, and on the other side the three divine modes of being which consist in the different relations of origin and in which we have come to know the truly incomprehensible eternal distinctions in God. In these analogies, which are not present in the world like the alleged *vestigia trinitatis* but which have been set up in the world by revelation, and by which the mystery is not as it were abandoned and solved but rather denoted, and denoted precisely as a mystery, we have the truth of the triunity as it is assigned and appropriate to us. We shall not overestimate this truth. If we did, if we confused the analogy with the thing itself, if we equated the distinctions that are comprehensible to us with those that are not, in other words, if we thought we had comprehended the essence of God in comprehending His work, we should be plunged at once into the error of tritheism. But why should we on this account underestimate this truth? Even though we acknowledge the inaccessibility of the thing itself, why should we not accept it as a reference to the thing itself? *Abusus non tollit usum* : why should we not use this reference as it is meant to be used as the creation and gift of revelation?

In the vocabulary of older dogmatics what falls to be said about this positive relation between Father, Son and Spirit in God's work and Father, Son and Spirit in God's essence is the doctrine of appropriations (attributions, assignments). By the specific assigning of a word or deed to this or that person of the Godhead, there should be brought to our awareness, as Leo the Great taught (*Serm.*, 76, 2), the truth of the triunity which is in fact undivided in its work and which still exists in three persons. *Ob hoc enim quaedam sive sub Patris, sive sub Filii, sive sub Spiritus sancti appellatione promuntur, ut confessio fidelium in trinitate non erret : quae cum sit inseparabilis, nunquam intelligeretur esse trinitas, si semper inseparabiliter diceretur. Bene ergo ipsa difficultas loquendi cor nostrum ad intelligentiam trahit et per infirmitatem nostram coelestis doctrina nos adiuvat.* Augustine (*De doctr. chr.*, I, 5) appropriated *unitas* to the Father, *aequalitas* to the Son and *connexio* to the Spirit ; Thomas Aquinas *potentia* to the Father, *sapientia* to the Son and *bonitas* to the Spirit (*S. theol.*, I, *qu.* 45, *art.* 6, *ad.* 2). Bonaventura (*Breviloq.*, I, 6) has a wealth of appropriations which he partly took over from older sources and partly indicated himself : unity to the Father, truth to the Son and goodness to the Holy Ghost, or eternity to the Father, appearance (*species*) to the Son and event (*usus, fruitio*) to the Spirit, or principle to the Father, execution to the Son and goal to the Spirit, or omnipotence to the Father, omniscience to the Son and benevolence to the Spirit. A particularly typical biblical appropriation was found quite early in the ἐξ αὐτοῦ, δι' αὐτοῦ, εἰς αὐτόν of Rom. 11[36]. We naturally have an appropriation before us when in Luther's Catechism the concepts of Father and creation, Son and redemption and Holy Ghost and sanctification are brought into the well-known close relation to one another, and in this regard it should be noted that whenever Luther comes to speak of the Trinity he never fails to refer to the real unity of what seem to be, and not just seem to be but actually are, threefold statements about God's work. Naturally we find another appropriation in the ternary which Calvin preferred, obviously borrowing from the great mediaeval tradition : *principium, sapientia, virtus.*

The clearest and most complete definition of the concept of appropriation is that given by Thomas Aquinas : *appropriare nihil est aliud quam commune trahere ad proprium . . . non . . . ex hoc quod magis uni personae quam alii conveniat . . . sed ex hoc quod id quod est commune, maiorem habet similitudinem ad id quod est proprium personae unius quam cum proprio alterius* (*De verit. qu.* 7, *art.* 3, cf. *S. theol.*, I, *qu.* 39, *art.* 7–8). The rules to be noted in this definition are as

C.D.—N*

follows according to Roman Catholic dogmaticians (cf., e.g., B. Bartmann, *Lehrb. d. Dogm.*, 7th edn., Vol. I, 1928, p. 215) :

1. The appropriation must not be arbitrary but must take place intelligibly. Not each and every triad, however significant in itself, is adapted even to denote truthfully the mystery of the triunity. There has to be a manifest kinship, similarity and analogy between the three things signifying and the three things signified, as there manifestly is between Father, Son and Spirit on the one hand and the three relations of origin on the other. If this is lacking the appropriation lacks significance.

2. The appropriation must not be exclusive. The appropriation of this or that quality or act of God to this or that mode of being must not be made a property of this mode of being or a distinction that is constitutive for it. What is appropriated belongs in fact to all the modes of being and the distinction between them cannot really be achieved by any appropriation, not even in the last analysis by the designations Father, Son and Spirit.

Evangelical dogmatics will have to add as a third and decisive rule that appropriations must not be invented freely. They are authentic when they are taken literally or materially or both from Holy Scripture, when they are a rendering or interpretation of the appropriations found there. If they are this they will certainly not be arbitrary or exclusive either.

Our statement concerning the comprehensibility of Father, Son and Spirit in God's work obviously requires—we are now enquiring into the unity of the three modes of being *ad extra* too—a dialectical counterpart. It may always be seen already on the margin of what has been said thus far, but it must now be emphasised, that also and precisely in God's work, in God's entry into the sphere of the creature and therefore into the sphere and the limits of our comprehensibility, God is one both in His eternal truth and also in the truth assigned and appropriate to us. It would be pagan mythology to present the work of God in the form of a dramatic entry and exit of now one and now another of the divine persons, of the surging up and down of half or totally individualised powers or forms or ideas, of a shifting coexistence and competition of the three hypostases. Again it is impossible to draw the line plainly and generally between permitted and commanded appropriations and this forbidden mythology. The one may often bear a confusing resemblance to the other. But the line has been drawn ; to the involution and convolution of the three modes of being in the essence of God there corresponds exactly their involution and convolution in His work. The fact that He is particularly manifest for us in this indissolubly and characteristically distinct act or attribute in this or that mode of being may not and must not mean that we have not to believe and worship God in the other modes of being even though they are temporarily hidden from us. Just as Scripture is to be read in context as the witness to God's revelation, just as, e.g., Good Friday, Easter and Pentecost can only say together what they have to say, so we must say that all God's work, as we are to grasp it on the basis of His revelation, is one act which occurs simultaneously and in concert in all His three modes of being. From creation by way of revelation and reconciliation to the coming redemption it is always true that He who acts here is the Father and the Son and the Spirit. And it is true of all the perfections that are to be declared in relation to this work of God that they are as much the perfections of the Father as of the Son and the Spirit. *Per appropriationem* this act or this attribute must now be given prominence in relation to this or that mode of being in order that this can be described as such. But only *per appropriationem* may this happen, and in no case, therefore, to the forgetting or denying of God's presence in all His modes of being, in His total being and act even over against us.

Materially, though not literally, the theological rule with respect to the Trinity : *opera trinitatis ad extra sunt indivisa*, is first found clearly in Augustine : *Sicut inseparabiles sunt, ita inseparabiliter operantur (De trin.*, I, 4). *Ad creaturam Pater et Filius et Spiritus sanctus unum principium, sicut unus creator et unus dominus (ib.*, V, 14). For : *Non potest operatio esse divina, ubi non solum aequalis est, verum etiam indiscreta natura (C. Adrian.*, 15). In the dogma of the Roman Catholic Church this insight has found its most precise expression in the statement of the *Conc. Florent.*, 1441 (Denz., No. 704) : *Pater et Filius et Spiritus sanctus non tria principia creaturae, sed unum principium.* The emphasis with which Luther supported this truth may be recalled again at this point. We must say of it, no less than of the doctrine of the perichoresis, that it is to some extent a proof by way of example in relation to the opposing statements about the *unitas in trinitate* and the *trinitas in unitate.* With the doctrine of appropriations it constitutes the other form of the dialectical outworking of the concept of triunity.

4. THE MEANING OF THE DOCTRINE OF THE TRINITY

By the doctrine of the Trinity we understand the Church doctrine of the unity of God in the three modes of being of Father, Son and Holy Ghost, or of the threefold otherness of the one God in the three modes of being of Father, Son and Holy Ghost. All that had and has to be expounded here in detail could and can expound only the unity in trinity and the trinity in unity. This doctrine as such does not stand in the texts of the Old and New Testament witness to God's revelation. It did not arise out of the historical situations to which these texts belong. It is exegesis of these texts in the speech, and this also means in the light of the questions, of a later situation. It belongs to the Church. It is a theologoumenon. It is dogma. We have asked (§ 8, 2) about its root, i.e., the possibility on the basis of which it could be a dogma in a Church which sought to regulate its doctrine by the biblical witness. And we have seen that this possibility lies in the fact that in the Bible revelation means the self-unveiling, imparted to men, of the God who by nature cannot be unveiled to men. According to the biblical witness this matter is of such a nature that in the light of the three elements of God's veiling, unveiling and imparting we have cause to speak of the threefold otherness of the one God who has revealed Himself according to the witness of the Bible. The biblical witness to God's revelation sets us face to face with the possibility of interpreting the one statement that " God reveals Himself as the Lord " three times in different senses. This possibility is the biblical root of the doctrine of the Trinity. But in the Bible it remains on the level of possibility. We are now asking about the meaning of its actualisation. With what necessity and right did the Church formulate this dogma ? It could do this. Did it have to do it ? What insight was it expressing in the dogma and what reason have we, then, to take pains to understand it ?

Now obviously we cannot discuss this question intelligently if the Church of earlier days which framed this theologoumenon and gave it the status of dogma has become so alien to us that we can view and evaluate it and its intentions only historically, i.e., in this case from outside, as strangers, not really thinking its thoughts with it.

This would be so, e.g., if we could not rise above the recollection that in the controversies before and after Nicaea a very considerable part was played by very non-theological antipathies in ecclesiastical and civil politics, in court relations, and in national and certainly economic matters as well ; or if we could not rise above the recollection that the development of the dogma of the Trinity is unquestionably a chapter in the history of the philosophy of later antiquity, an offshoot of Stoic and Neo-Platonic Logos speculation ; or if with the historical and systematic theologians of the school of A. Ritschl we could not rise above the recollection that the belief in revelation of the Christian world in which this dogma arose was shrouded beyond recognition in the mists of an ancient mystery religion nourished on Orientalisms of every possible kind, that it was embedded in a predominantly physical understanding of the revealed salvation, in a predominantly cosmic interest in the knowledge of revelation, in a predominantly sacramentally orientated piety with which we cannot really identify ourselves and the validity of which we shall perhaps have to call into serious question more from the standpoint of the Reformation than from that of the New Testament. If considerations of this kind, including perhaps a mere sense of reverence for a form sanctified by age, were to have the last word in regard to our participation in the rise of the dogma, what could this mean but that all these events, and the dogma as their result, and all later work attempted along the lines of the dogma, would be fundamentally alien to us? In relation to the decisive point of the dogma, namely, the Christian knowledge of God, we should then be faced by at least a deep suspicion if not an actual certainty that there is really nothing in it, that the only voice here is perhaps that of Byzantine politics, or Stoicism, or Neo-Platonism, or the ancient piety of the mysteries. And in this case any enquiry into the meaning of the doctrine of the Trinity could be pursued only with the aloofness of an astonished and disapproving spectator, and might just as well be abandoned.

We have to realise that if we adopt this attitude we are saying that the Church of earlier days lost, so to speak, its theme, that it need no longer concern us seriously in relation to what it was really intended to be, namely, the Church of Jesus Christ, and that its work does not have any relevance to us except perhaps as an object of contemplation from outside. If we evaluate it as we would evaluate a heresy or even an alien religion we are naturally in no position to ask seriously, i.e., sympathetically, about the meaning of its intention. But we have also to realise that this is a very daring and a very dangerous judgment. It is daring because in making it we are declaring that the Church of earlier days was basically a heresy or an alien religion—a judgment which is not indeed formally impossible, but which involves a heavy responsibility, especially when, as here, the issue is the line in dogmatic history along which, ever since the great and decisive battles of the 4th century, all the Church's significant theologians have unswervingly advanced, including the Reformers and their 17th century successors. And a judgment of this kind might well be dangerous because those in the Church who in this way want to see and understand others only from outside must face the question whether on the contrary it is not perhaps they themselves who are outsiders as the adherents of a heresy or even an alien religion. It is surely more normal and safer to start at least with the assumption that the Church of the earlier period, and specifically the Church of this earlier period, is one and the same as the Church which we know and which we like to call the Church, so that it makes sense to ask seriously, i.e., sympathetically, what it intended by this dogma. The assumption that Jesus Christ did not altogether abandon His Church in this age, and that, notwithstanding all the things that might justly be alleged against it, it is still in place to listen to it as one listens to the Church—this assumption would always seem to have a very definite advantage over its opposite. In any case we certainly need very weighty reasons if we decide to drop, as it were, the Church of any period, adopting that attitude of contemplation and evaluation from outside and no longer listening seriously to its voice. Are the reasons really so compelling in relation to the early period of the Church when the doctrine of the Trinity arose ?

In the dogmatic and theological history of every age, not excluding that of Protestantism, secular factors have played a part which tends to cover over all else. For all the gloating with which it was done, it was a good thing that the work of Pietism and the Enlightenment in Church History established so incontrovertibly the fact that even in such periods of supreme decision as that in which the dogma of the Trinity arose the history of the Church was anything but a history of heroes and saints. Yet in this case we should be just and perceptive and allow that not only the Church of Byzantium but also that of Wittenberg and Geneva, and finally the purest Church of any of the quiet in the land, have always and everywhere been, when examined at close range, centres of frailties and scandals of every kind, and that on the basis of the Reformation doctrine of justification at all events it is neither fitting nor worth while to play off the worldliness of the Church against the seriousness of the insights it has perhaps gained in spite of and in this worldliness. The same may be said about the indisputable connexion of the dogma with the philosophy of the age. By proving philosophical involvement we can reject the confessions and theology of any age and school, and we can do this the more effectively the less we see the beam in our own eye. For linguistically theologians have always depended on some philosophy and linguistically they always will. But instead of getting Pharisaically indignant about this and consigning whole periods to the limbo of a philosophy that is supposed to deny the Gospel—simply because our own philosophy is different—it is better to stick strictly to the one question what the theologians of the earlier period were really trying to say in the vocabulary of their philosophy. Caution is especially demanded when we insist on differences in the so-called piety of different periods and therefore claim that the piety out of which the dogma of the Trinity arose was completely different from our own piety with its sober focus, as they said some years ago, on " worldview and morality." What right have we to regard our own piety, even if its agreement with the Reformation and the New Testament seem ever so impeccable, as the only piety that is possible in the Church, and therefore to exalt it as a standard by which to measure the insights of past ages ? Let us be sure of our own cause so far as we can. But antithetical rigidity especially in evaluating the subjective religion of others is something against which we can only issue a warning.

There seem to be no compelling reasons why we should so distrust the Church of the 4th century and its dogma that we abandon the question as to the meaning of this dogma.

On the other hand, if any one wishes to advance such reasons, we cannot rebut them with counter-arguments. There can be no contesting the formal possibility that any Church might be an apostate church which does not concern us and has nothing to say to us. If we do in fact deny this possibility, this is, as in all similar cases, a decision of faith, or, as we might say more cautiously, a decision which must regard itself as a decision of faith, which can have meaning only as a decision of faith, and for the justification of which we can only appeal in the last resort to the dogma itself and to Holy Scripture confronting both us and the dogma, asking whether the dogma, for all the undeniable and ineradicable limitation of its origin, does not express an insight, which a Church with an ear for Holy Scripture not only could reach but had to reach at a specific time ; whether, by letting Scripture and the dogma speak for themselves, we can escape the conviction that divine truth is given human formulation here in a way in which it had to be formulated at some period, so that this formulation, once achieved, must never be lost or forgotten again ; whether what took place here, while it was certainly exegesis and not infallible revelation, was not still the kind of exegesis that can be confidently described as not merely correct but also important. And if we answer this question in the affirmative, if we thus confess the possibility of regarding ourselves as in the same sphere as the Church of the past which perceived and confessed this dogma as such, i.e., as being one and the same Church with it, if we thus enquire into the meaning of the doctrine of the Trinity, this does not imply a purely accidental personal decision. We should take into account the fact that even to this day this decision is that not merely of the Roman Catholic and Orthodox Churches but also basically of all the great Evangelical Churches as well.

None of them has actually revoked what took place when an express confirmation of the early symbols expressing the doctrine of the Trinity was made a constitutive part of the Reformation confessions in the 16th century. The liturgical recitation of the so-called Apostles' Creed, which is the practice in the Prussian and other territorial churches, repeats in its own fashion this significant event. And every baptism validly performed in our churches at least confronts us with the problem of the doctrine of the Trinity.

No one can say that he knows, and no one is competent to declare, that only pious reverence for a venerable landmark of Christianity has preserved some place for the doctrine of the Trinity in a more or less clear form even in the Evangelical Church as it is now ravaged by Modernism. This fact gives us the external right too, and indeed imposes upon us the task, of enquiring into its meaning at this point.

We should start with the fact that the rise of the doctrine of the Trinity, however varied the factors which contributed to it, was at least governed also by the need to clear up a question with which the Church saw itself confronted by Holy Scripture in the delivery of its message. Assuming that the Church is not only unfaithful by nature, as it has been, of course, in every age, but is also in some degree and sense faithful, so that in its proclamation it has tried to take up the · witness of the Old and New Testaments, there can be no cause for surprise that it has come up against the question which found an answer in the doctrine of the Trinity. Nor can there be any cause for surprise that it came up against this particular question in such a relatively early period, nor need we be surprised at the violence of the conflicts into which it was plunged by this question and the inexorability with which it has adhered through the centuries to the broad line achieved at that time. The question which arose for it out of the commitment of its proclamation to Scripture, and which it answered in the doctrine of the Trinity, was in fact a basic and vital question of the first rank for Church preaching and therefore for Church theology too. We thus regard it as right and proper to put discussion of this question at the head of all dogmatics. This is a practical outworking of what many have said theoretically about its significance from the very earliest times.

But the question that is answered by the doctrine of the Trinity is a very specific question regarding the basic concept of the revelation of God or the basic fact of it as attested in Scripture.

Even if it be regarded as a mere offshoot of the Logos speculation of later antiquity one must at all events concede that its occasion at least is the manifestation of Jesus Christ understood as the revelation of the Logos. It is trying to discuss the deity of this revealed, incarnate Logos. Its second theme, the concept of the Spirit, points in the same direction. And when it speaks of God the Father it is dealing with the point of origin and relation of these two, the Son and the Spirit.

The specific question about revelation which is answered by the doctrine of the Trinity is, however, the question who it is that reveals Himself, the question of the subject of revelation. One may sum up the meaning of the doctrine of the Trinity briefly and simply by saying that *God* is the One who reveals Himself. But if this meaning is to be fully perspicuous one must also reverse the emphasis and say that God is the One who *reveals* Himself. For the strictness and logic of the answer to the question about the subject of revelation consist in the fact that as we enquire into the interpretation of this answer we find ourselves referred back again to revelation itself. The Church doctrine of the Trinity is a self-enclosed circle. Its decisive and controlling concern is to say with exactitude and completeness that *God* is the Revealer. But how can it say this with exactitude and completeness unless it declares that none other than the *Revealer* is God ? One might put this more simply by saying that the doctrine of the Trinity states that our God, namely, He who makes Himself ours in His revelation, is really God. And to the question, But who is God ? there may then be given the no less simple answer, This God of ours. Is it not true that the main answer and the subsidiary answer are the simple but no less momentous presuppositions of all Christian thought and talk about God ? The first and last criterion of Christian proclamation is whether it moves in the circle indicated by these two answers. Christian theology can be only an exercise in this movement. The question of the subject of revelation and therefore of all God's dealings with man, which the Bible itself does not answer but poses in all its sharpness, calls indeed for an answer. Can we not understand the haste with which men felt called to answer it and the undoubtedly extraordinary zeal with which they set about this work ? Was this not precisely because it was such a simple and yet such a central matter ? And could the question be answered in any other way ? Or is this problem not really set in the Bible ? Could it be answered otherwise than it has been answered in the doctrine of the Trinity ?

The problem which we think we see posed in the Bible and which points towards the Church doctrine of the Trinity consists in the fact that the being and speech and action and therefore the self-revealing of God are described there in the moments of His self-veiling or self-unveiling or self-impartation to men, that His characteristic attributes are holiness, mercy and love, that His characteristic demonstrations are denoted in the New Testament by Good Friday, Easter and Pentecost, and that His name is correspondingly the name of Father, Son, and Holy Ghost. The Bible does not state expressly that the Father, Son and Holy Ghost are of equal essence and are thus in the same sense God Himself. Nor does it state expressly that thus and only thus, as Father, Son and Holy Ghost, God is God. These two express declarations, which go beyond the witness of the Bible, are the twofold content of the Church doctrine of the Trinity.

The doctrine of the Trinity means on the one side, as a rejection of Subordinationism, the express statement that the three moments do not mean a more and a less in God's being as God. The Father is not to be understood as the true God in distinction from the Son and the Spirit, and the Son and the Spirit are not, in distinction from the Father, favoured and glorified creatures, vital forces aroused and set in motion by God, and as such and in this sense revealers. But it is God who reveals Himself equally as the Father in His self-veiling and holiness, as the Son in His self-unveiling and mercy, and as the Spirit in His self-impartation and love. Father, Son and Spirit are the one, single, and equal God. The subject of revelation attested in the Bible, no matter what may be His being, speech and action, is the one Lord, not a demi-god, either descended or ascended. Communion with the One who reveals Himself there always and in all circumstances means for man that this God meets him as a Thou meets an I and unites with him as a Thou unites with an I. Not otherwise ! Totally excluded is a communion with this God of the kind that we can have with creatures, namely, of such a kind that the Thou can be changed by an I into an It or He over which or whom the I gains control. Also and particularly as Son and Spirit, the One who reveals Himself according to the witness of Scripture does not become an It or He, but remains Thou. And in remaining Thou He remains the Lord. The subject of revelation is the subject that remains indissolubly subject. One cannot get behind this subject. It cannot become object. All Subordinationism rests on the intention of making the One who reveals Himself there the kind of subject we ourselves are, a creature whose Thouness has limits we can survey, grasp and master, which can be objectified, in face of which the I can assert itself. Note well that according to Subordinationist teaching even the Father, who is supposedly thought of as the Creator, is in fact dragged into the creaturely sphere. According to this view His relation to Son and Spirit is that of idea to manifestation. Standing in this comprehensible relation, He shows Himself to be an entity that can be projected and dominated by the I. Subordinationism finally means the denial of revelation, the drawing of divine subjectivity into human subjectivity, and by way of polytheism the isolation of man with himself in his own world in which there is finally no Thou and therefore no Lord. It was against this possibility that the Church was striking when it rejected Arianism and every form of Subordinationism. We ask whether it did well in this regard or not.

The doctrine of the Trinity means on the other side, as the rejection of Modalism, the express declaration that the three moments are not alien to God's being as God. The position is not that we have to seek the true God beyond these three moments in a higher being in which He is not Father, Son and Spirit. The revelation of God and therefore His being as Father, Son and Spirit is not an economy which is foreign to His essence and which is bounded as it were above and within, so that we have to ask about the hidden Fourth if we are really to ask about God. On the contrary, when we ask about God, we can only ask about the One who reveals Himself. The One who according to the witness of Scripture is and speaks and acts as Father, Son and Spirit, in self-veiling, self-unveiling and self-imparting, in holiness, mercy and love, this and no other is God. For man community with God means strictly and exclusively communion with the One who reveals Himself and who is subject, and indeed indissolubly subject, in His revelation. The indissolubility of His being as subject is guaranteed by the knowledge of the ultimate reality of the three modes of being in the essence of God above and behind which there is nothing higher. Totally excluded here is all communion that means evading His revelation or transcending the reality in which He shows and gives Himself. God is precisely the One He is in showing and giving Himself. If we hasten past the One who according to the biblical witness addresses us in threefold approach as a Thou we can only rush into the void. Modalism finally entails a denial of God. Our God and only our God, namely, the God who makes Himself ours in His revelation, is God. The relativising of this God which takes place in the doctrine of a real God beyond the revealed God implies a relativising, i.e., a denying, of the one true God. Here, too, there is no Thou, no Lord. Here, too, man clearly wants to get behind God, namely, behind God as He really shows and gives Himself, and therefore behind what He is, for the two are one and the same. Here, too, we have an objectifying of God. Here, too, the divine subjectivity is sucked up into the human subjectivity which enquires about a God that does not exist. Here too, but this time by way of mysticism, man finally finds himself alone with himself in his own world. This possibility, which in its root and crown is the same as the first, is what the Church wanted to guard against when it rejected Sabellianism and every form of Modalism. And again we ask whether it did well in this regard or not.

The doctrine of the Trinity tells us—this is the positive thing which it was defending on the polemical fronts—how far the One who reveals Himself according to the witness of Scripture can in fact be our *God* and how far He can in fact be *our* God. He can be our God because in all His modes of being He is equal to Himself, one and the same Lord. In terms of the doctrine of the Trinity knowledge of revelation as it may arise from the witness of Scripture means in all three moments of the event knowledge of the Lord as the One who meets us and unites Himself to us. And this Lord can be our God, He can meet us and unite Himself to us, because He is God in His three modes of being as Father, Son and Spirit, because creation, reconciliation and redemption, the whole being, speech and action in which He wills to be our God, have their basis and prototype in His own essence, in His own being as God. As Father, Son and Spirit God is, so to speak, ours in advance. Thus the doctrine of the Trinity tells us that the God who reveals Himself according to Scripture is both to be feared and also to be loved, to be feared because He can be God and to be loved because He can be our God. That He *is* these two things the doctrine of the Trinity as such cannot tell us. No dogma and no theology as such can. The doctrine of the Trinity as such is not the Word of God which might tell us. But if there is a ministry to this Word of God, a proclamation which can become the Word of God, and a ministry to this ministry, dogmatics as critical reflection on the proper content of proclamation, then the question as to the subject of revelation, to which the doctrine of the Trinity is an answer, must be the first step in this reflection. Scripture, in which the problem of the doctrine of the Trinity is posed, is always the measure and judge of the solution to this problem. It stands above the dogma of the Church and therefore above the critical reflection to which we let ourselves be led by the dogma of the Church. But all things considered we venture to think that, pending better instruction, this leading is an appropriate one.

§ 10

GOD THE FATHER

The one God reveals Himself according to Scripture as the Creator, that is, as the Lord of our existence. As such He is God our Father because He is so antecedently in Himself as the Father of the Son.

1. GOD AS CREATOR

In the event which the Bible describes as revelation God deals with man as the Lord : not as a being of the kind and order to which man himself belongs and therefore not as a being over which man for his part might equally well be lord ; nor yet as a being which exists and remains in and for itself in its own kind and order. These are the two errors or lies about God which are set aside by revelation. God deals with man as the Lord, i.e., as the authority which in distinction from all others is absolutely superior to man, but which, even in this absolute superiority, also concerns and claims man with the same absoluteness. The fact that God reveals Himself, i.e., that He deals with man as Lord, is not equivalent to saying that He has and exercises power over man. Power is indeed the presupposition and means of lordship. We are speaking of lordship when one person brings himself to the awareness of another, an I to a Thou, as the bearer of power, when a superior will makes its power known. This is what takes place in the event that the Bible calls revelation. This is why the prevailing names for God are Yahweh in the Old Testament and Kyrios in the New.

But who is the Lord and therefore the God to whom the Bible is referring ? As we have seen already, it is typical of the Bible in both the Old Testament and the New that its answer to this question does not point us primarily to a sphere beyond human history but rather to the very centre of this history.

The answer is that at the climax of the biblical witness Jesus of Nazareth is the Kyrios. He is the One who approaches man in absolute superiority. He is the self-revealing God. We shall return in the next section to this confession which characterises the whole form and content of the biblical testimony and which is decisive as the presupposition of the Christian Church.

Even in the New Testament, however, the answer that Jesus of

Nazareth is the Lord is by no means self-evident. It never became this in the Church and it can never do so. Why not ? If this Jesus of Nazareth was a true and real man, there is an asymmetrical element about the answer. At all events its symmetry has to be disclosed. In the first instance the New Testament ascribes the true and real deity expressed by the predicate Kyrios to One who is quite other than Jesus.

In the name Christ, which it gives to Jesus, it reminds us of the prophets, priests and kings of the Old Testament as authorised and sanctified men of Yahweh behind whom and above whom there stands the One who is primarily and properly authoritative and holy. It calls Jesus the Word or Son of God, the One who was sent into the world by God as the light and life of men. It understands the dignity of Jesus, the lordship of Jesus and the superiority of Jesus as basically different and subordinate compared to that of the Other who is properly called θεός. In the so-called Synoptic Gospels this approach is especially prominent. It almost sounds like a false note, and is certainly an enigma, when even and precisely in these Gospels Jesus is called Kyrios. For what is Jesus here but a single pointer to the Lord whose kingdom (not His own) Jesus announces and declares by word and deed in a way that hardly distinguishes Him either formally or materially from John the Baptist, in relation to whom as the only One who is good (Mk. 10¹⁸) Jesus associates Himself with His disciples in the address : Our Father !, whose will He very definitely differentiates from His own (Mk. 14³⁶), to whom He prays, as is repeatedly emphasised, and obedience to whom seems to be in the last resort the whole meaning of His calling and work. He is thus called the *(ἅγιος) παῖς* of God like David and the Servant of the Lord of Isaiah 53 by what seems to be an ancient layer of the tradition, but one that was very highly regarded in the literature of the 2nd century, cf. Mt. 12¹⁸ ; Ac. 3¹³,²⁶ ; 4²⁷,³⁰. How could Jesus be more emphatically separated and distinguished from Him who is properly called God than by putting on His lips the doubly disconcerting : *Eloi, Eloi, lama sabachthani !* (Mk. 15³⁴) ? The One who is properly called God in the Synoptics seems unquestionably to be the " Father in heaven " who constitutes the background of the event recorded and therefore, with incomparable significance, the basis of its meaning. Even in John there not only stands the much-noted " The Father is greater than I " (Jn. 14²⁸) but once again Jesus consistently portrays Himself as the emissary of the Father (the *μόνος ἀληθινὸς θεός*, Jn. 17³) whose life is to do His will and speak His words and finish His work, whose triumph is simply to go to the Father, and through whom men come to the Father (Jn. 14⁶). With regard to all the Gospels, the Fourth included, A. von Harnack was surely right when he said of Jesus : " Aim, power, insight, result, and stern compulsion—all come to Him from the Father. This is how it is in the Gospels ; we cannot turn or twist it " (*Wesen d. Christentums*, 1906, p. 80). Similarly Paul is never tired of pointing to the Father, the " Father of Jesus Christ," who is side by side with Jesus and in some sense beyond Him and above Him. The greeting in nearly all his letters runs : Χάρις ὑμῖν καὶ εἰρήνη ἀπὸ θεοῦ πατρὸς ἡμῶν καὶ κυρίου Ἰησοῦ Χριστοῦ. Does this imply that he is expressly calling " God our Father " the Father of our Lord Jesus Christ too ? According to Eph. 1¹⁷, where He is called ὁ θεὸς τοῦ κυρίου ἡμῶν Ἰησοῦ Χριστοῦ, ὁ πατὴρ τῆς δόξης this might undoubtedly be the case. Or is it that the two, θεὸς πατήρ and κύριος Ἰησοῦς Χριστός, as is assumed in the Vulgate and Luther's translation, are set alongside one another as the common source of grace and peace ? What is beyond question is that the κύριος Ἰησοῦς Χριστός is separate from and subordinate to θεὸς πατήρ: Ἡμῖν εἷς θεὸς ὁ πατὴρ . . . καὶ εἷς κύριος Ἰησοῦς Χριστός (1 Cor. 8⁶) ; Ὑμεῖς δὲ Χριστοῦ, Χριστὸς δὲ θεοῦ (1 Cor. 3²³) ; Ἀνδρὸς ἡ κεφαλὴ ὁ Χριστός ἐστιν . . . κεφαλὴ δὲ τοῦ Χριστοῦ ὁ θεός (1 Cor. 11³). Jesus Christ is κύριος εἰς δόξαν θεοῦ πατρός (Phil. 2¹¹), He is the προσαγωγὴ πρὸς τὸν θεόν (Eph. 2¹⁸). He will finally hand over the kingdom τῷ θεῷ καὶ πατρί (1 Cor. 15²⁴). He is the εἰκὼν τοῦ θεοῦ (2 Cor. 4⁴; Col. 1¹⁵). And so Hebrews calls Him the ἀπαύγασμα τῆς δόξης (Heb. 1³), the πιστὸν ὄντα τῷ ποιήσαντι αὐτόν (Heb. 3²), who offered Himself without spot to God (Heb. 9¹⁴), and it gives a depiction of His passion which is very reminiscent of the Synoptic portrayal: ὃς ἐν ταῖς ἡμέραις τῆς σαρκὸς αὐτοῦ, δεήσεις τε καὶ ἱκετηρίας πρὸς τὸν δυνάμενον σῴζειν αὐτὸν ἐκ θανάτου μετὰ κραυγῆς ἰσχυρᾶς καὶ δακρύων προσενέγκας καὶ εἰσακουσθεὶς ἀπὸ τῆς εὐλαβείας, καίπερ ὢν υἱός ἔμαθεν ἀφ᾽ ὧν ἔπαθεν τὴν ὑπακοήν (Heb. 5⁷⁻⁸).

Looked at along these lines the lordship of Jesus as the Son of God is obviously only a manifestation, exercise and application of the lordship of God the Father. The essence of the deity ascribed to Jesus is to make clear and impart and give effect to who God the Father is, who God is in the true sense, and what He wills and does with man. It is to represent this God the Father.

Filius revelat agnitionem Patris per suam manifestationem (Irenaeus, *C. o. h.*, IV, 6, 3) . . . *ut in suis verbis non tam se quam Patrem adspiciamus . . . ut sic defixis oculis in Christum recta trahamur et rapiamur ad Patrem* (Luther, *Comm. on Gal.* 1⁴, 1535, *W.A.*, 40ᴵ, p. 98, l. 25). We should " know that Christ is the proper epistle, the golden book wherein we read, and learn to see before our eyes the will of the Father " (*Two German Fast Sermons*, 1518, *W.A.*, 1, p. 274, l. 41), " who is a mirror of the fatherly heart " (*Gr. Cat.*, 1529, *W.A.*, 30ᴵ, p. 192, l. 5). Along these lines A. von Harnack once formulated what was at the time a much disputed statement : " Not the Son but the Father alone belongs to the Gospel as Jesus proclaimed it " ; more explicitly his meaning here is that Jesus' witness to His own person did not belong to the Gospel proclaimed by Him as one ingredient or proposition along with others but it belonged to it as an expression of the fact that He knew Himself to be the way to the Father.

If in answering the question about Him who in Scripture is called the Lord it is right to start with the confession : Jesus is Lord, it is also right to let ourselves be pointed first in the different and as it seems opposite direction, and thus to ask : What is the goal to which Jesus is the way ? Whom or what does He reveal in so far as He reveals God the Father ? What do we see in Him to the degree that He is God's reflection and mirror ? Who is the Father of our Lord Jesus Christ ? The answer which the New Testament gives us here is a very different one from that which a natural and edifying but utterly arbitrary exposition of the word " father " might yield. What may be known as the manward will of the heavenly Father in what takes place through and to Jesus does not lie primarily in the direction of a genial affirmation, preservation and insurance of human existence but rather in that of a radical questioning and indeed abrogation of it.

Note that already in the Old Testament the term " father " is no less to be interpreted by " lord " than *vice versa* (Deut. 32⁶; Mal. 1⁶). That men are as such children of God, that God is a Father to them as such, is stated neither in the Old Testament nor the New. But according to the Old Testament Israel is chosen and called out of the multitude of nations to be the child of Yahweh. " Out of Egypt have I called my son " (Hos. 11¹).

And by a " new birth," and so by a re-establishment of natural existence which is totally inconceivable to man and beyond its dissolution, man is set in this sonship according to the New Testament (Jn. 1¹²ᶠ˙; 3³ᶠ˙). " Every plant, which my heavenly Father hath not planted, shall be rooted up," is the inexorable law which applies here (Mt. 15¹³). It is in fact the suffering Servant of the Lord of Isaiah 53 who is rediscovered in Jesus (Ac. 8²⁶ᶠ˙). In all four Gospels the story of Jesus' life is described as one which, strictly speaking, is from the very first a story of self-declaring and increasingly self-actualising death. Ἡμεῖς δὲ κηρύσσομεν Χριστὸν ἐσταυρωμένον, writes Paul (1 Cor. 1²³), well aware that this is God's wisdom which is necessarily an offence to the Jews and foolishness to the Greeks. It is as the High-priest of the new covenant who is Himself the victim that the author of Hebrews understands Him. His obedience is an obedience of suffering (Heb. 5⁸), obedience μέχρι θανάτου, θανάτου δὲ σταυροῦ (Phil. 2⁸). For this reason God has highly exalted Him and given Him the name κύριος Ἰησοῦς Χριστός (Phil. 2⁹⁻¹¹). The Lamb that was slain is worthy to receive power and riches and wisdom and strength and honour and glory and praise (Rev. 5¹²). Ἐν τῇ ταπεινώσει ἡ κρίσις αὐτοῦ ἤρθη. This is why the continuation of His life is unthinkable : ὅτι αἴρεται ἀπὸ γῆς ἡ ζωὴ αὐτοῦ (Ac. 8³³). He is the grain of wheat that must fall into the ground and die in order to bring forth much fruit (Jn. 12²⁴). Beyond the death of the man Jesus of Nazareth lies the place from which there falls on Him the light that makes Him the revelation of God the Father : ἐξ ἀναστάσεως νεκρῶν. He is instituted as the Son of God (Rom. 1⁴). God the Father acts on Him and through Him by raising Him from the dead (Gal. 1¹; 1 Cor. 6¹⁴; Rom. 4²⁴; 6⁴; Eph. 1²⁰). The believer calls Him who reveals Himself thus in Jesus Ἀββὰ ὁ πατήρ (Gal. 4⁶; Rom. 8¹⁵). He who sees Jesus sees this Father (Jn.14⁷ᶠ˙). The Jesus " who was delivered for our offences and was raised again for our justification " (Rom. 4²⁵) is the One to whom this applies. And since faith is faith in Jesus it is itself faith in the will and work of this Father. Being baptised into Christ is being baptised into His death, " being planted together in the likeness of his death " (Rom. 6³ᶠ˙, cf. Phil. 3¹⁰), being crucified and dead with Him in His crucifixion (Gal. 5²⁴; Rom. 6⁶; Col. 3³; Eph. 4²²). Already in the Synoptics, then, following Jesus is identical with self-denial and taking up one's cross (Mk. 8³⁴) and one can save one's life only by losing it for Jesus' sake (Mk. 8³⁵). Beyond this strait gate lies absolutely everything the New Testament can say about καινότης ζωῆς (Rom. 6⁴) in the baptised and believing. And the One who deals thus with men in Christ, who leads them along this way to this goal, is called by believers Father and " Father of the Lord Jesus Christ." He is the Father of the Son who was dead and is alive again, who was lost and is found (Lk. 15²⁹). Μετανοεῖν, to reverse one's thinking, to think afresh, to think through to God and His kingdom, really means in the New Testament too, and here especially, to consider the fact that we must die (Ps. 90¹², cf. Ps. 39⁵). Nor does it just mean this, but all else it might mean it can mean only if first and decisively it means this. Note that Thy name, Thy kingdom and Thy will are the objects of the first three petitions of the prayer directed to " our Father, which art in heaven " (Mt. 6⁹ᶠ˙), and it is on these that the three which follow rest. In the context of the New Testament the Thy makes these petitions absolutely equivalent to the saying : " Teach us to reflect that we must die."

The One whom Jesus reveals as the Father is known absolutely on the death of man, at the end of his existence. His will enters the life of man, not identically with death, nor merely in the same way as death, but really with death, executing death on man, impressing the signs of death upon man. Only in the sharply drawn boundary line of the cross, which is to be drawn again and again, is His will revealed as the will to quicken, bless, and benefit. The life that His will creates will be a life that has passed through death, that is risen from death ; it will be eternal life, truly a new birth.

What is the bearing of all this on our question : Who is God the Father ? As stated, this cannot mean that God the Father is identical with death, with the negation of human existence. Here rather death is vanquished in death and negation in negation. Resurrection is indeed the power of the cross and the gaining of life the power of the losing of life. But strictly and exclusively it is only as the power of the cross, of the losing of life, that there is resurrection here and the gaining of life. This implies at all events that God the Father is also not identical with what we know as our life or perhaps with its meaning and power, that His will stands over against our will to live, supreme, unbound, or rather in absolute control. Not only will it be impossible to establish what God the Father wills with us by the way of self-understanding, of analysis of our own existence. Rather it cannot be concealed from us that even to its deepest foundations and powers this existence of ours is set in radical crisis by the will of God, that as the will of God the Father is done upon it, it must become new. God the Father wills neither our life in itself nor our death in itself. He wills our life in order to lead it through death to eternal life. He wills death in order to lead our life through it to eternal life. He wills this transition of our life through death to eternal life. His kingdom is this new birth.

This is the reason for the remarkable relativising of the concepts of life and death which we find especially in Paul : 1 Cor. 3[22] ; Rom. 8[38] ; 14[8] ; Phil. 1[20]. Eternal life or resurrection life is undoubtedly for Paul the requickening of this life of ours—the requickening which is willed by God and is to be expected from God (1 Cor. 15[53] ; 2 Cor. 5[4]). But the requickening of this life of ours beyond the transition through death means that on this side of the gate it must lie on the scales with death and be jointly counterbalanced by the hope of faith.

We sum all this up by saying that God the Father, whose will and work on men these are, is the Lord of our existence. He is this in the strict sense to the degree that He is the Lord over the life and death of man. All other lordship which is not to be seen on this frontier of death cannot be lordship over our existence. At the very most it can only be lordship in our existence. The lordship of a God identical with our will to live would be limited by the lordship of death. And the lordship of a God identical with death would be only the frontier of our ability to live. Neither would be lordship over our existence. For our existence is our will and ability to live in its limitation by death, not just our life and not just its limitation by death. Not even then would it be real lordship. It would not be the bearer of a power which is really superior to us and which encounters us. The real Lord of our existence must be the Lord over both life and death. And this is precisely God the Father as we find Him attested in Scripture as the the One revealed in Jesus. But the Lord of existence is the Creator. For if God is the Lord of existence in the full sense of the term, this means that our existence is sustained by Him and by Him alone above the abyss of non-existence. It has no autonomous reality whether in its certainty as life or its imperilling by death. It is real in so far as He wills and posits it as real. It has an Author from whom as such it is absolutely distinct and to whom it is absolutely related, but not in such a way that it belongs essentially to this Author to have something really outside Himself, not in such a way that there is anything necessary for Him in this relation. It has an Author outside whom nothing is necessary, and who is not necessarily related to anything outside Himself. It has an Author who calls into existence and sustains in existence out of free goodness and according to His own free will and plan, in a free antithesis, determined only by Himself, to the nothing in which it might remain, but without anything being dependent on this. It has—this is what all these statements are describing—a Creator. And it is as the Creator that Jesus shows the Father to us. He also shows Him to us negatively : He whose will was done on Golgotha when in and with Jesus Christ the life of all of us was nailed to the cross and died in order that thereby and therein eternal life might be manifest—*He* is what the concept of Creator signifies.

Note how in Rom. 4¹⁷ the God of Abraham is called in one breath the ζωοποιῶν τοὺς νεκρούς and the καλῶν τὰ μὴ ὄντα ὡς ὄντα.

By the name " father " we do, of course, denote the natural human author of our existence. But our natural human father is not our Creator. He is not the lord of our existence, not even the lord of our life, let alone our death. When Scripture calls God our Father it adopts an analogy only to transcend it at once.

Hence we must not measure by natural human fatherhood what it means that God is our Father (Is. 63¹⁶). It is from God's fatherhood that our natural human fatherhood acquires any meaning and dignity it has. God is the Father ἐξ οὗ πᾶσα πατριὰ ἐν οὐρανοῖς καὶ ἐπὶ γῆς ὀνομάζεται (Eph. 3¹⁵).

God our Father means God our Creator (cf. for this Deut. 32⁶ and Is. 64⁷). And it should be clear by now that it is specifically in Christ, as the Father of Jesus Christ, that God is called our Creator. That God is our Creator is not a general truth that we can know in advance or acquire on our own ; it is a truth of revelation. Only as that which we know elsewhere as the father-son relation is transcended by the Word of Christ the Crucified and Risen, only as it is interpreted by this Word, which means, in this case, only as it acquires from this Word a meaning which it cannot have of itself, only in this way may we see what creation means. But in this way we can see. The Father of Jesus Christ who according to the witness of Scripture is revealed in Jesus His Servant has the qualities of a Lord of our existence. The witness to Him leads us to the place where the miracle of creation can be seen. It bears witness to the holy God, the God who alone is God, the free God. It is this witness that we have to understand with the help of the basic statements of the doctrine of the Trinity.

2. THE ETERNAL FATHER

The decisive statement by which the answer just given to the question : Who is God the Father ? is elevated to the status of an element in the knowledge of the triune God along the lines of Church dogma, must be as follows : God as the Father of Jesus Christ can be our Father because even apart from the fact that He reveals Himself as such He already is the One He reveals Himself to be, namely, the Father of Jesus Christ, His Son, who as such is Himself God. God can be our Father because He is Father in Himself, because fatherhood is an eternal mode of being of the divine essence. In the One whose name, kingdom and will Jesus reveals, in distinctive differentiation from the One who reveals Him and yet also in distinctive fellowship with Him, we have to do with God Himself.

How is it that with the Church dogma we reach this understanding of the biblical witness to God the Father ? The answer must simply be that we reach it as we accept the biblical witness and take it seriously to the degree that formally it absolutely conditions and binds the content of the revelation of the Father by its impartation in the person of the Revealer Jesus of Nazareth. Its content cannot be abstracted from this form. There can be no question here of distinguishing between content and form as though the content could be regarded as divine and necessary and the form as human and contingent, the former being the essence and the latter the historical manifestation of the revelation. The form here is essential to the content, i.e., God is unknown as our Father, as the Creator, to the degree that He is not made known by Jesus.

It is especially the Johannine tradition which expresses this exclusiveness with ever-renewed emphasis : Jn. 1[18] ; 5[23, 37] ; 6[46] ; 8[19] ; 14[6] ; 17[25] ; 1 Jn. 2[23] and 2 Jn. 9. Καθὼς γινώσκει με ὁ πατὴρ κἀγὼ γινώσκω τὸν πατέρα (Jn. 10[15]) and therefore ὁ ἑωρακὼς ἐμὲ ἑώρακεν τὸν πατέρα (Jn. 14[9]). But in the long run it is to be found with the same unmistakable clarity in the Synoptists too : Πάντα μοι παρεδόθη ἀπὸ τοῦ πατρός μου, καὶ οὐδεὶς ἐπιγινώσκει τὸν υἱὸν εἰ μὴ ὁ πατήρ, οὐδὲ τὸν πατέρα τις ἐπιγινώσκει εἰ μὴ ὁ υἱὸς καὶ ᾧ ἐὰν βούληται ὁ υἱὸς ἀποκαλύψαι (Mt. 11²⁷).

If this exclusiveness is accepted and taken seriously, if that abstraction between form and content is thus seen to be forbidden, this rules out the possibility of regarding the first article of the Christian faith as an article of natural theology. Jesus' message about God the Father must not be taken to mean that Jesus expressed the well-known truth that the world must have and really has a Creator and was venturing to give this Creator the familiar human name of father. It must not be taken to mean that Jesus had in mind what all serious philosophy has called the first cause or supreme good, the *esse a se* or *ens perfectissimum*, the universum, the ground and abyss of meaning, the unconditioned, the limit, the critical negation or origin, and that He consecrated it and gave it a Christian interpretation and baptised it by means of the name " father," which was not entirely unknown in the vocabulary of religion. In this regard we can only say that this entity, the supposed philosophical equivalent of the Creator God, has nothing whatever to do with Jesus' message about God the Father whether or not the term " father " be attached to it. Nor would it have anything to do with it even if the principle : Die and become ! were related and perhaps identified with the transcendent origin and goal of the dialectic of losing life and gaining it. An idea projected with the claim that it is an idea of God is from the standpoint of the exclusiveness of the biblical testimonies an idol, not because it is an idea but because of its claim. Even the genuinely pure and for that very reason treacherously pure idea of God in a Plato cannot be excluded. If the exclusiveness is valid, Jesus did not proclaim the familiar Creator God and interpret Him by the unfamiliar name of Father. He revealed the unknown Father, His Father, and in so doing, and only in so doing, He told us for the first time that the Creator is, what He is and that He is as such our Father.

In interpreting the address " our Father " it is thus important that in Jn. 20¹⁷ Jesus does not say : I go to our Father, but : ἀναβαίνω πρὸς τὸν πατέρα μου καὶ πατέρα ὑμῶν καὶ θεόν μου καὶ θεὸν ὑμῶν. It is not κατὰ φύσιν but κατὰ θεοῦ χάριν καὶ θέσει, ἀφάτῳ φιλανθρωπίᾳ, through the Son and the Holy Ghost, that we have God as Father (Cyril of Jerus., *Cat.*, 7, 7–8).

In relation to the knowledge of God the Father this implies that God is not just God the Father because He is the Creator and therefore our Father. He is so for this reason too, and this is the *opus ad extra* which is manifest in Jesus. But from the fact that in Jesus and Jesus alone He is manifest as the Creator and therefore as our Father it follows that He already is that which corresponds thereto antecedently and in Himself, namely, in His relation to the One through whom He is manifested, and therefore in His relation to Jesus. If it is true that we have to learn fatherhood from the will of God fulfilled on and by Jesus, and if it is also true that any abstraction of this will from the fact that it is fulfilled on and by Jesus is ruled out by the exclusiveness mentioned above, then we have to understand His fatherhood as that which applies previously to Jesus, and therefore as that which corresponds to a sonship in Jesus, irrespective of what it means for us. There is thus a fatherhood in God Himself whose truth does not first consist in the fact that He is the Creator and that we are His children by grace but already and primarily in the fact that a revelation of our new birth and therefore a revelation of creation, i.e., of His lordship over our existence, can take place. The possibility of this in God Himself is the Son of God who is identical with Jesus of Nazareth. In relation to Him and therefore as the Father of this Son God is antecedently Father in Himself.

Faith in God the Father must be proclaimed in such a way that implicitly at once, and unconfused by recollection of other fatherhoods, faith in the only-begotten Son may be impressed upon the hearers. Τὸ γὰρ τοῦ πατρὸς ὄνομα ἅμα τῷ τῆς ὀνομασίας προσρήματι νοεῖν παρέχει καὶ τὸν υἱόν. . . . Εἰ γὰρ πατήρ, πάντως ὅτι πατὴρ υἱοῦ (Cyril of Jerus., *Cat.*, 7, 3–4). *Per prius paternitas dicitur in divinis secundum quod importatur respectus personae ad personam quam secundum quod importatur respectus Dei ad creaturam* (Thomas Aquinas, *S. theol.*, I, qu. 33, art. 3c). God is Father *secundum relationem quam habet ad personam filii* (Polanus, *Syntagma theol. chr.*, 1609, III, 4, quoted from Heppe, *Dogm. d. ev.-ref. Kirche*, 1861, p. 92).

In relation to this original fatherhood of God the dogma of the Trinity speaks of the person or, as we should say, the mode of being of God the Father. It is not in this mode of being alone that God is God. He is so, too, in the possibility, or, as we must say, the possibilities in which He is revealed as the One who acts upon us in the new birth. He is so, if there is not really to be an abstraction between revelation and its content, in the modes of being of the Son and the Holy Spirit as well. But precisely if this is so, the content of revelation, inasmuch as it is also the revelation of creation, of the divine lordship over our existence, refers us back to a corresponding inner possibility in God Himself which, in order, is to be understood as the first and original possibility presupposed in all others. In this first original possibility He is God the Father in the sense of the dogma of the Trinity : the eternal Father.

Πρὸ πάσης ὑποστάσεως καὶ πρὸ πάσης αἰσθήσεως, πρὸ χρόνων τε καὶ πρὸ πάντων τῶν αἰώνων τὸ πατρικὸν ἀξίωμα ἔχει ὁ θεός (Cyril of Jerus., *Cat.*, 7, 5).

One should not say that the use of the name " Father " here is a transferred, improper and inadequate use. This could be said only if the standard of what is proper both here and generally were our language or the created reality to which our language is related. If the Creator is the standard of what is proper for the creature and therefore for our language too, then the very reverse must be said : Not merely the use of the name of father for the originating relationship in which one creature stands to another is improper, but in the last resort so is its use for the relation of God as Creator to the creature as we have read this off from the revelation of the new birth. God alone as He who He is by Himself, and therefore as the eternal Father of His eternal Son, is properly and adequately to be called Father. From the power and dignity of this only proper name of Father there flows by grace and for faith the improper—the really improper though certainly not on that account untrue—name of Father for God as the Creator, and from this again the naming of the intracreaturely originating relation, the thing that is called fatherhood in heaven and on earth (Eph. 3¹⁵). This, too, is to be regarded as a true but improper appellation dependent on the power and dignity of God's intratrinitarian name of Father.

Οὐ γὰρ ὁ θεὸς ἄνθρωπον μιμεῖται, ἀλλὰ μᾶλλον οἱ ἄνθρωποι διὰ τὸν θεόν, κυρίως καὶ μόνον ἀληθῶς ὄντα πατέρα τοῦ ἑαυτοῦ υἱοῦ, καὶ αὐτοὶ πατέρες ὠνομάσθησαν τῶν ἰδίων τέκνων (Athanasius, *Or. c. Ar.*, I, 23).

God's trinitarian name of Father, God's eternal fatherhood, denotes the mode of being of God in which He is the Author of His other modes of being.

Fons ergo ipse et origo est totius divinitatis (*Conc. Tolet.*, XI, 675, Denz., No. 275). In this mode of being the Fathers describe Him as αὐτόθεος, ἄναρχος, ἀγέννητος, θεὸς ἐπὶ πάντων, as *a nullo originem habens, a se ipso existens, ingenitus, innascibilis, principium sine principio*.

It must be strictly noted that this origination, which is the incomparable model of the relation between Creator and creature, which itself in turn is the incomparable model of all intracreaturely originating relations, refers to the mutual relations of the divine modes of being and is not, then, to be taken to mean that there is between the Father on the one side and the Son and Holy Spirit on the other a relation of super- and subordination regarding their deity. The divine essence would not be the divine essence if in it there were superiority and inferiority and also, then, various quanta of deity. The Son and the Spirit are of one essence with the Father. In this unity of divine essence the Son is from the Father and the Spirit from the Father and the Son, while the Father is from Himself alone. That is to say, the intradivine possibility in virtue of which God can be manifest to us as the Creator and as our Father is not a self-grounded and self-reposing possibility. It rather presupposes a possibility of this kind and it presupposes an event in God in virtue of which it is posited as a possibility. It arises out of a self-grounded and self-reposing possibility in God. It is—and all this is to be regarded as an intradivine relation or movement, as *repetitio aeternitatis in aeternitate*—the copy of an original, the issue from a source, the word of a knowledge and the decision of a will. This, the original, source, knowledge and will in God from which proceeds the second thing, the copy, issue, word and decision, in short, the fact that as the Creator and as our Father He can set Himself in relation to everything distinct from Him—this first thing in God Himself is the eternal Father in the sense of the doctrine of the Trinity. God is the eternal Father inasmuch as from eternity and in eternity He is the Father of the Son who from eternity and in eternity participates in the same essence with Him. In this relation and not in any other way God is God—the God who reveals Himself in the Son as the Creator and as our Father. From this insight arise two important conclusions especially with regard to this revelation of His through the Son.

1. From the eternity of the relation of the Father and the Son, in which that of the relation of both to the Holy Spirit is also contained, it necessarily follows first that not only God the Father is to be claimed as the Creator and as our Father, and that God the Father is not only to be claimed as the Creator and as our Father. We have said above that the use of the name Father for this relation and act of God *ad extra* is a derived and improper use. Revelation in so far as it is the revelation of God the Creator and our Father, and in so far as this its content is not to be separated from its form as revelation in Jesus, leads us to the knowledge of God as the eternal Father. But in this very knowledge we cannot separate the Father from the Son and from the Holy Ghost. In this knowledge, then, there necessarily becomes plain to us the purely relative significance of the way of isolation on which we have reached this knowledge. It implies an " appropriation " (cf. § 9, 3) when by isolation we regard specifically God the Father as the Creator and as our Father and when we regard God the Father specifically as the Creator and as our Father. The triunity does not mean that three parts of God operate alongside one another in three different functions. *Opera trinitatis ad extra sunt indivisa*, as also the essence of God is a single and undivided essence and the *trinitas* itself is an *individua trinitas*. Thus not only the subject of the first article of the Creed is the Father Almighty, Creator of heaven and earth, but with Him, in the order and sense pertaining to each, the subjects of the second and third articles too. And again the subject of the first article is not only the Father Almighty, Creator of heaven and earth, but also, again in the appropriate order and sense, the subject of reconciliation like the subject of the second article and the subject of redemption like that of the third article. Not the Father alone, then, is God the Creator, but also the Son and the Spirit with Him. And

the Father is not only God the Creator, but with the Son and the Spirit He is also God the Reconciler and God the Redeemer. The very knowledge of the intratrinitarian particularity of the name of Father is thus a guarantee of the unity of God which would be endangered by regard for the particularity of God's revelation as the Creator and our Father if this were not guided by this apparently—but only apparently —very speculative intratrinitarian insight. Because God is the eternal Father as the Father of the Son, and with Him the origin of the Spirit, therefore the God who acts in reconciliation and redemption, and who reveals Himself as the Reconciler and Redeemer, cannot be a second and third God or a second and third part of God ; He is and remains God *unus et individuus* in His work as in His essence.

All theological favouritisms are thus forbidden : the one-sided belief in God the Father which was customary in the Enlightenment ; the so-called Christo-centrism which Pietism loved and still loves ; and finally all the nonsense that is and can be perpetrated with isolated veneration of the Spirit. We cannot call God our Father apart from the Son and the Spirit, nor can we call the Son Saviour or the Spirit Comforter without also having the Father in view in both cases.

This insight safeguards the trinitarian dogma of the eternal Father, the Father of His only-begotten Son.

2. But from the same eternity of the relation between Father and Son, in which the eternity of the relation of both to the Holy Spirit is also expressed, it follows, secondly, that the necessary relativisation of the knowledge of revelation which leads us to perception of this eternal relation cannot imply any disparagement or discrediting of this way of knowledge. The fact that the understanding especially of God the Father as the Creator, and of God the Creator as the Father, is an improper understanding because God is One in His work and essence, does not mean that it is an untrue and illegitimate understanding which we must abandon. " Improper " here can only mean that it is not an exhaustive understanding, that it is one-sided, that it needs to be supplemented, that we cannot and should not adopt it exclusively, that we cannot and should not proclaim its exclusive validity, that it must imply what is not actually contained in it as such. The appropriation which we make when we understand God the Father and creation too in this particularity is not just permitted ; it is also commanded. And in all its relativity the knowledge based upon it is true knowledge. Without making this appropriation we could not even see that it is " only " an appropriation. It is on the way of knowledge founded upon it, and upon it alone, that we can reach the goal from which the relativity of the way as a way may be perceived. In fact the appro-priation simply corresponds to the reality of the revelation attested to

us in Scripture, and the impropriety of the knowledge based on the appropriation corresponds to the reality of the faith which apprehends the revelation, which is not sight. The dogma of the Trinity, which earlier reminded us of the unity of God's essence and work, will not lead us beyond revelation and faith, but into revelation and faith, to their correct understanding. It is quite out of the question, therefore, that the appropriation of especially God the Father for creation, or of creation for the Father, should be merely a provisional view which can be transcended and which will dissolve and disappear in a higher gnosis of the one God. In no sense does God's unity mean the dissolution of His triunity. God reveals Himself as the One He is. The dogma of the Trinity says this too. Because the relation of Father, Son and Spirit includes within it the unity and distinction of the three modes of being, the very eternity of this relation tells us that God's work *ad extra* too is no less truly distinct in its unity than united in its distinction. In regard to the work of Father, Son and Spirit *ad extra* we earlier applied the stipulation that they all work in the order and sense appropriate to them. This means that the unity of their work is to be understood as the communion of the three modes of being along the lines of the doctrine of " perichoresis " (cf. § 9, 3), according to which all three, without forfeiture or mutual dissolution of independence, reciprocally interpenetrate each other and inexist in one another. The unity cannot be taken to mean, then, that the truth with reference to God's work *ad extra* entails an extinction of the independence of the three modes of being in a neutral, undifferentiated fourth, so that with Modalism no statement relating to this *opus ad extra* can be seriously made about a specific mode of being, and all statements relating to this *opus ad extra* can be made indiscriminately about any individual mode of being. We are simply emphasising here an integral part of our theme, namely, that the Father is not the Son and is not the Spirit. This remains true in the *opus ad extra* too, so assuredly is it true from and to all eternity. Part of the distinction is the appropriation in which we equate the Creator with God the Father and God the Father with the Creator. It is only an appropriation to the degree that it does not also express the truth of perichoresis, of the intercommunity of Father, Son and Spirit in their essence and work. But it expresses the truth and imparts true knowledge to the degree that with the equation it touches upon and denotes the distinction which there is also in the *opus ad extra*, the order and sense in which God as the Triune is the subject of the *opus ad extra indivisum*. It expresses the truth to the degree that with its specific emphasis on the Father or Creator it points to the affinity between the order of God's three modes of being on the one hand and that of the three sides of His work as Creator, Reconciler and Redeemer on the other. There is an affinity between the relation of the

Father to the Son on the one hand and the relation of the Creator to the creature on the other. In both cases, though in a sense which differs *in toto coelo*, we are concerned with origination. In respect of this affinity it is not merely permitted but commanded that we ascribe creation as a *proprium* to the Father and that we regard God the Father *peculiariter* and specifically as the Creator. Conversely, the eternal truth of this distinction, which is valid for the *opus ad extra* too, yields the insight that certain statements about the work of the Son and the Spirit cannot be appropriated to the Father even though God the Father is no less the subject of reconciliation and redemption than the Son and the Spirit.

One cannot say of God the Father that He was conceived and born, that He suffered, died and rose again. One also cannot say of Him that there had to be prayer for His coming and that He was to be poured out on all flesh. For one thing, all these statements stand in affinity to the relation of the Son or Spirit to the Father and not *vice versa* ; their content thus applies *peculiariter* to the Son and Spirit and not the Father. Again, the statements in the second article especially relate to God the Son in so far as in His action as the Reconciler He assumed humanity and hence creatureliness. Applied to God the Father they would thus collide with His affinity to the essence and action of God as the Creator. It is true that in the incarnation of the Word the Creator became a creature. It is also true that the Holy Spirit for whom we pray is the *Creator Spiritus*. Hence we neither can nor should deny a presence of the Father also in the Son who was born and suffered and died and in the Spirit who was poured out at Pentecost. But it would be just as improper to say that God the Father died as to say that Jesus of Nazareth or the Spirit of Pentecost created heaven and earth.

It is, of course, impossible to draw an absolutely unambiguous line between what is commanded and what is forbidden. One can only say that the doctrine of perichoresis, which admits of misuse in a one-sided emphasis on the involution of the three modes of being, also contains the further element which should be a warning against misuse, namely, the understanding of the involution as a convolution, the presupposition of the eternal independence of the three modes of being in their eternal communion. And in any case one can say very definitely that any systematising of the one-sidedness such as is found in part in ancient Modalism (e.g., in the form of Patripassianism) is absolutely forbidden, since it would mean the dissolution of the triunity in a neutral fourth. The eternity of the fatherhood of God does not mean only the eternity of the fellowship of the Father with the Son and the Spirit. It also protects the Father against fusion with the Son and the Spirit. We must not arrive at this fusion on the basis of the principle *opera trinitatis ad extra sunt indivisa*. It would not only be contrary to the dogma of the Trinity. It would also be incompatible with any serious acceptance of the biblical witness which makes the Father and the Son one in their distinction. It is thus right and necessary that for all our awareness of the unity of the Father with the Son and the Spirit the knowledge of the Father as the Creator and our Father should always be a particular knowledge. Only when it is taken seriously in its particularity does it lead to that awareness, and the very awareness will lead us constantly to take it seriously in its particularity too.

GOD THE SON

The one God reveals Himself according to Scripture as the Reconciler, i.e., as the Lord in the midst of our enmity towards Him. As such He is the Son of God who has come to us or the Word of God that has been spoken to us, because He is so antecedently in Himself as the Son or Word of God the Father.

1. GOD AS RECONCILER

We return to the starting-point of the previous section where we began with the question : Who is the One whom Holy Scripture calls the Lord, who has dealings with man in revelation ? and where we gave the answer that at the climax of the biblical witness it is stated (obviously with the intention of stating what is true and valid for the whole of the biblical witness, including the Old Testament) that Jesus of Nazareth is this Lord. We then followed first of all the line in the New Testament message in which, in apparent antithesis to the statement, Jesus of Nazareth is understood rather as the Servant of the Lord who proclaims and does the will of His heavenly Father. But we then saw how also and especially the revelation of the Father might appear primarily as its pure Mediator Jesus, and how it cannot be abstracted in any sense from this Mediator according to the biblical witness. What God reveals in Jesus and how He reveals it, namely, in Jesus, must not be separated from one another according to the New Testament, and on the assumption that this prohibition is to be taken seriously we have to regard the concept of God as the Father in His relation to this Mediator of His revelation as a mode of being which truly and definitively appertains to Him ; we have to regard His fatherhood as an eternal one.

We now turn our attention again to the other line of biblical testimony which we touched on for a moment and then left again, namely, the line on which the emphasis lies, not on the distinction of Jesus from the Father, but, without denying this distinction, directly on His communion and even unity with the Father. To the statements about the relation of the Father to the Son to which we referred in the previous section there corresponds exactly a series of statements about the relation of the Son to the Father. The development of the dogma of the Trinity began with these statements and *a priori* it is to be expected that we shall have to follow the dogma again and specifically at this point too if the unity of the Son with the Father attested in these statements, and therefore the deity of Jesus Christ, is to be understood as definitive, authentic and essential.

In this regard we must refer already to the ascribing of the name of Kyrios to Jesus, even though this is, of course, wrapped in all manner of obscurity. Is apostolic usage adopting here the title of the divine world-ruler well-known in Hellenistic Egypt ? Or the title given in Syria to the cultic god in contrast to his slaves, the adherents of the cult ? Or the title of the emperor in the imperial religion of Rome ? Be that as it may, in the light of its significance beyond the confines of contemporary Judaism the name immediately removes the One described thereby far from the sphere of other men to the side of " deity " in the more or less serious sense of the concept as this might arise in the religious world in question ; it sets Him at the point where there should in every case be offered to Him that bending of the knee to which Paul refers in Phil. 2[10]. Furthermore— and this clarifies the matter at once—in view of the close connexion between the early Church and the Palestinian and Hellenistic Synagogue it cannot possibly have happened unawares and unintentionally that this word was at any rate used as well to translate the Old Testament name of God Yahweh-Adonai, and was then applied to Jesus. We are pointed in the same direction by the practical meaning of the name Jesus as the name in which they prophesied, taught, preached, prayed and baptised, in which sins were forgiven, demons driven out, and other miracles were done, in which His followers were to gather, in which they were to receive one another, in which they were to believe, on which they were to call, in which they were to be upheld, for the sake of which they were to be hated and despised, to renounce all their earthly possessions and even perhaps to die, in which again they are washed, sanctified and justified (1 Cor. 6[11]), and which is, so to speak, the place, the sphere, in which all they speak and do is to take place (Col. 3[17]). The name of Yahweh has precisely the same comprehensive and pervasive meaning in the Old Testament (cf. § 8, 2) ; the name of Yahweh is simply Yahweh revealed to men. Who, then, is Jesus if His name has this significance ? Is there really any need of the express declaration of Paul (Phil. 2[9]) that God has given Him the name that is above every name ?

As a second general phenomenon which points in the same direction—it is the merit of K. L. Schmidt (RGG[2], Art. " Jesus Christ ") to have brought this emphatically to our attention—we may cite the fact that the New Testament tradition has presented the revealing activity of Jesus as an inextricable inter-relation of word and act and indeed of word and miracle. Τὰ περὶ Ἰησοῦ τοῦ Ναζαρηνοῦ, apart from the final events in His life which are crucial for the meaning and direction of the whole, may be summed up in the words : ἐγένετο ἀνὴρ προφήτης δυνατὸς ἐν ἔργῳ καὶ λόγῳ (Lk. 24[19]), or : ἃ ἤρξατο ποιεῖν τε καὶ διδάσκειν (Ac. 1[1]). But these and similar summary accounts, which often enough (e.g., Ac. 2[22] ; 10[38]) seem to be acquainted only with Jesus the miracle-worker, simply formulate an impression which an impartial reading of, say, St. Mark's Gospel, cannot fail to leave, namely, that the teaching, which is, of course, presented here, is not meant to be understood apart from but only through the interpretation of the action which invariably accompanies it. It is a weakness of R. Bultmann's *Jesus* (1926) that he ignores this insistent demand of the texts and construes Jesus one-sidedly in terms of His sayings. The acts which invariably speak and are to be heard as well are miraculous acts. How they are connected with the central content of the words of Jesus may be seen from the story of the paralytic in Mk. 2¹⁻¹², where to the horror of the scribes—who immediately speak of blasphemy and not unjustly from their standpoint—Jesus not only speaks of the forgiveness of sins but actually forgives sins and, to show His authority for this act-word, cures the paralytic. God's act as it takes place visibly, the totality of a gracious act on man, emphasises that the word spoken is God's Word. This is the meaning of the miracles ascribed to Jesus (and expressly to His apostles too on the basis of the authority conferred on them by Jesus)—and it marks off these miracles, however we assess them materially, as at any rate something very distinctive amid the plethora of miracle stories in that whole period. Their distinctive feature, however, lies in their complete and indissoluble combination with the word of Jesus, a combination which distinguishes this word no less from mere prophesying than the miracles from mere thaumaturgy, a combination in which both word and deed in the same way give evidence of something above and beyond ethos (" history ") and physis, of a higher authority confronting the whole state of human and indeed cosmic reality. Who is the One who, obviously speaking representatively for this higher authority, can speak thus because He can act thus and act thus because He can speak thus ?

It might be said of the further titles ascribed to Jesus in the New Testament, the titles of Messiah-Christ, Son of Man and Son of God, that in themselves they are ambiguous or even obscure. Thus in the ancient Orient Son of God was a widespread term simply for the king. But the context of New Testament Christology makes this title, too, eloquent in a distinctive way. He whom the Gospel wants to depict, so the Fourth Evangelist begins, the Word which became flesh, tabernacled among us, and was seen by us in His glory (Jn. 1¹⁴), this Word, unlike all other words, was not a created human word only relating to God and only speaking of God and about God. As Word it was spoken where God is, namely, ἐν ἀρχῇ, *in principio* of all that is, πρὸς τὸν θεόν, belonging to God, therefore itself θεός, God by nature (Jn. 1¹), identical with the Word through which—πάντα δι' αὐτοῦ ἐγένετο—God called into being and existence everything that is (Jn. 1³). No more and no less than God Himself is there when this Word, οὗτος, i.e., Jesus, whose story the Gospel aims to tell, is there as light in the darkness which does not apprehend the light (Jn. 1². ⁴⁻⁵). The θεὸς ἦν ὁ λόγος is then expressly repeated in Jn. 1¹⁸ (according to the correct reading) : μονογενὴς θεὸς ὁ ὢν εἰς τὸν κόλπον τοῦ πατρός, He has revealed the invisible God. The same equation between the seen, heard and handled object of Christian proclamation and the ὁ ἦν ἀπ' ἀρχῆς is also made in 1 Jn. 1¹. Similarly Paul says : θεὸς ἦν ἐν Χριστῷ καταλάσσων (2 Cor. 5¹⁹), and : ἐν αὐτῷ κατοικεῖ πᾶν τὸ πλήρωμα τῆς θεότητος σωματικῶς (Col. 2⁹). The passage Heb. 1⁵ᶠ·, in which the majesty of the Son of God is established even above the angelic world, is noteworthy because in the words quoted from the Psalms even the distinction between θεός, which is perhaps still to be construed adjectivally and inexactly, and ὁ θεός disappears, and the Son is expressly called ὁ θεός. Jesus can be styled ὁ μέγας θεός (Tit. 2¹³), ἴσος τῷ θεῷ (Jn. 5¹⁸ ; Phil. 2⁷), ἐν μορφῇ θεοῦ ὑπάρχων (Phil. 2⁶), the ἴδιος υἱός of His Father (Rom. 8³²), the υἱὸς τῆς ἀγάπης αὐτοῦ (Col. 1¹³), the υἱὸς ὁ μονογενὴς (Jn. 3¹⁶· ¹⁸ ; 1 Jn. 4⁹), ὁ ἐκ τοῦ οὐρανοῦ καταβάς (Jn. 3¹³, ³¹). He can say of Himself : ἐγὼ καὶ ὁ πατὴρ ἕν ἐσμεν (Jn. 10³⁰). He has come from the Father (Jn. 16²⁸). He has already worked hitherto, as His Father has worked (Jn. 5¹⁷). He has life in Himself, as His Father has life in Himself (Jn. 5²⁶). Whoever has seen Him has seen the Father (Jn. 14⁹). He can say with the Father : Before Abraham was, I am (Jn. 8⁵⁸). And He can say to the Father : Thou lovedst Me before the creation of the world (Jn. 17²⁴). For He had glory before the existence of the world (Jn. 17⁵). Ὁ θρόνος σου ὁ θεὸς εἰς τὸν αἰῶνα τοῦ αἰῶνος is what Heb. 1⁸ has God say to His Son. He is the Alpha and Omega, the First and the Last, the ἀρχή and the τέλος (Rev. 22¹³, cf. 1⁸· ¹⁷), He who is and was and is to come ὁ παντοκράτωρ (Rev. 1⁸), the same yesterday, to-day and for ever (Heb. 13⁸). For this reason it may be said of Him, as the Prologue of John already emphasises, that through Him God made the aeons (Heb. 1²), that He is the Word of power by which He upholds all things (Heb. 1³), that in Him everything was made that is in heaven and on earth (Col. 1¹⁶ ; 1 Cor. 8⁶). He is πάντων κύριος (Ac. 10³⁶). He can say of Himself : All things are delivered unto Me of My Father . . . and therefore : Come unto Me, all ye that labour and are heavy-laden, and I will refresh you (Mt. 11²⁷⁻²⁸). Similarly the content of Peter's confession in Mt. 16¹⁶ : " Thou art the Christ, the Son of the living God," occurs again later (Mt. 26⁶³ᶠ·) as the " blasphemy " which leads Jesus to the cross.

This is the second line of the New Testament tradition that is found alongside the first line which we emphasised in the previous section. What is now meant by " Jesus the Lord " is the deity of Jesus Christ.

The New Testament statement about the unity of the Son with the Father, i.e., the deity of Christ, cannot possibly be understood in terms of the presupposition that the original view and declaration of the New Testament witnesses was that a human being was either exalted as such to deity or appeared among us as the personification and symbol of a divine being.

The essential understanding is threatened already if one agrees with M. Dibelius (RGG² Art. " Christologie ") in formulating the problem of New Testament Christology as the way in which " knowledge of the historical figure of Jesus was so quickly transformed into faith in a heavenly Son of God." The question is whether one can presuppose that knowledge of a historical figure came first and a transforming of this into faith in the heavenly Son of God came second, so that we have then to ask in terms of the history of thought how this came about. We see no possibility of this road ending anywhere but in a blind alley. If the question is put in this way there are in the main two modern historical attempts to explain the origin of the above formulation (cf. for a description of them K. L. Schmidt at the beginning and end of the article quoted, but already Schleiermacher, *Der. chr. Glaube*, § 22), and materially these correspond exactly and very remarkably with the two most important side-lines of christological thought which arose as early as the 2nd century and which were finally rejected by the Church.

First, the New Testament statement about Christ's deity can be taken individualistically as the apotheosis of a man, a great man, who as such, through the mystery of his personality and work, had such an effect on those around Him that there inevitably arose the impression and idea that He was a God. Such a man was Jesus of Nazareth, the author and preacher of a life-style unheard of in His own time and more or less in later times—a life-style of childlikeness, freedom, obedience, love and faithfulness even to death, so that He became the more or less willing or unwilling Founder of the Christian religion and the Christian Church. From the inspired and inspiring country Rabbi He was, and as whom His disciples originally respected Him, He rose in their eyes to the stature of an Elijah. From the political Messiah He originally was for them as well, He rose to the stature of the Son of David who as such could also be called the Son of God, of a heavenly being who attests His presence in visions even after death, who lives on in His " spirit," and is thus pre-existent, until, gaining in fervour in inverse ratio to its remoteness from the historical object, the claim transcends itself and equation between Jesus and God is no longer impossible. The idea now is that at some specific point, at His birth or baptism or transfiguration on the mount or resurrection from the dead, God appointed the man Jesus to this dignity and adopted Him as His Son. This could be a good symbol for what men themselves had done in the zeal of their Christ-enthusiasm. To the " eye of faith " a remarkable man who had once been known as such, and who strictly was always kept in view, was idealised upwards as God, as could happen and actually had happened to other heroes. This is Ebionite Christology, or Christology historically reconstructed along the lines of Ebionitism.

Secondly, the New Testament statement about Christ's deity could also be taken in just the opposite sense, collectively. In Him, the theory runs, we have the personification of a familiar idea or general truth, e.g., the truth of the communion of deity and humanity, or the truth of the creation of the world by God's word and wisdom, or the truth of redemption by the way of " Die and Become," or the truth of the juxtaposition of truth and goodness or forgiveness and claim. The fact that the manifestation of this idea was seen in Jesus of Nazareth was more or less accidental and indifferent, so indifferent that the concrete humanity of His earthly existence, or finally even its historical reality, could be queried. He was believed in as theophany or myth, as the embodiment of a general truth, as the familiar Son of Man of Daniel or the familiar pre-existent Logos or the familiar world-deliverer of whom all Hellenism thought it had some knowledge, or as an analogue of the divine hypostases taught by the Rabbis when they spoke of *Memra* (the Word), *Shechinah* (the glory) and *Metatron* (the supreme archangel of God). As and to the degree that the symbol of this idea was seen and venerated in Jesus of Nazareth, He was called Kyrios, Son of God, and finally, in full awareness of the implied dialectic, God Himself. The power of the Christ-enthusiasm which had both the ability and the need to make this equation was the power of the idea, the power of the concept of the condescending and self-manifesting God, which simply found in its connexion with Jesus of Nazareth its specific crystallisation, just as then and in other ages it has demonstrably found similar crystallisations. The general " eye of faith " had now also and specifically fallen on Him. But what was in view was the idea, not the Rabbi of Nazareth, who might be known or not known as such with no great gain or loss either way, whom there was at any rate a desire to know only for the sake of the idea. This is Docetic Christology, or Christology historically reconstructed along the lines of Docetism.

These two conceptions or explanations of the statement about the deity of Christ seem to be in greater self-contradiction than is actually the case. The former understands Jesus as the peak or a peak of history soaring into super-history. The latter understands Him as the sucker of super-history reaching down into history. According to the former He is the supreme manifestation of human life, while according to the latter He is the most perfect symbol of divine presence. Obviously it should not be very hard to relate these two conceptions to one another dialectically or to reconcile them with each other. Common to both is the notion that strictly speaking the New Testament statement about Christ's deity is a form of expression that is meant very loosely and is to be interpreted accordingly.

As early as the 2nd century the Church rejected both Ebionitism and Docetism and in so doing it also ruled out in advance the corresponding modern explanation. And the New Testament statement about Christ's deity can in fact be understood only on the assumption that it has nothing whatever to do either with the apotheosis of a man or with the personification of an idea of God or divine idea. It avoids these alternatives. But this takes place, of course, on a line in which the plane on which the Ebionite and Docetic lines intersect is itself cut by another plane, and therefore in a third dimension, perpendicular to it and to the two lines. If one thinks persistently on this plane with its two dimensions one can never escape the dialectic of history and super-history or super-history and history, the conception of a Christ-enthusiasm in which a heavenly essence arises out of a historical form or a historical form out of a heavenly essence. In this case one will persistently speak, not of the Christ of the New Testament, but of idealising and mythologising man, and of Jesus as the object of the thought of this man. But if so one is not speaking of God's revelation. The New Testament statement about Christ's deity makes sense only as witness to God's revelation. Any other exegesis is blatantly opposed to the opinion of the authors and in conflict with them. Ebionitism and Docetism are misunderstandings of a dialectic that is inevitably at work in the thought and utterance of the New Testament authors, for it is indisputable that men—because it has pleased God to assume humanity—are thinking and speaking here, and that the first plane with its two dimensions is the sphere in which they think and speak. (We shall return to the dialectic present in the New Testament itself in connexion with the doctrine of the incarnation of the Word.) Even on this plane, however, what they think and say has a different meaning from that it seems to have when seen from the standpoint of Ebionite and Docetic thinking. This other meaning is given by the fact that while the thought and utterance of the New Testament witnesses takes place on the first plane like all human thought, it is related to the second plane which falls upon it perpendicularly and which is identical with God's revelation. It is thus true that even in what the New Testament witnesses think and say one may plainly see and distinguish a kind of opposite movement. It is true that especially in the Synoptists we are presented on the whole with a christological thinking which finds *God* in Jesus and that especially in the Fourth Gospel we are presented on the whole with another christological thinking which finds God in *Jesus*. But the first does not mean that the Synoptists found God in a mere man, in the figure of a great man, in an impressive personality, in a hero. And the second does not mean that John found an idea, a general truth of an intellectual, moral or religious kind, personified specifically in Jesus. One will search the New Testament documents in vain for the fatal starting-point of Ebionite Christology, i.e., personality, or the fatal starting-point of Docetic Christology, i.e., idea. These can never be anything but an arbitrary construction behind the documents and in contradiction with them. The starting-point of Synoptic thought, which finds *God* in Jesus, is the fact, manifest to certain men, of the divine envoy as such. It is the unambiguous fact of the man who was among them teaching and healing, dying and rising again, as a reality which did not first have to be disclosed and interpreted and asserted, but which directly called to their lips the confession : Thou art the Christ, the Son of the living God (Mt. 16¹⁶), not as a synthetic but as an analytic statement. And the starting-point of Johannine thought, which finds God in *Jesus*, was the fact, manifest to certain men, of the divine mission, message and revelation which they found in Jesus, the enactment of " grace and truth," " resurrection and life," the actual event of their being fed with the bread of life (Jn. 6³⁵), their actual drinking of the living water (Jn. 4¹⁰). " We beheld—his glory." And this led again, though now in the reverse direction, as a synthetic and not as an analytic statement, to Peter's confession, which must be here : Κύριε, πρὸς τίνα ἀπελευσόμεθα; ῥήματα ζωῆς αἰωνίου ἔχεις· καὶ ἡμεῖς πεπιστεύκαμεν καὶ ἐγνώκαμεν ὅτι σὺ εἶ ὁ ἅγιος τοῦ θεοῦ (Jn. 6⁶⁸). In the light of these real starting-points of New Testament thought, and already with these starting-points, the common goal, the statement about Christ's deity, is easy to understand. It was not that a historical figure had first to be changed into a heavenly being or a heavenly being into a historical figure, and that either way knowledge had to be transformed into faith. The New Testament witnesses tell us how their unbelief, not their knowledge, was changed into faith, and the opposed movement of their thought then takes place within faith. This has in fact nothing whatever to do with the dialectic of Ebionitism and Docetism. For what is meant by the first step on a way at whose end a man is equated with God, and what is meant by the first step on another way at whose end God is a man ? Can this be the end of a way if it was not already its beginning ? Can the decisive assertion in the corresponding statements, or the corresponding statement which is to the same effect in both instances, be understood as a result of thought won in ascending or descending reflection or interpretation ? Can this assertion be anything but an explanation of the presupposition taken directly from the presupposition, a *petitio principii*, as a logician would unquestionably have to say here ? The material point in the New Testament texts is that *God* is found in Jesus because in fact Jesus Himself cannot be found as any other than God. And God is found in *Jesus* because in fact He is not found anywhere else but in Jesus, yet He is in fact found in Him. This factual element at the start of the two ways of New Testament thought is revelation, the point of reference which lies in another dimension and which distinguishes this thinking from that of the Ebionites and Docetics and their modern successors. Against the background of this factual material which is simply there in the New Testament texts one may certainly advance the following considerations too. When the Ebionite and Docetic Christologies presuppose that at the end of ascending or descending reflection—reflection on the man Jesus as such and reflection on deity in special relation to the man Jesus— we simply have a small or even a big exaggeration with whose help the statement about Christ's deity arises or is explained, they ascribe to the thought of the biblical witnesses an achievement which the latter themselves would have regarded as the blasphemy of which Jesus was accused, but falsely so, according to their records. If Jesus had called Himself, or the primitive Church had called Him the Son of God in the sense presupposed by these two conceptions, then He and His Church would have been rightly expelled from the Old Testament community. For what could the idealising of a man or the mythologising of an idea be but characteristically the very thing that the Old Testament understood by the setting up and worship of an idol, of an unworthy and empty rival of Yahweh ? Those who think, or hyperbolically allege that they think, that a man can really become God or that the real God could have a copy in a man have very little understanding of the word " God " in the Old Testament sense. If we can claim that the first generation of the witnesses of Jesus are in any degree true Israelites or Palestinian Jews ; if we can be confident that they understand the difference between God and man, not as a quantitative one that could be easily bridged, but as a qualitative one, then we can describe it as an *a priori* impossibility that they should have thought in the way they would have to have thought if they understood the statement about Christ's deity along the lines of those two conceptions. If they could make this statement at all as Palestinian Jews ; if they believed that they could not only reject the charge of blasphemy against Jesus as a frightful misunderstanding but also proclaim it as the end of the Old Testament, as the event in which Israel, by rejecting no more and no less than Yahweh Himself, finally renounced its own birthright, then on their lips the statement could not be the product of ascending or descending speculation but in its twofold movement it could be only the expression of an axiomatic presupposition, an explanatory statement about the absolute beginning of their thought which is posited in advance for their thought. The explanation of their statement that Jesus is Lord is to be sought only in the fact that for them He was the Lord, and was so in the same factual and self-evident and indisputable way as Yahweh was of old Israel's God. The utter embarrassment of a historical approach which on the one hand cannot conceal the fact that the statement " is already essentially present in the most ancient literary testimonies, the

C.D.—O*

epistles of Paul," and yet on the other hand will not take this presupposition into account, may be seen in the words of Johannes Weiss : " The fusion of hitherto unrelated conceptual elements at this centre presupposes a power of attraction which we cannot overestimate. How strong the indirect or direct effect of the personality of Jesus must have been on the souls of His followers if they were ready to believe this of Him and to die for this belief ! " (RGG[1], Art. " Christologie," I). What is the meaning of " power of attraction, of indirect or direct effect," in this case, in relation to this effect ? One may well ask whether apart from all else, the early Church did not perhaps have more sense of historical reality and possibility when it left it to heretics to wander to and fro along the beaten tracks of apotheosis and hypostasis Christology and thought it more natural to seek the meaning of the New Testament statement about Christ's deity in the corresponding factual presupposition as this is presented to us in the New Testament itself.

Jesus is Lord—this is how we think we must understand the New Testament statement in concert with the ancient Church—because He has it from God whom He calls His Father to be the Lord, because with this Father of His, as the Son of this Father, as " the eternal Father's only child," He *is* the Lord—an " is " which we deny if we are unable to affirm it with those who first uttered it, yet which cannot be deduced, or proved, or discussed, but can only be affirmed in an analytic proposition as the beginning of all thinking about it. In distinction from the assertion of the divinisation of a man or the humanisation of a divine idea, the statement about Christ's deity is to be understood in the sense that Christ reveals His Father. But this Father of His is God. He who reveals Him, then, reveals God. But who can reveal God except God Himself ? Neither a man that has been raised up nor an idea that has come down can do it. These are both creatures. Now the Christ who reveals the Father is also a creature and His work is a creaturely work. But if He were only a creature He could not reveal God, for the creature certainly cannot take God's place and work in His place. If He reveals God, then irrespective of His creaturehood He Himself has to be God. And since this is a case of either/or, He has to be full and true God without reduction or limitation, without more or less. Any such restriction would not merely weaken His deity ; it would deny it. To confess Him as the revelation of His Father is to confess Him as essentially equal in deity with this Father of His.

But what does it mean for us—for this must be our starting-point as well—to confess Jesus as the revelation of His Father and therefore as His true Son ? If now we consider this and stress that Jesus as the Revealer of the Father and His will and work does not merely proclaim to us our Lord but in so doing is Himself our Lord, so that He also reveals Himself as the Son of the Father, then to the degree that what takes place here is an act of God this obviously signifies something very different from the activity of God the Creator which we understood as the epitome of the content of the revelation of the Father. Over and above the reality of God's lordship over our existence it implies God's lordship in the fact that He turns to us, that indeed He comes to us, that He speaks with us, that He wills to be heard by us and to arouse our response. It signifies the reality of an intercourse which He has established between God and us. God does not just will and work. In His revelation in Jesus Christ He discloses to us His will and work. He does not treat us as dust or clay, even though we are this as His creatures. He does not just subject us to His power as Creator or cause us to be controlled by His power as Creator so as to fulfil His purpose in us. He seeks us as those who can let themselves be found. He converses with us as those who are capable of hearing, understanding and obeying. He deals with us as the Creator, but as a person with persons, not as a power over things. " Your brother is the eternal good." And this is by no means obvious. It is miraculous, and this not merely nor primarily as a miracle of power, as the mystery in which the principle *finitum non capax infiniti* is abrogated. Naturally this is true too. But the abrogation of this principle is not the real mystery of the revelation of the Son of God. The real mystery is the abrogation of the other and much more incisive principle : *homo peccator non capax verbi divini*. God's power to establish intercourse with us is also called in question of course, but in the long run not decisively, by the fact that He is infinite and we are finite, that He is Lord of life and death and we live as those who are limited by death, that He is the Creator and we are those who have been called out of nothing into being and existence. God's ability is decisively called in question, however, by the fact that we are God's enemies. How do we know that ? Certainly not of ourselves. Certainly not in and with the fact that we are aware of the problematic nature of our being and existence as men, of the conflict between the spiritual and the natural sides of our existence, or of the conflict between our theoretical ideals and our practical achievements, or of the antinomies generally in which the course of our thought and existence runs. The fact that we are God's enemies never follows from these intrinsically incontestable facts, and if we were to view it as only an expression of these familiar facts it could only be described as a misanthropic exaggeration. The insight that " I have sinned . . . and am no more worthy to be called thy son " (Lk. 15[18f.]) is not an insight of abstract anthropology. Only the son who is already recalling his father's house knows that he is a lost son. We know that we are God's enemies first and solely from the fact that God has actually established that intercourse with us. But precisely on the assumption of the factuality of this event we can regard this event itself only as miraculous. The Word of God whose revelation is attested in Scripture tells man that he is a rebel who has wantonly abandoned the fellowship between himself as creature and God as Creator and set himself in a place where this fellowship is impossible. It tells him that he wanted to be his own lord and therewith betrayed and delivered up himself to the sphere of God's wrath, the state of rejection by God, and therefore of being closed up against God. It tells him that contrary to its destiny by creation his existence is a contradiction against God, a contradiction which excludes listening to God. It thus tells him, strangely, that he cannot hear at all the Word of God which tells him this, and that he cannot hear it because he will not hear it, because his life-act is disobedience and therefore factually, in respect of the use he makes of his life, it is a refusal to listen to what God says to him. Indeed, this content of the Word of God spoken to man makes it quite inconceivable that man should even get to hear God's Word, that God should turn to him at all and address him. The fact that he is closed up to what God can say to him is simply an expression of the wrath of God resting upon him. If this wrath of God is serious—and God's Word will tell us no other than that it is really serious—then will it not consist primarily and decisively in the fact that God has turned away His face from us and therefore will not speak with us, that even objectively, then, there is for fallen man no Word of God at all? If we hear it nevertheless, and if this has the twofold implication that we can actually hear it and that we do actually get to hear it—and only on this presupposition shall we evaluate ourselves and our situation *vis-à-vis* God in this way and not another—then we cannot understand the Nevertheless of our hearing as a possibility which ("in some way") we still have left or which can still be fashioned by us. We could obviously do this only in flagrant absent-mindedness and forgetfulness of what we are told by God's Word about ourselves and our situation before God. This interpretation of the Nevertheless of our hearing would then mean quite simply that we have not yet heard at all or have already ceased to hear. If we have heard and heard again—if this self-understanding really relates to our hearing and not to the self abstracted from this hearing—then we can regard this possibility of our hearing as one which is given to us as a sheer miracle both subjectively and objectively, as the Nevertheless of grace which has on our side no complement or precondition.

Τὸ φρόνημα τῆς σαρκὸς ἔχθρα εἰς θεόν · τῷ γὰρ νόμῳ τοῦ θεοῦ οὐχ ὑποτάσσεται, οὐδὲ γὰρ δύναται (Rom. 8⁷). Ἐχθροὶ ὄντες κατηλλάγημεν τῷ θεῷ (Rom. 5¹⁰). Ἐν αὐτῷ ζωὴ ἦν, καὶ ἡ ζωὴ ἦν τὸ φῶς τῶν ἀνθρώπων καὶ τὸ φῶς ἐν τῇ σκοτίᾳ φαίνει, καὶ ἡ σκοτία αὐτὸ οὐ κατέλαβεν (Jn. 1⁵). Εἰς τὰ ἴδια ἦλθεν καὶ οἱ ἴδιοι αὐτὸν οὐ παρέλαβον (Jn. 1¹¹). Ὃ οἴδαμεν λαλοῦμεν καὶ ὃ ἑωράκαμεν μαρτυροῦμεν, καὶ τὴν μαρτυρίαν ἡμῶν οὐ λαμβάνετε (Jn. 3¹¹). Ὃ ἑώρακεν καὶ ἤκουσεν, τοῦτο μαρτυρεῖ, καὶ τὴν μαρτυρίαν αὐτοῦ οὐδεὶς λαμβάνει (Jn. 3³²).

This is how there comes into being the self-understanding of the real hearer with respect to the possibility of his hearing. He regards himself as one who continually robs himself of this possibility. He can regard God alone as the One who gives him this possibility, and by whose gift it is a possibility.

We shall have to speak of the subjective side of this possibility, and therefore of the possibility that we can hear what God says to us, in the next section, the doctrine of God the Holy Spirit. The fact that God can first tell us anything, this primary inconceivability in view of His wrath on sinful man, is in God's revelation the work of the Son or Word of God. The work of the Son or Word is the presence and declaration of God which, in view of the fact that it takes place miraculously in and in spite of human darkness, we can only describe as revelation. The term reconciliation is another word for the same thing. To the extent that God's revelation as such accomplishes what only God can accomplish, namely, restoration of the fellowship of man with God which we had disrupted and indeed destroyed ; to the extent that God in the fact of His revelation treats His enemies as His friends ; to the extent that in the fact of revelation God's enemies already are actually His friends, revelation is itself reconciliation. Conversely reconciliation, the restoration of that fellowship, the mercy of God in wrath triumphant over wrath, can only have the form of the mystery which we describe as revelation.

Paul describes Christ as Him δι' οὗ νῦν (i.e., in Paul : in the presence of the *regnum gratiae* denoted by revelation) τὴν καταλλαγὴν ἐλάβομεν (Rom. 5[11]). To God's good-pleasure to have His πλήρωμα dwell in Him there corresponds His will δι' αὐτοῦ ἀποκαταλλάξαι τὰ πάντα εἰς αὐτόν (Col. 1[20]). God was κόσμον καταλλάσσων in Him, 2 Cor. 5[19] says to the same effect. Hence the apostolic ministry is the διακονία τῆς καταλλαγῆς (2 Cor. 5[18]) which comes to a head in the challenge καταλλάγητε τῷ θεῷ (2 Cor. 5[20]). Thus the concept of reconciliation coincides with that of revelation though not with that of redemption (ἀπολύτρωσις, σωτηρία). In the New Testament redemption is from the standpoint of revelation or reconciliation the future consummating act of God which has still to come : νυνὶ δὲ ἀποκατήλλαξεν (ὑμᾶς) ἐν τῷ σώματι τῆς σαρκὸς αὐτοῦ (Col. 1[22]). Καταλλαγέντες σωθησόμεθα (Rom. 5[10]). For the eschatological use of ἀπολύτρωσις cf. Lk. 21[18] ; Rom. 8[23] ; Eph. 4[30] ; Heb. 11[35], and for the similar use of σωτηρία cf. 1 Thess. 5[8f.] ; Rom. 13[11] ; Phil. 1[19] ; 2[12] ; Heb. 1[14] ; 9[28]. In distinction from this reconciliation is the act of God which is the basis of this prospect of the future, the act in Christ as the μεσίτης between God and man (1 Tim. 2[5]) or of the new covenant (Heb. 9[15] ; 12[24]), the bearer and bringer of εἰρήνη as it is understood in Paul especially as the underlying purpose of God's gracious address to man (cf. the combination of χάρις and εἰρήνη in the greetings) and as it is explained as a divine act in Eph. 2[14-15].

The inconceivable element in revelation as such, in revelation as reconciliation which can be a reality only as it comes from God, is the fact of the Son of God who is the Lord in our midst, and therefore amid our enmity towards God. Because the love of God manifested in this fact cannot be identical with the love of God for the world which He willed to create and did create, for sin and death lie between this

world and our world ; because the love of God manifested in this fact
is rather His love for the lost world of man who has become guilty
before Him (Jn. 3[16]), for the world whose continuity with the original
one is completely hidden from us, therefore we cannot confuse God's
lordship in the one case with God's lordship in the other, or directly
identify them, but in relation to the one (creation) we must speak of a
first mode of God's being and in relation to the second (reconciliation)
we must speak of a second mode of His being. For as we have to say
that reconciliation or revelation is not creation or a continuation of
creation but rather an inconceivably new work above and beyond
creation, so we have also to say that the Son is not the Father but that
here, in this work, the one God, though not without the Father, is the
Son or Word of the Father.

It is hard to see how the distinction of the mode of being of the Son of God
from that of the Father—and the same distinction must also be made from that
of the Holy Spirit—can be denied without speculatively changing and weakening
the seriousness of God's wrath against sin, of the opposition between original
man and fallen man, of the world of creation and our world of sin and death,
into a mere tension within a totality which is known to us and can be surveyed
by us. On this assumption the inconceivability of revelation as a divine act of
reconciliation will naturally be contested. It will be seen to follow as a second
or third act in the same creation series which we can view as a totality, and God
the Reconciler can easily be identified with God the Creator. Thus Schleiermacher regarded sin quantitatively as a mere lack, and he then logically viewed
reconciliation (" redemption ") as the crowning of creation, and, again consistently, he interpreted the Trinity modalistically, regarding the three modes of
being as dissolved in the depths of God. A similar doctrine of the Trinity would
also seem to lie behind the even more unfettered gnosis of E. Hirsch in respect of
the synthesis of genesis and fall (*Schöpfung und Sünde*, 1932). It may also be
said conversely that such disasters will inevitably happen in the doctrine of
creation and reconciliation if the necessary safeguards are not provided by a
sound doctrine of the Trinity.

On the other hand we must also say that since the reference in God's
revelation is to His lordship amid our enmity against Him, and therefore
to the miracle of reconciliation, this work cannot be the work of a
superman or demi-god. The uniqueness of God's love for the world of
fallen man, the power of reconciliation, will be underestimated if the
true deity of the Reconciler is called in question. A superhuman or
semi-divine event, an event which is not strictly miraculous but in the
last resort self-evident, an event within the cosmos and therefore
creaturely, does not correspond to the seriousness of the problem it is
supposed to solve, nor to the character of omnipotent grace which the
event that Holy Scripture describes as the event of reconciliation or
revelation actually has. The character of omnipotent grace which this
event has, and in the light of which the problem that it solves is of
infinite seriousness, requires the acknowledgment that its subject is
identical with God in the full sense of the word.

It is in this light, with reference to the reconciliation whose subject can be no less than God Himself if its power and the seriousness of the problem that it solves are to be perceived, if it is not to be regarded as a mere appearance of reconciliation, that the knowledge of the true deity of Christ has rightly been asserted and proclaimed from time immemorial. The so-called Homily of Clement (I, 1) begins with the declaration that we are to think of Jesus Christ ὡς περὶ θεοῦ and forthwith it interprets this in the words : ὡς κριτοῦ ζώντων καὶ νεκρῶν.' One should not μικρὰ φρονεῖν περὶ τῆς σωτηρίας ἡμῶν. To think meanly of Christ is to show at once that one has only a mean hope too. There is interrelation and necessary correspondence in the knowledge πόθεν ἐκλήθημεν καὶ ὑπὸ τίνος καὶ εἰς ὃν τόπον. Similarly Gregory of Nyssa lays down that the benefactor can and must be known from his acts and the nature of one who does something must be disclosed by the event of his deed : 'Ἀφ' ὧν γὰρ εὖ πάσχομεν, ἀπὸ τούτων εὐεργέτην ἐπιγινώσκομεν, πρὸς γὰρ τὰ γινόμενα βλέποντες, διὰ τούτων τὴν τοῦ ἐνεργοῦντος ἀναλογιζόμεθα φύσιν. Those who ascribe creature-liness to the Son and Spirit, and thus subject themselves to a creature, are not placing their hope in God and are deceiving themselves in thinking that they are put in a better position as Christians (*Or. cat.*, 14 and 39). Luther constantly stressed this connexion too : *Vincere peccatum mundi, mortem, maledictionem et iram Dei* are not the works of a *humana aut angelica potestas* but *mera opera divinae maiestatis. Qua re cum docemus homines per Christum iustificari, Christum esse victorem peccati, mortis et aeternae maledictionis, testificamur simul eum esse natura Deum* (on Gal. 1³, 1535, *W.A.*, 40¹, p. 81, l. 18 ; on Gal. 1⁴, *ib.*, p. 96, l. 15 ; on Gal. 3¹³, *ib.*, p. 441, l. 16, 25, 31) . . . " for if sin is thus a big thing and its cleansing costeth so much that such a lofty person as Christ is here extolled must Himself set to and cleanse it Himself, what then in such great matters could avail our poor and helpless acts, for we are creatures, nay, sinful and wicked perishing creatures ? that were as if to undertake to set heaven and earth aflame with an extinguished firebrand. There must be here as great a payment for sin as God himself is who is injured by sin " (*Sermon on Heb.* 1¹ᵗ·, 1522, *W.A.*, 10¹¹, p. 161, l. 21). " Now God maketh none a king who is not God, for He will not let the reins out of His own hands, and will alone be lord over heaven and earth, death, hell, devil, and over all creatures. Since He then maketh Him a lord over all that is made, He must already be God " (*Sermon on Jn.* 3¹ᵗ·, 1526, *W.A.*, 10¹², p. 296, l. 37). " For if the person who offered himself for us were not God, it would help and avail nothing before God that he was born of a virgin and likewise suffered a thousand deaths. But it bringeth blessing and victory over all sin and death that the seed of Abraham is also very God who giveth Himself for us " (*Sermon on Phil.* 2⁵ᵗ·, 1525, *W.A.*, 17¹¹, p. 236, l. 25). " We men are all sinners and lost. If then we are to be righteous and blessed, it must come about through Christ. But because we are righteous and blessed through Christ alone, He must be more than a pure and simple man. For man's hand and power can make no one righteous and blessed, God must do it Himself " (*Sermon on the Passion, How Christ was Buried, and on Is.* 53, *E.A.*, 3, 276). The answer to qu. 17 of the *Heidelberg Catechism* is to the same effect : The Mediator must be true God " so that by virtue of His Godhead He might bear the burden of the wrath of God in His humanity, and acquire and restore to us righteousness and life."

Thus Jesus is Lord as the Son of God who has come to us or as the Word of God that has been spoken to us. We say here something which goes beyond the statement that God is the Creator or " our Father in heaven." Jesus reveals the God who is the Creator and " our Father in heaven." But as He does so, as that which is unheard of takes place, namely, that this God is revealed in Him, He reveals Himself to us, so assuredly does the fact of revelation signify a new thing *vis-à-vis* its content, so assuredly is reconciliation not to be understood as the completion of creation but as a miracle in and on the fallen world. We have seen in the previous section that in the context of the New Testament witness this new revelation of the Creator and our Father cannot be abstracted from the person of the Revealer. It was in the light of this unity of the content of revelation and the person of the Revealer that we then understood the original and proper sense of the fatherhood of God : He is Father because He is the Father of this His only-begotten Son. From the same unity we at once have the further result of the divine sonship of Jesus Christ. There is no abstract person of the Revealer, but the person of the Revealer is the person of Jesus Christ, who is subordinate to the Creator revealed by it, yet who is also indissolubly co-ordinate with Him, who is with Him ; in this person the revelation is a reality. In other words, there is no Jesus *per se* who might then acquire also the predicate of a bearer of the revelation of his Father. Nor is there any revelation of the Father *per se* which might then be apprehended in Jesus in exemplary and pre-eminent fashion. Jesus *is* the revelation of the Father and the revelation of the Father *is* Jesus. And precisely in virtue of this " is " He is the Son or Word of the Father.

Our criticism of Ebionite and Docetic Christology has shown us that in the New Testament witness the person and thing really constitute this unity and that the thinking of the apostles about Jesus Christ, whether it began with the person or the thing, never took the form of a syllogism but always ended with the knowledge of Christ's deity because it had already begun there. In this respect, too, we can only dodge the unity of the content of revelation and the person of the Revealer if we evade the New Testament witness and disregard the prohibition and command set forth therein.

And now in the light of what has been said about creation and reconciliation we can add that the divine sonship of Jesus also results from the fact that creation (the content of His revelation of the Father) and reconciliation (the content of His self-revelation) are completely different from one another in their significance for us and yet are also completely related to one another in their origin. In trying to follow the tracks of Holy Scripture itself we have already been able to grasp the concept of the Creator only on the apparent detour *via* knowledge of God as the Lord of life and death, as the God of Good Friday and Easter. And in trying to grasp the concept of the Reconciler we have had to presuppose that there is a world created by God even though fallen and lost and that there is a man created by God even though actually existing in enmity against Him. Only in the One who acts on us as the

Reconciler through the cross and resurrection could we perceive the Creator, and only in the Creator who remains the Lord of our being in spite of our enmity can we perceive the Reconciler.

Τῷ γὰρ ἐξ ἀρχῆς τὴν ζωὴν δεδωκότι μόνῳ δυνατὸν ἦν καὶ πρέπον ἅμα καὶ ἀπολομένην ἀνακαλέσασθαι (Gregory of Nyssa, *Or. cat.*, 8).

We must distinguish them, these two, and we must obviously distinguish them in such a way that we perceive and acknowledge the relation of subordination that is present here. We must say, then, that the Reconciler is not the Creator, and that as the Reconciler He follows the Creator, that He accomplishes, as it were, a second divine act— not an act which we can deduce from the first, whose sequence from the first we can survey and see to be necessary, but still a second act which for all its newness and inconceivability is related to the first. God reconciles us to Himself, comes to us, speaks with us—this follows on, and, we must also say, it follows from the fact that He is first the Creator. We can also say that it follows on and from the fact that He is " our Father in heaven." If He were not first the Creator and Father who is the Lord of our being, against whom we have sinned, whose wrath is thus upon us, but whose wrath is but the reverse side of His love as Creator and Father, how then could He be the Reconciler, the Peacemaker ? To this order of creation and reconciliation there corresponds christologically the order of Father and Son or Father and Word. Jesus Christ as the Reconciler cannot precede the Creator, " our Father in heaven." He stands to Him in the irreversible relation of following on Him and from Him as the son follows on the father and from the father and the word follows on the speaker and from the speaker. But again this subordination and sequence cannot imply any distinction of being ; it can only signify a distinction in the mode of being. For reconciliation is no more readily comprehensible and no less divine than creation. It is not as if reconciliation, unlike creation, could be made intelligible as a creaturely event. As creation is *creatio ex nihilo*, so reconciliation is the raising of the dead. As we owe life to God the Creator, so we owe eternal life to God the Reconciler.

Ipse est autem creator ejus, qui salvator ejus. Non ergo debemus sic laudare creatorem, ut cogamur, imo vere convincamur dicere superfluum salvatorem (August- ine, *De nat. et grat.*, 33, 39). *Creasti me, cum non essem, redemisti me cum perditus essem. Sed conditionis quidem meae et redemptionis causa sola fuit dilectio tua* (Anselm of Canterbury, *Medit.*, 12). " This fleeting corruptible life in this world we have through God, who, as we confess in the first article of our Christian creed, is the almighty Creator of heaven and earth. But eternal incorruptible life we have through the passion and resurrection of our Lord Jesus Christ, who hath sat down at the right hand of God, as we confess in the second article of our Christian creed " (Luther, *Sermon on Mt.* 22[34f.], *E.A.*, 5, 151). How could the second act be less great or miraculous than the first ? One might argue the very opposite and see the greater miracle in the second, in reconciliation. Thus

God is addressed as follows in the offertory of the Roman Mass : *Deus, qui humanae substantiae dignitatem mirabiliter condidisti et mirabilius reformasti . . .,* and in the Kyrie-Tropus " *Cuncti potens* " : *Plasmatis humani factor, lapsi reparator.* But the dispute is pointless. *Intelligant redempti tui, non fuisse excellentius, quod initio factus est mundus, quam quod in fine saeculorum Pascha nostrum immolatus est Christus* (*Oratio* after the 9th prophecy in the vigil on Easter Eve).

Here genuine miracle stands side by side with genuine miracle. On neither side can there be any question of more or less miracle and therefore of more or less deity. In both cases we simply have an either/or. Here, then, sonship as well as fatherhood, in and with the super- and subordination expressed thereby, is to be understood as unrestrictedly true deity.

2. THE ETERNAL SON

Who is the Son of God ? We have heard the provisional answer : Jesus Christ as the One who reveals the Father and the One who reconciles us to the Father is the Son of God. For as this One He reveals Himself to us as the Son who has come to us or God's Word that has been spoken to us. The dogma of the Trinity adds something new to this insight from Scripture's witness to revelation only to the extent that it adds the interpretation that Jesus Christ can reveal the Father and reconcile us to the Father because He reveals Himself as the One He is. He does not first become God's Son or Word in the event of revelation. On the contrary, the event of revelation has divine truth and reality because that which is proper to God is revealed in it, because Jesus Christ reveals Himself as the One He already was before, apart from this event, in Himself too. His sonship on the basis of which He can be the Revealer, the Mediator, the Reconciler, is not a mere contrivance of God behind which, in some higher essence of God which remains a mystery, there is no sonship or word-ness in God, but perhaps an inexpressible and speechless it-ness, a divine, a θεῖον with a different or unknown name. No, revelation has eternal content and eternal validity. Down to the very depths of deity, not as something penultimate but as the ultimate thing that is to be said about God, God is God the Son as He is God the Father. Jesus Christ, the Son of God, is God Himself as God His Father is God Himself.

How does this interpretation of the biblical witness to revelation arise ? We can give here only the very simple but momentous answer that it arises because as a final word we accept the truth and validity of the equal and incomprehensible divinity of both the work of creation and also the work of reconciliation, and therefore the truth and validity of the unity of the Father and the Son as the witness presents this to us as distinctive of the revelation attested by it. The Church dogma of Christ's deity as compared with the New Testament statement about Christ's deity says no other than that we have to accept the simple presupposition on which the New Testament statement rests, namely, that Jesus Christ is the Son because He is (not because He makes this impression on us, not because He does what we think is to be expected of a God, but because He is). With this presupposition all thinking about Jesus, which means at once all thinking about God, must begin and end. No reflection can try to prove this presupposition, no reflection can call this presupposition in question. All reflection can only start with it and return to it. The Church dogma of the deity of Christ arose out of this insight and it expresses this insight. For when it explicitly takes the deity of Christ to be eternal deity, when we say that the Son who has come to us or the Word that has been spoken to us is antecedently the Son or Word of God *per se*, we are simply saying in practice that the statement about Christ's deity is to be regarded as a basic and not a derivative statement. This is how the apostles understood it, the dogma says, and this is how we, too, must understand it if we are to understand the apostles. This is how we must understand the apostles and the statement, then, if our own understanding is not to be led astray from the understanding of the early Church which expressed and deposited this understanding in the dogma. Our own understanding as we have attempted it here has not so far led us astray from the dogma of the early Church but has rather led us to it. Things might have been different. The dogma does not have divine dignity for us but only human pedagogic dignity. We might have turned our backs on it, but we have no cause to do so. As an expression of our own understanding of the New Testament too we can and we must say what the dogma says. We cannot understand the New Testament statement about Christ's deity in any different or better way than by studying it in harmony with the early Church, i.e., by directly comparing with it the dogma of the eternal deity of Christ. The dogma as such is not to be found in the biblical texts. The dogma is an interpretation. But we can convince ourselves that it is a good and relevant interpretation of these texts. We thus accept it. The deity of Christ is true, eternal deity. We see it in His work in revelation and reconciliation. But revelation and reconciliation do not create His deity. His deity creates revelation and reconciliation.

Κύριος ὢν κατὰ ἀλήθειαν, οὐκ ἐξ προκοπῆς τὸ κυριεύειν λαβών, ἀλλ' ἐκ φύσεως τὸ τῆς κυριότητος ἔχων ἀξίωμα. Καὶ οὐ καταχρηστικῶς ὡς ἡμεῖς κύριος καλούμενος ἀλλὰ τῇ ἀληθείᾳ κύριος ὤν (Cyril of Jerusalem, *Cat.*, 10, 5).

Jesus Christ is the true and effective Revealer of God and Reconciler to God because God in His Son or Word does not posit and make known a mere something, however great or meaningful. He posits and makes known Himself exactly as He posits and knows Himself from and to all eternity. He is the Son or Word of God for us because He is so antecedently in Himself.

It is one of the many optical illusions of Modernist Protestantism to have imagined that it should and could interpret and discredit this " antecedently in himself," i.e., the confession of Christ's true and eternal deity, as the exponent of an untheological metaphysical speculation by claiming that the Reformers adopted a very different position in this matter from that of the ancient and mediaeval Church. What is usually adduced from the actual statements of the Reformers in support of this thesis is, however, quite inadequate to prove that they ever dreamed of attacking or even altering in the slightest degree the dogma of the deity of Christ.

The main passage to call for consideration here is in the first edition of Melanchthon's *Loci* (1521). In the introduction to this oldest Evangelical dogmatics Melanchthon distinguishes among the *Loci theologici* those which are *prorsus incomprehensibiles* and those which according to the will of Christ must be *compertissimi* to all Christian people. Of the first it must be said : *mysteria divinitatis rectius adoraverimus, quam vestigaverimus*. For the latter involves great danger, and God has veiled His Son in flesh *ut a contemplatione maiestatis suae ad carnis adeoque fragilitatis nostrae contemplationem invitaret*. Melanchthon is thus declaring that he sees no reason to spend too much time on the *loci supremi de Deo, de unitate, de trinitate Dei, de mysterio creationis, de modo incarnationis*. The Scholastics had become fools in investigating these things and the *beneficia Christi* had been obscured thereby. For the arguments (*e philosophia*, says the second edition, 1522) which they had presented had often been more worthy of a heretical than a Catholic dogma. The other *loci*, however, are vital : on the power of sin, the law, and grace. *Nam ex his proprie Christus cognoscitur, siquidem hoc est Christum cognoscere, beneficia eius cognoscere, non quod isti docent eius naturas, modos incarnationis contueri. Ni scias, in quem usum carnem induerit et cruci affixus sit Christus, quia proderit eius historiam novisse ?* As the physician must know more about plants than their nature, namely, their *vis nativa*, so Christ must be known as *salutare* as this is made plain precisely in these other *loci* of which the Scholastics did not speak. We should follow Paul's example in Romans, where, as though foreseeing *disputationes frigidae et alienae a Christo*, he did not deal with the Trinity, the incarnation, or *creatio activa et passiva*, but with the law, sin and grace, i.e., with the *loci, qui Christum tibi commendent, qui conscientiam confirment, qui animum adversus satanam erigant*. The Rationalists of the 18th and early 19th centuries (cf., e.g., J. J. Spalding, *Über die Nutzbarkeit des Predigtamtes*, 1772, p. 138 f. ; K. G. Bretschneider, *Handbuch d. Dogmatik*, Vol. I, 4th edn., 1838, p. 553), and in recent times especially A. Ritschl (cf. *Rechtf. u. Versöhnung*[4], Vol. 3, p. 374, *Theologie und Metaphysik*, 1874, p. 60) and his followers (e.g., B. M. Rade, *Glaubenslehre*, Vol. 1, 1924, p. 53 ; H. Stephan, *Glaubenslehre*, 2nd edn., 1928, p. 166, 240), are the ones who thought they had much to rejoice about in this passage. But we must not conceal the fact that the passage does not really say what they are pleased to find in it. It reflects a passing mood but not a theological position which became historically significant even for Melanchthon. And even the mood was not directed against the content of the trinitarian dogma but against its importance in relation to other dogmas which lay nearer to Melanchthon's own heart. Moreover it was not occasioned by Melanchthon's own, perhaps critical, preoccupation with the dogma of the Trinity. It was occasioned on the one hand by his intensive preoccupation with the other dogmas under the influence and inspiration of Luther and on the other hand by his indignation at the unchurchly theoretical way in which the Scholastics, i.e., the theologians of the later Middle Ages with whom he was primarily acquainted, had dealt with the doctrine of the Trinity. It was a passing mood. Only the later emergence of antitrinitarians was needed to change it at once and to make room for the dogma of the Trinity in his *Loci* in spite of the passage quoted. The mood never achieved significance in the confessions or the theological work of the Reformation.

Friends of the Melanchthon passage might do better to appeal to Calvin if they knew him better. In 1537, during his first stay in Geneva, the theological and ecclesiastical adventurer Petrus Caroli could publicly accuse Calvin of antitrinitarianism, and not without gaining a hearing even among serious people. The circumstances relating to the charge were as follows. The *Confession de la foy* of 1536 (in K. Müller, p. 111 f.), which was so authoritative at the beginning of the reformation in Geneva, though its contents are, of course, less characteristic of Calvin than of Farel, who was then the leader, has nothing at all to say about the doctrine of the Trinity either in its doctrine of God or its Christology. Furthermore the first draft of the *Institutio* of Calvin himself, which appeared rather earlier in the same year (*cap.* 2, *De fide*), does indeed give a very sound and respectful exposition of the doctrine of the Trinity, and shows that there is not a vestige of truth in Caroli's charge that Calvin avoided the terms *trinitas* and *persona*, but it should still be noted that the author hardly has a burning interest in the matter. Even in his defence against Caroli in 1545 Calvin himself writes that true knowledge of Christ's deity consists in putting all our confidence and hope in Him and calling on His name. *Quae practica notitia certior haud dubie est qualibet otiosa speculatione. Illic enim pius animus Deum praesentissimum conspicit et paene attrectat, ubi se vivificari, illuminari, salvari, justificari et sanctificari sentit* (*Adv. P. Caroli calumnias, C.R.,* 7, p. 312 f.). Calvin also seems to have had at that time various objections to the authority and authenticity of the symbols of the early Church (*C.R.*, 5, 337 ; 10², 84, 86 ; 7, 311 f.). And it is a fact that when Caroli demanded that he should subscribe to these symbols to prove his orthodoxy he strenuously refused to do so because of the " tyranny " of such a demand (*C.R.*, 7, 315 ; 10², 120 f.). From both the theological and the human standpoint the whole controversy is most obscure. What does emerge from the passage quoted, and especially from the first edition of the *Institutio*, is that Calvin at that period, like Melanchthon sixteen years earlier, was preoccupied with other matters, these being, as in the case of Melanchthon, the problems of appropriating salvation rather than its objective presuppositions. In the case of Farel one might well ask whether he had not really lost sight of the latter and was thus well on the way which would lead to antitrinitarianism, like many of his contemporaries. But one cannot say this of Calvin even in relation to this period. For even at this early time he had the presuppositions more plainly in view than the Melanchthon of the 1521 statements had. With the lack of a true and distinctive doctrine of the Trinity which he had traced back to Arianism, Caroli, who seems to have been rather confused, was also accusing Calvin of attributing to Christ the Old Testament name of Jehovah. Calvin naturally meant this as an *elogium divinitatis* (*C.R.*, 7, 312 ; 10², 121 ; 9, 708). Again one cannot speak of anything but a churlish mood (strengthened by Caroli's arbitrary accusation) even in the Calvin of this period, nor was it directed against the objective presuppositions, but against their doctrinal formulation by the ancient Church. How far he was from drawing antitrinitarian deductions from this mood is unequivocally attested by the structure of the *Institutio* and also by his attitude in the Servetus case.

The real issue in this whole matter is plain in Luther, to whom also appeal is usually made. It is Luther's insights that lay behind the statements of Melanchthon and indirectly behind those of Calvin too. From his perception that man's justification is in Christ alone and therefore by faith alone, Luther rightly concluded that all human theology can only be theology of revelation. As it is arbitrary and dangerous in the matter of justification to orientate oneself to a preconceived idea of the Law or one capriciously abstracted from the statements of Scripture ; so it is arbitrary and dangerous in theology generally to start with a preconceived idea of God or one capriciously abstracted from the statements of Scripture. The total theological question, like the question of justification in detail, can be answered only with reference to the God who reveals Himself in Christ. Already in 1519 Luther mentions a thought he was often to repeat : This is the *unicus et solus modus cognoscendi Deum* (shamefully neglected by the *doctores Sententiarum* with their *absolutae divinitatis speculationes*), that *quicumque velit salubriter de Deo cogitare aut speculari, prorsus omnia postponat praeter humanitatem Christi* (Letter to Spalatin, February 12, 1519, *W.A. Br.* I, p. 328 f.). About the same time we find him writing polemically : *Proinde, qui vult Deum cognoscere, schalam terrae infixam contueatur : cadit hic tota ratio hominum. Natura quidem docet, ut simus propensiores ad contemplanda magna quam abiecta. Hinc collige, quam inique, ne dicam impie, agant et speculantur, sua confisi industria, summa Trinitatis misteria : quo loco sedeant angeli, quid loquantur sancti, Cum tamen in carnem natus est Christus atque in carne mansurus sit. Vide autem, quid continget illis. Primo :* " If they should poke their heads into heaven and look around in heaven they would find no one but Christ laid in the crib and in the woman's lap, and so they would fall down again and break their necks." *Et ii sunt scriptores super primum librum sententiarum. Deinde adeo nihil consequuntur istis suis a speculationibus, ut neque sibi neque aliis prodesse aut consulere possunt.* " Start here below, Thomas and Philip, and not up above " (*Schol. in libr. Gen. on Gen.* 28, *W.A.*, 9, p. 406, l. 11). Even better known is the following passage : " For I have often said and say it again that when I am dead men should remember and guard against all teachers as ridden and led by the devil who in lofty positions begin to teach and preach about God nakedly and apart from Christ, as heretofore in high schools they have speculated and played with His works up above in heaven, what He is and thinks and does in Himself, etc. But if thou wilt fare securely and rightly teach or grasp God so that thou find grace and help with Him, then let not thyself be persuaded to seek Him elsewhere than in the Lord Christ, nor go round about and trouble thyself with other thoughts nor ask about any other work than how He hath sent Christ. Fix thine art and study on Christ, there let them also bide and hold. And where thine own thought and reason or anyone else leadeth or guideth thee otherwise, do but close thine eyes and say : I should and will know no other God save in my Lord Christ " (*Sermon on Jn.* 17³, 1528, *W.A.*, 28, p. 100, l. 33 ; cf. also *Comm. on Gal.* 1³, 1535, *W.A.*, 40¹, p. 75 f. ; *W.A. Ti.*, 6, p. 28). One should not fail to note that in so far as these statements of Luther are polemical in content they are not concerned with the doctrine of Christ's deity, and in so far as they are concerned with the doctrine of Christ's deity they are not polemical in content. What Luther wants—this is his point in this train of thought—is that deity in general and Christ's deity in particular should not be known along the path of autonomous speculation but along the path of knowledge of God's revelation, which means in practice along the path of knowledge of the *beneficia Christi* and therefore the *humanitas Christi*, i.e., His human reality as attested in Scripture, through which His benefits reach us. But Luther does want it to be known—and this must never be ignored or pushed into the background. More prudent than the Melanchthon of 1521, Luther does not fail to point out that in Jacob's dream we have angels both ascending and descending : *angeli ascendentes et descendentes : doctores precones verbi Dei.* The path is first from below upwards, from the *natura humana Christi* to *cognitio Dei.* But it does really lead upwards and therefore it leads downwards again too. *Deinde cum Χριστός in sic humilibus formis cognitus est, tum ascenditur et videtur, quod est Deus. Et tunc cognoscitur quod Deus benigne, misericorditer despectat* (*Sermon on Gen.* 28¹²ᵗ·, 1520, *W.A.,* 9, p. 494, l. 17 f.). Thus even knowledge of God's goodness depends again on the fact that the path leads from above downwards. " *Nos Christiani* do not have enough about how a Creator is to be compared with a creature. *Sed docemus postea ex scriptura* what God is in Himself . . . *quid est deus in seipso ?* . . . *quid* is He in Himself where He hath His divine being by Himself ? *Ibi Christiani : Is unicus dominus, rex et creator, per filium sic depinxit se, quod in deitate* He is so . . . *Non solum inspiciendus deus ab extra in operibus. Sed deus vult etiam, ut agnoscamus eum etiam ab intra.* What is He inwardly ? " (*Sermon on Jn.* 1¹ᵗ·, 1541, *W.A.,* 49, p. 238, l. 5).

What is left of the whole appeal to the Reformation in this matter is in the last resort the mere fact that the burning problem of the Reformation was a different one from that of the 4th century, and that in the urgency of the conflict about their own problem the Reformers did and perhaps had to permit themselves sometimes to set the problem of the 4th century aside and put it in its proper place in a somewhat impatient gesture. But no one can seriously maintain that for them it did not occupy this place, or that they did not know it as the natural presupposition of their own problem, or that they did not recognise it again at the very latest in the controversy with their radical adversaries who were emerging at that time. Whether we explain it (with Stephan, *op. cit.,* p. 140) as a lack of theological consistency that they not only did not attack the doctrine of the early Church but in its proper place very solemnly affirmed it, or whether (with A. Ritschl, *Rechtfert. u. Versöhnung*⁴, Vol. 1, p. 145 f.) we see in this attitude the results of their ecclesiastico-political regard for the mediaeval *corpus christianum,* the fact as such is plain, and we are right to stick to it. The Reformers never dreamed of allowing Christology to be resolved or dissolved in a doctrine of the *beneficia Christi.* Can we not agree once and for all that it is one thing when Melanchthon says (*Loci,* 1535, *C.R.,* 21, 366) : *scriptura docet nos de filii divinitate non tantum speculative sed practice, hoc est iubet nos, ut Christum invocemus, ut confidamus Christo,* and quite another when, as Ritschl and his disciples desired, the *speculative* is simply eliminated or simply transformed into the *practice?*

But the objection that we have only an untheological speculation in the dogma of Christ's deity is materially nonsensical and untenable and in the long run it is bound to recoil on its authors.

J. J. Spalding, who was perhaps the first to try to use the Melanchthon passage in this way, is typical of everything that is usually said along these lines even to our own day when he argues : " Not what the Son of God is in Himself, in His nature which is impervious to our understanding, is part of our true Christianity, of the religious knowledge which is generally necessary and fruitful, but what He is for us, that for which He was given to us, what we should thank Him for, how we should receive and use Him in order to attain to the blessedness to which He would lead us. And how definitely we can dispense with all those hard words and even harder concepts ! " (*op. cit.,* p. 142). " If there exists a clear divine declaration that after my offences a conversion is again granted to me and access to my blessedness is still open ; if in this declaration I am told that this is mediated and given to me in Jesus Christ, I do not see why this basis of my reassurance should not be sufficiently reliable for me. To regard such a generally declared assurance as inadequate, not to be ready to trust it with full confidence, until I myself first see how God could make this blessing possible, or whether He was even competent to forgive sins, would mean the assumption on my part of a kind of right of judgment on the holy laws of God's government that cannot possibly belong to me. He promises me forgiveness through Christ ; more I do not need. What my Redeemer had to do and had to be in order to accomplish this is no part of my religion whether in respect of my virtue or of my peace of mind ; I simply leave it to Him who has so clearly given me His word about my reacceptance. This declaration and assurance of the true God that He will forgive me is incomparably more necessary for me to know than the way in which He brings it about that He can forgive me ; and it would be hard to find adequate grounds for making both equally essential and important in religious knowledge " (p. 144 f.). In short, knowledge of what the dogma says gives to Christians " not the slightest addition to their blessedness and their solace, but a correspondingly greater one to the futile burdening of their understanding " (p. 147). This line of argument, which is typical of Enlightenment theology (in the broadest sense of the term), completely fails to see that the point of the dogma is not at all to enrich or obscure simple and self-sufficient religious knowledge by an explanation of the possibility of its content which is as subtle as it is superfluous, but that the issue in this religious knowledge— whatever burdening of the understanding this may involve and irrespective of the sense in which it may belong to my religion, virtue and peace of mind—is the mystery of the Word of God, i.e., that the truth of what Christ is for us, the truth of His *beneficia*, is the truth of the event of the divine manifestation and not the truth of a generally declared reassurance detached from this event. That the true God has forgiven me—this and not merely that He will forgive me is after all the content of the religious knowledge at issue here—can be heard and understood as truth only in the mystery of the way of God out of His divine majesty and into my sin-shattered creatureliness. What connexion is there between the general truth that there is divine reconciliation (as truth that can be heard and understood apart from the mystery of this way) and the truth of the grace of God ? The dogma of Christ's deity has to do with this truth, and therefore with the mystery of this way, and therefore with the distinction between the Whence and Whither of this way, and therefore with the distinction between the Son of God in Himself and for me. On the distinction between the " in Himself " and " for me " depends the acknowledgment of the freedom and un-indebtedness of God's grace, i.e., of the very thing that really makes it grace. It is this acknowledgment that is made in the Church dogma, whereas Enlightenment theology (in the broadest sense of the term) is obviously at war with it.

It is strange but true that the Church dogma of the true and eternal deity of Christ with its " antecedently in Himself " is the very thing that denies and prohibits an untheologically speculative understanding of the " for us." And the very man who thinks he must reject the Church dogma undoubtedly does this because he is in the grip of an untheologically speculative understanding of the " for us." This may be be shown in three respects.

1. If we will not listen to the fact that Christ is antecedently God in Himself in order that in this way and on this basis He may be our

God, then we turn the latter, His being God for us, into a necessary attribute of God. God's being is then essentially limited and conditioned as a being revealed, i.e., as a relation of God to man. Man is thus thought of as indispensable to God. But this destroys God's freedom in the act of revelation and reconciliation, i.e., it destroys the gracious character of this act. It is thus God's nature (*c'est son métier*, Voltaire) to have to forgive us. And it is man's nature to have a God from whom he receives forgiveness. That and not the Church dogma which forbids this thought is untheological speculation.

2. If we will accept only the Son of God for us without remembering that He is antecedently the Son of God in Himself this certainly cannot be called the knowledge of faith—if, that is, the knowledge of faith is the knowledge of a divine act, of an unveiling of the veiled God, and therefore of a coming forth or a way of God ; if the knowledge of faith is distinguished from other knowledge by the fact that it is knowledge of the mystery of the speech of God—the speech of God which arises out of a silence of God, which is truth as an actual event between a *terminus a quo* and a *terminus ad quem* and not otherwise. If we think we can understand the *beneficia Christi* apart from this event, then it is we, and not the Church dogma that reminds us of this event, who are engaged in untheological speculation.

3. If we want to restrict the task of theological reflection to an understanding of Christ in His revelation but only in His revelation in itself and as such, then what standard and criterion can there be for this understanding, this highly vaunted *beneficia Christi cognoscere* ? Obviously the criterion will have to be something man himself has brought. It may thus be, within the limit of our capability, either the evaluation of human greatness or the evaluation of the idea of God or a divine being. Since Christ is to be rated highly according to this humanly possible evaluation, we may to that extent, on the basis of our value judgment, call Him the Son of God. We are thus confronted again by the two christological types which we have learned to know as the Ebionite and the Docetic.

A. Ritschl—according to our classification his Christology, unlike that of the religious school which followed him, undoubtedly belongs to the Docetic type—has described as follows the process whereby there may be knowledge of Christ's deity on this presupposition : " If the grace and faithfulness and lordship over the world which are displayed both in Christ's mode of action and also in His bearing of suffering are the essential attributes of God that are decisive for the Christian religion, then in certain historical circumstances it was logical to establish the correct evaluation of the perfection of God's revelation through Christ in the predicate of His deity " (*Unterricht in d. chr. Rel.*, 1875, § 24 ; cf. *Rechtfertigung und Versöhnung*[4], Vol. 3, p. 370 f.).

But all this interpreting, estimating and evaluating by a standard cocksurely imported and applied to Christ by the theologian—is not this real untheological speculation (even though in result and in its actual wording it does seem to bring us back again to the content of the Church dogma) ? On the other hand, does not the Church dogma with its " antecedently in Himself " strike this standard out of our hands when it says to us that the knowledge of Christ's deity can only be the beginning and not the result of our thought ?

Undoubtedly the dogma of Christ's deity snaps any correlation between the divine revelation and human faith. The cycle of religious psychology, the theory of two accessible elements of truth in a unity of tension, and all such well-meant inventions no matter what we call them, can never lead us to what this dogma is seeking to say. And if everything that cannot be grasped by these instruments is for that reason illegitimate metaphysics, then certainly this dogma is metaphysics of that kind. But on the basis of the three points made above we may simply turn the tables and say that the illegitimate metaphysics in which the Reformers obviously did not indulge consists in absolutising the correlation that we suppose we can attain and survey and understand, in regarding it as the reality in which God has as it were delivered Himself up to man and human thought and speech, instead of remembering that our being in this relation may always be pure illusion, and our thought within it and speech about it may always be pure ideology, if they are not grounded in God Himself and continually confirmed by God Himself. Because and to the extent that what the dogma states is true, that God's Word is the Word of God, for that reason and to that extent the correlation is also true. Its truth hangs as on a nail on the truth of which the dogma speaks. Similarly all the truth of our thinking and speaking about it hangs on knowledge of the truth of the dogma. Without this it is empty dreaming and chatter even though it has for a long time called itself a theology of revelation and faith. Just because Christ is the Son of God antecedently in Himself, there are two elements of truth in mutual tension (the elements of truth in Ebionite and Docetic thought) in which we recognise that He is God's Son for us and not *vice versa*. How could a theology which does not know the freedom of God's grace, which does not know the mystery of His way, which does not know the fear of God as the beginning of wisdom, how could such a theology come to call itself a theology of revelation and faith ? How could it be knowledge of the *beneficia Christi* ? Is not this defiant arrogance, all the worse because it pretends to be so humble ? But there is no sense in scolding here. With particularly painful clarity we are faced here by the rift which divides the Evangelical Church. Those who are at loggerheads here can neither understand nor convince one another. They not only speak another language ; they speak out of a different knowledge. They not only have a different theology ; they also have a different faith. In the last resort we can only protest at this point as we can only protest against the assertions of Roman Catholic theology in other contexts.

For dogmatic science the most important record of the Church dogma of the deity of Christ is the portion of the second article of the so-called *Symb. Nicaeno-Constantinopolitanum* which relates to this problem.

The *Symb. Nic. Const.* is a baptismal creed of the last third of the 4th century, perhaps the baptismal creed of the Church of Constantinople (or Jerusalem ?), in which the decisive trinitarian decisions of the Council of Nicaea (325) were adopted and which according to a not wholly certain tradition is supposed to have achieved recognition at the Council of Constantinople in 381. It became an established part of the Eastern liturgy from 565 and of the Western from 1014. We say that it is for us the most important record of the dogma of the deity of Christ on the following grounds :

1. Of the three ancient creeds accepted by the Reformation Churches its definitions are at this point both the most trenchant and also the most succinct.

2. While simply repeating for the most part the ancient creed of Nicaea at this point, it offers us the definitive results of the patristic discussion of Christ's deity.

3. On account of its liturgical significance in the Eastern and Roman Catholic Churches, it is well adapted to remind us that over and above ecclesiastical divisions there was ecumenical consensus on the Christian confession, even though this was continually obscured.

4. It says unequivocally what Liberal Protestantism refuses to listen to, and for that very reason its validity must be recognised absolutely in an Evangelical dogmatics.

We shall conclude our consideration of the present problem with a short commentary on the relevant passage. It runs thus :

(Πιστεύομεν . . .)	*(Credo . . .)*
1. εἰς ἕνα κύριον Ἰησοῦν Χριστόν	1. *in unum Dominum Jesum Christum*
2. τὸν υἱὸν τοῦ θεοῦ τὸν μονογενῆ	2. *filium Dei unigenitum*
3. τὸν ἐκ τοῦ πατρὸς γεννηθέντα πρὸ πάντων αἰώνων	3. *et ex Patre natum ante omnia saecula*
4. φῶς ἐκ φωτός, θεὸν ἀληθινὸν ἐκ θεοῦ ἀληθινοῦ, γεννηθέντα οὐ ποιηθέντα	4. *Deum de Deo, lumen de lumine, Deum verum de Deo vero, genitum non factum*
5. ὁμοούσιον τῷ πατρί	5. *consubstantialem Patri*
6. δι' οὗ τὰ πάντα ἐγένετο	6. *per quem omnia facta sunt*
(Text, Denzinger, No. 86)	(Text, *Missale Romanum*)

1. We believe in the one Lord Jesus Christ. The term " Lord " points in the first instance to the significance of Jesus Christ for us. In relation to us He is the Bearer of authority and power. He has a claim on us and control over us. He commands and rules. But He does not do so accidentally and provisionally, nor partially and restrictedly, like other lords. His lordship is not derivative nor grounded in a higher lordship. It is lordship in the final and definitive sense of the word. It is self-grounded lordship. This is the point of the " one " Lord. Its meaning is that the confession " Jesus Christ is

Lord " is not just an analysis of the meaning of Jesus Christ for us as this is manifested to us in faith. It tells us that grounded in Himself, and apart from what He means for us, Jesus Christ is what He means for us, and that He can mean this for us because quite apart therefrom He is it antecedently in Himself.

How could faith (as the apprehension of what Jesus Christ means for us) succeed in regarding itself as the justification of that confession ? On the contrary, faith can regard itself as justified by the fact that prior to all apprehension of ours Jesus Christ is in Himself the very One as whom He gives Himself to be apprehended by us. *Christus quamquam sit coelestis et sempiternae conditor civitatis, non tamen eum, quoniam ab illo condita est, Deum credidit, sed ideo potius est condenda, quia credidit. . . . Roma Romulum amando esse Deum credidit, ista istum Deum esse credendo amavit* (Augustine, *De. civ. Dei*, XXII, 6, 1).

The phrase " the one " Lord relates Jesus Christ directly to the Father of whom the confession has said emphatically in the first article that He is the one God. If there can be no rivalry between the words " God " and " Lord " when they refer to the one being—to the one being in the same way as the statements about creation and reconciliation refer to the one work of this one being—then this phrase already makes the decisive point that Jesus Christ is Himself this being, that He is not just His legate or plenipotentiary, but that He is identical with Him. Because He is the one Lord, because He is the Lord in this strictest sense, His lordship for us, in His revelation, has no beginning and no end ; it breaks in upon us with the unique and incomparable thrust of eternal truth and reality itself ; it cannot be perceived or inferred from any standpoint whatever ; knowledge of it begins with its acknowledgment. Only if He were another Lord, one of the lords within our world, could things be different. But He is this Lord, the " Lord of all lords " (Deut. 10^{17} ; 1 Tim. 6^{15}). He has this significance for us because it corresponds to what His being is " antecedently in Himself."

2. We believe in Jesus Christ as the only-begotten Son of God. The term " Son " will be dealt with under point 4. The phrase " only-begotten " first emphasises the oneness, which means the exclusiveness and uniqueness of the revelation and reconciliation enacted in Jesus Christ. To believe in Him as the Son of God is to know no other Son of God alongside Him, i.e., to know no other revelations which would be for us the revelation of God Himself, to know no other reconciliations in which we would be aware of being reconciled to God Himself. There are indeed other, immanent revelations and reconciliations accomplished within the created world ; there are revelations of the spirit and revelations of nature. One man can reveal himself to another. And man can be reconciled to his destiny, even to death, and even— which is perhaps the greatest thing of all—to his fellow-man. But

none of all this is the act of the Son of God. At any rate if a man believes in Jesus Christ as the Son of God, if God is revealed to him in Him and he is reconciled to God through Him, he will not see works of other sons of God in all those revelations and reconciliations. If they are to be authentic revelations and reconciliations, they can only be identical with *the* revelation and reconciliation through *the* Son of God. Jesus Christ will have to be recognised as living and acting in them. The one revelation and reconciliation will not be one among others. Yet this is not all that the confession is saying in the clause about the only-begotten Son of God.

If this were all it might still mean that the New Testament υἱὸς μονογενής should be interpreted by υἱὸς ἀγαπητός, which also occurs in the New Testament. And this might mean that a being distinct from God was the object of God's special good-pleasure, favour, choice and adoption, that this being alone was called son by God and installed as God's son with the dignity and rights of sonship. And this would mean for us that he would have to be acknowledged and believed in by us as such. The exclusiveness of this belief, the so-called "absoluteness of Christianity," would then be the content of the confession. But if by μονογενής the confession is confessing the oneness and uniqueness of the revelation that took place in Jesus Christ, this is something very different from the absoluteness of Christianity. The confession is not saying that in faith, even in faith understood as a decision, we can and should choose one possibility among many others and label and claim it as absolute in distinction from the many others. How can this kind of exaltation of Jesus Christ attach itself to faith when the meaning of His exaltation by His heavenly Father is already quite different, when it is not an innovation but the confirmation of something original and intrinsic? The uniqueness of Jesus Christ as the Son of God, and therefore the uniqueness of the revelation and reconciliation enacted in Him, is not a predicate subsequently conferred on Him by God. It is to be understood as the content of an analytic, not a synthetic, statement. Μονογενής is not to be interpreted by ἀγαπητός but *vice versa*: *Non ideo* μονογενής *dicitur, quia* ἀγαπητός *sed ideo est* ἀγαπητός *quia* μονογενής (Quenstedt, *Theol. did. pol.*, 1685, I, cap. 9, sect. 1, th. 34).

The only-begotten Son is according to Jn. 1[18] the one God. God Himself, God in Himself, is in the mode of being of the only-begotten of the Father. This is why this Only-begotten is the object of the Father's love and this is why He can be the object of our faith. Before all revelation and all faith, before it is given to man to behold the glory of this Only-begotten (Jn. 1[14]), this glory is the glory of God Himself. And this is why it is " grace and truth " in its revelation. This is why its revelation has to be unique. The uniqueness of its revelation and of reconciliation corresponds to what God in His own being is antecedently in Himself : the Son of the Father, beside whom there can no more be a second Son of the Father than there can be a second God alongside the one God.

3. We believe in Jesus Christ as the begotten of the Father before all time. Our starting-point here, too, must be the fact that this is

said of Jesus Christ as the Revealer of God and therefore of the God who acts on us and for us in time. Hence the statement about God as such does not stand abstractly as a second statement alongside a first statement about God as the Lord of our history. The statement about God as the Lord of our history is underscored by the statement that He is God as such and not a mere analogy of God, even the highest, in a sphere of reality distinct from God. He does not signify God Himself; He is God Himself. The phrase " before all time " does not, then, exclude time, whether the *illic et tunc* of revelation as it is attested in Scripture or the *hic et nunc* in which it is to become revelation for us. It does not exclude but includes time, concretely this time, the time of revelation. Hence it does not exclude history; it includes it. But the fact that time (the time of our time, the time and history of the sinful creature—and this is also the time and history of revelation) is included in a divine " before all time " is not something that we can take for granted. It is grace, mystery, a basis that we must recognise in the fear of God. Hence the statement about God as such, about God Himself, must be explicitly made even at the risk of the misunderstanding that we might be speaking without revelation and faith, that we might be speaking " non-historically," at the very point where everything depends on our speaking correctly about revelation and faith, about history. Even the statement about God as the Lord of our history is not as such immune from misunderstanding. In itself it might be construed as a statement of anthropological metaphysics. But it, too, can and must be construed only as an underscoring of the statement about God as such. Certainly the statement about the pre-existence of Jesus Christ is only an explication of the statement about His existence as the Revealer and the Reconciler, as the God who acts in us and for us in time. But just as truly the statement about His existence is only an explication of the statement about His pre-existence. This One, the Son of God who exists for us, is the Pre-existent. But only this One, the pre-existent Son of God, is the One who exists for us. The dogma of the incarnation of the Son of God will elucidate the first statement. The dogma of the deity of Christ which is our concern here emphasises the second.

The second article of the *Nic. Const.* distinguishes very clearly between these two circles of knowledge. The dogma of the incarnation is not stated explicitly in the *Nic. Const.* but in the *Ephesinum* of 431 and the *Chalcedonense* of 451.

" Begotten of the Father before all time " means that He did not come into being in time as such, that He did not come into being in an event within the created world. That the Son of God becomes man and that He is known by other men in His humanity as the Son of God are events, even if absolutely distinctive events, in time, within the created world. But their distinction does not itself derive or come from time. Otherwise they would be only relatively distinctive events, of which there are others. Precisely because they have divine power, because the power of this world is here the power of the world to come, because the power of God's immanence is here the power of His transcendence, their subject must be understood as being before all time, as the eternal Subject, eternal as God Himself, Himself eternal as God. Jesus Christ does not first become God's Son when He is it for us. He becomes it from eternity; He becomes it as the eternal Son of the eternal Father.

" Before all time " should not be regarded, then, as a temporal definition. *Absque initio, semper ac sine fine : Pater generans, Filius nascens et Spiritus sanctus procedens*, says the *Conc. Lat.* IV, 1215, of God's three modes of being. On a passage often quoted in this context, namely, Ps. 2^7: " Thou art my Son, this day have I begotten thee," Cyril of Jerusalem has the pertinent comment : *Τὸ δὲ σήμερον, οὐ πρόσφατον, ἀλλ' ἀΐδιον · τὸ σήμερον ἄχρονον, πρὸ πάντων τῶν αἰώνων* (*Cat.*, 11, 5). *Vox " hodie " notat diem immutabilis aeternitatis*, is Quenstedt's paraphrase (*op. cit., th.* 15), and in regard to its relation to time he then interprets the concept of the generation of the Son from the Father as follows (*th.* 28) : *Haec generatio Filii Dei non fit derivatione aut transfusione, nec actione, quae incipiat aut desinat, sed fit indesinente emanatione, cui simile nihil habetur in rerum natura. Deus Pater enim filium suum ab aeterno genuit et semper gignit, nec unquam desinet gignere. Si enim generatio filii finem haberet, haberet etiam initium et sic aeterna non esset.* Of this divine " antecedently " (which decides the temporal event that affects us to-day), we can and must say equally, then, that it takes place to-day, that it took place yesterday, and that it will take place tomorrow. *Nec tamen propterea generatio haec dici potest imperfecta et successiva. Actus namque generationis in Patre et Filio consideratur in opere perfectus, in operatione perpetuus.* That is to say, the transcendence of the " antecedently " over all time cannot mean an emptying of the temporal event which is based on this " antecedently," for this is genuine and eternal transcendence. What is real in God must constantly become real precisely because it is real in God (not after the manner of created being). But this becoming (because it is this becoming) rules out every need of this being for completion. Indeed, this becoming simply confirms the perfection of this being.

4. We believe in Jesus Christ as light of light, very God of very God, begotten, not made. In this clause we have the true and decisive trinitarian definition of Christ's deity. It states two things : First, that in God's work and essence we have to distinguish light and light, God and God, to distinguish them in the same way that in the created world we have to distinguish a source of light and a light that emanates from it, or a light that kindles and a light that is kindled, or father and son, or speaker and the word spoken. Then we have to understand this distinction as a distinction in God Himself. We have not to understand it as though there were God on the one side and a creature on the other, but in such a way that the one God is found equally on both sides. We shall try to understand the two series that are discernible here together, in their mutual relationship to one another.

In the first instance the statements about distinction and unity in God are simply statements about revelation as the Church has found it attested in Holy Scripture. At this point, in this revelation, God is here and God is there, God is in this way and God is in that way, God is the Creator and God is the Reconciler, and yet He is one and the same God. We have here the concealed God and the revealed God, and yet the concealed God is no other than the revealed God and *vice versa*. In the first instance the dogma simply corresponds to the dialectic of revelation as such ; it repeats the distinction and the unification. But according to the preceding clause it is now incontestable that with reference to the revelation that took place in Jesus Christ, in interpretation of the revelation as such, we have to say something that is more than the revelation. By revelation we have to say something that is beyond and above the revelation. We have to say that, as Christ is in revelation, so He is antecedently in Himself. Thus He is antecedently in Himself light of light, very God of very God, the begotton of God and not His creature. We have to take revelation with such utter seriousness that in it as God's act we must directly see God's being too.

To say that our concern is with the distinction and unity of two modes of being in God is to say already that while we can and must try to define this distinction and unity we cannot expect to grasp it in these definitions. We can and must think them out and express them. To try to avoid doing so is to try to evade knowledge of them. But it is with the biblical witness to God's revelation, as we have felt we must understand it, that knowledge of them is imposed on us as at least the task of dogmatics. We have good reason to recall that knowledge of God's Word can only be knowledge in faith. Decisively, then, it can only be acknowledgment, man's responsibility to the question which is set by this object. This responsibility cannot be discharged by grasping this object or seizing control of it. The object will always remain an object for what we think and say. What we think and say will never be commensurate with it ; it will always be incommensurate (inadequate). Even though we reproduce the dogma or indeed the very statements of Holy Scripture it is only by God's grace and not intrinsically that the content of knowledge can be proper to what we think and say. Regarded immanently, what we think and say will always be in itself inadequate and broken thought and utterance.

(*a*) Relatively the least vulnerable of the three phrases in the clause is the middle one : " Very God of very God." The ἐκ denotes very briefly the distinction in modes of being : Very God grounded in and proceeding from very God—that is Jesus Christ. That is God only in this mode of being. The distinction of mode of being in which Jesus Christ is God consists, then, in the relation to another mode of being, a relation which the ἐκ shows to be a grounding in or proceeding from.

Conversely the unity of the two modes of being as *modes* of being of an absolutely identical *being* is denoted by the repetition of the noun θεός along with the emphatic repetition of the adjective ἀληθινός.

In what became the official Latin text the crescendo : *Deum de Deo, lumen de lumine, Deum verum de Deo vero,* is obviously intentional. In his controversy with Caroli, Calvin called the passage a *battologia,* a *carmen magis cantillando aptum quam formula confessionis, in qua syllaba una redundare absurdum est* (*Adv. P. Caroli calumnias, C.R.,* 7, 315 f.). But it is better to think that the intensification of thought from lesser to greater definition is meant to be achieved as it were *in actu.*

The difficulty in even this very simple formula consists in the fact that as soon as we try to explain the ἐκ either as above or similarly, it unavoidably gives rise to the idea of two autonomous beings in a specific relation of dependence to one another, or, if this concept is avoided, it becomes meaningless, so that there is no longer any reference to a distinction in the *Deus verus.* The truth signified actually lies beyond the words that signify it. *Deus verus* and *Deus verus* do not confront one another as autonomous beings but are twofold in one and the same autonomous being. This is what no language can render adequately ; even the language of dogma can render it only very inadequately.

(*b*) In the first phrase " light of light " we have a lofty but all the more parlous attempt at illustration. In the first instance what is probably in view is the image of the sun and sunlight, of which the fathers were particularly fond. Jesus Christ as one mode of being in God is related to the first mode of being in which it is grounded and from which it proceeds, in the same manner as sunlight is to the sun.

ὧν ἀπαύγασμα τῆς δόξης αὐτοῦ we read of the Son of God in Heb. 1³. *Cum radius ex sole porrigitur . . . sol erit in radio, quia solis est radius, nec separatur substantia sed extenditur. Ita de Spiritu Spiritus, et Deo Deus, ut lumen de lumine accensum* (Tertullian, *Apolog.,* 21).

We can only rejoice in what is indeed the loftiness and beauty of the figure used in this phrase, and yet we have to confess not only that it presupposes the existence in time and space of that denoted by it but also that it is exposed to very different physical interpretations of which probably not one would say what is really being said here. We incur similar difficulties if we find in the *lumen de lumine* a light that kindles and a light that is kindled. In this metaphor the confession is certainly not trying to offer a *vestigium trinitatis* in the created world. It is not trying to make a statement about the hypostatic character and the *homoousia* of light in that twofold possibility of meaning. But just because, strictly speaking, it is unable to do this, the metaphor remains inadequate as a statement about Jesus Christ and the object plainly continues to transcend the word.

(c) The decisive phrase is naturally the third : " Begotten, not made."

In the negative part, which we take first, it tells us that as a mode of being in God Jesus Christ is certainly from God, yet He is not from God in the way that creatures from the highest angel to the smallest particle of sun-dust are from God, namely, by creation, i.e., in such a way that He had His existence, as an existence distinct from God, through the will and word of God. This can, of course, be said of the human nature of Christ, of His existence as a man in which, according to Scripture, He meets us as the Revealer of God and the Reconciler to God. But it cannot be said of Him who here assumes human nature, of Him who here exists as man (" for us men," as *Nic. Const.* says later) but does not allow His being and essence to be exhausted or imprisoned in His humanity, who is also in the full sense *not* man in this humanity, who is the Revealer and Reconciler in His humanity by virtue of that wherein He is not man. He who becomes man here to become the Revealer and Reconciler is not made. Otherwise revelation and reconciliation would be an event within creation and, since creation is the world of fallen man, they would be a futile event. Because the One who here became man is God, God in this mode of being, therefore, and not otherwise, His humanity is effective as revelation and reconciliation.

We now turn to the positive side of the phrase. Surprisingly enough it denotes the real becoming of Jesus Christ, His eternal becoming appropriate to Him as God, His relation of origin and dependence as God in His distinctive mode of being. And it uses a figure of speech from the creaturely realm to do this. And, one might add, it uses the figure of speech which characterises this sphere as no other could. " Begotten," which means, in an eminent sense, that He has come into being as all living things in creation have come into being on the basis and presupposition of the divine Word of creation, that He has come into being in the context of sex and the nexus of the species, that He has come into being as the worm has come into being, that He has come into being as man comes into being, in the process in which creation and sin, in what is perhaps the most enigmatic way, are not interfused but opposed even as they exist together. We must not shut our eyes to this stumbling-block if we are to reach understanding here.

Thomas Aquinas thinks that what is properly expressed by the metaphor of generation is the *processio verbi* (*S. theol.*, I, *qu.* 27, *art.* 2). On this point we must say that *generatio* and the *processio verbi* are certainly to be regarded as terms for the same thing, yet not in such a way that one of the terms can be simply reduced to the other. *Processio verbi* may also be regarded as an important figure of speech but in its own way it is inadequate too. Both metaphors, that of the Son and that of the Word of God, point to an object with which they are not commensurate. But for that very reason each of them must be taken seriously, and neither should be abandoned with a reference to the other.

Obviously the natural character of the metaphor of begetting makes it clear at the outset that in all that is said about Father and Son in description of the two modes of being in God we have a frail and contestable figure of speech. We denote God in this way but we do not grasp Him.

The early Church, which did not invent the metaphor but found it in Holy Scripture, where it is the most prominent figure of speech for this fact, was by no means unaware of its inadequacy and often stated this. *Est in hoc mysterio generationis vocabulum ab omnibus imperfectionibus generationis physicae adhaerentibus purgandum* (Quenstedt, *op. cit., th.* 47). And already Cyril of Jerusalem demands expressly that not only the most patent physical sense of the term generation but also the sense of intellectual generation (e.g., in the teacher-pupil relation) and that of spiritual generation (as in believers when they become children of God) must be completely ruled out in this regard (*Cat.*, 11, 9).

But what, then, does the metaphor mean ?

In place of the categories of understanding which have been rightly rejected Quenstedt put a new one invented for the purpose when he spoke (*op. cit., th.* 47) of a *generatio hyperphysica, quae fit ab aeterno, sine omni temporis successione, materia et mutatione et in sola essentiae communicatione consistit.* But Irenaeus had made the same point in a more illuminating way when he declared : *Si quis itaque nobis dixerit : Quomodo ergo Filius prolatus a Patre est ? dicimus ei, quia prolationem istam, sive generationem, sive nuncupationem, sive adapertionem aut quolibet quis nomine vocaverit generationem eius inenarrabilem exsistentem, nemo novit, non Valentinus, non Marcion, neque Saturninus, neque Basilides, neque angeli, neque archangeli, neque principes, neque potestates, nisi solus qui generavit Pater et qui natus est Filius* (*C.o.h.*, II, 28, 6) and so had Cyril of Jerusalem when he declared that the Father begets the Son ὡς οἶδεν αὐτὸς μόνος: the only possible thing we can say of this begetting is how it did not take place (*Cat.*, 11, 11). Μὴ ἐπαισχυνθῇς ὁμολογῆσαι τὴν ἄγνοιαν, ἐπειδὴ μετʼ ἀγγέλων ἀγνοεῖς (*ib.*, 11, 12). Εἰπέ μοι πρῶτον, τίς ἐστιν ὁ γεννήσας, καὶ τότε μάνθανε ὃ ἐγέννησεν (*ib.*, 11, 14). Taken strictly, even the concept of *communicatio essentiae* says something which cannot be said without denying the unity of God's essence, and it becomes obscure or meaningless if it is not taken strictly. It does not carry us beyond the barrier which Quenstedt, too, had to admit in another passage (*op. cit.*, I, *cap.* 9, *sect.* 2, *qu.* 8, *font. sol.* 5) : *Satis est, nos hic τὸ ὄν tenere, quod scriptura docet, τὸ ποῖον vero reservare isti statui, qui mera lux erit.*

In all its secularity and inadequacy, which we cannot possibly overlook, the figure of the Father and the Son says that a similar—not the same but a very different, an inconceivably and inexpressibly different—nevertheless a similar distinction and continuity exists to that between the person of a father and the person of a son in the created world, that there is a similar being of the first for the second and a similar being of the second from the first, that there is a similar twoness and oneness of the same being, between the mode of being in which God is revealed to us in Jesus Christ and the mode of being from which He is as He who is revealed to us in Jesus Christ. The very thing which, veiled in the puzzling co-existence of creation and sin, we know only as the begetting of a son by a father, though it is not grasped but only denoted in its true How by this figure, being just as unfathomable to us in its true How as is the being of God generally—this same thing is God's self-positing in which He is also and through Himself alone indissolubly distinct, the Father of Jesus Christ and Jesus Christ the Son of the Father. Even this most forceful figure can do no more, and does not seek to do more, than summon us to knowledge, not trying even for a moment to tie us to itself but at once directing our gaze beyond itself to the object to which, powerless though it is in itself, it can respond, leading us to the acknowledgment in which alone knowledge can consist here. All the associations which might be meaningfully suggested by the image are legitimate, and none is legitimate. Everything we might think of in this connexion, the fruitfulness of the Father, the love that does not let Him want to be alone, the dependence of the Son's existence on the Father, the love He owes to the Father with His existence, the indestructible fellowship between the two which is not grounded in choice but in their two-sided existence—all this may be expressed and on all this we must be able to be silent again. The knowledge expressed in the metaphor is a non-knowing knowledge. It should regard itself as a knowing non-knowledge. Like every human word— though this is seldom so clear as here—it can only serve the Word which God Himself says about Himself. In this figure, which even in itself and as such denotes the deepest mystery of creaturely life, we can and should think of everything that can be meaningfully thought of in relation to the Father-Son relation in God, and we should then say : We are unprofitable servants, we have only thought and said in figures what we were under obligation to do, but we cannot claim that what we have thought and said is correct. Correctness belongs exclusively to that about which we have thought and spoken, not to what we have thought and spoken.

That the " begotten," along with the whole metaphor of father and son, says nothing, or does not say the truth, respecting God, does not in the least follow from all this. What it says is inappropriate, but it does say something and it says the truth. If we call what is said about Father and Son figurative, it should be remembered that this can apply only to our human speech as such but not to its object. It is not true, then, that the father-son relation is itself originally and properly a creaturely reality. It is not true that in some hidden depth of His essence God is something other than Father and Son. It is not true that these names are just freely chosen and in the last analysis meaningless symbols, symbols whose original and proper non-symbolical content lies in that creaturely reality. On the contrary, it is in God that the father-son relation, like all creaturely relations, has its original and proper reality. The mystery of begetting is originally and properly a divine and not a creaturely mystery. Perhaps one ought even to say that it is *the* divine mystery.

The *generatio ipsa* is *in divinis propriissima et longe verior et perfectior quam ullius creaturae* (Quenstedt, *op. cit., qu.* 8, *ekth.* 5).

But we know only the figure of this reality in its twofold inappropriateness as a creaturely figure and a sinful creaturely figure. We can speak of the truth only in untruth. We do not know what we are saying when we call God Father and Son. We can say it only in such a way that on our lips and in our concepts it is untruth. For us the truth we are expressing when we call God Father and Son is hidden and unsearchable.

The *modus generationis ipsae* is *in Deo longe alius quam in nobis estque nobis incognitus et ineffabilis* (Quenstedt, *loc. cit.*).

Nevertheless, in naming God thus we are expressing the truth, His truth. In this sense the " begotten " says precisely what a confession of faith can and should say at the necessary distance from but also in the necessary relation to its object. It explains God's mode of being in Jesus Christ as a real " Thence " and " Thither," as the bringing forth from a source which is real in God Himself. Though we cannot, of course, perceive it, this is the proper and original Father-Son relation, the fatherhood and sonship of God. And we must add that the force as well as the clarity of the " begotten " does at least also lie in its opposition to the rejected " made." Begetting is less than creating inasmuch as the former denotes the bringing forth of creature from creature whereas the latter denotes the bringing forth of the creature by the Creator. Yet begetting is also more than creating inasmuch as—and here the closed circle of creature and creature as we see it in what we know as begetting is a figure—it denotes the bringing forth of God from God, whereas creating denotes only the bringing forth of the creature by God.

Quenstedt differentiates as follows : *Generatio est entis similis secundum substantiam ex substantia gignentis productio. Creatio est entis dissimilis secundum substantiam ex nihilo extra essentiam creantis productio* (*op. cit., qu.* 8, *font. sol.* 16).

In the superiority of bringing forth from God in God over bringing forth by God, in the superiority of the freedom in which God posits His own reality over the freedom in which He posits a reality distinct from Himself, in the superiority of the love in which He is an object to Himself over the love in which the object is something that exists by His will in distinction from Himself—in this superiority lies the significance of the " begotten, not made."

This sheds light on a Scholastic thesis which is important here in helping to explain the purpose of the dogma. (J. Kuhn, *Kath. Dogmatik*, Vol. 2, 1857,

p. 464, can even call it " the supreme dogmatic definition and the climax of the Nicene faith.") Following Athanasius (*Or. c. Ar.*, 2, 29), John of Damascus (*Ekdosis*, I, 8) distinguished begetting as God's ἔργον φύσεως and creation as His ἔργον θελήσεως. Thomas Aquinas (*S. theol.*, I, *qu.* 41, *art.* 2), borrowing from Hilary (*Lib. de Synod. can.*, 24 f.), then explains that the begetting of the Son is certainly to be understood as an act of divine will, but only as the act of will in which *Deus vult se esse Deum*, as the act of will in which God, in freedom of course, wills Himself and in virtue of this will of His is Himself. In this sense, identically indeed with God's being Himself, the begetting of the Son is also an ἔργον θελήσεως for here θέλησις and φύσις are one and the same. But the begetting of the Son is not an act of the divine will to the degree that freedom to will this or that is expressed in the concept of will. God has this freedom in respect of creation— He is free to will it or not to will it—and creation is thus an ἔργον θελήσεως. But He does not have this freedom in respect of His being God. God cannot not be God. Therefore—and this is the same thing—He cannot not be Father and cannot be without the Son. His freedom or aseity in respect of Himself consists in His freedom, not determined by anything but Himself, to be God, and that means to be the Father of the Son. A freedom to be able not to be this would be an abrogation of His freedom. Thus the begetting of the Son is an ἔργον φύσεως. It could not not happen just as God could not not be God, whereas creation is an ἔργον θελήσεως in the sense that it could also not happen and yet God would not on that account be any the less God. Quenstedt sums it up concisely : *Filius Dei est obiectum volitum et amatum ipsius voluntatis divinae, non tamen per illam productus*. The Father begets the Son *volens*, but not *quia voluit* (*op. cit.*, qu. 8, *ofnt. sol.* 13). He does not beget Him *necessitate coactionis*, but *necessitate immutabilitatis* (Hollaz, *Ex. Theol. acroam.*, 1706, I, 2, 37).

It is pertinent to add here for the sake of completeness a reminder which is absent from the *Nic. Const.* The figure of the Father and the Son to whose express interpretation the *Nic. Const.* confines itself is not the only one by which we should try to understand the concept of the deity of Christ. Alongside it there is both in the New Testament itself and also in the vocabulary of the early Church another one, namely, that Jesus Christ is the Word of God. By this figure He is again a second mode of being in God which is distinct from the first one but again one in essence with this, just as the word that someone speaks is distinct from him and yet as his word is not different in essence from what he is. We are saying the same thing when we say either " Son of God " or " Word of God "—*Verbum suum qui est Filius eius* (Irenaeus, *C.o.h.*, II, 30, 9). One may perhaps say that the first term is more to the point when we understand God's action in Jesus Christ materially as reconciliation and the second is more to the point when we understand the action formally as revelation. But in the first instance the statement about Christ's deity as the Word of God simply relates to God's action on us in Jesus Christ as attested in Scripture. Thus primarily and simply we understand by this figure too the *beneficia Christi*. In its truth and clarity the Word of God that is spoken to us, like the Son who intercedes with us for God and with God for us, is no other and no less than God Himself.

When God speaks, then *Nous* and *Logos* share equal truth and dignity. *Deus totus existens mens et totus existens logos, quod cogitatur, hoc et loquitur et quod loquitur, hoc et cogitat* (Irenaeus, *C.o.h.*, II, 13, 8 and 28, 5). *Non enim se ipsum integre perfecteque dixisset, si aliquid minus aut amplius in eius Verbo quam in ipso* (Augustine, *De trin.*, XV, 14). *Etenim non potest aliud quam quod es aut aliquid maius vel minus te esse in verbo, quo teipsum dicis, quoniam verbum tuum sic est verum quomodo tu es verax* (Anselm of Canterbury, *Prosl.*, 23). " When Moses saith, ' In the beginning God made heaven and earth,' no person is yet specifically named or expressed, But as soon as he saith further, ' And God said, Let there be light,' he expresseth that there was a Word with God before light came into being. Now the same Word that God speaketh there could not be the thing that was created there, neither heaven nor earth, since God, just by speaking what He does, maketh heaven and earth with the light and all other creatures, so He hath done nothing more to create save His Word, therefore it must have been before all creatures. But if it was before, ere time and creatures began, it must be eternal and another and higher being than all creatures, whereupon it followeth that it is God " (Luther, *Sermon on Gen.* 1¹, 1527, *W.A.*, 24, p. 29, l. 4).

Jesus Christ, the Word of God, meets us as no other than God, but in another way, in a different mode of being compared with God in so far as God speaks the Word, in so far as the Word goes forth from Him.

" But if God speaketh and the Word falleth, He is not alone nor can He personally be Himself the Word that He speaketh. Therefore, because the Word is also God, it must be another person. Thus the two persons are expressed : the Father who speaketh the Word and hath essence of Himself, the Son who is the Word and cometh from the Father and is eternally with Him " (Luther, *op. cit.*, l. 14, cf. *W.A.*, 10¹, p. 183, l. 13).

The same revelation thus compels us to separate God and His Word and also to unite them.

" Who cannot here gather from these words of Moses how there must be two persons in the Godhead and yet but one Godhead ? unless he wisheth to deny clear Scripture. Again, who is so acute as he may here contradict ? He must allow the word to be something other than God its speaker, and must yet confess it was before all creatures and the creature was made thereby ; so he must certainly allow it also to be God, for apart from the creatures there is naught but God. So he must also confess, there is but one God. And so this scripture compelleth and concludeth that these two persons are one complete God, and each is the one, true, perfect, natural God who hath created all things, and that the Speaker hath not His being from the Word but the Word its being from the Speaker, yet all eternally and in eternity apart from all creatures " (Luther, *Sermon on Jn.* 1¹˙, 1522, *W.A.*, 10¹, p. 184, l. 6).

This distinction and unity in God which is inescapably presented to us in revelation itself is acknowledged and underlined by the dogma when it understands Jesus Christ, the Word of God, as the eternal Word. The Word of God in which He gives Himself to be known by us is none other than that in which He knows Himself. For this reason and in this way it is God's own Word, the Word of truth to us in His revelation. According to the preceding development in the history of the dogma, it is beyond question that whenever the *Nic. Const.* spoke of the Son of God it always meant the Word of God too. The Word is the one Lord. The Word is spoken by the Father before all time. The Word is light of light, very God of very God. The Word is spoken by God, not made. Alongside the statement that Jesus Christ is the eternal Son of the eternal Father one may thus put the statement that He is the eternal Word of the Father who speaks from all eternity, or the eternal thought of the Father who thinks from all eternity, the Word in which God thinks Himself or expresses Himself by Himself.

Jesus Christ is God's eternal *emanatio intelligibilis utpote verbi intelligibilis a dicente, quod manet in ipso* (Thomas Aquinas, *S. theol.*, I, qu. 27, art. 1).

As the Word which God thinks or speaks eternally by Himself and whose content can thus be no other than God Himself, Jesus Christ as God's second mode of being is God Himself.

Yet we must not disguise the fact that on our lips and in our concepts this way of speaking is also inappropriate. We do not know what we are saying when we call Jesus Christ the eternal Word of God. We know no word which, though distinct from a speaker, still contains and reproduces the whole essence of the speaker. We know no *Logos* with an adequate *Nous*-content and no *Nous* which can be exhaustively expressed in a *Logos*. We know no thought or speech which can transcend the antithesis of knowledge and being in triumphant synthesis. In short, we know no true word. Neither do we know, then, the true word about the true Word, God's Word. We must say once more what we said about the father-son relation. For us who think and speak in the doubly veiled sphere of creatureliness and sinfulness, the true word is strictly and exclusively the eternal Word concealed in God, Jesus Christ Himself. It is not that our creaturely thought and word has in relation to the creaturely reason which produces the creaturely logos a metaphorical aptitude which justifies the claim that we are thinking and speaking the truth when we call Jesus Christ the Word of God. It requires revelation and faith, and the connected gracious event of the incarnation of the eternal Word and the outpouring of the Holy Spirit, if what we know as word is to be continually awakened and raised up to this metaphorical aptitude, so that it may become the truth when we call Jesus Christ the Word of God.

" Now must we open wide the heart and understanding, that we regard not such a word as a man's petty and halting word, but as he is great that speaketh, so great must we consider his word. 'Tis a word he speaketh in himself, and it abideth in him and is never sundered from him. Therefore according to the apostle's thought we must so think as God speaketh with Himself to Himself and leaveth a word about Himself in Himself, but the same word is no mere wind or sound, but bringeth with it the whole essence of the divine nature, and as is said earlier in the epistle about appearance and likeness, the divine nature is so depicted that it is wholly present in the likeness and it becometh and is itself the likeness, and the clarity thus exceedeth the appearance and passes essentially into the appearance. Accordingly then God also speaketh His word about Himself that His whole godhead followeth the word and naturally abideth in the word and is essential. Lo, we see there whence the apostle hath his language that he calleth Christ an image of the divine being and an appearance of the divine honour, namely, from this text of Moses, who there teacheth that God speaketh a word about Himself which may not be other than an image that indicateth Him. For every word is a sign that signifieth somewhat. But here is that signified, naturally in sign or word, which is not in other signs ; therefore he rightly calls it an essential image or sign of his nature " (Luther, *op. cit.*, p. 186, l. 9).

On account of the inadequacy of this figure of speech it is inadvisable to bring the concept of the deity of Christ under the denominator of the image of " word."

There seems to be at least a strong tendency in this direction in Thomas Aquinas, cf. *S. theol.*, I, *qu.* 27, *art*, 2 and also *qu.* 34. Nor does this rest on any particularly high estimation of " word " as the epitome of revelation, Scripture or Church proclamation, but rather on his anthropology, i.e., on his high opinion of the process of knowledge as the *similitudo supremarum creaturarum* (*qu.* 27, *art.* 1). In regard to this it must be said that an *emanatio verbi manentis in dicente* is metaphorically apt, not because such a *similitudo* is immanent in it, but because it is awakened and raised up to be a *similitudo*, a likeness, and therefore to metaphorical aptness, in the event of revelation and faith. The same may naturally be said in opposition to Augustine's doctrine of the *vestigium* or the *imago trinitatis* in the three powers of the soul, *memoria, intellectus* and *amor*. There is no *analogia entis* but only an *analogia fidei*. But it is instructive to see how the preference which on the basis of his own theory Augustine, too, gives to the concept of word : *Eo quippe filius quo verbum*, is then reversed again : *et eo verbum quo filius* (*De trin.*, VII, 2). He is well aware, of course, that by " Son " something is said about Jesus Christ which cannot be said by " Word " and which must always be added in thought to what we know as word, namely, the continuity and oneness of essence between Speaker and Spoken. So he must combine the images : *Verbo quod genuit dicens est, non verbo, quod profertur et sonat et transit, sed. . . . Verbo aequali sibi quo semper est immutabiliter dicit seipsum* (*ib.*, VII, 1). *Seipsum dicens genuit Verbum sibi aequale per omnia. . . . Et ideo Verbum hoc vere veritas est* (*ib.*, XV, 14). And Thomas Aquinas, too, does not hesitate to admit that different *nomina* are needed to express the perfection of the divine origin of Christ : *Filius, splendor, imago, verbum. Non autem potuit unum nomen inveniri, per quod omnia ista* (namely, everything that is meant to be denoted by one or other of these terms) *designarentur* (*S. theol.*, I, *qu.* 34, *art.* 2, *ad.* 3). F. Diekamp's *conclusio theologica* that " the begetting of the Son from the Father is an intellectual one " (*Kath. Dogm.*, Vol. I, 6th edn., 1930, p. 329 f.) must be described as an unwarranted systematisation even of the view of Thomas. Cf. in this respect the more cautious attitude of B. Bartmann, *Lehrb. d. Dogm.*, Vol. I, 4th edn., 1928, p. 198 f., especially the references to Thomas given on p. 200.

It is when we use all the metaphors, including that of the Word, with an awareness of their limitations that in respect of the event of revelation and faith we shall always be the more confident to speak the divine truth in our human untruth : *peccatores iusti.*

C.D.—P*

5. We believe in Jesus Christ as being " of one substance (or essence) with the Father." Historically the incorporation of this phrase into the original Nicaenum was a bold anticipation, dubious in many respects, but ultimately justifiable both historically and materially.

Ecclesiastically, it was more than doubtful that Constantine I presumed to force this ὁμοούσιος on the council of 325 and that the majority of the council allowed the imposition of this imperial theology in spite of their well-considered persuasion to the contrary. Morally one is bound to sympathise, not with the orthodox minority who were given the victory in this way, and even less with the middle party of Eusebius which apparently yielded for the sake of peace, but rather with the unfortunate Arius and his few followers who preferred deposition and exile to abandoning their resistance. (There was a similar scandal to the detriment of the Nicene faith at Milan in 355.) Furthermore the meaning and intention behind the triumph of the ὁμοούσιος was far from clear ; before Nicaea, and for a long time afterwards, it was by no means obvious whether the concept of *homoousia* (a term already familiar to Valentinian Gnosticism according to Irenaeus, *C. o. h.*, I, 5, 1) did not involve subscription to Sabellianism or even a form of tritheism. In the 3rd and 4th centuries there was good reason to be opposed to this term. In 269 it had even been explicitly rejected at a council in Antioch in justifiable self-defence against Paul of Samosata. And even the group of theologians who eventually won the victory for the doctrine of Christ's eternal deity, the so-called Neo-Nicenes, finally accepted it only upon a very precise interpretation, i.e., in the sense of equality of essence along with distinction of the persons. It was understandable that the making of a dogma out of the hitherto relatively little discussed ὁμοούσιος should become the standard in a battle for or against it which occupied the whole period between 325 and 381 and in which, by wide detours and with many setbacks, the Church had later to learn to understand what it had intended and decided in 325 *hominum confusione et Dei providentia*. One may well ask whether the authoritative theologians at the time of the Council of Constantinople, the Cappadocians in particular, would themselves have devised this formula. Even the West, which was better able to resist Arianism, and which at certain points was the salvation of the Nicene faith, did not finally produce the ὁμοούσιος but accepted it as a *fait accompli*.

In fact one can understand and acknowledge this formula only after recognising quite fearlessly the problems of its origin. But in this way one can and must acknowledge it. One must do so historically, for with the ἀληθινὸν θεόν and the γεννηθέντα οὐ ποιηθέντα, but less ambiguously than either of these for the thought of the time, it proved to be the formula by which the Arian contradiction was finally bound to be unmasked as such and broken. Hilary (*De Syn.*, c. 83) once wrote not without humour : *Homousia si cui displicet, placeat necesse est, quod ab Arianis sit negatum.* One must also acknowledge it materially, for even if the Church had great difficulty in seeing what it meant by it, and was far from seeing this when it was made a dogma in 325, what it did positively mean by it is for us who come after expressed clearly enough in this formula along with the others in the symbol.

" Of one substance or essence," i.e., of identical essence, is the meaning of ὁμοούσιος or *consubstantialis* as a dogma.

This is how it was understood by Athanasius, who was virtually the leading man in the Church in this whole matter : ἀνάγκη γὰρ . . . τὴν ταυτότητα πρὸς τὸν ἑαυτοῦ πατέρα σώζειν (*De. decr. nic. syn.* 23), ἵνα μὴ μόνον ὅμοιον τὸν υἱόν, ἀλλὰ ταὐτόν τῇ ὁμοιώσει ἐκ τοῦ πατρὸς εἶναι σημαίνωσιν (*ib.*, 20), ἔχων ἐκ τοῦ πατρὸς τὴν ταυτότητα (*Or. c. Ar.*, I, 22), etc. This is also how it was understood in the West by Augustine in a way that was decisive for all later development. " In one and the same essence " is how Luther and the authors of the Book of Concord translated the phrase.

" Of equal essence " is included in this sense, for if the Son is of one essence with the Father He is also of equal essence with Him. On the other hand " of equal essence " does not have to mean " of one essence " ; it might be construed polytheistically.

The Neo-Nicenes, for whom the sense " equality of essence " was the dominant one, wished to draw attention thereby to the problem of the distinction and autonomy of the persons, which had received little emphasis in Athanasius. Polytheism thus became a constant threat to Eastern theology. On the other hand, it must be admitted that the idea of oneness of essence made Modalism a constant threat to Western theology. One must say, however, that it is plain enough from the total context in which alone ὁμοούσιος is intelligible that unity of essence is not to be thought of without equality of essence (which is implicitly expressed in the concept itself). In other words, the distinction of the modes of beings is not to be forgotten nor their autonomy surrendered. On the other hand when the opposite is missing there is no obvious safeguard against polytheism. On this ground we vote for Athanasius' ταυτότης i.e., for the Augustinian and Western interpretation of the ὁμοούσιος.

" Of one essence " is first and obviously a safeguard against the Arian understanding of Jesus Christ as a " demi-god from below " or a superman who is indeed like God but, being only like Him, is ultimately and in the last resort different from Him. It underlines and accentuates the γεννηθέντα οὐ ποιηθέντα. It places Jesus Christ on the side of the Creator in contrast to every creature, even the highest.

But " of one essence " is also secondly a safeguard against the idea, current from the days of Origen, that Jesus Christ is a " demi-god from above " on a lower stage and of lesser quantity within the Godhead itself. It underlines and accentuates the ἀληθινὸν θεόν.

" Of one essence " is thus directed against the two extremes which with reference to the situation in the 2nd century we called the Ebionite extreme on the one side and the Docetic on the other.

" Of one essence " is also thirdly a safeguard against the differentiation or multiplication of God's essence through the distinction in modes of being. That is, it is a safeguard against polytheism. If forces us really to understand the " persons " as modes of being, i.e., not as two subjects but as twice the same subject (in indissoluble twofoldness of course, as may be inferred from the context of the creed), as two who are two only in their mutual relations and not in themselves, not in their essence. Ὁμοούσιος τῷ πατρί means " I and the Father are one " —I and the Father, for only in this distinction does the " one " apply— yet " one," for only in this unity is there the I and the Father.

Of this most famous and, technically considered, most central concept of the dogma we may say what we have said of all the formulae in the preceding phrases. We do not even remotely grasp the object to which there is an attempt to respond in this concept. Precisely when we do not construe the concept of *homoousia* polytheistically nor modalistically, precisely when we interpret it with Athanasius and Augustine as identity of essence on the one side and when, taking up the concern of the Neo-Nicenes, we let it speak to us of two distinct but equal modes of being in the one essence on the other side, it is plainly referring to an essence of which we have no idea at all ; it thus becomes a concept of the type philosophy usually calls " empty concepts." We have stated often enough that distinction in unity and unity in distinction is the point in all trinitarian theology. In relation to the concept of *homoousia*, which is trying to express both at the same time, it is thus as well to grant that in the last resort we are familiar only with unities without distinction or distinctions without unity. All images fail at this limit of our thought and speech : the image of Father and Son, that of Speaker and Word, that of light and light, and that of original and copy, which is a metaphor too. For in these we never have one essence in what are really two modes of being or else we never have two modes of being in what is really one essence. Either we have one essence in what are only apparently and transitorily two modes of being or we have two modes of being with two corresponding essences. It all depends on our interpretation of the metaphors, and they can all be interpreted in two ways. The one real essence in two real modes of being is God Himself and God alone. He Himself and alone is both Father and Son, Speaker and Word, light and light, original and copy. From Him the created, sinful creature receives the truth of its relationships by revelation. It must confess Him, not independently or arbitrarily, but by His revelation in faith, if it is to know its own truth. The concept of *homoousia* is not an attempt at independent, arbitrary, so-called natural knowledge of God. It seeks to serve the knowledge of God by His revelation in faith. We have not concealed the historical and material ambiguity of this particular concept. Hence we neither can nor would hide the fact that considered in itself it serves the knowledge of God very badly. For philosophers and philosophical theologians it has always been easy game. But it may be that very little depends on its immanent soundness or unsoundness. It may be that even in its obvious frailty it was the necessary standard which necessarily had to be set up in the 4th century and which even to-day, as often before, has still to be kept aloft against the new Arians, not as the standard of a foolhardy speculative intuition of the Church, but as the standard of an unheard-of encounter which has overtaken the Church in Holy Scripture. If this is so, of what avail is anything that might be said against it ? Do we not have to be aware of all these objections, and yet still acknowledge it as the dogma which the Church, having once recognised, can never let go again ? For in all its folly it is more true than all the wisdom which has voiced its opposition to it. We have no reason to take any other view of it. We are under no illusion as to the fact that we do not know what we are saying when we take this term upon our lips. But still less can we be under any illusion as to the fact that all the lines of our deliberations on the deity of Christ converge at the point where we must assent to the dogma that Jesus Christ is ὁμοούσιος τῷ πατρί, *consubstantialis Patri*.

It is fitting that we should again listen to Luther, who by means of the distinction and unity of original and copy has also made the decisive point that must be made concerning the concept of *homoousia* : " Thus in these words 'tis powerfully taught that Christ is one true God with the Father, equal to Him in all things, without distinction, except that He is from the Father and not the Father from Him, like as radiance is from the brightness of the divine essence and not the brightness of the divine essence from the radiance." " So too when he says that He is the image of His substance he likewise attesteth powerfully that Christ must be true and natural God and yet there are not on that account many gods but one God. 'Tis said it is a counterfeit when a picture is made exactly like that of which it is a picture. But it is a lack in all pictures that they have not nor are the same essence or nature as that of what is depicted, but are of another nature or essence. As when a painter, or carver, or stone-mason depicts a king or prince on a canvas, block, or stone as exact and like as ever he can, so that all eyes must say : Lo, that is this or that king, prince, or man, etc. This is naturally an image or counterfeit. But it is not the essence or nature of the king, prince, or man, etc. It is a poor picture, image, or figure of it, and hath another essence, for its nature or essence is stone, wood, canvas, or paper, and whoso seeth or graspeth it doth not see nor grasp the essence, nature, or substance of the man, and every one saith, 'Tis a wooden or stone or canvas likeness. But it is not the living, essential likeness of the men. . . . But here Christ is the image of the Father, so that He is the likeness of His divine essence, and not made of another nature, but is (if one may so speak) a divine image which is of God and hath divinity in itself or of itself, as a crucifix is called a wooden likeness of Christ, being made of wood. And all men and angels are also made in the image of God. But they are not images of His essence and nature, nor made or arisen out of His divine nature. Christ, however, hath arisen from eternity out of His divine nature and is His essential image, *substantialis imago, non artificialis aut facta vel creata*, which hath His divine nature wholly in itself and also in it, not made nor fashioned of aught else, just as the divine essence is not made nor fashioned of aught else. For if He had not the entire Godhead of the Father in Himself and was not complete God, He could not be nor be called the likeness of His essence, for the Father would still have something wherein the Son was not equal nor like unto Him, so He would in the last resort be quite unlike and in no wise His image according to essence. For the divine essence is the most single of all, indivisible, it must be entirely where it is or not there at all " (Luther, *Die drei Symbola oder Bekenntnis des Glaubens Christi*, 1538, *W.A.*, 50, p. 276, l. 30 and p. 277, l. 19).

6. We believe in Jesus Christ " by whom all things were made."

We have here an almost literal quotation from Jn. 1[3], which says even more explicitly than the symbol itself : πάντα δι' αὐτοῦ ἐγένετο καὶ χωρὶς αὐτοῦ ἐγένετο

442 § 11. God the Son

οὐδὲ ἕν ὃ γέγονεν ; cf. also Jn. 1¹⁰ : ὁ κόσμος δι' αὐτοῦ ἐγένετο, 1 Cor. 8⁶ : δι'οὗ τὰ πάντα, Col. 1¹⁵ᶠ· : He is πρωτότοκος πάσης κτίσεως ὅτι ἐν αὐτῷ ἐκτίσθη τὰ πάντα . . . τὰ πάντα δι' αὐτοῦ καὶ εἰς αὐτὸν ἔκτισται, Heb. 1² : δι' οὗ καὶ ἐποίησεν τοὺς αἰῶνας.

It may be asked whether within the context of the creed this statement is one of the definitions of Christ's deity or whether it is not rather a pronouncement on His work as the Mediator of creation and thus a transition to the succeeding phrases on the incarnation and the work of reconciliation. The syntactical form, however, seems to point in another direction. And even if it were a pronouncement of the latter type, the content at any rate would still have to be understood strictly in terms of trinitarian theology, and, thus understood, it means that the Son of God, too, has a share in the work which is ascribed in the first article of the creed to God the Father, the work of creation. Thus understood, it is an indirect but all the more expressive confirmation of the ὁμοούσιος and therewith of all the preceding phrases. If the Son has a share in what was called the special work of the Father, if He works with the Father in the work of creation, then this means, at least in the sense of Athanasius and the theology which finally triumphed in the 4th century, that He is of one essence with Him. In order that all things might be made by Him, in order that He might be the Mediator of creation, He Himself had to be God by nature.

Rejection of the Arian view of Jn. 1³ and par. is not expressly voiced in the symbol. According to Arius the Son is itself the creaturely instrument of the divine Creator. This is completely ruled out by the ὁμοούσιος and γεννηθεὶς οὐ ποιηθείς. Thus the present clause interprets the ὁμοούσιος only to the degree that its own interpretation is governed by the context of the symbol.

Here again we have to remember the principle : *opera trinitatis ad extra sunt indivisa.* It implies at this point that an appropriation is involved when, as in the continuation in the creed, revelation and reconciliation are ascribed to the Son. This appropriation is right and necessary since it is grounded in revelation itself. But revelation cannot be understood correctly if we do not add that as this appropriation cannot exclude the Father from being also the subject of this event (to the degree that the Father is also present and at work with the Son in revelation and reconciliation), so it cannot exclude the Son being also the subject of the event to which the first article refers, that is, the subject of creation. We are following John 1 and Luther's expositions of Genesis 1 and John 1 (which we quoted earlier) when we offer the interpretation that Jesus Christ is the Word by which God created the world out of nothing. As this Word of the Father He is, in distinction from everything created by Him, equal to the Father, very God from all eternity.

Where has God created the world ? asks Augustine. In heaven ? On earth ?
In the air ? In the water ? In the universe ? But these are all themselves
created. Has He created them out of a being He first took in hand for the
purpose ? But *unde tibi hoc quod tu non feceras, unde aliquid faceres ? Quid
enim est, nisi quia tu es ? Ergo dixisti et facta sunt atque in verbo tuo fecisti ea
(Conf.,* XI, 5, 7). *Eo sempiterne dicuntur omnia (ib.,* XI, 7, 9). Thus : *Fecit
omnia per verbum suum et verbum eius ipse Christus, in quo requiescunt angeli et
omnes caelestes mundissimi spiritus in sancto silentio (De cat. rud.,* 17, 28). *Constat
. . . summam substantiam prius in se quasi dixisse cunctam creaturam quam eam
secundum eandem et per eandem suam intimam locutionem conderet* (Anselm of
Canterbury, *Monol.,* 11). *Cum ipse summus spiritus dicit se ipsum, dicit omnia,
quae facta sunt. . . . Semper in ipso sunt, non quod sunt in se ipsis sed quod est
idem ipse (ib.,* 34). In the same sense Thomas Aquinas gave an affirmative
answer to the question : *Utrum in nomine verbi importetur respectus ad creaturam ?
Deus enim cognoscendo se, cognoscit omnem creaturam. Uno actu* God knows
Himself and all that is outside Him, and so His Word is not just the precise image
of the Father but also the original of the world (*S. theol.,* I, *qu.* 34, *art.* 3). Similarly
Luther : *Filius enim in se habet exemplar non solum maiestatis divinae, sed etiam
exemplar omnium rerum creatarum (Comm. on Gen.* 1²⁰ᶠ·, 1535 f., *W.A.,* 42, p. 37,
l. 30). Even the bodily warmth with which a hen hatches her eggs is according
to Luther *ex verbo divino, quia, si absque verbo esset, calor ille esset inutilis et
inefficax (on Gen.* 1²², *ib.,* p. 40, l. 9). In contrast it is rather laboured and lacking
in humour when K. Bretschneider (*Handb. d. Dogm.,* Vol. I, 4th edn., 1838,
p. 659) assures us that we " must regard the whole idea of the creation of the
world by the Son as one which does not belong to religion but to Johannine and
Pauline theology," or when A. Ritschl, following in the footsteps of earlier
rationalism here, thinks he should comment on the relevant New Testament
passages as follows : " This combination takes us beyond the sphere of theology
proper and has no direct and practical significance for religious belief in Jesus
Christ " (*Unterricht in d. chr. Rel.,* 1875, § 24). In relation to the biblical references
and their exposition in the early Church we certainly can and should utter a
warning against the inference, which is not ruled out to full satisfaction in
Augustine or even Anselm, that the creation of the world was as essential to
God as the begetting of the Son, that it was not the result of a *nova voluntas*
(as Augustine says, *Conf.,* XII, 15, 18), that the existence of the world was
necessarily included in God's Word (as it might perhaps seem to be according
to the statement adduced from Anselm), that the world is thus an essential
predicate of God. Nevertheless, one cannot possibly suspect the thought itself
of being an unnecessary theologoumenon.

The idea does not have merely the abstractly trinitarian significance
of making it clear that the work and therefore the essence of the Father
and the Son are one and the same. In so doing, it also illumines and
explains once again who and what Jesus Christ is in His revelation :
not a stranger whom we might encounter as a stranger, interpreting
and choosing according to our own thought and evaluation ; not even
a semi-stranger whom we should judge according to a knowledge of
the God that sent Him which we have derived from some other source.
But " he came to his own possession " (Jn. 1¹¹), to the world, to us
whom He Himself created, who are from the very first His own, and
He theirs. The Word which we hear in revelation, the Word by which

we are summoned to the unmerited and from our standpoint impossible fellowship of God with sinners—this Word is none other than the Word by which we who should hear it are called into being along with all the reality that is distinct from God, without which we would not be either sinners or righteous, without which we would not be at all. The One who in revelation calls us out of our enmity against Him to Himself, who calls us out of death into life, is the One who in so doing also makes Himself known as the One who previously called us out of nothing into existence, into existence as *pardoned sinners*, yet into *existence* as pardoned sinners. We cannot hear the Word of justification and sanctification without being reminded that it is through this Word, in no other way and from no other source, that we who are justified and sanctified by this Word even exist. This Word is the ground of our being beyond our being ; whether we hear it or not, whether we obey it or not, it is in virtue of its superior existence that our existence is a reality. This Word came to us before we came or not, and as we come or not. Our coming or not coming is possible only because this Word is real. The same Jesus Christ through whom God unites us to Himself even while we are His enemies has already united us to Himself as those who belong to Him because He alone holds us over the abyss. And it is by this first union with Him, manifested to us in and by the second, by revelation, that the significance of the second for us is measured. To be sinners, as we are shown to be in the revelation of Jesus Christ, means that we have separated ourselves from the One without whom we would not be even in this separation and yet, separated from whom, we cannot be in any true or proper sense. To be sinners means that we have come to a place where our existence is absolutely inconceivable because at this place it can be only a plunge into nothing, where our existence can be understood only as an event of inconceivable kindness, or it cannot be understood at all. And to attain to grace, as we are again shown to have done in the revelation of Jesus Christ, means that notwithstanding our separation He without whom we would not be, and yet from whom we have separated ourselves, not only does not let us fall into the nothing from which He called us, but also, addressing and claiming us as sinners, He grants to us over and above existence no less a gift than Himself, fellowship and intercourse with Himself. What does this mean ? It means that in His revelation Jesus Christ the Word of God does not need to get from some other source the authority to address and claim us ; He already has it antecedently in Himself. It is not a question of whether we want to respond to Him or not. We are already responsible to Him and in different ways our whole being is response to Him. In relation to Him there is no possibility of appealing or withdrawing to some domain of our own where we were once alone and where He does not yet reach us or does so no longer, to a neutral human existence, as it were, where it is first up to us to place ourselves or not under the judgment and the grace that He declares to us, and from which we might comfortably come to an understanding with Him. In fact we do not know anything about our human existence except through the Word which declares to us judgment and grace. In declaring this, it tells us that it is itself the ground of our being as men ; on this ground alone are we men, and not otherwise. It comes to us because it already applies to us even before it comes. It is the hand that already holds us even as it grasps us. It is the ruling act of the king who was already a king before and who has both the might and the right to perform this act. It encompasses us on every side (Ps. 139⁵). It is the Word which has power, the Word of the Lord. And it is the Word of the Lord because it is the Word of the Reconciler who is also the Creator.

In our investigation of the New Testament doctrine of the deity of Christ we ended with the tautology that for the men of the New Testament Jesus Christ is the Lord because He is the Lord. Though we cannot avoid this tautology we can now put it this way : He is for them God the Reconciler as He is God the Creator. His judgment and grace concern them as He concerns their existence. We should, of course, immediately reverse this and say also that He concerns their existence as He comes to them with His judgment and His grace. The point cannot be that in their existence, in their creaturely humanity, they had a previously given criterion by applying which they then accepted His judgment and His grace and thus believed in Him as the Lord and the Son of God. On the contrary, His judgment and His grace bar every exit or escape to a humanity which is already given and assured as such. They take away every private criterion and spoil every private judgment. These men have found themselves, their being, and also the possibility of their own judgment only at the place where His wrath and His kindness have reached them. But there they have in fact found themselves and their being and therewith the possibility of their own judgment. They are as men who are judged by Him, And as men who are judged by Him they now judge ; they judge concerning Him. They thus judge concerning Him : He is the Son of God. In saying this they are saying that He is our Reconciler as He is our Creator. They might just as well abandon the judgment " We are " as the judgment that " He is God's Son." For them the two are inseparable, for their knowledge of themselves, their existence, their creatureliness and their Creator is not from another source than knowledge of their reconciliation. For them there can be no question of any gap between a known Creator God and Jesus Christ as a Redeemer and Saviour who perhaps stands in some relation to God. As they know their reconciliation through Jesus Christ, they know themselves, their existence, their creatureliness, the Creator. There is thus taken away from under their feet the ground on which they would have to stand to ask, to seek, and to discover whether Jesus Christ is the Lord and the Son of God. So they can only begin with this knowledge and this confession. One would have to abstract again between the Creator and the Reconciler ; one would have to make two words again out of what is for the men of the New Testament one word, to be able to find Ebionite or Docetic Christology in the New Testament.

In this sense, then, the statement illumines and explains who and what Jesus Christ is in His revelation. It says of Him that in His revelation He has the immediate power of the Creator over men. But in acknowledging this we shall not limit His power as Creator to His revelation.

Already in the 2nd century writers like to compare with the δι' οὗ τὰ πάντα the insight that the Church is the first creature of God made before the sun and moon καὶ διὰ ταύτην ὁ κόσμος κατηρτίσθη (Hermae Pastor, *Vis.* II, 4, 1 ; Clem. *Hom.*, 14, 1). And in the 20th century R. Seeberg has interpreted this biblical concept as follows : " If God created the world with the resolve that the Church should come into being in it, then the will of God—and this is Christ—was already at work in the creation and formation of the world. . . ." In so far as the natural world was to be " the theatre of a spiritual historical world, the divine will that there be a history which leads to the Church . . . was already at work in such a way at the creative fashioning of the world that the natural possibility was provided for the existence and continuity of a spiritual world " (*Chr. Dogmatik*, Vol. I, 1924, p. 463 f.). Even if we ignore the fact that the Church is hardly the same thing as a " spiritual historical world," we must still comment as follows. Certainly Jesus Christ as the One by whom all things were made is also the κεφαλὴ τοῦ σώματος, τῆς ἐκκλησίας (Col. 1[18]). As the former He can be and is the latter. But it is not as the latter that He is the former. It is not as the Head of the Church, not first and only in revelation, that He is the One by whom God made all things. Certainly He is so powerful in His revelation because He is already the Creator. But He is not first the Creator in the fact that He is so powerful in His revelation, nor is He the Creator only on this ground. If we permit reversals here, if we are not content to find the Creator again in the revelation, if we at once take the further step of deducing creation as such from revelation and basing it on this, this is just as much an illegitimate speculation as the attempt, which we criticised earlier, to understand revelation as *creatio continuata*. To attribute the Church or revelation directly to creation or the creative will of God as such is to forget or ignore the fact that the Church or revelation can be an event only as an answer to the sin of man, or it is to be forced to try to integrate the sin of man into creation. It is also to forget the free loving-kindness of God which gives this answer, or to make it a necessary member in a dialectical process. Then this speculative synthesis of God's works—in a way which is no less unavoidable in Seeberg than Schleiermacher—finds appropriate expression in the abrogation of the distinction of the divine persons, in a modalistic doctrine of the Trinity. Only thus can one say that the world was created for the sake of the Church or revelation, and that this purpose is the meaning of the participation of the Son of God in creation. These conclusions are the necessary price of such syntheses. If we do not want to pay the price— and we have good reason not to want to pay it—then we must refrain from the syntheses.

The truth of the recognition that Christ in His revelation has the power of the Creator depends on its being the acknowledgment of a fact and not an arbitrary combination. When the power is experienced there is nothing to combine. Creation and revelation are not truths which are to be held alongside one another and compared to one another and set in relation to one another. They are the one reality of Jesus Christ as the Revealer with the power of the Creator. And this power of the Creator cannot be regarded as one that is specifically related or restricted to revelation alone.

Augustine is thus right when he has it that the angels, too, were created by the Word, and so is Luther when he says that the broody hen was created by the Word.

Creation, then, means deity in its originality above and beyond all creatureliness. To come back to the theology of the Trinity, this is what the creed is saying with its δι' οὖ τὰ πάντα. By the δι' οὖ it completely distinguishes the Son from the Father. By the τὰ πάντα it completely unites Him here too to the Father. It is thus the first and last word of the dogma. It is the first and last word on who and what Jesus Christ is " antecedently in Himself." It is also the first and last word in the account of the reality of revelation as this may be seen quite plainly in the mirror of the witness of Holy Scripture.

GOD THE HOLY SPIRIT

The one God reveals Himself according to Scripture as the Redeemer, i.e., as the Lord who sets us free. As such He is the Holy Spirit, by receiving whom we become the children of God, because, as the Spirit of the love of God the Father and the Son, He is so antecedently in Himself.

1. GOD AS REDEEMER

We begin a third time with the New Testament witness : Jesus is Lord. But this time we add the query : How do men come to say this ? We are presupposing that they believe and therefore speak. They are to be taken seriously in what they say. They are to be nailed to it. In other words, they do not say it as the result of arbitrary reflection but in acknowledgment of a fact. They do not say it out of a desire to give the man an office or to give the office a man, but because the man has an office and discharges it. They say it as the beginning and not the end of their thinking about Him. They say it because He is the Lord. They do not say, then, that He is a demi-god from above or from below—the incarnation of a divine idea or a superman. They say that He is God. But on this presupposition we are inevitably confronted by the question : How do they come to say this ? How do they reach this beginning of their thinking about Him ? How does it happen that they believe the Father through the Son and the Son through the Father ? How do these contents get into this vessel ? How does this predicate, this faith, come to this subject, the subject man ? How can anyone have this faith ? Can men believe ?—if faith means meeting the Lord who is God, meeting Him as the New Testament witnesses met Jesus, in hard objectivity, in the world which is the world of men, in which everything is problematical, in which everything must first be tested, in which nothing, when tested, will yield the result that it is identical with God, and yet also meeting Him in such a way that nothing is problematical, that nothing is to be found by the way of testing, but the encounter with Him is as such encounter with God. This is what revelation means in the New Testament. But in the New Testament does not the man to whom it happens also belong to revelation ? And how can a thing like this happen to a man ?

1. God as Redeemer

Might it not be said that at this point the whole concept of revelation is problematical if the presupposition is that faith in revelation consists in that absolutely unproblematical knowledge of God in Christ? It is not as if a new question requiring a new answer did not arise at this point for the New Testament.

In the New Testament too and especially the possibility of faith is not automatically given with the fact that Jesus is present as the revelation of the Father or as the One He is, as the Son or Word of God. In relation to Him man, too, is always, and for the first time properly, the one he is. How does he come to see and hear at this point? When the First Epistle of John begins with the declaration : We attest and proclaim to you ὃ ἀκηκόαμεν, ὃ ἑωράκαμεν τοῖς ὀφθαλμοῖς ἡμῶν, ὃ ἐθεασάμεθα καὶ αἱ χεῖρες ἡμῶν ἐψηλάφησαν (1 Jn. 1¹ᶠ·), this is the indication of a reality whose possibility is by no means self-evident in the New Testament. Οὐχ ὅτι ἀφ᾽ ἑαυτῶν ἱκανοί ἐσμεν λογίσασθαί τι ὡς ἐξ ἑαυτῶν (2 Cor. 3⁵). " He that hath ears to hear, let him hear," says the Synoptic Jesus with reference to His preaching (Mk. 4⁹). " Flesh and blood hath not revealed it unto thee," is His reply to Peter's confession (Mt. 16¹⁷). In face of the incarnate Word at the heart of revelation there seems to be a kind of delaying or questioning or limiting of revelation. Will revelation, this revelation, real revelation, reach its goal after all? Will it get at man? Will it become manifest to him? This does not seem to lie only with the good or bad will of man. For if this manifesting takes place, if there are ears to hear, this means : " Unto you it is given to know the mystery of the kingdom of God. Ἐκείνοις δὲ τοῖς ἔξω ἐν παραβολαῖς τὰ πάντα γίνεται. Seeing they shall see, and not perceive ; hearing they shall hear, and not understand, so that they shall not be converted, and it cannot be forgiven them " (Mk. 4¹¹⁻¹²). When the givenness is not present, it must be in virtue of a supreme material necessity.

Becoming manifest has to be something specific, a special act of the Father or the Son or both, that is added to the givenness of the revelation of the Father in the Son.

The Father must reveal it to man (Mt. 16¹⁷). The Father must draw him (Jn. 6⁴⁴). The Father must give it to him (Jn. 6⁶⁵). Man must be given to the Son by the Father (Jn. 10²⁹). He must hear and learn from the Father (Jn. 6⁴⁵). But it can also be said that the incarnate Word of God Himself gives to those who receive Him the ἐξουσία to be the children of God and as such to believe in His name, so that as such they are what they are, not in virtue of their first and natural generation and birth, but in virtue of their second and divine generation and birth (Jn. 1¹²⁻¹³ ; 3³). There can also be reference to a stream of living water, clear as crystal, flowing forth from the throne of God and the Lamb (Rev. 22¹). This is the added element of becoming manifest in revelation. The riches of grace are not just present for us in Jesus Christ but : ἐπερίσσευσεν εἰς ἡμᾶς ἐν πάσῃ σοφίᾳ καὶ φρονήσει γνωρίσας ἡμῖν τὸ μυστήριον τοῦ θελήματος αὐτοῦ (Eph. 1⁸· ⁹).

This special element in revelation is undoubtedly identical with what the New Testament usually calls the Holy Spirit as the subjective side in the event of revelation.

Jn. 20²² says of the disciples that Jesus breathed on them, saying : λάβετε πνεῦμα ἅγιον, and by this λαμβάνειν, in full material agreement with Ac. 2, they become what they are, His apostles, His envoys. The πνεῦμα is what makes alive (Jn. 6⁶³ ; 2 Cor. 3⁶). " No man can say that Jesus is the Lord, but by the holy πνεῦμα " (1 Cor. 12³). Because we have received the πνεῦμα that is of God, we know for what they are the things that are freely given to us by God (1 Cor. 2¹³). Sealed with the holy πνεῦμα of promise you heard the word of truth, the gospel of your salvation, and you came to believe (Eph. 1¹³). God must give us the πνεῦμα of wisdom and revelation to know Himself (Eph. 1¹⁷). Except a man be born of water and the πνεῦμα he cannot enter into the kingdom of God (Jn. 3⁶). Εἰ δέ τις πνεῦμα Χριστοῦ οὐκ ἔχει, οὗτος οὐκ ἔστιν αὐτοῦ (Rom. 8⁹). Therefore Ac. 19²ᶠ· tells us that the most striking mark of those who have been baptised only in the name of John but not in the name of Jesus is that they know nothing of the Holy πνεῦμα.

Πνεῦμα θεοῦ or Χριστοῦ is a figure of speech, like υἱὸς θεοῦ. According to Jn. 3⁸ ; Ac. 2² πνεῦμα means wind, which comes from one place and moves mysteriously to another. More precisely it is in 2 Thess. 2⁸ ; Jn. 20²² breath, which comes out of the mouth of a living creature and can reach another living creature, invisibly, without removing the spatial distance between them. This little and removable paradox becomes in the New Testament and already in the Old Testament a metaphor for the great and irremovable paradox of divine revelation. The fact that God gives His πνεῦμα to man or that man receives this πνεῦμα implies that God comes to man, that He discloses Himself to man and man to Himself, that He gives Himself to be experienced by man, that He awakens man to faith, that He enlightens him and equips him to be a prophet or apostle, that He creates for Himself a community of faith and proclamation to which He imparts salvation with His promise, in which He binds men to Himself and claims them for Himself, in short, in which He becomes theirs and makes them His. As this incomparable thing the πνεῦμα is τὸ πνεῦμα τὸ ἅγιον. It is holy because only thus is it God's πνεῦμα, and because its purpose is the sanctification, i.e., the setting apart, the seizing, appropriating and distinguishing of the men who receive it, the distinguishing by which they become that which in and of themselves they neither are nor can be, men who belong to God, who are in real fellowship with Him, who live before God and with God. One may regard Gen. 2⁷ as the model for all the biblical use of references to the divine πνεῦμα. Here we are told that God breathed into man's face the breath of life and that in this way man became for the first time a living soul : *et inspiravit in faciem eius spiraculum vitae et factus est homo anima vivens* (Vulg.).

In both the Old Testament and the New the Spirit of God, the Holy Spirit, is very generally God Himself to the degree that in an incomprehensibly real way, without on this account being any the less God, He can be present to the creature, and in virtue of this presence of His effect the relation of the creature to Himself, and in virtue of this relation to Himself grant the creature life. The creature needs the Creator to be able to live. It thus needs the relation to Him. But it cannot create this relation. God creates it by His own presence in the creature and therefore as a relation of Himself to Himself. The Spirit of God is God in His freedom to be present to the creature, and therefore to create this relation, and therefore to be the life of the creature. And God's Spirit, the Holy Spirit, especially in revelation, is God Himself to the extent that He can not only come to man but also be in man, and thus open up man and make him capable and ready for Himself, and thus achieve His revelation in him. Man needs revelation, for he is certainly lost without it. He thus needs to have revelation become manifest to him, i.e., he himself needs to become open to revelation. But this is not a possibility of his own. It can only be God's own reality when it does happen, and therefore it can lie only in God's own possibility that it can happen. It is God's reality in that God Himself becomes present to man not just externally, not just from above, but also from within, from below, subjectively. It is thus reality in that He does not merely come to man but encounters Himself from man. God's freedom to be present in this way to man, and therefore to bring about this encounter, is the Spirit of God, the Holy Spirit in God's revelation.

The work of the Holy Ghost is *nos aptare Deo* (Irenaeus, *C.o.h.*, III, 17, 2). He is the *doctor veritatis* (Tertullian, *De praescr.*, 28). He is the *digitus Dei, per quem sanctificemur* (Augustine, *De spir. et lit.*, 16, 28). *Intelligo spiritum Dei, dum in cordibus nostris habitat, efficere, ut Christi virtutem sentiamus. Nam ut Christi beneficia mente concipiamus, hoc fit Spiritus sancti illuminatione: eius persuasione fit, ut cordibus nostris obsignentur. Denique, solus ipse dat illis in nobis locum. Regenerat nos, facitque ut simus novae creaturae. Proinde, quaecunque nobis offeruntur in Christo dona, ea Spiritus virtute recipimus* (Calvin, *Catech. Genev.*, 1545, in K. Müller, p. 125, l. 16). He is the *applicator, illuminator, sanctificator* (*Syn. pur. Theol.*, Leiden, 1624, *Disp.* 9, 21).

The Holy Spirit is not identical with Jesus Christ, with the Son or Word of God.

Even in the saying in 2 Cor. 3¹⁷ : ὁ δὲ κύριος τὸ πνεῦμα, we do not have an identification of Jesus Christ with the Spirit but rather a statement that to the Spirit belongs the κυριότης, the deity of the Lord, to whom there is reference in v. 16. The continuation is that where this Spirit is, who is the Lord, who is God, there is liberty, namely, liberty from the veiling of the heart which had continually made the reading of Moses unprofitable in the worship of the Jews, liberty to see and to hear. Then according to v. 18 there is reflected in us—our face is uncovered—the glory of the Lord, and so we are changed into His image, from His glory to a glory of our own, namely, ἀπὸ κυρίου, πνεύματος, through the Lord who is the Spirit. We are forbidden not merely by usage elsewhere but also by the meaning and context of the passage itself to identify the Spirit with Jesus Christ even here. Other passages in which the Spirit is clearly mentioned (1 Cor. 12⁴ᶠ· ; 2 Cor. 13¹³ ; 1 Pet. 1² , etc.) along with the Father and Christ, or (1 Cor. 6¹¹) with Christ alone, need only be recalled at this point.

In the context of the New Testament witness the non-identity between Christ and the Holy Spirit seems to be as necessarily grounded as possible. Thus we find the Holy Spirit only after the death and resurrection of Jesus Christ or in the form of knowledge of the crucified and risen Lord, i.e., on the assumption that objective revelation has been concluded and completed. We have seen already that Christ is the revelation of the Father in His passage through death to life. Those who believe in Him and confess Him believe in Him and confess Him as the exalted Lord. Thus the Spirit in whom they believe and confess and He who is the object of this faith and confession stand as it were on two different levels. What comes over or down to us from above, from the exalted Lord, is, therefore, the Spirit.

This " descent " of the Holy Ghost is a concept found especially in Acts (cf. Ac. 2^2; 10^{44}; 11^{15}). Thus the " Receive ye the Holy Ghost " in Jn. 20^{22} can only be a saying of the risen Christ. For the same reason the outpouring of the Holy Spirit is depicted in Ac. 2 as a work which is added to the completed *kerygma* of the life, death and resurrection of Jesus by Him of whom this *kerygma* speaks. For the same reason again John's Gospel has the distinctive doctrine, but one which is important for an understanding of the New Testament as a whole, that Jesus is, in distinction from John the Baptist, ὁ βαπτίζων ἐν πνεύματι ἁγίῳ (Jn. 1^{33}). Streams of living water are to flow from the body of him that believes in Him, says the difficult passage Jn. $7^{38f.}$, with the addition that Jesus was referring to the Spirit whom those that believe in Him should receive, and with the important explanation : οὔπω γὰρ ἦν πνεῦμα, ὅτι Ἰησοῦς οὐδέπω ἐδοξάσθη. In Jn. 14^{16} the Spirit then appears as the (again future) gift of the Father to the disciples, the gift for which Jesus will ask the Father on their behalf. The Father will send Him in Jesus' name (Jn. 14^{26}). On the other hand in Jn. 15^{26} Jesus Himself will send from the Father Him that proceedeth from the Father (ὁ παρὰ τοῦ πατρὸς ἐκπορεύεται). But to this end Jesus according to Jn. 16^7 must first leave the disciples : συμφέρει ὑμῖν ἵνα ἐγὼ ἀπέλθω. ἐὰν γὰρ μὴ ἀπέλθω, ὁ παράκλητος οὐ μὴ ἔλθῃ πρὸς ὑμᾶς. ἐὰν δὲ πορευθῶ, πέμψω αὐτὸν πρὸς ὑμᾶς. Finally Jn. 16^{13} is just speaking of His coming in a general way. What we find in Jn. 20^{22} is obviously the fulfilment of this repeated promise.

In spite of all this, it can hardly be the idea of the New Testament that chronologically it was only after Good Friday and Easter that there were men who received the Holy Ghost. If so, what could it mean that faith is in all seriousness ascribed to many disciples and non-disciples even before Good Friday and Easter ? What would Jesus' reply to Peter's confession mean (Mt. 16^{17}) ? The story of the transfiguration in Mk. $9^{2f.}$ and par. shows that the Synoptists at least reckoned with the possibility that chronologically there might be anticipation of the conclusion and completion of revelation, that there might be revelations of the exalted Christ, even before His appearing. And one might well ask whether the miracles of Jesus are not all to be regarded as, so to speak, backward-striking rays of the glory of the risen Lord, whether ultimately the entire life of Jesus is not meant to be considered in this retrospective light. Even in John, where the chronological schematism seems to be more consciously and strictly applied, the temporal relationship between Him who lived as a man among the disciples and the exalted Christ, and hence also between the promised Spirit and the given Spirit, is undoubtedly more complicated than might appear at a first glance. How are we to understand Jn. 2^{11} if the future is not also thought of as already present here even as the future ? Similarly Jn. 20^{22} and the story of Pentecost in Ac. 2 are surely to be understood as explicit and solemn testimony to an event which chronologically was not restricted either forwards or backwards to Pentecost.

We must now add at once that while the Spirit is the element of revelation which is different from Christ as the exalted Lord, while He is revelation to the extent that it becomes an event on us and in us, nevertheless He is still to be regarded wholly and entirely as the Spirit of Christ, of the Son, of the Word of God. He is not to be regarded, then, as a revelation of independent content, as a new instruction, illumination and stimulation of man that goes beyond Christ, beyond the Word, but in every sense as the instruction, illumination and stimulation of man through the Word and for the Word.

It is true that the Holy Spirit is expressly called the Spirit of Christ only in relatively few passages (Gal. 4⁶ ; Rom. 8⁹ ; Phil. 1¹⁹ ; 1 Pet. 1¹¹). Usually He is simply the Spirit of God, which in a whole set of passages must be taken to mean the Spirit of the Father. But no incongruence can be shown between Christ and the Spirit. John's Gospel again reproduces the meaning of the New Testament as a whole when it has Jesus say of the Spirit : ἐκεῖνος μαρτυρήσει περὶ ἐμοῦ (Jn. 15²⁶), οὐ γὰρ λαλήσει ἀφ' ἑαυτοῦ ἀλλ' ὅσα ἀκούει λαλήσει καὶ τὰ ἐρχόμενα ἀναγγελεῖ ὑμῖν. ἐκεῖνος ἐμὲ δοξάσει, ὅτι ἐκ τοῦ ἐμοῦ λήμψεται καὶ ἀναγγελεῖ ὑμῖν (Jn. 16¹³ᶠ·).

The statements about the significance and work of the Holy Spirit in the event which is called revelation in the New Testament can be arranged in three groups.

1. The Spirit guarantees man what he cannot guarantee himself, his personal participation in revelation. The act of the Holy Ghost in revelation is the Yes to God's Word which is spoken by God Himself for us, yet not just to us, but also in us. This Yes spoken by God is the basis of the confidence with which a man may regard the revelation as applying to him. This Yes is the mystery of faith, the mystery of the knowledge of the Word of God, but also the mystery of the willing obedience that is well-pleasing to God. All these things, faith, knowledge and obedience, exist for man " in the Holy Spirit."

Ἐν τούτῳ γινώσκομεν ὅτι ἐν αὐτῷ μένομεν καὶ αὐτὸς ἐν ἡμῖν, ὅτι ἐκ τοῦ πνεύματος αὐτοῦ δέδωκεν ἡμῖν (1 Jn. 4¹³). The specific Pauline view of the Holy Spirit demands special attention here. The Spirit dwells in us (Rom. 8⁹· ¹¹). He is thus the ἀπαρχή (Rom. 8²³) or ἀρραβών (2 Cor. 1²²; 5⁵; Eph. 1¹⁴). He is also the projected light of the salvation assigned to us by God. To participate in the Holy Ghost is to have " tasted the good word of God and the powers of the world to come " (Heb. 6⁵ᶠ·). With Christ or the Word the Holy Spirit bears witness to our spirit that we are the children of God : αὐτὸ τὸ πνεῦμα συμμαρτυρεῖ τῷ πνεύματι ἡμῶν (Rom. 8¹⁶). God reveals to us διὰ τοῦ πνεύματος what He wills to reveal to us because the Spirit searches all things, even τὰ βάθη τοῦ θεοῦ, and because He, the Spirit, does this for us and in us (1 Cor. 2¹⁰). He helps our infirmities (συναντιλαμβάνεται) ; we do not know what proper prayer is, but He intercedes for us (ὑπερεντυγχάνει) with His groanings that cannot be uttered (ἀλαλήτοις) by us, and so, since quite apart from our weakness or strength, our ability or inability to pray, there takes place in us something that is according to God (κατὰ θεόν), God hears and answers our prayer (Rom. 8²⁶ᶠ·). Through the Holy Spirit the love of God (or love for God) is shed abroad in our hearts (Rom. 5⁵). In short, because and so far as a man receives the Holy Ghost, he is a temple of God (1 Cor. 3¹⁶ ; 6¹⁹ ; 2 Cor. 6¹⁶) ; because and so far as he has received the Holy Ghost, he may be told to his face that the Word is " nigh thee, even in thy mouth and in thy heart " (Rom. 10⁸). The very common Pauline formula ἐν πνεύματι describes man's thinking, acting and speaking as taking place in participation in God's revelation. It is an exact subjective correlate of ἐν Χριστῷ, which denotes the same thing objectively.

2. The Spirit gives man instruction and guidance he cannot give himself. A point that we should remember in what has been said already is made quite explicit here : the Spirit is not identical, and does not become identical, with ourselves.

When Paul uses the term πνεῦμα in his anthropology he is not saying that the Holy Spirit either wholly or partially, either originally or subsequently, is part of man's own essence. When used thus πνεῦμα denotes at best the place (beyond σῶμα and ψυχή) where reception of the Holy Spirit can become a reality (1 Thess. 5²³).

He is absolutely other, superior. We can only note what His Yes is to the Word of God. We can only repeat this Yes of His. As our Teacher and Leader He is in us, but not as a power of which we might become lords. He remains Himself the Lord.

In the main the Johannine doctrine of the Paraclete is especially relevant here. The term reminds us of Paul's important concept of *paraclesis*. This word, for which there is no real equivalent, denotes the combination of the admonition and comfort which God causes His people to experience and which the apostle has, as it were, to accept and pass on (cf., e.g., 2 Cor. 1³ᶠ·). This is what Jesus portrays as the special work of the Holy Ghost according to John's Gospel. As the Paraclete the Spirit is the " spirit of truth " (Jn. 14¹⁷ ; 15²⁶ ; 16¹³). Ἐκεῖνος ὑμᾶς διδάξει πάντα καὶ ὑπομνήσει ὑμᾶς πάντα ἃ εἶπον ὑμῖν ἐγώ (Jn. 14²⁶). Ὁδηγήσει ὑμᾶς εἰς τὴν ἀλήθειαν πᾶσαν (Jn. 16¹³). Also identical with the Paraclete and therefore with the Holy Ghost is what is called the *chrisma* in 1 Jn. (and also 2 Cor. 1²¹). 1 Jn. 2²⁰ says of this : Ἔχετε ἀπὸ τοῦ ἁγίου καὶ οἴδατε πάντες. " Ye need not that any man should teach you : but as the same anointing teacheth you of all things, and is in truth, and is no lie " (2²⁷). Also pertinent here is the fact that Paul ascribes to the Spirit an ἄγειν and to believers an ἄγεσθαι by the Spirit (Gal. 5¹⁸ ; Rom. 8¹⁴), and we should compare here the very direct instructions in which this ἄγειν can take concrete shape, especially according to Acts, e.g., Ac. 8²⁹ ; 10¹⁹ ; 13² ; 16⁶, etc.

Along these lines the Spirit is obviously not so much the reality in which God makes us sure of Him as the reality in which He makes Himself sure of us, in which He establishes and executes His claim to lordship over us by His immediate presence.

3. Exegetically most obscure but materially of crucial importance is the fact that the Spirit is the great and only possibility in virtue of which men can speak of Christ in such a way that what they say is witness and that God's revelation in Christ thus achieves new actuality through it. Has God's personal coming to us, in the twofold sense in which we have viewed it, any independent signification as a work of the Holy Spirit alongside the fact that by the Holy Spirit man can and should become a real speaker and proclaimer of real witness and therefore of the real Word of God ? Does not the New Testament doctrine of the Holy Ghost point beyond all that the Spirit can mean for the believer in this personal relation with God to that which, in the power of the Spirit, ought to happen in the believer and through the

believer for God, i.e., in the service of God ? Is not the relation
between the Spirit and the Church, or the relation between the Spirit
and the will of the Lord of the Church which is to be executed, the
dominating factor which governs all the rest ?

A Whitsun sermon cannot be an exposition of Ac. 2$^{1-14}$ if it does not see and
show that the outpouring of the Holy Spirit to which this passage refers consists
very concretely in the fact that cloven tongues are seen and that the disciples
on whom these alight begin to speak in other tongues : καθὼς τὸ πνεῦμα ἐδίδου
ἀποφθέγγεσθαι αὐτοῖς. (Repetitions of this event are reported in Ac. 10^{46} and 19^{6}.)
The second effect of this Whitsun miracle then consists in the fact that γενομένης
τῆς φωνῆς ταύτης the members present from every possible nation both near and
far hear the disciples declare τὰ μεγαλεῖα τοῦ θεοῦ in their own tongues (Ac. 2$^{7f.}$).
A Whitsun sermon which aims to be an exposition of Ac. 2$^{1f.}$ will have to talk
about this speaking of the disciples and this hearing by Parthians, Medes and
Elamites, etc. The impact of the address of Peter which follows in Ac. 2$^{14f.}$, in so
far as this is not a presentation of the *kerygma* itself, also consists purely and
simply in the fact that what has happened is declared to be a fulfilment of the
prophecy of Joel about the outpouring of the Spirit on all flesh, which will mean
that men—both men and women is the surprisingly strong emphasis—will
" prophesy." This is what is fulfilled at Pentecost. Over against the Lord Jesus,
absolutely subordinate to Him but distinct from Him, there is another element
in the reality of His revelation, an apostolate, men commissioned, authorised and
empowered by Him to witness, men whose human word can be accepted by
all kinds of people as proclamation of the " wonderful works of God." This
is the doing of the Holy Ghost. The difficult exegetical question here is how
this gift of " tongues " at Pentecost is related to the special gift of individual
members of the Christian community to which Paul gives the same name in
1 Cor. 12 and 14, and which he takes very seriously and values highly, but in
respect of which he has many reservations and even criticisms. We do not
have to pursue this question in the present content. But there is no doubt
that what Paul knew by this name did not have either for himself or, on his view,
for the community, the same central significance as that which is recorded in
Ac. 2. There is also no doubt that what gives the thing recorded there its central
significance, the commissioning, authorising and equipping of the apostolate,
is for him too—and for him too as the work of the Holy Ghost—the presupposition
of his own activity and message. Πρὸς φωτισμὸν τῆς γνώσεως τῆς δόξης τοῦ θεοῦ ἐν
προσώπῳ Χριστοῦ God caused it to shine in our hearts as at the first day of
creation (2 Cor. 4^{6}). " Ye shall receive the power of the Holy Ghost coming
upon you, and ye shall be my witnesses," says the risen Lord to His disciples
(Ac. 1^{8}). We find the same combination of πνεῦμα and μαρτυρεῖν in Jn. 15^{26} :
The Holy Spirit shall testify of Me to you, and you also shall bear witness.
Another saying of Jesus is to the effect that in the hour of trial the disciples are
not to be anxious about what they shall say on their own behalf ; they are to
say what is then given them to say. Οὐ γάρ ἐστε ὑμεῖς οἱ λαλοῦντες ἀλλὰ τὸ πνεῦμα
τὸ ἅγιον (Mk. 13^{11} and par., with the variation in Lk. 12^{12} that the Holy Spirit
διδάξει ὑμᾶς . . . ἃ δεῖ εἰπεῖν).

The Holy Spirit is the authorisation to speak about Christ ; He is
the equipment of the prophet and apostle ; He is the summons to the
Church to minister the Word. To the extent that everything in which
this authorisation, equipment and summons consists—we discussed

this under 1. and 2.—is directed to this goal, to the extent that it cannot be a private affair but only the affair of the Church, or rather the Lord of the Church, if there are individuals to whom the Spirit guarantees that God's revelation comes to them, individuals whom the Spirit constrains—to that extent we shall have to call this third operation of the Spirit the decisive one. If we ask concerning the mind of the Spirit (τὸ φρόνημα τοῦ πνεύματος, Rom. 8²⁷), we must answer that it consists in the fact that He is the gift of speaking about the " wonderful works of God." But if we ask what it means to receive and possess this gift, we shall constantly have to read off the answer from the first two definitions of our concept.

In the thesis we have described the nature and work of the Holy Spirit in revelation by two expressions which carry allusions to biblical statements : He is " the Lord who sets us free " and " by receiving Him we become the children of God." We may claim that these two expressions are a summary of what we must infer from the witness of Holy Scripture to the nature of the Spirit as an element of God's revelation in Jesus Christ.

The word " freedom " implies first and formally that when Scripture speaks of the Holy Spirit as an element in revelation we are dealing with an ability or capacity or capability which is given to man as the addressee of revelation and which makes him a real recipient of revelation. The problem by which we found ourselves confronted was : How can man believe ? How does *homo peccator* become *capax verbi divini* ? The New Testament answer is that it is the Holy Spirit who sets man free for this and for the ministry in which he is put therewith.

Christ has " set us free for freedom," we read in Gal. 5¹. Here and everywhere the term is undoubtedly contrasted with the idea of the servitude overcome in Christ. Primarily—but only primarily—this servitude consists in bondage to a law of God which man has misunderstood and misused, a law to which man ascribes divine authority and which he makes every effort to observe, although in practice he does not recognise in it the voice of the God who commands and is far from letting it serve him as real revelation. But the nature and curse of this servitude lies deeper. Because man is bound in this way he is not able nor free to receive real revelation. The converse is also true : Because he is not free for real revelation, he is in bondage. At all events, although in appearance, but only in appearance, he believes in God and hearkens to Him and strives diligently to serve Him, he is in fact powerless in relation to the living God, i.e., powerless to know Him as He is and to obey Him as He desires. The freedom for which Christ sets us free cannot, then, consist merely in freedom from that servitude. It must also consist—and decisively so—in freedom from that powerlessness, in freedom for the real revelation of God. This is confirmed by a glance at the important passage Jn. 8³⁰⁻⁵⁹. The Jews think they are free as the people of Abraham (v. 33). Jesus contests this : " Whosoever committeth sin, is the servant of sin " (v. 34), and so not free. Why and to what extent ? " If the Son therefore shall make you free, ye shall be free indeed " (v. 36). But this is the very thing that is impossible. Their sin is that the Word of Jesus finds no place in them (οὐ χωρεῖ ἐν ὑμῖν, v. 37), that they cannot hear it (οὐ δύνασθε ἀκούειν, v. 43). " He that is of God heareth God's words ; ye therefore hear them not, because ye are not of God " (v. 47). Hence the freedom for which the Son (v. 36) or the truth (v. 32) makes them free cannot possibly be the mere negation of false bondage (which is hardly mentioned in this passage). Understood thus, freedom would immediately serve as a " pretext to give free rein to the flesh " (Gal. 5¹³), as a " cloke of maliciousness " (1 Pet. 2¹⁶). Thus understood, it would obviously be nothing but a new unfreedom. The truly free are free rather as the servants of God (1 Pet. 2¹⁶). It is not impossible that the paradox of 1 Cor. 7²² about the Christian slave who by his calling is the Lord's freedman, and the Christian freeman who by his calling is Christ's slave, also points in this direction in addition to its most obvious sense. Certainly the freedom which is there where the Lord, the Spirit, is (2 Cor. 3¹⁷) denotes exclusively the freedom to turn to the Lord, to God, in contrast to the Jews, from whom the face of God remains hidden even as and although they read the sacred texts. No less plainly the " law of liberty " referred to in Jas. 1²⁵ ; 2¹² is the order which is directly contrasted, but positively so, with the law of the Jews, an order under which a man stands who is not just a hearer but also a doer—and in James this means, not a forgetful nor a merely reputed hearer, but a real hearer of the Word of God who is claimed in his life-act, in his existence. The man who is capable of being a doer of the Word of this kind, i.e., a real hearer, is free in the New Testament sense of the term. The reference is not to any kind of freedom or any kind of ability. In accordance with the freedom of God Himself, His freedom to be Himself, what is at issue here is a man's freedom for God, for the " glorious liberty " of the children of God (Rom. 8²¹), the *analogia fidei* of the divine freedom which alone really deserves to be called freedom. This, then, is a formal summary of the work of the Spirit in God's revelation. His work consists in freedom, freedom to have a Lord, this Lord, God, as Lord.

On the other hand the concept of divine sonship declares materially that when Scripture speaks of the Holy Spirit as an element in revelation the reference is to a being of the man to whom this freedom or ability belongs. These men are what they can be. They can be what they are. It is thus that they are real recipients of revelation. It is thus that they can believe. We ask again how *homo peccator* can become *capax verbi divini*. The second answer, which comprehends the first, must now be that he does not first become this in order to be it ; he is it, and in virtue of this being he becomes it. He is the child of God. As such he is free, he can believe. And he is God's child as he receives the Holy Ghost. One can and should also say conversely : He receives the Holy Ghost as he is God's child. At all events, in receiving the Holy Ghost he is what in himself and of himself he cannot be, one who belongs to God as a child to its father, one who knows God as a child knows its father, one for whom God is there as a father is there for his child. This is the second and material summary of the operations of the Holy Spirit in God's revelation.

Linking up with our formal definition of the matter, we first repeat that freedom for God is the freedom of the children of God (Rom. 8²¹). Obviously the New Testament concept of divine sonship cannot compete in any sense with that of the divine sonship of Jesus Christ. On the contrary, it is absolutely dependent on this. The fathers made the distinction that Jesus Christ is *Filius Dei natura* while believers are *filii Dei adoptione*. They can be this *adoptione* because Jesus Christ is so *natura*. Because the Reconciler was the Son of God reconciliation or revelation consists for its recipients in being sons of God in the irremovable distinction between the blessed and Him who blesses them. " A man can receive nothing, except it be given him from heaven " (Jn. 3²⁷). While this does not apply to the divine sonship of Jesus it does apply to the divine sonship of those who believe in Him. " By faith, in Christ Jesus, ye are the sons of God, because ye have been baptised into Christ, and have (as such) put on Christ " (Gal. 3²⁶ᶠ·). To be God's child, a man must be called to the κοινωνία τοῦ υἱοῦ αὐτοῦ Ἰησοῦ Χριστοῦ (1 Cor. 1⁹). He must be begotten "with the word of truth" (Jas. 1¹⁸), and when this happens it is the " good gift " which comes to him " from above " (Jas. 1¹⁷). The birth in virtue of which he is God's child is emphatically a " birth from above " (Jn. 3³), distinct from his natural birth and resting on the ἐξουσία which the Logos Himself must give him. Yet all this does not imply a limitation, but rather an underlining, of the constant indicatives in which the New Testament says of believers that they are (Rom. 8¹⁴), we are (Rom. 8¹⁶), we are called and are (1 Jn. 3¹), we are now (1 Jn. 3²), you are (Gal. 4⁶), and even you all are (Gal. 3²⁶) sons or children of God, and therefore not servants (Gal. 4⁷), who are only for a time part of the household (Jn. 8³⁵), but heirs (Rom. 8¹⁷ ; Gal. 4⁷), not Ishmael but Isaac (Gal. 4³⁰ᶠ·), not " strangers and foreigners " but " fellow-citizens with the saints, and of the household of God " (Eph. 2¹⁹). To be such a child of God and to receive the Holy Spirit is one and the same thing. The Holy Spirit is τὸ πνεῦμα τοῦ υἱοῦ (Gal. 4⁶) and hence the πνεῦμα υἱοθεσίας (Rom. 8¹⁵).

How does He show Himself to be such ? In a decisive passage Paul mentions only one thing in which everything is obviously included for him. In the Holy Spirit, and therefore as children of God, we cry, κράζομεν: Ἀββά, ὁ πατήρ (Rom. 8¹⁵ ; Gal. 4⁶). Remarkably, and certainly not by accident, this is the same cry as the Gospel narrative (Mk. 14³⁶) puts on the lips of Jesus when He is at prayer in Gethsemane. So then, in this form, the Son of God is the prototype of the sonship of believers. The children of God have put on this Christ. This child, sinful man, can meet this Father, the holy God, as a child meets its father, only where the only-begotten Son of God has borne and borne away his sin. His reconciliation does not consist in his being placed with the Son of God. It consists in what the Son of God has done and suffered for us. But in his being placed with the Son of God reconciliation is achieved in him. Herein consists his participation in the atonement effected in Christ. This is what it means to have the Holy Spirit. To have the Holy Spirit is to be set with Christ in that transition from death to life. The form of a real recipient of God's revelation, the form which gives the law to his thought, will and speech, will always be the form of the death of Christ (Rom. 6⁵ ; Phil. 3¹⁰). And so his freedom, ability and capacity for God can be understood only as the power of the resurrection of Christ, not as an immanent freedom of his own, but as that which is conferred on him by God, which he can neither manipulate nor understand, which can only be understood as factual, and factual indeed only as the fact of God. In this fact God makes us sure of Him and makes Himself sure of us, and He teaches us what we are to say as His witnesses. All statements about the Holy Spirit, like all statements about the Son of God, can relate only to this divine fact. For us as in the New Testament itself, they are comprehensible or incomprehensible only in the light of it.

The present exposition should be compared with Luther's remarks on Gal.

4 ⁶ᵗ· (*W.A.*, 40ᴵ, pp. 579–597) : He calls ' Abba Father ' the cry of the Holy Ghost in our hearts amid the very severe, the total powerlessness and despair of this heart of ours at its radical sinfulness, at its doubting even of God's graciousness, at the devil's accusation : *Tu es peccator*, at the wrath of God who threatens us with eternal damnation, in the temptation in which there is no experience of the presence and help of Christ, where even Christ only seems to chide us, where we can only cling to the *nudum verbum*. Then that cry rings out, pierces the clouds, fills heaven and earth, rings out so loudly that the angels when they hear it think they have never heard ought at all before, in fact that God Himself hears nought else in the whole world but this sound. And yet *quantum ad sensum nostrum attinet* it is but a trifling sigh in which we do not hear at all this cry of the Spirit. What we experience is the temptation that what we hear are the voices of hell and what we see is the face of hell. If we were now to trust our experience we could only give up ourselves for lost. There and thus—though those who speak *speculative tantum* of the Holy Ghost like Papists and fanatics do not, of course understand this—Christ is almighty, regnant and triumphant in us. The word, nay that unassuming little sigh (*gemitulus*), that *affectus*, in which in spite of everything and with no basis in experience we can still say " Father," this word now becomes more eloquent than any Cicero or Vergil. Curiously enough, in this same passage (*op. cit.*, p. 586, l. 13) Luther strikes his strongest blow against the *pestilens error* of Roman Catholic doctrine that there is in this life no true and impregnable assurance of the grace of God. When and where is there such assurance ? Certainly not in relation to ourselves but in relation to the *promissio et veritas Dei, quae fallere non potest. Aversis oculis a lege, operibus, sensu et conscientia* this assurance becomes an event as appropriation of the divine promise. The promise brings us this assurance in so far as it brings us the possibility of that cry " Abba Father " which in our mouth and heart is the smallest thing but before God is the greatest thing, the one thing, as the cry of His own Spirit in us. *Tum certo definitum est in coelo, quod non sit amplius servitus sed mera libertas, adoptio et filiatio. Quis parit eam ? Iste gemitus.* But this takes place as I accept God's promise. And as for my accepting God's promise, *hoc fit, cum isto gemitu clamo et respondeo corde filiali isti voci : Pater. Ibi tum conveniunt pater et filius* (p. 593, l. 18). But : *quanta magnitudo et gloria huius doni sit, humana mens ne quidem concipere potest in hac vita, multo minus eloqui. Interim in aenigmate cernimus hoc, Habemus istum gemitulum et exiguam fidem, quae solo auditu et sono vocis promittentis Christi nititur. Ideo quoad sensum nostrum res ista centrum, in se autem maxima et infinita sphera est. Sic Christianus habet rem in se maximam et infinitam, in suo autem conspectu et sensu minimam et finitissimam, Ideo istam rem metiri debemus non humana ratione et sensu, sed alio circulo, scilicet promissione dei, Qui ut infinitus est, ita et promissio ipsius infinita est, utcunque interim in has angustias et, ut ita dicam, in verbum centrale inclusa sit. Videmus igitur iam centrum, olim videbimus etiam circumferentiam* (p. 596, l. 16).

In what has been said we have stated already that according to the testimony of Scripture the Holy Spirit is no less and no other than God Himself, distinct from Him whom Jesus calls His Father, distinct also from Jesus Himself, yet no less than the Father, and no less than Jesus, God Himself, altogether God.

We again recall 2 Cor. 3¹⁷ : ὁ κύριος τὸ πνεῦμα, the Lord is the Spirit. We also think of the well-known πνεῦμα ὁ θεός, God is Spirit (Jn. 4²⁴). In both these verses the reverse, the Spirit is the Lord, the Spirit is God, while it is not actually in the passages, is not only permitted but commanded as an inference from what is said. The same equation is presupposed in Ac. 5³¹· where Ananias is accused of having lied to the Holy Ghost and then immediately after we read : οὐκ ἐψεύσω ἀνθρώποις ἀλλὰ τῷ θεῷ. Similarly in Mk. 3²⁸ᶠ·—however we may understand it—there could not possibly be a blasphemy against the Holy Ghost which makes man guilty of an unforgivable, eternal sin, if the Spirit were less or something other than God Himself.

That not only these and similar verses but the whole New Testament doctrine of the work of the Holy Spirit implies the deity of His essence can properly be contested only if one has first explained away the fact that with its Ἰησοῦς Κύριος the New Testament community confessed its faith in Jesus Christ as faith in God Himself. If the Christ of the New Testament is a demi-god from above or below, then naturally faith in Him becomes a human possibility. Then, extraordinary though the phenomenon may be, one can show how faith in Him has arisen on certain grounds and presuppositions which we ourselves can perceive and control. But in this case there is in fact no need for the deity of the Holy Spirit who creates this faith. On this view the name " Holy Spirit " may very well be a mere name for a particularly profound, serious and vital conviction of truth or experience of conscience, or one may equally well omit it altogether when describing the basis of faith according to the New Testament.

Along these lines one may, with Karl Holl, describe as follows the experience and reflection of those pagan contemporaries of the primitive community who became believers : " This concept of God advanced by Jesus (namely, the concept that God is first and basically the God who forgives and only on that ground the God who demands), which ran so sharply contrary to all natural religious feeling, had nevertheless a hidden, irresistible power. It penetrated more deeply than any other concept of God. For it spoke to the conscience. Was it not convincing that the man who was reaching upwards to God should take his standard, not from human respectability or heroism, but from the unconditioned, from God's own moral nature, from His goodness ? But those who seriously attempted this involuntarily lost sight of the distinction between right and wrong, pure and impure. The solemn initiatory saying of the mysteries : ' Whoso hath lived well and righteously,' became a superficiality. In place of it the γνῶθι σεαυτόν now acquired its full stringency. . . . From the depths of such introspection there then grew up an understanding of Jesus' concept of God. Was it not really the case that the God by whose gifts man lived always sustained man with forgiving loving-kindness ? The only problem was that man had lost awareness of Him. And was not the God who sought the heart of man, and even knew how to win back the lost, greater and holier and mightier in this love than all the gods of high Olympus ? Thus everything fell into place to yield coherent sense. If a man grasped it, he had the feeling of waking from a dream. The boldness, the utter novelty, or, as one might say to-day in an overworked slogan, the irrational element in the preaching of Jesus, would not have done it alone. What is only irrational has at most the limited and transitory attraction of the forcefully arbitrary. But here the irrational produced an illuminating sense. What was a stumbling-block to sound common sense commended itself to the thoughtful as the revelation as a deeper and convincing truth about God and man.

This was the victorious element in Christianity " (" Urchristentum und Religions-geschichte," *Ges. Aufs. z. KGesch.*, Vol. 2, 1928, p. 18). This analysis of Holl's, which purports to be exegesis of the New Testament, should be compared with Rom. 8[16f.] ; Gal. 4[6f.] and Luther's exposition of these passages. One can hardly try to argue that in both cases the same thing is being said in different words. No, in Holl's analysis there is clearly substituted for the Holy Spirit man's own faculty of distinction and judgment. It is by means of this that Jesus' concept of God can " penetrate " like any other, though more deeply than any other. It is in virtue of this that man, waking as from a dream, can in profound introspection become aware of something he was not aware of before. It is in virtue of this that he can establish as illuminating and meaningful that which at first offended him. It is in virtue of this that he can in a word convince himself of the " truth about God and man " which is expressed in Jesus' concept of God. The measure-ment here is not by the infinite circle of the divine promise but altogether *humana ratione et sensu.* The " victorious element in Christianity " consists here, not in the fact that Christ is powerful in the powerlessness of man, not in the centre with no visible or palpable periphery, but in the fact that Christ's (or Jesus') " concept of God " has an illuminating and " coherent sense " for man, or at least for " the thoughtful." The expression " Holy Spirit " does not need to be used here, and the doctrine of the deity of the Holy Spirit is certainly not advo-cated. Obviously the New Testament has to be read in this way here because even where it speaks of Christ it is construed as if it were referring to the bearer of a particular concept of God of which man was unaware but which he can properly grasp, the bearer of the deep and convincing truth that the relation of forgiveness and demand, contrary to sound common sense (i.e., superficial Greek self-knowledge), is the reverse of what it is usually taken to be.

If we may now presuppose that this is not a tenable exegesis of New Testament Christology, then the transformation of the New Testament doctrine of the Spirit into a doctrine of a very profound and very conscientious conviction of truth is also untenable. For if it is true that the men of the New Testament perceived the deity of Christ, not on the basis of their knowledge and choice, but on the basis of their being known and chosen (not as the result but as the beginning of their thinking about Him), then the faith, or the basis of the faith of these men, cannot be regarded as a faculty which was unfortunately hidden from themselves, nor can the rise of faith be understood formally as waking up from a dream or materially as a recollection of how things always were at root. In this case the category of faith does not have any place in the history of religion and conscience cannot be evoked to explain its possibility as δός μοι ποῦ στῶ. Faith, New Testament πίστις, is rather to be understood as a possibility which derives from a mode of being of God, from a mode of being which is in essential unity with Him who in the New Testament is described as Father and as Son.

In faith an " anointing " or " sealing " is presupposed which can have no resemblance to the creature " anointed " or " sealed " (Athanasius, *Ep. ad Serap.*, I, 23 ; III, 3). If this presupposition, the Holy Spirit, were a creature, he could not mediate to us any μετουσία θεοῦ. Ourselves creatures, we should then be dealing with a mere creature, and would remain remote from the θεία φύσις.

But if it is true that by the Holy Spirit we are made worthy of that μετουσία, would it not be mad to try to deny His deity ? (*ib.*, I, 24). One may certainly question the vocabulary used here. But can one on that account question whether this is correct exegesis of the New Testament doctrine of the Spirit in contrast to the Modernist Protestant theologian cited above ? If we look back at the results of our analysis of the New Testament doctrine of the Spirit, i.e., at the predicates which we have ascribed to the Spirit and His work in revelation, what else can we say but that *Spiritus vox hic a creaturae notione plane sub-movenda est ?* (*Syn. pur. Theol.*, Leiden, 1624, *Disp.*, 9, 2).

But this also means that the creature to whom the Holy Spirit is imparted in revelation by no means loses its nature and kind as a creature so as to become itself, as it were, the Holy Spirit. Even in receiving the Holy Ghost man remains man, the sinner sinner. Similarly in the outpouring of the Holy Ghost God remains God. The statements about the operations of the Holy Spirit are statements whose subject is God and not man, and in no circumstances can they be transformed into statements about man. They tell us about the relation of God to man, to his knowledge, will and emotion, to his experience active and passive, to his heart and conscience, to the whole of his psycho-physical existence, but they cannot be reversed and understood as statements about the existence of man. That God the Holy Spirit is the Redeemer who sets us free is a statement of the knowledge and praise of God. In virtue of this statement we ourselves are the redeemed, the liberated, the children of God in faith, in the faith we confess with this statement, i.e., in the act of God of which this statement speaks. This being of ours is thus enclosed in the act of God. Confessing this faith in the Holy Ghost, we cannot as it were look back and try to contemplate and establish abstractly this being of ours as God's redeemed and liberated children as it is enclosed in the act of God. We may, of course, be strong and sure in faith—that we are so is the act of God we are confessing, the work of the Holy Spirit— but we cannot try specifically to make ourselves strong and sure again by contemplating ourselves as the strong and the sure. To have the Holy Spirit is to let God rather than our having God be our confidence. It lies in the nature of God's revelation and reconciliation in time, it lies in the nature of the *regnum gratiae*, that having *God* and our *having* God are two very different things, and that our redemption is not a relation which we can survey in its totality, i.e., which we can under-stand in both its aspects, God's and our own. Paradoxically enough we can understand it only in its divine aspect, i.e., in faith we can understand it only as it is posited by God. Faith is understanding it as posited and indeed fulfilled and consummated by God, but not by us, not in such a way that we may see ourselves in the being which corresponds to this fulfilment and consummation by God, i.e., in our redemption or beatitude or eternal life. If we could also understand it thus, this would mean that all the difficulty of faith would be behind us. It would no longer have to be a Nevertheless. It would no longer have to be obedience and venture. It would no longer have to be faith at all. It would be sight. For it is sight when we can survey and see in its totality how what is true from God's standpoint is also true from ours. This would be more than God's revelation and reconciliation in time. It would be our being with Him in eternity, in the *regnum gloriae*. If we cannot erase this distinction, if we cannot anticipate what lies beyond revelation and faith, this means necessarily that in so far as redemption implies our own being in addition to God's act we can regard it only as future, i.e., as the redemption that comes to us from God. We have it in faith.

But to have it in faith means that we have it in promise. We believe that we are redeemed, set free, children of God, i.e., we accept as such the promise given us in the Word of God in Jesus Christ even as and although we do not understand it in the very least, or see it fulfilled and consummated in the very least, in relation to our present. We accept it because it speaks to us of an act of God on us even as and although we see only our own empty hands which we stretch out to God in the process. We believe our future being. We believe in an eternal life even in the midst of the valley of death. In this way, in this futurity, we have it. The assurance with which we know this having is the assurance of faith, and the assurance of faith means concretely the assurance of hope.

Ἐλπιζομένων ὑπόστασις, πραγμάτων ἔλεγχος οὐ βλεπομένων (Heb. 11¹). Hence the concept of sonship, which is very important as we have seen, is often elucidated, especially in Paul, by the concept of an inheritance (κληρονομία) into which we have not yet entered but which is legally in prospect, and sure and certain as such (Rom. 8¹⁷; Gal. 3²⁹; 4⁷; Tit. 3⁷; also Jas. 2⁵). Hence Gal. 5⁵ says that in the Spirit we wait for the righteousness which is hoped for (and which precisely as such is present in Jesus Christ), ἐλπίδα δικαιοσύνης ἀπεκδεχόμεθα. Hence again 2 Cor. 5 says that we walk in faith and not in sight. Hence Rom. 8²³f·, in a passage we can never consult too often, says that we, the same (note the twofold καὶ αὐτοί), who have the ἀπαρχὴ τοῦ πνεύματος, groan with all creation in expectation of sonship to the degree that this is to be understood as the fulfilment and consummation of the promise, the ἀπολύτρωσις τοῦ σώματος. Τῇ γὰρ ἐλπίδι ἐσώθημεν· ἐλπὶς δὲ βλεπομένη οὐκ ἔστιν ἐλπίς· ὃ γὰρ βλέπει τις, τί καὶ ἐλπίζει; εἰ δὲ ὃ οὐ βλέπομεν ἐλπίζομεν, δι᾽ ὑπομονῆς ἀπεκδεχόμεθα. God has regenerated you. How? Through the resurrection of Jesus Christ from the dead. To what? To a living hope, namely, the inheritance incorruptible, undefiled, that fadeth not away, reserved in heaven for you (1 Pet. 1³f·). We are called and are God's children. We are this now . . . but it has not yet appeared what we shall be. We know that when He shall appear we shall be like Him (1 Jn. 3¹f·). Your life (i.e., your salvation) is hid with Christ in God. When Christ, our life, appears, then you too will appear with Him in glory (Col. 3³f·). Abraham is the father of all believers because he did not consider his own sterile body nor that of Sarah but gave God the glory in the certainty that what He promised He could do (Rom. 4¹⁹f·).

Thus the Holy Ghost Himself is called the πνεῦμα τῆς ἐπαγγελίας (Eph. 1¹³) and His office in relation to us is our sealing εἰς ἡμέραν ἀπολυτρώσεως (Eph. 4³⁰, cf. 1¹⁴).

In the New Testament sense everything that is to be said about the man who receives the Holy Spirit and is constrained and filled by the Holy Spirit is an eschatological statement. Eschatological does not mean in an inexact or unreal sense but in relation to the ἔσχατον, i.e., to that which from our standpoint and for our experience and thought has still to come, to the eternal reality of the divine fulfilment and consummation. It is precisely eschatological statements and these alone, i.e., statements which relate to this eternal reality, that can claim real and proper meaning as statements about temporal relations. For what can be more real and proper for man than truth in this particular relation ?

The New Testament speaks eschatologically when it speaks of man's being called, reconciled, justified, sanctified and redeemed. In speaking thus it speaks really and properly. One has to realise that God is the measure of all that is real and proper, that eternity comes first and then time, and therefore the future comes first and then the present, just as the Creator undoubtedly comes first and then the creature. Those who realise this will not take offence here.

Only of God Himself, which means at this point the Holy Spirit and His work as such, can one speak non-eschatologically, i.e., without this reference to something other, beyond, and future. It might be said, of course, that even our talk about God Himself and His work is eschatological to the extent that all our thoughts and words as such cannot grasp this object but can only point beyond themselves to it. But that to which they point when we are speaking of God and His essence and work has itself no margin or border. It is not related to an ἔσχατον but is itself the ἔσχατον. This is what we cannot say of the man we know even and precisely in faith. The man we know does not live an eternal life. This is and remains the predicate of God, of the Holy Spirit.

The Holy Spirit is Lord over every creature but is not lorded over. He deifies but is not deified. He fills but is not filled. He causes to participate but does not participate. He sanctifies but is not sanctified (John Damasc., *Ekdos.*, I, 8).

Of ourselves, however, we must say that God so gives Himself to us in His revelation that we are and remain and indeed only truly become rich in Him and poor in ourselves. Both become our experience : that we are rich in God and that then and only then we truly become poor in ourselves. But we do not have the divine and spiritual riches and the divine and spiritual poverty in our experience. What we have in our experience, what can be changed and extended and developed quantitatively and qualitatively in us, what moves up and down or perhaps forwards in a straight line or in spirals, what can be the theme of the anthropology, psychology or biography of the believer, is a human sign of the fact that God has given Himself to us by His revelation in faith, and as such it is certainly not to be treated lightly. It would be strange indeed if such signs were not in evidence at all. Yet it is still true that " the things which are seen are temporal, but the things which are not seen are eternal " (2 Cor. 4[18]). Man remains man, the man who can deceive himself and others ; the sign remains a sign, which may fade again and disappear. But the Holy Spirit remains the Holy Spirit, wholly and utterly the Spirit of promise. Even and especially the child of God in the New Testament sense will never for a moment or in any regard cease to confess : " I believe that I cannot of my own reason or power believe in Jesus Christ my Lord or come to Him." God remains the Lord even and precisely when He Himself comes into our hearts as His own gift, even and precisely when He " fills " us. No other intercedes with Him on our behalf except Himself. No other intercedes with us on His behalf except again Himself. No one else speaks from us when He speaks through us except Himself. " In thy light we see light " (Ps. 36[9]). The deity of the Holy Spirit is thus demanded. The essentiality, the directness of the work of the Holy Spirit is demanded. We are not grasping at more but at less, and ultimately at nothing at all, if in addition to the guarantee which is identical with God Himself we think we must grasp at an unequivocal experience, at a guarantee of the guarantee so to speak, in order that we may then decide for certainty of faith, as though a certainty for which we must first decide could be the certainty of faith. " If I have but thee, I ask naught of heaven and earth," and further : " Though body and soul languish within me, yet thou, God, art the strength of my heart and my portion for ever " (Ps. 73[25f.]) This is how we think and speak ἐν πνεύματι. But if we grasp at another, at ourselves, if we seek strength and confirmation in ourselves, we simply show thereby that we are still far from thinking and speaking ἐν πνεύματι, or have long since ceased to do so. We can comprehend God in *ourselves* only as we comprehend ourselves in *God*, just as we can, of course, comprehend *ourselves* in God only as we comprehend *God* in ourselves. It is precisely ἐν πνεύματι that we shall be ready either way to turn from ourselves to God and to pray to Him, not to contemplate God and manipulate Him. But again only the man who seeks everything in God prays to Him. And yet again only the man who seeks nothing in himself seeks everything in God.

Μακρόθεν ἑστώς, not daring to lift his eyes to heaven, the publican in the temple prays : " God be merciful to me, a sinner." And this man went down to his house justified (Lk. 18[10f.]). Did Jesus go into the ship to Simon or not ? Did He fill his ship with blessing or not ? But what did Simon say to this ?

" Depart from me, for I am a sinful man " (Lk. 5¹ᶠ·). " It should be understood that . . . all that is not Christ is altogether unclean and damned with birth and all life, And no purity or holiness cometh into us or out of us, but over and above us and far beyond us, yea, above all our sense, wit and understanding, in Christ alone by faith 'tis found and attained " (Luther, *Sermon at Torgau*, 1533, *W.A.*, 37, p. 57, l. 32). This is how a man thinks and speaks ἐν πνεύματι.

What we have to offer, to sacrifice to God in order to pray aright, is ourselves in this total lack of any claim.

We have to sacrifice " a broken spirit," " a broken and a contrite heart " (Ps. 51¹⁷), a heart that knows it must be created by God in us as a new heart, a spirit that knows it must be created by God in us as a new spirit, and must be sought in prayer for this reason (Ps. 51¹⁰).

Whether prayer is made aright and answered depends on this total lack of any claim.

Rom. 8 is unthinkable without Rom. 7 (including Rom. 7²⁴), and indeed without Rom. 7 understood, not as a glance back at the past, but as an assertion about the present and about the whole temporal future even and especially of the Christian.   The *Veni Creator Spiritus* is true and will be heard when it is persistent beseeching, when no present or perfect *venit* stands behind it to spoil everything.   That simple *venit* is the truth just because it is in God and from God.

The impregnable basis of faith, the assurance of faith by God's revelation, depends on whether this basis, not just at the beginning but in the middle and at the end too, is sought in God alone and not anywhere else, not in ourselves.   Grace is the Holy Spirit received, but we ourselves are sinners.   This is true.   If we say anything else we do not know the deity of the Holy Spirit in God's revelation.

2. THE ETERNAL SPIRIT

The Holy Spirit does not first become the Holy Spirit, the Spirit of God, in the event of revelation.   The event of revelation has clarity and reality on its subjective side because the Holy Spirit, the subjective element in this event, is of the essence of God Himself.   What He is in revelation He is antecedently in Himself.   And what He is antecedently in Himself He is in revelation.   Within the deepest depths of deity, as the final thing to be said about Him, God is God the Spirit as He is God the Father and God the Son.   The Spirit outpoured at Pentecost is the Lord, God Himself, just as the Father and just as Jesus Christ is the Lord, God Himself.   Once more, if we are asked how this statement comes to be made, we can only answer that to make it no special dialectical effort is required ; we have only to allow the biblical statements to stand ; we have only to accept their validity and take them seriously. According to these statements the work of the Holy Spirit in revelation is a work which can be ascribed only to God and which is thus expressly ascribed to God. The dogma of the Holy Spirit to which we now turn adds nothing new to this. Here again the dogma does not invent anything. It simply finds what was and is more or less plainly hinted at in the New Testament even though it obviously was not and is not to be found there. The dogma itself, then, is not in Scripture ; it is exegesis of Scripture. It does not speak of any other deity of the Holy Ghost than that in which He is revealed to us according to Scripture. It insists, however, that this deity is true, proper and eternal deity. The Spirit is holy in us because He is so antecedently in Himself.

The doctrine of the deity and autonomy of the Spirit's divine mode of being achieved general understanding and acknowledgment in the Church much later than the corresponding doctrine of the Son. One can see it intimated from the very beginning, of course, in the primitive threefold structure of the creed. But in the main the 2nd and 3rd century Fathers confined themselves to speaking of the operation and gifts of the Holy Spirit, and there was often approximation to, or at all events no clear exclusion of, the Subordinationist view that He is a creature or creaturely force on the one hand and the Modalist view that He is identical with the Son or Logos on the other. At that time the position which later prevailed in both respects was understood with relative clarity and lack of ambiguity only by Tertullian (in his work against Praxeas), perhaps not without some connexion to the high regard he had for the Spirit as a Montanist. Even the Nicene Creed, though it uses ὁμοούσιος of the Son, is content, like the older symbols, simply to mention the Holy Ghost as an object of faith without opposing Arianism at this point as well. It was again Athanasius (in his letter to Serapion opposing Macedonius of Constantinople) who saw the connexions and spoke the decisive word in this regard. Not without some hesitation the Neo-Nicenes and the Council of 381 followed him. The dogma found precise formulation, corresponding to the definitions of the Son in *Nic.-Const.*, only in the 5th century (*Symb. Quicunque vult*). But for the full development of the doctrine we shall have to look as late as the final reception of the *filioque* into the creed of the Western liturgy (1014) and the schism of the Eastern Church occasioned by the rejection of this addition.

It is deeply rooted in the matter itself that Christian knowledge about the Holy Spirit permeated the Church so slowly and with such difficulty. The fact that the Holy Spirit is the Lord, that He is wholly and utterly God, the divine Subject, in the same sense as the Father of Jesus Christ and in the same sense as Jesus Christ Himself, is without doubt the harder and more exacting demand, not just or chiefly for formal thought, but in face of man's ideas about himself also and precisely in relation to God. He himself, his presence at God's revelation, is indeed the issue in the problem of the Spirit within the concept of revelation. Even though man may accept the fact that the author of revelation, the Father, is fully God, and perhaps that the Revealer, the Son, is also fully God in order to be able to be God's Revealer, the question remains open whether God has said that man's own presence at revelation, the reality of his encounter with the Revealer, is not his own work but is again in the full sense God's work. If the Spirit, the Mediator of revelation to the subject, were a creature or creaturely force, then it would be asserted and maintained that in virtue of his presence at revelation along with God and over against God, man, too, is in his own way the lord in revelation. For even in circumstances that are unfavourable to us our relation to creatures and creaturely forces is a reciprocal one, a co-operation of freedom and necessity, a relation between one pole and its opposite. Even Modalism in relation to the Spirit, the identification of the Spirit with Christ, would imply that man confronts revelation as an object. Even as it gains control over him, he can also gain control over it. Even as a recipient of the fulness of grace man could still regard his faith as an active instrument (cf. A. Ritschl, *Rechtf. u Vers.*[4], Vol. I, 1900, p. 157). By the doctrine of the deity and autonomy of the Spirit's divine mode of being man is, as it were, challenged in his own house. It is now clear that his presence at revelation cannot be the presence of a partner or counterpart, that from this presence no claims or privileges can arise *vis-à-vis* God, that this presence can only be a factual, incomprehensible and miraculous presence, factual because God is there, as we have already said, not just objectively but also subjectively, not just from above but also from below, not just from without but also from within. The dogma of the Holy Spirit means recognition that in every respect man can be present at God's revelation only as a servant is present at his master's work, i.e., following, obeying, imitating and serving, and that this relation—as distinct from that of human servant and master—cannot be reversed in any way or at any point. This developed recognition of the unconditionality and irreversibility of the lordship of God in His revelation is what makes the dogma of the Holy Spirit difficult, difficult, of course, intellectually too, but difficult intellectually only because man does not want the very thing that it states to be true.

It is logical that this doctrine had to be the last stage in the development of the trinitarian dogma. It had to be reached before the doctrine of grace, which then became the distinctive theme of the Western Church, could become a problem, before the struggle and victory of Augustine over Pelagius could take place. The Reformation with its doctrine of justification by faith alone can also be understood only against the background of this specific dogma. Its true and total significance, of course, has never been understood in Catholicism (not even in Augustine), and only very partially even in post-Reformation Protestantism. Modernist Protestantism in its entirety has simply been a regression to pre-Nicene obscurities and ambiguities regarding the Spirit.

For a more precise exposition of the dogma we shall now turn here again to the Nicaeno-Constantinopolitan Creed.

(Πιστεύομεν . . .)	(Credo . . .)
1. εἰς τὸ πνεῦμα τὸ ἅγιον, τὸ κύριον	1. *in Spiritum sanctum Dominum*
2. τὸ ζωοποιοῦν	2. *et vivificantem*
3. τὸ ἐκ τοῦ πατρὸς ἐκπορευόμενον	3. *qui ex Patre Filioque procedit*
4. τὸ σὺν πατρὶ καὶ υἱῷ συνπροσ- κυνούμενον καὶ συνδοξαζόμενον.	4. *qui cum Patre et Filio simul adoratur et conglorificatur.*

1. We believe in the Holy Ghost, the Lord. The underlying Greek text uses κύριον adjectivally here. This implies no limitation of the statement as we have it in the Latin *Dominus* and English " Lord." Like the Father and the Son, the Spirit is not *Dominus*, Lord, as one Lord side by side with two others. He is Lord in inseparable unity with the Father as Lord and the Son as Lord. Our first point, with a backward glance at the ἕνα κύριον of the second article, is that the Holy Spirit, with the Father and the Son, is the bearer of the lordship of God which is not based on any higher lordship. With the Father and the Son He is the one sovereign divine Subject, the Subject who is not placed under the control or inspection of any other, who derives His being and existence from Himself. But the adjectival use of κύριος, along with a fact that we have not yet taken into account, and which is not evident in Latin (or German), namely that πνεῦμα itself is a neuter, forces us to note at once the special way in which the Holy Spirit is all this. These two circumstances indicate that He is it all in a neutral way, neutral in the sense of distinct, i.e., distinct from the Father and the Son whose modes of being are reciprocal, but neuter also in the sense of related, i.e., related to the Father and the Son, whose reciprocity is not a being against, but a being to and from and with one another. This togetherness or communion of the Father and the Son is the Holy Spirit. The specific element in the divine mode of being of the Holy Spirit thus consists, paradoxically enough, in the fact that He is the common factor in the mode of being of God the Father and that of God the Son. He is what is common to them, not in so far as they are the one God, but in so far as they are the Father and the Son.

Spiritus sanctus commune aliquid est Patris et Filii (Augustine, *De trin.*, VI, 5, 7). He stands " in the middle between the Begotten and Unbegotten " (John of Damasc., *Ekdos.*, I, 13). *Nomen Spiritus sancti non est alienum a Patre et Filio, quia uterque est et spiritus et sanctus* (Anselm of Canterbury, *Ep. de incarn.*, 2).

Thus, even if the Father and the Son might be called " person " (in the modern sense of the term), the Holy Spirit could not possibly be regarded as the third " person." In a particularly clear way the Holy Spirit is what the Father and the Son also are. He is not a third spiritual Subject, a third I, a third Lord side by side with two others. He is a third mode of being of the one divine Subject or Lord.

C.D.—Q*

In this regard it is worth noting that the Church has forbidden the portrayal of the Holy Ghost in human form (Bartmann, *Lehrb. d. Dogm.*⁷, Vol. I, 1928, p. 194).

He is the common element, or, better, the fellowship, the act of communion, of the Father and the Son. He is the act in which the Father is the Father of the Son or the Speaker of the Word and the Son is the Son of the Father or the Word of the Speaker.

He is *communio quaedam consubstantialis* (Augustine, *De trin.*, XV, 27, 50). He is the *vinculum pacis* (Eph. 4³), the *amor*, the *caritas*, the mutual *donum* between the Father and the Son, as it has often been put in the train of Augustine. He is thus the love in which God (loves Himself, i.e., loves Himself as the Father and as the Son, and) as the Father loves the Son and as the Son loves the Father. *Si charitas qua Pater diligit Filium et Patrem diligit Filius, ineffabiliter communionem demonstrat amborum, quid convenientius quam ut ille dicatur charitas proprie, qui Spiritus est communis ambobus* (Augustine, *De trin.*, XV, 19, 37). To this extent—the figurative nature of the expression does not need to be emphasised—He is the "result" of their common "breathing," *spiratio*. *Amborum sacrum spiramen, nexus amorque*, as we read in the Kyrie-Tropus "*Cuncti potens*" (L. Eisenhofer, *Handb. der kath. Liturgik*, Vol. 2, 1933, p. 89).

How far is this act to be understood as a special divine mode of being ? It is obviously to be regarded as a *special* divine mode of being because this common being and work of the Father and the Son is a special and distinct mode of divine being as compared to that of the Father and the Son. It is obviously to be understood as a *divine* mode of being because in this act of His divine being as Father and Son, in this reciprocal love of His, God cannot be or do anything other or less than what is equal to Himself. There cannot be any higher principle from which and in which the Father and the Son must first find themselves together. They can find themselves together only in their own principle. But this principle is the breathing of the Holy Spirit or the Holy Spirit Himself. Again the work of this love is not the created world ; it is the reciprocal love of the Father and the Son. The work, then, must be what is equal to them, and this equal is the Holy Spirit.

Father and Son are *non participatione, sed essentia sua, neque dono superioris alicuius, sed suo proprio servantes unitatem Spiritus in vinculo pacis* (Augustine, *De trin.*, VI, 5, 7). *Nam ideo amor non est impar tibi aut Filio tuo, quia tantum amas te et illum et ille te et seipsum, quantus es tu et ille, nec est aliud a te et ab illo* (Anselm of Canterbury, *Prosl.*, 23). *Si nulla umquam creatura, id est si nihil umquam aliud esset quam summus spiritus Pater et Filius : nihilominus seipsos et invicem Pater et Filius diligerent. Consequitur itaque hunc amorem non esse aliud quam quod est Pater et Filius, quod est summa essentia (Monol.*, 53).

Thus God—and to this degree He is God the Holy Spirit—is "antecedently in Himself" the act of communion, the act of impartation, love, gift. For this reason and in this way and on this basis He is so in His revelation. Not *vice versa* ! We know Him thus in His revelation. But He is not this because He is it in His revelation ; because He is it antecedently in Himself, He is it also in His revelation.

He is in His revelation the *donator doni* because in Himself, as the Spirit of the Father and the Son, He is the *donum donatoris* (Augustine, *De trin.*, V, 11). *Donum vere dicitur non ex eo tantum, quod donetur, sed ex proprietate, quam habuit ab aeterno. Unde et ab aeterno fuit donum. Sempiterne enim donum fuit, non quia daretur, sed quia processit a Patre et Filio . . . temporaliter autem donatum est* (Peter Lombard, *Sent.*, I, dist. 18 D). *Donum non dicitur ex eo quod actu datur, sed in quantum habet aptitudinem ut possit dari. Unde ab aeterno divina persona dicitur donum, licet ex tempore detur* (Thomas Aquinas, *S. th.*, I, *qu.* 38, *art.* 1 and 4.) *Amor habet rationem primi doni, per quod omnia dona gratuita donantur. Unde cum Spiritus sanctus procedat ut amor . . . procedit in ratione doni primi* (*ib.*, *art.* 2c).

The Holy Spirit, says the dogma with its τὸ κύριον, is the Lord who acts on us in revelation as the Redeemer, who really sets us free and really makes us the children of God, who really gives His Church the words to speak God's Word, because in this work of His on us He simply does in time what He does eternally in God, because this mode of being of His in revelation is also a mode of being of the hidden essence of God, so that it really is the hidden essence of God Himself, and therefore the Lord in the most unrestricted sense of the term, who, in all His inscrutability, is revealed in revelation in this respect too.

2. We believe in the Holy Ghost, the giver of life. This statement, too, teaches the deity of the Holy Spirit. Like the *per quem omnia facta sunt* of the second article, it does so by referring to the fact that the Holy Spirit is with the Father (and the Son) the subject of creation. He is not just the Redeemer, so surely does redemption stand in indissoluble correlation with reconciliation, so surely does reconciliation reach its consummation in redemption. He is thus the Reconciler too, with the Son, and as the Spirit of the Son. And just as in reconciliation, and as its presupposition, God the Father is revealed through the Son, i.e., God the Creator, and the work of creation is shown to have happened through the same Word who became incarnate in Jesus Christ, so now the Holy Spirit is revealed as the One who in His own way co-operates in creation too.

In the first instance the ζωοποιοῦν, which reminds us of two New Testament verses Jn. 6⁶³ ; 2 Cor. 3⁶ that have been quoted already, is certainly to be understood soteriologically. But behind these passages there is again a reminiscence of the significance which the Old Testament assigns to *ruach* and *neshamah* for the *regnum naturae*, of Gen. 2⁷, where Adam, though he is not himself a πνεῦμα ζωοποιοῦν as Christ the second Adam is said to be in 1 Cor. 15⁴⁵, is still a " living soul " through the " living breath " of God. And this leads us at once to the " Spirit " who according to Gen. 1² hovered (" brooded ") over the " ocean " of creation when it was as yet without form and neither filled nor fashioned by any life, to the Spirit through whom the " host of heaven " is made according to Ps. 33[6], who is in all flesh according to Gen. 7[15], and who is in every place to which man might go according to Ps. 139[7], to that " breath " in every creature which according to Ps. 150[6] puts it under obligation to praise the Lord because according to Ps. 104[29f.] it is His, the Lord's breath, by which the creature is created and without which it would inevitably vanish away at once.

Already at the beginning of the section we have given thought to this general meaning of the term " spirit." In order it is the primary meaning. But epistemologically it can only be secondary. For as it is only through revelation (and therefore through the Spirit in the soteriological sense of the term) that we see that we and all that is in general the creation of God are, the same applies in particular to our creation by the Word and Spirit (now in the primary and general sense of the term). This general meaning " spirit," the significance of the Spirit as the Creator Spirit, consists, however, in the fact that creation in its own existence as distinct from God's existence is not only there according to the will of the Father effected by the Word but in and of itself it is and remains capable of this existence of its own, as it must always be sustained objectively too in its existence by the Word of God. The Holy Spirit is the Creator God with the Father and the Son in so far as God as Creator creates life as well as existence. From this standpoint we cannot avoid speaking of a presence and operation of the Holy Spirit which is presupposed in revelation, which is first and general, and which is related to the created existence of man and the world as such. This can as little be the object of a general and independent knowledge preceding revelation as can the *per quem omnia facta sunt* of the second article or the dogma of creation generally. It cannot, then, be the theme of a natural theology. It can be known and confessed only on the basis of revelation and in faith. But on the basis of revelation and of faith it must be confessed, already as a necessary consequence of the deity of the Holy Spirit, already in the light of the principle *opera trinitatis ad extra sunt indivisa*, but also on account of its significant content.

'Η δὲ τοῦ ἁγίου πνεύματος μεγαλωσύνη ἀδιάλυτος, ἀπέραντος καὶ πανταχοῦ καὶ διὰ πάντων καὶ ἐν πᾶσιν ἀεί ἐστιν. πληροῦσα μὲν τὸν κόσμον καὶ συνέχουσα κατὰ τὴν θεότητα, ἀχώρητος δὲ κατὰ τὴν δύναμιν, καὶ μετροῦσα μέν, οὐ μετρωμένη δέ (Didymus of Alexandria, *De trin.*, II, 6, 2). *Spiritui sancto . . . attribuitur quod dominando gubernet et vivificet quae sunt creata a Patre per Filium.* He is the *bonitas*, and so the goal, and so the *primum movens* of creation (Thomas Aquinas, *S. theol.*, I, qu. 45, art. 6, ad. 2). Therefore in the *Offertorium* of the vigil before Pentecost, with a clear reminiscence that the Holy Ghost in baptism is also the Holy Ghost in creation, the Roman Church prays according to Ps. 104[30] : *Emitte Spiritum tuum et creabuntur et renovabis faciem terrae.* And in the Introit for Whitsunday : *Spiritus Domini replevit orbem terrarum, allelujah : et hoc quod continet omnia scientiam habet vocis.* And in the familiar Whitsuntide hymn :

Veni Creator Spiritus,
mentes tuorum visita,
imple superna gratia,
quae tu creasti pectora.

And in the *Oratio* for the Ember Day (Saturday) in Whitsun week : *Mentibus nostris . . . spiritum sanctum infunde cuius et sapientia conditi sumus et providentia gubernamur.* Luther, too, can speak of a *duplex Spiritus quem Deus donat hominibus : animans et sanctificans.* Thus all *homines ingeniosi, prudentes eruditi, fortes, magnanimi* are impelled by the *Spiritus animans. Soli autem christiani ac pii habent Spiritum sanctum sanctificantem* (*W.A., Ti.,* 5, p. 367, l. 12). And Calvin in his general definition of the three modes of being of God could even describe the Holy Ghost as God's *virtus per omnia quidem diffusa, quae tamen perpetuo in ipso resideat* (*Cat. Genev.,* 1545, in K. Müller, p. 118, l. 28). He interpreted Gen. 1² as follows : Both the existence of things, created first as chaos (*inordinata moles, massa indisposita*), and also their nature or form (*pulcher ac distinctus ordo*), in order not merely to be created but also to be, to persist, needed an *arcana Dei inspiratio,* a *vigor* imparted to them by God (*Comm. on Gen.* 1², 1544, *C.R.,* 23, 16). And Calvin regarded the thought which follows as an important expression of the doctrine of the deity of the Holy Spirit : *ille enim est, qui ubique diffusus omnia sustinet, vegetat et vivificat in coelo et in terra. Iam hoc ipso creaturarum numero eximitur, quod nullis circumscribitur finibus ; sed suum in omnia vigorem transfundendo essentiam vitam et motionem illis inspirare, id vero plane divinum est* (*Instit.,* I, 13, 14). Again J. Gerhard teaches : *Quemadmodum in prima creatione Spiritus sanctus aquas fovendo iisque incubando fuit efficax, ita in rerum creatarum conservatione idem cum Patre et Filio efficaciter agit ;* in springtime *qua cuncta revirescere et frondescere incipiunt, postquam per hiemem fuerunt emortua,* but also in the coming into being of each new individual in which its species is renewed (*Loci,* 1610, L. III, 10, 132). And Paul Gerhardt in the Whitsun hymn " Enter then thy gates " :

> In thine own hands Thou bearest
> The whole wide world, O Lord,
> The hearts of men Thou turnest
> By thine own will and word.
> Thy grace, then, O vouchsafe us
> . . . .

3. We believe in the Holy Ghost, who proceedeth from the Father and the Son.

This clause corresponds to the *genitum non factum* of the second article. It is meant in the first instance as a negation : the Holy Spirit is not a creature. No creature can be said to have proceeded from God, i.e., to be an emanation of the divine essence. The creation of the world and man is not a procession or emanation from God. It is the establishing of a reality distinct from God with an essence of its own and not the divine essence. What proceeds from God can only be God once again. And since the essence of God cannot be divisible, what proceeds from God—and this is how the dogma describes the Holy Ghost—cannot go out from Him ; it cannot, then, be an emanation in the common sense of the term but only a mode of being of the one essence of God which intrinsically remains and is the same. In this case, obviously, the procession is not from the one essence of God as such but from another mode of being or other modes of being of this essence. Primarily, then, the clause is a description of the Holy Spirit, not now with reference to the *opus ad extra* common to the three modes of being, but with reference to His reality as a divine mode of being, i.e., to His reality in His relation to the other divine modes of being. This reality is of a kind that marks it out as being of divine essence with the Father and the Son. This is the first point made by the *qui procedit*.

> *Processionis vox accipienda est . . . juxta actionem Dei ad intra . . . id est qua ita agit Deus in essentia sua, ut reflexus in seipsum, divinae essentiae communione relationem realem constituat (Syn. Theol. pur.* Leiden, 1624, Disp., 9, 10).

The second point is that the Holy Spirit is differentiated from the Son or Word of God. The work of the Holy Spirit in revelation is different from that of the Son or Word of God. Though never separated from it, and to be distinguished only *per appropriationem*, it is still not to be confused with it. If we are to refrain from going beyond revelation, we shall interrelate the objective element of the Word in revelation and the subjective element of the Spirit, only in the essence of God but not as modes of His being. We shall acknowledge that the Holy Ghost, both in revelation and also antecedently in Himself, is not just God, but in God independently, like the Father and the Son. Again there is no special and second revelation of the Spirit alongside that of the Son. There are not, then, two Sons or Words of God. In the one revelation, however, the Son or Word represents the element of God's appropriation to man and the Spirit the element of God's appropriation by man. But by analogy, if our thinking is not to leave the soil of revelation, a distinction must be acknowledged in the reality of what the Son and the Spirit are antecedently in Themselves. Secondly, then, the *qui procedit* means that the divine mode of being of the Spirit is to be differentiated from that of the Son, which is denoted by *genitus*, and implicitly, therefore, from that of the Father as well.

> It is an isolated oddity that the *Pastor Hermae (Sim.,* V, 5, 2 ; 6, 5 f. ; IX, 1) calls the Holy Ghost the Son of God. In the dogma itself the need to distinguish the Spirit not merely from the creature but also from the Son or Word of God follows logically from the *unigenitus* of the second article. Both distinctions are included in the saying of Gregory of Nazianzus : ὃ καθ᾽ ὅσον μὲν ἐκεῖθεν ἐκπορεύεται, οὐ κτίσμα · καθ᾽ ὅσον δὲ οὐ γεννητόν, οὐχ υἱός (*Or..* 31, 8), and also in the statement of the *Quicunque vult : Spiritus sanctus a Patre et Filio, non factus nec creatus nec genitus, sed procedens.*

But what does the term " procession," ἐκπόρευσις, mean here ? It is neither chance nor carelessness that this term is one which in itself might well be applied to the origin of the Son from the Father, so that it does not specifically denote the distinctiveness of the origin of the Holy Spirit, but strictly and properly says only that alongside the begetting of the Son or speaking of the Word the Holy Spirit has His own and " in some way " different " procession " in God. The peculiarity of this procession as compared with the first one might be denoted by the term " breathing," *spiratio*, though in the strict sense it could only be " denoted " thereby. For what is the difference between breathing and begetting if in the same unconditional way both are meant to denote the eternal genesis of an eternal mode of being of God ? Would not any conceivable or expressible distinction entail a denial once again either of the deity or of the autonomy of the divine mode of being of the Holy Spirit ? The difficulty which confronts us here is in fact insurmountable.

Distinguere inter illam generationem et hanc processionem nescio, non valeo, non sufficio (Augustine, *C. Maxim.*, II, 14, 1). John of Damascus made a similar declaration (*Ekdos.*, I, 8), and it was often repeated later. *Quo modo a generatione differat, explicabit nullus* (M. Leydecker, *De veritate rel. reform.*, 1688, p. 28, quoted from H. Heppe, *Dogm. der. ev. ref. Kirche*, 1861, p. 94) ; often with the warning : *istud discrimen tutius ignoratur quam inquiritur* (so F. Turrettini, *Inst. Theol. el.*, I, 1679, L. III, qu. 30, 3). And for good reason the Church has never defined the more precise meaning of the *processio*.

The feeling one involuntarily has here, that the difficulty which faces us at this point might have a significance that is more than accidental, and that goes beyond this particular question, is correct. Why are we unable to express the distinction between the begetting of the Son and the breathing of the Spirit even though—assuming again that our thinking is not leaving the soil of revelation but we are regarding the revealed God as the eternal God—we are forced to maintain it ? The moment we measure what for the sake of definition we call the *spiratio Spiritus* by what we call the *generatio Filii*, something we established plainly in our discussion of that *generatio* obviously takes on clarity and force, namely, that the *generatio* or *loquutio*, too, is just an attempt to express what man cannot essentially express, what his language is unable to achieve. How is the Son of God begotten ? How is His Word spoken ? We do not know, either when we are speaking of the eternal reality or when we are speaking of the temporal reality which can be denoted by these metaphors, for both are only metaphors. Our knowledge can be only an acknowledgment of the fact. This is why we are now in difficulties when, in order to learn what *spiratio* is, we try to compare it to *generatio*.

Augustine (*loc. cit.*) gave a reason for his definite *nescio*. It was as follows : . . . *quia et illa (generatio) et ista (processio) est ineffabilis.* In next to the last chapter of his work on the Trinity (*De trin.*, XV, 27, 50) he did, of course, return to the question, and he now seems able to give, at least by indication, a positive answer. Using his well-known doctrine of the *imago trinitatis* in the human soul he proposes for consideration the possibility that the genesis of the Spirit might be related to that of the Son in the same way as will or love is to knowledge in the soul. The will proceeds from knowledge without being an image of knowledge (*voluntatem de cogitatione procedere—nemo enim vult, quod omnino quid vel quale sit nescit—non tamen esse cogitationis imaginem*). Similarly the Spirit from the Son! This suggestion was taken up and greatly expanded by Thomas Aquinas (*S. theol.*, I, *qu.* 27, *art.* 3 and 4). The procession of the Holy Spirit is the *processio secundum rationem voluntatis* which is distinguished from the *processio secundum rationem intellectus* by the fact that it proceeds from this and is related to this, presupposing it. *Ideo quod procedit in divinis per modum amoris, non procedit ut genitum, vel ut filius, sed magis procedit ut spiritus* (*art.* 4c). Modern Roman Catholic dogmatics (cf., e.g., F. Diekamp, *Kath. Dogm.*[6], Vol. I, 1930, p. 345 f.) seems to regard this explanation as a real answer to the question and so it does not make any further use of Augustine's *nescio*. On the other hand one should not forget that in relation to the suggestion, Augustine, unlike Thomas, did not fail to point out that the light which is thrown on the question by the *imago trinitatis* which we ourselves are, is always opposed by the *infirmitas* which our *iniquitas* has caused and only God can heal, so that he preferred to close his book *precatione quam disputatione*. We for our part were unable to accept the entire theory of the *imago trinitatis* and we are thus forced to say that we cannot regard the question about the Spirit as answered by it. As we have seen, the understanding of *generatio* as knowledge or of the Son as the Word of God, while it is true and significant, is an inadequate understanding, whose real import is hidden from us when we think we understand, or really do so to the best of our ability. Hence the related explanation of the Holy Ghost as the will which proceeds from knowledge cannot help us at all except by furnishing another and rather arbitrary analogy. It is better that the impossibility of making a distinction, which Augustine conceded in the first saying, should remind us, if we have forgotten, that the *processio* of the Spirit and the Son may indeed be denoted but cannot be comprehended.

This means no more and no less than that we cannot establish the How of the divine processions and therefore of the divine modes of being. We cannot define the Father, the Son, and the Holy Ghost, i.e., we cannot delimit them the one from the other. We can only state that in revelation three who delimit themselves from one another are present, and if in our thinking we are not to go beyond revelation we must accept the fact that these three who delimit themselves from one another are antecedently a reality in God Himself. We can state the fact of the divine processions and modes of being. But all our attempts to state the How of this delimitation will prove to be impossible. In our hands even terms suggested to us by Holy Scripture will prove to be incapable of grasping what they are supposed to grasp. What has to be said will obviously be said definitively and exclusively by God Himself, by the three in the one God who delimit themselves from one another in revelation. Nor can there be any repetition of this by us, not even the repetition in which we are aware of our own inability, in which we are constantly referred to the truth of God beyond the totally questionable truth of our own thoughts and words. The *ignoramus* which we must confess in relation to the distinction that we have to maintain between begetting and breathing is thus the *ignoramus* which we must confess in relation to the whole doctrine of the Trinity, i.e., in relation to the mystery of revelation, in relation to the mystery of God in general. If we could define this distinction we could define the Son and the Spirit and then we could define the Father as well, and therewith God Himself. For God Himself is the Father, the Son, and the Spirit. Only if these were not God could we achieve a definition here, the kind of definition that is more than description of the fact that God Himself is there in His revelation. But what is there in God's revelation is the Father, the Son, and the Spirit. Hence there could be a successful definition of these three only on the assumption that the Father, the Son, and the Spirit are not God. Therefore for the sake of what the doctrine of the Trinity must state, namely, that the Father, the Son, and the Spirit are God, no more must be said at this point and no definition must result here. This is the general significance of the *qui procedit* in trinitarian theology.

Τίς οὖν ἡ ἐκπόρευσις; Εἰπὲ σὺ τὴν ἀγεννησίαν τοῦ πατρός, κἀγὼ τὴν γέννησιν τοῦ υἱοῦ φυσιολογήσω καὶ τὴν ἐκπόρευσιν τοῦ πνεύματος, καὶ παραπληκτίσωμεν ἄμφω εἰς θεοῦ μυστήρια παρακύπτοντες (Gregory of Nazianzus, *Or.*, 31, 8).

But according to the Latin text of the creed, which we follow here, the procession of the Holy Ghost is His procession from the Father and the Son (*ex Patre Filioque*).

The main point to be noted here is that the creed, which has ἐκ τοῦ πατρός in the original, is not involved in the dispute that arose on this matter. It follows Jn. 15²⁶ in saying "from the Father," but without saying : "and not from the Son." It could not say this, for at the time, even among Greek theologians, there was no opposition to the material content of the addition. Thus, no less unconditionally than the addition, Epiphanius would say : πατὴρ ἦν ἀεί, καὶ τὸ πνεῦμα ἐκ πατρὸς καὶ υἱοῦ πνέει (*Ancoratus*, 75), or Ephraem : The Father is the Begetter, the Son the Begotten from the bosom of the Father, the Holy Ghost He that proceedeth from the Father and the Son (*Hymnus de defunctis et trinitate*, 11), and as late as the 5th century Cyril of Alexandria : τὸ πνεῦμα τὸ ἅγιον . . . πρόεισι δὲ καὶ ἐκ πατρὸς καὶ υἱοῦ (*Thes. de trin.*, 34). Again the creed could not exclude the *Filioque* because it is hard to see against what heresy the exclusion could have been directed. The opponents at whom the clause is aimed are again the Macedonians, who denied the deity of the Holy Spirit, but who affirmed His procession from the Son too, although in an Arian sense, i.e., as the procession of a creature from a creature. By ruling out the ἐκ τοῦ υἱοῦ the creed would have conceded, in glaring contradiction to its second article, that ἐκ τοῦ υἱοῦ implies less than ἐκ τοῦ πατρός. Yet in this dispute with the Pneumatomachi the creed had also not to teach the *Filioque* explicitly. With a backward glance at the γεννηθέντα ἐκ τοῦ πατρός of the second article, it wanted to make the origin of the Spirit parallel to that of the Son as regards consubstantiality with the Father. This could be achieved by the ἐκ τοῦ πατρός but by this alone (for the opponents were confessing the ἐκ τοῦ υἱοῦ in their Arian fashion). We may conclude, then, that there was no necessary reason—the factual reason adduced is not a necessary one—why the *Filioque* should not have been in the original creed.

The fact that the *Nic. Const.* did not have for many centuries a sacrosanct character in the West, and even then not to the degree that this was very soon accorded to it in the East, provided the formal possibility for the acceptance of the *Filioque* first of all into the liturgical use of the creed (beginning, as far as is known, in the early 6th century in Spain), while the fact that in the West the trinitarian doctrine of Augustine increasingly established itself as an expression of the common insight served as the positive reason. Approval of this practice by the Roman Curia had to wait a full five centuries. Almost at the very time when a quarrel arose between Frankish and Greek monks in Jerusalem (808) over the singing of the *Filioque* in the Mass, and when Pope Leo III defended the legitimacy of the disputed addition, the same Pope at a synod in Rome (810) disapproved of its insertion into the creed, and he had expressed a wish to Charlemagne (809), who championed the *Filioque* at the Synod of Aachen, that its use should be discontinued in the royal chapel. The general trend of thought in the West was still against it. But as the opposition of the Eastern Church to the doctrine enshrined in the addition became clearer, i.e., as the material negation which is not in the creed, and cannot be explained by it, came to light, the *Filioque* found official endorsement. The creed which became an acknowledged part of the Roman Mass in 1014 contained it. It thus became a dogma of the Western Church. Yet even in negotiations for union in later centuries the popes (cf. expressly Benedict XIV in the Bull *Etsi pastoralis*, 1742) did not insist that what was for the Greeks an addition to the liturgical text should be treated as a *conditio sine qua non* for the ending of the schism but only that the truth stated in the addition should be confessed. The Reformation in its trinitarian theology was also strongly enough orientated to Augustine to accept quite naturally and without further ado the general Western confession, so that implicitly or explicitly the expression became an integral part of the Evangelical confessional writings. Some in the older Protestant theology (e.g., J. Cocceius, *S. theol.*, 1662, 12, 8) might occasionally judge that it had been a mistake for the Roman Church to alter the creed when Leo III had solemnly endorsed it in its ancient form—the business is not in fact a shining testimonial to the Roman Catholic theory of the certainty of the Church's teaching authority as concentrated in the hands of the pope. It might be declared (so Quenstedt, *Theol. did pol.*, 1685, I, *c.* 9, *sect.* 2, *qu.* 12, *object. dial.* 16) that in this matter the orthodox decision belongs *non ad fidem simplicem, sed ad peritiam theologicam*, so that what matters is that it should not be flatly rejected by anybody. Even more generously it could be explicitly stated (so F. Turrettini, *Inst. theol. el.*, I, 1679, L. III, *qu.* 31, 6) that the Greek view of the matter was not to be regarded as a heresy but the Western view was simply to be regarded as better. Both Lutheran and Reformed, however, were almost completely unanimous that materially we should accept this decision even though it was reached in so unusual a way, apart from either council or pope.

In this whole affair the battle has really been fought sharply and seriously only by the Eastern Church, while the Western Church has on the whole confined itself to the defensive. (Cf. in this regard the formula of the *Conc. Lugd.*, II, 1274, Denz., No. 460 : *Damnamus et reprobamus qui negare praesumpserint, aeternaliter Spiritum Sanctum ex Patre et Filio procedere.*) In this regard it should also be noted that strictly speaking sharp feelings and statements are found in the East only from the time of Photius (9th century), whose real interest in the schism was very different, and always primarily in the form of indignation at the unlawful and unloving way in which the West acted when it changed the creed. (Cf. in this regard the moving complaints of A. St. Chomjakow in

Östl. Christentum. Dokumente, edited by H. Ehrenberg, Vol. 1, p. 156 f.) As for the significance of the conflict at any rate in modern Russian orthodoxy, we find on the one side—even if he is not to be taken too seriously—L. P. Karsavin, who somewhat obscurely makes the *Filioque* responsible for the doctrine of the immaculate conception and the papal infallibility, for Kantianism, for the belief in progress, and for many other evils in Western culture (*Östl. Christentum.* Vol. 2, p. 356 f.), and on the other side we find the Archimandrite Sylvester of Kiev, who at the time of the negotiations for union between the Orthodox and the Old Catholics was prepared to agree on historico-dogmatic grounds that the *Filioque*, in any possible sense, can be said only with regard to the *opus trinitatis ad extra*, but not the inner life of God (*Answer to the Note on the Holy Spirit contained in the Old Catholic Scheme*, 1875), and then the incomparably saner V. Bolotow of St. Petersburg, who did indeed take the view that the Augustinian *Filioque* was a private opinion which had been wrongly given the status of dogma, but who still regarded Sylvester's thesis as quite untenable, pointing out that there is no negation of the *Filioque* in the creed, and finally concluding that the whole question had not been the cause of division and could not constitute an *impedimentum dirimens* to intercommunion between the Orthodox and Old Catholics (" Thesen über das Filioque," *Revue intern. de théol.*, 1898, p. 681 f.). This final standpoint may be regarded as the prevailing view in Eastern Orthodoxy to-day.

We have reasons for following the Western tradition as regards the *Filioque*, and since the East-West schism is now a fact and this is one of the issues—whether rightly or wrongly is another question—there is cause to give some account of the matter.

Fundamentally what has brought us to this side is no less than the whole thrust of our attempted understanding of the doctrine of the Holy Spirit and the Trinity generally. Even supporters of the Eastern view do not contest the fact that in the *opus ad extra*, and therefore in revelation (and then retrospectively in creation), the Holy Spirit is to be understood as the Spirit of both the Father and the Son. But we have consistently followed the rule, which we regard as basic, that statements about the divine modes of being antecedently in themselves cannot be different in content from those that are to be made about their reality in revelation. All our statements concerning what is called the immanent Trinity have been reached simply as confirmations or underlinings or, materially, as the indispensable premises of the economic Trinity. They neither could nor would say anything other than that we must abide by the distinction and unity of the modes of being in God as they encounter us according to the witness of Scripture in the reality of God in His revelation. The reality of God in His revelation cannot be bracketed by an " only," as though somewhere behind His revelation there stood another reality of God ; the reality of God which encounters us in His revelation is His reality in all the depths of eternity. This is why we have to take it so seriously precisely in His revelation. In connexion with the specific doctrine of the Holy Spirit this means that He is the Spirit of both the Father and the Son not just in His work *ad extra* and upon us, but that to all eternity—no limit or reservation is possible here—He is none other than the Spirit of both the Father and the Son. " And the Son " means that not merely for us, but in God Himself, there is no possibility of an opening and readiness and capacity for God in man—for this is the work of the Holy Ghost in revelation—unless it comes from Him, the Father, who has revealed Himself in His Word, in Jesus Christ, and also, and no less necessarily, from Him who is His Word, from His Son, from Jesus Christ, who reveals the Father. Jesus Christ as the Giver of the Holy Spirit is not without the Father from whom He, Jesus Christ, is. But the Father as the Giver of the Holy Spirit is also not without Jesus Christ to whom He Himself is the Father. The Eastern doctrine does not contest the fact that this is so in revelation. But it does not read off from revelation its statements about the being of God " antecedently in Himself." It does not stand by the order of the divine modes of being which by its own admission is valid in the sphere of revelation. It goes beyond revelation to achieve a very different picture of God " antecedently in Himself." We must object already at this point quite apart from the results. What gives us the right to take passages like Jn. 15^{26}, which speak of the procession of the Spirit from the Father, and isolate them from the many others which equally plainly call Him the Spirit of the Son ? Is it not much more natural to understand opposing statements like this as mutually complementary, as is freely done in the reality of revelation, and then to acknowledge the reality disclosed thereby as valid to all eternity, as the way it is in the essence of God Himself ? For us the Eastern rejection of the *Filioque* is already suspect from the formal standpoint because it is patently a speculation which interprets individual verses of the Bible in isolation, because it bears no relation to the reality of God in revelation and for faith.

This formal defect, however, takes on at once material significance. The *Filioque* expresses recognition of the communion between the Father and the Son. The Holy Spirit is the love which is the essence of the relation between these two modes of being of God. And recognition of this communion is no other than recognition of the basis and confirmation of the communion between God and man as a divine, eternal truth, created in revelation by the Holy Spirit. The intra-divine two-sided fellowship of the Spirit, which proceeds from the Father and the Son, is the basis of the fact that there is in revelation a fellowship in which not only is God there for man but in very truth—this is the *donum Spiritus sancti*—man is also there for God. Conversely, in this fellowship in revelation which is created between God and man by the Holy Spirit there may be discerned the fellowship in God Himself, the eternal love of God : discerned as the mystery, surpassing all understanding, of the possibility of this reality of revelation ; discerned as the one God in the mode of being of the Holy Spirit.

Missio haec temporalis (Spiritus sancti) praesupponit aeternum illum Spiritus sancti (aeque a Filio atque Patre) processum estque eius declaratio et manifestatio (Quenstedt, *Theol. did. pol.,* 1685, I, *cap.* 9, *sect.* 2, *qu.* 12, *beb.* 3).

This whole insight and outlook is lost when the immanent *Filioque* is denied. If the Spirit is also the Spirit of the Son only in revelation and for faith, if He is only the Spirit of the Father in eternity, i.e., in His true and original reality, then the fellowship of the Spirit between God and man is without objective ground or content. Even though revealed and believed, it is a purely temporal truth with no eternal basis, so to speak, in itself. No matter, then, what we may have to say about the communion between God and man, it does not have in this case a guarantee in the communion between God the Father and God the Son as the eternal content of its temporal reality. Does not this mean an emptying of revelation ?

It would be even worse if the denial of the *Filioque* were not restricted to the immanent Trinity but were also applied to the interpretation of revelation itself, if, then, the Holy Spirit were to be one-sidedly and exaggeratedly regarded as the Spirit of the Father even in His *opus ad extra*. We must be very careful here, for this is theoretically contested. Yet we cannot avoid asking whether, if that denial, the exclusive *ex Patre* is to obtain as an eternal truth, it is not inevitable that the relation of God to man will be understood decisively from the standpoint of Creator and creature, and that it will thus acquire a more or less developed naturalistic and unethical character, so that the Mediator of revelation, the Son or Word, will be set aside as the basis and origin of the relation, and it will take on the nature of a direct and immediate relation, a mystical union with the *principium et fons Deitatis*.

The distinctively unrestrained manner of thought and utterance of the Russian theologians and religious philosophers as it is presented to us in Ehrenberg's documents, obliterating the frontiers of philosophy and theology, of reason and revelation, of Scripture, tradition and direct illumination, of spirit and nature, of *pistis* and *sophia* (but also the distinction between the economic Trinity and the immanent Trinity), may not have anything to do with the omission of the *Filioque*, but even if not, one would still have to speak of a remarkable coincidence between this omission and these characteristics, which could be very readily understood as the results or the necessary parallels of this omission.

But be that as it may, in the Eastern view of the relation between the divine modes of being we cannot recognise their reality as we believe we know it from the divine revelation according to the witness of Scripture.

We do not recognise it even in the version in which it does indeed rule out the ἐκ τοῦ υἱοῦ but is prepared to accept a διὰ τοῦ υἱοῦ as a possible interpretation of the ἐκ τοῦ πατρός. For even this διὰ τοῦ υἱοῦ does not lead, and according to the intent of Eastern theology it is not meant to lead, to that on which everything seems to us to depend, namely, to the thought of the full consubstantial fellowship between Father and Son as the essence of the Spirit, corresponding as a proto-type to the fellowship between God as Father and man as His child the creation of which is the work of the Holy Spirit in revelation.

Διὰ τοῦ υἱοῦ, per filium, has on its side the usage of most of the Greek and Latin Fathers before the schism. Neither can it be contested that in so far as the Son Himself is the Son of the Father the procession of the Spirit from the Son may be finally traced back to the Father. The Latin Fathers never disputed this. Augustine himself declared unequivocally : principaliter the Spirit pro-ceeds from the Father, and the Son has it from the Father, ut et de illo procedat Spiritus sanctus (De trin., XV, 26, 47 ; cf. 17, 29 ; In Joann. tract., 99, 8). But Eastern teaching after the schism, and even the older Eastern teaching in so far as it was later construed in a schismatic sense, says more than this. It takes ἐκ τοῦ πατρός in the sense of ἐκ μόνου τοῦ πατρός, and hence it does not see in διὰ τοῦ υἱοῦ a direct procession of the Spirit from the Son on the presupposition of the begetting of the Son, but sees in it rather a continuation or extension or prolongation of the procession of the Spirit from the Father. It found classical expression in the metaphor of the three torches in Gregory of Nyssa, the second of which was lit from the first and the third from the second (De Spir., s. 3). It is also expressed (according to Bolotow, op. cit., p. 692) in another comparison, that of the Father to the mouth, the Son to the word, and the Spirit to the breath that gives sound to the word : to the degree that the breath is breathed out for the sake of the word, to the degree that the pronouncing of the word inevitably entails the breathing, the word is the logical prius of the breathing and to that degree διὰ τοῦ υἱοῦ is valid. But to the degree that the word does not produce the breath, the breath coming from the mouth and not the word, ἐκ τοῦ πατρός is true but not ἐκ τοῦ υἱοῦ. According to a saying of Athanasius (Ad Serap., I, 20) which is often quoted, the secondary derivation of the Spirit is not an ἐκπορεύεσθαι but an ἐκλάμπειν παρὰ τοῦ λόγου τοῦ ἐκ πατρός. According to this view of the διὰ τοῦ υἱοῦ, begetting and breathing are thus presented " as a straight-line movement in which the second proceeds from the first " (M. J. Scheeben, Hand-buch der kath. Dogmatik, new impr., 1925, Vol. I, p. 820). The Son is a mediating principle, the Father alone being αἰτία or principle in the strict sense of the word.

Though in itself διὰ τοῦ υἱοῦ goes without saying, it must obviously be rejected if interpreted in the above sense. And in opposition to this interpretation the adherence of the West to ἐκ τοῦ υἱοῦ seems both logical and necessary. Where διὰ τοῦ υἱοῦ is taken in such a way that it does in fact rule out a true derivation of the Spirit from the Son as well, this means that there is no relatio originis between Son and Spirit, and that only improperly can the Spirit be called the Spirit of the Son, i.e., not in the way that the Son is called the Son of the Father. Furthermore, if the Son is not also the true origin the Spirit, the Father and the Son do not have all things in common, the one being the origin of the Spirit in a primary sense and the other only in a secondary sense. Even the unity of God the Father is called in question if implicitly He is not already the origin of the Spirit as the Father of the Son, the origin of the Spirit from Him being a second function along with His fatherhood. Finally and above all, the Spirit on this view loses His mediating position between the Father and the Son and the Father and the Son lose their mutual connexion in the Spirit.

Possibly an unsubdued remnant of Origenist Subordinationism may be regarded as one of the sources of error in the Eastern conception. But above all it is the unity of the Trinity which we must see to be endangered at every point by the denial of the *Filioque*. We have seen elsewhere that tritheism was always the special danger in Eastern theology and we cannot escape the impression that when the Trinity is constructed in such a way that the *Filioque* is denied the *trinitas in unitate* is very perilously overemphasised as compared with the *unitas in trinitate*. It was for the sake of the *unitas* that the *Filioque* forced itself on Augustine and then carried the West. Our decisive reason for adhering to this view is to be found in the fact that only in this *unitas*, and not in the strange juxtaposition of Father and Son with respect to the Spirit which may be seen in the Eastern doctrine, do we have anything corresponding to the work of the Holy Spirit in revelation. If the rule holds good that God in His eternity is none other than the One who discloses Himself to us in His revelation, then in the one case as in the other the Holy Spirit is the Spirit of the love of the Father and the Son, and so *procedens ex Patre Filioque*.

In accordance with what has been said, the positive meaning of the Western version of the dogma may be summarised as follows.

As God is in Himself Father from all eternity, He begets Himself as the Son from all eternity. As He is the Son from all eternity, He is begotten of Himself as the Father from all eternity. In this eternal begetting of Himself and being begotten of Himself, He posits Himself a third time as the Holy Spirit, i.e., as the love which unites Him in Himself. As He is the Father who begets the Son He brings forth the Spirit of love, for as He begets the Son, God already negates in Himself, from eternity, in His absolute simplicity, all loneliness, self-containment, or self-isolation. Also and precisely in Himself, from eternity, in His absolute simplicity, God is orientated to the Other, does not will to be without the Other, will have Himself only as He has Himself with the Other and indeed in the Other. He is the Father of the Son in such a way that with the Son He brings forth the Spirit, love, and is in Himself the Spirit, love. It is not, course, to satisfy a law of love, nor because love is a reality even God must obey, that He must be the Father of the Son. The Son is the first in God and the Spirit is the second in God, that is, as God is the Father of the Son, and, as Father, begets the Son, He also brings forth the Spirit and therefore the negation of isolation, the law and the reality of love. Love is God, the supreme law and ultimate reality, because God is love and not *vice versa*. And God is love, love proceeds from Him as His love, as the Spirit He Himself is, because He posits Himself as the Father and therefore posits Himself as the Son. In the Son of His love, i.e., in the Son in and with whom He brings forth Himself as love, He then brings forth in the *opus ad extra* too, in creation, the creaturely reality which is distinct from Himself, and in revelation the reconciliation and peace of the creature that has fallen away from Him. The love which meets us in reconciliation, and then retrospectively in creation, is real love, supreme law and ultimate reality, because God is antecedently love in

Himself : not just a supreme principle of the relation of separateness and fellowship, but love which even in fellowship wills and affirms and seeks and finds the other or Other in its distinction, and then in separateness wills and affirms and seeks and finds fellowship with it. Because God is antecedently love in Himself, love is and holds good as the reality of God in the work of reconciliation and in the work of creation. But He is love antecedently in Himself as He posits Himself as the Father of the Son. This is the explanation and proof of the *qui procedit ex Patre.*

But just because we explain and prove it thus, we must now continue that similarly, as God is the Son who comes forth from the Father, He brings forth the Spirit, He brings forth love. In this mode of being, too, He negates loneliness in His absolute simplicity ; He is orientated to the Other ; He does not will to be without the Other out of whom He is. How else could He be the Son but as the Son of the Father ? How could He be less the origin of love in being the Son than in being the Father ? Distinct as Father and Son, God is one in the fact that His distinction is that of the Father and the Son, so that it is not the kind of distinction which might also arise in a supreme principle of separateness and fellowship, a loveless distinction, but the distinction which affirms fellowship in separateness and separateness in fellowship. How, then, can the breathing of the Spirit belong less essentially, less properly and originally, to the Son than to the Father ? In relation to the *opus ad extra* we must also ask : If it is true that God reveals Himself to us through His only-begotten Son, if it is also true that God's only-begotten Son is no less and no other than God the Father, if it is true again that God's revelation is also the revelation of His love, if revelation would not be revelation without the outpouring and impartation of the Spirit through whom man becomes the child of God, can it be that this Spirit is not directly the Spirit of the Son as well ? Is it only indirectly, only derivatively, that the Son is here the Giver of the Spirit, of the revelation of love ? But if He is this immediately and directly, how can this be if He is not so in reality, in the reality of God antecedently in Himself ? If here, and already in creation when seen from here, love is God's reality in the Son and through the Son, we have no reason and no warrant to think beyond that which is valid here. It is also the love of the Son antecedently in Himself, in eternity. As the Son of the Father He, too, is thus *spirator Spiritus.* He is this, of course, as the Son of the Father. To that extent the *per Filium* is true. But here *per Filium* cannot mean *per causam instrumentalem.* This Son of this Father is and has all that His Father is and has. He is and has it as the Son. But He is and has it. Thus He, too, is *spirator Spiritus.* He, too, has the possibility of being this. This is how we explain and prove the *qui procedit ex Patre Filioque.*

At this point it might be asked whether, to correspond with the procession of the Father from the Son, there should not also be asserted a procession of the Son from the Father and the Spirit. In favour of this one might on the one side argue exegetically that in more than one respect the work of the Holy Spirit in revelation is presented as a work of creating or begetting. In particular one might adduce the birth of the Spirit (Jn. 3⁵ᶠ·) which is a condition of seeing and entering the kingdom of God. If, one might ask, the children of God are born of the Spirit, might we not say something of the same regarding the Son of God too ? And in fact is not something of the same said about the Son of God in revelation ? In the story of the baptism of Jesus in the Jordan (Mk. 1⁹ᶠ· and par.), is not His divine sonship shown to be established by the Spirit alighting upon Him ? Does not Rom. 1³ also say that Jesus Christ was instituted the Son of God with power κατὰ πνεῦμα ἁγιωσύνης ἐξ ἀναστάσεως νεκρῶν ? And what are we to say especially about Lk. 1³⁵, where the angel's prophecy of the impending conception of the Virgin Mary contains the words : πνεῦμα ἅγιον ἐπελεύσεται ἐπὶ σέ, καὶ δύναμις ὑψίστου ἐπισκιάσει σοι, διὸ καὶ τὸ γεννώμενον ἅγιον κληθήσεται υἱὸς θεοῦ, or Mt. 1¹⁸, which says of Mary : εὑρέθη ἐν γαστρὶ ἔχουσα ἐκ πνεύματος ἁγίου, or Mt. 1²⁰, where we read : τὸ γὰρ ἐν αὐτῇ γεννηθὲν ἐκ πνεύματός ἐστιν ἁγίου ? If we apply at this point our rule that material dogmatic statements about the immanent Trinity can and must be taken from definitions of the modes of being of God in revelation, are we not compelled to accept a relationship of origin between the Spirit and Son which is neither begetting nor breathing but a third thing ? And one might also wish to add that the circle of mutual relations in which God is one in three modes of being is only then closed and complete, and that already for this reason one should postulate an origin of the Son from both the Father and the Spirit.

This second, systematic argument may be dismissed at once. If the circle or *perichoresis* between the three modes of being of God had really to be a circle of mutual origins, and if it had to be complete as such, then an origin of the Father from the Son and from the Spirit would also have to be discovered. But the *perichoresis*, though it is complete and mutual, is not one of origins as such, but a *perichoresis* of the modes of being as modes of being of the one God. It is a further description of the *homoousia* of Father, Son, and Spirit, but has nothing to do with begetting and breathing as such, and therefore needs no supplementation in this direction, so that the postulate cannot be said to have, formally, a legitimate basis.

It is more difficult to meet the first, exegetical objection. To do this we must note throughout that the work of the Holy Spirit in relation to the Son in revelation, to which all the passages refer, is not of such a kind that it can be described as commensurable with the eternal begetting of the Son by the Father or the eternal breathing of the Spirit by the Father and the Son, so that another eternal relation of origin can and should be read off from it. What the commensurability lacks is as follows. The begetting and breathing are a bringing forth from the essence of the Father, or of the Father and the Son, but not from another essence. But the bringing forth of the Holy Spirit described in the passages quoted is always a bringing forth from some other essence whose existence is presupposed. This may be seen very clearly in Jn. 3. Birth of the Spirit is a new birth, a regeneration, and the man to be born of the Spirit as a child of God is already there when this happens. He, this man, is born of the Spirit as a child of God. But one obviously cannot say that the child of God this man becomes is created or begotten by the Spirit. The child of God is what it is in fellowship with Jesus Christ, the eternal Son of God. The same applies to the story of the baptism in the Jordan, which is undoubtedly to be viewed as a parallel to the story of the Virgin Birth. It is this man Jesus of Nazareth, not the Son of God, who becomes the Son of God by the descent of the Spirit. Again the installation of Jesus

Christ as the Son of God by the Holy Spirit in Rom. 1 is expressly related to the resurrection. The ὁρισμός is the exaltation and revelation of Him who was crucified and who died to the glory of the Son of God. It denotes the participation of the One hitherto called Jesus Christ according to His humanity, in the majesty of the eternal Son. This Son of God as such does not derive His being from this ὁρισμός, nor from the Holy Spirit. But the One called Jesus Christ according to His humanity derives it from the Holy Spirit that He should be the Son of God. The situation is much the same in the references to the Virgin Birth which also call for consideration here. The incarnation of the Word of God from Mary cannot consist in the fact that here and now the Son of God comes into being for the first time. It consists in the fact that here and now the Son of God takes to Himself that other which already exists in Mary, namely, flesh, humanity, human nature, being as man. Furthermore the dogma of the Virgin Birth does not in any sense imply that the Holy Spirit is the father of the man Jesus and thus becomes, in the incarnation of the Son of God, the Father of the Son of God as well, It tells us that the man Jesus has no father (just as He has no mother as the Son of God). What is ascribed to the Holy Spirit in the birth of Christ is the assumption of human existence in the Virgin Mary into unity with God in the mode of being of the Logos. That this is possible, that this other, this being as man, this flesh, is there for God, for fellowship and even unity with God, that flesh can be the Word when the Word becomes flesh, is the work of the Holy Spirit in the birth of Christ. This work of the Spirit is prototypal of the work of the Spirit in the coming into being of the children of God ; in the same way, not directly but indirectly, *per adoptionem*, in faith in Christ, we become that which we are not by nature, namely, children of God. On the other hand, this work of the Spirit is not ectypal of a work of the Spirit on the Son of God Himself. What the Son " owes " to the Spirit in revelation is His being as man, the possibility of the flesh existing for Him, so that He, the Word, can become flesh. How could one derive from this that He owes His eternal sonship to the Spirit ? He is the eternal Son of the essence of the eternal Father which is also His own, not by the assumption of another essence. Therefore what we may infer from these passages as regards understanding of the eternal Trinity has nothing whatever to do with an origin in God. It is rather a confirmation of what has been said already, namely, that as the Holy Spirit in revelation unites God and man, Creator and creature, the Holy One and sinners, so that they become Father and child, in the same way He is in Himself the communion, the love, which unites the Father to the Son and the Son to the Father.

With this explanation and proof, however, we have already said the final thing that has always been said, and must necessarily be said, in explanation of the Western view, namely, that the *ex Patre Filioque* denotes, not a twofold, but rather a common origin of the Spirit from the Father and the Son. The fact that the Father is the Father and the Son the Son, that the former begets and the latter is begotten, is not common to them ; in this respect they are different divine modes of being. But the fact that between them and from them, as God's third mode of being, is the Spirit, love—this they have in common. This third mode of being cannot result from the former alone, or the latter alone, or co-operation of the two, but only from their one being as God the Father and God the Son, who are not two " persons " either in themselves or in co-operation, but two modes of being of the one being of God. Thus the one Godness of the Father and Son is, or the Father and the Son in their one Godness are, the origin of the Spirit. What is between them, what unites them, is, then, no mere relation. It is not exhausted in the truth of their being alongside and with one another. As an independent divine mode of being over against them, it is the active mutual orientation and interpenetration of love, because these two, the Father and the Son, are of one essence, and indeed of divine essence, because God's fatherhood and sonship as such must be related to one another in this active mutual orientation and interpenetration. That the Father and the Son are the one God is the reason why they are not just united but are united in the Spirit in love ; it is the reason, then, why God is love and love is God.

Tertius enim est Spiritus a Deo et Filio (Tertullian, *Ad Prax.*, 8). In revelation it is true, says Augustine, that *Spiritus et Dei est qui dedit, et noster qui accepimus* ; it is true that the Spirit of God can also be called the spirit of Elijah, or the spirit of Moses, or the spirit of a man. This wonderful truth has its basis in God Himself in the fact that Father and Son (even if the Son from the Father and the Father *principaliter*) are the *principium* of the Holy Ghost : *Non dua principia, sed sicut Pater et Filius unus deus et ad creaturam relative unus creator et unus dominus, sic relative ad Spiritum sanctum unum principium* (*De trin.*, XV, 14, 15). This unity of origin of the Spirit was given the status of a dogma at the *Conc. Lugd.*, II, 1274 : *Non tanquam ex duobus principiis, sed tanquam ex uno principio, non duabus spirationibus, sed unica spiratione procedit* (Denz., No. 460). And the *Conc. Florent.* in 1439, adopting Augustine's exposition of the *per Filium* quoted earlier, added : *Quoniam omnia quae Patris sunt, Pater ipse unigenito Filio suo gignendo dedit praeter esse Patrem, hoc ipsum quod Spiritus sanctus procedit ex Filio, ipse Filius a Patre aeternaliter habet a quo etiam aeternaliter genitus est.* In this sense, it was held, the *Filioque* was added to the creed *veritatis declarandae gratia et imminente necessitate* (Denz., No. 691).

4. We believe in the Holy Ghost " who with the Father and the Son together is worshipped and glorified." This final clause of the creed to call for consideration here again defines the deity of the Holy Spirit. To some extent it links up with the first one. This said that as the Father and as the Son is the one Lord, so, too, is the Spirit. Now we read that as the one Lord is to be worshipped and glorified as Father and as Son, so He is also as Spirit. Note that the Latin text, by adding *simul*, rules out the tritheistic appearance which would not have been avoided by a mere *cum* and is perhaps not altogether avoided by the Greek compounds. " With " here does not mean " alongside "—the divine modes of being are not alongside one another—but " together with " or " in and with," yet again not in such a way that the Spirit is a mere attribute or relation of the Father and the Son, but in such a way that one might equally well say of the Father or the Son or both that they are to be worshipped and glorified together with the Holy Ghost. The meaning, then, is " like " the Father and the Son.

One may compare the *Gloria Patri et Filio et Spiritui sancto* in the Roman Mass or the Evangelical liturgy, or Luther's hymn to the Trinity :

> " We believe in Holy Ghost,
> God with Father and the Son . . .,"

or the third stanza of M. Rinckart's " Now thank we all our God " :

> " All praise and thanks to God,
> The Father now be given,
> The Son and Him who reigns
> With them in highest heaven . . ."

What is obviously stressed here is the deity of the Spirit as it must now be established from the human standpoint. One might ask why the emphasis should be made in a phrase with a liturgical character as it were ? Why does it not say, who with the Father and the Son is to be believed in or to be loved ? Whatever the historical explanation may be, we must say at least that the reference does in fact carry with it a twofold safeguard in this particular form. By being denoted as object of worship (*proskynesis*) and glorification the πνεῦμα, which is, abstractly considered, neuter, is brought into relation to the personality of God as this is denoted by the terms πατήρ and υἱός. Not intrinsically —the same applies to the Father and the Son as well—but by identity with the one God, the Spirit, too, is not a neuter, an It, but a He, the great, original, incomparable He, over whom man has no power but who has all power over man. And by being denoted object of worship and glorification the Spirit, who in revelation is the Spirit of God and man (*Spiritus Dei et noster*), the consummation of the fellowship between God and man, is again very emphatically withdrawn from man's sphere. He dwells in us and there is a being of man in the Spirit, but this must not leave us even for a moment under any illusion as to the fact that the qualitative and not just quantitative distinction between God and man is not abrogated even or especially in revelation, but that it is rather established in revelation, this distinction being the presupposition of fellowship between God and man. The Holy Spirit, in distinction from all created spirits, is the Spirit who is and remains and always becomes anew transcendent over man even when immanent in him. Worship and glorification mean approach to Him on the presupposition and in observance of distance from Him, not just any distance, not the cold mathematical distance of the finite from the infinite, but the distance of man as creature from God as Creator, of man as sinner from God as Judge, of man as pardoned from God as the One who is freely and causelessly merciful. Hence *proskynesis*, glory to God in the highest ! Nowhere is there more obvious danger of confusing the subject and object of faith or love than in relation to this third mode of God's being in revelation. But all such confusion is ruled out by the clause : " Who with the Father and the Son together is worshipped and glorified." This gift, the *donum Spiritus sancti*, refuses to be abstracted from its Giver. But the Giver is God. We can have the gift only when and as we have God. At this point we may simply refer again to the significance of this particular clause for the whole doctrine of the operations of the Spirit, and especially for the whole doctrine of faith. One would think a blind man would have to see here that if man's presence at God's revelation, the *Deus in nobis*, is to be stated with real content, it can be understood only from the standpoint of the divine Subject, of the Subject who cannot be set aside as such. Even and especially the doctrine of the *gratia Spiritus sancti applicatrix* cannot lead to an independent anthropology. Justification and sanctification are acts of this divine Subject precisely as this Subject makes Himself ours. He makes Himself ours as the *Spiritus sanctus, qui cum Patre et Filio simul adoratur et conglorificatur.* Thus and not otherwise He becomes our salvation. We have had this clause constantly before us in all that has had to be said about the appropriation of grace and salvation in our discussions thus far, and we shall have to keep it before us in the future. Hence we hardly need to give it special emphasis again at this juncture.

One can hardly conclude an exposition of God's triunity in any better way than Augustine did at the end of his work on this subject (*De trin.*, XV, 28, 51). There he declares again in simple terms that he believes in God the Father, Son and Holy Spirit because God has revealed Himself thus in Scripture. The " Truth " would not have expressed itself in this way *nisi trinitas esses. Ad hanc regulam fidei dirigens intentionem meam, quantum potui, quantum me posse dedisti, quaesivi te, et desideravi intellectu videre quod credidi et multum disputavi et laboravi.* And now he finds himself constrained to pray : *Libera me, Deus, a multiloquio quod patior intus in anima mea, misera in conspectu tuo et confugiente ad misericordiam tuam.* He knows how hazardous is not just what he says but also what he thinks. Hence he prays that he may not grow hard or sleepy in what he has said or thought in what is only man's much-speaking. He realises that only God Himself can be the consummation of what man thinks and speaks about Him. R. Seeberg (*Lehrb. d. Dogmengesch.*, Vol. 2, 1923, p. 163) concludes from these words of Augustine that at the end he was worried about the " fulness of visions." Now that might very well be. There are theologies whose authors have no need to be worried at the end, since for good reasons the " fulness of visions " has been spared them. Augustine was not in this happy position. He had run the risk and the " fulness of visions " had in fact come upon him. When this risk is run, one may come to grief. And a theologian who runs the risk may not only come to grief himself but also bring destruction on others. This explains Augustine's final prayer and also the closing words of the book : *Dominus Deus une, Deus Trinitas, quaecumque dixi in his libris de tuo, agnoscant et tui : si qua de meo, et tu ignosce, et tui. Amen.*

INDEXES

I. SCRIPTURE REFERENCES

C.D.—R

II. NAMES